ALL CHILDREN

READ

TEACHING FOR LITERACY IN
TODAY'S DIVERSE CLASSROOM

CHARLES TEMPLE
Hobart and William Smith Colleges

DONNA OGLE
National Louis University

ALAN CRAWFORD
California State University, Los Angeles

PENNY FREPPON
University of Cincinnati

PEARSON
A and B

Boston   New York   San Francisco   Mexico City

Montreal   Toronto   London   Madrid   Munich   Paris

Hong Kong   Singapore   Tokyo   Cape Town   Sydney

Senior Acquisitions Editor: Aurora Martínez Ramos
Senior Development Editor: Mary Kriener
Series Editorial Assistant: Erin Beatty
Senior Editorial-Production Administrator: Beth Houston
Editorial-Production Service: Kathy Smith
Senior Marketing Manager: Krista Groshong
Composition and Prepress Buyer: Linda Cox
Manufacturing Buyer: Andrew Turso
Cover Administrator: Linda Knowles
Photo Research: Kathy Smith
Interior Design: The Davis Group, Inc.
Electronic Composition: Monotype Composition

Library of Congress Cataloging-in-Publication Data

All children read : teaching for literacy in today's diverse classrooms / Charles Temple . . . [et al.].
    p. cm.
  Includes bibliographical references and index.
  ISBN 0-321-06394-5
    1. Reading (Elementary)—United States. 2. Language arts (Elementary)—United States.
    3. English language—Study and teaching (Elementary)—United States—Foreign speakers.
    4. Limited English-proficient students—Education—United States. I. Temple, Charles A.

LB1573.A435 2005
372.41—dc22   2004053450

11/22/04

About the Authors

Charles Temple stays busy teaching education courses at Hobart and William Smith Colleges in Geneva, New York; consulting on literacy throughout the world; and writing books for children. Dr. Temple studied with the late Edmund Henderson at the University of Virginia, where he explored reading instruction, invented spelling, reading disabilities, and what was to become emergent literacy with many others who have gone on to do good work in the literacy field. He has written books on emergent literacy, invented spelling, writing instruction, language arts, diagnosis and remediation of reading disabilities, and children's literature.

Donna Ogle is professor of education at National Louis University in Evanston, Illinois, and has been involved in staff development work in the Chicago public schools and in other urban areas. She recently finished her term as the president of the International Reading Association (IRA) and continues to give workshops around the United States and the world on teaching for comprehension and higher order thinking, as well as using the arts in teaching. Her K-W-L procedure has become so recognized and popular that teachers all over the world use it.

Alan Crawford is now Emeritus Professor of Education at California State University at Los Angeles. He has been busily involved in the California State Reading Association (of which he is a former president) and has done extensive teaching, consulting, and writing on teaching reading in the elementary school, especially for English language learners. Alan has written curriculum for teaching reading in Spanish. He served as IRA's representative to UNESCO for many years, and frequently presents workshops on a volunteer basis for international development projects in Latin America, Asia, and Africa.

Penny Freppon is professor of education at the University of Cincinnati. Her professional work has focused on workshop-based and literature-rich instruction that attends to children's skill development, as well as working with teachers of young children, especially in urban classrooms. Those who are afraid that current trends in reading instruction run the risk of dismantling much that is good in child-centered instruction will be much encouraged by Dr. Freppon's thoughtful attention to skills in the context of meaning-centered instruction.

Brief Contents

Preface

Teaching all children to read is the most demanding challenge facing elementary schools in the United States. Reading instruction takes the most time and easily commands the most public scrutiny of any school subject. With the greater diversity of our schools, especially in terms of the home languages of the children, the challenge of helping all children succeed in reading will only increase. As authors of *All Children Read,* we accept this challenge and are dedicated to helping you help *all children read.* As you read these words:

- Making all children readers has become a primary concern not just of teachers and parents but of the President of the United States, the U.S. Congress, and the daily news.

- In country after country, an unprecedented emphasis is being placed on making *all children readers* through UNESCO's worldwide initiative called "Education for All" [See http://www.unesco.org/education/efa/index.shtml]. Diplomats from the most powerful countries in the world gather to talk about ways to extend quality primary school instruction—and especially literacy—to every child on the planet.

- The major professional associations and the state education departments of forty-nine states have passed learning standards that specify what children should know about reading and writing, and what teachers should know about teaching to make all children readers and writers. Children and prospective teachers are being tested as never before on their knowledge of literacy and literacy instruction. The standards, and the tests, promise to shine light into every corner of American education—we have, after all, one of the most socially stratified education systems in the world—with the ultimate hope of assuring quality education for all. But some educators warn that the present versions of the standards and the tests threaten teachers' creativity; and they also worry that the resources will not follow the needs that are uncovered.

- Scholars in the evolving field of literacy studies are sharing fascinating insights on the way reading and writing influence the way people think and learn, and how they view the world. New scholarship is changing the way we think about the ways members of different cultural groups use language, and respond to language and literacy instruction in the classroom. These insights have direct consequences in the classroom.

- American classrooms are inhabited by children who speak many languages other than English, and whose ancestral cultures come from every corner of the world. Legislation affecting children with special learning needs requires that children be educated in the "least restrictive environment." Children who were formerly educated in separate special education classrooms are now taught in blended classrooms, often with teams of teachers present. The task of making all children readers now means working effectively with children with different languages, different cultural backgrounds, and different learning needs.

- Our children's performance in literacy tasks is being compared not only with children in previous generations, but with children all over the world, in countries with which we are both interdependent and in economic competition.

- Disagreements among educators over approaches to teaching reading—beginning reading, in particular—have led to the formation of a national commission to study the issue. But attempts to settle disagreements among educators with appeals to science have raised new questions. What constitutes the scientific study of literacy, and who has claim to expertise in the field?

- The past decade has been a wonderfully inventive time for new insights into children's literacy learning. Our knowledge of emergent literacy, developing word knowledge, the writing process, literature-based instruction, strategic instruction, workshop approaches to teaching, and teaching for comprehension have both expanded and matured. We have a much more thorough understanding than ever before of the ways children learn to read and write. We also have a better appreciation of the roles played by differences in language and culture, and ways those can be accommodated in the classroom to make all children readers.

- We also have a richly supplied "tool kit" for teaching. A host of approaches exist for encouraging children's emergent literacy, promoting language development, teaching word recognition in ways that honor children's developmental processes, teaching comprehension, encouraging and teaching thoughtful and critical reading, and teaching students to use strategies for reading, writing, and learning.

It is a challenging time, a fascinating time, a wonderful time to take up the challenge of teaching reading in North America, and your four authors are pleased to prepare you and guide you as you take up the challenge. *All Children Read: Teaching for Literacy in Today's Diverse Classrooms* is not a book about special education. It is not a book about teaching English as a second language. It is a book about teaching reading and writing to every child who walks through the door of your classroom. They include children who need to learn English, children who have a flair for reading and writing, and children for whom literacy is a challenge. This is a book about helping all of them become readers and writers.

⭐ How This Book Is Organized

Incorporating a "whole-part-whole approach," *All Children Read* is organized in three parts. Part 1 helps you develop a broad understanding of the processes by which students learn to read and write. It situates reading and writing instruction in the context of the schools of today and the students you serve. Part 2 looks in depth at the different aspects of reading and writing. Finally, Part 3 describes, level by level, how to put all of this information together into an effective reading program that helps all children become readers and writers.

Part 1: The Literary Process

- Chapter 1, "Teaching Reading," provides an overview of the reading process, exploring the aspects of it and the stages through which readers grow. *All Children Read* addresses the questions "How well are we doing in teaching literacy in America?" and "What can we do to improve?" Some of the answers may surprise you.

- Chapter 2, "The Social and Cultural Contexts for Teaching All Children to Read," looks closely at the diverse group of students that many of you teach or will teach in your classrooms. After developing a deep understanding of how children's home language and home culture, as well their special learning needs, must factor into planning and teaching, the chapter provides suggestions for working effectively with students, other school personnel, and families. Because many of the topics introduced in this chapter are revisited in later chapters, Chapter 2 also establishes the foundation for understanding the concepts of struggling readers and writers, assessment, language diversity, and families and literacy.

- Chapter 3, "What Teachers Need to Know about Language," provides a basic understanding of linguistics, and what you should know about language in order to teach reading and writing well. You will find a thorough discussion of phonological awareness and awareness of phoneme-to-grapheme correspondences, as well as the stages of word recognition. Language and thought are discussed, as well as language diversity.

Part 2: Aspects of Reading

- Chapter 4, "Emergent Literacy," looks at emergent literacy and details the many concepts about language and print, including phonemic awareness, that children develop from early childhood on, as they lay the basis for learning to read and write. There are many ideas, systematically arranged, that you can use to nurture children's emerging literacy.

- Chapter 5, "Building Word Knowledge," explores word knowledge, including a thorough coverage of phonics and developing fluency in children. In *All Children Read,* the authors approach teaching phonics both explicitly and in context. You will find a variety of strategies to make sure that children apply what they are learning about phonics as they read for meaning and write meaningfully.

- Chapter 6, "Comprehension and Response to Literature," lays down a theoretical background in schema theory and reader response theory, and then helps you build a large and diverse repertoire of teaching techniques for reading comprehension.

- Chapter 7, "Reading to Learn: Content and Study Reading," extends the discussion of comprehension to the task of teaching students the special demands of reading and learning from informational texts.

- Chapter 8, "The Writing Process," explores the phases and components of the writing process and explains the writing workshop approach, as well as other approaches to teaching writing, from those that offer the most support to those that give the students the most leeway to create. Suggestions are made for helping students who have difficulty learning to write, and for involving their families to support them.

Part 3: Organizing and Managing the Literacy Program

- Chapter 9, "Putting Effective Literacy Instruction into Practice: K–2," explains how to set up and manage a literacy program for emergent and beginning readers. This chapter shows how to weave together the concepts and strategies that have been introduced earlier in the book. It includes "survival knowledge" for new teachers, providing hints for working with all students, and what to do when problems arise.

- Chapter 10, "Putting Effective Literacy Instruction into Practice in Grades Three to Five," picks up the discussion with third-grade children and shows how to build their reading and writing fluency, and help them read for meaning and learn from texts. This chapter also stresses ways to work with diverse learners.

- Chapter 11, "Reading in the Middle Grades," continues with middle school students and adds a strong emphasis on reading and writing to learn.

- Chapter 12, "Models and Strategies for Teaching ESL and for Teaching Reading in the Mother Tongue: A Focus on Spanish," shows you how to set up instructional programs for English learners. The chapter puts primary emphasis on teaching Spanish speakers, since they constitute the majority of our English learners, but also covers other English learners, too.

Special Features

Throughout the book, special features have been provided to provide a focus on issues of recurring importance to teachers of reading as well as to aid with review and understanding of key concepts in reading instruction.

- Central to this text are **six overriding themes** interwoven throughout the book that are critical in reading instruction today. Special marginal icons call your attention to points in the text that specifically address these themes.

Language & Diversity

Writing & Reading

Technology

Family & Community Literacy

Struggling Reader

Phonics & Phonemic Awareness

- **In-depth coverage of assessment** spread across the chapters integrates formal and informal assessment methods for each of the topics described, rather than relegated to one chapter. Major sections of most chapters specifically address assessment in the context of the chapter discussion. (See list of Assessment coverage on features p. xxvi)

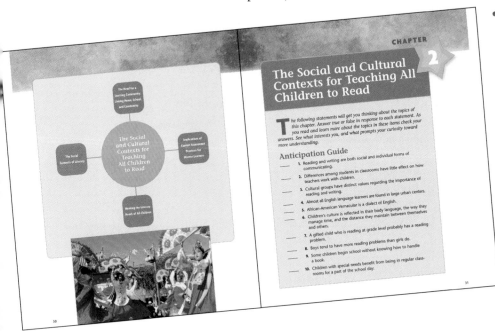

- A **graphic organizer** and **anticipation guide** at the start of each chapter provide readers with an overall perspective of the chapter and the opportunity to assess their level of understanding prior to reading the chapter.

- Every chapter begins with a narrative **vignette** that shares a reading teacher's experience in an active classroom. Each vignette models key concepts from the chapters and demonstrates the challenges of today's classrooms and considerations for addressing children's needs.

- **Correlation to critical standards in literacy.** Throughout this book, the impact of standards on literacy is discussed in a special **Standards & Literacy** feature. These boxes explore standards from an objective perspective and openly discuss the pros, cons, and considerations surrounding their use in literacy education. In addition, the book includes a special appendix outlining the *IRA Standards for Reading Professionals-Revised 2003*, including a discussion of how these new standards differ from the previous IRA standards and how *All Children Read* perfectly correlates to these changes. This special appendix also includes a table of the NCTE Standards for Language Arts (similar to the IRA

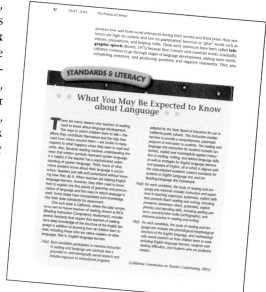

table located on the inside cover of the book) and a correlation of where those standards are addressed within *All Children Read*.

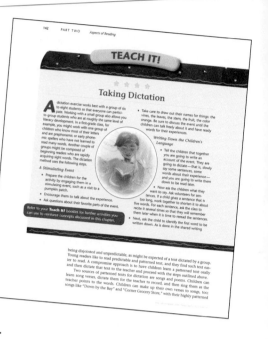

- **TEACH IT!** boxes provide readers with ready-made teaching tips for skill development, as well as for introducing new approaches to the teaching of literacy. Additional Teach It! activities and lesson plans can be found in the *Teach It!* booklet that accompanies each copy of *All Children Read*. As you read through the text, look for *Teach It!* icons in the margin that identify correlating activities from the *Teach It!* booklet that can be used to teach the concepts discussed.

- **World of Reading** boxes investigate a wide array of subjects as they pertain to the field of reading.

- Each chapter ends with a review of the key concepts and literacy terms from the chapter; a list of readings that can extend your knowledge of literacy issues; and special exercises that can be recorded in a reflective journal, that link you with contemporary technology programs and organizations that aid in reading and writing instruction. In addition, **Taking It to the World** exercises challenge readers to apply the material in the chapter, and **Being a Professional Reading Teacher** exercises provide you with suggestions for taking steps to advance your professional growth.

Expand your knowledge of the concepts discussed in this chapter by reading current and historical articles from the *New York Times* by visiting the **Themes of the Times** section of the Companion Website (www.ablongman.com/templeall children1e).

- *All Children Read* also includes two special Internet connections that encourage you to go beyond the text to learn all that you can about literacy instruction. The first can be seen at the start of each chapter in the form of a **Themes of the Times** icon that directs you to the Companion Website (www.ablongman.com/templeallchildren1e) and a direct link to specially selected *New York Times* articles, which present differing perspectives on contemporary topics on literacy and education.

The second connection appears at the end of each chapter in **Connect with Research** sections that prompt you to use **Research Navigator**. This powerful research tool allows you to investigate key concepts and terms from the book using a collection of resources available to you online at http://www.research-navigator.com, including EBSCO's Content Select Academic Journal Database and the *New York Times*. Purchase of this book allows you free access to this exclusive pool of information and data. Your personal code and access instructions are included in the *Teach It!* booklet that came packaged with this copy of *All Children Read*.

✦ Supplements and Learning Aids

To get the most use of *All Children Read: Teaching for Literacy in Today's Diverse Classroom,* a number of useful supplements are available for students and instructors. Speak with your representative about obtaining these supplements for your class!

For the Instructor:

- **Instructor's Manual with Test Items** provides a variety of instructional tools, including chapter summaries, student objectives, activities and discussion questions, vocabulary, test questions, and reflections inspired by the text.

- **VideoWorkshop,** a new way to bring video into your course for maximized learning! This total teaching and learning system includes quality video footage on an easy-to-use CD-ROM plus a Student Learning Guide and an Instructor's Teaching Guide. The result? A program that brings textbook concepts to life with ease and that helps your students understand, analyze, and apply the objectives of the course. VideoWorkshop is available for your students as a value-pack option with this textbook. (Special package ISBN required from your representative.)

- **Computerized Testbank**   The printed Test Bank is also available electronically through our computerized testing system: TestGen EQ. Instructors can use TestGen EQ to create exams in just minutes by selecting from the existing database of questions, editing questions, or writing original questions.

- **Allyn & Bacon Digital Media Archive for Literacy**   This CD-ROM offers still images, video clips, audio clips, weblinks, and assorted lecture resources that can be incorporated into multimedia presentations in the classroom.

- **PowerPoint™ Presentation**   Ideal for lecture presentations or student handouts. (Available for download from Supplement Central at www.suppscentral.ablongman.com)

- **Professionals in Action: Literacy Video**   This 90-minute video consists of 10- to 20-minute segments on Phonemic Awareness, Teaching Phonics, Helping Students Become Strategic Readers, Organizing for Teaching with Literature,

Discussions of Literacy and Brain Research with experts.. The first four segments provide narrative along with actual classroom teaching footage. The final segments present, in a question-and-answer format, discussions by leading experts in the field of literacy.

- **Allyn & Bacon Literacy Video Library**   Featuring renowned reading scholars Richard Allington, Dorothy Strickland and Evelyn English, this three-video library addresses core topics covered in the Literacy classroom: reading strategies, developing literacy in multiple intelligences classrooms, developing phonemic awareness, and much more.

(mylabschool) LEARN MORE ▸

- **My Lab School**   Discover where the classroom comes to life! From videoclips of teachers and students interacting to sample lessons, portfolio templates, and standards integration, Allyn & Bacon brings your students the tools they'll need to succeed in the classroom—with content easily integrated into your existing courses.

    Delivered within Course Compass, Allyn & Bacon's course management system, this program gives your students powerful insights into how real classrooms work and a rich array of tools that will support them on their journey from their first class to their first classroom.

For Students:

- The **_Teach It!_** lesson plan booklet, written by classroom teacher and author Jean Gillett of the Orange County Public Schools in Virginia, contains a wide variety of ready-to-use, classroom-tested activities for teaching critical concepts in Literacy Education. All activities are correlated to lessons in the text itself. This free supplement, packaged with the book, is the perfect resource for first-time and experienced literacy teachers. The Teach It! booklet also contains students' personal access codes and instructions for gaining access to Research Navigator.

- A **Companion Website** (www.ablongman.com/templeallchildren1e) provides a link to additional study items, special _New York Times_ articles, annotated weblinks, and a complete guide to conducting research on the Internet.

- A **Literacy Zone Website (access code required)** (www.ablongman.com/literacy) A website with a wealth of information for pre-service and in-service teachers—whether you want to gain new insights, pick up practical information, or simply connect with one another! It includes State Standard Correlations; Teaching Resources; Ready-to-Use Lesson Plans and Activities for All Grade Levels; Subject-specific Web links for further research and discovery; Information in A&B professional titles to help you in your teaching career; up-to-date "In the News" features and Discussion Forum, and much more.

Acknowledgments

The four of us have enjoyed writing this book, although we have to confess, this manuscript probably set a record for miles traveled before completion. We were brought together in the first place in Brasov, Romania, several summers ago by the Reading and Writing for Critical Thinking Project, which is facilitated by the International Reading Association and funded by the Open Society Institute. Ever since then, we have been offering workshops in Eastern Europe, Russia, Central Asia, Africa, and Latin America, as well as the United States. The authors would like to thank the RWCT volunteers and overseas partners who helped us lift up this great enterprise, Liz for believing in us, and G.S. for being so generous. We learned a ton from all of you.

We thank all teachers, educators, researchers, and our students who contribute so much to this team of authors' learning. In particular, we'd like to recognize the professional contributions of three people without whom this project would not have been complete. Jean Gillet, a long-time friend, author, and reading specialist in the Virginia school system who compiled the *Teach It!* booklet that accompanies *All Children Read* as well as the Instructor's Manual and Test Bank; and Dr. Darlene Michener at California State University–Los Angeles and Sue Kawell, Director of the California State–Los Angeles RICA Rescue project, for their specialized efforts on the compilation of the special RICA material packaged with the book for California educators.

We also would like to thank the reviewers who took time out from busy schedules to share with us their support and expertise and provided us with the valuable feedback that helped to shape this project: Rebecca S. Anderson, University of Memphis; Diane Barone, University of Nevada-Reno; Marian S. Beckman, Edinboro University of Pennsylvania; Charlotte Black, California State University–San Bernardino; Melise Bunker, Palm Beach Atlantic College; Margaret Bell Davis, Eastern Kentucky University; Deborah Doty, Northern Kentucky University; Darlene Michener, California State University–Los Angeles; Michael Moore, Georgia Southern University; John Savage, Boston College; James Zarrillo, California State University–Hayward.

Charles Temple wants to thank his colleagues and students at HWS for good cheer at all hours, the International Reading Association and the Open Society Institute for all their support over the years, and his (oh so) extended family. Donna Ogle wants to thank her husband and her colleagues for their contributions to this book. Bud has provided incredible support for their project and takes ideas right into the field, testing them in his work in Good News Ministries and as a part of the Reading and Writing for Critical Thinking Project. The teachers with whom Donna works in Chicago and in international contexts energized her to share their ideas and hers in this book. Special thanks to Elizabeth Meyers who helped in the development of chapters 7 and 11, to Debbie Gurvitz, Marge Harter, and the rest of the RLI team, and to colleagues on the faculty at NLU. Alan Crawford wants to thank his colleagues and students in the public schools of Los Angeles and Cal State Los Angeles for inspiration over the years; the teachers with whom he's worked—in California, Latin America, Central Asia, Central Europe, and Africa; good friends at UNESCO, the International Reading Association, and the Open Society Institute; and of course, Linda. Penny Freppon wishes to thank Dr. Jill Dillard and Linda Headings for their friendship and professional guidance. Penny also thanks her family, in particular, Don, her husband and intellectual partner with whom all things are possible.

Last but not least, a special thank you to everyone at Allyn & Bacon for their dedication to this project: Senior Acquisitions Editor, Aurora Martinez for being gracious and enthusiastic; Senior Development Editor, Mary Kriener for her patience; Senior Production Editor, Beth Houston for her project coordination; Sara Holliday for her assistance with the standards correlations, and to Kathy Smith for her good eye and detailed oversight.

Contents

3   What Teachers Need to Know about Language   76

Anticipation Guide   77

PART 2   Aspects of Reading   117

⭐4 Emergent Literacy   118

Anticipation Guide   119

⭐5 Building Word Knowledge   156

Anticipation Guide   157

6 Comprehension and Response to Literature   204

Anticipation Guide   205

7 ★ Reading to Learn: Content and Study Reading   252

Anticipation Guide   253

8 ▸ Chapter 8: The Writing Process   302

Anticipation Guide   303

PART 3   Organizing and Managing the Literacy Program   343

9 ▸ Putting Effective Literacy Instruction into Practice: Grades K-2   344

Anticipation Guide   345

10 ⭐ Putting Effective Literacy Instruction into Practice in Grades Three to Five   394

Anticipation Guide   395

⑪ Reading in the Middle Grades   444

Anticipation Guide   445

Models and Strategies for Teaching ESL and for Teaching Reading in the Mother Tongue: A Focus on Spanish   494

Special Features

The Process of Literacy

My biggest reward is having meaningful work to do. I know there's the potential to make a difference as a teacher. Since I am so new, I can't claim that I have made a difference yet, but I do anticipate it!

— ELIZABETH. FIRST-YEAR EIGHTH GRADE TEACHER
CHICAGO

If I had one piece of advice for new teachers it would be, just stay patient. Your first year will be overwhelming, but give it time. The children are getting used to your presence, your teaching style, and your routine. . . . They are eager to read words. When they sit in the literacy area, they read the pictures and imagine that they are reading.

— JOEL, HEAD START TEACHER
BOSTON

If I have a student whose primary language in not English, should I teach that child in her own language sometimes? Should the entire class learn their language as that child learns English? Can I expect her to learn to read in English when she is just learning to speak the language? Does my action depend upon the age of the child?

— CURREY, STUDENT TEACHER
GEORGIA

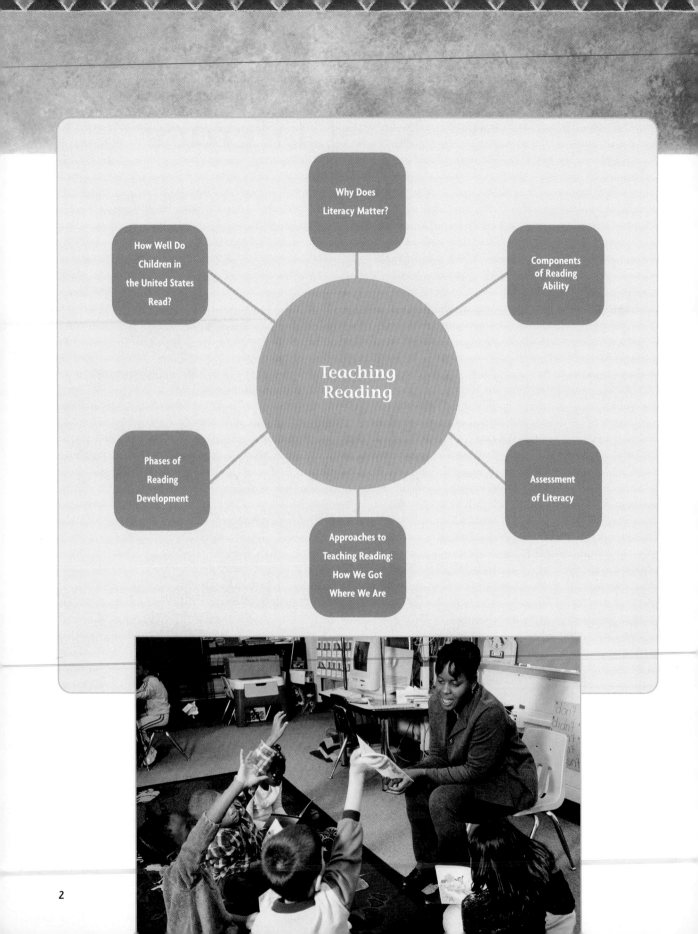

Why Does
Literacy Matter?

How Well Do
Children in
the United States
Read?

Components
of Reading
Ability

Teaching
Reading

Phases of
Reading
Development

Assessment
of Literacy

Approaches to
Teaching Reading:
How We Got
Where We Are

Teaching Reading

*T*he following statements will help get you thinking about the topics of this chapter. Answer true or false in response to each statement. As you read and learn more about the topics in these statements, double-check your answers. See what interests you and prompts your curiosity toward more understanding.

Anticipation Guide

_____ **1.** Literacy makes you smarter because the vocabulary, the information, and the habit of learning from text make you better able to learn new things.

_____ **2.** Among adults, there is little correlation between people's level of reading ability and their income level.

_____ **3.** American children read fairly well. Nine-year-olds scored second in the world on one recent international comparison of basic reading skill.

_____ **4.** Most reading disabilities are caused by malfunctions of the brain, and children with reading problems need a wholly different kind of teaching from what normally developing readers need.

_____ **5.** Research shows that more than 86 percent of the children who get a poor start in learning to read do not catch up with their peers.

_____ **6.** Differences in the amount of reading children do are not significant. What matters in teaching reading is the skill.

_____ **7.** Giving parents ideas for helping their children at home with literacy experiences makes a considerable difference in the children's success in school.

_____ **8.** Reading ability develops through stages in this order: beginning reading, emergent literacy, reading to learn and for pleasure, building fluency, and mature reading.

_____ **9.** The debate between advocates of phonics instruction and advocates of whole-word instruction began in the 1980s in the United States, during the Reagan Administration.

_____ **10.** Testing is the only worthwhile means of assessing children's literacy.

What Makes a Good Teacher
of Reading and Writing?

Good teachers of reading and writing are multitalented people. They do know a great many teaching methods; but they also have a solid background in the science of language and literacy, and they manage to keep up with new developments in their field. They are keen observers of children's learning and inventive designers of lessons and techniques. They can connect with children, and children of all backgrounds like them, trust them, and are inspired by them. They make unusual efforts to connect with their students' families and help the families feel comfortable with the school environment and process. Good teachers of reading and writing love to read and write, and they gladly demonstrate their enthusiasm and share their knowledge with their students.

Good teachers of reading and writing are everywhere—in classrooms from Los Angeles to New York City, from the Rio Grande Valley to the fields of Saskatchewan, and all around the world. Some work in carpeted classrooms equipped with gleaming rows of computers, but just as many make cheerful places out of storage rooms, hallways, or even tropical shelters with rattling tin roofs and open walls—always thoughtfully orchestrating the learning of an individual child or of many different children. You will find them teaching in English, Spanish, French, Tagalog, Arabic, or many languages at once. You will find them in the offices of school principals and districtwide administrators, pondering the best ways to help all the children make progress in reading; you will also find them huddled in deliberations with a parent and a school psychologist, trying to unlock the puzzle of a child's reading difficulty. You will find them in a school or community library, sharing just the right book with a child who is on the threshold of becoming a reader. You will find them creating a lesson without books or paper in a classroom in any one of scores of developing countries for children whose parents never knew the craft of literacy or strategizing in a committee room at the United Nations to help spread literacy to all of the children in the world.

The authors of this book hope that you will share with those good teachers a passion for bringing the gift of literacy to young people, that you will have a fascination for the intricacies of the task and an appreciation of the scholarship necessary to understand how reading works and how it is taught, and that you will continue to grow in your knowledge of reading and reading instruction.

Teaching every child to read and write is the most important mission of the elementary and middle school teacher. Science, mathematics, and social studies; art, physical education, and vocational preparedness; anti-drug abuse and conflict resolution education; civic education and education for self-awareness—all contribute to the making of the well-rounded child. But teaching children to read and write and to use the thinking processes that go with literacy prepares them to learn their other school subjects and to educate themselves for the rest of their lives. The skills of literacy are centrally important for other reasons, too: Being able to read and write makes children smarter and ultimately makes their lives better.

Why Does Literacy Matter?

Teaching children to read not only gives them access to knowledge from print, but also makes them better able to use that knowledge. Children who read store up background knowledge about the things they read about, whether it be nature, science, history, current events, or geography (Stanovich, 1992). This knowledge helps them make sense of the new things they read (Anderson & Pearson, 1984; Hirsch, 1985). Children who read gain bigger vocabularies, too (Smith, 1997), and having bigger vocabularies enables them to notice things (Brown, 1955) and to make finer distinctions in their perceptions of the world (Beck et al., 2002).

Literacy helps children to think in more sophisticated ways. Studies have shown that being readers makes profound differences in people's reasoning, their awareness of language, their awareness of themselves, and even their ability to formulate questions and learn about things they didn't know (Luria, 1976). Children who read and talk about books with others show greater self-awareness and critical thinking (Almasi, 1995), tend to engage ideas more deeply (Eeds & Wells, 1989; Goatley, Brock, & Raphael, 1995), and are more likely to perceive themes in stories: that is, they are more likely to get the message (Lehr, 1988).

Among adults, literacy is associated with better health, better jobs, and better income (National Center for Educational Statistics, 1993, 1992). Surveys show that people who can read and write well tend to have a wider range of options in life. This fact is important to teachers of the lower grades, because students' early experiences as readers will probably have a determining effect on their eventual success or failure to learn to read and write.

Those of you who are fortunate enough to be teachers are in a privileged position to make sure your children have better choices available to them. You can teach them to read and write. But be aware that people with limited literacy do not usually see themselves as having a literacy problem (National Center for Education Statistics, 1993). The task of a teacher of reading, then, will not only be to teach, but also to motivate. Even though reading ability is a ticket to a better future for all students, they might not know that, and their families might not know it either. The teacher will have to make special efforts to encourage every child to *want* to be a reader.

How Well Do Children in the United States Read?

For years, the media have clamored about the poor state of reading in American schools. But the critics have mostly gotten it wrong. They have missed both the considerable achievements as well as the most serious challenges in our nation's efforts to teach all children to read (Klenk & Kibby, 2000). In a nutshell, three things are true about the way children read in the United States:

Because literacy is associated with better health and better socioeconomic standing, ESL programs for adults are important services in all communities.

- **On average, American students excel at basic reading skills.** In terms of basic reading (that is, reading text with essential understanding) taken as a whole, American school children do very well. On the International Educational Achievement study done in the early 1990s (Elley, 1992), American nine-year-olds scored second in the world, surpassed only by children from Finland. Fifteen-year-olds performed respectably: They tied for fifth place, behind New Zealand, France, Sweden, and Finland.

- **Success in reading is spread unevenly, however.** The most successful American students do well in basic literacy tasks, but there are many students who do not perform well. The National Assessment of Educational Progress (NAEP) defines fourth graders with a "basic reading level" this way: These readers should "demonstrate an overall understanding of what they read . . . . [T]hey should be able to make relatively obvious connections between the text and their own experiences, and extend the ideas in the text by making simple inferences." (National Center for Education Statistics, 1994, p. 42; quoted in Snow, Burns, & Griffin, 1998, p. 97). But in 1996, 40 percent of U.S. fourth graders could not read on this basic level. For black students and Hispanic students, the results were even worse: 69 percent of black fourth graders and 64 percent of the Hispanic fourth graders could not read on a basic level. At higher grades, the numbers for the total student populations are still disturbing: 30 percent of the eighth graders and 25 percent of the twelfth graders on the 1996 NAEP survey lacked basic reading ability.

- **Differences in reading achievement are often related to economic circumstances.** Schools in the United States fare worse than those in two thirds of the countries in the industrialized world when it comes to helping all children succeed regardless of their family income (Willms, 1999; Organization of Economic and Community Development, 2000). This fact is especially significant because, with a poverty rate of over 21.5 percent, American schools have by far the highest proportion of children living in poverty—twice as high as children's poverty rate in the United Kingdom (9.9%), and eight times as high as that in Sweden (OERI, 2000). Poorer children may be harder to educate:

    > As a result of their living in poverty, children may bring a variety of challenges to the classroom that necessitate the provision of additional services such as remediation or after school tutoring programs. These children may require basic provisions from the school, such as breakfast and/or lunch, and may lack essential supplies such as pencil and paper. (National Center for Educational Statistics, 2000, p. 14)

- **American students do not excel at thinking through reading.** American students score right at the international average when asked to do higher-order thinking with what they read: to reflect on it, interpret it, or evaluate it drawing on their own prior information. In a recent international comparison of life-skills reading (reading and reasoning for everyday life outside of school), American fifteen-year-olds scored sixteenth out of thirty-two countries, midway between Finland and Brazil (Organization of Economic and Community Development, 2001). Students from Canada, by contrast, ranked in third place, behind Finland and Korea. Results like these matter for many reasons, especially because the job market is increasingly requiring people with skills in communication and problem-solving and analytical skills (Organization for Economic Co-operation and Development, 1995).

Who Are the Struggling Readers?

Struggling Reader

If success in reading in the United States is spread unevenly, how many of our children have "reading disabilities"? A reading disability is said to be present when a child with normal intelligence who has had adequate instruction fails to learn to read. By this definition, experts have estimated that 10–20 percent of all school children have specific reading disabilities (Shaywitz et al., 1992). Some researchers suggest that the figure might be much lower and that deficiencies can be overcome or prevented through appropriate reading-related experiences at home and proper instruction in kindergarten and first grade. (See the World of Reading box.)

Why are such early reading experiences so important? The importance of a good beginning in reading—and the damage that can be done by a poor beginning—was underscored by Connie Juel (1988). Juel surveyed a group of first graders in a Texas public school, found the 20 percent who read least well, and carefully tracked the reading progress of fifty-four of them for three years. At the end of the study, 86 percent of those children were still in the bottom half of the class. Although reading problems had not been severe in first grade, they were serious by fourth grade. There was little reason to hope that these children would close the gap in later years. Why?

Stanovich (1986) has shown how relatively mild deficits in the early years are compounded and grow into severe reading disabilities after three or four years. It is

THE WORLD OF READING

Do Specific Reading Disabilities Exist?

Are problem readers constitutionally different from normally competent readers? The United States has a huge industry devoted to the identification and treatment of learning disabilities, the largest number of which are specific reading disabilities. These disabilities have traditionally been treated as a categorically different set of problems from normal reading development. However, a growing body of evidence suggests that nearly all instances of specific reading disability, including dyslexia, are just extreme cases of difficulty in normal reading development (Snow et al., 1998). Children with reading problems look much like children who can read; they just don't read as well (Stanovich & Siegel, 1994; Vellutino et al., 1996).

When Frank Vellutino and his associates (1996) identified a large number of struggling first graders and tutored them intensively using conventional best practices, only 3 percent of them continued to have difficulty learning to read, and only 1.5 percent had severe difficulties. Vellutino and associates concluded that the difficulties in learning to read

may well be caused by deficits in certain of the cognitive abilities underlying the ability to learn to read, especially phonological abilities such as phoneme analysis, letter-to-sound decoding, name encoding and retrieval, and verbal memory. However, ... the number of children impaired by basic cognitive deficits represents a relatively small percentage of beginning readers compared with the substantially larger percentage of those children whose reading difficulties are caused by experiential and instructional deficits. (Vellutino & Scanlon, 2001, p. 317)

Vellutino and his colleagues (1996) concluded that most of the children who had been identified as possibly having specific reading disability did not suffer from abnormal brain function. Rather, what those children needed was a program of instruction that was carefully tailored to their strengths and needs—one that included meaningful reading and writing as well as attention to word study and (as needed) attention to sounds in words and sound-to-symbol relationships.

known that the more children read, the better they get at reading. The reverse is also true. Whatever mild deficit a child has makes reading difficult, and the difficulty breeds aversion. When Juel asked a fourth-grade subject whether he would rather do chores than read, he responded, "Lady, I'd rather scrub the mold around the bathtub than read!" (Juel, 1988). Children learn to read by reading. But studies of reading habits show huge differences in the amount of reading children do. One study showed that the most prolific three or four readers in a fifth-grade classroom read 100 times as much as the least prolific did (Anderson, Wilson, & Fielding, 1988).

Family and Community Involvement

Family & Community Literacy

Families make a difference in children's preparation to learn to read and write. On the average, children from poor families with little education have more difficulty learning to be literate than children from middle-class homes do (Vernon-Feagans et al., 2001). But the exact reasons for this can be difficult to tease out. If a family is poor—and one fourth of America's children live in families that are poor—then poverty itself presents a complex set of stress factors (Ehrenreich, 2001). If you are poor, it is hard to raise a healthy and competent child. It is hard to buy and prepare nutritious food. It is hard to afford good-quality childcare. It is hard to find the time and energy between jobs to spend time with your child.

Nonetheless, researchers have identified family literacy practices related to children's success in learning to read and write. Many of these may be influenced by the school or by the school working in concert with community partners. Here is a set of factors that the National Research Council (Snow et al., 1998, p. 123) has identified:

1. **Value placed on literacy**: By reading themselves and encouraging children to read, parents can demonstrate that they value reading.
2. **Press for achievement**: By expressing their expectations for achievement by their children, providing reading instruction, and responding to the children's reading initiations and interests, parents can create a press for achievement.
3. **Availability and instrumental use of reading materials**: Literacy experiences are more likely to occur in homes that contain children's books and other reading and writing materials.
4. **Reading with children**: Parents can read to preschoolers at bedtime and other times and can listen to schoolchildren's oral reading, providing assistance as needed.

Family literacy projects that encourage families to read to children and talk with children can have success (Vernon-Feagans et al., 2001). But helping families nurture their children's literacy is not a simple matter. Communication patterns in families are hard to change. Poor African-American families offer children less verbal interaction than middle-class families do, and the shortage of interaction has a strong effect on the children's vocabulary size (Hart & Risley, 1995), which in turn affects learning how to read and write. Here is another problem: It is known that children's preschool experiences with books and print also contribute to their success in learning to read once they arrive in school (Teale & Sulzby, 1987; Snow et al., 1998). But low-income families visit the library half as often on average as middle-class families do (Baker, Serpell, & Sonnenschein, 1995). Nearly all families in the United States have some contact with literacy materials (Teale, 1986), but many low-literacy families really do not seriously engage with print enough to provide experiences for children that teach them (Purcell-Gates, 1995).

Components of Reading Ability

What goes into teaching a child to read? At its simplest, reading is the act of getting meaning from a written text. To read successfully, readers must be able to collect or construct meaning through written symbols. Readers recognize squiggles of ink on a page as letters and words. This activity is called ***word recognition***. To become skilled at word recognition, readers need to be aware of the smallest sounds in language, called *phonemes*. In turn, **phonemic awareness**, as this aptitude is called, prepares readers to look for matches between sounds and letters. Learning letter-to-sound correspondences is the study of **phonics**.

Readers work with the words they recognize, and somewhere in the interplay between what they see on the page and what they expect from what is in their heads, they construct an understanding of what they read. This activity is called **comprehension**. Comprehension is made up of several processes and kinds of knowledge, including knowledge of **vocabulary** and the pronunciation and meaning of words.

Readers eventually come to recognize words quickly and accurately, while comprehending. This activity is called ***reading fluency***. It is hoped that as they have learned to read, they have made books a part of their lives and found authors they especially enjoy and have developed a habit of reading. Eventually, they may learn to hone their minds by weighing an author's words, reflecting on arguments, and coming up with their own interpretations of what they have read, a skill known as interpretation, or **critical reading**.

Here is an illustration of these components in action. Suppose a third grader is asked to read this passage.

> *"Come quick," whispered Mother, from across the street. "The guard is looking the other way."*
>
> *Rebecca clutched her doll close to her chest, crouched low, and scrambled across the empty street toward the lamppost that hid her mother. Just then a search light from atop a darkened building swept the street she had just crossed.*
>
> *"Gestapo," said her mother, hugging the panting child. "They're everywhere." Rebecca squeezed the Star of David around her neck and trembled.*

A number of things have to happen for this passage to be read successfully.

Word Recognition

Of course, readers have to recognize most of the words for the meaning of the passage to be easily available to them. If they are reading the passage on their own, they should find *no more than four* words in this passage that they did not recognize (That is, they should easily recognize 95 percent of the words). If they are reading the passage with the support of a teacher, they would be expected to find *no more than eight* unknown words (a 90 percent recognition rate), according to many reading specialists (e.g., Gillet, Temple, and Crawford, 2004). As will be seen, understanding a passage is much more than the sum of understanding the words. Nonetheless, if readers have to pause and puzzle over the meanings of more than a few words in a passage, their comprehension will be impaired.

How is this word recognition done? By the time they have reached third grade, children will have stored thousands of words in memory that they can recognize instantly. Reading specialists call this store of instantly recognized words their **sight vocabulary**. These readers have been accumulating these words since they were in kindergarten, and as they progress through the grades, they will be learning more new words—thousands more new words—every year.

How do readers go about learning new words? In several ways. For example, if a child failed to recognize *clutched* on a first exposure, the teacher would remind the child to break the word into parts: *cl + utch + ed*. A third grader would be highly skilled at **phonemic segmentation** and would have no difficulty breaking the words in her speech into separate sounds, and she would be able to find matches between letters on the page and speech sounds. But also because she is a third grader, her knowledge of phonics would be a matter not just of matches between individual letters and sounds, but also of matches at the level of patterns of letters combining vowels and consonants. Therefore, she would be able to find the pattern *-utch,* which she would be able to pronounce by relating it to a word she knows: *Dutch.* She would know the *cl-* consonant blend from many words she can read, such as *clap, click, clock*, and *cloud*. She would also know the past tense ending *-ed* from her past reading and study of words.

**Phonics &
Phonemic
Awareness**

Once she worked out the pronunciation of this unfamiliar word, *clutched*, she would recognize it as a word that she has heard and used in speech but not read before. A third grader would be using phonics, but her word knowledge would include not just letter-to-sound relationships, but also knowledge of larger spelling patterns and even of grammar as a factor in word structure.

The word *Gestapo*, on the other hand, would present a different problem. Here she would have to work out the pronunciation of this unfamiliar word, but once she could pronounce the word or an approximation of it, she still would not be able to associate the written word with a word she uses in speech. She would have to use other strategies—in this case, context clues—to decide what the word means. The sentence in which the word appears is

"Gestapo ... They're everywhere."

She would know that Gestapo are referred to as "they," meaning that Gestapo are most likely people. From the context of the passage, she would know to equate Gestapo with the guards who were scanning the street with their searchlights. Having surmised that the girl in the passage with the Star of David was Jewish, this reader would reason that Gestapo were guards or police who hunted Jews at some time in history. Perhaps they were German soldiers or police, and perhaps the setting was the time around World War II. In this second example, this reader not only learned to pronounce a previously unfamiliar word, but also derived an approximation of its meaning. From the context of the passage, she learned a new item of vocabulary.

This example illustrates how recognizing words is a complex business involving several strategies. The example features a third grader who is a reasonably successful reader; when younger children are just beginning to recognize words, still more strategies enter the picture.

Comprehension

It was said that understanding a text is more than the sum of understanding the words. Now consider the processes by which a reader does come to understand the text. Look again at the passage on page 10. How would readers go about understanding it?

First, they would be helped by their knowledge of vocabulary (Pressley, 2000). They use their knowledge of words such as *guard, searchlight*, and *Star of David* to help them construct the meaning of the text; as was just seen, one reader reasoned that the word *Gestapo* provides a new name for a concept she already had: the Nazi police. Knowing vocabulary provides readers with building blocks to help them construct their understanding of the passage. But items of vocabulary are not enough by themselves. Although vocabulary is necessary to understanding the text, readers must also create a context in which choices among competing meanings of words can be made. Without a context to give these words meaning, a reader does not know whether a *chest* refers to a box or a rib cage, whether *scrambling* is a way of preparing eggs or of moving our bodies, whether *post* refers to a job or a pole, or whether *sweeping* is an act of cleaning or a kind of motion across a surface. Here, then, is something of a paradox: Although knowing the vocabulary helps a reader to construct a meaning for the text, the meaning that is constructed for the text also helps the reader to understand the words.

Second, readers have background knowledge or **cognitive schemes** that help them to understand the passage. Words such as "whispered," "guard," and "search light" are more than vocabulary items. Together, they help young readers to construct mental frameworks for understanding that the situation described in the passages is one of danger, of stealth, of the neccessity to avoid detection. It is important that readers be able to supply this framework themselves, because the situation of needing to avoid detection is not stated explicitly by the text. From the mention of Star of David, readers might also suppose, without being told explicitly, that the passage has to do with the flight of Jews from persecution by the Nazis during World War II—something they know about because they have read about it in other books, such as Lois Lowry's *Number the Stars* and Carol Matas's *Daniel's Story*.

Third, readers make **inferences** about what is going on in the text. Although the text never said that Rebecca was a young girl, a reader might notice the details of Rebecca's clutching her doll and depending on her mother for guidance and infer that Rebecca was young. And although the text left a gap between Rebecca's scrambling across the dangerous street and her being hugged by her mother, a reader can infer that she made it safely across the street into her waiting mother's arms.

Fourth, young readers can **visualize**, or form mental images of, what the words in the text describe. They can picture a darkened street (even though the text never said explicitly that the street was dark), with silent, unlit buildings on each side. They might imagine a nearly silent scene. If they were asked, they could draw a picture of the street.

Fifth, if the teacher asked the young readers to say what they had read, the readers would be able to say, "A young Jewish girl snuck across the street and got away from the guards." In other words, they were able to find the **main idea** of the passage.

Sixth, in retelling what they just read about, our young readers make it clear that they think the girl was the main character—the hero, or the protagonist—of this text and that the rest of the text might tell about her attempts to escape from the Gestapo, the Nazi police. In other words, readers assume that they are reading a story, and they use their knowledge of the **structure of stories** to make predictions about what will follow in the coming pages. Their knowledge and use of the structure of the text make up one more important part of their comprehension of it.

Reading Fluency

Another aspect of reading that is related to word recognition and comprehension together is reading fluency. A child would not be considered a competent reader of this passage unless he or she could read it fairly **quickly and accurately** and with some **inflection**—some changes in the tone of voice that roughly paralleled the emotional or meaningful contours of the text. Reading fluency is both an indicator of and a contributor to successful reading. If you hear a child reading smoothly and accurately, you can infer that the child recognizes the words efficiently. If the child also reads with appropriate inflection, you can also infer that the child is comprehending the text to some degree (although occasionally a child will concentrate on rendering a text aloud with accuracy and pay little attention to the meaning). In this case, fluency is an indicator of the child's ability to recognize words and to comprehend text. It is also known that if readers read the text fluently, their fluency will contribute to their understanding. That is because having the ability to read strings of words smoothly and accurately leaves the mind plenty of capacity to appreciate the meaning of the text (Perfetti, 1992; Pressley, 2000). To illustrate this point, imagine two bicycle riders, one to whom riding comes naturally and a novice who is still struggling to balance, pedal, and steer the bicycle all at the same time. Which one do you suppose will enjoy the scenery?

Reading experts have found it worthwhile to give children practice in reading for fluency because a well-developed capacity for relatively fast and accurate reading facilitates understanding. It is also a transferable ability: Becoming a fluent reader carries over from one text to another. That is why thoughtful teachers provide children plenty of opportunities to read texts that are fairly easy for them.

Critical Literacy

Critical literacy is another aspect of literacy that our third graders might or might not call into play. Critical literacy means reading with polite skepticisms, examining a text's hidden assumptions and bringing to light the devices by which the text might be intended to work its effects on the reader (Luke & Freebody, 1999).

Critical reading leads us to ask questions such as the following:

- Why is the author telling us this?
- Whose voices are left unheard?
- What is this text trying to do to me?
- What questions can be asked about the message?

Critical insights that our young readers might reach could include some like these: Just as Indians used to be commonly portrayed as riding on horseback and shooting arrows at wagon trains, Jewish children are frequently and stereotypically portrayed as trying to escape persecution. Surely there are other interesting things about their lives that could be written about. Also, in American children's books, the example of ethnic persecution that is most often given has to do with Jews more than fifty years ago. Of course, the Holocaust was consummately important and should not be forgotten. But there are cases of ethnically motivated persecution going on in the world in our own time that get much less attention, particularly children's attention. Shouldn't the focus on issues of justice be broadened to include contemporary problems that one can still do something about?

In summary, it has been shown that the act of reading has several components and that each of them has its own complexity. To read, readers must recognize words, and word recognition entails not only having words stored in memory for instant recognition, but also knowing how to pronounce a word from its sequence of letters and word parts and being able to infer the meaning of words from their context. Reading also involves comprehension, which in turn includes knowing vocabulary, having and appropriately calling to mind frameworks of prior knowledge, making inferences, visualizing, getting main ideas, and knowing and making use of the structure of the text. Furthermore, skilled reading also includes fluency: reading quickly, accurately, and with appropriate inflection. Fluency is a sign of skilled reading, and the ability to read fluently also enables meaningful reading. Finally, reading ability can include critical reading. In the chapters that follow, you will see all of these aspects of reading in more detail. But first, it must have occurred to you that the issues involved in reading might look different if one were describing youngsters just learning to read or middle school students using their reading ability to study a science text. Now look at the way reading ability develops as children progress through the grades.

Phases of Reading Development

Using the word *development* to describe reading implies that the learner doesn't simply wait passively to take in reading instruction from a teacher, but rather undertakes the interaction among growth, experience, and discovery that can be called **developmental learning**. Developmental learning proceeds according to these factors:

- Cognitive growth of learners, which opens up capacities for learning
- The provision of relevant models of skilled performance and challenges in learners' own performances from their surroundings
- Active discoveries initiated by the learners themselves

To say that learning to read is developmental implies that all children go through roughly the same set of stages as they learn to read. It implies that their maturation plays a part but that the stimulation, encouragement, and modeling of reading and writing behavior they receive are important, too. It also implies that while the teaching that learners experience can be beneficial, teaching alone will not result in meaningful learning without the learners' reorganizing and expanding their own powers through activities of discovery. Developmental learning follows predictable pathways, although a learner's development along those pathways is more predictable in the early stages than in later ones.

Emergent Literacy

The earliest period or stage of learning to read and write has come to be called **emergent literacy**. In early childhood, before children enter formal instruction, they discover useful insights about literacy; and these insights become the basis on which their later learning can be built, even the learning that is orchestrated by their teachers in school. In the emergent stage, learning about literacy involves the following:

- Learning about the nature of reading
- Learning what books are, what kinds of experiences come from them, and how they are put together
- Learning about language itself, that it comes in patterns like stories and poems, and that even though you cannot see it, it is real enough to be captured in books and revisited again and again
- Learning that language comes in units of words and even smaller units and that the language one speaks while reading bears some kind of relationships to marks on a page

As awareness of emergent literacy has grown, teachers have promoted practices among families that help children's literacy to emerge. Head Start, the federally funded early childhood education program for disadvantaged children, now includes as part of its programming reading to children and other literacy activities that are embedded in children's daily play and learning activities. In some communities, parents are given a children's book when they leave the hospital with a newborn, to underscore the importance of reading to children and to make the point that it is never too early to begin reading to a child.

With their growing awareness of emergent literacy, teachers have developed means of observing and assessing children's early concepts of literacy. These include approaches such as Marie Clay's *Concepts about Print* test, Elizabeth Sulzby's Emergent Storybook Reading Inventory, Darrell Morris's *Early Reading Screening Inventory*, and studies of invented spelling, as described by Richard Gentry or Temple, Nathan, Burris, and Temple. (You will see all of these presented in detail later in the book.) Using these investigative approaches yields often amazing profiles of what children have discovered about literacy. However, they also give cause for concern when they show that important concepts about literacy have not yet emerged in a child, because it is known that those concepts will be important to the child as he or she learns to read. That point leads to the third contribution of our understanding of emergent literacy.

Learning to read in school without a fully developed foundation of emergent literacy concepts has been likened to trying to climb stairs when the first several steps are missing. Because teachers are aware of the importance of emergent literacy, they are now able to teach all children in a way that gives them another chance to develop emergent concepts about literacy. They can also provide finely tuned tutoring to children who need it so that more children can get off to the best possible start in learning to read and write.

Beginning Reading

In late kindergarten and first grade, most children enter the phase of beginning reading. Most prominent in this stage is their learning to read words, but children are also learning to understand what they read. The task of learning to make words emerge from different combinations of letters on the page is so challenging that teachers often must remind children to "go back and read that line so it sounds like talk" or ask them, "Does that make sense?"

That children are ready to learn words and coordinate reading them with making sense of what they read shows that this stage of beginning reading comes after much prior learning. After all, emergent readers must come to understand that print, and not pictures, talks (Clay, 1985) and that a reader is not free to say just any words when paging through a text but must come up with pronunciations of the words whose representations are printed there (Sulzby, 1985). They have a sense of the patterns of stories and poems, and they know how to follow them to make meaning.

With these understandings in place, children are able to concentrate on words and develop strategies for sounding them out, as well as develop sight vocabularies (stores of words in memory that they can recognize at sight, or without having to work them out letter by letter). They are ready, though they often need reminding, to find humor, suspense, and surprise in what they read—in other words, to make meaning.

Building Fluency

By late first grade or early second grade, children have enough experience in reading words and following messages that their reading is becoming fluent: more rapid and more accurate. For children who have often been read to, this period can be a joyful affirmation of their own competence. After a period of struggling to read texts that were far simpler and less meaningful than the stories they had long heard read to them, chidlren are at last able to do for themselves what adults had to do for them. For children who are not so lucky, however, this period can be a hard trek through unfamiliar territory, as the fascinations of reading materialize only gradually. For the first type of child, teachers will find that their main task is to keep providing more books to a hungry reader. For the second type of child, the teacher will have to celebrate gains but also gently and insistently push the child to read—and to read more challenging texts.

If the teacher is successful, then both types of children will rapidly amass sight words and steadily increase both the quantity and speed of their reading. They will be preparing themselves for the next stage of reading, which is called *reading to learn and for pleasure.* Even so, wide differences will begin to open up here in the amount of reading children do and the size of their sight vocabularies.

Reading to Learn and for Pleasure

By the beginning of third grade and increasingly in fourth grade, a threshold is crossed, and the emphasis shifts from learning to read to reading to learn—and, one might add, reading for pleasure. By now, children will be expected to read and follow directions and to gain information from texts. At the same time, they may be expected to read chapter books and novels and have something to say about them in their response journals and in their book clubs or whatever their discussion groups are called.

Reading for pleasure opens up a child's world and encourages imagination and inquiry.

A period for reading and writing instruction is still provided every day, but more and more time is given to free reading and discussion, as well as to writing workshops. These activities are useful, even essential, because children must practice literacy to develop it. Nonetheless, there is still a place for teaching the students *how* to comprehend, interpret, and compose. There is also still a need to make students aware of the structure of written words and the way our English vocabulary works. This is because word knowledge is not gained in the early years and then is done with. On the contrary, because the collection of words children encounter in text change significantly at around fourth grade (from mostly words derived from Anglo-Saxon to words derived from Latin and Greek), there are new concepts to be learned about words though this period.

It is in fourth grade that problems in reading have traditionally become obvious. That is because reading shows up as a problem that is affecting students' learning in other subjects. It is also because the unsuccessful struggles to learn to read well have led children to frustration and poor motivation. Indeed, children's self-esteem might have begun to suffer because they haven't succeeded in a skill that is highly valued in school (Stanovich, 2002). Although troubled readers can and certainly should be helped to overcome their difficulties, doing so is time consuming at this stage, especially since there is much content to be learned by now throughout the school day. Because they now understand how earlier experiences contribute to children's reading abilities, many teachers, and whole programs such as Reading Recovery, are placing their greatest emphasis on getting children off to a good start in reading, so that the problem of the "fourth grade slump" can be avoided wherever possible.

Mature Reading

After fifth grade and certainly by sixth grade, children who have made normal progress as readers have gradually shown other abilities that are characterized as mature reading. They read with an appreciation of the author's style, and they enjoy reading passages aloud to friends or try to imitate an author's style in their own writing. They read with an awareness of issues and themes and see a novel not only as a series of events, but also as a metaphorical commentary on life. They might read several books on a theme and talk perceptively on the ways the authors' views affected the different presentations. They might practice critical literacy, argue back against the theme of a book, or be offended by its sexist or racist overtones. In any case, they are more analytical and more philosophical in what they look for in texts and in the ways they respond to them.

They are also more strategic. They can read for information, and they have strategies for previewing, questioning, marking, note taking, reviewing, and studying books they read for information.

As we noted at the outset of this section, one characteristic of developmental learning is that the earlier periods of development are more predictable and more commonly experienced than the latter ones. That is certainly true with respect to mature reading. Some readers show evidence of mature reading by the time they enter fourth grade. Many more show it by seventh or eighth grade. But many others rarely do this kind of reading.

In summary, this chapter has discussed reading in terms of some of its core processes: *word recognition, comprehension, fluency,* and *critical literacy*. It has also looked at reading in terms of the stages children pass through: *emergent literacy, beginning reading, building fluency, reading to learn and for pleasure,* and *mature reading*. Later sections of this book will revisit each of the aspects of reading that must be developed. Then you will see how teachers help children lean to read and write at every grade level.

Approaches to Teaching Reading: How We Got Where We Are

In 1908, Edmund Burke Huey (1908) chronicled the major approaches to teaching reading that were practiced in American schools in his time. He found an unreconciled difference between teachers who preferred to emphasize words as wholes and teachers who taught students the relationships between letters and sounds. As Huey noted, this distinction was already very old—perhaps 350 years old, according to one of his sources. Huey offered research—his own and that of others—that showed that the eye and brain take just as long to recognize a single letter as they do a whole word. This finding, building on a reaction to the heavy drill orientations of reading approaches in the late nineteenth century, encouraged a movement toward whole-word teaching approaches that lasted through the mid-1960s. Even then, the issue was not settled, and between Huey's time and ours, there has been an intense outpouring of research on the issue and hundreds of conferences have been attended by thousands of educators, yet the tension between different approaches to teaching beginning reading remains.

In the 1960s, Jeanne Chall (1967) reviewed the available research on the question of the best approaches to beginning reading. She found that in the decades leading up to the time when she was writing, most children in the United States were taught to read in basal reading programs, that is, in textbooks composed of short reading passages with graduated difficulty levels. For the most part, the basal reading programs, such as the popular Dick and Jane series, used whole-word approaches (what Chall called a "meaning emphasis") and did not teach phonics (what Chall called a "code emphasis"). According to the studies she reviewed, however, reading approaches that *did* use phonics showed better results than programs that did not. Following the publication of Chall's influential book, publishers began to include phonics instruction in their basal reading programs.

But that did not settle the matter. Many teachers, such as New Zealander Sylvia Ashton-Warner (1963), continued to favor whole-word approaches and argued that their use emphasized meaning, whereas the phonics approaches could lead children to focus on the small parts of reading—the letters and sounds—without an adequate appreciation of what the letters were supposed to add up to. Indeed, some of the reading materials that came into use during the 1960s focused so much on letter-to-sound regularities that they left very little meaning to be pursued. "Linguistic readers" contained text like this: "A man had a tin pin. It's a pin for a cap. It's a cap for Dan." Advocates of meaning-centered reading instruction worried that if children mostly read text that was so devoid of meaningful content, they could easily become confused about the true purpose of reading: to construct meaning from print.

Cognitive Revolution

The 1970s saw a revolution in the way scholars thought of language learning. The field of psycholinguistics was developing, largely under the influence of an ingenious linguist named Noam Chomsky. The researchers whom Chomsky inspired began to accumulate evidence that children learn language by exercising a built-in capacity for discovery. As long as they are in the company of people who talk to them and who model language, and as long as those around them honor children's own needs to communicate, children will learn to talk. Gradually, by stages, through an amazing exercise of finely tuned linguistic discovery processes, children learn language.

Almost immediately, theorists began to see applications of psycholinguistic theory to the acquisition of reading. Frank Smith wrote an influential book called *Psycholinguistics and Reading* (1973), in which he and others argued that children could learn to read, in large part, by discovery and encouragement. One of the contributors to that book, Kenneth Goodman (1967), had offered a conception of reading as "a psycholinguistic guessing game." Goodman's work, along with that of some imaginative Australians such as Don Holdaway (1979) and Andrea Butler and Jan Turbill (1985) gave rise to what came to be known as the *whole language movement.*

Whole language advocates embraced many child-centered approaches to teaching. The writing process approach of Donald Graves (1982) and Lucy Calkins (1996) was taken up by whole language advocates and became part of the movement. So did the literature-based approaches of Dorothy Strickland (1991) and Nancie Atwell (1985). Whole language classrooms were (and are) bursting with children's creativity, as children have rich experiences that stimulate talk, as they read and listen to much good literature, and as they write out and act out their own ideas.

On the psychological front, the new field of cognitive psychology yielded studies of comprehension that were relevant to reading. A U.S. government grant to the University of Illinois created the Center for the Study of Reading, where Richard Anderson and David Pearson (1984) and others elaborated a theory of comprehension called *schema theory.* As was seen in the example of children reading the passage on pages 10–13, schema theory stresses the reader's active role in making meaning. Schema theory was highly compatible with the work of both the psycholinguists inspired by Noam Chomsky and the constructivist theories of intellectual development inspired by Swiss psychologist Jean Piaget and others. The theory found ready acceptance in the 1970s and 1980s, and most reading experts still accept it today in some form or another as our guiding theory of how comprehension works. Like psycholinguistic research before it, schema theory seemed to lend support to the child-centered, discovery-oriented beliefs of the whole language movement.

Research-Based Emphasis

Still, the disagreements between the meaning-centered advocates and the code-centered advocates continued. In the late 1980s, the U.S. Department of Education commissioned another examination of beginning reading instruction. The resulting work was *Beginning to Read* (1990), by a psychologist, Marilyn Jager Adams. In it, Adams concluded that exposure to print and enthusiastic encouragement might work in some cases but that they were not sufficient to teach all children to read. Like the evidence Jeanne Chall had reviewed twenty years before, the evidence Adams collected led her to conclude that reading approaches that explicitly and systematically taught children the code that links speech sounds to patterns of letters in words were more successful than those that did not. Adams urged teachers to give primacy to teaching children to decode and recognize words, even as they immersed the children in print and encouraged them to write.

Adams also passed along another finding from late twentieth century research on reading: the importance of children's awareness of **phonemes**, the smallest sound units in words. In a host of studies, phonemic awareness in first grade was found to make a critical difference in whether or not children learned to read successfully, and Adams made a strong suggestion that teachers emphasize phonemic awareness and letter-to-sound correspondences in their early reading instruction. She said in her conclusion,

> *In summary, deep and thorough knowledge of letters, spelling patterns, and words, and of the phonological translations of all three, are of inescapable importance to both skillful reading and its acquisition. By extension, instruction designed to develop children's sensitivity to spellings and their relations to pronunciations should be of paramount importance in the development of reading skills. That is, of course, precisely what is intended of good phonics instruction. (Adams, 1990, p. 416)*

In the 1980s, Vice President George H. W. Bush assembled fifty governors at the University of Virginia to work out a plan that would use U.S. schools to make American students more competitive in the world. In an initiative called Education 2000, led by their chairman, then-Governor Bill Clinton of Arkansas, the group agreed to specify explicit performance standards for reading and other subjects at intervals throughout the grades and to test students' abilities to meet those standards. Many states added standards for what schools of education should teach new teachers to teach. (See the Standards and Literacy box.) As individual states designed their standards, many drew on the work of Marilyn Jager Adams and like-minded writers and called for the teaching of letter-to-sound correspondences and the development of phonemic awareness. In 1996, for example, the California State Legislature passed a bill that specified that the training of all elementary teacher certification candidates include:

(i)   The study of organized, systematic, explicit skills including phonemic awareness, direct systematic, explicit phonics, and decoding skills.

(ii) A strong literature, language, and comprehension component with a balance of oral and written language.

(iii) Ongoing diagnostic techniques that inform teaching and assessment.

(iv) Early intervention techniques.

(v)   Guided practice in a clinical setting. (quoted in Snow et al., 1998, p. 302)

Also in the late 1990s, a study of early reading difficulties was undertaken by the Committee on the Prevention of Reading Difficulties in Young Children, a group of reading experts assembled under the auspices of the National Science Foundation. The resulting report, entitled *Preventing Reading Difficulties in Young Children* (Snow et al.,

STANDARDS & LITERACY

★ ★ High-Stakes Testing ★ ★

Twenty years ago, the U.S. government publication *A Nation at Risk* seriously called into question the quality of American schools. The report and its claims surprised many, because the trend in American students' achievement scores throughout the twentieth century had always shown small but steady increases. Besides, international comparisons of industrialized countries showed American students performing at or above average of industrialized countries in the world. In reading, U.S. students did better than average, and one study from the early 1990s showed that American fourth graders performed second in the world.

Nonetheless, although there might not have been grounds to declare a crisis twenty years ago, a nearly flat line in educational improvement was still worrisome, and the demands placed on education were escalating quickly. Changes in employment demographics throughout the country identified a need for more advanced literacy skills. The sharp rise in the need to teach students to read and think skillfully required urgent attention, even if the sudden demand did not constitute a massive failure of the schools, as the federal report alleged.

Historically, the governance of education in the United States has been the responsibility of the states, but the initiation of America 2000 began a movement toward standards-based education that continues today. As a result of this initiative, most states set performance standards for children, and by the year 2000, seventeen states had developed tests for those standards. At present, there is considerable variety from state to state in what children are expected to learn and what teachers are expected to teach. For instance, in Virginia, there are specific standards for children in each grade, such as the following for first graders:

The student will orally identify and manipulate phonemes (small units of sound) in syllables and multisyllabic words.

    a. *Count phonemes (sounds) in syllables or words with a maximum of three syllables.*

    b. *Add or delete phonemes (sounds) orally to change syllables or words.*

    c. *Create rhyming words orally.*

    d. *Blend sounds to make word parts and words with one to three syllables.*

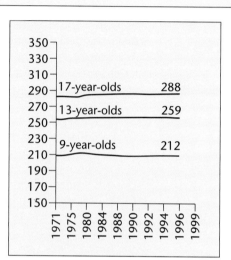

Performance level descriptions:
150: Simple, discrete reading tasks
200: Partially developed skills and understanding
250: Interrelate ideas and make generalizations
300: Understand complicated information
350: Learn from specialized reading materials

FIGURE

Reading Proficiency

Average reading proficiency on a scale of 0–500 for various age groups, 1971–1999, based on nationwide tests given by the National Assessment of Educational Progress.

Source: "The Condition of Education 2001." June 2001. National Center for Education Statistics.

The student will apply phonetic principles to read and spell.

    a. *Use beginning and ending consonants to decode and spell single-syllable words.*

    b. *Use two-letter consonant blends to decode and spell single-syllable words.*

    c. *Use beginning consonant digraphs to decode and spell single-syllable words.*

    d. *Use short vowel sounds to decode and spell single-syllable words.*

    e. *Blend beginning, middle, and ending sounds to recognize and read words.*

    f. *Use word patterns to decode unfamiliar words.*

    g. *Use compound words.*

    h. *Read and spell common, high-frequency sight words, including the, said, and come.*

(Virginia State Department of Education, 2002, pp. 6–7).

In New York State, by contrast, the standards are specified only for students at "elementary," "intermediate," and "commencement" levels. They are expressed in broad terms that leave more to the teacher's discretion than Virginia's standards do. For example, the New York standard for reading and decoding that parallels the standard from Virginia simply states that the "elementary" student should be able to:

> *Make appropriate and effective use of strategies to construct meaning from print, such as prior knowledge about a subject, structural and context clues, and understanding of letter-sound relationships to decode difficult words.*

(New York State Education Department, 2002, p. 2.)

Although the federal government has not required a single set of tests for use nationwide, connecting results with federal monies through the No Child Left Behind Act has placed great pressure on states and schools to comply. But that does not mean that everyone agrees with the standards movement. Richard Allington (2000), a prominent reading expert and leader in the International Reading Association, has noted two major omissions from the government's list of required areas of focus. One is *the habit of reading*. Allington argues that no amount of skills instruction is as effective as simply motivating children to read a lot, and children will not become proficient readers unless they read. The other is the absence of what Allington calls *thoughtful reading*: reading to solve problems, to generate ideas of one's own, to think critically, and to think interpretively. Allington points out that, although not required by the federal government, many state standards do include these two concerns. For example, New York State expects every student to read twenty-five books a year at her or his grade level.

Another issue surrounding standards education is what to do if children do not pass the state tests. In what has been called *high-stakes testing,* many states have ruled that children will not be promoted to the next grade, that teachers and principals will not get pay raises, or even that schools will lose their accreditation or be closed if scores fail to meet the standards. The federal government has offered parents the right to transfer their children out of a low-achieving school to a higher-achieving one or to a public charter school. They have also offered vouchers that are good for tutoring services for children who do not pass the tests. Many observers have complained that these are severe consequences to base on a one-time event such as an examination, but polls show that a majority of parents support having standards and the tests that go with them (Public Agenda On-Line, 2002). Learning standards are here to stay, and those who teach, as well as those who train teachers, must be mindful of them.

1998), recommended that teachers encourage students' growth in language and general knowledge, their exposure to and appreciation of literature, and their opportunities to write, while also providing instruction to boost phonemic awareness, knowledge of letter-to-sound relationships, fluency, vocabulary, and comprehension.

In 1997, Congress commissioned yet another group of experts to "assess the effectiveness of different approaches used to teach children to read" (National Reading Panel web site, 2003). This was the National Reading Panel, organized by the National Institute of Child Health and Human Development (NICHD) at the National Institutes of Health. After reviewing what they considered to be evidence-based studies of reading over a two-year period, the National Reading Panel published their findings in *The Report of the National Reading Panel: Teaching Children to Read* (2000). In it, the panel made a number of recommendations, including a strong push for skills instruction, especially in the recognition of words and the skills that support word recognition: awareness of speech sounds and knowledge of phonics. (See the web site of the National Reading Panel at www.nationalreadingpanel.org.)

With the reauthorization of the Elementary and Secondary and Education Act (U.S. Department of Education, 2001), called *No Child Left Behind* (signed into law on January 8, 2001), the administration of President George W. Bush insisted that every state develop learning standards in the basic subjects, including reading, and test every child annually from third grade up. (Testing is being phased in over a four-year period.) The act requires that schools receiving federal funding use "evidence-based" instructional practices, and for its source of evidence, the Administration embraced the recommendations of the National Reading Panel, with special focus on five particular recommended areas of focus: phonological awareness, phonics, fluency, vocabulary, and comprehension.

Programs such as Head Start and Jumpstart help prepare children for learning by promoting an interest in reading at a very young age.

However, there are other important aspects of literacy instruction to be considered. As was noted in the Committee on the Prevention of Reading Difficulties in Young Children (Snow et al., 1998) recommendations, teachers need to take care to "develop children's language" and help them gain "a holistic understanding of reading." The research of Vellutino and colleagues (1996) and Dahl and Freppon (1992, 1994) lends weight to those recommendations. The Committee urged that renewed efforts be made to involve families in their children's literacy and called for teachers to understand and accommodate cultural and linguistic differences in literacy learning. In addition, many teachers and specialists worry that teaching reading skills without immersing children in plentiful opportunities to speak, listen, read, and write could be unproductive. Children need skills, but they also need to understand the purposes of reading and writing and to be practitioners of both.

Today, many reading educators speak of the need for **balanced instruction** (Raphael, 1998) in teaching literacy. The term refers to an approach that, on the one hand, pays due attention to the need for giving children meaningful encounters with written language so that they will understand its purposes and forms and come to enjoy it. On the other hand, *balance* also means that teachers must ensure that children learn skills that make reading possible. The Teach It! box introduces a four-part model for literacy instruction that can help to promote the teaching of skills while integrating them into meaningful literacy practices.

TEACH IT!

* * * *

A Framework for Literacy Development

Intense scrutiny of the reading process over the past several decades has greatly increased our understanding of how children learn to read. We now know that, given the right instruction, nearly all children can learn to read (Vellutino et al., 1996). We know that what teachers do makes an enormous difference, particularly when there is a schoolwide movement to improve reading (Hoffman, 1991; Taylor et al., 1999). In addition, providing balanced literacy instruction creates a meaningful literacy experience for students. The following four-part approach outlines the shape of lessons that encourage children's discoveries while also offering careful guidance, practice, and, above all, the free use of reading and writing for children's own uses.

Students who are learning to read and write benefit from a program of instruction that devotes time to these four kinds of activity every day:

1. ***Demonstration and Immersion:*** *Seeing the acts of reading and writing carefully demonstrated to them as they are drawn into meaningful literacy activities*

   In the parts of lessons devoted to modeling acts of reading and writing, the teacher shows students how books are laid out, how words are read, and how writing is done. At the same time, students realize that reading is "talk written down" as they create texts that they can read for practice and to see how speech relates to print. Classroom activities include shared book reading with big books, language experience activities in which children's talk is written down; "thinking aloud" with one's own comprehension processes; demonstrating the writing process; and reading aloud to children

and leading discussions of authors and their styles, of genres, and of their demands on the reader.

ACTION: *The teacher reads a book or shares a piece of writing, thereby showing the whole from which the part (the skill) will be taken. The purpose is to show the context in which the skill makes sense.*

2. ***Attention to Detail:*** *Paying attention to detail, and developing their knowledge of the structure of written language*

   Research shows that learning the structure of written language— the ways in which letters spell words—should not be left to chance. Nor should strategies for comprehending and interpreting or for composing texts in the writing process. Although meaningful reading and writing should get the bulk of attention in reading instruction, brief, focused, and carefully sequenced lessons can help students become better readers and writers in the long run. When you begin lessons with demonstration and immersion and proceed to attention to detail, children see the context out of which a detail is taken and understand it as part of a meaningful whole. Then they should take the part—the literacy skill—and relate it back to a meaningful act of reading.

ACTION: *The teacher highlights the skill—the part—and makes sure students understand what it is and how it works.*

3. ***Guided Practice:*** *Having guided practice in meaningful reading and writing so that they may internalize effective strategies*

(continued on next page)

Continued

During guided practice, students work closely with the teacher, watching how literacy task are carried out, and then do it themselves. Through this practice, they learn effective strategies for reading and writing texts and constructing and communicating meaning.

ACTION: Students practice a skill under the teacher's supervision, with prompt correction and reteaching if needed.

4. ***Application and Extensions:*** Carrying out independent activities in which they apply and extend their reading and writing abilities and develop lifelong habits of literacy

The goal of reading and writing is meaningful (and enjoyable, purposeful, and edifying) communication. Students need plenty of opportunities to exercise their reading and writing abilities for their own

Refer to your **Teach It!** booklet for futher activities you can use to reinforce concepts discussed in this chapter.

purposes. Students learn much of what they need to know about literacy by practicing it. They learn vocabulary, text structures, and background information by reading; and they learn how words are structured as well as rhetorical devices for writing clearly for real audiences. Indeed, it is an empty exercise to teach reading without encouraging children to become people who read or to teach writing without encouraging them to become writers.

ACTION: Students are encouraged and reminded to use the skill in context as they read and write independently.

Teachers who dedicate themselves to becoming adept at providing the kind of reading education described in this basic four-step model will be effective in the classroom. However, truly effective teachers add to those abilities ongoing assessment of what students learn and how they go about learning, involvement of parents in learning, and respectful treatment of all children regardless of their cultural background.

Assessment of Literacy

Assessment is a vital part of teaching reading and writing. Assessment allows teachers to determine how well a particular child is learning and how well an individual lesson succeeded and to evaluate the effectiveness of the whole program of instruction. Assessment enables children to see for themselves how they are performing as they learn to read and write and what they can do to improve. It helps school administrators to make decisions about the placement of individual children in special assistance, about the design of a curriculum, and about the in-service training needs of their faculty. Assessment also provides parents with feedback on their children's progress and identifies areas where they can provide support. It can even help parents and communities to know how their schools are performing in comparision to other schools.

Assessment can take many forms, including testing. Although some formal and informal tests of reading and writing ability can be useful, some of the most informative kinds of assessments involve watching very carefully as children read and write under natural circumstances. The type of assessment that is used depends a great deal on what needs to be known and who needs to know it.

External Audiences

Assessment of children's literacy may be undertaken for external audiences, that is, for groups outside the immediate classroom. Within particular states or communities, standards-based assessments are used to judge whether students are eligible to pass from one grade to the next. Standardized tests—tests of achievement on which children's performance is compared against the performance of many other children across the country—are sometimes used to tell parents, administrators, and teachers how well students are faring in reading performance. These tests can be used to compare children, classes, schools, states, and even entire countries. Results of standardized tests may be used to determine whether a child is eligible for special education services.

Standardized testing received a boost from the U.S. federal government with the enactment of the "No Child Left Behind" education act in 2001. Now state education agencies are required to set explicit learning standards for reading and other subjects and to test all children on their abilities to satisfy those standards. By the 2005–2006 school year, schools will be required to test children in each of grades three through eight. Schools' scores are reported in the media, and parents of children in schools that do not meet the standards may be given vouchers to send their children to other schools, private or public. The standards-based tests are keyed to skills and abilities that have been chosen by curriculum developers in each state and that are made available to teachers and parents. Therefore, it is possible for teachers in each school to examine their students' performance levels and modify their own teaching to improve performance where necessary.

Internal Audiences

Assessment also is often undertaken for internal audiences: classroom teachers and other teachers within the school, as well as students. When teachers gather some quantitative data on how well students are reading, these can form the basis for discussions that can help teachers to compare the effectiveness of teaching methods, and improve their instruction. Taylor and colleagues (1999) found that when teachers made periodic assessments of their students' performance and shared the results with other teachers at their grade level and with the principal, schoolwide planning for improving reading instruction began to be undertaken.

Some assessments for internal audiences focus on isolated aspects of reading and writing; for example, they might examine children's phonemic awareness or stage of spelling development. Other assessments, such as informal reading inventories and running records, look at many aspects of literacy at once. Work sampling is another kind of assessment for internal audiences, as teachers collect samples of children's writing or written responses to readings for examination and discussion. Additionally, engaging students in assessment of their own work can help them to become more purposeful and strategic.

In this book, to show the importance of ongoing assessment in the reading classroom and demonstrate its connection with all aspects of reading, the important topic of assessment is integrated within each chapter rather than being singled out in one chapter. Suggestions for assessment will be provided for every aspect of literacy: including emergent literacy, word recognition, fluency, vocabulary, comprehension, response to literature, and writing. Suggestions for assessment will also be given at every level of schooling, from lower primary to upper elementary to the middle grades.

FOR REVIEW

Reading and writing are important parts of the school curriculum. They are tools that help students learn nearly everything else in the school day and continue to learn when they leave school. However, literacy is valuable as something far more than a school subject. Literacy leads to habits of language and mind that take readers beyond what they would find it natural to notice, think about, and communicate if they were not literate.

International comparisons show that U.S. students read fairly well—second in the world, according to one recent study. But another international comparison finds that they do not do as much deep thinking or problem solving with what they read. The benefits of literacy are not shared very equitably among students from different income groups or ethnic groups. When the National Assessment of Educational Progress has assessed reading ability, unacceptably high numbers of elementary age students have been found not to read with adequate comprehension. At the same time, studies show that few disabled readers have problems related to cognitive function. Ninety-seven percent or more, according to one study, could be remediated with appropriate instruction, although that instruction should be judiciously planned and intensively applied when necessary. These findings cast doubt on the still-continuing practice of treating so many children with "specific reading disabilities" as if there were something wrong with their brains.

The history of research on reading instruction is nearly as old as the scientific study of psychology. But debates over instructional methods in literacy—such as the whole word versus phonics debate—have lasted for many generations. Arguments between advocates of holistic approaches and skills-based approaches have been heated in the past decade but appear to be easing with the emphasis on a balance of both. Research supports holistic instruction so that children see that literacy is meaningful; it also supports instruction in the alphabetic writing system—in phonics and the awareness of the sound system that underlies it—at least to those students who don't intuit the system.

The components of reading are interrelated, but reading can be viewed in terms of word recognition, comprehension, reading fluency, and critical literacy. Reading develops normally through stages: emergent literacy, beginning reading, building fluency, reading to learn and for pleasure, and mature reading.

To teach reading well requires that the teacher keep several things in mind. Effective reading instruction means immersing children in real literature, teaching decoding skills and coaching children in their use, attention to comprehension and to higher-order thinking skills, teaching learning strategies to children, frequent assessment, involving parents in their children's learning, and respecting cultural differences.

Assessment of reading and writing ability is done for external and internal audiences. External audiences include parents, school administrators, and the general community—all of whom have a stake in knowing how well the literacy instruction program is working. External audiences usually want results from standardized tests. Assessment is also done for internal audiences, who are the children themselves and their teacher. Assessments for internal audiences typically include careful observations of children's reading and writing performance at real tasks, and are intended to shed light on what learners are doing well and what aspects of their literacy need improvement.

For Your Journal

Go back to the Anticipation Guide that opened this chapter, and consider your answers to the questions posed. Divide a page of your journal with a vertical line. On the left side, write down one of your answers that you want to think about more. On the right side, write what you think about that topic now. Repeat the exercise with at least two more questions. Take your journal to class with you, and share your comments with your classmates.

★ Taking It to the World

1. Interview three primary grade teachers, and ask them how they have seen the emphases in reading instruction change in the past ten years. What aspects have stayed the same? What changes have they witnessed?
2. Many adults who have poorly developed reading skills don't see their limited literacy as a problem. Call the local chapter of Literacy Volunteers of America, and ask whether this is their experience. Do many of the adults in the community who need help with literacy seek help? (A class might choose to appoint a committee to do this so as not to inundate the chapter with phone calls.)
3. The National Adult Literacy Survey noted that prisoners are more likely than the rest of the population to have reading problems. Have a member of your class interview the person in charge of education at a local or regional prison. To what extent are literacy issues tied up with the problems the inmates have faced?

★ Being a Professional Reading Teacher

Reflecting on the Chapter

You are about to enter a very exciting and challenging profession. Change will be a constant in your professional life. There is no more dynamic area of educational change than reading instruction. Your perceptions of the nature of reading and of reading instruction will evolve as you read each chapter of this text. Your professional portfolio provides an opportunity for you to document that evolution of your thinking.

Your Professional Portfolio

Most college and university teacher preparation programs now require that candidates prepare portfolios that reflect their professional development. In addition, many principals and school district personnel directors make new teachers' portfolios a focus of their pre-employment interviews. Finally, your portfolio can be a means of self-evaluation, a record of past achievement, and a plan for future professional development.

As you begin this course, you should begin thinking about your own portfolio. Because reading instruction is such an important part of your new career, it should be highlighted in your portfolio. There are many formats for teacher portfolios. Most include some or all of the following:

- Sample lesson plans
- Thematic units
- Videotapes of lessons
- Descriptions of cooperative learning activities used in your lessons
- Photographs or hand-drawn plans of your classroom environment
- Student, teacher, and participant products, such as writing assignments, self-evaluations, projects, lesson plans, maps, experiments
- Plans for and evidence of continuing education or professional development, such as courses, workshops, conference attendance, and activities in professional organizations
- Descriptions of mentoring activities, both as mentee and mentor
- Peer observations and evaluations
- Letters of reference, commendations, and recommendations from supervisors
- An essay about your teaching philosophy (how you teach and why)
- Written reflections about planning (why artifacts are included in the portfolio); many teachers write them on stick-on notes that can be attached to items in the portfolio

Your portfolio is a dynamic, living document. It should change over time. It should reflect you as you are, which means that you should periodically remove items that no longer reflect your current status, interests, and capabilities. How large should your portfolio be? Only you can answer that. But it should be functional and useful, not a burden to you or to the person reviewing it.

Two final cautions:

- Ensure that all examples presented in your portfolio are your own original work. If you use or adapt the work of someone else, be sure to give credit.
- Proofread everything carefully; you are presenting your best face in your portfolio, including your ability to write and spell in English.

You can read more about portfolios in McLaughlin, M., & Vogt, M. (1996). *Portfolios in teacher education*. Newark, DE: International Reading Association.

Technology Connections

1. On the Internet, log onto the Web pages of the International Reading Association (www.reading.org) and the National Council of Teachers of English (www.ncte.org). From what they say on these pages, can you tell what the emphases of these two organizations are?
2. The International Reading Association publishes an electronic journal called *Reading On-Line*. Log on and read an issue. What topics are of most interest to the readership at the moment?

Connect with Research

Research
Navigator.com

Review the following key words from the chapter and then connect to Research Navigator (www.researchnavigator.com) through this book's companion web site to conduct a search into research on each of the various topics as they relate to reading and literacy education today.

balanced instruction   emergent literacy   phonemic segmentation
cognitive schemes   inferences   phonics
comprehension   inflection   reading fluency
critical literacy   main idea   sight vocabulary
critical reading   phonemes   vocabulary
developmental learning   phonemic awareness   word recognition

Further Readings

Allington, R. *What Really Matters for Struggling Readers: Designing Research-Based Programs.* Boston: Allyn and Bacon, 2001.

A knowledgeable reading specialist, Allington rounds out what he argues is an incomplete picture of reading ability and best practices in reading instruction that have been conveyed by the National Reading Panel and others.

National Reading Panel. *Teaching Children to Read: An Evidence-Based Assessment of the Scientific Research Literature on Reading and Its Implications for Reading Instruction.* Washington, DC: National Institute for Literacy, 2000.

This report forms the theoretical basis for the federal government's policies on reading education.

OECD. *Reading for Change: Performance and Engagement Across Countries.* Available online at www.pisa.oecd.org.

Reports an international comparison of how well students read for meaning.

Smith, F. *Reading without Nonsense* (Revised Edition). New York: Teachers College Press, 1997.

Smith's writing was very influential, especially in the 1970s and 1980s. He is one of the most articulate presenters of the case for holistic reading instruction.

Snow, C. E., Burns, M. S., and Griffin, P. (Eds.). *Preventing Reading Difficulties in Young Children.* Washington, DC: National Academy Press, 1998.

This report of the National Research Council summarizes in a readable way a great many findings about young children's reading abilities and their problems with reading.

Spear-Swerling, L., and Sternberg, R. J. *Off Track: When Poor Readers Become "Learning Disabled."* Boulder, CO: Westview Press, 1997.

A special educator and a noted cognitive psychologist attempt to set the record straight on reading disabilities.

The Need for a
Learning Community:
Linking Home, School,
and Community

The Social
and Cultural
Contexts for
Teaching
All Children
to Read

Implications of
Current Assessment
Practices for
Diverse Learners

The Social
Contexts of Literacy

Meeting the Literacy
Needs of All Children

The Social and Cultural Contexts for Teaching All Children to Read

The following statements will get you thinking about the topics of this chapter. Answer true or false in response to each statement. As you read and learn more about the topics in these statements, double-check your answers. See what interests you and prompts your curiosity toward more understanding.

Anticipation Guide

_____ 1. Reading and writing are both social and individual forms of communicating.

_____ 2. Differences among students in classrooms have little effect on how teachers work with children.

_____ 3. Cultural groups have distinct values regarding the importance of reading and writing.

_____ 4. Almost all English language learners are found in large urban centers.

_____ 5. African-American Vernacular is a dialect of English.

_____ 6. Children's culture is reflected in their body language, the way they manage time, and the distance they maintain between themselves and others.

_____ 7. A gifted child who is reading at grade level probably has a reading problem.

_____ 8. Boys tend to have more reading problems than girls do.

_____ 9. Some children begin school without knowing how to handle a book.

_____ 10. Children with special needs benefit from being in regular classrooms for a part of the school day.

Getting Parents and the Community
Involved in the Classroom

Marguerite has been teaching seventh grade for several years. Recently, she has begun to follow the new state standards for her reading and language arts classes. Just this last year, her state, Pennsylvania, provided a model unit on Community Biography that integrates language arts and history as students study their own community members. Knowing that her students always seemed to do better when there were connections between what she did in her classroom and what they did outside of school, she found this to be a natural way to get students more interested in developing their oral and written language skills and processes in interviewing, collecting data, and writing biographies. She got the CD-ROM that provides ideas for how to develop the unit and found a great deal of useful information and many teaching suggestions. After reviewing these and thinking of her other plans for the fall, she decided to try this new unit, which involves students selecting a special person about whom they will write a biography. To complete the project, they need to select the special person, develop questions to use in their interview, conduct the interview, and write up their findings. In addition, they conduct research on the national and international events that occurred during this person's life, create a time line of important events that correlate with the person's life, collect pictures and other artifacts that pertain to the report, and then represent the results on a three-part bulletin board to be shown at the Special Persons' Fair, which will be open to the public. Doing this unit permits students to use their language arts skills in reading, writing, and oral communication, as reflected in state standards.

Marguerite decided to check with some of her students before putting too much time into planning the unit, just to be certain that the idea of doing this elaborate unit would appeal to them. After she explained the basic structure of the unit, the students gave her very enthusiastic feedback, and she proceeded with the planning. As she read more and began to organize the time frame for this unit, she visited with the school librarian to see what resources were available to help students gain more information about local history and community leadership. The librarian introduced her to the collection of local newspapers on file and suggested that the public library also had a wealth of materials that students could use. Because this was a new unit, Marguerite decided to follow the unit through the experience of one student in each of her sections of language arts to ensure that she was clear and that the activities were appropriately explained and taught. She didn't want just to assign and test, but really to develop students' competence. The guide materials suggested that teachers introduce the skill of interviewing in this unit as part of meeting the state standards. Marguerite knew that this would be a new skill for her students, and she decided to emphasize it in her teaching. She looked through the materials for how to introduce the process, what steps were involved, and how to give students some practice before having them conduct their actual project interviews. She decided to conduct a demonstration interview for students and began to think of whom she could ask to help her with this demonstration. This strategy fit into the planning model Marguerite preferred to follow: Demonstration and Immersion, Attention to Details, Guided Practice, and Application. As she thought more about the project, she decided that she would create her own community biography with her students so that she could share the experience and fun of the project.

With her planning done and with resources well organized, she was able to begin the unit with a sense of confidence. The students benefited from her careful preparation and became very excited about what they learned about their own community during their research and interviewing. In fact, by the third week, Marguerite had allotted time for students to share what they were learning. The enthusiasm and insights gained by one student often sparked new ideas and questions from others. By the special community night when students shared their displays of their community subjects, the success of the project was clear. Both students and community members were proud of the students' accomplishments. The activity created a positive connection between the various parts of the community—those in leadership roles and many less-noticed, but important, contributors.

Most people spend a great deal of time trying to do the things that family, friends, and those considered important are doing. Think of how, as an infant and young child, you learned to speak by following the models of those who nurtured you or how, as a teenager, you watched and then tried to dress and look just like your friends. The power of the social context is also very strong as people develop their literacy interests and behaviors. Children who come from families in which reading is a part of the fabric of their lives—in which family members keep books by their beds to read in quiet moments, newspapers arrive daily and are read avidly, and even bathrooms have piles of magazines that can be picked up for short periods—know that reading is important. They come to school with the expectation that they will become readers like the rest of their family members. Some children, however, come to school without a strong social foundation for becoming literate; this can occur in all socioeconomic, linguistic, ethnic, and cultural groups. No one might ever have read to them, there might be no books and magazines in their homes, and their family members might never read or write in their presence. It is particularly important to ensure that these students become part of a social network of children and adults who value literacy and who use it for a variety of purposes.

Teachers also need to be cognizant of the importance of the social nature of literacy as they deal with the impact of the range of literacy experiences and abilities of the children when they are in the classroom. Children continually compare themselves to those around them. Just ask students who the best readers are in their class—they know. Ask who should write the letter of thanks to the author who visited the school, and they will direct you to the best writer. Teachers must be sensitive to all the children so that each one gains confidence in being a capable part of the literacy community. All children have strengths that can and must be celebrated so that they will continue to put their energies into the challenges of developing as readers and writers. The social context of the classroom becomes more and more important as students develop many levels of social comparison. Even the positive small group learning opportunities that teachers suggest can lead to domination of the less assertive students if care is not taken. Teachers therefore need to be aware of how powerful the social forces are in the participation in school life of students and families and in their sense of self-confidence and willingness to take risks in the classroom.

At the start of the new century, fewer and fewer classrooms are composed of children from one ethnic or cultural group who all speak English as their mother tongue and who are otherwise similar to each other. As cultural and linguistic diversity are increasing, most schools are now finding ways to make the regular classroom the center for the diverse universe of children. This chapter highlights the research and best practices that emphasize the importance of reading and writing as social activities, not just as individual skills to be acquired. Literacy happens in cultural contexts, and awareness of the power of these contexts is basic to creating the kinds of settings that support literacy efforts.

⭐ The Social Contexts of Literacy

Communities and families vary in their approaches and orientations to literacy, and many of these variations are grounded in historical and cultural circumstance. Not all Americans value literacy in their lives. Not all use reading and writing in the same ways. Research in mainstream American communities, as well as in varied cultural set-

**Family &
Community
Literacy**

tings, has highlighted both the commonalities and differences across families and communities.

A classic study of variations in literacy is that done by Heath (1983) and reported in her book *Ways with Words*. In this comparison of literacy in three different cultural groups in Appalachia, Heath illustrates how the two working-class communities, Tracton and Roadville, provided their children with different cultural experiences related to reading and writing from those of the Townspeople, whose use of literacy was more compatible with that of the schools. Roadville families saw literacy as very concrete and functional, and the students from this community had difficulty with more abstract learning. Tracton families viewed literacy as important for real, practical tasks. In neither of these communities was literacy important for the residents' jobs, yet the parents did want their children to read and would often help with the worksheet and skill assignments teachers gave the children. Reading for enjoyment and pleasure as a family event, however, was not part of these cultures.

Since that early work of Heath, others have explored underlying values and styles associated with literacy. Delpit (1995) has provided insights about African-American cultural variations in literacy. She argues that African-American children are accustomed to a more direct form of teaching and discipline and that they need that kind of clarity for all to succeed. According to Delpit, the more indirect forms of teaching and discipline preferred by many middle-class teachers leave some students out. They often don't understand the cues that teachers provide about what is important and what the students' roles should be.

Research by Kelly (1999) on a group of Mexican-American mothers revealed the high level of respect they accord teachers and schools. Even when they have had few opportunities for formal schooling themselves, they want their children to succeed. Their high regard for teachers, however, has a potential negative effect. They do not want to interfere with the teachers' role by helping their children learn to read before going to school. Because of this respect for teachers and their lack of a tradition of home literacy, their children often do not enter school with the same story reading and writing experiences that other children have. These families also thought that their children could learn English in school but that Spanish would remain the language used at home. This has both advantages and disadvantages. It poses a problem in giving English language learners enough opportunities to speak and use English to become proficient. It also means that the language of intimacy and familiarity is not English, so the school associations with English need to be very positive if students are going to learn it easily. Students who speak languages other than English can be encouraged to work and talk together so that they can practice English more regularly.

Because students are coming from increasingly diverse cultural traditions with varying literacy experiences, it is valuable to try to understand something of their family and cultural values, particularly those related to literacy and schooling. It is also important to find good ways to communicate with the parents and adjust to their needs. For example, some Hispanic parents feel intimidated when asked to come to school for parent conferences. They are unfamiliar with the traditions of U.S. schools and the customary relationships between teachers and families in this country. In an attempt to honor the different experiences of the parents, one school district in California changed its format for parent nights. Instead of having each family come alone for conferencing, the schools have small group conferencing. After the teachers lead a discussion of students' work and curriculum expectations, they answer questions from the parents. The teachers then make themselves available to individual families who wish to talk privately. This format has worked very well. The parents feel much more secure discussing issues of school learning in a group setting rather than alone with a teacher. Instead of creating high levels of anxiety among the parents, there is much more comfort and willingness to participate.

The more teachers learn about the social contexts of their community, the better able they are to respond appropriately to their students and to build new expectations and competence so that all students can attain the levels of literacy needed today. Despite the traditional values that many communities place on literacy, all teachers need to expand their horizons and become versatile in their use of literacy in a wide variety of settings.

The Need for a Learning Community: Linking Home, School, and Community

Becoming aware of the relationship between community values and students' motivation and focus is a starting place for understanding the setting in which one teaches. The cultural importance of literacy activities and the ways adults and children communicate affect how teachers can help their students most effectively.

New teachers should think of themselves as working in a community, not just in a school. Before entering the school door and closing out the rest of the world, take time to become acquainted with the resources around you. For example, are there libraries you can link with to help provide the variety of reading materials you will want your students to have available to them? What resources are particular to the families you will be working with, such as community clubs, religious and ethnic centers, and local leaders?

Your most powerful opportunities, however, come within the school. As a teacher, you have a very important role for the parents and families of the children in your classroom. How you meet and relate to them is critical. Understanding the families' attitudes and values will help you work with the parents as partners in developing children's literacy. You want to know them as well as possible to communicate effectively with them. Think of their needs and ways to build bridges between the school and their homes. What do they want to know? How can you support them in their efforts to help their children? Think of how you can involve them in the life of the school and the classroom. What is appropriate and beneficial for both you and them?

As a teacher, you will be part of a school community, too. The more you can participate as part of the professional team, sharing your own literacy and learning and growing with others in the building, the more successful you will be as a teacher. Do not wait until you have your classroom under control before you think about building your roles within this larger support team. Begin to envision yourself as a committed professional sharing with others.

Inside the Classroom

Along with the variation among communities in how they express the values and functions of literacy, there is also great variation within schools in how the value of literacy is expressed. A part of creating a community is creating an inviting and purposeful space in the classroom—one that maximizes the possibilities for creating a real literacy community among students. Whether adjusting the physical environment or adapting the structure of reading and writing activities, each teacher can do a great deal to contribute to a school culture that stimulates literacy and honors students' contributions.

CREATE A LITERATE CULTURE.   One of the first statements you make to students about what is important in school is what they see in the classroom. Are desks grouped together? Are books and print materials displayed and easily accessible? Think about the classroom environment you want to create during your first year of teaching. What will the classroom look like? Remember, you will have a great deal to do in determining what kind of context you create for your students. Think of your classroom space as a visual and physical opportunity to invite your students to enjoy reading and writing. Think about some of the classrooms you have visited in recent years. How did the teachers make a clear statement that they valued reading and writing? Table 2.1 identifies things teachers can use in their classrooms to enhance the value of literacy.

TABLE 2.1

Visual Survey of a
Literate Classroom

The classroom contains:
1. A special place for reading and writing—a reading corner, a writing corner, etc.
2. A classroom library of books students can use regularly
3. A collection of books students have written either individually or in groups (these could be big books, bound books added to the classroom library, etc.)
4. A rack with magazines and newspapers appropriate for the students
5. An author's chair and/or a reader's and writer's chair from which the students read to the rest of the class
6. Books and magazines the teacher is reading, both professional and personal
7. Examples on the walls or ledges of students' responses to materials they are reading—reviews of books, story maps of key points, sketches of interesting parts of stories, shared responses, etc.
8. Charts and other visuals that serve as strategy guides for students learning to read and write—reading strategies, fix-up strategies, steps in writing, word walls to guide spelling using key patterns, etc.
9. Visual "in process" charts of students' work—I-charts, matrices of learning, K-W-L charts, responses to questions for reflection, etc.
10. Illustrations of what students are studying and learning in content areas—science process journals and social studies artifacts
11. Books, magazines, and other materials that reflect cultures represented in your class or school
12. Examples of writing in different orthographies so that students can explore the varieties of written languages

One of the easiest and most important ways in which you can invite your students into literacy is by providing them with places where they can participate with others in literate activities. Every classroom with a library of appropriate books, magazines, and newspapers encourages the habit of reading. As you begin to create a library, identify the range of reading levels likely among the students, identify key themes and authors that children of this age enjoy, and begin building the collection. Many schools provide sets of books for each classroom. However, you will still want to evaluate the collection and make it as appealing as possible. It should contain material on a wide range of topics of interest to your students, and some of the collection should connect to the science, social studies, and special topics that the children will study. Ensure that there are books representing the various cultures from which students in the school come. All students deserve to find and see themselves in the books and magazines in their classrooms.

Another important step is to create an attractive place for literacy activities. If space is available, create both a reading corner and a writing corner. In the reading corner, house the classroom library and additional inviting reading materials in a space where students can browse through the books and curl up on the floor or in comfortable chairs to read. Some teachers find soft chairs, pillows, or even bathtubs in which children can relax and read. You can add a small paper bin for students to make notes about special ideas they find while reading and for sticky notes so that they can mark places for sharing with each other. Some teachers involve students in creating bookmarks so that they can easily access their point of reading and have extra bookmarks available in the reading center.

Writing &
Reading

The writing space needs a table and comfortable chairs. The space becomes more attractive when students can enjoy a range of writing tools and a supply of writing materials. Depending on the students' age, these will vary, but a selection of colored pencils and pens, some wooden ink blocks with special designs, and a variety of kinds of paper, some with designs, make writing more fun. Computers in this area can be used for writing and editing support by parents and volunteers in early primary classes and by students as they become adept in using computers. In addition, dictionaries, thesauruses, and other writing aids should be displayed prominently for students' use. This area can house students' writing folders so that when they are ready to write, they can enter the process easily and, when finished, can refile their works in process.

ENSURE THE SHARING OF LITERACY. A key to helping students become lifelong readers and writers is to develop the social nature of literacy by providing regular opportunities for children to engage with each other around literacy events. Too often, as students move up in the grades, opportunities to talk with others about what they are reading and writing disappear. Yet it is through the sharing with others that students realize how central literacy can become in their own lives as part of their own enjoyment and learning. As you begin to plan for your literacy program, think carefully about including regular opportunities for students to engage with each other without the teacher dominating the discussion or exchange. Students need opportunities to work in paired reading and writing activities. They need to learn how to function as part of small cooperative literacy groups, knowing that they should be prepared with their own ideas to share and willing to listen and link to what others say. They also need to have experiences in larger groups and whole class discussions that build from their partner or small group experiences.

For many students who are new to this country, talking in a whole class setting is extremely difficult, since they lack confidence in their command of English and of the culture of the school. Teachers can ease these students into the classroom academic life by using paired reading and talking as a first step before involving the students in larger group activities. One variation of this is called Think-Pair-Share (McTighe & Lyman, 1988). As you think about all the literacy learning activities you will structure for your students, make sure that there are frequent and regular opportunities for students to talk and share with their peers in nonthreatening settings. Don't assume that students know what it is like to discuss a book or piece of text. You might need to spend a significant amount of time getting students familiar with "talk about text." One way to develop more book discussion is to begin a Great Books program. There is full training for teachers and group leaders in this program and materials that guide students' thinking about the rich stories and texts that are included at each grade level (Plecha, 1992). Many teachers now use some form of book club (Raphael & McMahon, 1994) or literature circle (Daniels, 2002) as a way of involving students in focused talk about what they are reading. (Strategies for engaging students are discussed in Chapter 6, "Comprehension and Response to Literature.")

Another support for book talk is to help parents learn how to elicit reflection from their children. Some school districts have developed videotapes of the kinds of questions and follow-up comments that parents can use to help children talk about their reading. Others have prepared guides for parents to follow. One example is shown in Figure 2.1 on page 40.

TEACH IT!
11

It is useful to help students share literacy with each other at all ages and grade levels. In this way, the shared, cultural aspects of reading and writing can become more alive for all the students in the school. A very simple way to do this is for two grades to become partners in which students form buddy pairs for reading and writing and meet regularly (e.g., weekly, every two weeks, monthly). The children begin to share their literate activities with children older and/or younger than they are. The older readers help the younger ones as they read from books they want to share; the older students might also help write responses to the reading—what the two like about the story, characters, or information. When the younger students write their own descriptions of a trip to the nature center, the older student buddies take dictation and help to create personal accounts of the experiences.

TEACH IT!
10

In some schools, the students who struggle with reading also get help from older students who are trained in some basic reading strategies. In this way, both groups of students gain, and the shared understanding of literacy develops naturally. One particular program, Tall Friends, pairs middle-grade below-level readers with second graders who are also having trouble. The reading teacher helps the older students develop some activities to help the second graders focus on the phonic regularities of English by doing controlled word sorts and by learning to listen to and support students as they read orally from their instructional-level materials.

If a school does not have a vibrant, shared literacy culture, think about how to bring in some new focus to stimulate students' attention to reading and writing. There are many ways in which this can be done. One is to celebrate special days—from International Literacy Day, September 8, to Dr. Seuss's birthday in March. Some states have their own awards for good children's books. Illinois holds a contest each year to select students' favorite books as part of the Rebecca Caudill Awards Program. California's Young Reader Medal, sponsored by the California Reading Association, is

---

1. Find a relaxed time and setting.

2. Talk about the book as you read.
   *Look over the cover, title, author and picture and predict
   what you think may happen and why you like the book.
   *As you read, share connections to your life.
      "Doesn't this seem like Aunt Dorothy?"
      "This picture reminds me of our trip."
      "Oh, I remember feeling like this!"
   *Ask questions of your child. For example:
      "Do you know anyone like this?"
      "How would you feel?"
   *After reading, share your favorite parts. For example:
      "I really liked . . ."
      ". . . was so funny!"

3. Reread favorite books.

4. Read many kinds of books—real world, poetry, folk tales, humor,
   & fiction.

FIGURE 2.1

Tips for Reading with Your Child.

similar. School participation in the selection of these books creates a new focus for the celebration of books. Other programs that recognize student writing can also help to add emphasis to school literacy. Inviting authors to visit the school and speak with different groups of students can make literacy and the process of writing and reading very real. Most states have some beloved and respected authors who are willing to visit schools, and bookstores will often help to bring authors to area schools.

Each of these examples highlights the importance of thinking of literacy as a community activity in the school. The more there is a climate of support for and interest in how students read and write, the more all students benefit. In addition, the more students talk with each other about their reading, the more they identify with books and reading.

START THE YEAR OUT RIGHT.   Just as teachers can do much to create a warm, supportive literacy climate in the classroom, what they do even before students start the year can help to model the importance and joy of literacy. Consider writing a letter to each of your new students before the year begins, introducing yourself and telling a little about your expectations for the fall. You can suggest that students bring with them an example of their own writing (if they are beyond the second grade) or a favorite book or poem. Some teachers ask students to bring pictures of themselves doing something they enjoy to put on a board for the first day. Each of these activities is an example of using literacy as a bridge to building relationships. Students love to receive mail, and some of the apprehension of starting a new year can be melted away with such simple, yet profound, gestures.

Teachers can also involve parents in events at the start of the year. By sending a letter home during the first week explaining who they are and what they will be doing in the classroom, teachers can build a bridge from school to home. Parents respond positively to an introduction from the teacher explaining what to expect for the fall. After an initial letter, the teacher might publish a weekly or monthly newsletter of the class events, with explanations of aspects of the reading and writing programs. Parents need to know how they can contribute. Figure 2.2 on page 42 shows an example of a home-school letter that a multiage team sent to help parents understand their approach to reading development. Figure 2.3 on page 43 provides an example of a letter a kindergarten teacher sent to parents and children asking them to identify favorite poems and bring them to class for all to share. This simple activity set the stage for monthly units that involved some parent participation. Knowing that they were important and were helping their children extend the resources of the class, most parents participated eagerly.

During the first week of school, literacy activities can also help the class to become better acquainted. Ask each student to bring a favorite book or magazine to share, give the students time to explain why they have selected the particular material, and listen carefully to them. This can be a good way to find out even more about the students' personal and home uses of literacy. For students for whom such selection and sharing might not be comfortable, conduct a book talk about several books and magazines in the classroom library and ask students to select the one they think they will like most. Having time to scan the materials gives each student an opportunity to share responses.

Getting to know the students quickly is important. Asking them to draw or write something about themselves is another way to elicit shared literacy activity. The bulletin board that can be created from this activity then becomes an invitation to read and learn about classmates. In one school, parents created the covers for the writing journals that the kindergarten and first-grade children were given the first week of school. Imagine the children's surprise when they realized that they would be holding a creation of their parents each time they wrote! Parents knew their children would be using their developmental spelling abilities as well as drawing to write messages each day when they spent time at the writing table.

Involving Parents in the School

Family & Community Literacy

It is impossible to discuss social contexts of literacy without focusing on parents, for they are the children's first and most important teachers. Teachers need to know as much about the parent's cultural values and styles of communicating with their children as possible so that the adjustments to the school culture and style of each teacher can be made. Even the ability to talk about different ways of thinking, talking, reading, and writing can be useful to students, parents, and teachers. For example, you might suggest to a parent, "At school, we are trying to get the children to be independent in their reading by giving them time to figure out unfamiliar words for them-

Research to Practice

"Research is an effort to do things better, it is the problem-solving mind— it is the tomorrow mind, it is a natural extension of good teaching."
(Hubbard & Power)

Welcome to *the Research to Practice* segment of our bi-monthly class news. This is the place where we hope to clarify terms, strategies, theory, research, district expectations and how it connects to what we do in our classrooms. Each newsletter will focus on a particular area of instruction, learning, and/or curriculum. It is our professional obligation to not only keep you abreast with current research, but also to align it to what we do in our classrooms. We hope that you find this portion of the newsletter informative and helpful.

Rainbow Reading

<u>Reading Levels</u> (Jerry Johns, 2001)

<u>Independent</u>   The independent reading level is the level at which the student can read fluently without teacher assistance. Materials should be read with near perfect accuracy (95–100%) and 90% comprehension.

<u>Instructional</u>   The instructional reading level is the level at which the student is <u>challenged</u> but not <u>frustrated</u> with teacher guidance. The student can read accurately (90–95%) with 75% comprehension.

<u>Frustration</u>   The frustration level is the level at which the student should not be given materials to read. Students at the frustration level (<90% accuracy and <50% comprehension) are unable to read the materials even with the support of the teacher.

<u>Rainbow Reading</u>

Rainbow Reading is one component of our Balanced Reading Program.* The Rainbow Reading books in our classroom are grouped into four colors: <u>Red</u> (Beginning), <u>Orange</u> (Developing), <u>Yellow</u> (Transitional), and <u>Green</u> (Fluent).

During Rainbow Reading, (independent reading) students choose books from one of the four levels that are at their **independent** (95% accuracy, 90% comprehension) level. "Independent reading is essential for the development of fluency. Fluency comes from the ability to immediately and automatically identify most frequent words. This is key to the success of a lifelong reader." (Cunningham, 1998)

During Reading Workshop, students are placed in materials at their **instructional** (90–95% accuracy) level. Teacher guidance provides a scaffold where students are challenged but not frustrated.

*A Balanced Reading Program provides opportunities for pleasurable, independent reading (Reading Rainbow), reading for a specific purpose (Reading Workshop, learn content, skill, strategy), and interaction through discussion, response to literature, research and inquiry. (Pinell & Fountas, 2000)

<u>AT HOME . . .</u>

Continue to set aside a special "reading time." During that time your child might be reading from the Rainbow Reading collection from school, reading a library book or other book of choice, reading to another child, or listening to you read. It is extremely important that children **hear** the language and pattern of text in the higher-level books adults read to them. Remember that reading should be **pleasurable**. Allow time for "easy" reading!

Happy Reading!

FIGURE 2.2

Home-School Newsletter.

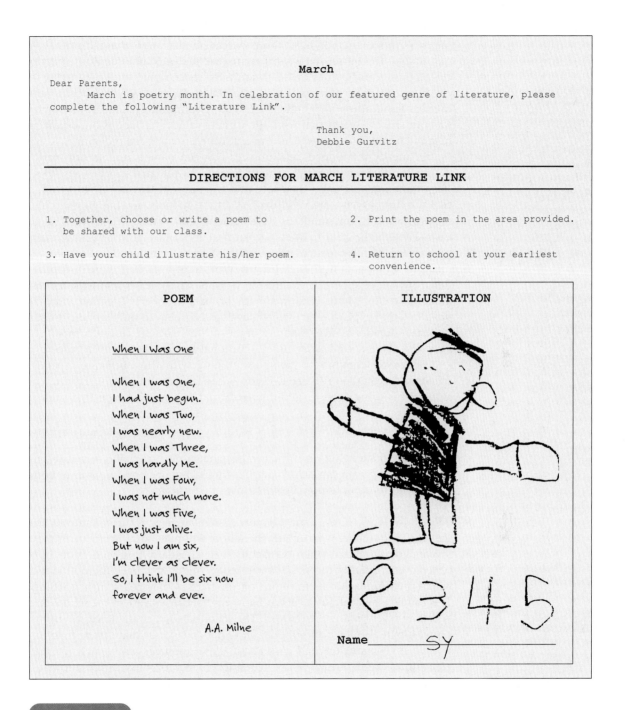

March

Dear Parents,

   March is poetry month. In celebration of our featured genre of literature, please complete the following "Literature Link".

                    Thank you,
                    Debbie Gurvitz

DIRECTIONS FOR MARCH LITERATURE LINK

1. Together, choose or write a poem to be shared with our class.

2. Print the poem in the area provided.

3. Have your child illustrate his/her poem.

4. Return to school at your earliest convenience.

POEM   **ILLUSTRATION**

When I Was One

When I was One,
I had just begun.
When I was Two,
I was nearly new.
When I was Three,
I was hardly Me.
When I was Four,
I was not much more.
When I was Five,
I was just alive.
But now I am six,
I'm clever as clever.
So, I think I'll be six now
forever and ever.

                    A.A. Milne

Name   SY

FIGURE 2.3

Home-School Newsletter.

selves. We ask them to look for three sources of information: visual, grammatical, and meaningful. Of course, you want them to read perfectly and fluently. Giving them the correct pronunciation of words helps this. However, right now we are trying to get the children to be more independent. If you could help reinforce our teaching strategy for the next few months, your child will feel more comfortable and, I think, reach the goal we both share." Accept that what the parents value and think is important, and then help them understand how they can assist the instructional program.

As already mentioned, relationships between parents and schools vary tremendously. In some communities, parents feel too intimidated to join the school culture. They want teachers to do their jobs and will support this as best they can. In other communities, parents are very involved in the schools, serving on curriculum committees, working on standards development, and visiting classrooms on a regular basis. They might want to know a great deal about how reading is taught and might have a wealth of experience themselves guiding their own children's literacy development. In this situation, the teacher will want to give parents some in-depth explanations. Figure 2.4 shows an example of a home-school letter that explains the importance of spelling and word study for primary students. Creating videotapes and programs that explain how literacy develops can help to build good communication in these situations. Even sharing some of the current research reports, such as *Preventing Reading Difficulties* and the National Reading Panel report, can be useful to knowledgeable community members. Dealing with the variations depends on the school and should be a shared decision of the faculty and administration. A key in all situations is being open to, and interested in, the parents' perspectives and concerns.

Become Part of a Professional Community

Teaching is challenging work and can be exhausting, especially for new teachers. One of the best ways you can help yourself is by seeking out opportunities to become part of the multilevel professional community of educators.

WITHIN THE SCHOOL.   At the most immediate level is the community within the school. If the teacher is fortunate, the school will have some structured times for professional development when the faculty meets regularly to discuss issues of common concern and to learn together. New teachers might also have the option of working with a mentor teacher in an induction program as they begin their teaching careers. This can be a helpful way to get to know the specific culture of the school and district and can prevent many frustrations. The school district or the larger county or service center might also have an optional set of good activities that can be used to increase our effectiveness as teachers. Ask about these resources, and watch for special programs that are advertised. Many new teachers feel too busy to add another commitment, but the rewards can outweigh the time demands.

OUTSIDE OF SCHOOL.   Outside of school, teachers can seek out groups that meet regularly for discussions both of adult recreational books and of professional ones. Some book clubs also read and discuss new children's books, which can help teachers become aware of new possibilities for students. With so many new books published each year, it is difficult to keep up with the ones that might be appropriate for your students. You can attend book discussions hosted by bookstores and distributors with your teaching colleagues as well. They can help to identify special books and upcoming

Learning and Growing Together at Home

Word Study

"The purpose of word study is two-fold. Through active exploration, word study teaches students to examine words to discover regularities, patterns, and rules of English <u>orthography</u> needed to read and <u>spell.</u> Second, word study increases specific knowledge of words—the <u>spelling</u> and meaning of individual words." (Bear, Invernizzi, Templeton, Johnston, 2000)

Educators in District #34 conducted year long spelling study (1999–2002) . . .

After a comprehensive review of the research in spelling, the committee recommended **Word Study** as a method to study spelling. While memory does play an important role in learning to spell, it does not play the *only* role. (Henderson, 1990). Learning to spell should *also* be a process of coming to understand how words work—the conventions that govern structure and how their structure signals sound and meaning. (Berninger, 1994, 1995; Brown & Ellis, 1994; Read & Hodges, 1982; Templeton & Bear, 1992; Templeton & Morris, 2000)

The goals for our District Word Study Program are:

- **Students will learn spelling strategies to assist in spelling unknown or unfamiliar words.**
  - We want your child to be able to rely on "sounding it out" as ONE of several strategies to use when writing a challenging or new word. Additional strategies that will be taught are using word sorts, other references, applying knowledge of vowel patterns, and discovering how our alphabetic system works. (Cunningham & Cunningham, 1992) and decoding by analogy (Goswami & Bryant, 1998)
- **Students will learn how to memorize words. Each grade level has identified words that should be memorized.** (See attached grade level list.)
  - Expecting students to memorize every word **just does not work.** However, there are key words from our Word Wall that we call the NO EXCUSES LIST! These are words that may not follow a spelling pattern and are words that we use in our daily writing. These words are like math facts—they need to be practiced and memorized. (Routman, 1999)
- **Students will learn common patterns used in spelling.**
  - Word sorts and make a word are strategies that reinforce vowel and blend patterns. (Cunningham, 1998)
- **Students will develop a spelling consciousness and competence.**
  - As your child explores words through spelling and meaning, your child will develop a curiosity and interest in words that will carry over into reading and other academic areas. Students gradually will move from inventive spelling to traditional spelling.
  - Good spellers attribute their spelling proficiency to reading and writing, not spelling lessons or tests. Good spellers are more likely to conceptualize how words look and think about what they mean. (Hughes & Searle, 1997)

At Home . . . Encourage your child to "Do What Good Spellers Do" (Routman, 2000)

- Read a lot, enjoy reading, have a fascination with new words
- Integrate sound, visual, and meaning to words
- Use what you already know about words to find out new words . . . utilize strategies and resources
- PRACTICE often—learn 5 words from the Grade Level Spelling list then learn 5 more and so on . . .
- Take pride in doing your best work!

FIGURE 2.4

Home-School Newsletter.

events to link into the classroom. If teachers share their search for books, magazines, and computer materials with each other, they can enjoy learning together as they find materials that are of interest to a wide variety of young people.

As you begin your journey of professional growth, share what you are doing with your students, who might not think of teachers as learners, too. Children might be intrigued to see the professional journals and books that help their teachers evaluate their own teaching and that encourage them to stretch in new directions. Keep some of your professional materials in the classroom as a visible reminder that adults are readers and learners, too. Talk about your own reflection and questions.

PROFESSIONAL ORGANIZATIONS. New teachers are also nurtured when they join professional organizations that hold conferences and publish journals and books designed to help them become better teachers. For literacy teachers, that means becoming a member of the International Reading Association (www.reading.org) and/or the National Council of Teachers of English (www.ncte.org). These organizations have local and state groups that meet periodically to bring speakers to the area and sponsor special events; they also may offer grants to teachers wishing to attend a conference or develop some special student project. These professional organizations also provide many opportunities for teachers to develop leadership skills by speaking, being an officer, and working on advocacy when the need arises. Teachers enjoy their challenges most when they become part of the larger professional community. At a personal level, membership often results in new friends and a valuable support network. Local affiliates can be found by checking the web sites of the national groups. Participation with other teachers in the building or district can help to create a strong professional "learning community."

Meeting the Literacy Needs of All Children

An Urban Classroom

Farah's fourth-grade class is located in a low-income area of a major urban center. Her thirty-six students represent, in about equal numbers, four major ethnic groups: African-American, Asian, Hispanic, and Anglo. Almost half entered kindergarten speaking another language or dialect of English. Although all are at least minimally proficient in English now, many have gaps in their oral language vocabularies and in the background knowledge that corresponds to that of the middle-class children for whom the school curriculum and textbooks are typically designed. According to the results of informal reading inventories that Farah administered in the fall, many are reading below grade level, and a few are reading markedly below grade level.

Today, one group of ten children, all reading at grade level, is beginning to read a novel by Spinelli (1990a) entitled Maniac Magee, *which was awarded the prestigious Newbery Award. It is not a particularly difficult story, but there are many vocabulary words that are new to the children. In addition, some lack background knowledge about substantive issues that underlie the story. As Farah planned this lesson and several to follow, she had in mind the state reading standards she would be addressing, the*

California State English–Language Arts Standards (California State Board of Education, 1997):

Reading

2.3 *Make and confirm predictions about text by using prior knowledge and ideas presented in the text itself, including illustrations, titles, topic sentences, important words, and foreshadowing clues*

3.3 *Use knowledge of the situation and setting and of a character's traits and motivations to determine the causes for that character's actions*

Writing

1.1 *Select a focus, an organizational structure, and a point of view based upon purpose, audience, length, and formal requirements*

In addition, Farah ensured that she was applying the elements of the reading model she applies in her classroom: demonstration and immersion, attention to details, guided practice, and application. Before the children read, she leads them through several brief anticipatory reading activities that prepare them to read the story with good understanding. First, she says, "Let's read the title of the book and look at the illustration on the cover," demonstrating and modeling how she makes predictions about text she will read. She asks, "What predictions can you make about this book?" One child tries to sound out the word "maniac," saying "m-m-maniac— What does it mean?" Another child quickly responds, "It's a word for a crazy person, somebody out of control." Another notices the shoes on the cover and asks, "Do those shoes belong to a boy or a girl?" Farah says, "Let's find out." She reads the two-page foreword of the book aloud to the children; it ends with a short poem:

> Ma-*niac*, Ma-*niac*
> *He's so* cool
> Ma-*niac*, Ma-*niac*
> *Don't go to* school
> *Runs all* night
> *Runs all* right
> Ma-*niac*, Ma-*niac*
> *Kissed a* bull.

She then explains, "The main character is Jeffrey Magee, but they call him 'Maniac Magee.' He's a boy about your age. Now what do you think the story might be about?"

Farah has already prepared the beginning of a semantic map to introduce the term dump, which the children will encounter early in the story. She asks, "What do you know about this word?" The children share the information they already have, and Farah records it in appropriate categories on the graphic organizer, reflecting attention to details.

She then has the children close their books with their finger in place at the first page of the first chapter, and she asks them a question that will *guide their silent reading of that page, beginning the guided practice part of her lesson where they will build knowledge through reading. She asks, "How does Jeffrey's life suddenly change?" They listen to the question, then open their books and begin reading silently. (Jeffrey is orphaned when his parents are killed in an automobile accident. He lives with an aunt and uncle for a short time and then runs away to live in a dump.)*

As they read, Farah circulates around the group, motivating them by touching shoulders, smiling, and offering encouraging comments. Some children ask for assistance with words that are unfamiliar, even after the anticipatory reading activities. Farah quickly provides that help so that they can maintain their comprehension. This activity also provides an opportunity for her to briefly circulate around the classroom and supervise the work of other children who are working independently as they wait for their own small group lessons.

As the children finish reading the page and begin to raise their hands to respond to the question, Farah returns to her seat. She repeats the question and calls on a child who says, "He went to live with his aunt and uncle—they weren't too cool." Another adds, "His mom and dad were killed in a car accident." Yet another says, "He ran away." Other children add new information and share other points of view. Finally, Farah asks one student to read aloud the sentence that provides evidence for the answer that all the students finally agreed on. She then asks another comprehension-level question about the same page, following this procedure through the three pages of this first chapter of the story.

In a consolidation activity at the end of the lesson, Farah asks, "How did the story begin?" A child responds, "Jeffrey's parents were killed, and he went to live with his uncle and his aunt." Farah asks, "What happened next?" The children continue to retell the story up to that point in their own words. Farah then says, "Write a short paragraph, and predict what you think will happen in the next chapter of the story." As they begin to think about that, she moves on to work with another small group of children that is reading from an anthology.

Writing &
Reading

TEACH IT!
19

Farah has exhibited many behaviors that tell us she is an outstanding teacher, some of which relate to her strong instructional program—one that uses teaching strategies that support or scaffold their comprehension and that help them build confidence. She has also demonstrated all of the elements of the framework described in the Chapter 1 Teach It. In reading aloud the preface of the book, she provided a model both of fluent reading and of thinking about what she read, as revealed in her follow-up question. She gave attention to detail in analyzing a crucial word in the story, *dump*, the meaning of which was a key to understanding the circumstances in which Maniac Magee was living. She provided guided practice in the silent reading that was directed and scaffolded by the higher-order questions she asked before they read. Finally, she provided an application and extension activity: writing a short paragraph to predict what might happen in the next chapter.

Equally important are aspects of her approach that motivate the children, that indicate her high expectations and affection for them, and that demonstrate her deep understanding of the cultures from which they come. Choosing literature for the children's lessons is an important part of her planning. The main character of *Maniac Magee* is a boy who has very positive interactions with African-American children in the story. She has also provided a large-print version of the book from LRS Large Print Publications (Spinelli, 1990b) for a partially sighted student in the group. Farah's next literature choice for this group is *By the Lake of Sleeping Children: The Secret Life of the Mexican Border* (Urrea, 1996), about life in a dump in Tijuana, Mexico, which parallels and connects with the setting of *Maniac Magee*. Farah takes much care to ensure that all children in her class see themselves in many different roles in the literature she provides for them. She directs the major part of her small discretionary budget each year to the purchase of sets of trade books to supplement her basal reading program.

Valuing Diversity or Coping with Differences?

Creating an inviting environment in your classroom can help promote a literacy community for all students.

Diversity in the classroom can be viewed from at least two perspectives. On the one hand, teachers can consider that associating with people who are different enriches everyone. On the other hand, because diversity means that differences between children are greater than just the ordinary individual differences found among homogeneous groups of children, some teachers see it as a problem. Different languages can make it difficult to meet needs, group students efficiently for instruction, and provide materials that are appropriate for all children. Cultural differences arise, making teaching a complex and demanding act. These are legitimate concerns, but they should be viewed as challenges instead of problems. Teachers who take the first perspective, the positive one, see diversity as an asset to be exploited for the benefit of the children, an asset that enriches the learning of all—the students and the teacher.

CULTURE DIVERSITY, BACKGROUND KNOWLEDGE, AND LITERACY.   The pervasive culture in U.S. schools, according to Gollnick and Chinn (1998), is essentially "based on the knowledge and perspective of the West (Northern and Western Europe)." Many believe that this culture is apparent in textbooks and curricula and in the cadre of teachers that staff most schools. It characterizes what teachers expect students to know when they come to school, and it serves as the basis for teachers' assessment of student outcomes. It often characterizes how teachers reinforce children's behavior, both positively and negatively; how they ask children questions and accept their responses; how they correct children; how they do, or do not, make the classroom safe for children; and how they use gestures and time. Clearly, schools cannot adopt the culture of each and every child, but they can accept the culture of every child, accommodate that culture, and use its presence and teachers' knowledge of it to help teach all children. According to Fitzgerald (1995), teachers must make reading instruction congruent with the background culture that children bring to their lessons.

THE ZONE OF PROXIMAL DEVELOPMENT.   The work of Vygotsky (1978) provides another view of social constructivism that underlies children's cognitive development, with particular applications to the teaching of reading and language. The learning community includes culture, language, and important adults who guide children in their learning.

Vygotsky's concept of the **zone of proximal development** is especially important. According to his view of learning, there are tasks that can be performed by a student independently, others that cannot be performed at all, even with help, and those that fall within the "zone"—that can be performed with help from others. Those others in the classroom are usually adults, such as teachers, paraprofessionals, and parent volunteers, but they can also be other more capable students in cooperative learning group settings.

Many implications for the classroom emerge from these concepts.

- Teachers need to design instruction that is at an appropriate level for each child —not so difficult that they fail, not so simple that there is no gain, but at a level where, with **scaffolding** (i.e., a support system), they can learn. A one-size-fits-all approach is not appropriate.
- Learning activities need to be done in meaningful contexts, not in isolation.
- Children need to construct their own meaning with the help of the teacher and other adults and peers in the role of facilitators.
- Children need to see relationships between what they are learning and the communities in which they live.

CULTURALLY RESPONSIVE CLASSROOM COMMUNICATION.   Children's language develops in a sociocultural context. How children use language in their homes and communities also has important effects on their use of language in classrooms, especially when they are learning to read and write. Although language arts and reading curricula often reflect a linear assumption about the development of language and literacy in all of its iterations, ethnographers remind teachers that they must view how parents use language in rearing their children, the range of types of language use in the home, and the amount of exposure that children experience with respect to the diversity of languages, to the diversity of speakers of languages, and to the diversity of ways of using language outside of their homes (Heath, 1986). Culturally responsive teachers apply their knowledge of the many cultures in their classroom to how they address children and how they respond to them, both verbally and nonverbally.

Verbal Communication.   Providing feedback to students is a vital teacher activity. When feedback is provided across cultures, there is always potential for misunderstanding. Scarcella (1990) provides several categories of feedback behavior:

- Interpreting student feedback (how they indicate that they are paying attention). Most Americans nod their heads to indicate that they are listening. Asian students often nod to indicate that they are listening, but this does not necessarily indicate understanding.
- Complimenting and criticizing (how this is interpreted from both perspectives). Asian students might reject too many compliments as being insincere, whereas Hispanic students will usually welcome praise.

- Teacher correction of student errors (how students view the way the teacher corrects errors). Students from some cultures want to be corrected and are concerned at a lack of correction. In other cultures, correction can be a humiliation for the student. It is important for the teacher to consider how to treat this issue with each student in the classroom.

- Student requests for clarification (how, or if, students ask for help and how teachers interpret these requests). Teachers should carefully monitor the comprehension of their students, checking for understanding and watching for nonverbal behavior that might indicate a question that has not been expressed.

- Spotlighting, or calling attention to a student's behavior in front of others. Many children do not appreciate having attention called to them, especially from across the room. Teachers might be more effective if they walk over to students and softly give instructions, especially if student misbehavior is involved or even praise for older students. The teacher can avoid turning a small problem of inattention into a major problem of defiance.

- Questioning and answering (the purpose of questions). Asking questions is an important teacher instructional behavior. American teachers tend to ask many questions for the purpose of motivating critical thinking on the part of the students. But Heath (1983) has found that African-American children are often confused by the way teachers ask questions when the teachers already know the answers to them. She recommends that these children be asked questions of the type they are asked at home, such as "What's that like?" or "What's happening?" To promote higher-order thinking, teachers often ask for opinions about what a character did in a story or how an author expressed an idea. Children from some cultures are uncomfortable in offering opinions; they can gain experience and confidence in acquiring this ability in small group work before they express themselves in front of the entire class.

- Pausing (wait-time). Teachers tend to provide insufficient wait-time for students. They need to allow students time to think about their responses before going on to another student or accepting a response from students who always seem to know the correct answer before anyone else. According to Rowe (1974), teachers usually wait little more than one second. She found that when children were provided with at least three seconds of undisturbed wait-time, they responded more completely and correctly, the number of nonresponses decreased, and the number of volunteered responses increased.

Nonverbal Communication.   Communication is often thought of only as a verbal process, but the important impact of nonverbal communication should also be considered, especially when teachers work with children from many different cultures. For example, a frequent type of interaction between teacher and child is the teacher's need to correct the inappropriate behavior of a child. To show respect, an Anglo child will usually look in the teacher's eyes when being corrected. The same child will show defiance by looking at the floor instead of looking the teacher in the face. Conversely, a Hispanic child will often show respect to the teacher by looking at the floor, whereas defiance is shown by looking the teacher in the eyes. What message does the teacher send by saying to the Hispanic child, "Look me in the eye when I talk to you"? In this case, the teacher might be asking the student to demonstrate defiance. This is only one of many examples of the potential for cross-cultural misunderstandings between teacher and child, even when both are behaving appropriately for their own cultures.

These nonverbal aspects of communication are a form of **paralanguage**, which includes many aspects of nonverbal behavior that are very useful for teachers to understand (see Table 2.2). These behaviors are the clues that tell us someone is from another culture, sometimes even what country they are from, although we might not be able to hear them speaking. You cannot be expected to be familiar with all of the nonverbal behaviors of all of the cultures of the children in your classroom, but you can begin to reflect about the reactions of children to your own nonverbal behaviors and about your own reactions to puzzling nonverbal behaviors of students. When student reactions to a teacher's behavior are counterintuitive, there is often a cultural explanation.

As children's experiences with life in the United States expand, they also begin to learn the appropriate nonverbal behaviors of the new language and culture they are acquiring. When they are successful, they are able to function comfortably in two cultures, making them **bicultural**. Teachers need to be sensitive to children as they go about the complicated task of becoming bicultural.

TABLE 2.2

Selected Components of Paralanguage

COMPONENT	OBSERVABLE BEHAVIORS	SELECTED CLASSROOM EXAMPLES
Kinesics (Pennycook, 1985)	Gestures and other movements of the body, including facial expression, movements of the eye, and posture	American children often show respect with eye contact; other cultural groups of children frequently show respect by looking down.
Proxemics (Hall, 1966)	Social distance	Hispanic children often cling closely to the teacher and like a hug; Asian children tend to maintain a greater social distance and are less comfortable with touching.
Haptics (Pennycook, 1985)	Arm and hand movements	Americans indicate the height of a person with the hand held horizontally at the appropriate level; Hispanics hold the hand vertically for people, but horizontally for animals.
Paraverbal features (Pennycook, 1985)	Nonlexical aspects of verbal communication, such as pitch variation, the use of silence, how space is filled in a conversation (e.g., *uh* in English, *este* for many Spanish speakers)	Asian children often giggle when embarrassed, such as when they are caught misbehaving.
Chronism (Hall, 1983)	Monochronic use of time in a linear mode in Western cultures, with sequential scheduling and tasks completed one at a time; polychronistic use of time in a cyclical mode in non-Western cultures, with less precise time commitments	*Monochronic:* Western children tend to line up to be helped by the teacher one at a time. *Polychronic:* Non-Western children often gather around the teacher's desk, all wanting to be helped at the same time, unconcerned that the teacher helps each one a little bit so that everyone is eventually completely helped.

Language & Diversity

Linguistic Diversity: Today's Classroom Demographics

Who are the English language learners? Where are they? Everywhere! The 2000 census revealed a significant and growing diversity in American classrooms in almost all parts of the country. Perhaps the most important aspect of this change is the number of children classified as **English language learners**, children who arrive in American classrooms with no English or insufficient English for learning to read and write in English. When teachers think of English language learners, they likely think of Hispanic children; indeed, Hispanics make up the largest population of English language learners. They also think first of California, Texas, Florida, and New York as the states that are most affected by the presence of Spanish-speaking English language learners. But schools in most areas of the country are now beginning to experience an influx of Spanish-speaking English language learners.

According to the 2000 U.S. census, the Hispanic population of the United States has nearly doubled since the 1990 census, rising from 9 percent to 12.5 percent of the total population (U.S. Census Bureau, 2000; Campo-Flores, 2001). Some of the largest percentage increases have occurred in surprising areas of the country, from 10.4 percent to 19.7 percent in Nevada, from 1.2 percent to 4.7 percent in North Carolina, from 1.2 percent to 2.8 percent in Iowa, and from 6.5 percent to 9.4 percent in Connecticut. The meatpacking and processing industry has attracted many Spanish-speaking workers and their families to such states as Nebraska, Iowa, Minnesota, Arkansas, Kentucky, Tennessee, the Carolinas, Alabama, and Georgia, accounting for major changes there.

The most dramatic difference in the growth of Hispanic populations in the 2000 census, however, was the rapid dissemination to smaller population centers and suburbs (Suro & Singer, 2002). Almost half of Hispanic population growth was in fast-growing Hispanic hubs and new Hispanic destinations; the other half occurred in established metropolitan areas.

Similar growth is seen in other language groups as well, and not only are these groups growing, but they are also appearing in states where they were not as numerous in previous years. For example, most Hmong immigrants from Laos began their American experience near Fresno, California, but many of them have moved to Minnesota and Wisconsin (University of Wisconsin–Eau Claire, 2000). There are many other significant populations of English language learners, and how their needs are met in American schools depends not only on how many people there are in these populations, but also on how concentrated they are. Clusters of children with a mother tongue in common present special challenges—but also unique opportunities.

English language learners are not a monolithic population. Some are very proficient in speaking and understanding their mother tongue, and some are literate in that language. Some became literate in their home countries; others do so in programs of bilingual education here in the United States. As a result of living in refugee camps, some upper elementary and adolescent children have arrived in this country with little or no school experience at all. Some English language learners are migrant children from rural areas without educational opportunities, and others were working and contributing to the family income. Some English language learners have limited proficiency even in their mother tongue, just as some native English speakers are limited in their English proficiency. As teachers consider the challenges today's students represent, they also must think in terms of possible solutions.

BILINGUAL EDUCATION. Perhaps the most sweeping policy change to affect the education of English language learners in recent years was the 1974 *Lau* v. *Nichols* decision of the U.S. Supreme Court, which ruled that equal education did not result from providing exactly the same education to all children (*Lau* v. *Nichols*, 1974; J. Crawford, 1989). It required that school districts take positive steps to overcome the educational barriers experienced by students who did not speak English. Soon afterward, the Elementary and Secondary Education Act was amended with Title VII to make limited English proficient students eligible for federal funds and to permit their enrollment in **bilingual education** programs.

A 1981 court decision (*Casteñeda* v. *Pickard*, 1981) established three criteria for determining how programs of bilingual education were to be held accountable for meeting requirements of the Equal Education Opportunity Act of 1974. The criteria included the following:

- The program must be based on sound educational theory.
- The program must be effectively implemented with adequate resources for personnel, instructional materials, and space.
- Following a trial period, the program must be shown to be effective in overcoming language handicaps.

Although the *Lau* v. *Nichols* decision did not mandate bilingual education as a remedy, school districts did find it to be one of the few ways to ensure that English language learners had equal access to education, that is, education in their mother tongue while they were learning English. Most of such programs have taken the transitional form, in which children learn to read and write and also study the other subjects of the academic curriculum, mathematics, social science, and science in the mother tongue. Simultaneously, the children study English as a second language, a process that typically takes from two to five years or more. Through a transition process called *positive transfer of skills,* children can then do in English what they learned to do in the mother tongue. Even learning to read in English as a second language is a relatively smooth and effortless process—we learn to read only once. When children do not have the opportunity to learn academic subjects in the mother tongue, they fall behind in those subjects during the period of time when they are learning English.

Children in transitional bilingual programs usually continue their academic studies only in English after the onset of transition to English, although they typically receive continuing support in the mother tongue as needed. More infrequently, children are placed in maintenance bilingual education programs and continue to receive instruction in the mother tongue even after transition, with the goal of being a bilingual, biliterate, and bicultural individual at the end. Because of the lack of instructional materials in the mother tongue and often a lack of trained bilingual teachers in many languages, non–Spanish language bilingual education programs are less common and usually limited in scope.

TEACH IT!

39

ENGLISH LANGUAGE LEARNERS AND LITERACY. Bilingual education, however, is a subject of much controversy. In recent years, initiatives in a number of states, including California, Arizona, and Massachusetts, have discouraged most bilingual education in those states. They require instead a one-year period of **immersion instruction** in English as a second language, although the efficacy of this approach is not supported in

Because of the changing demographic of the U.S. population, strategies for meeting the needs of non-English-speaking students have become a focal point of discussion in many communities.

the literature. In fact, there is abundant evidence that children need two to five years of instruction in English as a second language before they are ready to learn to read in English (Thomas & Collier, 1997). An analysis of test scores from the 2002 California Stanford 9 test scores reported by the influential League of United Latin American Citizens (LULAC) (O'Leary, 2002) suggested that English language learners were not developing English fluency and that many were falling further behind in academic subjects. O'Leary reported that four years after the passage of California's Unz English Initiative, Proposition 227, more than a million limited English immigrant students in second through eleventh grades in California still had not been mainstreamed in English-only classes, an indication of the failure of the policy.

In a major meta-analysis of the effectiveness of bilingual education, Greene (1998) carefully selected eleven studies that had comparison groups of children not in bilingual education programs, in which initial assignment to groups was random or statistically controlled, in which results were based on standardized test scores in English, and in which differences between the scores of treatment and control groups were determined with appropriate statistical tests. He found that the bilingual programs in studies that met these criteria were effective in increasing standardized test scores in reading and mathematics that were measured in English.

Goodman (1986) reminds us that bilingual children are not disadvantaged in some academic way. They are disadvantaged only if their linguistic strengths are not appreciated and if schools fail to build on their strengths. The International Reading Association (IRA) has recognized the efficacy of teaching children to read in the mother tongue while they learn to understand and speak English and before they begin learning to read in their second language, English. The IRA's resolution of support includes three major elements: (1) initial literacy instruction should be provided in the child's native language whenever possible; (2) although initial literacy instruction in a second language can be successful, there is a higher risk of reading problems than beginning with a child's first language; and (3) instructional decisions should support the professional judgment of the teachers and administrators who are responsible for teaching students whose first language is not English and oppose any restrictive federal, state, or local initiatives (International Reading Association, 2001).

Dialects of English and Literacy

English language learners, those whose mother tongue is not English and whose English proficiency is limited, are not the only children whose reading instruction is affected by linguistic factors. African-American Vernacular English is a major dialect of English that is spoken by urban African-American children in the United States. There are other dialects, including Southern Regional Dialect, a mostly rural dialect of both Anglo and African-American children.

THE WORLD OF READING

Children's Secret Languages

Most people remember the joys of confounding their childhood friends, or perhaps being confounded by them, when they first encountered Pig Latin. It was a secret language that was easily learned, once the principle of moving the first letter to the end of the word and adding the sound of "ay" was grasped. When the skill was shared with friends, it allowed them to communicate with each other while leaving adults perplexed.

Children are intrigued with the possibilities of understanding, speaking, reading, and writing in another language, although they often do not have the opportunity until secondary school. Today, more and more children across the country encounter classmates who speak another language in addition to English. Sometimes the other language is that person's only language. Children who speak only one language might not have an appreciation of the advantages of speaking another language or of the disadvantages of not speaking English. Teachers can gently address both issues by using secret languages as an example. Children's secret languages are a nice language play activity that usually has the added bonus of providing practice in syllabication and letter-sound correspondence.

If you have children in your class from other countries, you could ask whether they have a secret children's language and whether they would teach it to the class. This activity places them in a position of leadership that they might not often have, so you need to be sensitive to their comfort level in front of groups and help them with the process. If you you do not have children in your class from other countries, or wish to explore a variety of secret languages, you could use Alvin Schwartz's book *The Cat's Elbow and Other Secret Languages* (1982), a collection of thirteen secret children's languages, including Pig Latin and Boontling.

AFRICAN-AMERICAN VERNACULAR ENGLISH.   African-American Vernacular English, also known as *Black Dialect* and *Ebonics*, is the dialect of the English language that is probably most frequently encountered in American classrooms. According to Labov (1970, 1972), African-American Vernacular English is as logical and consistent as Standard English, it can be reproduced, and it makes sense. It is merely different from Standard English. A policy statement of the TESOL Board of Directors (1997) stipulates that African-American Vernacular English has been demonstrated in research to be a rule-governed, linguistic system that has its own lexical, phonological, syntactic, and discourse patterns and that it therefore deserves pedagogical recognition. It is not a substandard dialect of English, and it is not poor English. It is a dialect that is widely understood and spoken among many inner-city African-Americans.

There are many phonological and syntactical differences between African-American Vernacular English and Standard American English. Some of those identified by Johnson and Simons (1974) are presented in Table 2.3.

These characteristics of African-American Vernacular English appear so consistently that they occasionally appear in the oral reading of children who superimpose

TABLE 2.3

Selected Phonological and Syntactical Differences between Standard American English and African-American Vernacular English, based on Johnson & Simons (1974)

LINGUISTIC FEATURE	STANDARD AMERICAN ENGLISH	AFRICAN-AMERICAN VERNACULAR ENGLISH
Phonological features	(as pronounced)	(as pronounced)
Initial and final sounds of /th/ (modified)	that, these both, breathe	dat, dese bof, breave
Medial /v/ (modified)	seven	seben
Medial or final /r/, /l/ (deleted)	door help	doe hep
Consonant clusters (deleted)	desk told	des tol
Syntactical features	(as expressed)	(as expressed)
Past tense marker	I talked to him.	I talk to him.
Copula (deleted)	She is tall.	She tall.
Use of verb *be* (habitual)	Julie reads every day.	Julie be reading.
Subject-verb agreement	We were there.	We was there.
Double negative	Henry doesn't have a football.	Henry don't have no football.
Possessive (deleted)	The girl's dress	The girl dress
Question (reversal of subject and verb)	What is that?	What that is?

their dialect over the words written on the page (Johnson & Simons, 1974). Teachers must consider whether or not there is a negative effect on reading comprehension or only on oral reading accuracy, since both are possible, even in a single reading episode by an individual child.

ADDING STANDARD AMERICAN ENGLISH.   Teachers demonstrate that they value the language of children when they accept the way the children communicate with each other and with members of their families and communities. In classrooms, however, teachers also need to help students add a second dialect of English: Standard American English, a dialect that supports the children's continuing academic learning and that offers access to higher education and desirable employment opportunities. The resulting bidialectical children resemble bilingual children in that they can readily switch back and forth between dialects according to the educational or social situation in which they find themselves. Part of the process of being bidialectical is knowing when and where to use each dialect.

Where an ESL program is already in place for English language learners, many ESL activities will be of value for children whose home and community language environment is African-American Vernacular English. Teachers can use many intermediate and advanced ESL instructional strategies to add Standard American English to the children's repertoire. The children will not require instruction at the basic stages of the natural approach for English language learners (described in Chapter 12), but participation in activities at the third stage of the natural approach will be helpful because they focus on communication, not on grammar. In addition, the activities described for "sheltered English" in Chapter 12 will support and enhance the children's development of **background knowledge** and vocabulary needed for effective reading comprehension. Where such a program is not in place because there are no English language learners, an oral language development program should be provided to help children acquire Standard American English in much the same way that English language learners acquire English. This is not an English-as-a-second-language or ESL program, but rather a program of oral language development.

Rickford and Rickford (1995) suggest a very direct approach, beginning with an agreement among students that Standard American English is appropriate for classroom interaction and writing. With that understanding, teachers should provide focused activities based on language needs that children demonstrate. Delpit (1990) suggests that these include dialect contrast activities in which students and teachers agree that learning Standard American English is a goal, probably in the upper elementary grades and beyond. These dialect contrasts can be incorporated into dialogue journals, class logs, and student portfolios.

LITERACY ISSUES FOR AFRICAN-AMERICAN CHILDREN.   The issue of mother tongue instruction has important implications for children who speak African-American Vernacular English. If learning to read in Spanish while learning to speak English is the most effective program for Spanish-speaking children, then it could follow that speakers of African-American Vernacular English should learn to read from materials written in that dialect while they are acquiring Standard American English as a second dialect (Simpkins, Holt, & Simpkins, 1974). Indeed, there are educators who have advocated for this approach. There are, however, some significant barriers:

- There is not broad acceptance in the African-American community for the use of African-American Vernacular English as a language of instruction.

- Although some reading instructional materials have been written in African-American Vernacular English through the years, they have not been broadly or systematically used.

- There is limited research evidence at present to support the use of reading materials written in African-American Vernacular English (Simpkins et al., 1974).

- There is a sense among some African Americans and others that the use of African-American Vernacular English might be a tool for minimizing opportunities for success among African-American children (Williams, 1991).

Given the highly controversial nature of the issue, there are several ways in which teachers can make effective and positive use of the undeniable presence of

African-American Vernacular English—and other dialects of English—in American classrooms:

- Value and accept positively the communication efforts of children who use African-American Vernacular English in the classroom.
- Avoid "correcting" pronunciation and syntactical structures from African-American Vernacular English and other dialects of English used by children in their ordinary classroom discourse; such attempts betray a negative valuing of the way the children speak and, by implication, of the children themselves and of their family members and communities.
- Demonstrate valuing of the dialect by accepting it in the dictations of children in key vocabulary and language experience approach activities.
- In addition to using children's literature in which dialogue is in Standard American English for read-aloud activities, incorporate children's literature that includes dialogue in African-American Vernacular English and other dialects spoken by children in the classroom.
- In activities that are designed to help children acquire the Standard American English, avoid references to the standard dialect as the "correct" or "better" way to speak.
- Use traditional cultural literary structures of the African-American community, such as the *praise song* and the *praise poem* (Johnson-Coleman, 2001) and trickster tales, which are also a part of the Native American oral tradition. An Internet search at www.google.com will yield dozens of praise song, praise poem, and trickster tale resources.
- As an important part of the literacy program for African-American children, include Afrocentric children's literature that reflects the culture and linguistic traditions of children who speak African-American Vernacular English.
- Ensure that phonological, morphological, lexical, and syntactical features of African-American Vernacular English and other dialects of English are not used to penalize children in assessment activities, especially those that are not related to the purpose of the assessment (see Chapters 9 and 10).

Delpit (1991) provides nine factors that teachers should consider in educating children of color who are too often failed by our schools. She recommends that teachers do the following:

- Teach these children more, not less
- Provide critical thinking experiences for them
- Challenge the racist view of some that these children are incompetent
- Recognize and build on the children's strengths
- Use metaphors, analogies, and experiences that are familiar to the children to connect them to school knowledge
- Ensure that the children feel cared for, as in a family
- Identify the children's needs and meet them with a variety of strategies
- Honor and respect the culture the children bring to school
- Connect the children to their community, something that is greater than themselves

TEACH IT!

1

Phonics & Phonemic Awareness

TEACH IT!

Incorporating Authentic Children's Literature

The Language Experience Approach (LEA) to reading is a powerful tool for addressing culture and beginning reading that is based on the oral language of children. The approach centers on language as the vehicle for communicating thoughts and ideas. This Teach It! explores the approach with a lesson that incorporates authentic children's literature.

The first step is for the teacher to conduct a read-aloud of a piece of children's literature that is culturally appropriate—in this case, for a group of African-American first graders—and that is also ideal as a stimulus for a language experience dictation. The book in this example is Patricia McKissack's *Ma Dear's Aprons* (1997), about a little boy living with his mother in a single-parent situation. In the story, David Earl's mother has a different apron for each day of the week, and David knows which day of the week it is by observing the apron his mother is wearing. Although there are seven days and seven aprons, the teacher might decide to read only up through the first three days and aprons. During the read-aloud, share the wonderful illustrations by Floyd Cooper, asking questions about the activities of the three days and the aprons that Ma Dear wears.

Then have the children dictate their brief version of the story. They might come up with something sim-

ilar to the example seen in the figure. Accept the dictations of the children as stated, regardless of any cultural affectations. In this collaborative chart story strategy, other children might suggest changes that result in a dictation in Standard American English. The example shows two past tense verbs, "wash" and "iron," that were written as dictated by the children because no child suggested a change. The word "next" was pronounced as "nex"; the teacher should spell it correctly according to best practice in the language experience approach. The children should have many opportunities to read the text in a shared reading mode as the dictation is recorded and after the children's rendition of the story is completed.

On Monday, Ma Dear put on the blue apron.
She wash the clothes.

The next day she wore a yellow apron.
She iron the clothes on Tuesday.

David likes the green apron on Wednesday.
It had a treasure pocket.
There was candy in it.

Refer to your **Teach It!** booklet for further activities you can use to reinforce concepts discussed in this chapter.

**Struggling
Reader**

Supporting At-Risk Readers

Another aspect of diversity in American classrooms is a more generic category that incorporates children from all groups, that of the student who is at-risk of not learning to read. Through the years since the Coleman Report (Coleman et al., 1966), many terms have been used to describe students whose school achievement is below expectation, including at-risk, disadvantaged, low-income, and others. The constellation of factors often associated with **at-risk students** includes the following: low-income; inner-city or rural; ethnic and/or language minority; non-English-speaking; nontraditional family structure, including frequent absence of father; and high rate of school dropout.

There are many students who exhibit the characteristics above who have satisfactory or above-average achievement in school, and there are students who exhibit none of the characteristics who do experience failure in school. But it is fair to say that these factors are strongly associated with low school achievement.

As a result of the Coleman Report (Coleman et al., 1966), a variety of federally funded efforts were initiated to alleviate the effects of the above factors on low school achievement, especially in reading. These included Head Start, Title I and Title VII of the Elementary and Secondary Education Act (ESEA), and other so-called compensatory education programs.

The rapidly increasing influx of English language learners and other so-called disadvantaged students in U.S. schools provides a greater challenge than ever before to teachers whose charge is to promote the equitable access of all students to high-quality instruction in reading and writing. These students have generally been placed in compensatory or remedial programs, where they are expected to learn to read and write by acquiring isolated skills through interaction with incomplete fragments of language. Rarely do they emerge successfully from these programs into the mainstream; instead, often they leave the programs only when they leave school—all too often as early leavers or dropouts (A. N. Crawford, 1993).

COGNITIVE, AFFECTIVE, AND PSYCHOMOTOR FACTORS.   Cultural and linguistic diversity are major factors for teachers to consider in planning reading instruction for children. But there are cognitive, affective, and psychomotor aspects of diversity that also have an effect on reading.

The increasing diversity of our classrooms seems to bring with it an increase in the numbers of children who are struggling to read. Duffy-Hester (1999) examined several model reading programs for such children and found common guiding principles that should serve teachers well in working with troubled readers. Among these guiding principles are the following:

- Reading programs should be balanced, drawing on more than a single theoretical perspective. A one-size-fits-all approach to reading instruction inevitably seems to miss meeting the needs of some children. A balanced program touches on all of the learning modalities that diverse groups of children bring to the classroom

- There should be a well-supported role for every element in a balanced reading program. Several currently popular direct instruction reading programs, for example, make heavy use of decodable text, fragments of unconnected text in which the students are to practice word recognition elements they have been studying. Yet there is little research to support the use of such text, whereas there is abundant research to support the use of connected text, especially in the promotion of reading comprehension (Allington, 1997).

- Word recognition, comprehension, and vocabulary development should be taught in the context of authentic reading and writing activities, not in isolation.

- Teacher read-aloud activities serve to build background knowledge and vocabulary, preparing children to understand their own reading of the text later.

- Authentic assessment provides valuable information that teachers can use to inform their instruction. Some assessment does not provide this type of information and takes up valuable time that could be used for children to read and write. We are reminded of two traditional dictums about assessment: "You don't fatten a pig by weighing it," and "You don't help a plant grow faster by ripping it up to look at the root development from time to time."

- Teachers should use their professional preparation to make instructional decisions about reading programs they use.

- Staff development activities should provide time for reflection and opportunities to share experiences about best practices.

- The learner-centered goals and strategies that are most effective for troubled readers will serve other children well, too.

There are other factors that affect the plight of troubled readers. Allington (2001) offers several research-based accommodations that relate to the organization of the school. Class size is an important factor, with research demonstrating that achievement is higher when classes are smaller, especially with children from low-income families (Achilles, 1999). Allington recommends a class size of twenty. Access to appropriate instructional materials is also important. In agreement with Duffy-Hester, he feels that programs should be designed to fit children, not forcing children to fit into programs. He recommends that no more than 20 to 30 percent of instructional time be devoted to single-source materials, that is, materials that all children in the classroom use in common. A third factor is that of honoring instructional time. There should be no interruptions of the period for teaching reading, not even public address announcements from the principal's office.

Allington then turns his attention to the question of access to intensive, expert instruction. He suggests that one-on-one tutoring is the most intensive type of instruction but that very small group instruction (four to seven students) is much more effective than traditional large-group or whole-class instruction is. He further observes that pullout remedial reading programs, such as those underwritten by federal funds, frequently offer instruction for too short a time but over too long a period of duration. He recommends offering a semester of very frequent and intensive support instead of a year of less intensive support. Finally, Allington suggests expanding instruction time for troubled readers. This can be accomplished by adding a second daily lesson, providing extended-day reading instruction through after-school programs, and providing summer school reading support to minimize summer reading loss.

READERS WHO ARE MAINSTREAMED.   Federal law calls for inclusion for many children identified for special education services, who are now **mainstreamed** in regular classrooms, although sometimes for only part of the school day. They are educated, to the maximum extent possible, in the same setting as their classmates without disabilities. This means that regular classroom teachers must address the needs of some children who are physically disabled, mentally retarded, visually or hearing impaired, emotionally disturbed, and from other special needs categories.

Under provisions of the law, students are identified as requiring assessment if they have a disability such as mental retardation; a hearing impairment, including deafness; a speech or language impairment; a visual impairment, including blindness; a serious emotional disturbance; an orthopedic impairment; autism; traumatic brain injury; a specific learning disability; deaf-blindness; or multiple disabilities. These children's needs must be assessed, and an individual educational plan must be developed for each student (Individuals with Disabilities Education Act, 1997). The plan must include the following elements:

- Current levels of educational performance
- Annual goals and short-term objectives
- Need for special education and related services
- Explanation if the child cannot be mainstreamed in the regular classroom
- Description and schedule of special education services provided
- Description of transition services provided
- Assessment of student progress, including needed accommodations.

Support services from experienced special education teachers are often provided to the regular classroom teacher who is working with mainstreamed children, but they are often not sufficient or timely.

Individualized plans for mainstreamed students is one strategy for addressing the needs of at-risk students.

There is also great concern about the overrepresentation of children from linguistic and ethnic minorities in special education (Hill, Carjuzaa, & Baca, 1993). Historically, children were often assigned to special education classes on the basis of supposed language disorders and/or mental retardation that might be nothing more than limited English proficiency. Under provisions of *Diana* v. *State Board of Education* (1970) and subsequent special education legislation, such as P.L. 94-142, this is no longer permitted. Damico (1991) suggests that care be taken to ensure that referral to special education is not based on the following:

- Other factors that might explain the child's learning and language difficulties, including lack of opportunity to learn, cultural dissonance, and stressful life events, for example, among refugee children
- Language difficulties that the student has at school but not at home or in the community
- Ordinary needs of children to acquire English as a second language or the Standard American English dialect
- Cross-cultural interference
- Bias in the assessment process, including data analysis that does not take into account the child's culture, language, and life experiences

There are many strategies that can be used very effectively in teaching children with these needs. According to Gersten and Baker (2000), teachers should do the following:

- Build children's vocabulary and use it as a curricular anchor

- Use visual representations to reinforce major concepts and vocabulary
- Use the children's mother tongue as a support system
- Adapt cognitive and language demands of instruction to the children by using sheltered English strategies

It is not only the physical needs of these students that should be addressed in inclusion efforts, but also the content of the curriculum. If students of color or girls need to see themselves in the literature they read, then so should students with disabilities. According to Landrum (2001), this benefits not only those students, but also students without disabilities, who need to learn about and accept differences. Landrum has developed a set of criteria for the evaluation of novels that feature characters with disabilities. Among her criteria are the following:

- Plot: Story events are realistic, not contrived; disabled characters are active participants
- Character development: Disabled characters are presented as strong and independent, not passive and dependent; the focus is on what they can do, not on what they cannot do.
- Tone: The text avoids using such terms as *retarded*, *handicapped*, and *crippled*.

READERS WHO ARE GIFTED.   **Gifted** children as diverse learners are not as frequently a challenge for classroom teachers. Many have learned to read at home as a result of being read to, and most of those who don't learn to read at home very quickly learn to read in kindergarten or first grade. But there are three assumptions that teachers sometimes erroneously make about gifted children. The first is that gifted children don't have reading problems. The gifted child who is reading at grade level might have a reading problem that should be diagnosed and treated. Ordinarily, gifted children will be reading above grade level, often several grades above their age-expected level.

A second assumption is that all children will benefit from the same reading program. Children who already read, often far above grade level, will be bored if they are required to proceed laboriously through instructional content designed for children who read at grade level or even below. Teachers must find opportunities to challenge such children, usually by modifying the reading program for them and certainly by providing alternative activities when other children are learning something that was mastered long ago by gifted children or other children who are advanced in their reading abilities.

A third assumption is that gifted children have already mastered all the basic skills. Fragmentation of basic skills is not unusual among gifted children, who can be integrated into reading groups that are addressing these areas of weakness at the time when those lessons are offered.

READERS WHO ARE BOYS.   Much attention has been given to the roles of girls in literature for children in recent years—and with good effect. Whereas stories in basal readers and current literature anthologies tended to focus on boys in the most active roles in past years, there is now balance in the stories that the children read, not to mention representation of major cultural and linguistic groups as well. You might wonder why boys would be listed as a category of diversity among readers, but boys continue to have problems in reading that are out of proportion to their numbers in the population. Why do boys make up an almost overwhelming proportion of troubled readers? Among the many factors associated with this finding are the greater frequency of left dominance; lack of physical and emotional maturity compared to girls; greater frequency of attention deficit disorder; different cultural expectations for boys, including more physical activity and action; fewer positive reading models for boys; interest levels of books for boys; and female-dominated environment in schools, with teachers also favoring realistic fiction and character-related stories.

There are many steps teachers can take to ensure that boys do not continue to be overrepresented among the ranks of troubled readers:

- Provide more time in the initial stages of reading instruction for immature boys, especially those who exhibit signs of left dominance
- Provide positive role models for boys—men and older boys who read
- Provide books of interest to boys, such as the highly irreverent *Captain Underpants* series (Pilkey, 2000) and nonfiction informational books about nature, history, biography, and sports
- Provide magazines and newspapers that have more real world interest and shorter texts
- Permit more physical movement, for example, letting the children sprawl out on the floor when reading
- Provide structured opportunities for children to discuss the text they are reading and writing about (Young & Brozo, 2001)

Finding the Books They Want to Read

Diversity is important with respect not only to the learning characteristics of all students, but also to their need for appropriate text to read and from which to learn to read.

THE PRINT ENVIRONMENT OF STUDENTS AT HOME.   As might be expected, the print environment of the home and community is closely related to the factors of diversity described in this chapter. The newspapers, magazines, books, calendars, checkbooks, notes on the refrigerator door, web site pages on the computer screen, and instructional manuals found in most middle-class homes may be absent from or less frequently encountered in the homes of children from low-income families. There might not be a tradition of reading and writing in the family, or perhaps a Bible or other religious book is the only representation of print in the home.

In a study, Halle, Kurtz-Costes, and Mahoney (1997), found that access to print was an important factor related to the reading achievement of African American children. In an international study of the relationships among reading achievement, home literacy environment, and school and public library availability of reading material in several countries, Elley (1992, 1996) reported that access to print was the most powerful factor associated with reading achievement, including the size of the school library. He found that frequent silent reading was the next most significant variable affecting reading achievement.

Beyond the presence of text to read, the need for models reading in the home is also of great importance, especially when it is recognized that men and older boys are often less likely to read than are women and girls in the family.

Besides often being a factor in the low-income home, the absence of text also characterizes the low-income communities in which the homes are located. In a study of print resources in two low-income and two middle-income neighborhoods,

Neuman and Celano (2001) surveyed the availability of reading materials for purchase, such as newspapers, magazines, and children's books; the quantity of signage; public places where reading took place, such as laundromats and bookstores; the availability of books in child-care centers; and the quality of services and materials provided by school and public libraries. They found an overwhelming advantage of print resources in the middle-income neighborhoods, and they concluded that children in the low-income neighborhoods would have difficulty finding books of good quality, while those in the middle-income neighborhoods would have difficulty avoiding them.

In addition, the provision of a full-time or even part-time librarian is often related to the income levels of students in the schools. Neuman and Celano (2001) found that there were no trained school librarians in the low-income communities they studied, while the schools in the middle-income communities had well-trained and highly experienced school librarians. School libraries in the middle-income communities were also open more days and hours per week than those in the low-income communities. The same disparities were found in public libraries in the communities studied.

They concluded, as did Cunningham and Stanovich (1997), that the children who are most in need of a print-rich environment are the least likely to encounter it, resulting in a spiraling down of environmental opportunities for reading in the community, which in turn results in less motivation to read and yet fewer opportunities to read. Allington (1983) adds that this is aggravated when these same children are enrolled in public schools in which low-level programs are provided to address the reading problems of the children, resulting in these children doing less reading of text than do children who read well. These programs involve major time commitments to studying about reading instead of time devoted to reading connected text.

GETTING BOOKS, MAGAZINES, AND NEWSPAPERS INTO CHILDREN'S HANDS.

Given the diversity of children in our schools, especially children who are at risk of being troubled readers, teachers should take special pains to find books and other print materials that they will enjoy, books with characters and settings with which they can identify, books in which they can see themselves in positive roles, and materials that are of high interest and have visual appeal. A valuable resource of books and other sources of connected text that reflect cultures of diversity is found in Banks and Banks's *Teaching Strategies for Ethnic Studies* (1996). Banks and Banks categorize many dozens of books in English for teachers and for children in the following groups: First Americans (American Indians, Native Hawaiians, and African Americans); European Americans (European ethnic groups and Jewish Americans); Hispanic Americans (Mexican Americans, Puerto Rican Americans, and Cuban Americans); and Asian Americans (Chinese Americans, Japanese Americans, Filipino Americans, and Indochinese Americans).

An abundance of books available in Spanish exist for children who want and need to read in that language (Schon, 2000, 2001; Schon and Berkin, 1996). Even when children do not have the opportunity to learn to read in the mother tongue, those who learned to read in the mother tongue in another school or country should be provided with opportunities to read more books in that mother tongue. It improves self-concept, offers evidence that the school and teacher value that mother tongue, and provides practice in reading that builds background knowledge and skills that transfer positively to reading in English later. Teachers should also be very careful about the use of so-called bilingual books that are written in two languages, usually with English and Spanish versions on facing pages. This practice ensures that children will acquire

English in terms of Spanish, that is, a very ineffective translation approach. It is better for children to read a story in Spanish from one book and then read the same story in English from another book, as elaborated in later chapters. The children can use their background knowledge from the first experience to support their comprehension, and learning, of English in the second book.

Technology

Gifted children require a rich variety of books and other text materials to maintain their many and changing interests. They will often tackle books at a much higher level than the level at which they are reading because of their motivation and willingness to persist. Given good guidance, they can use the Internet very productively, too. Many sites are now available that are geared to younger children's reading abilities. Teacher sites like MarcoPolo (see www.marcopolo-education.org) can also help teachers locate stimulating project ideas and resources for them. This is less of a problem for children in the lower grades of a multigraded school because they will find reading resources for older children in the school library. But it can be a problem for the sixth-grade gifted child in a K–6 school. This child needs access to a middle or secondary school library or an understanding teacher who is willing to check out books at the public library.

Finding materials that are high-interest and low-vocabulary enough for troubled readers, especially for boys, is a perennial problem for teachers. The teacher who is always conventional might have difficulty finding books that meet both criteria. A good resource for magazines is *Magazines for Kids and Teens* (Stoll, 1997), which provides descriptions of the content and the reading and interest levels of over 200 magazines on a wide variety of topics, including some that publish students' own writing.

In addition, boys will enjoy recent offerings in the immensely popular Captain Underpants series (Pilkey, 2000): *Captain Underpants and the Invasion of the Incredibly Naughty Cafeteria Ladies from Outer Space, Captain Underpants and the Wrath of the Wicked Wedgie Woman, Captain Underpants and the Attack of the Talking Toilets,* and *Captain Underpants and the Perilous Plot of Professor Poopypants.* Teachers who understand and appreciate the sense of humor of nine-year-old boys will recognize the appeal of these titles and the opportunities for stimulating those boys' creative writing instincts.

School budget problems are often a factor that affects the numbers of books, magazines, and newspapers available to children in the classroom. Some sources of text that teachers can exploit to augment those supplied by the school district are the following:

- School storage rooms, where surplus books are often hidden away
- Secondhand stores, public library book sales, yard sales, and swap meets, where teachers can often negotiate low prices with vendors "for the children." Returning to vendors at the end of the day and offering to buy all remaining books for a bulk price is often an effective way to maximize scarce teacher resources, since many teachers spend much of their own money on books for children.
- Child-made books that result from collaborative chart stories, language experience approach activities, and other student writing activities
- Local public libraries that are usually available for walking field trips and that permit children to request library cards so that they can check out their own books
- Commercial book clubs, which offer children's books at quantity discounts, usually with paper covers instead of hard covers. Depending on the number of books ordered by the children, many book clubs provide additional books for the teacher's classroom library.

- Newspapers that often sponsor programs to adopt a classroom and also often provide newspapers at no cost
- Support from parent groups, service clubs, and other community sources
- *Reading Is Fundamental* (RIF.org), which provides sets of books to schools at no cost

Finally, teachers should ensure that a wide variety of text is readily available for children to take home to read. Too many resources are so protected from loss or abuse that they are never used.

Equity and Access to Computers

Technology

As was noted, library resources for children from low-income neighborhoods are limited, and certainly the same is true with respect to access to computer technology. According to Becker (2000), only 22 percent of children of low socioeconomic status have a computer at home, while 91 percent of high socioeconomic status children do. This digital divide is particularly acute for African-American and Hispanic families. A report of the Children's Partnership (2000) indicates that the percentage of Caucasian households with Internet access is 29.8 percent, that of African-American households is 11.2 percent, and that of Hispanic households is 12.6 percent.

Access to the Internet at school has improved dramatically during the past several years. According to the National Center for Education Statistics (1999), 95 percent of all public schools provide Internet access, including 90 percent of those where 71 percent of students are eligible for free or reduced-price school lunch, a frequently used measure of a school's socioeconomic status.

Even as the gap in providing access to computer technology and Internet access to all students is closed, teachers should consider the value of this access in terms of instruction in reading and writing. According to Krashen (1997), computer technology and the Internet might not have a great deal to offer in teaching children to read. He found no evidence that computer-based reading management programs such as Accelerated Reader or the IBM Writing to Read program provide any benefits to children. He concluded that funds should instead be directed to trade books for free voluntary reading, as time invested in this activity is very effective in increasing reading achievement. Becker (2000) reported that, in elementary grades from 4 to 8, most teachers who used computers in the classroom used them for skill practice games, for word processing, and to access CD-ROMs. He also reported that computers were used slightly more frequently in low socioeconomic status schools than in high socioeconomic status schools, but that their use in low socioeconomic status schools involved more traditional drill and practice activities, whereas their use in high socioeconomic status schools reflected teaching strategies that are more constructivist and innovative.

When utilized properly, specially designed educational software or access to the Internet can offer a variety of opportunities for working with all children, regardless of their needs.

Children who surf the Net are reading, usually with high motivation. Children without access to the Internet are probably not reading something else instead of surfing the Net, the result being less practice in reading for those children, another example of the Matthew effect, according to which the rich get richer, and the poor get poorer (Stanovich, 1986). This could be a motivation to ensure that all students have access to computers with focused purposes so that even the least affluent have opportunities to sample the wealth of information on the Net.

Although the contributions of computer technology to reading instruction are still being assessed and ways of using computers effectively may be limited, there is broad recognition of the need to provide access to disadvantaged children and to narrow the digital divide between them and advantaged children. Computer technology can be a powerful tool for hearing-impaired students and visually impaired students, since there are voice-synthesizing programs and good visual tools for the hard of hearing. Students who have come to this country with little familiarity with English can also use some of the basic decoding programs and talking books to build their familiarity with this language.

As was noted earlier, boys are much more likely to experience difficulties in learning to read than girls are. A helpful source of ideas for boys, and for other identifiable groups of children, is the List category on the Amazon web site (www.amazon.com), which recently included a Gross-Out Books for Boys list. Among the irreverent books listed there were *Dragon's Fat Cat* (Dragon Tales); *Pigs Aplenty, Pigs Galore!*; *Dogzilla; Kat Kong; Everyone Poops; Parts; The Gas We Pass: The Story of Farts; Captain Underpants Boxed Set (Four Books and a Whoopie Cushion);* and *Dog Breath: The Horrible Trouble with Hally Tosis*.

For example, in Gomi's (1993) *Everyone Poops*, facing pages with illustrations of an elephant and a mouse have the following text:

An elephant makes a big poop. A mouse makes a small poop.

The girls in the class might react with "Eeww," but that will only heighten the boys' interest as they read the very predictable text in this book. Interested teachers should check the Amazon web site from time to time for lists that are provided by parents and other teachers. Of course, teachers are free to contribute their own lists of children's books that meet "gross-out" or other criteria.

Finally, early and full communication with parents will be necessary before children are introduced to this type of book, with alternative options for children of parents who object to the books. Some of these titles might be most appropriate for small-group reading lessons and individual conferences and less appropriate as whole-class read-aloud activities. Parents with troubled readers at home, however, are usually thrilled to find that their children are interested in reading something and that they are enjoying it.

Teachers need to know the community of which they are a part and respect the values parents hold. Always check with other teachers and the school librarian, when there is one, before recommending any books. The lists of books recommended by the International Reading Association, the National Council of Teachers of English, and the American Library Association are good places to start. Give a book you are unsure of to some parents to review as a way of gauging their feelings. Usually, when people read the books that might be in question, the concerns dissipate. However, you do need to know the books and magazines that you recommend, and the more you know about particular interests and resources, the more students will come to you as a resource when they want to find something to read.

STANDARDS & LITERACY

★ ★ Finding Resources ★ ★

There is a tendency in some areas of the country to limit what is taught to only the standards that are assessed. As you think about how to motivate students and engage them in becoming independent learners, ensure that your classroom activities are rich in complexity and challenge and that they continue to broaden children's interest in and understanding of the world. There are ways to achieve these goals while meeting most states' standards. You will need to think carefully about what you know about students' motivation and ways of learning so that your classroom is both structured and goal-oriented and also stimulating to all students. Many positive resources have been developed to help teachers implement the state standards. You saw one example in the vignette about Marguerite, a Pennsylvania teacher, at the beginning of this chapter. The integrated unit on community biography comes with a rich set of resources for teachers to use in making this unit come alive. You need to find resources and support available in the state in which you teach and within your school district and use them well.

★ Implications of Current Assessment Practices for Diverse Learners

In recent years, calls for increased accountability of schools for academic achievement have resulted in a number of reforms, some with positive outcomes and some with negative ones. In almost all states, standards for reading achievement have been established, usually according to expectations for grade level. Some states have also established students for English language proficiency. The establishment of standards can be a positive step in that teachers, school administrators, and the school board are provided with a clear vision of what children should accomplish. Schools are held accountable for meeting children's needs. Tests are developed and adopted to assess progress in achieving established standards; some states even adopt the dubious practice of financially rewarding schools and districts that are successful and penalizing those that are not.

Because of the priority placed on standards and the assessments that are derived from them, teachers need to be familiar with the standards in their states and know how their districts have designed the instructional program to reflect those standards and benchmarks. Teachers also need to review the state assessment tests and become familiar with what will be asked of students when they have to take these tests. The more teachers can help students feel comfortable with the language that is used in the state programs and the format of testing, the less they have to focus on specific lessons targeted to outcomes or do practice testing. It is helpful to think through your own experiences and ideas with state or professional standards and assessments, since parents will also probably involve you in conversations about them. Both positive and negative outcomes are associated with the standards and assessment movement.

Positive outcomes of such practices include a clear focus on educational goals; staff development based on those goals; high motivation to improve; and the provision of data to support changes in curriculum, staff development, instructional materials, and funding. Negative outcomes include extraordinary pressure to raise test scores at all costs, dishonesty in testing programs in some areas, instruction focused on fragments of language instead of on reading connected text, and narrowing and dilution of the curriculum to teach only what is tested.

With respect to the last outcome, a particular concern relates to the development of students' vocabulary. When areas of the curriculum are eliminated because they are viewed as less important, students are deprived of the rich vocabulary that is associated with these areas. In this way, the more school-dependent students are deprived of a key tool in their own learning: vocabulary knowledge. Their knowledge of vocabulary is limited by the elimination of areas of the curriculum that are sometimes viewed as less important than reading and mathematics, and sometimes even as frills.

There are two important aspects of vocabulary development for English language learners and speakers of African-American Vernacular English. One is the richness—or, often, the lack of richness—of the language that surrounds them. Students become familiar with the meanings of words when those meanings are highly contextualized, not when they are studied as isolated vocabulary words. It follows, then, that a richer language environment should result in increased exposure to contextualized vocabulary and therefore to understanding of their meanings. Teachers are often obligated to cut back or even eliminate instruction for these students, however, in the very areas of the curriculum where new vocabulary words will be offered in the most highly contextualized ways, such as science, social studies, art, music, physical education, and health. Teachers must ensure that these areas of the curriculum are present for at-risk students and that they are presented in such a way that contextualized exposure to a rich vocabulary is promoted, including such strategies as cooperative learning, problem solving, and other language-rich strategies.

In a related vein, Nagy, Anderson, and Herman (1987) found that a major factor in vocabulary development by third-, fifth-, and seventh-grade students was the sheer volume of reading that students did and the amount of vocabulary they were exposed to, even though the proportion of words learned was low. Stanovich (1986) elaborates this idea further in his treatment of individualized differences and the Matthew effect, the idea that those who read more (the rich) read better (get richer). Smith (1986) has added that good readers read and poor readers take tests and do drill sheets.

FOR REVIEW

In Chapter 2, the social and cultural contexts of literacy for children in grades K–8 were considered. Different social and cultural groups have views of literacy that reflect their own realities and needs, which might vary from the mainstream view. It is important to acknowledge the validity of the various views of literacy as instruction is planned for children from these social and cultural groups.

Teachers can often create their own cultures of literacy within their classrooms by the way they value those points of view and by the way they organize the physical environment of the classroom and select instructional materials and trade books for their students. A shared literacy environment creates the most effective tone for extending literacy to all.

To involve parents and extended families in our shared literacy community, teachers must begin early in the school year with communications that welcome families to the classroom and request their support for classroom efforts. Teachers should also become a part of the professional community through induction activities, professional meetings, and involvement in major professional organizations in our field, such as the International Reading Association and the National Council of Teachers of English.

Because of the diversity that is found in U.S. schools today, it is the rare classroom in which the children all come from a single cultural, ethnic, or linguistic group. A typical classroom in the coming years will have children from several cultures and ethnic groups; most will have some children who speak another language at home, usually Spanish. Most classrooms will have mainstreamed children with special needs for at least part of the school day. This diversity can be viewed as a problem, but a more healthy viewpoint is to appreciate the richness of the diversity and use it as an asset in teaching.

This diversity also provides many challenges for teachers. They must be aware of cultural differences far beyond holidays and foods. Aspects of nonverbal communication are particularly important in determining how teachers relate to their students and their families. Teachers will encounter children who speak another language or dialect of English at home and who might not be able to communicate effectively in Standard American English in the classroom; recent demographic trends indicate that teachers who have not yet encountered these children in their classrooms will find them there soon. The needs of our English language learners can best be met with mother tongue instruction coupled with a strong program of ESL, but teachers must also recognize that the most efficacious approach to meeting these studends needs might be counter to laws or policies of some states.

It is clear that many children struggle to learn to read in our classrooms. Some of them are at risk of failure because of environmental factors, such as living in low-income inner-city or rural areas and coming from ethnic or linguistic minority groups. It is sometimes tempting to address the needs of these children with one-size-fits-all approaches to literacy instruction, but their strengths and needs vary greatly, and so should the programs that are provided to teach them to read and write. Some children struggle with reading because of cognitive, affective, and psychomotor factors. Teachers must be flexible about children with needs for accommodations that are new to them and also to the need to work closely with colleagues from special education so that these children can have a school experience that is as similar to that of most students as possible.

In addition, it is necessary to find print materials for children to read that are interesting and culturally appropriate for them. Children need to see themselves in what they read. They need large numbers of books and other sources of text at many levels. This includes access to computer technology resources and the Internet for the children from many groups who have very limited access to technology.

Finally, assessment is important for planning instruction, selecting instructional materials, and making adjustments in our instruction when needed. But it is also necessary to be cautious about letting assessment become the tail that wags the dog. Assessment should emerge from the curriculum, which should in turn emerge from the needs of students and the standards established by state and local governing authorities.

For Your Journal

1. Now that you have read Chapter 2, return to the anticipation guide at the beginning of the chapter. What differences are there in how you would answer the open-ended questions now?
2. The true-false questions in the anticipation guide addressed many myths about the demographics of children in our schools and about children's learning. After you read and found answers to the questions, which one(s) surprised you the most? Why?

★ Taking It to the World

Now that you have considered the implications of classroom diversity, think about your classmates when you were in the third grade. In terms of diversity, how does the student population of the classroom to which you are assigned now compare to that of your own third-grade classroom? Make a list of positive outcomes that the children of today exhibit as a result of the increased classroom diversity they experience.

★ Being a Professional Reading Teacher

Reflecting on the Chapter

The typical classroom in this era is a community of children from many cultures and languages. How can you take advantage of that diversity?

Culture

1. The children in your classroom will likely reflect many cultures. How can you use authentic children's literature to build mutual respect for a variety of cultures in your classroom?
2. The power of social interaction is the major vehicle of cooperative learning strategies. As you form cooperative learning groups for language and reading activities, how does your knowledge of culture help you to get children ready for this experience?

Language

3. Some parents who come for parent conferences do not speak English or don't speak it well. How do you make these parents feel comfortable and welcome?

4. Some African-American children speak another dialect of English. How do you show respect for the way they speak while helping them add the standard dialect of the language?

Children At Risk of Failure in Reading

5. Some children are at risk of failure in learning to read; they are often boys in inner-city and rural schools. What are some specific steps that you can take to ameliorate this problem?

6. Most teachers have children with special needs in their classrooms, at least for part of the day. What steps would you take for welcoming and integrating a new child who has a vision problem?

Your Professional Portfolio

An important dimension of your professional development will be diversity. Potential employers want to know how you will address diversity in their classrooms. How can you use your portfolio to document your experiences with the diversity of students we have in our classrooms now? Here are some ideas that you might consider:

- Thematic literature units that reflect diversity
- Photographs of children in the classroom where you might complete a practicum or student teach, volunteer, or work as a paraprofessional
- Lesson plans that reflect gender equity, cultural sensitivity
- Descriptions or journal accounts of community experiences
- Descriptions of workshops and university classes about multicultural issues that you have completed
- Photographs of bulletin boards you have prepared that reflect diversity in the classroom where you volunteer or work as a paraprofessional

Teaching Resources

This is a good time to begin reading and evaluating children's books that reinforce multicultural themes. Make a list of books appropriate for the grade levels you are interested in. Start looking for these books at swap meets, garage sales, used bookstores, and thrift shops. Building your own classroom library is a good way to ensure that children have easy access to good literature.

Technology Connections

1. Literacy Access Online offers connections to book and electronic initiatives for literacy access, including assistive devices and low-vision aides for the impaired. Visit their web site at http://chd.gse.gmu.edu/LiteracyAccess/prototype/resources/ and explore at least two of the listed resources. What is the primary focus of each site and how might each help you as a teacher?

2. Visit the "Guys Read" web site (www.guysread.com), a web site that focuses on supporting boys' reading. How does this web site help to encourage "guys" to explore connections to feelings through reading? Identify three books recommended by other guys as appropriate for early readers.

Research
Navigator.com

Connect with Research

Review the following key words from the chapter and then connect to Research Navigator (www.researchnavigator.com) through this book's companion web site to conduct a search into research on each of the various topics as they relate to reading and literacy education today.

at-risk students	English language learner	paralanguage
background knowledge	gifted	scaffolding
bicultural	immersion instruction	zone of proximal development
bilingual education	mainstreamed	

Further Readings

Cunningham, P. M., Moor, S. A., Cunningham, J. W., & Moore, D. W. (2000). *Teachers in Action*. New York: Longman.

The authors follow an elementary class through five years of literacy instruction using a detailed review of teachers' journals.

Morrow, L. M. (Ed.) (1995). *Family Literacy: Connections in Schools and Communities*. Newark, DE: International Reading Association.

In Morrow's edited volume, teachers will find articles on the issue of family and school literacy connections by significant authorities in the field.

Nieto, S. (2002). *Language, Culture, and Teaching*. Mahwah, NJ: Erlbaum.

Nieto provides a very positive view of language diversity and how it should be viewed as an asset in the classroom.

Ogle, D. (2002). *Coming Together as Readers*. Arlington Heights, IL: Skylight Professional Books.

Ogle's book is full of examples of how schools create communities of readers at all grade levels.

Suárez-Orozco, C., & Suárez, M. (2001). *Children of Immigration*. Cambridge, MA: Harvard University Press.

Suárez-Orozco and Suárez offer an in-depth analysis of immigrant children's experiences and how these experiences affect them in U.S. classrooms.

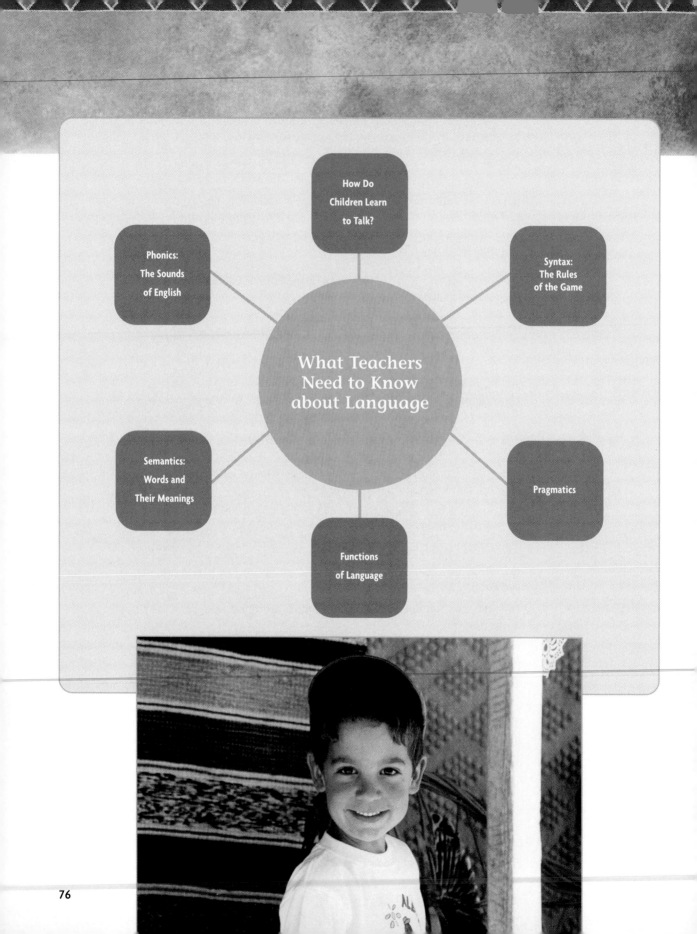

How Do
Children Learn
to Talk?

Phonics:
The Sounds
of English

Syntax:
The Rules
of the Game

What Teachers
Need to Know
about Language

Semantics:
Words and
Their Meanings

Pragmatics

Functions
of Language

What Teachers Need to Know about Language

The following statements will get you thinking about the topics of this chapter. Answer true or false in response to each statement. As you read and learn more about the topics in these statements, double-check your answers. See what interests you and what prompts your curiosity toward more understanding.

Anticipation Guide

_____ 1. Children are taught their first language through careful instruction.

_____ 2. The major components of language study are the sounds, the grammar, the meanings, and the uses of language.

_____ 3. The ways in which children learn to talk and the ways in which they learn to read are more different than similar.

_____ 4. The syllable is the smallest unit of sound in a language.

_____ 5. The English language is ideal for teaching word recognition by syllables.

_____ 6. The English spelling system is a hodge-podge of irregularity.

_____ 7. One must be fully aware of the parts of a language in order to learn it.

_____ 8. Understanding the alphabetic nature of English spelling—that is, realizing the relationships between letters and sounds—is an important aspect of learning to read.

_____ 9. A morpheme is a kind of ritual insult.

_____ 10. For some children, part of the challenge of learning to read is getting used to how language is used in school instruction.

Iuliu's Questions

Iuliu, age five, has some questions:

"Why don't those birds over there fall out of the sky?"

"What are those birds saying to each other?"

"Why is that grass short and that tree tall?"

His eleven-year-old sister Ana is exasperated. "Iuliu, *why* do you ask so many questions?"

Iuliu looks at her as if the answer were obvious. "So I'll know the answers when *I* have a curly-haired boy."

Talking is a miracle, you have to admit. The biggest, most powerful computers in the world cannot look around and make interesting conversation about the world the way a child who barely comes up to your waist can.

"Reading is talk written down," teachers say, and in many ways the statement is true. Therefore, to teach reading well, you need to understand children's talk—children's language. This chapter takes a look at the ways in which children learn to talk, because those learning processes are a lot like the processes children use when they learn to read. It also examines the major parts of language that children learn when they learn to talk—such as learning about sounds, rules, words, and uses—because those parts of language skill become aspects of reading skill. Finally, it examines *how* talk gets written down and becomes print—that is, the relationship between spoken and written language. By the time you finish reading this chapter, you should know a great deal about the structure of the English language, including its phonological-morphological structure as well as how children learn that language—and yes, that includes English language learners.

How Do Children Learn to Talk?

That is a good question—one that has intrigued people for thousands of years. The answer surely has some bearing on how teachers should help children learn to read and write. Over the centuries, two main answers have been offered: The first, from ancient Greek historian Herodotus, suggests that language is innate. Children are born with language inside, ready to come out and grow. The second, a mid-twentieth century American psychological approach, proposes that children are taught to talk. They need "stimuli" and "responses" from adults in order to learn to talk said behaviorists, such as B. F. Skinner (1957). Contemporary understanding of how children learn to talk combines both perspectives. Learning language relies on some things that *are* innate. Babies appear to come into the world "pretuned" with a set of capacities that makes it virtually inevitable that they will learn language. For example, newborn babies just a few days old do the following:

- Turn their heads and look toward the source of a sound
- Prefer patterned and varied sounds, such as human voices, to random noises like buzzes and clicks
- Synchronize the movements of their bodies so that they track along with the rhythms of the speech they hear
- Perceive extremely subtle distinctions in speech, such as the difference between the beginning consonant sounds in "bat" and "pat"—a difference that equals 40/1000ths of a second delay in the vibration of the vocal cords
- Prefer high-pitched voices to low-pitched voices

In addition to these features of perception, linguist Noam Chomsky (1993) has argued that babies are "prewired" with a basic grammar, or system of order for language. That is, from a very early age, they understand on some deep level that language is constructed according to meaningful patterns organizing its units and that at their simplest, these patterns dictate that meaningful utterances should have a subject and a predicate (or a "topic" and "comment" or a "noun phrase" and a "verb phrase").

Infants and older children are equipped with one other essential capacity: the ability to examine the language they hear around them, tease out its patterns, and use those patterns to shape their own utterances. This is not the same thing as imitating what they hear adults say, because children often say things that adults *wouldn't* say, and that is when their ability to discover patterns in language is revealed. For instance, a six-year-old boy says, "Don't worry, Mom. I'm hold-onning," after his mother told him to "hold on" during a windy sailboat ride. You can see that he is aware that verbs add *-ing* to show that action is going on in the present. His unique demonstration of this rule shows that he is not merely parroting back what he has heard others say in his presence. He has figured out a rule of grammar all on his own. This act of discerning and learning patterns of grammar is a significant achievement, and it is accomplished by virtually all children. It is no wonder that literacy educators come back to this amazing language-learning ability and look for its contributions to children's learning to read. They conclude that children may possess the following qualities that allow them to learn language:

1. Children are born with a highly developed set of sensory capacities that preadapt them to perceive and respond to human language.

2. Children might also be equipped with a rudimentary grammar for language. (This claim is still controversial, as the evidence for it is indirect.)
3. Children have the ability to analyze language for its features and for its patterns and to construct an organized understanding of those findings. (Linguists call this construct a *grammar*.)

All this is still a far cry from being born with a built-in vocabulary, but it does support the claim that much of a child's capacity for language is innate and not taught. Linguist Steven Pinker writes:

> *The complexity of language, from the scientist's point of view, is part of children's biological birthright; it is not something that parents teach their children or something that must be elaborated in school—as Oscar Wilde said, "Education is an admirable thing, but it is well to remember from time to time that nothing worth knowing can be taught." A preschooler's tacit knowledge of grammar is more sophisticated than the thickest style manual or the most state-of-the art computer language system, and the same applies to all healthy human beings, even the notorious syntax-fracturing professional athlete and the you know, like, inarticulate teenage skateboarder. (Pinker, 1994, p. 6)*

But Oscar Wilde underappreciated his teachers, and Dr. Skinner was not entirely wrong. Unless adults provide some kind of support for their efforts to learn language, children will not learn to listen and speak. History has some horrifying examples of children reared in isolation from adults who never really learned to talk, even after being placed later in normal environments. Children need us, or they will not learn language. But what do they need from us?

How Adults Support Children's Language Learning

When adults help infants learn to talk, it is remarkable how much of this "help" comes naturally and unconsciously. Take the case of a mother engaged in face-to-face play with a six-month-old child. The mother gazes into the child's face and raises the pitch of her voice to a high register. She makes swooping changes from low to high, from soft to loud. She exaggerates consonant sounds and stretches out vowel sounds. She speaks in sentences with few words and simple structures. She leaves pauses in her utterances: She speaks and waits, speaks and waits, as if she were inviting the baby into a conversation and demonstrating where to slot utterances. In short, she is speaking **"Motherese"** (Newport, Gleitman, & Gleitman, 1977).

When a parent speaks with a toddler, similar interactions take place that help the child learn language. A parent might read a book to a young child at bedtime, turn to a picture of a dog, point to it, say to the child, "What's that?," and wait for the child to answer, "Dog!" (although the response more likely sounds like "Dock" because young children's speech usually gives voiced consonants at the beginning of a word and unvoiced consonants at the end of a word). Like Motherese, this book-reading exchange teaches the child important lessons about language: that words are names for things, that the same thing is labeled by the same word each time it appears, and that words are real and can be represented in print. This insight will be of help as the child begins to wonder about printed language and how it works.

Even in instances in which direct language instruction might seem called for, the path of indirect teaching seems to be the one that teaches the most about language. Psycholinguistic research literature is full of examples of parents who correct their young children's speech repeatedly, only to have the children continue saying things their own way.

Nonetheless, research is very clear on one point: Children benefit from having adults talk to them. The benefit to syntactic development is considerable (McCartney, 1984), and the impact on vocabulary development is still greater (Hoff-Ginsburg, 1998). However, research also indicates that the amount and quality of language support young children get from their families differ greatly depending on families' socioeconomic status.

Struggling Reader

One research team (Hart and Risley, 1995) made monthly one-hour observations of the language directed to children in professional families, working-class families, and families on welfare. The differences were dramatic. Children in working-class families had twice as many words spoken to them as children in families on welfare. But children in professional families had twice as many words spoken to them as children from working class families, and nearly *four times* as many words as children in families on welfare.

There also were differences in the kinds of speech addressed to children. Comparing verbal encouragements ("Yes, that's good!"), children in working-class families received three times as many encouragements as children from families on welfrae. But children from professional familes received *7.5 times* as many encouragements as children from families on welfare.

Looking at prohibitions that children received from their parents ("Stop!" "Don't do that!" "Quit!"), the rates were just the reverse, with children in families on welfare receiving nearly twice as many prohibitions as children in working-class families, and almost three times as many as children from professional families received. This means that children from families on welfare were told not to do things three times more often than they were encouraged. Children from working-class families were encouraged twice as often as they were discouraged. And children from professional families were encouraged *six times* as often as they were discouraged (Hart and Risley, 1995, pp. 252–253).

Less verbal interaction in the family means less developed vocabulary in the child. By the age of three, there are large differences in vocabulary size between children from poor familes and those from professional families (Hart and Risley, 1995). By the age of six, children from low-income undereducated families come to school with well below half the vocabulary as those from middle-class families, and the differences continue to grow after that (Beck, McKeown, and Kucan, 2002). Having a limited vocabulary—and limited structures for language—limits children's concept formation and their "world knowledge," and it certainly creates problems for children learning to read and write (Droop & Verhoeven, 2003; Snow et al., 2001).

Children begin to hear speech patterns from early on and benefit greatly when adults make an effort to speak with them directly and often.

The Nature of Language Acquisition

Children's growth in language ability unfolds through stages. In the first twelve to eighteen months of life, children cry, coo, babble, babble with intonation, and produce one-word utterances. These one-word utterances have been called **holophrases** (Brown, 1973) because they pack a lot of meaning into one word. As children begin to produce two- and three-word utterances during their second and third years, their sentences are high on content and low on grammatical function or "glue" words such as articles, prepositions, and helping verbs. These early sentences have been called **telegraphic speech** (Brown, 1973) because they contain only essential words. Gradually, children continue to go through stages of language development, adding more words, completing sentences, and producing questions and negative statements. They also

STANDARDS & LITERACY

★ ★ What You May Be Expected to Know about Language ★ ★

There are many reasons why teachers of reading need to know about language development. The ways in which children learn to talk—the efforts they contribute themselves and the help they need from others around them—are similar in many respects to what happens when they learn to read and write. Also, because reading involves understanding the ways that written symbols represent spoken language, it is helpful if the teacher has a sophisticated understanding of spoken language. Third, much of what native speakers know about their language is unconscious: Speakers just talk and understand without knowing how they do it. When teachers are helping English language learners, however, they often need to know how to explain the fine points of grammar and pronunciation of language and the ways in which language is used. Some states have incorporated such knowledge into their state standards for assessment.

One such state is California, where the state competency test for future teachers of reading, known as RICA (Reading Instruction Competency Assessment), includes several standards that require that teachers of reading have deep knowledge of the structure of the English language in addition to knowing how all children learn to read, including those who are native speakers of other languages, that is, English language learners:

7A(a) Each candidate participates in intensive instruction in reading and language arts methods that is grounded in methodologically sound research and includes exposure to instructional programs adopted by the State Board of Education for use in California public schools. This instruction enables her/him to provide a comprehensive, systematic program of instruction to students. The reading and language arts instruction for students includes systematic, explicit and meaningfully-applied instruction in reading, writing, and related language skills, as well as strategies for English language learners and speakers of English, all of which is aligned with the state-adopted academic content standards for students in English Language Arts and the Reading/Language Arts Framework.

7A(d) For each candidate, the study of reading and language arts methods includes instruction and experience in teaching organized, systematic, explicit skills that promote fluent reading and writing, including phonemic awareness; direct, systematic, explicit phonics; and decoding skills, including spelling patterns, sound/symbol codes (orthography), and extensive practice in reading and writing.

7A(f) For each candidate, the study of reading and language arts includes the phonological/morphological structure of the English language, and methodologically sound research on how children learn to read, including English language learners, students with reading difficulties, and students who are proficient readers.

(California Commission on Teacher Credentialing, 2001)

seem to go through something of a common sequence of adding grammatical inflections to words.

What controls the order and the rate of language learners' progress through the stages of language learning is not entirely clear, but the fact that so many children go through the stages in the same order suggests a strong innate or biological base for language learning. Children are able to learn to talk, it seems, because they have a built-in capacity for language. This capacity is so central to humans that it has been called "the language instinct" (Pinker, 1994).

Still, in the course of learning to talk, children seem to need adults to talk to them. Adults serve as more than models of language. As you saw in the discussion of Motherese, adults provide **scaffolding,** or carefully aimed support, for children's efforts to learn language. By scaffolding, adults help children pay attention to words and their meanings. They invite them into conversations and show children how to take turns sharing meaning with others. They ask questions and offer suggestions and help children learn to stretch out their utterances and weave their reported experiences into narratives. By scaffolding, adults help children articulate their ideas so that they can think the ideas through and eventually engage in more complex thinking on their own.

Reading teachers need to take note of children's language-learning processes, first, because reading ability is based on language knowledge, and second, because similar dynamics are at work when children learn written language. As you will see in Chapter 4, when children read storybooks, they discover and use a series of strategies that get more and more complex (Sulzby, 1985); and as children begin to write, they invent strategies for spelling words and these strategies, too, go through stages of increasing complexity (Temple et al., 1992). Therefore, because children's language-learning strategies are at work when they learn to read and write, including when they learn a second language (see Chapter 12), it is important to understand what children learn when they learn language. Many states now require some understanding of basic linguistics in their state standards, such as those shown in the Standards and Literacy box. Linguists often speak of five aspects of language: **phonology,** the sounds of language; **syntax,** the ordering of words and other grammatical bits into meaningful language; **semantics,** the meaning system of language; **morphology,** the way words are built; and **pragmatics,** the way speakers use words on the basis of social contexts.

Phonics: The Sounds of English

The word *phonics* sends teachers scrambling to take positions. Should teachers teach children letter-to-sound rules explicitly? Should they encourage students to pick up phonics generalization by inference? Or should they downplay phonics and just teach words as wholes? Disagreement is rife among people who hold these three positions or variations of them.

No doubt, part of the reason teachers disagree about phonics is that the matches between letters and sounds in English seem so variable. It is a daunting task to teach phonics generalizations—the rules that link letters and sounds—because so many generalizations are called for to capture the whole system. Look, for example, at the many ways in which the same vowel sound is spelled in these words: *cake, bait, break, eight, may, obey,* and *a.*

In the face of the complex relationships between letters and sounds, some people have argued that the spelling system should be reformed (Venezky, 1999). But the problem is not that English spellings fit the sounds of English imperfectly, but rather that the sound patterns of English are themselves complex (Chomsky & Halle, 1968; Cummings, 1988; Snow, Burns, & Griffin, 1998; Venezky, 1999). Understanding phonics—that is, knowing how to teach children to render English spellings into sounds and vice versa—requires attention to the English sound system. Later you will see how this understanding helps children as they learn to write.

Learning the Sounds of English

TEACH IT!
5

A sleepy baby in her father's arms looks into his eyes and says, "Mbwalah ngouby dwat, thah thah?" The father is almost certain that the baby has said something; he just wishes he could understand it. These occurrences are typical of babies from six months to a year old. Their "babbling with intonation," as linguists call it, fascinates us, especially for the variety of the sounds babies produce. Children at six to ten months of age babble very nearly all of the speech sounds used in all of the languages in the world. In fact, until babies are a year old, one usually cannot tell from their babble what language their parents speak (Hoff, 2001). Then an odd thing happens: The children gradually stop making any but the sounds used in the language they hear around them. The Tanzanian baby keeps making "*mb-*" and "*ng-*" sounds but stops making the "*-ou-*" and "*th-*" sounds; the American baby does just the opposite.

What is going on here? Well before they begin to talk, these babies are realizing that the language they hear every day has its own store of meaningful speech sounds, sounds that are used over and over again as constituents of talk. Linguists call these constituent sounds **phonemes**. In English, phonemes are the sounds that roughly correspond to the letters. In the spoken word *cat*, for example, the phonemes are the sounds represented by the *C*, *A*, and *T*. In the spoken word *chip*, the phonemes are the sounds represented by the *CH, I,* and *P*. The two main classes of phonemes are **vowels** and **consonants**. Let's look more closely at both.

A CRASH COURSE IN ENGLISH VOWELS.   The way teachers of the primary grades talk about vowels is not quite the same way that linguists do. First of all, linguists would point out that vowel sounds are simply *voiced air*: The sounds you produce vibrate your vocal cords while you breathe across them. But what makes the difference between one vowel sound and another? That is, what are you doing when you produce the sound of "EEEE" as opposed to "AHHH"? Say those two sounds aloud, one at a time. The answer is in how and where you hold your tongue in your mouth while you breathe past your vibrating vocal cords. The sound of "EEEE" is made with the tongue high in the front of the mouth, while the sound of "AHHH" is made with the tongue low in the back of the mouth. But of course, there is more.

Vowels: Long and Short and Tense and Lax.   Reading teachers use the terms *long* and *short* to refer to the distinction between the sound represented by the letter *I* in *kite* (a "long" vowel sound) and the sound represented by the letter *I* in *kit* (a "short" vowel sound). But those terms do not describe at all what you do when you make those sounds.

To make this point, say *feet* and *fit* aloud, and stretch out the vowels as you pronounce them. Notice what your mouth does when you say each. If you can't tell the difference, then poke your finger firmly into the muscle under your jaw and say them again, very slowly. This time you should feel your tongue muscle tense up when you say the vowel in *feet* and relax when you say the vowel in *fit*. Because of the tensing and relaxing of the tongue muscle when you make the sound of *ee* and *ĭ*, linguists call these vowels *tense* and *lax*, rather than *long* and *short*.

The sounds of the vowels in *feet* and *fit* might seem completely unrelated, but that wasn't always the case. During the fourteenth century, the time when Geoffrey Chaucer wrote *The Canterbury Tales*, the vowel sounds of *ee* and *ih* were spelled by using the same letter. So were the vowel sounds *ay* and *eh*. These sounds, linguists would say, are tense and lax variations of each other.

But after Chaucer's time, a strange thing happened. The way people pronounced English words changed, so the vowel sound that used to be pronounced *ay* changed its pronunciation to *ee*, and the sound that was pronounced *eh* stayed the same. Similarly, the sound that had been pronounced *ee* was now pronounced *iy* (as in *my*), while the sound that had been pronounced *ih* stayed the same. All of these changes resulted in the situation we have today. Now the letters *a, e,* and *i* each represent pairs of sounds that do not sound at all like each other because the pronunciation of the tense members of the original pairs of sounds changed but the pronunciation of the lax vowels did not. This phenomenon was so important in the history of the English language that it earned a name: the **Great Vowel Shift**.

These facts matter for two reasons. First, they show why reading English vowels is puzzling to speakers of many other languages, especially of the Romance languages such as Spanish, Portuguese, French, Italian, and Romanian. Because those languages did not undergo the Great Vowel Shift, children who speak them and have learned to read in them will still associate the vowel sounds in *bait* and *bet* and expect them to be spelled by the same letter—and that letter will be *e*. They will expect the same of *beat* and *bit* (expecting them to be spelled with the letter *i*).

Second, the fallout from the Great Vowel Shift shows up in native English speakers' first attempts to write: that is, in their **invented spelling**. Most children go through a period when they use the same letter to spell the sounds of *ay* and *eh*, and the same letter to spell the sounds of *ee* and *ih* (see Figure 3.1). Awareness of tense and lax vowels and having some knowledge of the Great Vowel Shift will help you make sense of children's early spellings and will put you in a position to help young writers.

Diphthongs. Native English speakers do something else with their pronunciation of English vowels that other languages do not: They make double pronunciations of them. Look in the mirror as you say the word *so* and pay attention to what your lips do. You start out saying the vowel "*Oh*," then you end up by pronouncing the vowel "*u*," and you round your lips as you do so. That is, you run two vowel sounds together, even though

FIGURE 3.1

The Amazing Vowels of Invented Spellers.

Brian, Grade 1
Translation: "My fish is red."
Source: Temple, Nathan, Burris, and Temple, 1992.

you might think you are pronouncing only one. You do the same thing when you pronounce the vowel "i": You actually run together "ah" and "ee." The long sound of "a" is really "eh" plus "ee," and even the sound of "eeee" starts off as one kind of "eeee" and ends up with another pronounced with the tongue a little more tense and a little higher in the mouth. These are called **dipthongs**.

What difference does all of this make? For one thing, it confounds people for whom English is not their first language and whose languages don't contain these unconscious diphthongs. It also confuses young writers who accurately hear diphthongs that adults have long since ceased to hear and might try to represent them in their early attempts at spelling. As a teacher, you need to be aware of these matters so that you can guide children past their confusion. Otherwise, features of the language that you no longer notice will puzzle children, who are more sensitive to sound differences than adults are.

Reduced Vowels.   One more phenomenon that is common in English but rare in other languages is **vowel reduction**. In words of more than one syllable, vowels in the unstressed syllable are given an indistinct pronunciation called *schwa*. Schwa occurs, for instance, in the second syllable of the word *fatal*. The vowel in that unstressed syllable is said to be reduced. Vowel reduction is a fact of English pronunciation that presents major difficulties to spellers. How do you spell the second syllable of *fatal*? It might be spelled "-*le*" as in *table*, "-*ile*" as in *futile*, or "-*el*" as in *label*. Challenges like these raise roadblocks for those who seek regularity in letter-to-sound relationships.

A CRASH COURSE IN ENGLISH CONSONANTS.   Earlier in this chapter, vowels were defined as what happens when you vibrate your vocal cords while breathing out. Consonants are what happen when that breath flow is interrupted in some way. There are many ways to interrupt the breath flow. If you stop it momentarily, you produce what are called *stop consonants*, such as the sounds represented by *p, b, d, t, k,* and *g*. If you whistle or hiss the breath flow, you produce *sibilant consonants*, such as the sounds represented by the letters *s, z,* and *zh* (the sound made by the second *g* in *garage*). If you do two things to the airflow, that is, if you stop it and then hiss it, you get *affricate consonants*, such as the sounds represented by the letters *ch* and *j*. If you buzz it slightly, you get the *fricative* sounds represented by the letters *th, f,* and *v*. If you direct the airflow out through the nose, you get *nasal consonants*, such as the sounds represented by the letters *m, n,* and *ng*.

The nature of the consonant sounds you produce depends on two more factors: where in the mouth you produce them and whether or not the vocal cords are vibrating. Let's illustrate. If you stop the airflow through your mouth with the back of the tongue raised against the top of the mouth toward the rear, you get the sound of *g* or *k*. If your vocal cords are vibrating while you do it, you get the sound of *G*. If they are not, you get the sound of *K*. Similarly, *b* and *p* are made by closing the lips. *B* is voiced (that is, the vocal cords vibrate the whole time it is made), and *p* is unvoiced (the vocal cords don't start vibrating until 40 thousandths of a second after you start producing the sound).

The sorts of details about speech sounds that we just touched on are most useful to speech pathologists and teachers of foreign languages, including those who teach English to speakers of other languages (and this could well mean you!). But this knowl-

FIDI I SOR THE BLA AJLS TA R APRLNS TACRT IHOVR AD FOL UP NTU VE CLALS

FIGURE 3.2

Invented Spelling of Consonants.

Joey, Grade 1
Translation: "Friday I saw the Blue Angels. They are airplanes. They crossed each other and flew up into the clouds."
Source: Temple, Nathan, Burris, and Temple, 1992.

TEACH IT!

6

edge is also useful to teachers of primary grades, because as children begin to experiment with spelling, you will see that they are sensitive to similarities in sounds that are related to the ways they are made. For example, children who wish to spell the voiced consonant sound represented by *th* and do not know the conventional way to do it will often use the letter *v* to spell the sound they want, because the letter name *v* sounds like the sound it makes, while the sound represented by *th* does not closely resemble either a *t* or an *h*. Note the spelling in Figure 3.2 of V for /th/ in IHOVR ("each other") and in VE ("the").

Consonant Blends and Consonant Digraphs.

As the example just given illustrates, there are some consonant sounds that are easier for young children to write and read than others. The easiest are single consonants. More difficult are **consonant blends**: two or more consonants pronounced closely together, like the beginning element of *slip* or the ending part of *help*. Still harder are the **consonant digraphs**: single-consonant phonemes that are spelled with two letters. The beginning elements in *then, chip,* and *shirt* are consonant digraphs. (The word *digraph* comes from two Greek words meaning "double writing.") Note the difference between blends and digraphs. In blends, each of two or more consonant letters is clearly heard; but the two-consonant letters in digraphs make only one sound—they are not separately pronounced.

Digraphs emerged because the Roman alphabet, which was based on the sounds of Latin, was used to write English. English had some sounds that did not occur in Latin; therefore, the Roman alphabet had no letters to stand for the uniquely English sounds of /sh/, /ch/, or /th/. Something had to be done to indicate when those sounds were intended by writers, and early scribes came up with the convention of writing an *H* after certain Roman letters: *sh, ch,* and *th*.

The spelling of *wh* is a strange exception. *WH* is a consonant blend and not a digraph: One really does hear two consonant sounds in words that begin with *wh*—but the sounds are heard the other way around: "*hw.*" In fact, *hw* is the way those sounds were spelled, until scribes in the twelfth and thirteenth centuries turned the letters around, perhaps to make them resemble *ch, sh,* and *th.*

Consonants are difficult for beginning writers to spell. When children use the strategy of spelling sounds by matching them to the sounds contained in the names of alphabet letters (Read, 1975; Temple et al., 1993), they often seek one letter to spell the sound that is conventionally spelled by a digraph (that is, two letters that spell one sound). Thus, you see spellings like *h* for the sound of /ch/ and *v* for the sound of /th/, as you did in Figure 3.2.

Consonants, Coarticulation, and Phoneme Segmentation.

If you look up the word *consonant* in a good dictionary, you will see that it came from two Latin words *con* or "together" and *sonare* "to make sound." It is often said that words are composed of phonemes (sounds) and phonemes are represented by letters, but this is only partially true. Consonant phonemes make recognizable sounds only when they are pronounced

"Deep Phonology" and English Spelling

Many people complain from time to time about the lack of regularity of English spelling. English playwright George Bernard Shaw summed up what he saw as the absurdity of the spelling system when he suggested that *GHOTI* could spell *fish*. (*GH* makes the sound of /f/ in *tough*, *O* makes the short /i/ sound in *women*, and *TI* makes the /sh/ sound in *initial*). Fortunately, the English spelling system does have regularity, but on a different level from where you might expect it. The regularity in English spelling is found partly in the relationships between letters and sounds and partly in the relationships between words that have different sounds.

English words come in families, and the scribes and printers who devised the English spelling system deliberately encoded those family relationships. For an example, let's return to the word *fatal*. The vowel in the second syllable is unaccented and is therefore reduced to schwa—which, as you saw, is difficult to spell, because the schwa sound can be spelled in many different ways. But *fatal* has a cousin word, *fatality*, in which the second syllable *is* accented, and the vowel in it is clearly pronounced as a short (lax) /a/. Remembering the related word *fatality* can help you spell the troubling reduced vowel in *fatal* (and vice versa: Note that the vowel in the first syllable of *fatality*

is also reduced and unrecognizable from its sound, but you know it must be spelled with an *A* if you remember the first syllable in its cousin word *fatal*). The fact that *fatal* and *fatality* are spelled in similar ways gives writers a useful clue for writing them, and it also helps readers recognize that the meanings of the words are related. These same principles apply to words such as *sign* and *signature*, *sane* and *sanity*, *photograph* and *photography*, and *bomb* and *bombard*.

It should be remembered that the relationships between words such as *fatal* and *fatality* and *sane* and *sanity* are not there because of spelling, but the sound system of spoken English has regular ways of deriving one word from another. For example, some words such as *sane*, *malign*, and *sign* are pronounced with long vowel sounds. But these words have derivative forms that have short vowel sounds: *sanity*, *malignant*, and *signature*. English speakers can be shown to "know" these rules, on a tacit level. By the time they are sixth graders, many students playing a word game like the one in the figure will show a tacit knowledge of the phonological changing rules being discussed (Templeton, 1989).

It would be possible to spell words such as *sign* and *signature* in ways that honored their sounds, but the people responsible for much of the English spelling system chose a different path. Here a bit of history

together with vowels. Spoken words—at least those words with consonant sounds in them—cannot be pronounced so slowly and carefully that all of their phonemes are distinctly audible. If you tape-record someone reading the word *cat* into a microphone, it turns out to be impossible to divide the tape into segments in which a listener can recognize the sounds of the beginning consonant, the vowel, and the final consonant. The vowel can be recognized by itself, but the consonant is recognizable only when it is coarticulated, or pronounced together, with a vowel.

These facts have implications for children who are learning to read. Teachers of beginning reading often assume that children can hear the three phonemes in *cat*. But those distinct phonemes cannot really be heard. Adults know that the phonemes are there, but their knowledge is based on inference rather than direct perception. For one

FIGURE

Phonological Word Game

Instructions: *Fill the blank with a form of the nonsense word in italics that sounds right.*

1. This woman is very *blane*. Her _____*ity* is clear for all to see.

2. This man is very *blimous*. His _____*ity* can be annoying.

3. The workers threatened to *cobign*. Their _____*ation* would have stopped work on the project.

Note: Many respondents pronounce the first vowel in *blane* with a long vowel sound but supply a short vowel sound in the derived form. Many respondents give *-osity* as the derived form of *blimous*. Many respondents pronounce the second syllable in *cobign* with a long vowel sound and a silent *G*. In the derived form, they pronounce the *G* and give the second vowel a short sound.

might help. As printing expanded in sixteenth century England, typesetters found themselves in a position to decide how English words should be spelled. Before their time, words were spelled many different ways, and nobody much minded because books were scarce, all having to be copied by hand, and readers read them aloud anyway. But with the advent of metal type, books became more plentiful, and readers began to read silently and more rapidly. Rapid silent reading required consistency in spelling (Scragg, 1974).

The typesetters made what might seem a curious choice: They chose spellings to honor not their pronunciations, but the history of words and their family relationships to other words. That is, they wrote the spellings of words to reflect their deep orthography. This choice made sense, and in spite of the occasional campaigns to "reform" English spelling by making it more regular (that is, to tie letter spellings more closely to sounds of words), our current system of spelling has many defenders. The great linguist Noam Chomsky wrote that the modern English spelling system is "nearly optimal for the language" (Chomsky & Halle, 1968). If you know these things, you will be in a position to help your students when they are puzzled by what appear to be the eccentricities of English spelling.

thing, you can substitute a /b/ phoneme for the /k/ phoneme and get *bat*, and you can substitute an /n/ phoneme for the /t/ phoneme and get *can*. For another thing, once you began to read, you see that letters tend to be matched with phonemes in words such as CAT. But you still are not hearing the consonant phonemes separately from the vowels.

As you will see later in this chapter and the next, becoming aware of phonemes is important in learning to read. Often referred to as **phonological awareness,** this ability normally emerges in late kindergarten and first grade (Goswami, 2000). However, some children have trouble with phonological awareness, and this difficulty appears to complicate learning to read (Snow et al., 1998). Conversely, teaching children to be aware of phonemes seems to help them learn to read (Bradley & Bryant, 1985).

**Struggling
Reader**

Syllables, Onsets, and Rimes

Syllables are rhythmic pulses in words. The word *final* has two of them, *fi* and *nal*, while *awareness* has three: *a + ware + ness*. In the example of the word *awareness*, you can see that a vowel can stand alone as a syllable but consonants cannot (at least not in English; they can in some Slavic languages).

Some languages such as Spanish, Japanese, and Kiswahili have relatively few syllables. Teachers of reading in these languages often teach children to read by learning a few syllables at a time and learning to combine these into words (which is not a recommended practice if it is done without taking the meanings of the words into account). In Spanish, for instance, children might be asked to memorize these syllables:

ma   me   mi   mo   mu

Then the teacher asks the children to read *"Mi mama me mima,"* a rather awkward sentence that means "My mother imitates me."

TEACH IT!

6

The English language, however, has thousands of different syllables. Few teachers of English would bother to have students learn groups of syllables, as teachers of Japanese, Spanish, Portuguese, and Kiswahili sometimes do. Instead, when children are struggling to read words of more than one syllable—such as *along, ahead,* or *baseball*—it helps to have young readers break those words into syllables, read each syllable, and reassemble them into a word. The teacher should always remind the children to make sure the word makes sense in the context of the passage.

Syllables can be broken into two smaller units that Rebecca Trieman (1985) has called *onsets* and *rimes*. The **onset** is the initial consonant of a syllable, and the **rime** is the vowel plus any consonant that comes after it. For example, in *cat*, the sound of *C* is the onset and the sound of *AT* is the rime. Trieman has found evidence that children find it natural to mentally divide syllables into onsets and rimes—or at least good readers do. Bradley and Bryant (1985) found that children who knew more nursery rhymes and were better at thinking up rhymes had an easier time learning to read than did children who knew less.

Rimes are also known as *phonogram patterns*. They are the rhyming portions of families of words such as *bug, dug, rug, tug,* and *mug*. As it turns out, the English language makes repeated use of a relatively limited set of phonogram patterns or rimes. Wylie and Durrell (1970) found a group of thirty-seven phonogram patterns that make up many hundreds of English words (see Table 3.1)

Although the words in English cannot be generated from a small set of standard syllables as can the words in Japanese, Spanish, or Kiswahili, our language does offer a very learnable set of phonogram patterns. Not every language has this. For example, while devising a program of word study in their language, a group of first-grade teachers in Slovakia were asked to think of groups of words that rhymed with each other and were spelled with the same phonogram pattern. None of the teachers could think of groups that had more than two words. For any of the words in Wylie and Durrell's list, though, you can probably think of at least six words that share the same phonogram pattern.

Because English has these common phonogram patterns, it makes sense to call children's attention to them. Activities such as word sorting and word making, which you will read about in Chapter 5, make children aware of phonogram patterns and use them to read many words after learning to read just a few exemplars of the phonogram patterns.

TABLE 3.1

Phonogram Patterns, or Rimes

b<u>ack</u>	m<u>eat</u>	n<u>ice</u>	cl<u>ock</u>	d<u>uck</u>
m<u>ail</u>	b<u>ell</u>	st<u>ick</u>	j<u>oke</u>	r<u>ug</u>
r<u>ain</u>	cr<u>est</u>	w<u>ide</u>	sh<u>op</u>	j<u>ump</u>
c<u>ake</u>		l<u>ight</u>	st<u>ore</u>	j<u>unk</u>
s<u>ale</u>		<u>ill</u>	n<u>ot</u>	
g<u>ame</u>		w<u>in</u>		
pl<u>an</u>		l<u>ine</u>		
b<u>ank</u>		br<u>ing</u>		
tr<u>ap</u>		th<u>ink</u>		
cr<u>ash</u>		tr<u>ip</u>		
c<u>at</u>		f<u>it</u>		
pl<u>ate</u>				
s<u>aw</u>				
st<u>ay</u>				

Invented Spelling

Understanding speech sounds and how words are constructed helps us to understand how children make sense of these sound patterns and how they incorporate that information into their reading and writing. One of the most fascinating discoveries in the past century with regard to literacy has been children's ability to invent and discover the ways in which letters represent sounds in print. This discovery of invented spelling was a natural extension of the research on children's spoken language acquisition: Children see people around them communicating in some medium (in this case, print); decide to try out their own versions of such communication; organize their versions according to rules or patterns that are logical, though incorrect by adult standards; and gradually, stage by stage, modify their strategies so that they grow closer and closer to the versions they hear and see adults using.

Sure enough, children appear to go through stages as they experiment with invented spellings for words (Gentry, 1989; Temple et al., 1992). Progress through the stages depends on two things: children's own developing concepts of how the English spelling system works (what we call their **word knowledge**) and the levels of challenge that system presents to them as they move through the grades. The stages of spelling development that we examine, modified from Gentry (1989) and Henderson (1990), are *the prephonemic stage, the early phonemic stage, the letter name stage,* and *the transitional stage.* Looking at children's progress through stages of invented spelling shows us a great deal about children's knowledge of words, which is important to their learning to read.

SPELLING AT THE PREPHONEMIC STAGE.   When children first begin to write, they often fill entire pages with a lot of unconnected letters (see Figure 3.3 on page 92). Although what the child has written has no meaning, what he or she has demon-

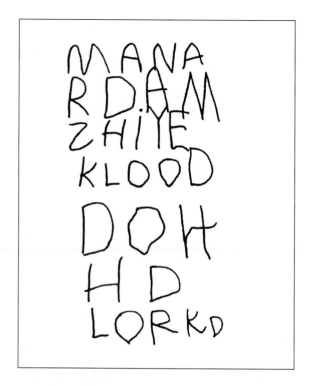

FIGURE 3.3

Prephonemic Spelling.

Jessie, Age 4
Source: Temple, Nathan, Burris, and Temple, 1992.

strated is called ***prephonemic spelling***. It is a kind of writing that uses letters without regard to their sounds. In this stage, children write down letters at random or possibly with some early notion of how they might represent ideas.

Children at the prephonemic stage of spelling know how to make many letters (and often many more pseudo-letters). They know what writing looks like and might know how it is arrayed on the page. But children at this stage have not yet discovered the **alphabetic principle**: the understanding that spelling represents words by relating written letters to spoken phonemes. If this is the case, this means that much reading instruction in which children are expected to learn to recognize words by being exposed to them will not be effective yet. Neither will phonics instruction that focuses on learning particular letters and sounds, which requires an understanding of the fundamental idea that words are real, they consist of phonemes, and those phonemes are represented by letters.

SPELLING AT THE EARLY PHONEMIC STAGE. Figure 3.4 represents a child in the **early phonemic stage** of spelling. This child has used letters to represent some of the sounds in words but not all of them. That is why we call this stage *early* phonemic: The child is just beginning to represent words by their phonemes. Children at this stage typically represent only the first and last and possibly a middle consonant in the word. They usually leave out vowels unless the whole word is a vowel, such as *a*. Children who spell in the early phonemic stage sometimes spell the first sound in a word with a sensible choice of a letter, then add random letters to make the word longer and hence make it look like a word (Ferreiro & Teberosky, 1982). But note carefully what we mean by a sensible choice. When children do use letters to represent sounds, rather than to use letters for sounds in conventional ways, they spell intuitively, matching as best they can a letter with a letter name that sounds closest to the

FIGURE 3.4

Early Invented Spelling.

Daryl, Grade 1
Source: Temple, Nathan, Burris, and Temple, 1992.

sound they want to spell. Thus, for example, they are likely to choose the letter *H* to spell /*ch*/, and the letter *Y* to spell /*w*/.

If children are spelling in the early phonemic stage, we know that they have discovered the alphabetic principle. They are not yet very proficient, however, at breaking words into phonemes and matching them with letter sounds. Matching letters to sounds contains at least four operations: making the word hold still in the mind, breaking it down into phonemes, matching each phoneme with a letter, and writing down that letter. All of these steps may be difficult for a beginner.

Determining the number of sounds children can represent in their spelling yields important diagnostic information. Bear in mind Ehri's hypothesis that a child's memory for storing images of written words for later recognition consists of a number of "slots" (Ehri, 1991, 1997). A child with more memory storage "slots" for word recognition will store a more complete memory of that word and will recognize it more accurately when seen in print. The number of "slots" a child has available seems to correspond to the depth to which that child can segment a word into its phonemes.

Examining a child's invented spelling is a good indication of his or her ability to segment words into phonemes. A child who writes "HK" for *truck* (that is, the early phonemic speller) shows a limited ability to segment phonemes in words. When it comes to recognizing words in print, that child will try to say the word on the basis of very shallow processing, typically looking at the first letter and calling out a word the child knows that begins with that letter. Because the child does not yet focus on all of the letters and phonemes in the word (Morris, 1998), he or she can easily confuse the words being read with other words that share one or two of the same letters.

SPELLING AT THE LETTER NAME STAGE.   At a slightly more advanced stage, a child offers spelling like that in Figure 3.5. This child is in the **letter name stage** of spelling. Here, the child represents all or nearly all of the phonemes in a word but does so intuitively. Logical judgments were made in choosing letters to represent sounds, but that logic still diverges quite a bit from the conventions of English spelling.

Children use names of the letters of the alphabet as if they were building blocks of sound out of which words can be constructed. In the case of some sounds, the letter name strategy results in spellings that look conventional; in others, the spellings can look bizarre. Especially in these cases, examining children's letter name spellings gives us a window into the ways children think about words and into the eccentricities of the English spelling system.

YUTS A LADE YET FEHEG AD HE KOY FLEPR

FIGURE 3.5

Letter Name Stage of Spelling.

No Name, Age 4 From Carol Chomsky.
Translation: "Once a lady went fishing and she caught Flipper."
Source: Temple, Nathan, Burris, and Temple, 1992.

- **Spelling Most Consonants.** As the sample in Figure 3.5 demonstrates, many consonant letters are spelled intuitively in ways that look conventional. Note the spellings of *F, L,* and *P* in *FLEPR (Flipper)* and of *D* in *AD (and).* The spelling *K* in *KOT (caught)* could be correct. The names of these letters are close enough to their corresponding phonemes to make the letter name strategy successful or nearly successful.

- **Spelling Nonintuitive Consonants.** The spelling of *Y* for the /*w*/ sound in *YUTS (once)* and *YET (went)* reveals very clearly that the child has chosen the *Y* for the sound of its name, rather than for its conventional value. But the letter name for *W* ("double U") doesn't sound at all like /*w*/, while the name of *Y* ("wye") is close, so this choice of *Y* for the /*w*/ sound is not surprising for the child who is using the letter name strategy.

- **Spelling Digraph Consonants.** Young spellers are troubled by the spellings of digraphs, since they do not know about the conventions for spelling them. Note the invented spelling of the *SH* digraph is *FEHEG (fishing)* and *HE (she).* In both cases, the letter *H* was chosen because the name of that letter sounds closest to the phoneme that is usually spelled by *SH*. The letter *H* is often used by children in the letter name stage of learning to spell the sound of /*sh*/ and /*ch*/.

- **Spelling Ns and Ms before Stop Consonants.** As we see in the spellings of *YUTS* for *once* and *AD* for *and,* letter name spellers often leave out *N*s and *M*s when they come before other consonants, especially before stop consonants, such as /*p*/, /*b*/, /*t*/, /*d*/, and /*k*/. The problem is not that children don't know how to spell the /*n*/ and /*m*/ sounds. It is rather that they are used to feeling the consonants produced in the mouth as they sound out the word in order to spell it (Read, 1975). When *N*s and *M*s are pronounced before stop consonants, you cannot feel them in the mouth, because the tongue goes to the same position to form the stop consonant anyway. Say the words *wet* and *went* aloud, and you will see what we mean: the activity of the tongue in the mouth is the same in both cases. What is different when *N* or *M* is present is that the whole syllable is pronounced through the nose. The omission of *N* and *M* in this position is prevalent in the spellings of kindergarten and first-grade children and in older children who are advancing slowly as spellers.

- **Spelling Word-Final *R, L, M,* and *N*: "Syllabic Sonorants."** The spelling of *FLEPR* for *Flipper* shows another common feature of children's letter name spelling. Unstressed syllables ending in *R, L, M,* and *N* often lack vowels when they appear at the ends of words. Thus it is common to see *TABL* for *table, LEDL* for *little,* and *BIDM* for *bottom* in the writing of children in the letter name stage of spelling. English has a convention that all syllables must be spelled with vowels. Even though children in the letter name stage represent most vowels, they leave them out of these words, presumably because they expect every letter they write into a word to be clearly sounded, but in these syllables, no distinct vowel sound is heard (Read, 1975).

- **Spelling Long Vowels.** As the spelling of *A* for *A, LADE* for *lady,* and *HE* for *she* demonstrates, long vowels in words usually "say their names"; that is, the sound to be spelled sounds much like the name of the letter we would use to spell that sound. In the spelling of *LADE* for *lady,* the spelling of the second vowel makes it clear that the child intends for the *E* to "say its name."

- **Spelling Short Vowels.** Spelling short vowels presents problems to letter name spellers. As was discussed earlier, short vowels do not sound very much like the "long" vowels spelled by the same letter. There are no vowel letter names that have short vowel sounds; so the speller must choose the letter name that is the best fit with that short vowel. This in practice is the long vowel sound that sounds the most like, or is produced in the mouth in the manner most like, that short vowel sound. This principle explains the spelling of *E* for the short vowel /ĭ/ in *fishing*. It also explains why children write *A* for /ĕ/ and *I* for /ŏ/.

Children who are letter name spellers represent nearly all of the phonemes (the smaller speech sounds) in words. But they represent those speech sounds intuitively, using a letter name strategy, rather than conventionally, using the kinds of spellings for sounds that are seen in books. Letter name spellers' ability to segment words into all of their phonemes gives them many corresponding "slots" in word memory storage for the parts of the words they see in print. Letter name spellers are usually beginning readers who are making progress acquiring sight words.

Letter name spellers have a means at their disposal to write many words, and children enjoy this freedom to create. Their spelling ability is still limited, of course. Because they spell words by relating letters to their individual sounds, they are not yet taking advantage of onsets and rimes and phonogram patterns. Nor are letter name spellers yet aware of the conventions for marking vowels "long" or "short." They also are not aware of the standard spellings of grammatical endings such as *-ing* or *-ed*, which explains why *fishing* was spelled *FEHEG* in Figure 3.5.

When it comes to recognizing words, because letter name spellers look for matches between letters and phonemes, they often use a strategy that some researchers call *sophisticated guessing*. Letter name spellers try to sound out all of the letters in a word and sometimes produce bizarre readings such as */ree add/* for *read* and */lie vee/* for *live*.

Research shows that the practice of invented spelling is good for kindergarten and first-grade children. Children who are encouraged to invent spellings learn to recognize more words than do children who do not use invented spelling. But children should not persist in letter name spelling much beyond the end of first grade. To help them make progress, teachers need to be careful to remind children that invented spelling is "temporary spelling," the way that they write some words before they learn the way words are spelled in books. They also need to be careful to give students correctly spelled material to read and take opportunities to call children's attention to standard spelling patterns in print.

SPELLING IN THE TRANSITIONAL STAGE.   Spellers in the transitional stage are beginning readers who are becoming aware of conventional spellings for sounds. They are learning phonogram patterns (onsets and rimes) and are trying to master the marking systems for long and short vowels, although not always correctly, as seen in Figure 3.6 on page 96. Transitional spellers may be keen observers of the English spelling system, and the difficulties they face in spelling correctly often reflect the eccentricities of the system. For example, transitional spellers may write *LUV* and *ABUV*. The correct spellings, *love* and *above*, thwart their expectations.

Transitional spellers have learned the common patterns of spelling, but some words don't conform because they aren't pronounced the way they are spelled, such as *NACHER* and *GROSHRY* for *nature* and *grocery*. In casual speech, we often say,

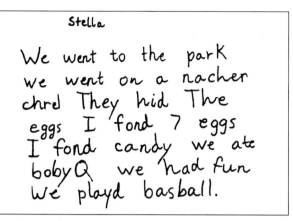

Stella

We went to the park
we went on a nacher
chrel They hid The
eggs I fond 7 eggs
I fond candy we ate
bobyQ we had fun
We playd basball.

FIGURE 3.6

Spelling in the Transitional Stage.

Stella, Grade 1. Note spelling of "nature trail"
Translation: We went to the park. We went on a nature trail. They hid the eggs. I found 7 eggs. I found candy. We ate barbeque. We had fun. We played baseball.
Source: Temple, Nathan, Burris, and Temple, 1992.

"Dincha?" for "Didn't you?" The /t/ and /y/ sounds between those two words get run together as /ch/. Exactly the same thing happened to the pronunciation of *nature*, which went at some point from a pronunciation like /natyur/ to /nachər/. *Special, initial, grocery,* and many other words go through similar sound changes, that linguists call *palatalization.* It is no wonder children grapple with these phenomena!

What children who spell in the transitional stage show us, however, is that they have learned many things about the way the English writing system works, and this knowledge can help them both in writing and in reading. These children show a grasp of common onsets and rimes in their writing, indicating that they should be able to use knowledge of these patterns to read unfamiliar words. Children who are aware of onsets and rimes can use the strategy of *reading by analogy.* For example, if they encounter the unknown word *sill,* they can recognize its similarity to the known word *pill* and will read *sill* by mentally taking away the /p/ sound and substituting the /s/ sound in front of the *-ill* rime. Such reading by analogy leads to more rapid and accurate deciphering of words than does puzzling out words letter by letter.

Spelling in the transitional stage presents challenges, though, that many students never move beyond. A student who has learned to spell *gate,* for example, might still be unsure how to spell *great, bait, straight,* or *eight.* It will take a habit of studying words carefully plus an act of memory to master these challenges. Of course, encouragement and reminders from the teacher don't hurt!

Syntax: The Rules of the Game

Syntax, another term for *grammar,* refers to the set of rules that order words and their inflections meaningfully in sentences. Syntax is what enables you to read the sentence "The veterinarian bit the dog" and understand who was bitten and who did the biting. Syntax can be thought of as a kind of code that enables speakers to encode meaning and for hearers to decode it.

Syntax occurs on two levels. At the *conscious* level, we think of syntax as the common set of rules taught in school, such as

> *"A verb must agree with its subject in person and number."*

But conscious syntactical knowledge represents only a fraction of the knowledge that enables you to produce and understand sentences. Consider, for example, the following sentences:

- *I would go bike riding if I weren't tired.* (But I won't go bike riding because I am tired.)
- *I will go bike riding if I'm not tired.* (I don't know yet if I will go bike riding.)
- *I go bike riding if I'm not tired.* (When I'm not tired, I usually go bike riding.)

- *I'm going bike riding, and I'm not tired. (I expected to be tired, but I'm not.)*
- *I did go bike riding, and I'm not tired. (Somebody asserted that I didn't go bike riding.)*

If you have ever taught English as a second language, you have surely found that although the differences between these sentences were clear to you, it was difficult to explain the differences to nonnative speakers and nearly impossible to tell nonnative speakers how to produce sentences that convey those different shades of meaning. That is, you have knowledge of grammar, but you cannot explain what you know. Linguists call this *tacit knowledge,* and the lion's share of your knowledge of syntax is of this variety.

Word Order and Inflectional Endings

In English, it makes a difference whether you say "The veterinarian bit the dog" or "The dog bit the veterinarian." The order of the words in those sentences determines the grammatical function of its parts and lets you know who did the biting and who was bitten. In other languages, however, word order does not indicate grammatical function but inflectional endings do. Consider these sentences from English and German:

| *English:* | *The boy* | *gave* | *the* | *girl* | *the book.* |
| *German:* | *Der jünge* | *gab* | *dem* | *madchen* | *das büch.* |

In the case of the English sentence, listeners know from the word order that the boy was the giver, the book was what was given (that is, it was the object of the act of giving), and the girl was the receiver of the gift (or the indirect object of the act of giving). The German sentence means the same thing as the English one. German syntax, however, also provides inflectional endings that indicate the cases of nouns and hence tell you which one is the subject, which is the indirect object, and which is the direct object in the sentence. Depending on the intended emphasis of the words, the speaker could say:

Dem madchen gab der jungen das büch

or

Das büch gab der junge dem madchen.

The giver, the receiver, and the thing given would remain the same, even though the ordering of the words had changed.

Like German, English has inflectional endings, but relatively few of them: *-s, -ed, -ing, -er,* and *-est* are the most common. English speakers don't rely as heavily on grammatical inflections to tell them what words mean as do speakers of highly inflected languages such as German.

Grammatical Morphemes

Inflectional endings are a kind of **grammatical morpheme**, which is a small word or word form that carries meaning. In the word *cats,* for example, *cat* is a morpheme and so is *-s.* The *-s* is a morpheme because it is a piece of a word that carries the meaning of "more than one." We call it a *grammatical* morpheme because issues such as person and number are issues of grammar.

When children learn English as a first language, they learn inflectional endings and other grammatical morphemes one at a time and—remarkably—almost always in the same order. According to Roger Brown's painstaking research (1973), between

TABLE 3.2

Order of Acquisition of Grammatical Morphemes

1. Present progressive verb tense (verbs ending in *-ing*)
2. The preposition *in*
3. The preposition *on*
4. The noun plural marker *-s*
5. Irregular past verb tenses *(ran, went)*
6. The possessive of nouns *'s*
7. The linking verbs *am, is, are, was, were*
8. Articles *a, the*
9. Regular past tense verb markers *-d*
10. third person regular verb markers *-s* (as in "It shouts")
11. Third person irregular verbs *(does, has)*
12. Auxiliary verbs *am, is, are, has, have*
13. Linking verb contractions *'m, 's, 're*
14. Auxiliary verb contractions *('m, 's, 're)* combined with verbs ending in *-ing* ("We're sleeping")

the ages of two and four, children tend to acquire grammatical morphemes (not just inflectional endings but also auxiliary verbs such as *is, are,* and *can* and articles such as *a* and *the*) in the order shown in Table 3.2.

There is no reason to believe that children are exposed to these grammatical morphemes in that order. So this fourteen-step ordering of the acquisition of inflectional endings is taken as another piece of evidence that language acquisition is a stage-bound process, internally governed by the learner. The ordering of the stages seems to be determined by the unfolding of language-processing abilities in the child.

The acquisition of syntax is said to begin when children string together two words in a sentence. For most children, this occurs at the age of eighteen to twenty-four months. From then until about the age of four, children add to their repertoire not only the grammatical morphemes just listed, but also control over the main sentence patterns of English. By the time they enter kindergarten, most children can make statements *(I'm taller than you)*, negate statements *(You aren't being nice to me)*, ask questions *(Why won't the boat go?)*, and give commands *(Come here a minute)*. They can speak in simple sentences *(I like my skates)*, compound sentences *(My dog is nice and I love him)*, and complex sentences *(We're going to eat ice cream when we get home)*. Many linguists consider that children know the basic grammar of their language by the age of four, although there are still a few grammatical constructions they have not mastered.

Syntax and Reading

Syntax is important in reading, both to word recognition and to comprehension. Often, teachers will ask a reader who struggles over an unknown word, "What would make sense there?" If the child is reading the sentence, "The pilot was hoping the parachute would open, but i__ d____n't," the word *but* will help the reader figure out that the next two words should say *it didn't*. The conjunction "but" tells the reader to expect those words to convey a meaning counter to the beginning phrase. Therefore, the syntax of the sentence is a strong clue to the identity of the obscured words.

Syntax helps children learn organizing principles for longer units of language as well. The most interesting of these sets of principles is called **story grammar**. Consider the story "The Frowning Princess" in Figure 3.7.

The Frowning Princess

In a faraway time and a distant place, there lived a king and his daughter. She frowned. From morning to night, she frowned and frowned and frowned. Even if you saw her in her sleep, she would still be frowning.

The royal advisor worried. "This is terrible, your majesty. A frowning princess is like a cloudy day," he said. "The people will think there is something wrong with your kingdom if the princess doesn't stop frowning."

"I pay you well, so I guess you are right," said the king. "We must find a way to make my daughter stop frowning."

The king and the royal advisor told the princess every joke they knew. But kings and royal advisors are not funny people, and after they had told both of their jokes, the princess was still frowning.

They brought a dozen monkeys and three trained hyenas to the palace. Nobody got any sleep for days. The princess frowned even harder.

Then it happened that a chambermaid put her head between her legs to clean under the princess' bed. Seeing the princess from this odd position, the chambermaid discovered something. "The princess is smiling," she thought. She told the princess to stand on her head and look into the mirror. When the princess saw her reflection, she tried to turn her upside-down frown right-side up. So, of course, she smiled.

Now the princess smiles all the day long. The king, his advisor, and the people are happy. It may be that the princess is still trying to frown, but I won't tell if you won't.

FIGURE 3.7

The Frowning Princess.

TABLE 3.3

Story Grammar Applied

ELEMENTS OF STORY GRAMMAR	EXAMPLES
The **setting** contains • Characters • A place and time	*… a king and his daughter* *In a faraway time and a distant place*
There is one or more **episodes** that contain • An initiating event—something that sets up a disequilibrium in the situation that sets further events in motion • A problem that must be solved—the goal that the character seeks to fulfill, as well as the impediments to reaching that goal	*She frowned. From morning to night, she frowned and frowned and frowned. Even if you saw her in her sleep, she would still be frowning.* *The people will think there is something wrong with your kingdom if the princess doesn't stop frowning.*
• An attempt to solve the problem • Which has an outcome • Possibly another attempt • Which has an outcome • Possibly another attempt	*The king and the royal advisor told the princess every joke they knew.* *… after they had told both of their jokes, the princess was still frowning.* *They brought a dozen monkeys and three trained hyenas to the palace.* *Nobody got any sleep for days. The princess frowned even harder.* *A chambermaid put her head between her legs to clean under the princess' bed. Seeing the princess from this odd position, the chambermaid discovered something. "The princess is smiling," she thought. She told the princess to stand on her head and look into the mirror.*
• Which has an outcome • There is a resolution to the problem—the state of affairs at the end of the story, as a result of the preceding events.	*When the princess saw her reflection, she tried to turn her upside-down frown right-side up. So, of course, she smiled.* *Now the princess smiles all the day long.*
There is a **consequence** of all the events	*The king, his advisor, and the people are happy.*

Stories such as this one have a set of identifiable elements, or slots, into which the particulars of the story are placed; these slots are almost always organized in a particular order. (The terms *identifiable elements* and *particular orders* are signs that one is talking about grammar or syntax.) For example, a story consists of a *setting,* one or more *episodes,* and a *consequence.* An analysis of the story "The Frowning Princess" using this story grammar model is found in Table 3.3 (Stein & Glenn, 1979).

Children as young as kindergarten age have a sense of story grammar, and they appear to use it to comprehend stories (Stein & Glenn, 1979). Teaching children story grammars improves their comprehension (Olson & Gee, 1988). Such instruction has been found to be especially helpful for children with learning disabilities (Gersten, 1998).

Struggling Reader

Semantics: Words and Their Meanings

After phonology (the sounds of language) and syntax (the grammar or ordering of language), the third main division of language learning is semantics, or the system of meanings in a language and the way those meanings are encoded in words.

Words as Symbols

TEACH IT!
36

All languages come in units of words. Words have sounds and meanings, and they fit into elaborate webs and hierarchies of meanings. They have *nuances,* or fine shades of meaning. Words have associations—other words, things, and feelings that they remind you of. They enable you to pay attention to things easily, but they also direct attention in some ways and not others. Words have histories, and their histories show how our ancestors have thought about things. Good readers and writers have a fondness for words, and good teachers know enough about words to help kindle students' curiosity about them.

The collection of words used in any people's language is a collection of the names of things those people have thought about. Words are symbols for the things people notice, the things that have seemed important enough to be carved out of the restless flow of experience, named, recalled, and noticed again (Ogden & Richards, 1923). Each word you have is a flashlight that illuminates some aspect of experience. Studies have shown that people are more likely to remember images if they already have a word they can associate with the particular image (Brown, 1958).

Words and Categories

Words vary in their level of generality and specificity. Take a family pet whose name is Phoebe. She is a springer spaniel, and that is a breed of dog. A dog is called a canine, like foxes, wolves, and jackals but not cats or gerbils. However, canines, cats, and gerbils—but not snakes or lobsters—are all called mammals; and all of these—Phoebe along with the foxes, gerbils, lobsters, and snakes—are called animals, unlike ferns and pine trees. Yet along with Phoebe, the foxes, cats, gerbils, lobsters, snakes, ferns, and pine trees are called living things, unlike peat moss. Still, peat moss—just like Phoebe, the foxes, cats, gerbils, lobsters, snakes, ferns, and pine trees—is called organic matter. So this furry companion you call Phoebe is also called a springer spaniel, a dog, a canine, a mammal, an animal, a living thing, and a mass (a lovable mass) of organic matter.

The mental exercise you did to identify Phoebe in the world of names of things is called *categorization* or *classification*. This sort of activity does not come easily to children. The Swiss psychologist Jean Piaget (1926) observed that most children reach the age of six or seven before they can easily think on all levels of generality and specificity at once. To demonstrate Piaget's point, if you ask a six-year-old whether he or she is from Omaha or Nebraska, the child is likely to answer one or the other but not both.

Russian psychologist Lev Vygotsky (1986) noted that children have another kind of difficulty with classification. Vygotsky pointed out that classifications like the one demonstrated in the Phoebe exercise are implicit in all of the concepts people hold. That is, when you store words in your memories, you naturally store them in relational hierarchies, and these hierarchies are part of your understanding of the meanings of the words. Imagine that you are planning a catered dinner party and you have been discussing the appetizers, the soup course, the entrée, and the dessert courses with the chef, who asks, "And will you want coffee with the crepes?" You know immediately that the chef is asking about the dessert. Vygotsky would call your use of the word *crepe* as a member of the class of dessert as an example of a *scientific concept*, one that allows for the word's location in a hierarchy of concepts. Vygotsky found, however, that young children often make *spontaneous concepts*. Jill and Peter DeVilliers (1975) gave a fine example of a spontaneous concept in the language of their one-year-old. The boy called the family dog, Nancy, by his original name for her, Nunu; but he also said "Nunu" when he rubbed his hand on the shag carpet in the living room (because it was soft and furry like Nancy?), when he had his hair brushed (because it scratched him like Nancy's claws?), and even when he saw a ripe olive atop a neighboring diner's salad in a fancy restaurant (because the olive was wet, black, shiny, and round like Nancy's nose?). This child was not thinking "Nancy—St. Bernard—dog—canine—mammal" at all, but rather associating a group of otherwise unrelated impressions with the word or name *Nunu*.

Knowledge of the way objects in the world have been classified—that Phoebe the family pet is at the same time a springer spaniel, a dog, a canine, a mammal, and an animal—does not come to children through their senses. This is knowledge that has to be learned from older language users—learned by observation and imitation rather than direct teaching, most likely, but learned from others nonetheless. Children need many opportunities to talk meaningfully with fluent language users and to do so in active and interesting situations so that they will hear words used properly and with proper relationships to their referents. In this way, they can learn not just words, but also the hierarchies of meanings within which the words fit.

How Do Words Get Meaning?

"When I use a word," Humpty Dumpty said in a rather scornful tone, "it means just what I choose it to mean—neither more nor less."

"The question is," said Alice, "whether you can make words mean different things."

"The question is," said Humpty Dumpty, "which is to be master—that's all."

from *Through the Looking Glass* by Lewis Carroll (1875/1992)

The author who put those words into Humpty Dumpty's mouth taught logic at Oxford University, and he was professionally interested in the question of how words get their meanings. Words have definitions that are written into dictionaries, but as lexicographers—those who compile definitions—will tell you, those definitions are not just dictated from the dictionaries to the people who use them. The process also works the other way around, and definitions are collected from the ways in which many people are observed using words. One self-important egg-man does not have enough influence to coin a new word or give an old one a new meaning, although some people occasionally do; for instance, Steven Jobs of Apple Computers invented and named the "mouse," and the definition of *mouse* as a hand-held device for aiming a cursor on a computer screen is now in your dictionary. But it usually takes many people to use a new word, and especially to use it in print, before that new word or new definition of an old one will find its way into a dictionary.

Still, words have histories, too, and how words have been used in the past matters—from a little to a lot. It is mostly a historical oddity that the words *bank* and *bench* are related, but they are: Bankers or moneychangers originally did their work sitting on a bench (originally called a *bank*) in medieval villages. It is more important to know that the phrase *to decimate* came from an act of discipline practiced by Roman commanders when their troops failed to fight valiantly: They lined them up, called out every tenth man, and killed him. (That's why *decimate* is considered a cousin of *decimal* and *decade*.) These days many people use the word *decimate* incorrectly when they mean "get rid of a great many."

Etymologies: Word Origins

In many dictionaries, you will find listings for words that look like this:

give. (giv). vt *gave, giv'en, giv'ing. [OE* giefan*]*

TEACH IT!
37

What do these notations mean? The part in parentheses is the pronunciation; *vt* means that the word is a transitive verb—that is, a verb that takes an object to complete the meaning. *Gave, given,* and *giving* are the past, past participle (the form used in compound verbs like *have given* or *had given*), and present participle (the form used in compound verbs like *is giving* and *were giving*). The part in brackets means that the word came down to us from an earlier word—in this case from Old English (OE). Words in English are derived from many sources. Nonetheless it is possible to map out a rough lineage for a great many of the words you use in English. When you trace the origins of words or look at their histories, you are dealing with their **etymologies**.

The English language traces its origin to Anglo-Saxon. In the fifth and sixth centuries of the common era, Germanic peoples from northern Germany and the Netherlands invaded England and pushed the indigenous Celts north into Scotland and west to Wales and Ireland. They brought their Germanic language with them, and it came to be called Anglo-Saxon (*Anglo* comes from Angles, the name of one of the Germanic tribes, and *Saxon* comes from another of those tribes). In the eighth and ninth centuries, Vikings raided from Scandinavia, and Old English became a mixture of Germanic, Norse, Danish, and Dutch words.

In 1066, the Normans from France conquered England and brought with them not only an early version of the French language but also Latin, which became widely used in the church, the government, and other places of higher culture—to the exclusion of English, which remained the language spoken around the hearth, on the farm, and in the market. Hundreds of words from Latin and Greek (Greek was read in the monasteries), as well as French, were absorbed into English in this period.

In 1477, William Caxton brought the first printing press to England and began printing books in English, giving an enormous boost to the language. The language he wrote, Middle English, had a sort of dual structure, consisting of Anglo-Saxon words and Latinate words. You can see this duality in the English words for food. The animal you call a *pig* (an Anglo-Saxon word) on the farm is called *pork* when it reaches the dining room table. *Pork* is a French word, from Latin. The cow (Anglo-Saxon) in the pasture became beef (French and Latin) in the dining room. Sheep on the farm (Anglo-Saxon word) became mutton (French and Latin) in the dining room. This all came about because English was spoken on the farm by farm workers but French was spoken in the dining rooms of the ruling class. To this day, our language has a core of words that came through Old English from Anglo-Saxon. These are very often the common, basic items in our vocabulary; the words children learn first, the words you use when you are being most direct. But there is another body of words, from Latin and Greek, that are more specialized, more scientific, and more limited to educated usage. Thus, you find the Anglo-Saxon words *cat* and *dog* and the corresponding Latin words *feline* and *canine;* you also find the Anglo-Saxon word *feel,* the related Latin word *sensitive,* and the related Greek word *sympathy.*

Morphology

As you saw earlier in this chapter, words can have smaller meaningful parts, called *morphemes.* The word *cats,* for example, has two morphemes: *cat* and *-s.* The word *runners* has three morphemes: *run + (n)er + -s,* and the word *roadrunners* has four:

road + run + (n)er + -s. Each additional part provides a change to the original word to create a new meaning. All of these morphemes are of slightly different kinds.

FREE MORPHEMES.   Free morphemes are words minus any grammatical endings. They are called "free" morphemes because they can stand alone. *Cat* is a word and a single free morpheme. Free morphemes can be combined to make compound words, such as *housecat, fireplace,* and *chainsaw.* Young children find it natural to use compound words in speech. At age two, Annabrook, who had seen a chainsaw and a bicycle, saw her first motorcycle and said, "Look! Chainsawbicycle!" Children who are beginning readers usually need to be shown to "look for two little words you know within this big word" when they confront compound words such as *doghouse* or *screwdriver.*

INFLECTIONAL MORPHEMES.   Bound morphemes such as *-s, -ed,* and *-ing* change the sense of a word from singular to plural or from present to past, but otherwise they do not make a new word out of the original one. They are called *inflectional morphemes* because they are used to make grammatical inflections. Children as young as two and three years of age learn inflectional morphemes as part of the process of language acquisition. Earlier in this chapter, there was an example of a child's spontaneous application of an inflectional morpheme when the six-year-old boy mentioned earlier said to his mother, "Don't worry, Mom. I'm hold-onning."

As children explore words on their own, they begin to find meaning in the words and to learn how to use words for different purposes.

DERIVATIONAL MORPHEMES.   A different kind of bound morpheme makes a new word out of the word to which it is joined. When you attach *-er* to the verb *run,* you create *runner,* "someone who runs." When you attach *-ist* to drug, you get *druggist,* "someone who prepares and sells drugs." Both *runner* and *druggist* are new words that are derived from the original words *run* and *drug.* Thus, *-er* and *-ist* are called *derivational morphemes* because they help to derive a new word from an original one. How do you know whether a word is an inflectional morpheme or a derivational morpheme? Jean Aitchison (1987) gives a simple test: An inflectional morpheme can be attached to a derivational morpheme, but a derivational morpheme cannot be attached to an inflectional morpheme. Thus, you can say *runners* but not *runser.* Children find it more difficult to manage derivational morphemes than inflectional ones. Research has shown that even up to middle school age, children show uncertainty over derivational morphemes in speech (Hoff, 2001). When learning to read, children need to be taught the effects of derivational morphemes on the meanings of the words to which they are attached.

HISTORICAL MORPHEMES.   Another kind of morpheme that can be useful for children to recognize is *historical* or *etymological morphemes.* Look at these words:

disrupt	*abrupt*
eruption	*rupture*

All have in common a word stem *-rupt-,* which came from a Latin word meaning *to break or to burst.* Note the morphemes attached to the stem in each case: *dis-, e-, cor-,* and *ab-.* All of these combine with the *-rupt-* stem to form new words in predictable ways:

dis- ("apart") + *rupt* = break apart or break up

e- ("out") + *rupt* = break or burst out

ab- (away from) + rupt = breaking away from, that is, a sudden shift

rupt + -ure (a state of) = the state of something breaking or bursting.

Many English words that came from Latin and Greek origins are made up of ancient bound morphemes and ancient stem words. Some are repeated often and with reasonably obvious meanings. These are worth teaching to children because they build children's power over vocabulary and help their spelling. As you will recall, the most basic vocabulary in English consists of words from Anglo-Saxon, and it is only at fourth grade and up that words with Latin and Greek roots and affixes begin to appear regularly in children's reading vocabulary. At that point, it is worthwhile to teach students Latin and Greek stems and affixes for the sake of their word recognition, their vocabulary, and their spelling development. Table 3.4 shows more stems and bound morphemes that appear in enough words to make them worth teaching.

TABLE 3.4

Some Common Word Stems and Affixes from Latin and Greek

LATIN STEMS	MEANING	WORD USAGE
Manu	Hand	Manual, manufacture
Stell-	Star	Stellar, interstellar, constellation
Mand-	To order	Command, remand, demand, mandate, mandatory
Miss-	To send	Missile, mission, transmission, dismiss, commission
Duce, duct	To lead	Conduct, reduce, introduce, deduction
Loc-	Place	Local, locate, collocate
Scrib, script	To write	Scribe, scripture, manuscript, conscript
Grad-	Step	Graduate, gradual, grade, degrade
LATIN AFFIXES		
Ab-	From, away from	Abstract, abrupt, abject
De-	Down	Demote, deride, demand, derogatory
Con (cor-, com-)	With, together	
Re-	Again, back	Remit, reduce, retarded
Trans-	Through, across	Transmit, transit, transcribe
Inter-	Between	Interrupt, international, intermission
Super-	Above	Supervise, supersonic, supersede
Ad- (al-, ac-)	To or toward	Admit, address, allot, access, allusion
GREEK STEMS		
Therm-	Heat	Thermometer, thermal
Geo-	Earth	Geography, geology, geometry
Metr-	Measure	Metric, geometry, meter
Scop-	To look at	Telescope, microscope
Path-	To feel or suffer	Sympathy, psychopath
GREEK AFFIXES		
Sym-	Together	Sympathy, symphony
-logy	The study of	Geology, psychology
Tele-	At a distance	Telescope, telephone
Mono-	Single	Monograph, monocle
Micro-	Small	Microphone, microbe

Pragmatics

Of course, language ability is made up of more than making appropriate sounds, speaking in words, and stringing words together with understandable syntax. Young people can have full power over none of those things and still get their point across. Hymes (1972) defined having power with language as **pragmatics:** the ability to do things with words. Since then, linguists have come to make a distinction between knowing language and knowing how to use language, or having *communicative competence.*

Speech Acts

Several decades ago, linguists began to talk of language not only in terms of grammar and meaning, but also in terms of **speech acts**: attempts to accomplish things with language. When language is described as speech acts, according to Austin (1962) and Searle (1969), each utterance has three aspects

- *Illocutionary force,* which means its intended outcome, what the speaker seeks to achieve by saying it
- *Locution,* which is the form in which the speaker words it
- *Perlocution,* which is its effects or what it accomplishes

Here is an example:

> *Iuliu hovers near the elbow of his stepfather, who is typing away on a manuscript at the computer.*
> "Mama got me a computer game," Iuliu says.
> "That's very nice," says his stepfather without looking up from the screen.
> *Iuliu says nothing for a minute and a half. Then he says, "Hey, Charlie, can you tell me when you're finished so I can play my computer game?"*
> *His stepfather laughs and says, "Hey, Buddy. Let's play your computer game."*

You can guess from this exchange that the *illocutionary force* of both Iuliu's utterances, that is, what he intended to achieve by making the utterances, was to get his stepfather to abandon the computer so that Iuliu could play his computer game. The *locution,* the verbal form Iuliu chose for his first utterance, was a statement about his new computer game. But that utterance did not achieve Iuliu's intention, since its *perlocution,* its effect, was to evoke a vague acknowledgment from his stepfather but not access to the computer. For his second locution, Iuliu chose a question, an indirect request. This utterance was understood for its intention by his stepfather, and it achieved Iuliu's goal: Its perlocution was an invitation to play the computer game, which matched the illocutionary force of Iuliu's utterance.

Pragmatics is an aspect of language that tends to keep people guessing. You might sometimes think, "I know what she said, but what did she mean? *Why* did she say what she just said?" Children have mastered many essentials of pragmatics before they enter school; that is, they know how to do things with words. They have a beginning awareness that language is used to achieve the speaker's purpose, but they still have much to learn about the strategizing that can go into language use. Discussions of literature often turn on questions of language use. What was the character's intent?

Pragmatics and Critical Literacy

A step beyond looking at what motivates the speech of a character in a story is to question what motivates the writer of the work. The discussion of pragmatics and speech acts should make clear that the meaning a listener or reader takes from an utterance or a written text is more than the sum of its sounds, syntax, and word meanings. A text can be seen as a set of words someone has crafted with the intention of having some effect on readers: having readers change their beliefs or actions.

The writer's intentions might be noble—wanting the reader to see, to notice, to understand, to enjoy, to beware of some part of experience—but sometimes a writer's words serves intentions that are not made clear, and those intentions might not be benign. For example, much of the advertising aimed at young people in North America promotes habits of (often unhealthy) consumption rather than self-development and social relationships. Although such advertising might be good for business, it can be bad for children.

Why might it be important to teach young children to become critical readers? What benefits does the child gain from this skill?

Given the fact that all of us—children included—live in a language environment that is full of messages whose intentions and possible effects are both healthy and harmful, many teachers are using techniques of critical literacy (Siegel & Fernandez, 2000) to encourage students to ask questions about things they hear, see, and read. Some of those questions are as follows:

Who created this text?

Why did they create it?

What is this text trying to do to me?

In whose interest is the text trying to do this?

What is not being said in this text?

What counterargument could I make to this text?

Whose point of view is not being heard?

What kind of person would have no problem accepting the claims of this text?

⭐ Functions of Language

The Scottish linguist M. A. K. Halliday (1975) studied what his young preverbal son Nigel seemed to be trying to do with his unconventional utterances and gestures and identified seven functions of language that were obviously present before the child could utter recognizable words or use syntax (see Table 3.5). These seven functions grow

TABLE 3.5

Classroom Language Practice

LANGUAGE FUNCTION	CHILDREN USE UTTERANCES AND GESTURES . . .	CLASSROOM PRACTICE ACTIVITY
Instrumental	as if they were extensions of their arms, to get things for themselves, such as to be handed something or to be lifted up.	Students write letters to agencies such as state chambers of commerce requesting information to use in a report.
Regulatory	to control other people's behavior, such as to get someone to stop playing with a toy.	Students explain to others how to do a procedure through verbal and written exercises.
Interpersonal	to set up and maintain relationships with other people, as in face to face play with a mother, or in teasing (tormenting?) the family dog.	Students are given training for working together in cooperative groups; students take turns being the class or school hosts, to greet and escort visitors.
Personal	to express how they are feeling, whether it is joy or loneliness.	Students write in personal journals.
Heuristic	to express curiosity and to find things out, such as to find out where an absent parent went or what a noise was.	Students keep learning logs; students write KWL charts.
Imaginative	to play with language and create sounds for one's own and others' enjoyment.	Students write poems, songs, stories, and plays.
Representational	to communicate knowledge about the world, such as to announce that a guest has arrived.	Students give oral reports; students write reports; students use the I-Search Procedure (see Chapter 2).

with the child and remain the areas of language use in which children continue to develop competence. Thus, even after developing a vocabulary of conventional words and a grasp of syntax and beginning to learn various verbal strategies for addressing different audiences, a child will continue to add skills at using language to get things, to regulate others' behavior, to build relationships, and so on. Table 3.5 identifies activities language arts teachers can utilize to encourage language development.

Cultural Differences in Language Use

Family & Community Literacy

Families in various cultural groups differ from each other in another way when it comes to their use of language, particular written language. Anthropologist Shirley Brice Heath lived for ten years in Piedmont, South Carolina, among economically marginalized African-American and working-class white families. In her book *Ways with Words* (1983), Heath demonstrated differences between these families that included not only dialects (different words, syntax, pronunciation, and styles of language), but also ways of using language.

Heath found that the white families had a literal approach to language that was rooted in their fundamentalist Christian faith and made interpretation of texts, and

TEACH IT!

★ ★ ★ ★

Sheltered Instruction for English Language Learners

English language learners and other students who need extra support in the classroom can be helped to learn the content of the curriculum if the right kind of scaffolding is supplied. A comprehensive approach to scaffolding for such students described by Mary Ellen Vogt is called sheltered instruction. Sheltered instruction requires that the teacher carefully think through the demands that the language of the lesson, the content of the lesson, and the learning tasks will place on the student. Then the teacher takes steps to make all three accessible. As Vogt writes,

For ELL's [English Language Learners] to become successful in learning content, they need to learn not only English grammar and vocabulary, but also "the language of school." ... What we have learned from these students is that they need assistance with all three knowledge bases: knowledge of English, knowledge of the content topic, and knowledge of how tasks are to be completed. Together, these are the key components of academic literacy. (Vogt, 2000, pp. 335, 336)

To teach students in Sheltered Instruction, teachers must do the following:

- Make the objectives of the lesson—for both the language to be used and the content to be learned—very explicit, including writing it on the board.
- Engage the students in active and meaningful activities (not just seatwork), and use various means to communicate information: graphic organizers, examples, analogies, repetitions. Communication between teacher and student and among students is frequent.
  - Relate the lessons to the students' prior experiences and background knowledge.
  - Choose key vocabulary for the lesson and introduce it in advance, highlight it during the lesson, and review it at the lesson's end and periodically thereafter.
  - Word lessons carefully and speak clearly and distinctly.
- Explain how tasks are to be carried out, then give examples of the kinds of responses that are expected, and explain why.
- Scaffold writing assignments with graphic organizers and other outlining aids; scaffold reading assignments with study guides, written questions, and outlines for note taking.
- Encourage higher-order thinking by means of many techniques that are described elsewhere in this chapter.
- Use group work, including paired work.

Refer to your **Teach It!** booklet for further activities you can use to reinforce concepts discussed in this chapter.

even storytelling, suspect. The black families engaged in verbal sparring even with very young children, showing an approach to inducting young children into language practice that was strikingly different from the intricate patterns of turn-taking and Motherese that was described earlier in this chapter. Also striking was the way groups of adults would chime in to interpret a text, such as an announcement received in the mail inviting them to enroll their four-year-olds in a Head Start class. The words were shouted from porch stoop to porch stoop and interpreted by several mothers before people were satisfied that they had fully explicated their meaning. The African-American children were inventive storytellers and were especially adept at helping each other construct, each one building on the others' contributions.

Children from both groups experienced degrees of mismatch with the culture of the school when they entered first grade. The white children tended to sit in mute embarrassment when asked to interpret a story or to write one, and the black children drew disapproval from the teacher when they alternately teased each other, helped each other construct stories, and read passages aloud during reading lessons. The teachers responded as if the children were somehow deviant or at fault. But as Heath recognized, there was a mismatch between the children's home culture and the culture of the school—specifically in the ways in which the children's families used language.

Social Variations in Language Use

The focus in this chapter has moved from understanding language as a way of making meaningful utterances toward language as it is used in social situations. Three ways in which language use differs in social situations is in the use of dialects, registers, and social languages or discourses.

DIALECTS.   Members of different geographic, social, and cultural groups use language in unique ways. Part of the uniqueness is captured in dialects that the groups use. *Geographic* dialects are reflected in the differences in the word pronunciations, word choice, and conversational styles of speakers from northern Minnesota; Goliad, Texas; or Ocracoke, North Carolina. *Social* dialects are reflected in the speech of people from different social classes. *Ethnic* dialects are reflected in the speech of people from different racial groups. Of course, all these dialects overlap, as in the speech of a professional African-American family from the southern Appalachian Mountains. Differences in dialects can result in children experiencing difficulties learning to read, especially if they aren't aware of sounds in the standard pronunciations of words reflected in the spellings.

From the choice of words and the structure of sentences to the patterns in which information is presented, written language differs significantly from spoken language. The language of books is probably closer to urban educated white middle-class speech than to any other dialect. Therefore, when it comes to reading and writing, that gives a big advantage to people who already speak that dialect—and a disadvantage to those who speak a different regional, social, or ethnic dialect.

REGISTERS.   Another way in which speakers use language differently is the many social registers all people employ when talking to people they hold in different degrees of intimacy and respect. Even a kindergarten child uses different forms of address when she is talking to another child, her mother, or her teacher. In English, different degrees of intimacy and formality are signaled by the amount of indirection that is used. Compare the following sentences:

"Hey, open the window!"

"Please open the window."

"Would you mind opening the window?"

"Don't you think we need some fresh air in here?"

Other languages signal these differences with grammatical forms. Spanish has the familiar form of the pronoun *tu,* used with close friends and family members, and the formal *usted,* used with adults. Romanian has *tu,* which is familiar, but also *dumnea-voastra,* which is more formal and distant, and *dumneata,* which, as one Romanian explained, is "so polite that it's insulting." Linguists use the term *registers* to refer to the ranges of speech speakers have for expressing themselves in different social situations:

- A *ceremonial register,* used in religious functions and formal affairs such as school graduations
- A *professional register,* used in giving an explanation at school such as discussing a lesson in science or language arts
- A *polite register,* used in informal situations with people the speaker does not know well
- A *casual register,* used when telling a story or sharing jokes with close friends

DISCOURSE.   As was mentioned earlier, families put language to different uses, and some of those uses can lead to mismatches in children's accommodation to the routines of classroom reading instruction. James Paul Gee (1999, 2000, 2001) points out that all real uses of language occur in a social setting. Discourses—forms of language that are used in social situations—involve a *who* and a *what.* The *who* refers to the socially recognized role people play at the time they use language. The *what* refers to the thing they are trying to accomplish when they use language. (Think of speech acts here.) In any setting, speakers and listeners use a *discourse,* a form of language that occurs within the boundaries of shared understandings of what roles they are playing and what they are trying to accomplish. Classroom instruction is a special kind of social setting that uses its own discourses, such as when a teacher asks children questions about readings, even when it is obvious the teacher knows the answers. But the questioning is a method of instruction, and the children quickly learn to play along with this "game." Teachers need to be aware of the special demands that learning school discourse places on students. Such awareness allows them to help their students learn the "language of school" while also helping them to learn the content.

FOR REVIEW

As children learn to talk, they gain much of their power to use language through their own discovery processes, aided by the special support—but not the direct instruction—of the adults and older speakers around them. As they learn to use language, children infer the patterns of regularity or "rules" that govern speech, and gradually construct their own versions. Do children learn to read and write in the same way? Clearly, discovery helps, but because written language is a deliberate contrivance that bears peculiar relationships to speech, several conventions of reading and writing need to be taught.

The aspects of language important for teachers to know include the following:

- Phonology, or the sound system of language
- Syntax, or the rules and patterns that string words together meaningfully
- Semantics, or the meaning system of language, including morphology
- Pragmatics, or the social uses of language

Much of the irregularity in the English spelling system can be explained by the system of English speech sounds. Because of historical changes in pronunciation, words such as *sign* and *signal* that used to be pronounced similarly now have different pronunciations. The spelling system has been designed to honor these historical relationships between words rather than to carefully match their sounds. Word study, as will be seen later in this book, can help children become aware of the complexities of the sound and spelling system as they learn to recognize words and also learn their meanings.

The meanings of words were also discussed in the sections on semantics, including etymologies, or word histories, and morphology, or the way words are constructed.

For Your Journal

1. Review the answers to the anticipation guide on the first page of this chapter. What answers would you give to those questions now that you have read this chapter?

2. If you still need proof that you have *tacit* knowledge of English grammar, that is, knowledge that enables you to talk and listen but of which you are largely unaware, try this exercise. Explain what is wrong with this sentence: *Ignacio is playing with a red big ball.* State the rule that you would use in writing the sentence correctly.

3. Families from different social backgrounds think of literacy in strikingly different ways. How did you use literacy in your family when you were growing up? What materials did the people around you read? Did they share or discuss them with each other? If so, how? Was there bedtime reading? If so, what was it like?

⭐ Taking It to the World

1. Look up your own state's standards for elementary and reading teachers' knowledge of language. You can find them on your state department of education's web site, usually by using the key word *standards*. What do you think teachers need to know about language besides what is mandated in the state standards?

2. Halliday's functions of language constitute a menu of ways in which people of every age need to learn to use language. Interview a kindergarten or first-grade teacher and ask whether he or she consciously tries to help children develop their ability to talk and listen for different purposes—that is, to use language for different functions. If so, what purposes does the teacher emphasize? How does the teacher help children learn to use them well?

3. Interview a guidance counselor at a middle or high school or a counseling psychologist who treats adults. Interview a foreman or manager at a business or manufacturing plant. With regard to their clients or the people they supervise, to what extent do these professionals find that people's problems are related to their difficulties in using language for different purposes—for self-awareness, for getting along with others, for giving and receiving directions clearly? Do these people believe that schools have a role in teaching communication for different purposes?

4. After you have written in your journal about your own family's uses of literacy, interview a first- or second-grade teacher. What differences does that teacher notice in different children's expectations of and approaches to literacy tasks? That is, what do different children do when they are asked to make up a story or to discuss one? How do the teacher's accounts compare with the recap of Heath's findings on pages 108–110?

★ Being a Professional Reading Teacher

Reflecting on the Chapter

Chapter 3 provides valuable background information about language and how it underlies the development of children's reading. What are some examples of how this knowledge contributes to a teacher's effectiveness in teaching reading?

Teacher Examinations

Many states now require that teachers take formal examinations that reflect the content of all or part of their teacher preparation programs. States with undergraduate teacher preparation programs often require Praxis I. California requires the Reading Instruction Competence Assessment (RICA). Both of these examinations focus heavily on information found in Chapter 3. Other states can be expected to add their own similar requirements in the future.

Your Professional Portfolio

As you review material for one or more of the examinations that many prospective teachers must take, you might identify a particularly salient piece of research or an article about best practice. Consider including such an article in your portfolio, along with a written reflection about its importance to you and your teaching.

Technology Connections

There are several sites on the Internet that provide rich examples of how sounds are made, including diagrams of the mouth, recordings of sounds, and even spectrographic displays of sound waves produced with sound.

1. Professor George Dillon at the University of Washington has a wonderful site (`http://faculty.washington.edu/dillon/PhonResources/PhonResources.html`) that provides information about speech sounds and also links to numerous other sites that provide detailed information and tutorials.

2. Visit the "Vocal Vowels" exhibit at the San Francisco Museum of Science's online Exploratorium (`www.exploratorium.edu/exhibits/vocal_vowels`) to see how a duck call can be made to produce human vowel sounds by modifying the production chamber.

3. Noted linguist Peter Ladefoged provides a comprehensive site devoted to speech sounds at `http://hctv.humnet.ucla.edu/departments/linguistics/VowelsandConsonants`

4. A site made available by the University of California at Los Angeles features an interactive chart of the sounds of the Internationl Phonetic Alphabet (IPA), which covers English as well as most other languages in the world. Click on a symbol to produce specific sounds `http://hctv.humnet.ucla.edu/departments/linguistics/VowelsandConsonants/course/chapter1/chapter1.html`

Connect with Research

Research Navigator.com

Review the following key words from the chapter and then connect to Research Navigator (`http://www.researchnavigator.com`) through this book's Companion web site to conduct a search into research on each of the various topics as they relate to reading and literacy education today.

allophones	invented spelling	rime
alphabetic principle	letter name stage	scaffolding
consonant blends	morphology	semantics
consonant digraphs	Motherese	speech acts
consonants	onset	story grammar
diphthongs	phonemes	syntax
early phonemic stage	phonics	telegraphic speech
etymologies	phonological awareness	vowel reduction
grammatical morpheme	phonology	vowels
Great Vowel Shift	pragmatics	word knowledge
holophrases	prephonemic spelling	

Further Readings

Pinker, S. (1995). *The Language Instinct.* New York: Harper Collins.

A lively introduction to the topic of language and language acquisition by a linguist from MIT.

Hart, B., and Risley, T. (1995). *Meaningful Differences in the Everyday Experience of Young American Children.* Baltimore: Brookes.

Children from different social groups vary tremendously in their language experience before they reach school, and these differences translate into differences in the size of their vocabulary and the complexity of their sentences.

Stanovich, K. (2002). *Matthew Effects in Reading.*

The term "Matthew effects" refers to the statement in the Gospel according to St. Matthew that the rich get richer and the poor get poorer. Stanovich traces a research-based scenario in which difficulties in phonological awareness can lead step by step to general reading disability.

Temple, C., Nathan, R., Burris, N., and Temple, F. (1992). *The Beginnings of Writing,* 3rd Edition.

Originally written in 1982, this book describes children's stage-by-stage processes of discovering the writing, spelling, and compositional patterns of English writing and relates the whole enterprise to the process of language acquisition.

Vellutino, F. R., Scanlon, D. M., Sipay, E., Small, S., Pratt, A., Chen, R., and Denckla, M. (1996). Cognitive Profiles of Difficult to Remediate and Readily Remediated Poor Readers: Early Intervention as a Vehicle for Distinguishing between Cognitive and Experiential as Basic Causes of Specific Reading Disability. *Journal of Educational Psychology,* 88, 601–638.

How many children have reading disabilities so profound that they will not respond to the regular palette of good reading instruction? These authors sought an answer to that question in an amazingly practical way: They took a large number of children with reading disabilities, gave them excellent instruction, and saw how many had not been helped.

Venezky, R. L. (1999). *The American Way of Spelling: The Structure and Origins of American English Orthography.* New York: Guilford.

For anyone who wants the last word on what turns out to be a fascinating subject, a noted authority on the English spelling system takes you through a comprehensive explanation of the sound system of English and the way it is spelled, including a history of English spelling. When all is said and done, there are irregularities in the system, but Venezky makes the whole of English spelling much more understandable.

Aspects of Reading

How do I start a writing workshop? I have never actually seen a class-room (except for one of my college courses) use a writer's notebook and implement it to produce finished pieces of writing. I just need some practical tips for getting started in my classroom next year.

— CURREY, STUDENT TEACHER
GEORGIA

I'm worried about the self-esteem of my students. They need to develop English, but there is a danger of their losing the language and culture of their homes. How can I help them develop self-esteem so that they recognize the value of two languages and cultures?

— LEONORA, PRESERVICE TEACHER CANDIDATE
CALIFORNIA

Remember why you are doing this. Keep in mind the power of starting from the beginning with young chil-dren, as opposed to trying to fix the world of adults. . . . Literacy is the key to success in all subjects. It opens the gates to communication, know-ledge, and imagination. The greatest reward I've gotten from teaching is hearing them get excited about a book and hearing them resolve con-flicts peacefully and independently.

— SARAH, PRESCHOOL READING TEACHER
WASHINGTON

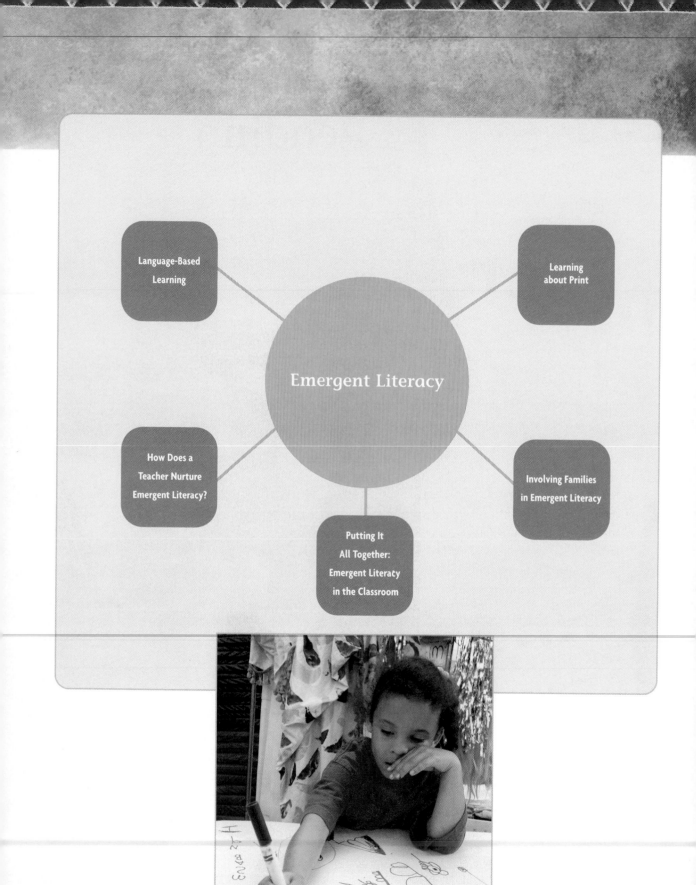

Emergent Literacy

Language-Based Learning

Learning about Print

How Does a Teacher Nurture Emergent Literacy?

Involving Families in Emergent Literacy

Putting It All Together: Emergent Literacy in the Classroom

Emergent Literacy

T*he following statements will get you thinking about the topics of this chapter. Answer true or false in response to each statement. As you read and learn more about the topics in these statements, double-check your answers. See what interests you and what prompts your curiosity toward more understanding.*

Anticipation Guide

_____ 1. When you get right down to it, learning to read is "natural."

_____ 2. Children's scribbles are a window into their thinking about how print works.

_____ 3. Concepts about print, such as the arrangement of print on the page or the fact that people read the print and not the pictures, rarely need to be taught.

_____ 4. Children should never be allowed to write words incorrectly.

_____ 5. Invented spelling provides teachers with insights into children's knowledge of phonics.

_____ 6. We can teach children a lot about reading and writing through passive means, such as labeling items in the classroom.

_____ 7. When children imitate adults reading storybooks, they teach themselves important concepts about the way reading works.

_____ 8. Reading aloud to children is a waste of valuable instructional time. If it is to be done at all, it should be left up to parents.

_____ 9. Teaching reading is such a complicated undertaking that parents should be discouraged from taking any part in it.

_____ 10. There are no significant differences in the amount of time that parents from different social groups spend reading to their children.

Vignette of a Kindergarten Classroom

It is the second Monday in November, and Ignacio Diaz's kindergartners know the morning routine very well. As they enter, they take off their coats, stuff their lunch boxes into their cubbies, then check the job board to see who will give the weather report, who will lead the Pledge of Allegiance, and who will line the children up to go to lunch. Then they go to the task board and see what their rotations are for the language block. Their names are pasted in quadrants with symbols, indicating who will go to the independent study center, who will work with the teacher in the reading circle, who will write, and who will have reading time. Charmaigne enters the room and hands her teacher a book baggie, a plastic bag that holds a book and a group of games and activity sheets.

"Mama said she liked the drawing I did of Toad. Or maybe it was Frog. … How do you tell them apart again?" she says. "And she said to tell you we finally figured out how to do the alphabet game."

Ignacio laughs and puts the book baggie into a bin to be repacked for another child to take home.

As children come in from various buses, Charmaigne wanders to the library corner and begins reading a little book about frogs. It is one of her favorites, written by Henry, the boy who taught them all to draw cartoons. Henry's penciled letters make dubious spellings that flow across the page in pencil, but Charmaigne focuses on the neat black letters her teacher has written with a felt-tipped pen. She can read some of the words, and she likes finding the ones she knows. Henry's drawings always make clear what is going on in his books, so when Charmaigne wants to, she can hold the book up and tell the story aloud as if she were reading it, even though she does not yet know many of the words.

The class is all here, and Charmaigne's time has come to lead the Pledge of Allegiance. She knows what a flag is, but the word *flag* is taped underneath it anyway. It begins with *F*, just like the title of Henry's book, *Frogs*. Now Mr. Diaz calls the children to the rug in front of the chart stand.

"Who knows what today is?" he asks.

"Monday," says Henry.

"Right," says Ignacio. "And I'm going to write '*Today is Monday*' right here on the chart. Let's say that sentence: '*Today is Monday.*'"

"Today is Monday," chants the class.

"What's the first word I need to write?"

"*Today*," Charmaigne offers.

"Good. What's the first sound we hear in '*Today*'?" Some children, including Charmaigne, chant the "*tuh*" sound, over and over. After a moment's hesitation, other children join them.

"Aw, you're champions. Now, what letter will we use to spell the "*tuh*" sound?"

With the children and Mr. Diaz taking turns offering up sounds and naming letters to spell them with, the morning news is written on the chart. It covers four lines. Ignacio is careful to show the children that he begins writing over on the left side, then writes across to the right, then returns to the left but down one line, and continues writing to the right again.

The children read the sentences through three times as Ignacio points to every word with his "Harry Potter wand," the stick he uses for pointing to words.

I n science, observations often follow theory. As you saw in Chapter 3, children learn to talk through their own efforts at discovery (Pinker, 2000). Shortly after psycholinguists began to publish their studies of children's language acquisition, researchers began to take a close look at children's literacy learning, too. They wondered whether children might learn about the features of written language and how reading and writing work by being immersed in an environment of readers and writers. These assumptions turned out to be largely true. Children learn a great deal about reading and writing years before they enter school and even before they are taught to recognize their first letter (Clay, 1975; Temple, Nathan, & Burris, 1982; Teale & Sulzby, 1986; Neuman & Dickinson, 2000). They learn many of these insights by their own efforts, but they learn better with the support of adults who orchestrate opportunities for discovery. We call this ***emergent literacy,*** which refers to the following:

- A period in children's learning to read and write that begins when children first notice print and wonder what people are doing when they work with it
- Early instruction that children receive in preschool and kindergarten at the hands of careful teachers who make sure that all children gain the insights about literacy they will need in order to profit fully from formal reading instruction once it begins

Because print represents spoken language, learning how to read requires that children simultaneously understand print and be conscious of the features of language that it represents. Learning about language, learning about print, and learning how reading and writing work are the main aspects of emergent literacy that will be explored in this chapter.

Language-Based Learning

With our speech, we can pledge love, declare war, or forecast blizzards—all without being conscious of the language we use to do these things. When children learn to read, however, they have to be conscious of language. Because print represents spoken language, emergent readers need to be aware of the words of which language is built. They also need to be aware of the sounds. If their language is Japanese, emergent readers need to be aware of sounds at the level of syllables. If their language is English (or German or Finnish), readers must be aware of sounds at the level of onset and rimes and phonemes.

The Concept of Word

The first unit of language of which young readers need to be aware is the word. Distinguishing words in speech is not a simple matter, because speech usually comes to us all run together. We more often hear someone say "Whuzapnin?" than "What is happening?" If we can sort an utterance into individual words, it is because, as experienced learners, we can already think of those words in units. For children in kindergarten and even first grade, separating speech into word units is not so simple.

Not being aware of words in speech puts children at a disadvantage when they are learning to read. Suppose a teacher teaches the children the song "The Corner Grocery Store" and then writes the words on chart paper. The teacher then asks the children to look at the printed words as they sing the words from memory. Children who are aware of word units—who have a **concept of word**—can look at the word *corner* at just the instant they sing it. Children who do not have the concept of word might scan their eyes across a whole line of text as they sing the word *corner*, or they might look at only a single letter. In either case, at the conclusion of the activity, a child who lacks the concept of word is unlikely to have learned to recognize any new words from it. The child who has the concept of word, who looks at the written words at the instant each is sung, will be in the position to associate the written version of the words with the spoken versions and is likely to learn to read several of them from the activity.

Phonological Awareness

**Phonics &
Phonemic
Awareness**

Beyond the level of words, there are other levels of speech of which emergent readers must be aware. These are syllables, onsets and rimes, and phonemes. **Syllables** are the "pulses" of language. They are the "beats" we hear in *elbow* (two syllables), *love* (one syllable), and *popsicle* (three syllables). As was discussed in Chapter 3, onsets and rimes are two parts of most single syllables: The onset is the beginning consonant sound (if the syllable has one), and the rime is the vowel sound plus any consonant sound that follows. In *cat,* the onset is *k* and the rime is *-at*. In *step,* the onset is *st* and the rime is *-ep*. As the smallest speech sounds in language, phonemes roughly correspond to letters. *Dig* has three phonemes: /d/, /i/, and /g/. *Clam* has four phonemes: /k/, /l/, /æ/, and /m/. (Note that we conventionally represent phonemes with slashes on either side.) As a good deal of research has shown (e.g., Adams, 1991; Snow et al., 1998), children who are aware that words can be broken into onsets and rimes and phonemes are more likely to learn to read words successfully than those who are not.

Hall and Moats (1999) present the following as abilities of normally developing children in kindergarten and first grade:

At the end of Kindergarten:

- *At the syllable level:* Most children can distinguish single-syllable words from words with two syllables when they hear them.

- *At the onset and rime level:* Most children can match a target word with a rhyming word.

- *At the phoneme level:* Most children can pick out words that begin with the same sound as a target word and can tell you the odd word out—the one that does not begin with the same sound as the others.

Two months into first grade:

TEACH IT!

5

- Given two letters on cards, most children can combine them and pronounce the word they spell (*in, on, at, it, up*)

- Given a three-phoneme word, most children can say the word that is left when the beginning consonant is deleted: *bat/at, sit/it, cup/up*.

By the end of first grade:

- Most children can pronounce two-phoneme words slowly and separate the phonemes: /t/ - /oo/; /b/ - /y/.

- Given longer words, most children can leave off the first consonant and pronounce what is left: *b - utterfly*.

- Given three isolated phonemes, most children can combine them to make a word: /s/ /æ/ /t/ = *sat*.

Again, if children are aware of sounds in words, they will have an easier time matching letters and sounds when they begin to read.

**Struggling
Reader**

Reasonably short periods of exclusive phonemic awareness instruction embedded in reading, writing, and oral discussions improve children's phonemic awareness learning. Research by Iversen and Tunmer (1993) shows that adding a phonemic awareness component to already successful **Reading Recovery** programs is of benefit. Reading Recovery is a program of intense, individualized tutoring for struggling readers (Clay, 1985). Iversen and Tunmer demonstrated that a focus on systematic

Short periods of dedicated instruction can help struggling readers improve their reading skills.

TEACH IT!

3

phonemic awareness skills within the 30-minute Reading Recovery session improved learning. Clearly, this phonemic awareness addition was short (and highly focused) because it fit within the 30-minute period. The study included three groups of teachers working with struggling first graders. One group had Reading Recovery training, one had Reading Recovery training and additional phonemic awareness training, while the third group had a different intervention. The results showed that the group of teachers with Reading Recovery training and additional phonemic awareness training helped children achieve more than did the other groups.

In another study, O'Connor, Jenkins, and Slocum (1995) examined the phonemic awareness learning of two groups of at-risk kindergartners. One group received a broad-based (not as explicit) phonemic awareness training, while another group received focused training (explicit) on letters and sounds that included work with words and letter patterns embedded in a book or in writing. The second group engaged in manipulating and segmenting (combining letters to make a word such as *sp - out* and pulling them apart) and deleting phonemes (Remove the letters *sp,* and what do you have?). The children were given phonemic awareness instruction for ten weeks in two fifteen-minute sessions per week, totaling five hours. This is not a lengthy time. The children with the focused training in this study achieved greater phonemic awareness knowledge.

Various exercises to help emergent readers develop a concept of word and become aware of sounds in words are discussed later in this chapter.

Dialogic Reading

Family & Community Literacy

When working with individual children, one approach to reading with children called **dialogic reading** helps put the child in the active role as a storyteller and not just a listener. Dialogic reading has shown gains in children's language acquisition and growth in concepts about print (Whitehurst & Lonigan, 2001).

Dialogic reading is intended to be used by parents, teachers, and volunteer tutors, such as college students working in special literacy programs such as America Reads or Jumpstart. In some communities, training in dialogic reading is available through family literacy programs offered by public libraries. The training is supported by twenty-minute videotapes (Whitehurst, 1994). Adult readers are taught to read interactively with the child. Two acronyms, PEER and CROWD, are used to remind the adult readers of the steps. PEER is a mnemonic for a strategy used to nurture language development with younger children as they read a book together with an adult. The letters stand for:

> ***Prompt*** the child to name objects in the book and talk about the story;
>
> ***Evaluate*** the child's responses and offer praise for adequate responses and alternatives for inadequate ones;
>
> ***Expand*** on the child's statements with additional words; and afterward
>
> ***Repeat***—Ask the child to repeat the adult's utterances.

CROWD identifies five kinds of questions adults ask:

1. *Completion prompts.* Ask the child to supply a word or phrase that has been omitted. (For example, "I see a yellow duck looking at ___.")
2. *Recall prompts.* Here the child is asked about things that occurred earlier in the book. ("Do you remember some animals that Brown Bear saw?")
3. *Open-ended prompts.* Here the child is asked to respond to the story in his own words. ("Now it's your turn: You say what is happening on this page.")
4. *Wh- prompts.* The adult asks *what, where, who,* and *why* questions. ("What is that yellow creature called? Who do you think Brown Bear will see next?")
5. *Distancing prompts.* Here the child is asked to relate the content of the book to life experiences. ("Do you remember when we saw a yellow duck like that one swimming in the lake? Was it as big as this one?")

⭐ Learning about Print

Children's emergent literacy involves both the development of language and the development of children's awareness of language. Simultaneously, children also gain awareness of aspects of print. Print awareness includes the following:

- *Graphic principles*: a set of discoveries about the features of print that are often displayed in children's scribbles
- *Awareness of the alphabetic nature of writing*: the idea that, in languages such as English, German, Spanish, and Kiswahili (but not Japanese or Chinese), writing works by using units of letters to represent language at the level of phonemes
- *Concepts about print*: a constellation of realizations about what print is and how it works
- *Alphabet knowledge*: being able to recognize and produce many letters of the alphabet
- *Orthographic concepts*: an understanding of the particular rules and relationships that relate letters to sounds

Graphic Principles

When examining the scribbles of four-year-old children from literate families whose languages were English, Arabic, and Chinese, educator Jerry Harste and his colleagues (Harste, Woodward, & Burke, 1984) found that they could easily tell which scribbles came from which child. Even though the scribbles did not use any actual letters or characters from any of the languages, the children's scribbles nonetheless looked like their parents' writing and not like those of the other children. Although the children did not yet know how to make any graphemes from their languages, the children nonetheless managed to capture many of their visual features.

Marie Clay (1975) carefully examined the patterns in children's scribbles and identified **graphic principles** that emerge as they begin to experiment with writing. Understanding these principles will not necessarily tell you what to teach next, anymore than listening to a child's baby talk will. Nonetheless, following the emergence

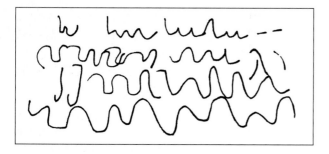

FIGURE 4.1

The Recurring Principle.

Carlene, Age 4

Source: Temple, Nathan, Burris, and Temple, *The Beginnings of Writing.*
Copyright © 1992. Allyn & Bacon Publishers, Inc.

of these graphic principles will increase your appreciation of a preschool and kindergarten child's growth in emergent literacy

THE RECURRING PRINCIPLE. As the scribbles in Figure 4.1 make clear, a young child's mock-writing is often composed of the same mark, roughly the same size, repeated again and again, usually in a linear arrangement. Children whose language is English will sometimes show a preference for linked and continuous marks that resemble cursive writing or for discrete marks that resemble print. Children who are used to other writing symbols might produce recurring marks that resemble those.

THE GENERATIVE PRINCIPLE. When children realize that they can add some variety—but not too much variety—to their mock-writing, they have discovered the *generative principle*: the idea that a few marks or characters can be combined and recombined in different orders to produce a whole page or more of writing. We often see children taking advantage of the generative principle when they have learned to write a few letters, such as those that spell their own name. Then they combine and recombine those letters to generate many lines of text (see Figure 4.2).

The generative principle, of course, is real. It is a key advantage to alphabetic writing. Whereas speakers of Chinese must learn to write and read some 6,000 characters by the time they finish grade school, speakers of English need only twenty-six letters (fifty-two counting the uppercase ones) to write. Don't be surprised to hear a child who has generated a page of mock-writing show it to you and ask, "What did I write?" As Marie Clay observed in her book by that title (1975), children at this stage believe that they can now generate writing, but because they cannot yet read, they rely on the adults around them to tell them what their creations mean.

FIGURE 4.2

The Generative Principle.

Four-year-old

Source: Temple, Nathan, Burris, and Temple, *The Beginnings of Writing.*
Copyright © 1992. Allyn & Bacon Publishers, Inc.

THE FLEXIBILITY PRINCIPLE. To a child, letters must be arbitrary-looking things. Some have straight lines, and some have curves. Some have loops that flop to the left, and some have loops that flop to the right. Some are vertical staffs with one, two, even three horizontal arms. To adults, the combinations of lines that make up letters, with their straightness or their curves, with the directions of their slants and their slopes, with the numbers of their parts, constitute the closed system of the alphabet. To children who do not yet know the system, these variations in lines are an open field of possibilities. Consider that children are trying to learn the set of features that make up particular letters. What makes matters confusing is that often even letters they know are sometimes being presented to them in forms they do not yet recognize, as occurs when they see new words in different typefaces.

good   good   *good*   good   good   *good*

good   *good*   **good**   good   good

It should not be surprising, then, that children experiment with the forms of letters and sometimes produce original forms. A strategy that many children seem to use is to take a letter they know how to make and add things to it to make letters they never made before (see Figure 4.3). Sometimes this works: An *L* with two extra arms becomes an *E*. But suppose we add *five* extra arms? What letter will that be?

DIRECTIONAL PRINCIPLES.   A particular instance of the flexibility principle is the set of **directional principles**. Directional principles have to do with learning to associate the identity of letters with the directions they face. We refer to "principles" because they include the horizontal orientation of both individual letters and of words.

Letters are nearly the only things in children's experience whose identity changes with their orientation in space, so it is not surprising that children find it hard to remember what direction they should face. What is surprising, from an adult point of view, is how easily children can shift from one orientation to another. As you see in Figure 4.4, a five-year-old child who starts writing on the right-hand side of the page might find it natural to reverse the letters and write a whole line of text from right to left.

In past years, children's tendency to reverse letters was taken as a sign of a dysfunctional brain, but now it is seen as a sign of intellectual immaturity and inexperience with print. Reversing letters and whole lines of print is natural for kindergartners and first graders who are learning the directionality principle (Temple, Nathan, Burris, & Temple, 1992). In the writing of older students whose literacy is not advancing as quickly as their classmates', reversals can still appear, but they are evidence of delayed literacy development rather than neurological problems. Students who are diagnosed with dyslexia make no more reversals of letters than do normally developing younger children who read at the same level (Vellutino, 1979). Kindergarten and first-grade teachers need to take every opportunity to remind children of the orientation of letters and avoid materials, like

FIGURE 4.3

The Flexibility Principle.

Carlene, Age 4

Source: Temple, Nathan, Burris, and Temple, *The Beginnings of Writing.* Copyright © 1992. Allyn & Bacon Publishers, Inc.

FIGURE 4.4

Directionality.

Annabrook, Age 5

Writing backwards was easy for her.

Source: Temple, Nathan, Burris, and Temple, *The Beginnings of Writing.* Copyright © 1992. Allyn & Bacon Publishers, Inc.

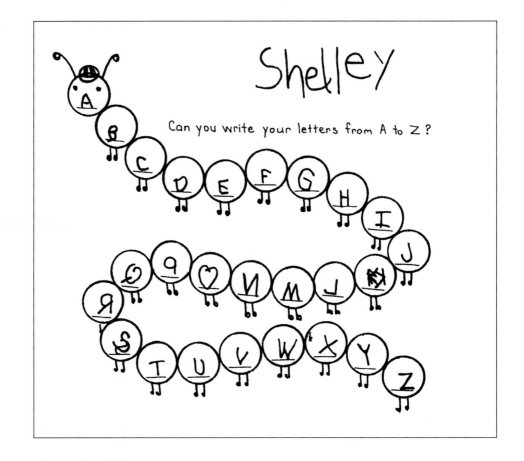

The Snake Picture.

Shelley, Kindergarten
The "A" and "Z" were already printed.

Source: Temple, Nathan, Burris, and Temple, *The Beginnings of Writing.*
Copyright © 1992. Allyn & Bacon Publishers, Inc.

the one shown in Figure 4.5, that aren't sensitive to the challenges directionality poses to children.

Concepts about Print

New Zealander Marie Clay has long been the literacy field's favorite example of a *kidwatcher*, Yetta Goodman's term for a teacher who observes children very, very carefully and appreciates how they see the tasks of learning and what they do to learn. Kidwatchers make good teachers because they help children solve puzzles and they adjust their instruction to fit nicely with children's own efforts to discover how literacy works and how to become good at it. Clay offers us this account of a novice teacher giving a reading lesson to a group of beginning readers:

Suppose the teacher has placed an attractive picture on the wall and has asked her children for a story, which she will record under it. They offer the text, "Mother is cooking," which the teacher alters slightly to introduce some features she wishes to teach. She writes:

Mother said, "I am baking."

If she says, "Now look at our story, 30% *of the new entrant group* [children who are just beginning reading instruction] *will attend to the* picture. *If she says, "Look at the words and find some that you know," between 50 and 90% will be looking for* letters. *If she says, "Can you see Mother?" most will agree that they can, but some see her in the picture, some can locate* M, *and others will locate the word* Mother.

Perhaps the children read in unison, "Mother is ..." and the teacher tries to sort this out. Pointing to said, *she asks, "Does this say* is?*" Half agree that it does because it has* s *in it. "What letter does it start with?" Now the teacher is really in trouble. She assumes that the children will know* that a word is built out of letters, *but 50% of the children still confuse the verbal labels* word *and* letter *after six months of instruction. She also assumes that the children know that the left-hand letter following a space is the "start" of a word. Often they do not. (Clay, 1975, pp. 3–4)*

As this example makes clear, there are many concepts about print that children must have in place so that in a reading lesson, they can orient themselves properly to a book and direct their attention appropriately. These concepts include understandings of the layout of books; the relative roles of print and pictures; the orientation of print on the page; the meanings of terms used in reading instruction, such as *beginning, end, first,* and *last*; where to find the "top" and "bottom" of a page; the terms *word* and *letter*; uppercase and lowercase letters; and at least a beginning understanding of punctuation. The Teach-It! box identifies some ways in which you can assess students' knowledge of the concepts of print.

Alphabet Knowledge

Alphabet knowledge is considered part of a child's emergent literacy because a great many children learn to recognize and even produce letters of the alphabet before they enter first grade. Children's knowledge of the alphabet is both an indicator of their exposure to print (Walsh, Price, & Gillingham, 1988) and a facilitator of learning to read (Morris, 1999). Although children can start learning to read and write without knowing all of the letters of the alphabet, they do need to know most of them to make progress. Thoughtful teachers will want to know how many letters each of their students can recognize and produce, especially when they are concerned about a particular student's progress.

An inventory of children's letter knowledge should be taken from one child at a time. Show the child a set of randomly ordered letters, such as the one given in Figure 4.6 on page 131. Prepare a sheet on which to record the child's responses. To administer the inventory, point to each letter and ask the child to name it. Go through the uppercase letters and the lowercase letters. Record the child's responses by circling letters the child does not know and write in letters the child substitutes above the appropriate letters. Then give the child a blank sheet of paper and ask the child to write the letters as you call them out. For scoring purposes, accept both uppercase and lowercase letters. Tally the responses on the record sheet.

Assessing Concepts about Print

A child's knowledge of concepts about print can be tested by showing the child a book that contains both pictures and print and asking a series of questions to probe the child's ability to orient to the book and the print it contains. You will need a book that has the following features:

- A double-page spread with print on one page and a picture on the other
- A page with a single line of print
- A page with two or more lines of print
- A page that has both uppercase and lowercase versions of two different letters
- Several punctuation marks, including periods, a question mark, an exclamation point, and quotation marks

You will also need two index cards. It is advisable to prepare a record sheet ahead of time for keeping track of the child's responses.

Concepts to Be Tested:

- **Knowledge of the layout of books:** Hold the book out to the child so that the child is looking at the spine. Say, "We're going to read this book. Show me the front of the book." Note whether the child lays the book in front of himself or herself so that the front of the book is properly facing up.

- **Knowledge that print, not pictures, is what we read:** Show the child a double-page spread with text on one page and a picture on the other. Say, "Show me where we read. Point to the spot where we begin reading." Note whether the child points to the text or to the picture.

- **Directional orientation of print on the page:** Show the child a page with at least two (and preferably three) lines of print. Say, "We're going to read this page. Show me where we begin reading. Point to the place. Show me where we

go after that. Now show me where we go after that." Note whether the child points to the upper left-hand word, then sweeps across to the right, then goes the whole way back to the left and down one line, then across to the right. (A correct response will include this entire Z-like pattern.) Then you read the page.

- **Knowledge of the terms, *beginning, end, first,* and *last* with respect to words on a page:** Turn to a new page and say, "Show me the *beginning* of the story on this page. Show me the *end* of the story on this page. Show me the *first word* on this page. Show me the *last word.*" Note if the child points to the appropriate words. Then read that page.

- **Orientation to "top" and "bottom" of a page:** Turn to a new page. Say, "Point to the *top* of this page. Point to the *bottom* of this page." Note whether the child points to the right places. Then read the page.

- **Understanding of the terms *word* and *letter:*** Turn to a page that has one line of print. Take an index card in each hand and say, "Look. I can hold these cards so you can only see one or two words or one or two letters. Here. You try it." Hand the cards to the child and say, "Show me *one word.* Now show me *two words.* Show me *one letter.* Now show me *two letters.*" Note whether the child responds correctly. Then read the text.

- **Knowledge of uppercase and lowercase letters:** Turn to a page that has uppercase and lowercase versions of two different letters. Point to an uppercase letter and say, "Find me a little letter like this." Then point to the lowercase version of the other letter. Say, "Find me a big letter like this." Note whether the child responds correctly. Then read the text.

- **Knowledge of punctuation:** Find a page with a period on it. Say, "What is this? What are we supposed to do when we get to it?" In turn, find quotation marks, a question mark, and an exclamation point. As you point to each one, say, "What is this? What does it tell us?" Note which ones the child understands.

Refer to your **Teach It!** booklet for further activities you can use to reinforce concepts discussed in this chapter.

—After Clay (2000).

| A | F | P | W | K | Z | B | C | H | O | J | u | |
| M | D | L | Q | N | S | X | I | G | R | E | V | T |

++

| a | f | p | w | k | z | b | c | h | o | j | u | y |
| m | d | l | q | n | s | x | i | g | r | e | v | t |

_____ Uppercase Recognition
_____ Lowercase Recognition
_____ Production

FIGURE 4.6

Alphabet Inventory.

Family & Community Literacy

LETTER-TO-SOUND CORRESPONDENCE: LEARNING PHONICS. A child realizes that language is real and comes in units of words, syllables, and phonemes. The child can now produce not just letterlike forms, but also many actual letters. The child has learned to orient himself or herself to books. The child realizes that ours is an alphabetic writing system that works not by showing pictures of things, not by representing syllables, but by matching letters with phonemes. Now what?

Now comes the process of discovering the system by which writing spells words and letters and clusters of letters represent sounds or groups of sounds. This kind of knowledge is called *phonics*. It is also called *orthographic knowledge* and *letter-to-sound relationships*. The patterns that relate letters to sounds are complex. They come in layers that are peeled back, essentially in stages, by the child who is encouraged to be an active explorer of written language.

INVENTED SPELLING AND WORD KNOWLEDGE. One of the best ways to observe children's growth in their orthographic knowledge—that is, knowledge of the spelling structure of words—is through their invented spelling (see Chapter 3). As

THE WORLD OF READING

The Development of Storybook Reading: Language and Print Together

A line of development that combines both language awareness and concepts about print is children's progress in storybook reading. Researcher Elizabeth Sulzby (1985) has shown us that having children pretend-read a favorite storybook can be a very useful way to observe their concepts of what reading is about and how language is captured in print.

When we read a storybook to children at the age of four or five, they often ask to have it read again. A storybook that is read to a child three or more times, especially when it is requested, can be said to be a favorite storybook. What happens if we ask the child to read that favorite storybook back to us? With a little encouragement, most children will pretend-read the book; when they do, they are demonstrating for us their conception of what reading is. Sulzby (1985) has observed hundreds of children rereading favorite storybooks and has documented stages or advancing strategies that children use to read books. Her stages are repeated by other children so reliably that watching for them can give us a developmentally based assessment tool.

- **Picture naming.** At the earliest of the book-reading strategies, the child points at the picture, shouts the name of the depicted object, then points to the next page and does the same thing. As Sulzby notes, such a child is repeating a ritual he or she has been through many times with a parent or other adult reader, who often opens a book, points to a picture, says, "What's that?," waits for the child's answer, then says, "Right! That's a _____!"

- **Verbal storytelling with conversation.** Slightly later, some time around the age of four or five years, the child will point to the pictures and then weave an oral story around them in a conversation with the adult. This is not a stand-alone story yet, as it still relies on an adult for support. It also is cued by the pictures rather than by the print on the page or the exact words the child remembers from the adult's reading.

- **Verbal storytelling without conversation.** At a slightly later time, often around age five, a child will tell a story while paging through the book from picture to picture. The story is clearly a *told* story, and if the child pretend reads this book more than once, no attempt will be made to keep the wording the same.

- **Talking like a book.** Still later, the child will use a singsong, rather distant voice that sounds like a reader's—sometimes even complete with stumbling over words—while creating a monologue to accompany the pictures. Amazingly, the child is still not actually reading the words, which you will note when the monologue bears little resemblance to what is on the page.

- **Refusal to read.** At a still later stage, when asked to read the book aloud, the child will become troubled by the request. Why? Because the child doesn't know how to read the words. This is actually a breakthrough. Not knowing the words did not prevent pretend-reading of the book before. But now the child seems to have realized that to read a book, one has to look at the print and know how to pronounce it as spoken language.

- **Reading a word or two.** Still later, when asked to pretend-read the book, the child will look for known words and read them aloud.

This fascinating sequence of strategies shows the child moving from a series of isolated verbal responses to pictures to a woven verbal text—first with the support of conversation and then without support, followed by a phase of talking like a book and then leading to the realization that to truly read, one must know how to bring to life exactly the words that are written on the page. Once that last discovery has been made, the child is ready to match the expected words with the words on the page (and doubtless bringing into play other knowledge, such as the concept of word and knowledge of letters) and read a few words aloud. The child has gone from playful imitation of the whole of reading to a careful study of the details. Bit by bit, especially if given books written on an accessible level, the child will be able to return to the whole while reading the entire book aloud.

Writing &
Reading

Tom Gill (1992) and others (Mann, Tobin, & Wilson, 1987) have noted, when children spell words they have not been taught, that is, when their spelling is the result of invention and not of memorization, their invented spelling gives us a window into the complicated issues of how children understand the relationships between spoken words and written symbols, also known as their ***word knowledge***. Word knowledge consists of more than the sum total of correct spellings the child has memorized. It more accurately refers to their awareness of the units of language such as words, syllables, onsets and rimes, and phonemes and of the many ways in which words are represented by letters and groups of letters.

Research and experience show that it can be useful to encourage even beginning readers to venture their own ideas of how letters can represent sounds. This practice helps in several ways:

1. It leads children to focus carefully on the spoken language they want to write down and practice finding its units of sound.
2. It challenges children to think of the relationships between letters and sounds.
3. It provides useful diagnostic information to the teacher about the children's growth as writers and even as readers.

TEACH IT!

6

Looking at children's invented spellings can help to answer questions like these:

*   Does this child appear to have a concept of word? Can the child make words "hold still" in his or her mind while the child examines their parts and decides how to spell those parts?
*   Can this child segment words into phonemes?
*   Can this child match letters to phonemes? Which ones?
*   Which principles of the English writing system does this child understand? Letters-to-sounds? Onsets and rimes? Marking of long and short vowels? Grammatical endings? Word families?

How Does a Teacher Nurture Emergent Literacy?

Classrooms where literacy emerges are set up and managed by thoughtful teachers who understand how children learn to read and write and who carefully follow each child's development and provide each child the opportunities to learn what she or he needs to know at a given time. These teachers make literacy—listening, reading, and writing—a rich part of every school day. Let us look at a few active and passive ways in which you can help literacy grow in an early childhood classroom.

Arranging Classrooms for Literacy Learning

To promote literacy, reading and writing must be made part of the classroom environment. The classroom itself should demonstrate both the importance of literacy and the way literacy works while also providing many opportunities for children to observe and use written language. There are many ways in which classrooms can be arranged passively to immerse children in print.

LABELS.   Label objects around the classroom with written letters that are readable from far off. Every several days, take time to "read the room" with the children together (Fountas & Pinnell, 1996) as you or a student points to the labels with a pointer or ruler. Remind students to listen for the first sounds in the words, such as in *door* and point out that the first letter in *door* is *D*.

LITERACY PLAY.   Make props readily available to support children's dramatic play. Some of these props might include reading and writing. For example, the doctor's office has an eye chart and a pad for the doctor to write prescriptions. Shelves in a grocery store center might have labels (*fruit, soup, bread*) where the grocer would stock the items and pads handy for the customers to use for writing grocery lists.

Allowing children to act out stories encourages interpretive imagination, and the active involvement adds fun.

CLASSROOM LIBRARY.   Create a classroom library in a corner of the room. It should have a carpet and comfortable chairs (such as beanbag chairs) for creating an inviting reading environment. Include a space for displaying books so that children can see their covers, and change the books on display every few days to catch the children's eyes. Books should accommodate a range of tastes, from informational books with bright illustrations to simple patterned books. On a regular basis, read a book or part of a book aloud and then place it on display in the library corner to entice children to look it over. The classroom library should include books written by individual classroom authors and books written or dictated by the whole class—perhaps books of favorite jokes and riddles, books about animals, and books about the seasons.

CHARTS AND POSTERS.   Display on the walls around the classroom posters of children's books and pictures of authors. You can solicit these directly from children's book publishers. Children know authors such as Rosemary Wells, Dr. Seuss, Arnold Lobel, Cynthia Rylant, and Alma Flor Ada, and the children are excited when the teacher announces that the class has a new book by one of these or other authors they know and like. You can also display charts of interesting things, such as volcanoes and maps of the town or neighborhood with the children's street names labeled. You could also include autobiographical posters with each child's name and something special that each child has dictated. Children love to see their own works posted.

CLASSROOM POST OFFICE.   Include in your classroom a post office where children can mail letters. Each child could have a mailbox (constructed from three-inch cardboard tubes) for receiving mail. Have children write each other letters at least once a week; the teacher should also make a point of writing something to put in each child's box every few days.

WRITING CENTER.   Create a writing center with paper, markers, and pencils. Include magazines as sources of pictures that can be cut out and glued to attach them as illustrations for children's compositions.

Reading Aloud to Children

Reading aloud is one of the most useful, active things adults can do to nurture children's literacy growth. Many of the abilities that are considered essential to literacy can be developed as children listen to a book read aloud by a parent or teacher. Among the main benefits of being read to are the following:

- *It expands their vocabulary.* As Stanovich (1992) has pointed out, there are words that are more commonly encountered in books—even children's books—than in conversation or from watching television. Listening to books being read aloud helps children learn a literate vocabulary.

- *It develops their ability to comprehend written language.* Research on reading comprehension tells us that it involves component skills that include perceiving main ideas and supporting details, making inferences, venturing predictions and confirming them, and visualizing in the mind's eye what the words suggest. Children have the opportunity to develop all of these abilities from listening to a book being read aloud and discussing it.

- *It encourages enthusiasm for literacy as they participate in the teacher's excitement.* When children first learn to talk, parents slow down and exaggerate their speech and their gestures as if to say, "This is how language works. This is how we show excitement and interest. This is the way we soothe each other." Similarly, when adults read books aloud with expression, they have the opportunity to show children how written language conveys the full range of emotions. This not only will make literacy appealing to children, but also will show them how to derive meaning and associate emotions with the language of print.

- *It makes them aware of the structure of stories and of other kinds of texts.* Skilled readers learn to find questions and pursue answers according to the structure of whatever text they are reading. A story shows characters in settings and the problems they have and how those problems are solved. Expository writing frames questions about topics and goes about answering those questions. By reading texts aloud and commenting on them, a careful teacher can help students to become aware of the recurring structures of different texts and use them to guide their comprehension.

TEACH IT!

2

Reading aloud at least twenty minutes each day should be a regular feature of every classroom from preschool through the primary grades and on through the elementary grades. Even when children are learning to read, it is not until fourth grade that many children's reading ability approaches the speed and fluency with which teachers can read to them. Many children's reading rate will take much longer to develop. Therefore, the teacher's reading aloud is a necessary source of language, of stories, and of information for children.

You certainly do not need advanced training to read a book aloud successfully with children! Nonetheless, good preparation is rewarded by a more satisfying experience all around. We suggest following these steps when reading aloud to children:

[1] *Prepare the Book for Reading.* Read the book through yourself before you read it to children. Decide whether it is suitable for this group. Does it have enough excitement or depth to hold the interest of a whole group? If it is suitable, decide *how* you want to read it—with humor, with drama, with questions to whet curiosity? If there are voices to bring to life, decide how you want to make each one sound. If you decide

to stop reading to ask for predictions or discussion, decide where the stopping places should be. If there are any words or ideas that will be unfamiliar to the children, make a note to pronounce them carefully and explain them to the children.

If the book has illustrations large enough for the children to see, practice reading the book through while you hold it in front of and facing away from you, where the children will be able to read it.

(2) *Prepare the Children.* Make sure the children are seated comfortably where they can see and hear you. Most teachers prefer to have the children sit on a carpet or cushions in front of them. Remind the children, if you need to, of the behavior you expect of good listeners: hands to themselves, eyes on the teacher, and ears for the story.

(3) *Begin to Read.* Show the children the cover of the book. Ask them what they know about the topic. If you want to arouse more curiosity, quickly show them some other pictures in the interior of the book (but not the last pages—keep the children in suspense about those). Ask the children to make predictions about what will happen or what they expect to find out in the book.

Turn to the title page. Read the author's name and the illustrator's. Talk about what each contributed to the book. It might help to point out that if only one name is given, then the illustrator and author are the same person. Otherwise, the children should know that the author and illustrator both have important things to do to bring the book into being (Publishers usually pay authors and illustrators equally and usually encourage them to work independently of each other.) Remind the children of any other books they know by this author or this illustrator.

(4) *While Reading.* As you read the book through the first time, ask for comments about what is going on. How is the character feeling? What is the character's problem? What do they think the character can do to solve the problem? Ask the students to predict what will happen. Read a few pages, then stop again. Ask how things look for the character now. What is the character doing to solve the problem? How is it working? What do the children think will happen now? Why do they think so? Stop right before the end and ask for last predictions. You can add to the suspense if you take an obvious quick look at the last page, but don't let the children see it. Then ask the children to predict what will be on the last page.

(5) *After the First Reading.* Ask the children whether the book turned out the way they thought it would. What made them think it would turn out that way, or why were they surprised? What did they like about the book? How did it make them feel? Why?

(6) *Rereading.* Read the book a second time through. This time, you might want to take more time to look at the ways the illustrator pictured the action. If there are any chants given in the book, ask children to repeat them. If there is time, ask questions about characters, motives, and other things you and the students find interesting about the book.

(7) *After Reading.* Put the book on display in the library corner, and encourage children to read it later during scheduled time in the reading center or between other activities. The children might especially enjoy taking turns reading it to each other.

Extending Reading Experiences for Younger Children

The meanings of books can loom larger in children's imaginations by providing them opportunities to respond to the books in various ways. Although children of all ages can talk about what they read (Martinez & Roser, 1991), younger children find it most natural to respond to books with their whole bodies: by getting up and moving around, by chanting chants, by acting out parts, and by drawing key scenes (Hickman, 1992). English language learners have more opportunities to participate if meaningful responses to stories are encouraged through drama, music, and art rather than through discussion only.

USE CHANTS.   A very engaging form of response to a story is to repeat a key phrase or chant every time it occurs in a book. English language learners profit from repeating shorter chants, which become nuggets of remembered language that are useful models of grammar and good for pronunciation practice. Children listening to Mem Fox and Patricia Mullins's *Hattie and the Fox* (1992) love to repeat the animals' refrains:

"Good grief!" said the goose.

"Well, well!" said the pig.

"Who cares?" said the sheep.

"What next?" said the cow.

USE DRAMA.   Many children's books have clear patterns of actions that are easy for children to act out. Some books, such as Michael Rosen's *We're Going on a Bear Hunt* (2003) and Frances Temple's *Tiger Soup* (1992), are already scripted for children to act out. Both have chants and movements that the children will enjoy. *The Three Billy Goats Gruff* is not scripted as a play, but it has simple, repeated actions and chants that are easy for children to practice and perform. The whole story can be rehearsed and staged in a single class period. Single scenes of longer stories can be acted out, too, if time is short.

Acting involves interpretation. You can encourage children to interpret stories imaginatively as they rehearse the dramatizations: "How does the little goat feel when he sees the troll? How might he look at that point? What would his voice sound like?"

Props help children get into character. In *The Three Billy Goats Gruff*, horns made of construction paper bring the goats to life, and a robe and a club add to the troll's fierceness. Construction paper masks indicate which character is Tiger and which one is Anansi the Spider in *Tiger Soup*.

USE ART.   Drawing is a favorite way for children to respond to a story. The drawings may be extended by asking the children to leave space at the bottom of their papers and think of one line they want to dictate to the teacher. The children can rehearse reading these lines and then take them home to read to family members. Another activity, "Sketch to Stretch" (Short, Harste, & Burke, 1996), is a wonderful way to add interpretation when children draw in response to a story. After they have listened to a story, the children draw their favorite part or the most important part. Then one child is invited to be the *artist* and display his or her work for the *critics* (classmates) to interpret. After the critics have noted the features in the drawing and commented on what they think each one means, the artist then gets to interpret his or her own work, telling the critics why the story was depicted as it was.

Teaching Phonological Awareness

As we noted earlier in this chapter, children who are aware of the sound constituents of language have an advantage when it comes to reading words because they will sense the elements of words that are matched with letters. The National Reading Panel

(2000) recommends that teachers teach phonological awareness in kindergarten through grade 2. This teaching may occupy a short part of each day—six or seven minutes—to yield the 20 hours-a-year of phonological training that the NRP recommends. Activities to boost phonological awareness can take place at several levels.

At the syllable level:

- Children can clap along to the syllables in their names—"Bet-ty," "Ta-kee-sha," "Da-vid."
- Children can raise their hands when the teacher says a word with one syllable, two syllables, or three syllables.
- When the teacher says "One syllable!", a child must say a one-syllable word; when the teacher says, "Two syllables!" and calls on a child, that child says a word with two syllables; and so on.

At the onset and rime level:

TEACH IT!

6

- Children are asked to supply rhymes to complete couplets such as the following:

  Ding, dong, dell
  Kitty's in the _____ (well)
  Ding, dong, dasement
  Kitty's in the _____ (basement)
  Ding, dong, dimming pool
  Kitty's in the _____ (swimming pool)

- When the teacher says a target word, such as *boy*, the children raise their hands when they hear a word that rhymes with it when the teacher says a list of words such as "tea, tock, tack, *toy*."

- When the teacher says a word such as *bat* and then pronounces the sound /k/, the children say a new word that begins with the sound /k/ and rhymes with *bat*: *cat*.

At the phoneme level:

- The children sing a song that substitutes the vowel sounds:

  I like to eat, eat, eat, apples and bananas
  I like to eat, eat, eat, apples and bananas.

  I like to oot, oot, oot, ooples and bonoonoos
  I like to oot, oot, oot, ooples and bonoonoos

  I like to oat, oat, oat, oples and bononos
  I like to oat, oat, oat, oples and bononos.

- The children practice taking words apart into their phonemes:

  "If I say dog /d/ /o/ /g/*, you say* cat, ball, *and* foot *the same way."*

- The teacher pronounces a series of speech sounds and asks children to say the word they form:

  /f/ /e/ /t/ = feet;   /s/ /o/ /p/ = soap

- The children place letter markers into boxes as they pronounce each letter sound. Then they say the word that is formed by the sounds (Elkonin, 1965).

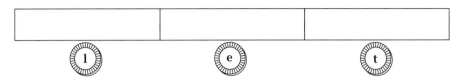

For example, given a card marked with three boxes, and the three letter chips, **l**, **e**, and **t**, the child places each letter into the box, pronouncing its sound at the same time: *ull, ehhh, tuh* and then saying the whole word *let*.

Teaching the Alphabet

Children pay closer attention to the letters of the alphabet after they have come to notice writing as a holistic display (Gibson & Levin, 1975). That means, as we saw earlier in this chapter, that children will spend considerable time doing pretend-reading of books and producing scribbles and mock writing before they come to focus consistently on individual letters. Nonetheless, teachers can encourage children's learning processes by pointing out individual letters and by making displays of letters prominent in the classroom. If teachers hold off teaching children letters of the alphabet until children show "readiness" to learn, they might inadvertently penalize children who have not been given alphabet books or taken to the library. Children will undeniably learn the alphabet more quickly and easily when they have pretend-read and scribbled their way to the point at which they are paying close attention to letters. Nonetheless, it is important to show all children the letters anyway, as this kind of learning is too important to delay.

Even as you invite children to write inventively, including mock-writing, or read to them and show them print, you also need to show them individual letters and demonstrate how the letters are formed. There are many ways of doing this:

TEACH IT!
5,35

- Alphabet letter cards can be posted around the room, with pictures of objects that feature that letter.
- Letter-sorting and letter-matching games can be arranged for children to play with at center time.
- Children can practice writing letters at their desks as the teacher writes a model. They may use large-ruled paper for this or individual slates and chalk. Later, they may practice writing letters with a grease pencil on a transparency film overlaid on sample words with large letters.
- Alphabet strips can be taped to children's desks. A strip of tagboard with the letters of the alphabet carefully printed in lowercase can be attached to each child's desk in front of the pencil tray. Such strips are available commercially, or they can be produced by the teacher or by an aide.
- The alphabet song can be taught, with the teacher pointing to the letter cards as the children sing the song slowly.
- Children's names can be written on cards and taped to their desks, with the first letter of the first name written in a bright color. Then the children can practice saying, "A is for Ana, B is for Bart," and so on.
- Plastic letters can be placed in centers to match with printed letters to form words.
- Sandpaper letters on cards can be used in centers for children to trace with their fingers.

- Letter cards can be sent home so that parents can play letter recognition games with the children.
- Alphabet books can be made. Prepare a blank book for the class and print a letter on the top of each page, *A* to *Z*. The children think of objects that begin with the sound of that letter and take turns drawing pictures of those objects on the appropriate page.

Inviting Early Writing

The practice of writing can and should begin well before children know how to spell words or even to form letters. When children produce their own versions of writing and when they invent spellings, they are led into exploring how the writing system works and putting forth their own hypotheses about what writing looks like, how it is arranged on a page, how writing represents ideas, and how the spelling system works. The child who is actively investigating these questions is alert to the ways the system actually works. With encouragement and some lessons from the teacher, that child should progress step by step and stage by stage to standard writing and spelling and fluent and meaningful reading. Teachers can encourage early writing in several ways.

WRITING WORKSHOP.   Beginning in kindergarten, many teachers conduct writing workshops three or four days per week. (Writing workshops are described in greater detail in Chapter 8.) For emergent readers and writers, teachers begin by reminding children of the topics they want to write about. Children who are reluctant to begin writing immediately might draw a picture of their topic. The teacher reminds the students to leave space at the bottom of the drawing for their writing. The children then have a period of ten to fifteen minutes for writing and drawing at their seats. Those who have drawn pictures write captions underneath their drawings. Then, one at a time, they take the page to the teacher and read it aloud to her or him. The teacher writes the words correctly above the child's words and might take this opportunity to show the children how letters represent sounds. During sharing time, children share their works with the rest of the class.

The writing workshop should have a period of time set aside for focused lessons that show students how to handle particular aspects of writing. A very useful focused lesson for young children is shared writing, an effective strategy for demonstrating how spoken words are broken into sounds and spelled with letters and for encouraging writing (Tompkins, 2000). A sample lesson in shared writing might go as follows:

Sample Lesson:

> *After discussing an exciting event with his students, a teacher gathers late kindergarteners around an easel and invites them to help write about the event. First they agree on a short sentence they want to write:*
>
> ### A fireman came to school.
>
> *They practice saying the sentence several times so that everyone is aware of the words. The teacher then tells the students that they will write the first word and asks,*
>
> > *"Who can tell us what letter we need to write?"*
>
> *A child suggests the letter* A, *and the teacher accepts it, writes it slowly on the easel, and then says,*

"We wrote A. *Now what's the next word we want to write?"*

After someone says, "Fireman," the teacher says,

"Right. It's 'fireman.' That's a new word, so I'm going to leave space between the word A *and the first letter of this new word."*

The teacher puts his or her finger after the A to identify the space and says,

"What is the first sound we hear in 'fireman'?"

When the students identify the first sound, the teacher asks,

"What letter are we going to use to write the 'fuh' sound in 'fireman'?"

The teacher pauses for responses and then says,

"Right. It's F. *Who can come up and write the letter* F *for me?"*

This process continues as the group works through the entire sentence. When they are finished, the teacher might end up with

A FIRMN CAM TO SKOL.

The teacher concludes by saying,

"This could say 'A fireman came to school.' Later on, I will show you another way to write it."

The teacher recognizes that these kindergarten children—most of whom are pre-phonemic or early phonemic spellers—will not be ready to focus on the silent letters in *fireman* and *came* or on the uncommon spelling of *sch* in *school*. Later, when the children can produce letter name spellings, the teacher will show them where silent letters and other conventional spellings would be added to these words to show the students the next challenges they will need to master. But for now, matching letters with phonemes is sufficient challenge for these children. Shared writing lessons can be conducted almost daily with a class. In the meantime, children should be encouraged to use writing every chance they get.

Language & Diversity

DICTATION.   Taking dictations from children, long considered part of the language experience approach (Stauffer, 1970), is one of the most effective techniques for teaching children about literacy. The technique is especially useful for English language learners because it provides an opportunity to attach language to meaningful concepts and then shows how that talk can be represented in print.

Using the dictation method can demonstrate very directly the whole purpose of writing and reading: to encode and decode meaningful messages and to help record experiences that can be retrieved and reviewed later. Taking dictations enhances children's language awareness by slowing down their words and capturing them in print. The teacher can show children how print is laid out on the page, that language comes in units of words, and that words come in phonemes. The teacher can also show how letters represent sounds and words. In short, using dictations teaches language awareness, phonemic segmentation, and phonics. Taking and rereading dictations teach children to recognize words, too. The Teach It! box demonstrates the steps in a typical dictation exercise.

TEACH IT!

1

Dictated experience accounts have the advantage of recording children's own experiences in their own words—which is a source of excitement and motivation for many children (Ashton-Warner, 1963). But dictated accounts have the drawback of

TEACH IT!

★ ★ ★ ★
Taking Dictation

A dictation exercise works best with a group of six to eight students so that everyone can participate. Working with a small group also allows you to group students who are at roughly the same level of literacy development. In a first-grade class, for example, you might work with one group of children who know most of their letters and are prephonemic or early phonemic spellers who have not learned to read many words. Another couple of groups might be composed of beginning readers who are rapidly acquiring sight words. The dictation method uses the following steps.

A Stimulating Event

- Prepare the children for the activity by engaging them in a stimulating event, such as a visit to a pumpkin patch.
- Encourage them to talk about the experience.
- Ask questions about their favorite parts of the event.

Refer to your **Teach It!** booklet for further activities you can use to reinforce concepts discussed in this chapter.

- Take care to draw out their names for things: the vines, the leaves, the stem, the fruit, the color orange. Be sure to discuss the event until the children can talk freely about it and have ready words for their experiences.

Writing Down the Children's Language

- Tell the children that together you are going to write an account of the event. They are going to dictate—that is, slowly say some sentences, some words about their experience—and you are going to write them down to be read later.

- Now ask the children what they want to say. Ask volunteers for sentences. If a child gives a sentence that is too long, work together to shorten it to about five words. For each sentence, ask the class to recite it several times so that they will remember them later when it is time to reread the sentences.

- Next, ask the child to identify the first word to be written down. As is done in the shared writing

being disjointed and unpredictable, as might be expected of a text dictated by a group. Young readers like to read predictable and patterned text, and they find such text easier to read. A compromise approach is to have children learn a patterned text orally and then dictate that text to the teacher and proceed with the steps outlined above.

Two sources of patterned texts for dictation are songs and poems. Children can learn song verses, dictate them for the teacher to record, and then sing them as the teacher points to the words. Children can make up their own verses to songs, too; songs like "Down by the Bay" and "Corner Grocery Store," with their highly patterned exercise, have students repeat the word slowly and invite the other children to identify the first sound they hear in that word. Then ask them to name the letter that makes the sound and write down the letter. Note that this part of the exercise can be extended for children who are just discovering the alphabetic principle and letter-to-sound relationships. More advanced children require less time to sound out the spellings of words. The goal of the exercise is to capture the whole text and read it back several times, all in this one sitting. If you want to emphasize breaking words into sounds and matching those sounds to letters, you will need to work with a shorter text.

- Ask the children for four to five sentences (though very early readers might give only one sentence), and write each one up in the way just described. Once the sentences have all been recorded, go back and ask the children to come up with a good title for the account. Write the title above the lines on the chart paper.

Rereading the Dictation

Rereading the text is usually done in four steps, each being repeated twice.

1. *Read the text at a slow, normal reading rate, pointing to each word with a stylus as it is read.*

2. *Invite the children to **choral-read** the text; that is, teacher and students read the text in unison as the teacher points to the words.*

3. *Have the children **echo-read** the text while pointing to the words. That is, read the line aloud and then silently point to the words as the children read the line aloud.*

4. *Ask an individual child to read a line or more of the text.*

You may work more with the text at this point. Pointing to a word in a line and having a child read it is a good way to exercise a child's concept of words. (Early readers will silently mumble through the lines, word unit by word unit, until they reach the indicated word to be read aloud.) You also might ask a child to come forward and point to a word that he or she already recognizes.

Finally, ask for volunteers to illustrate the class text and pass out markers for them to use. The illustration will help to remind children of the topic of the text when they revisit the text on subsequent days.

verses, are easy and inviting to innovate on. Another source of patterned text are retold stories. After the children have heard a story read aloud to them a couple of times, they can retell a short and memorable version for the teacher to record and read back with them.

Following a group dictation, teachers can prepare smaller versions of texts to give each student for individual reading. These texts, typed by the teacher or a parent volunteer on a word processor and photocopied, can be used in many ways. Pairs of students might "buddy-read" two copies of the text with each other. Children might take

Dear parent,

   Today our class learned a new poem. Your child has brought home a copy of it to read to you. We hope you will enjoy hearing it. We are still learning to read in our class, so if your child has trouble reading the poem, here is what you can do to help:

- Hold the copy of the poem so that both of you can see it.
- Read the poem in a slow but natural voice and point to the words as you read them.
- Now ask your child to read the poem with you.
- Then ask your child to read the poem by himself or herself.
- Give your child lots of opportunities to read the poem aloud.
- Praise your child for a job well done!

Sincerely,

FIGURE 4.7

A Letter to Parents.

the texts home with them, with instructions to the parents such as those found in Figure 4.7. Children's collections of readings can be put on loose-leaf paper and clipped in a binder. Children enjoy rereading songs, poems, and stories together well after they were originally dictated, and this repeated reading makes the words more familiar to the children.

Using Books

USING BIG BOOKS. Big books were the brainchild of New Zealand educator Don Holdaway (Holdaway, 1979). Holdaway wanted to be able to teach children to read from well-composed, patterned texts, yet have texts that were big enough to allow the teacher to guide the children's attention to features of the text as they read them. At first, Holdaway produced his own versions of big books, and many teachers still make their own; but now trade book publishers and textbook publishers alike are producing big book versions of many simply written picture books, especially those with highly patterned texts that are especially good for emergent and beginning readers.

   Big books can be used to show children the layout of books and also to practice reading and rereading text. In a typical lesson with emergent readers, the teacher reads the book twice.

On the First Reading

- Put the big book on an easel, and call the children's attention to the cover. Point to the title, and have the students read it aloud with you. Ask the students to say what they think the book will be about, given the title, and invite their ideas and predictions.

- Point to the cover illustration, and invite the students to say what they see. When they think of the title and consider the picture, what do they think will happen in the story?

- Open to the title page, and point to the author's name. Make sure the children understand that this is the person who wrote the book. Do the same with the name of the illustrator. Do the children know any other books by either one of them?

- Now turn to the first page of text, and read it aloud, pointing to the words as you go. Read several more pages this way, pausing to discuss a picture or to comment on an action.

- Ask the children to make predictions, even predictions about what will happen on the other side of a page. Sometimes rhyming books have a phrase on one page that ends in a word that is matched with a phrase on the next page ending in a rhyming word. You might pause at the page turn and ask the children what will come next. For example, on one page of John Langstaff's *A Hunting We Will Go* are the words:

Using big books is a valuable way to introduce students to reading and to help them become familiar with all the elements in books.

A hunting we will go
A hunting we will go
We'll catch a fox

Before turning the page, pause and ask the children to predict what comes next. The text continues:

And put him in a box
And then we'll let him go.

On the Second Reading

Follow the process described for dictations:

- Go back to the beginning of the book, and invite the children to read it again with you. Using a stylus or something similar, choral-read a page with the children.

- Still pointing to the words, echo-read the next page with the children.

- Silently point to the words in a repeated phrase, and invite the children to read them.

- Finally, invite individual children to come up and read a line of text as you point to the words.

Following the reading with the group, leave the big book available for children to read individually and to each other.

USING LITTLE BOOKS   Little books are short, patterned, and predictable texts supported by pictures and written at carefully graduated levels of difficulty. The lowest difficulty levels include one or two words on a page, with an illustration that strongly suggests what the words might be. Several titles are available on each level so that child readers can practice reading in material that is accessible. The difference in challenge between levels is so slight that children can find progressively more difficult material within their reading competence.

Reading Levels of Little Books.   Publishers of little books provide their own system of levels. The Wright Group/McGraw-Hill, publisher of the Story Box and the Sunshine Series, has twenty levels of books, ranging from "Early Emergent" through "Upper Emergent" and "Early Fluency" to "Fluency." These levels would cover most children from kindergarten through late second or early third grade, and they are designated by letters.

The Reading Recovery Program (Clay, 1993) makes regular use of little books and has identified twenty difficulty levels from late kindergarten to late second grade. Reading Recovery levels are given in numbers and not letters, and they roughly correspond to the Wright Group/McGraw Hill levels. Reading Recovery levels are widely accepted by teachers in organizing their books by difficulty level.

To complicate matters further, Informal Reading Inventories and basal reading textbooks report reading levels as grade equivalents: "PP" (pre-primer), "P" (primer), 1 (second half of first grade), 2-1 (first half of second grade), and so on. Table 4.1 provides a rough correlation of these leveling systems.

Matching Children with Little Books.   The first point in using little books with children is to match the child with the proper level of book. To make sure the book matches the child's reading level, preview a book with a child and then ask the child to read it through. If the child misses at least one but no more than two words in twenty, the book is at the right level for the child to read with supervision. That is, the book challenges the child at an appropriate **instructional reading level**, the level at which the child experiences moderate challenges and learns to read new words and practice new strategies without being overwhelmed by difficulty.

TABLE 4.1

Systems of Leveling Books for Young Readers.

BASAL READING LEVELS	SUNSHINE BOOK STAGES	SUNSHINE BOOK LEVELS	READING RECOVERY LEVELS
PP–P	Early emergent	Levels A B C D	1–10
1–2-1	Upper emergent	Levels E F G H I J	11–12
2-2–3-1	Early fluency	Levels K L M N	13–20
3-2–4	Fluency	Levels O P Q R S T	

Teaching with Little Books.   Using little books helps children to learn concepts about print, strategies for reading, and sight words. Because little books are real books—complete with text, pictures, pages that turn, author, and illustrator—and because they are written simply at the lower levels, with graduated degrees of complexity, they make it easy to call children's attention to the features of text and to practice a few reading strategies at a time. Typically, a teacher has a child read a little book three or more times:

- The first time, the child reads to preview the book to reduce the difficulty of reading it. With the teacher, the child pays attention to the title and the cover illustration, sampling pictures inside and reading a few words and repeated phrases.

- On the second reading, the child grapples with the text, attempting to read the words and derive meaning from the words and the pictures. The teacher provides scaffolding to support the child's reading and teaches and reinforces the child's use of strategies for reading (see below).

- On the third (and possibly fourth and fifth) reading, the child, alone or with minimal support from the teacher, reads the book for pleasure, for practice, and to gain fluency.

Little books are designed to make children successful readers at some level from their very first encounter. To support a child's success, the teacher can use several strategies to scaffold the child's reading activity—that is, to provide just enough support to make it possible for the child to make sense of the book but not so much as to stifle individual motivation for learning. One scaffolding technique that has already been mentioned is to preview the book: to page through and look at the pictures, reading aloud any repeated phrases so that the child will come to expect them. Another kind of scaffolding is to take turns reading parts of the text. For example, the teacher reads a line and the child reads a line; the teacher reads a passage and the child reads a passage; the teacher reads a page and the child reads a page. As the child gains confidence and ability to read on his or her own, the teacher reduces the scaffolding, that is, takes a lesser role in reading the text.

At the same time, children should be taught to use helpful reading strategies, such as the following, and should be praised when they use those strategies correctly:

Struggling Reader

- Reading an unknown word by sounding the first letter and thinking of a word that begins with the letter and that would make sense in the passage

- Skipping an unknown word, reading to the end of the passage to get the meaning of the sentence, and then going back and reading the unknown word.

- Using the grammatical context of the sentence to narrow down the choices of an unknown word.

CLASSROOM-PRODUCED BOOKS   Classroom-produced books provide a useful and enjoyable way to showcase children's authorship and to share their works with each other. Single-author books typically are written or dictated by a child (if written, they have corrected text pasted or written in by the teacher or parent volunteer) and, of course, are illustrated by the child-author. Composite books are collections that all of the children in a class contribute to. The range of such books is very broad; but for emergent readers, the following are recommended. These can be

TEACH IT!

4

written by the children themselves (with corrections written in darker ink) or simply dictated. Remember that because the books are intended to be read repeatedly by children, the text should be spelled correctly.

Alphabet books: Every child is assigned a letter and writes a word that begins with that letter and draws a picture of it.

Counting books: A group of children are assigned numbers 1 through 10. They draw pictures of 1, 2, 3 (and so on) of something and then write the name of the things (e.g., birds, pennies, cars) next to or under each drawing.

Riddle books: Children contribute individual riddles. The riddle is written on one side of the page and the answer on the other.

Joke books: The jokes of five- and six-year-old children are funny, if only for their lack of obvious humor. Individual children can contribute jokes to a whole class book.

Concept books: Concept books focus on one or a few specific topics, such as kinds of animals, sports, famous people, things to be thankful for, or images we associate with each season. Ideas for topics are limitless.

Involving Families in Emergent Literacy

Family & Community Literacy

The day a child leaves home to enter kindergarten is a poignant one for families. Many parents feel the shock of having well-meaning strangers take over the intellectual and social parts of their child's upbringing; for parents who feel "different" from the school because of language, culture, or income, the feeling of estrangement can be particularly pronounced. Kindergarten and first grade are especially important times for teachers to reach out and invite parents to take part in their children's education.

Keeping parents involved in their children's education is important for the children, too. Parental involvement in school is positively associated with everything from children's academic achievement to good behavior (they will be less likely to be disruptive) and even eventual resistance to using drugs (National Center for Educational Statistics, 1999, 2002). The amount of time parents devote at home to reading to their children, telling them stories, and teaching them songs is clearly related to the gains children make in literacy. Likewise, a child's level of reading ability in English is related to the mother's reading ability in English.

Not surprisingly, parents' involvement in their children's education and their practice of literacy at home increases with the income and the educational level of the parents. In 1996, at least 80 percent of three- to five-year-old children were read or told stories in the past week by a parent or family member. Children whose parents had a bachelor's degree or more education were more likely to read to their children than were parents whose highest educational level was a high school diploma or less. Also, white children were more likely to have been read to in the past week (about 90 percent) than were African-American children (about 75 percent) and Hispanic children (about 65 percent) (National Center for Educational Statistics, 1999).

For emergent readers, families can be involved in their children's literacy instruction in two ways: in the school and at home.

In the Classroom

First, it is desirable for parents to come into the classroom and take part in activities. They can help move instruction forward by reading to children, taking dictation, and helping publish and bind books. They can also tell stories, especially family stories; and they can demonstrate family traditions and crafts. In this latter way, they can make their families' lives part of the curriculum.

Some parents might be more willing than others to come into the class and participate. Parents of children who have been through Head Start might well have been involved in classroom activities already and might have been trained to conduct activities such as reading aloud. For other parents, special invitations and special orientations will probably be required. The National Center for Family Literacy has developed a program to recruit and orient parents to help out in classrooms. A description of the program, called PACT (Parents and Children Together), can be found on the center's web site at www.Famlit.org.

Technology

At Home

Family literacy initiatives can also be reinforced at home by sending home to parents materials and ideas for helping develop their children's literacy. Two good examples of home-directed family literacy initiatives are *home books* and *book baggies*.

HOME BOOKS.   Simple books with very short and predictable texts can be written and sent home for children to read aloud to their parents. Eight-page home books can be made from one sheet of paper, printed on both sides, and assembled with the two double pages stapled one inside the other. Pictures are added to remind the children of what the text says. A sample text for a home book is shown in Figure 4.8 on page 150.

The teacher reads the book through twice with the children before they take it home so that they will be able to read it on their own. Instructions go home with the book for parents to read the book with their children and to read many times, if possible. Home books can go home once a week. They provide useful practice in reading and help children to acquire concepts about print and even sight words.

BOOK BAGGIES.   A book baggie consists of a simple paperback book in a bag with an accompanying activity sheet (such as instructions to draw a favorite character, a word hunt, or an alphabet matching game) and perhaps a recording of the book on tape. Parents are encouraged to read the book with the child and take time to do the accompanying activity. Children should be told how to take care of the book bags when they go home. A book bag may spend several days at a time with each child and then be repacked with a new activity sheet and passed along to a different child.

Help with Family Literacy

A parent who was a regular volunteer in a Head Start classroom worried aloud because her child was going into kindergarten the next fall.

"But you can still volunteer in the kindergarten," the teacher pointed out. "They will be happy to have you."

"Me? Suppose they hand me one of those school books to read?" the troubled mother said.

Like this mother, there are parents who do not volunteer to help in school and do not read to their children because they cannot read well themselves. For those parents, the

Where is my dog?	In the yard?
No.	In the closet?
No.	In the kitchen?
No!	He is under my bed!

FIGURE 4.8

A Sample Home Book.

agencies that used to provide adult literacy services are now offering family literacy programs, in which parents who are English learners are taught basic English and parents who need help with reading are taught to read to their children. These programs can be quite successful, since the imperative of helping the children can serve as a motivation for parents to improve their own literacy skills, and the stories they practice to read to their children can be appropriate fare for developing their own reading fluency. For information on programs that offer literacy services to parents, contact the following organizations:

Technology

- Literacy Volunteers of America at www.literacyvolunteers.org
- The Barbara Bush Literacy Foundation at www.barbarabushfoundation.com
- The National Center for Family Literacy at www.famlit.org
- The Even Start program at www.evenstart.org

Putting It All Together: Emergent Literacy in the Classroom

Children's literacy begins to emerge at home, well before they enter school. Once they enter kindergarten and first grade, their literacy develops through a combination of children-driven discoveries and experiences orchestrated by a teacher. A successful teacher of reading and writing in the early years must be part psychologist—a kid-watcher, a careful observer of what children have discovered and are discovering for

STANDARDS & LITERACY

★ ★ Invented Spelling ★ ★

The International Reading Association (IRA) and the National Council for Teachers of English (NCTE) have developed a set of standards for certifying reading specialists. The standards are quite specific with regard to what reading professionals should know about invented spelling.

According to Standard 3.3, teachers should:

understand that spelling is developmental and is based on students' knowledge of the phonological system and of the letter names, their judgments of phonetic similarities and differences, and their ability to abstract phonetic information from letter names. (NCATE, 2000)

This is a tall order, but you should be able to master it from studying this chapter and the previous one. The idea that "spelling is developmental" has just been covered—and you know what language development means: children's discoveries, finding patterns in the language they hear used around them, positing invented rules for language use that unfold in stages: these things occur as children learn to talk as well as write. The "phonological system" is the system of meaningful speech sounds of words: syllable, onsets and rimes, and phonemes. It also includes the ways consonants and vowels are produced, including *digraph consonants* and *tense* and *lax vowels.*

"Judgments of phonetic similarities and differences" is what children are making when they spell a lax vowel like the one in "pet" with the acoustically most similar vowel letter name A (as in PAT for "pwet"), or the consonant phoneme that is conventionally represented by the digraph *sh* with the single letter H (as in HEK for "chick."

themselves—and part bridge builder, carefully constructing experiences that will lead children from where they are to where they are going as readers and writers.

Although all children develop concepts about print before they enter school, the amount of experience they have with literacy varies widely. A teacher of kindergarten and first grade must both provide lavish opportunities for children to learn about print and target help for children to learn what they need to know. The teacher can also reach out to the home, both to invite families to contribute material from their lives—family stories and traditions, for example—and to enlist the help of parents in helping children practice their literacy. This teacher would do well to follow the four-part model for teaching literacy introduced in Chapter 1.

- Demonstrate acts of reading and writing, and immerse children in print.
  Example: While taking a class dictation, show children how words are written down.

- Pay attention to detail.
  Example: Point out how a certain word is spelled in a class dictation.

- Provide guided practice.
  Example: Arrange classification games that call children's attention to the first sounds in words.

- Provide for application and extension.
  Example: Encourage children to use invented spelling to write captions for their pictures in a writing workshop.

FOR REVIEW

Emergent literacy refers to the period from early childhood through the first year of school in which children learn about language and print and about reading and writing. In recent years, scholars have come to recognize the role of the child's own discoveries in learning to read and write, and research in literacy has identified aspects of literacy that teachers can help children to develop.

Children must learn about the features of print and how print works. Marie Clay has provided a set of concepts about print that children must honor in their reading. She has also described a set of graphic principles that children try to master in their writing even before they can form recognizable letters. The English writing system is alphabetic—letters of the alphabet represent words by their smallest sounds, called phonemes. This concept, too, must be discovered or otherwise understood by children. Once children recognize the alphabetic principle, they are ready to figure out how letters represent sounds, or phonics. On the writing side, they may discover the mirror image of phonics as they invent ways to use writing to represent words. Understanding children's invented spelling yields valuable insights into their word knowledge—the knowledge they use to read and to spell words.

Teaching for emergent literacy should support and encourage children's processes of discovery, call children's attention to details, and give them guided and independent practice in reading and writing. Parents are children's first teachers, and careful teachers include parents in the school's efforts to help children's literacy emerge.

For Your Journal

1. Take a moment to review your answers to the questions on the Anticipation Guide that opened this chapter. Has your thinking changed? If so, write about the changes in your journal.
2. Recall the discussion in Chapter 3 of children's language learning, and consider those points along with the discussion about emergent literacy. What are two ways in which learning to read and write is like learning to talk? What are some ways in which the processes are different?
3. Teachers and literacy experts differ in the degree to which they expect children to learn about literacy from being immersed in print—that is, being read to and having chances to read and write on their own level—and from being taught the skills of reading. Where along this continuum would you place yourself?

★ Taking It to the World

1. What are your first memories of reading and writing? Can you remember not being able to read and write? Were you curious about these activities? What things did you do to teach yourself about them?
2. Visit a preschool—a Head Start program, if possible. Ask the teachers what they do to support children's early literacy. How and when are reading and writing used during the day? How have their approaches to supporting children's early literacy changed over the last ten years?

3. To learn about efforts to involve parents in supporting children's literacy, interview an elementary school teacher or administrator. How are parents' ideas and volunteer efforts brought into the classroom? What things are sent home to help parents help their children? What special efforts are being made toward increasing family literacy?

4. Continuing with the interview in item 3, how are English learners being supported as they learn to read and write? How is the school working with their parents?

5. Ask a teacher of kindergarten or first grade to show you samples of children's mock-writing and invented spelling. Using the discussion in this chapter of graphic principles and invented spelling, do a careful analysis of two writing samples from children who appear to be at different points of development.

6. Speak with a kindergarten or first-grade teacher about how he or she assesses students' concepts about print and what types of screenings are used to assess students' reading skills.

7. Visit the Jumpstart Website (www.jstart.org/about/) to determine whether there is a Jumpstart program near your community. What are some possible ways in which you might be able to volunteer some time?

★ Being a Professional Reading Teacher

Reflecting on the Chapter

Print represents spoken language, and learning how to read requires that children understand print and be conscious of the features of language that print represents. What is the print environment of children that brings them to reading?

Early Signs of Literacy

- A common occurrence during parent conferences is a parent question about how to ensure that a younger sibling does not have the same problems with reading that the child under discussion is experiencing. What advice would you give such a parent about getting that next child ready for reading at home?
- Everyone knows about the importance of reading aloud to young children, especially at home. Describe some strategies that parents can use to enrich this activity and keep it fresh so that children do not tire of it.

Integrating Emergent Literacy across the Curriculum

- Many schools and school districts restrict the primary grade curriculum to reading and mathematics to raise test scores. What arguments would you use to support the importance of art, music, physical education, dramatic activities, and other areas of the curriculum in improving early reading (and also test scores)?

Sources of Text for Emergent Literacy

- Big books are quite expensive. What are some of the advantages of using big books over regular-sized books that make the extra expense worthwhile?

Your Portfolio

What happens in children's lives before they go to school is a very important determiner of their success in reading years later. Consider writing an advice column for a parent newsletter in which you make recommendations about what they can do at home to support reading for their younger children. It can be a publication suitable for inclusion in your portfolio.

Teaching Resources

Begin to accumulate chants, finger plays, stories that lend themselves to dramatization, puppets, and other resources that you can use to support emergent literacy. Even if you do not teach in a primary grade, they will be useful with your own children or those of friends and relatives. You might expand on some these in a regular feature for the parent newsletter described above. Your principal will definitely mention this positively in your annual review.

Technology Connections

1. Visit the literacy homepage of the North Central Regional Educational Laboratory at www.ncrel.org/litweb and do a search for "emergent literacy." Examine the numerous articles and connections to useful information and materials. A search of Professor "Elizabeth Sulzby" walks you through an evaluation of children's emergent writing.
2. The National Right to Read Foundation (www.nrrf.org) provides thorough information and support on phonics instruction. The site also raises a number of concerns about issues such as emergent literacy and invented spelling. Visit the "Topical Essays" page to read the critiques of these and other topics.
3. The University of Idaho's Center for Disabilities and Human Development provides training materials for promoting emergent literacy in Head Start centers. Their Web page can be found at www.idahocdhd.org/cdhd/emerlit.
4. Investigate the "Read to Me" program run by the Idaho State Library. (www.lili.org/read/readtome/index.htm) What programs do they offer to promote family literacy?
5. The Center for Research in Early Reading Achievement is a federally funded consortium of five universities. Its web site (www.ciera.org) might be the single best site on emergent literacy, with research reports, book reviews, news of conferences, and links to other sites.

Connect with Research

Research
Navigator.com

Review the following key words from the chapter and then connect to Research Navigator (www.researchnavigator.com) through this book's companion web site to conduct a search into research on each of the various topics as they relate to reading and literacy education today.

choral-read	emergent literacy	Reading Recovery
concept of word	graphic principles	syllables
dialogic reading	instructional reading level	word knowledge
echo-read		

Further Readings

Clay, M. *What Did I Write?* Portsmouth, NH: Heinemann, 1975.

A must-read, richly illustrated exploration of the scribbles of four- to six-year-old children by an internationally famous literacy educator.

Committee on the Prevention of Reading Difficulties in Young Children, Catherine E. Snow, M. Susan Burns, and Peg Griffin (Editors). *Preventing Reading Difficulties in Young Children.* Washington, DC: National Academy Press, 1998.

A congressionally commissioned review of the literature on the early beginnings of reading failure, with recommendations for teachers.

Goelman, H. (Editor). *Awakening to Literacy.* Portsmouth, NH: Heinemann, 1984.

This early collection of papers on emergent literacy blazed the trail for much that was to follow.

Morrow, L. M. (Editor). *Family Literacy: Connections in Schools and Communities.* Newark, DE: International Reading Association, 1995.

This very useful volume combines thought-provoking pieces that help us to conceptualize family literacy and understand some of its human dynamics. It includes practical accounts of several different models of family literacy programs.

Neumann, S., Copple, C. and Bredekamp, S. *Learning to Read and Write: Developmentally Appropriate Practice.* Washington, DC: National Association for the Education of Young Children, 2000.

A discussion of a key focus of the National Association for the Education of Young Children by a leading researcher on early literacy.

Scheckedanz, J. *Much More than ABC's: The Early Reading and Writing of Young Children.* Washington, DC: National Association for the Education of Young Children, 1999.

A thorough discussion of preschool children's development as readers and writers with helpful teaching suggestions.

Strickland, D. S., and Morrow, L. M. (Editors). *Emerging Literacy: Young Children Learn to Read and Write.* Newark, DE: International Reading Association, 1989.

A highly useful collection of practical articles on nurturing the literacy of children from early childhood to age eight.

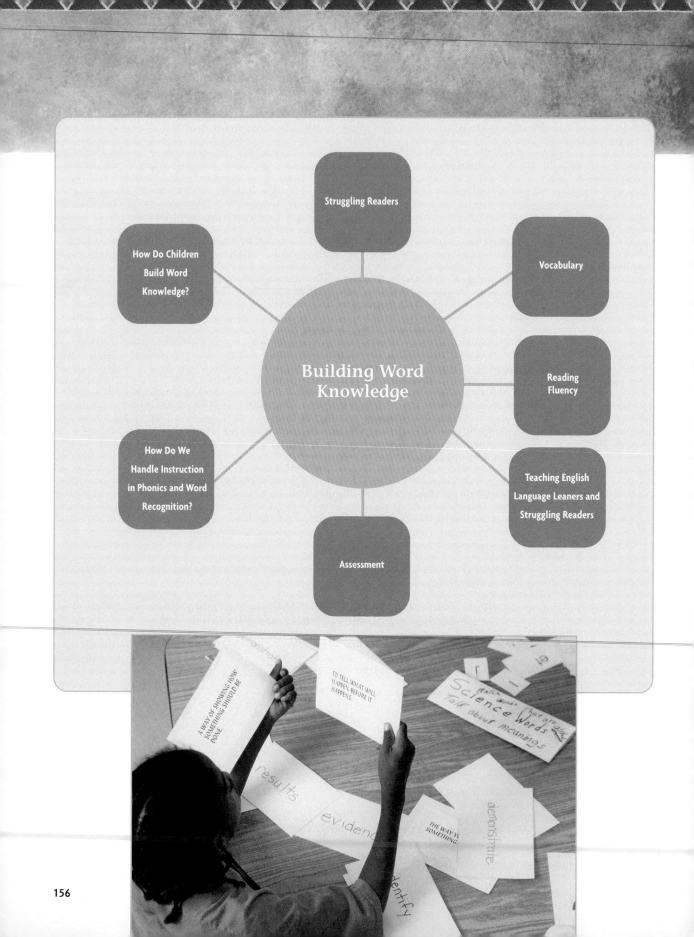

Struggling Readers

How Do Children Build Word Knowledge?

Vocabulary

Building Word Knowledge

Reading Fluency

How Do We Handle Instruction in Phonics and Word Recognition?

Teaching English Language Leaners and Struggling Readers

Assessment

Building Word Knowledge

The following statements will get you thinking about the topics of this chapter. Answer true or false in response to each statement. As you read and learn more about the topics in these statements, double-check your answers. See what interests you and what prompts your curiosity toward more understanding.

Anticipation Guide

_____ **1.** *Sight words* are words that are not decoded, but are recognized instantly.

_____ **2.** *Phonics* is an umbrella term for a variety of explicit, implicit, and systematic ways to show children how the print-to-speech/speech-to-print system works.

_____ **3.** Decoding requires the skill of transforming written words into spoken words. Spelling requires exactly the same thing.

_____ **4.** Knowledge of phonics is essentially all that children need to be able to read well.

_____ **5.** It is incorrect to assume that all vocabulary is learned from reading. Vocabulary can and should be taught.

_____ **6.** Vocabulary is an all-or-nothing proposition: A child either knows a word or doesn't.

_____ **7.** Instruction in phonemic awareness has been shown to help kindergartners and first graders recognize words.

_____ **8.** The high-frequency words students read in higher grades are more meaningful than are the words in lower grades.

_____ **9.** Research has not been able to tell us very much about the value of computer technology in teaching reading because the software changes more quickly than researchers can study its effects.

Building Word Knowledge
in a First-Grade Classroom

irst-grade teacher Ms. Gupta sits at her desk planning a lesson on word recognition for her diverse group of students, who range from emergent to beginning readers. The children are catching on to using beginning consonant blends to decode words, but a few are not yet reading well enough to manipulate parts of words or make words with letter cards. For this lesson, Ms. Gupta will move these less experienced readers and three new Spanish-speaking learners into the writing center, where they can practice writing. The children will choose to either write personal letters or make signs about books for the class library.

For the other students, Ms. Gupta will use words from the book *The Eensy Weensy Spider* (Hoberman, 2000) to focus on a limited number of initial blends. Ms. Gupta added this lesson because she noticed that many beginning readers and those who are in transition to the next level often struggle with consonant blends. So she gathers sets of previously made word cards, including some "/g/ /l/ gl as in *glue*" cards from a previous lesson on blends so that the children can compare and contrast the target *sp* blend in today's lesson with the *gl* blends. Ms. Gupta also sets aside some of the more challenging words for the more advanced readers. With overhead transparencies, she makes matching target *sp* word cards to show on the projector. She sets up two large charts and puts the book *The Eensy Weensy Spider* on her desk.

The next morning, Ms. Gupta calls specific children to the writing center and helps them get started. She then asks the others to turn around in their chairs so that they can see the overhead screen clearly and says, "Children, do you remember reading the *The Eensy Weensy Spider?*"

The children nod yes and then read along as Ms. Gupta points to each of the words in the poem on the "spider chart." From time to time, she demonstrates and discusses how fluent reading sounds and has the children reread some lines as fluently as possible. Following this reading, the children and Ms. Gupta sing the poem and participate in the finger-play for the *Eensy Weensy Spider.*

Ms. Gupta then points the children's attention to the words *water* and *spout.* "If you think you know what a spout is, whisper it in your neighbor's ear," she says. The children do so with plenty of interaction. With a vocabulary teaching point in mind, Ms. Gupta goes to the chalkboard and sketches a waterspout pipe that carries rain away from a house and another picture of water coming up out of a pool and ending in a fountain. "Here are two kinds of water spouts," she says. "Which do you think is in our poem?" The children whisper their ideas to one another and then state their guesses aloud. The class settles on the water pipe because that makes more sense in the poem.

"Right," exclaims Ms. Gupta. "Did you picture in your head what it would look like for a spider to climb up a pipe? Good readers make pictures in their minds when they read; they really think about what they are reading. As you can see, sometimes the same word can have different meanings. Thinking about what you're reading can help you identify the correct meaning."

"Here is something else I've noticed about some of the words in the spider poem," Ms. Gupta continues. "With what two letters does the word *spider* begin?" Ms. Gupta writes the word *spider* in large letters on the board and points to the *sp* blend as children respond by giving the letters. "And how about *spout?*" She writes, points, and the children respond again. Ms. Gupta draws a line under the <u>sp</u> in each word and says, "This <u>sp</u> is a blend. Blends are letters that work together to make a beginning or ending sound in a word. When you say the blend, <u>sp</u>, it sounds like /*sp*/. Try it with a partner—remember to whisper."

The children practice saying the <u>sp</u> blend, and Ms. Gupta reviews. "Blends are interesting spelling chunks. Even though they work together, you can still hear each letter sound if you listen carefully. For today's word sort, we will work mostly on beginning blends, although some of you may have some ending blends, so watch carefully."

Ms. Gupta continues to talk as she puts the word *spider* on the overhead and underlines the <u>sp</u>. With several blank transparency cards nearby, Ms. Gupta asks the children to think of some words that begin with the *sp* sound. The children's responses, guided as needed by her prompts and questions, are written on the transparency cards and placed under the word *spider*.

Drawing the discussion to a close, Ms. Gupta reviews: "Excellent thinking. You've come up with *spell, spend,* and *spot,* and we found out that *see* and *snow* won't work. And why is that?" Children respond by talking about letter/sound differences, and Ms. Gupta confirms. She adds, "I also made the words *spill* and *space* [she shows each of these word cards on the overhead], and you have these words in your new word sort bags."

Ms. Gupta has some of the children help her make cards for each of the words the children provided and adds them to the word sort bags. She then has the children get started on word sorts by having them work in pairs to compare and contrast words and watch for the target blend.

As the children begin working on their word sorts, Ms. Gupta checks on the children at the writing center and then moves quietly around the room, speaking and questioning the children as she guides them toward success. During this sort, Ms. Gupta checks to see that the children are working at their developmental levels, which helps to ensure success. To complete this lesson, she will have the children self-assess their consonant blend word sorts using classroom checklists or rubrics. When the children are finished, Ms. Gupta will assign as homework fifteen minutes of reading for pleasure (or being read to) and a minimum of five to eight minutes of adult/child word sorts (or longer if the child is having a good time).

At various points throughout the lesson, Ms. Gupta jots down some assessment notes about the children's responses to the lesson. Later, she will elaborate on these notes and put them into children's individual files. Five assessment notes on the focal children for that day help to keep the children's files up to date.

I n the primary grades, students learn to recognize and pronounce printed words, developing the skills that serve as the foundation for independent reading. They learn to use these skills to figure out new words and build up their word knowledge, all the while working toward becoming fluent readers. **Fluency** is the ability to read strings of words rapidly and effortlessly and with meaningful intonation. The more words children recognize quickly, the more fluent they become. This chapter explores children's development of reading ability at the word level as they move toward fluency.

How Do Children Build Word Kno

Word recognition refers to a reader's ability to identif
orally or silently. When a reader recognizes a word autor
recognize a familiar face, that word is said to be a **sight**
vocabulary. But if the reader must use his or her know
to decipher a word's identity, the person is using phonics anu u...
an umbrella term for a variety of explicit, implicit, and systematic ways to show chi...
dren how the print-to-speech/speech-to-print system works (Beck, 1998, p. 28).
Phonics instruction focuses directly on letter/sound relationships and involves the use
of word analysis strategies. **Decoding** is the act of transforming written words into
spoken words, using phonics. It is the opposite of spelling, which is the act of rendering spoken words into written words.

Phonics instruction comes in two varieties. **Analytic phonics** shows readers
how to take whole words and break them down into their constituent sounds. For
example, a teacher might ask a child to take the first sound from *small* and pronounce the word that is left (*mall*) or pronounce *cat* slowly so as to stress all three of
its sounds: /k/ /æ/ /t/. **Synthetic phonics**, on the other hand, teaches readers how
to combine speech sounds to make up words. It involves working with letter/sound
relationships to blend, segment, and manipulate the letters to make words. For example, a reader who knows the sounds made by the letters *T*, *U*, and *B* combines them
to pronounce the word *tub*. Through the process of synthetic phonics, children learn
to pronounce unknown words and understand what the words mean. (See the World
of Reading box.)

Word Recognition

TEACH IT!

7

The teaching of word recognition has long been the most hotly debated aspect of reading instruction. On the topic of word recognition, either/or propositions abound.
Teachers ask:

- Should we emphasize word recognition or comprehension?
- Should the teaching of word recognition emphasize words as meaningful wholes
  or focus on the rules that relate letters to sounds?
- Should instruction on word recognition be done in isolation, or should it be integrated with reading meaningful text?
- Should phonics instruction be taught systematically—that is, following a prede-
  termined sequence of skills—or should it be taught situationally, as needs for
  instruction appear among the children?

As we saw in Chapter 1, these are not new questions. Nearly a century ago, when
Edmund Burke Huey (1908) summarized what was known in his day from research
about reading instruction, these questions already divided the professional community. In our day, we can offer confident answers to most of these questions.

WORD RECOGNITION EMPHASIS.   It is apparently true that some teachers
emphasize word recognition so much that they give short shrift to children's reading
comprehension (Durkin, 1983; Pressley, 2000). But it does not follow that we can teach

THE WORLD OF READING

Synthetic Phonics and Spelling

Synthetic phonics was described by Jeanne Chall in her book *Learning to Read: The Great Debate* (1967), which, along with Rudolf Flesh's book *Why Johnny Can't Read* (1995), is often cited as part of the great debate over reading and spelling instruction. This debate has raged for years and continues today.

For years, the "look-say" method of learning words dominated the teaching of reading in the United States. The best-known look-say reading series was the Dick and Jane series. These texts helped millions of children learn to read by repeating words in stories until children learned them as sight or known words. However, although these children demonstrated good comprehension and vocabulary in first grade, they were not as accurate in word recognition as were children taught with a phonics approach. Some children picked up enough knowledge to become good readers and spellers for life, but many did not.

Some teachers of the look-say approach included a phonics component, teaching parts of words (letter/sound relationships) after the children knew them on sight. However, some teachers included no phonics component in their instruction. Fewer still taught phonics that connected children with the English language spelling patterns, let alone with their teaching of reading or writing. Spelling was a subject unto itself.

Historically, spelling instruction has gone through several notable shifts. From the 1920s to the 1960s, spelling was a process of rote memorization. Learning to spell depended on word memorization and weekly tests prescribed by the spelling book. It was not grounded linguistically and had nothing to do with language learning. In the 1960s and 1970s, spelling was seen as a language-based process that involves abstracting, or learning, regular sound/spelling patterns. Beginning in the late 1970s and continuing today, spelling has been seen more as a developmental process, one in which there are definable patterns of learning, and spelling is taught based on those developmental patterns (Templeton & Morris, 2000).

None of these approaches were totally wrong. In fact, the memorization and abstraction approaches laid the groundwork for the developmental recommendations in this book. The period of linguistic abstraction showed that spelling was a language process (including memory) that is involved in all learning. We now know better how to implement synthetic phonics in language-centered and developmentally appropriate ways that make sense to children. We know that spelling instruction supports orthographic knowledge and that spelling and word recognition are important to reading comprehension (Perfetti, 1985; Stanovich & Cunningham, 1993). Thus, attention to spelling instruction should not be left to be done on an as-needed basis (Templeton & Morris, 2000, p. 537). Spelling and phonics should be viewed as a means of studying and seeing words as tools that serve reading, writing, and vocabulary development (Templeton, 1991). Research continues to search for more understanding of how children learn to spell and read and how we can improve all children's literacy instruction.

children to comprehend what they read without making sure they can read the words efficiently. Word recognition and comprehension need to advance together. As Charles Perfetti (1986) pointed out, being able to recognize words rapidly and efficiently makes it easier for children to comprehend the meaning of what they read, because efficient word recognition frees the mind to concentrate on the message. Research bears this out: Better readers are better at both comprehension and word recognition (Stanovich, 2000).

WHOLE WORDS VERSUS PHONICS.   The pendulum has swung on the question of whether to use the whole-word method or teach phonics many times over the centuries. Johann Comenius, the famous seventeenth century Slovak educator who wrote the first book specifically for children, favored teaching reading by the whole-word method. In eighteenth century America, Noah Webster favored the phonics method (though he assumed that knowledge of Latin and Greek would form part of phonics knowledge). An energetic debate has continued on this issue ever since.

Jeanne Chall's influential book *Learning to Read: The Great Debate* (1967) came down strongly on the side of teaching phonics. So did Marilyn Adams's survey of research in the early 1990s, *Beginning to Read* (1990), the National Research Council's report *Preventing Reading Difficulties in Young Children* (Snow et al., 1998), and the report of the National Reading Panel, *Teaching Children to Read* (2000).

Why, then, do so many teachers resist the conclusion that teaching children to read words is simply a matter of teaching phonics? On grocery store intercoms and television commercials, popular phonics programs are hawked to parents as the "key to unlocking reading success." But in teachers' planning discussions, teachers express less confidence in phonics instruction as the only path or even the main path to success.

Their hesitation is justified. It is true that children need to understand the relationships between letters and sounds (although these relationships are not always simple and consistent). It is also true that many children do not learn these relationships without instruction and that phonics instruction helps children learn to read. But it also matters *when* instruction is provided and *what kinds* of phonics instruction are given. That is because children's ability to recognize words is learned in a developmental sequence and because the kind of instructional support children need varies with their level of development.

Stages in Children's Development of Word Recognition

Reading experts have disagreed for centuries over whether teachers should take a **whole-word approach** or a phonics approach to teaching reading. When we consider how children develop the ability to recognize words, it is clear that children favor whole words at some times and their parts at other times. The stages of children's development of word recognition have been described by Uta Frith (1985) and summarized by Usha Goswami (2000). According to these scholars, children go through a set of stages of word recognition that can be called *logographic, transitional, alphabetic,* and *orthographic*. As you consider these stages, think about the kind of instruction that will help children at each stage.

LOGOGRAPHIC READING.   Young children—preschoolers and kindergartners—who are just beginning to see familiar words around them tend to recognize words as whole displays. Children recognize McDonald's restaurants by their golden arches. They may recognize the word *look* by associating the two O's with eyes. Children in this stage may call the same word with different but related names, calling a Crest toothpaste label at one time "Crest" and at another time "toothpaste" (Harste, Woodward, & Burke, 1985). They are not yet reading the letters in the words, but are trying to find any identifiable feature that will help them remember the words, almost as if the words were faces. Logographic readers often give no response at all when faced with a word they do not know, because they do not yet have strategy for sounding out words.

Marshall (1977) called this stage of word recognition "glance and guess," because children would look at a word and call it by the few names of words they knew or say nothing at all. They had no way to begin to recognize words by puzzling out their letters.

When they are writing with invented spelling (see Chapter 3), children who are logographic readers may produce one or two memorized words—usually their names—and also symbols such as heart shapes. They will also produce prephonemic spelling: strings of letters that might resemble words but whose letters have no phonetic value.

How does one teach such readers to recognize words? Many years ago, Russell Stauffer (1975) offered what is still good advice: Use various means to familiarize children with print, and help them learn words as wholes until they can recognize at least fifty words as wholes.

TEACH IT!

3

TRANSITIONAL ALPHABETIC READING.   More advanced children—usually in early first grade—begin to read words by their letters, but not by very many letters. The child might read the first consonant of a word and call it by the name of another word she or he knows that begins with that sound. It is as if a word such as *ball* appeared to children like this: *bxxx*. They might correctly read the word, especially if they are helped by the context, but they might readily confuse it with *bat, bark*, or *beep* (Morris, 1999).

As writers using invented spelling, alphabetic readers produce what we call early phonemic spelling (see page 92); that is, they write a few letters to represent only the most salient sounds—usually consonant sounds. Thus, they might write *LDL* for *little* and *BT* for *boat*.

How does one teach such readers to recognize words? Teachers now can begin to help children learn more associations between letters and sounds. Techniques such as word sorting with picture cards can focus on teaching children to associate individual letters and sounds.

ALPHABETIC READING.   By the middle of first grade and into early second grade, most children begin to read more and more letters in words. When they attempt to read a word, rather than calling out the name of another word that begins the same way, a child might sound out every letter, even if it means pronouncing something that doesn't make sense. A child might say, "We went to the fire *sta-t-yon*" instead of "fire station." With practice, students produce fewer nonsense word readings and read words more accurately.

Children are acquiring a growing body of sight words—words that they can read accurately and quickly without having to decipher them. This rapid word identification occurs after a period of sounding out the words, or **phonological recoding**, as linguists call it. Ehri (1991) suggests that the earlier practice of reading words alphabetically—figuring them out letter by letter—lays down pathways to the memory that makes it easier for children to recognize the words when they see the words later. She explains:

> When readers practice reading specific words by phonologically recoding
> the words, they form access routes for those words into memory. The access

> *routes are built using knowledge of grapheme-phoneme correspondences that connect letters in spellings to phonemes in the pronunciation of words. The letters are processed as visual symbols for the phonemes, and the sequence of letters is retained as an alphabetic, phonological representation of the word. The first time an unfamiliar word is seen, it is read by phonological recoding. This initiates an access route into memory. Subsequent readings of the word strengthen the access route until the connections between letters and phonemes are fully formed and the spelling is represented in memory. (Ehri, 1991, p. 402)*

As writers using invented spelling, alphabetic readers produce examples of what we call letter name spelling or phonemic spelling. Now children's spellings represent all or most of the phonemes in a word. Yet, because they focus on matching one letter to one sound at a time, they are not aware of silent *e*'s or other ways of marking vowel letters long or short. Thus, *BET* can spell either *beat* or *bit*. Children usually do not spell consonant digraphs either; they might write *IHOVER* for *each other*. In fact, because their reading exposure is still very limited, they are only gradually noticing conventional ways in which letters represent sounds in spelling.

How does one teach such readers to recognize words? Word study can intensify, and phonics instruction can show children the common onsets and rimes, or **phonogram patterns**. Instruction usually follows a sequence such as the one found in Figure 5.1. The teacher can help these children by working with the first three levels of word patterns.

ORTHOGRAPHIC READING.   By late first grade to the middle of second grade, most children are moving into another stage. Now they are looking at words in terms of spelling patterns—not just one letter to one sound, but also familiar patterns such as *-ake, -ight,* and later *-tion.* Children who can separate words into onsets and rimes and who are taught by means of word sorts (Temple & Gillet, 1979; Bear, Invernizzi,

---

Word Features in Order of Introduction

- Short vowel rimes, such as **-at, -id,** and **-ock** words
- Then long vowel rimes, such as **-ate, -ide,** and **-oke** words
- Then the contrast between long and short vowel rimes, such as words with **-at/-ate; -id/-ide;** and **-ock/oke**
- Then various words with short vowels, such as **-at, -ack, -ab,** and **-ad; -it, -id,** and **-ick**
- Then words with long vowels, such as **-ate, -ake, -ail,** and **-aid; -ite, -ight, -ide,** and **-ike**
- Then **consonant blends,** such as **bl-, tr-, sp, -st, -nd,** and **-mp**
- Then **consonant digraphs** such as **th, ch, sh,** and **-ng**
- Then **two-syllable words,** such as **mother, table, kitten,** and **happy**
- Then **compound words,** such as **intro, cowboy, steamboat,** and **football**
- Then words with **inflectional endings,** such as **-er, -est, -ing,** and **-ed**

FIGURE 5.1

Word Features in Order of Introduction.

Templeton, & Johnston, 2000) can read by analogy; that is, if they can read *bake* and *take*, they can also read *rake* and *stake*. As they move further into the orthographic phase, children read not just by phonogram patterns, or onsets and rimes, as Trieman (1985) calls them, but increasingly by root words and even historical morphemes.

Children's spelling now passes through the transitional stage. They are spelling words in conventional ways, although not always correctly. For example, they might write *baisball, fase, trane,* and the like.

How does one teach such readers to recognize words? The teacher continues to work with them on word patterns such as the later seven levels of word patterns in Figure 5.1, calling their attention to more and more sophisticated spelling patterns through word study and reminding them of those patterns during reading activities.

Phonics in Isolation or Contextual Reading and Writing

There has been considerable debate recently on the question of whether phonics should be taught in isolated or dedicated lessons or in the context of reading and writing meaningful text. The National Reading Panel (NRP, 2000) recommends that children be given phonics instruction from kindergarten through second grade. The National Reading Panel, as you might remember from Chapter 1, is a group of reading experts and educational psychologists commissioned by the U.S. government to recommend best practices for reading instruction. One panel member recommends thirty minutes of phonics instruction each day in kindergarten through second grade (Timothy Shanahan, personal communication, 2003). The thirty minutes of instruction would include specific instruction in word work, with the teaching of phonics and spelling, and decoding practice with child-centered materials during various periods or mini lessons.

The principle that motivates the recommendation for dedicated phonics instruction is this: Teachers should make sure that phonics instruction is systematic and deliberate, not just an offshoot of other reading lessons. In our view, this principle is compatible with another principle: Young readers need to know how to apply the phonics skills they learn when they read meaningful text. In this vein, we remind you of the four-part instructional model we set out in Chapter 1 with some examples:

1. *Demonstration and immersion:* reading aloud, shared book reading, language experience, etc.
2. *Attention to detail:* teaching a phonics generalization showing students a spelling pattern (a rime); teaching about compound words, etc.
3. *Guided practice:* assigning practice with the phonics generalization or other phonics skill, as in a word sort or a making and breaking words activity (see below).
4. *Application and extension:* applying the phonics skill in the act of independent reading or writing of a meaningful text.

By this model, students first read or are read to from an interesting text that contains words with the pattern or patterns to be studied. That is the demonstration and immersion part of the lesson. Then the teacher calls the children's attention to a phonics pattern they will study (attention to detail). They do an exercise such as word sorting or making and breaking words to practice the phonics pattern (guided practice). Then they read or write another meaningful text, applying to the extent possible the phonics generalization they have been studying (application and extension).

Should We Teach Sight Words?

Reading teachers use the term *sight words* in two ways. One way is to refer to words that readers recognize instantly and do not need to decode. Because most children enter first grade with more than 6,000 words in their spoken vocabulary, it is expected that in the primary school years, children will learn to recognize most of those words in print, as well as a growing number of words they encounter in print but not in speech. Once the children can confidently read them, the words will be sight words, part of children's sight vocabulary.

The other meaning of the term *sight words* is the body of high-frequency words that populate children's texts. One hundred high-frequency words account for nearly half of the words primary-age children encounter in print, and 300 words account for 72 percent of the words they encounter (Eldredge, 1995). Note that many of these are "glue words"—words such as *the, and, in,* and *though.* Because they are meaningless in isolation, they can be difficult for children to learn. Note, too, that the lower-frequency words—words such as *dinosaur, escape, helicopter, football, cave, computer,* and *party*—number in the tens of thousands by the end of sixth grade, and these are the words that convey most of the meaning in texts. Table 5.1 identifies the 100 most frequently used words in primary school texts.

How are children taught the high-frequency words? Primary-grade children learn words through meaningful practice. Instruction in vocabulary helps (see below). So does independent reading with predictable books, which provides repeated exposure to these words. Incorporating high-frequency words in word study activities such as word sorts, making and breaking words, and word walls (see below) is also recommended. Word games such as novice and expert Scrabble, crossword puzzles, and word-search games are useful.

TABLE 5.1

The 100 Most Frequently Used Words

A: about, after, all, am, an, and, are, around, as, at, a
B: back, be, because, but, by
C: came, can, could
D: day, did, didn't, do, don't, down
F: for, from, fun
G: get, go, got
H: had, have, he, her, him, his, home, house, how

I: I, if, in, into, is, it
J: just
K: know
L: little, like, no, not, now
M: man, me, mother, my
O: of, on, one, or, our, out, over
P: people, put
S: said, saw, school, see, she, so, some

T: that, the, them, then, there, they, things, think, time, to, too, two
U: up, us
V: very
W: was, we, well, went, were, what, when, who, will, with, would
Y: yes

Reading Fluency

Since fluency (phrasing/prosody, reading rate, and word recognition) is strongly linked to reading comprehension (Rasinsky, 2000; Richards, 2000), children must attain fluency to read successfully. Fluent readers demonstrate smooth phrasing and a good pace, no longer sounding "mechanical." They use intonation and punctuation well. While it may seem as if some children become fluent overnight; for others the period of "word reading" can last for months as they plod along sounding choppy while focusing on each and every word.

With beginning readers, five to ten minutes of instruction each day can help them become fluent. Older readers (third and fourth grade and up), as well, can benefit from fluency instruction. Fluency lessons can be explicit and deliberate, or they may be embedded in other tasks so that children hardly notice they are being pressed to read fluently.

Explicit Fluency Instruction

With first or second grade children, use a familiar book to demonstrate and model what *dis*-fluent and fluent reading sound like. To demonstrate fluent reading with the children you need to have enough book copies for each child or a piece of chart paper, and then invite them to read along as you read.

- Read smoothly, making it "sound like talk"
- Pause for commas and stop for periods
- Make sentences sound like questions (the voice goes up), exclamations (the voice gets louder), or statements (the voice goes down).

Then model dis-fluent reading by reading word-by-word, skipping punctuation, and making every sentence sound alike. Invite the children to comment on how the dis-fluent reading sounds. Then read fluently again and ask the children to describe how fluent reading sounds.

Now invite the children to practice reading and re-reading sentences fluently. They can buddy-read in partner groups and practice reading the same sentences over and over again. Walk around and listen to each child read, offering encouragement and praise, and also modeling fluent reading as necessary.

For further practice, have the children take a book home with them to practice with an adult. Adults are asked to have their children practice until the children can read the sentences fluently. You might send along a letter with pointers to the adults, such as the one in Figure 5.2.

Embedded Fluency Instruction

Fluent reading is accomplished when students re-read materials until it sounds meaningful. Students can practice reading for fluency even when they are reading for other purposes, like bringing a text to perform through readers' theater or dramatizing poetry through voice choirs.

READERS' THEATER.   Readers' theater is performing a text while reading it aloud. To do readers' theater, choose a text with plenty of speaking parts. Assign one child to

Dear Parent —

Today we are practicing reading fluently. By fluent reading we mean:
- Reading smoothly, so that the reading sounds like talk;
- Pausing at commas and stopping at periods.
- Making the sentences sound like questions, statements, or exclamations. You can help by fluently reading a page of the book first, and then listening while your child reads it. Invite the child to read each page at least three times. Challenge your child to read fluently—but keep it fun. With practice, all children will learn to read fluently—especially if the practice is enjoyable.

FIGURE 5.2

Letter to Parents about Reading Fluently.

read each part, and assign one more child to read the narrator's part (all the text that is not in quotations).

Practice reading a passage with the entire class in a "fishbowl" arrangement, where the readers sit in the middle of a circle and the observers sit around them. After the reading, ask the observers if they could tell how each reader felt. Ask if they thought the situation was funny, happy, scary, sad, or exciting—and if they could tell the mood of the scene for the readers' voices. Invite the original group to read the passage again and to display the mood more clearly. Then you can invite other children to be the readers while their peers take turns being observers.

After children have gotten the idea of readers' theater, have them practice reading their own scenes in small groups. Invite them to take turns performing their scenes for the class.

VOICE CHOIRS.   Remind children that the spoken voice can have many of the same effects as a singing voice. We can read loudly or softly. We can build from soft to loud or diminish from loud to soft. We can read several lines as a whole choir, or we can alternate lines between small groups, or between a solo and the group. We can "sound like popcorn popping" as a line is read with one person reading each word.

After choosing a poem to read, tell the children to imagine a situation before they read it together. For example, before they read the poem, "The Grand Old Duke of York," have them imagine a platoon of soldiers marching down the road. We first hear them far off and quiet, but they get louder and louder as they approach, until the tramp of their boots is almost deafening; but then they get softer as they move away, so that we can barely hear them. Now, read the whole poem through as a whole group, starting very softly in a whisper, then building to very loud (their outdoor voices) as they reach the line "And when they were up they were up," and then diminishing to a whisper again by the last line.

The grand old Duke of York
He had ten thousand men,
He always marched them up the hill
Then he marched them down again.
And when they were up they were up,
And when they were down they were down.
And when they were only half way up,
They were neither up nor down.

They can read a poem in alternate groups of voices, too. For example, this poem of A.A. Milne's can be read with one group reading the words on the left and the others reading the words indented right:

John had
    Great big
Waterproof
    Boots on
John had a
    Great big
Waterproof
    Hat.
John had a
    Great big
Waterproof
    Macintosh
And that
    (Said John)
Is
    That.

A more challenging task for a voice choir is to read a poem as a round. This traditional poem can be read by three groups. After practicing reading the poem through several times in unison so that the readers get the rhythm, assign the class to three groups, and have them start reading the poem with each group starting one line behind the other. Tell them to read the whole poem through twice when they perform it. The first two groups should repeat the last line until the third group reads it, so they will all end together. You will likely need to clap your hands to keep everyone on the beat. The results can be good fun.

Can you dig that crazy music?
Can you dig it, can you dig it, can you dig it, can you dig it?
Can you dig that crazy music?
Can you dig it, can you dig it, can you dig it, can you dig it?
Oh, look—there's a chicken come struttin' down the road.
Now, now, there's another on a barbed wire fence.
Ma—ma!
Ma—ma!
Get that son-of-a-gun off my porch!

After practicing several poems with the class, groups of students can prepare poem readings to share with others.

Ongoing Assessment

For a quick test of oral (or silent) reading fluency take a words-per-minute (WPM) sample. Use a stopwatch or a watch with a second hand and have the child read text at an easy and instructional level. Have the child read one, two, or more pages (depending on the amount of print, 50 to 200 words) and time the reading. Count the number of words in the sample, multiply by 60 and divide it by the amount of time it took for the child to read. This provides a WPM check. Part of fluency is the speed at which readers process print. However, as mentioned earlier, speed says nothing about comprehension or how the reading sounds (intonation). Keep checking reading rate (WPM) along with comprehension and intonation (smooth versus choppy, it sounds like good reading). If improvement does not occur after you have modeled and demonstrated fluency repeatedly and the child engages in many rereadings of a favorite book, you might need to consult a reading specialist.

Vocabulary

Every word we have in our vocabulary is a flashlight that illuminates a corner of our experience. Indeed, a famous research study showed that we most readily know—and most readily notice—what we can name (Brown, 1958). But the benefits of vocabulary are distributed unevenly among schoolchildren. Children from the lower socioeconomic groups enter school with half the vocabulary of children from the upper ones. By twelfth grade, students with larger vocabularies know four times as many words as do their least proficient classmates, the size of whose vocabularies is even exceeded by that of many third graders (Beck, McKeown, & Kucan, 2002). It is not surprising, then, that the National Reading Panel (2000) made the teaching of vocabulary a top priority for literacy educators.

Vocabulary is important in reading. As Carl Smith puts it, "Most people feel that there is a common sense relationship between vocabulary and comprehension—messages are composed of ideas, and ideas are expressed in words" (Smith, 1997, p. 1). But the relationship between children's vocabulary and their reading comprehension points in more than one direction, and the means of helping *develop* vocabulary have been subject to dispute, even while the teaching of vocabulary has not commanded much attention from elementary teachers (Beck et al., 2002). Therefore, we need to explore the relationship between vocabulary instruction and reading.

Vocabulary development interacts with word recognition as children try to recognize in print words they already know—or partially know—in speech. But although younger children have in their spoken vocabulary most of the words that they are likely to encounter in print, there are still many words that occur in young children's picture books that children do not hear in the spoken language around them (Stanovich, 1992). By fourth grade, the vocabulary that is found in books is considerably richer than the words children use in speech.

Certainly, children can grow larger vocabularies from doing wide reading (Stanovich, 1992). As Nagy et al. (1985) point out, however, readers who encounter 100 unknown words will learn perhaps five of them. Children must do a great deal of reading, in at least moderately challenging texts, to learn large vocabularies from reading. Huge disparities exist, however, in the amount of reading children do. As we saw in Chapter 1, in one study (Wilson, 1992), the top 20 percent of a fifth grade class read

20 times as much as the bottom 20 percent. The bottom 20 percent read very little. If we count on children to learn vocabulary from reading, we will surely continue to see the huge disparities in vocabulary size described above.

One way to help children learn vocabulary is to show them how to learn more words from context (Szymborski, 1995). Another way to help their vocabularies grow is to give them systematic vocabulary instruction (McKeown & Beck, 1988).

Levels of Vocabulary Knowledge

What do we mean by *knowing* vocabulary? Knowing vocabulary well means not just understanding what words in a book mean, but also knowing words in a range of contexts, in associations with other words, and in connection with one's experience—to have words as one's own. Beck et al. (2002) suggest a continuum of word knowledge that looks like this:

- No knowledge
- General sense, such as knowing that *mendacious* has a negative connotation
- Narrow, context-bound knowledge, such as knowing that a *radiant* bride is a beautifully smiling happy one but being unable to describe an individual in a different context as radiant
- Having knowledge of a word but not being able to recall it readily enough to use it in appropriate situations
- Rich, decontextualized knowledge of a word's meaning, its relationship to other words, and its extension to metaphorical uses, such as understanding what someone is doing when they are *devouring* a book (Beck et al., 2002, p. 10)

A Closer Look at the Vocabulary Challenge

The job of teaching vocabulary seems truly immense. Nagy (1985) estimates that by ninth grade, students are having to cope with a written vocabulary of 88,500 words (Nagy & Anderson, 1984). Were we to try to teach all those words, the prospect of teaching children nearly 10,000 words a year would be daunting indeed. But Beck and colleagues (2002) have found a useful way to break down those numbers by dividing words into three tiers:

- *Tier One Words.* There are many thousands of words already in children's spoken vocabulary that don't usually have to be taught. These words Beck and colleagues call Tier One words; they include words such as *mother, clock,* and *jump.*
- *Tier Three Words.* Then there are many more thousands of words that are so highly specialized that they are almost never used outside of the disciplines in which they are encountered. These Tier Three words—such as *monozygotic, tetrahedron,* and *bicameral*—are best learned in science, social studies, and other classes in which they are tied to the content under study.
- *Tier Two Words.* That leaves the Tier Two words, the words with wide utility that most children do not have in their spoken vocabularies—words such as *dismayed, paradoxical, absurd,* and *wary.* Beck and colleagues (2002) estimate that there may be about 7,000 Tier Two words, and even if they teach children only half of them —or about 400 words a year—reading teachers will have gone a long way toward growing children's vocabularies and equalizing children's access to learning.

Approaches to Teaching Vocabulary

There is a wide consensus among researchers that vocabulary is best learned in the context of ideas under consideration. There is also agreement that learners should be actively involved in making meaning with new vocabulary, that vocabulary be related to other words, and that new words be tied to the learners' own experience (Smith, 1997).

WORD CONVERSATIONS FOR K–1.   When young readers (kindergarten and first grade) are learning new words, Beck and colleagues (2002) suggest that teachers conduct a rich discussion of words that includes these six steps:

1. Contextualize words, one at a time, within a story. For example, with kindergartners, the teacher could use Don Freeman's perennially popular *Corduroy* (1978) as a pretext for introducing the words *insistent, reluctant,* and *drowsy.* The teacher says, *"In the story, Lisa was* reluctant *to leave the department store without Corduroy* [her new teddy bear]."

2. Ask the children to repeat the word so as to make a phonological representation of it.

3. Then explain the meaning of the word in a child-friendly way: "Reluctant *means you are not sure you want to do something."*

4. Now provide examples of the word in other contexts: "I am *reluctant* to go swimming in the early summer when the water is cold."

5. Next ask children to provide their own examples: "What is something you would be *reluctant* to do?"

6. Finally, ask the children to repeat the word they have been talking about, so as to reinforce its phonological representation.

Word conversations are not as easy as they look. Teachers need to do the following:

- Choose books carefully to provide a meaningful context for introducing the vocabulary
- Think carefully about the words, and formulate child-friendly explanations of the word meanings
- Plan questions to relate the words to the children's experience
- Remind the children of the words they are studying, giving them several opportunities to pronounce the words (See Beck et al., 2002, for further discussion of this approach.)

EXERCISES FOR SECOND GRADE AND UP.   Activities to teach vocabulary should relate words to a meaningful context, to other words, and to the students' own experiences. The following exercises satisfy these requirements by making connections (to self, personal stories, and other books); collaborating with peers (interpersonal dynamics through all the language arts); exploring meaning (asking questions, making statements, interpreting, higher-level thinking such as application, synthesis and evaluation); and participating as an active reader (summarizing, predicting, confirming, and clarifying).

- *Semantic webs:* A **semantic web** is a way to organize information graphically according to categories. There are several ways to use semantic webs. The most open-ended way is to draw a circle on a page and write a topic word in it. Then, together with the students, the teacher thinks of aspects of the topic and comes up with examples or aspects of that subtopic.

TEACH IT!

8

TEACH IT!

9

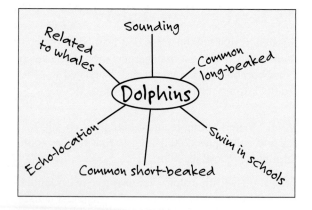

One approach to semantic webs is the *character web,* in which the name of a character is written in the circle in the middle of the display. Then words that describe the character are written as satellites around the character's name. Examples that illustrate each attribute are then written as satellites around the descriptive words. Figure 5.3 depicts a semantic web on dolphins. Schwartz and Rafael (1985) suggest guiding the students' responses to a semantic web and asking them to offer answers to three questions asked about the target word, as shown in Figure 5.4:

- What is it?
- What is it like?
- What are some examples of it?

FIGURE 5.3

A Semantic Web.

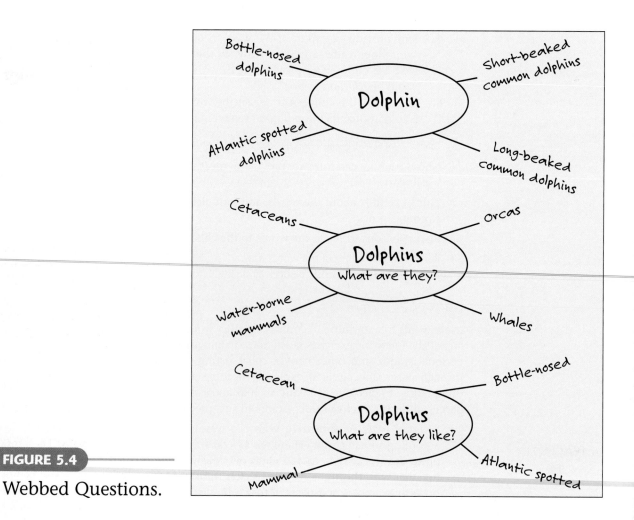

FIGURE 5.4

Webbed Questions.

What kind of thing is this?	What is it a part of?	What causes it?
_____ _____	_____ _____	_____ _____
What are the kinds of it?	What are its parts?	What does it cause?
_____ _____	_____ _____	_____ _____

FIGURE 5.5

A Concept Ladder.

	Bear live young	Have gills	Cold-blooded	Have milk
SHARKS				
DOLPHINS				

FIGURE 5.6

A Semantic Feature Analysis.

- *Concept ladders:* Concept ladders provide yet another way for children to organize their thinking and to categorize thus supporting comprehension. The concept ladder shown in Figure 5.5 would be useful in a study on volcanoes and earthquakes.
- *Semantic feature analysis:* Semantic feature analysis enables students to compare several terms at once and make judgments about them. The terms are placed in a grid like the one shown in Figure 5.6, and students are asked to write in a plus sign if the answer to the question is positive and a minus sign if the answer is negative.

Struggling Reader

Struggling Readers

Because fluency is strongly linked to reading comprehension (Rasinsky, 2000; Richards, 2000), children must attain fluency to read successfully. Fluent readers demonstrate smooth phrasing and a good pace (although fluency is not just reading fast), no longer sounding mechanical and now using intonation and punctuation well. Although it might seem as if some children become fluent overnight, for others the period of "word reading" can last for weeks or months as they plod along sounding choppy while focusing on each and every word. They struggle with processing words with the degree of ease needed for reading comprehension.

Struggling readers can take a year or more to become fluent as they stay stuck at the word level. Often they overuse phonics, sounding out words without discernible use of other strategies. Overuse of phonics often indicates a lack of full understanding of the English language phonics/spelling system and may be combined with a lack of other strategy knowledge. Nonfluent readers might not be able to put the units of letter/sounds (the chunks) together, and thus lack sight word recognition.

Listening to struggling readers can be heartbreaking for the teacher. Their labor is great, and reading exhausts them and is frustrating for them; as a result, avoidance can set in. Therefore, the teacher needs to intervene quickly and provide additional fluency practice and instruction in word recognition. Help from home and from school specialists is often needed at this critical phase of reading development.

As little as five minutes of fluency instruction each day can be helpful. Teach and practice phrases and short sentences and implement repeated readings using basal stories, nonfiction, trade books, and poetry and reader's theater. Make this practice purposeful, collaborative, and gamelike to avoid boredom.

How Do We Handle Instruction in Phonics and Word Recognition?

Earlier in this chapter, we responded to a series of questions about phonics instruction. Among our conclusions was that phonics instruction works best when students are shown how to apply what they learn about phonics when they are reading words. This conclusion is borne out by research. When Barbara Taylor and her associates sought to find out what teachers did in schools that "beat the odds"—that is, schools that succeed in teaching high-risk children to read—they discovered that the teachers did teach phonics, but they also coached children to apply phonics generalizations when they were reading words in texts (Taylor et al., 1999).

How does one help children apply what they learn about phonics? It is recommended that in teaching phonics, teachers use a **whole/part/whole approach**, in which they show children words that contain a phonics principle in a whole context of meaningful text, then call children's attention to the part, or the phonics generalization, and then return their attention to the whole again by having them read more words in connected text that exhibit the phonics generalization that has just been taught. A more elaborate version of the whole/part/whole approach is the four-part model used in this book:

1. *Demonstration and immersion:* Show students whole text that contains words that use the phonics generalization.
2. *Attention to detail:* Call attention to the phonics generalization.
3. *Guided practice:* Have students do activities to practice using the phonics generalization.
4. *Application and extension:* Encourage children to apply their knowledge of the phonics generalization when they read and write.

STANDARDS & LITERACY

★ ★ A State Standards Lesson Plan ★ ★

Many educators question whether standards are determining instruction, feeling that they are used to force teachers to teach "correctly" when in reality no standard can accomplish this. Effective teaching flows from knowledgeable, highly skilled, and dedicated individuals who study the literature, watch the development of children closely, attend conferences, engage in professional development, and learn from their students throughout their careers (Freppon, 2001). Effective classrooms are highly motivating (students are intrinsically motivated), have few if any discipline problems, and provide many varied techniques for teaching reading and writing. All children have a right to this kind of classroom and multiple, research-based opportunities to learn (Pressley et al., 2001).

Many critics of state and national standards believe that standards are more politically driven than based on child development and literacy research. The field of literacy serves as a good case in point in which the emphasis of the standards varies greatly from state to state as well as among all the various national organizations. This is particularly true with regard to instruction in phonics, emergent literacy, whole language, and invented spelling. An example of conflicting information in standards are some differences between the California State Standards and those of the New Standards for Primary Literacy Committee (1999) and the 1998 joint position statement from the International Reading Association and the National Association for the Education of Young Children with regard to invented spelling.

The California standards discuss phonemic awareness and concepts of print, letter recognition, word analysis, explicit phonics instruction, and spelling assessment. However, invented spelling and its role in assessment and instruction are absent.

In contrast, the NAEYC and IRA statement says, "Some educators may wonder whether or not invented spelling promotes poor spelling habits. To the contrary, studies suggest that temporary invented spelling may contribute to beginning reading; Clarke, 1988)." Clark's work in particular found that invented spelling benefited children more than having the teacher provide correct spellings in writing. Invented spellings encourage and support children's exploration of the letter/sound relationships in written language. As children engage with these spellings, they learn to segment words so that they can spell them into constituent sounds. (NAEYC/IRA, 1998, p. 5). The standards of the New Standards for Primary Literacy Committee (1999) also discuss invented spelling positively. In addition, these standards stress the vital role of teachers' understanding and use of children's invented spellings for accurate assessment.

Ultimately, the best way to approach standards-based teaching is to learn the standards for your state and school district and use them in conjunction with your knowledge or research-based information on children's development. The standards can be a guiding factor in your instruction. The following example shows one way to develop a lesson to meet a particular standard (Teaching the English Language Arts: A Sample Standards-Based Lesson Plan, 2002):

Grade Level Indicator: First grade

Standard (from Ohio): Recognize, say, and write the common sounds of letters.

Teacher's decisions and lesson plan:

Focus of Instruction: Initial consonant sounds for *m, f,* and *t.*

Description of Lesson: Students will sort pictures according to initial consonant sounds.

Required Materials: Picture and letter cards for initial consonant sounds of /m/, /f/, and /t/

Before the lesson:
Sing the alphabet song "Alligators All Around."
Review sounds and letter names for *m, f,* and *t.*

(continued on next page)

STANDARDS & LITERACY

★ ★ Continued ★ ★

During the lesson:

Focus attention on the task by naming the pictures.

Explain the /m/, /f/, and /t/ categories for sorting.

Model how to say the name of the picture to listen for initial sound.

Show one picture at a time, say the name of the picture, and place it under the correct letter category.

Encourage talk about why the picture fits the category.

Rename the pictures after sorting all pictures. Restate the categories.

After the lesson:

Provide opportunities for children to practice sorting on their own.

Reflection: Think about what has happened and what the children have done, as well as your teaching (What didn't happen that you planned? What do you need to work on? What do you wish you had done that slipped away?). Move your thinking into assessment and planning.

Ongoing assessment: Observe how students perform the picture sort, and document your observations.

As you consider the teaching strategies that follow, bear in mind the need to coach children in the application of the phonics generalizations they learn.

We can handle phonics through knowledgeable teachers' ongoing assessment, sound planning, and grouping for instruction. In the hands of effective teachers, grouping becomes a broad form of individualization. Many classrooms have needs-based groups; however, other classrooms have multileveled small groups, consisting of children with various needs and strengths. Instructional groups must be carefully monitored and changed according to children's growth or struggles. With struggling readers or English language learners, some one-on-one instruction must occur. Include all resources in your recommendations and practice for these children. For example, help parents get every assistance available at school, encourage them to enroll their children in summer programs, and at times arrange for private tutoring. Teach parents how to work with their child at home.

Specifically, what are children taught? They are taught frequently used words (at least through third grade), decoding (until about grade three or four for average and below-average readers), and spelling and vocabulary (in every grade). Word recognition skills and strategies are taught daily in explicit, systematic, and child-centered ways.

The following word recognition activities are appropriate for learners across the elementary grade levels. The examples of instruction and recommended books are aimed toward the primary grades. However, nearly all recommendations are applicable to older children. Additional suggestions and examples for middle and upper grades are provided in later sections.

Word Recognition Activities

Children learn better if they physically manipulate letters and words. The following activities focus on helpful developmentally appropriate activities. The section is aimed toward children in grades one to four; however, many of these suggestions work well in fifth to eighth grades.

The use of manipulatives allows emerging readers to experiment with word families and engage in developmentally appropriate phonics practice.

TEACH IT!
10

WORD SORTING AND WORD MAKING. Word sorting activities include sorting words by letter/sound relationship characteristics (see Figure 5.7) and by the concepts that words represent—for example, sort all the weather-associated words in one row (rain, snow, ...), and sort all the cooking-associated words in another row (stove, bowl, ...). Word sorting by affixes and word roots in the middle and upper grades also provides sound practice and the kind of hands-on activity that older children appreciate.

Sorting instruction provides more opportunity for seeing words as objects that children manipulate and "own" by organizing and classifying them. Jerry Zutell (1999, p. 105) notes, "Organizing objects, events, and experiences into categories and classes is a fundamental way we make sense of the world around us." The act of sorting makes words concrete objects of study. Word sorts are made easier or more challenging in various ways:

- *Easier:* The teacher repeats the lesson several times before the children work with word cards, or the teacher works with only one set of word cards. Children work in pairs with the same set of cards used in the demonstration lesson, or the teacher and children use picture cards with word cards for additional support. Include self-assessment.

- *More challenging:* Introduce blends, digraphs, and mixed sorts as noted above, for example, different short vowels, blends, and digraphs sorts. Use the information in this and in other chapters in this book to guide your decisions. Have children work on their own more often, but always include some collaborative work.

Children learn to make words by using the spelling patterns in known words. The following example works well for most first and second graders. You can see how word

Blends for as bl, fl, gl		Blends for br, dr, tr	
Bl	black, blue, blank	Br	brag, bread, brick
Fl	flag, flop, flew	Dr	drop, dream, drive
Gl	glue, glad, glow	Tr	tree, trap, trip

FIGURE 5.7

Word-Sorting Guides.

making is applied to grades three to five (intermediates spellers) and sixth to eighth graders (advanced spellers). For example, older children can make words by combining root words (on one set of word cards) with various affixes (on another set of cards).

The children put the known word *then* up for all to see. The teacher or children point out the spelling pattern *(th - en)*. Children work at their tables with spelling pattern cards: *th, sh, wh,* and so on. You'll need to preselect the cards or ask the children to do this by telling them to draw specific spelling patterns from their individual collections—for example, "Take out your *th, sh,* and *wh* cards." It is also helpful to have children select additional cards; they find the misfits and real words. With support, children grow to love word play.

Card collections are built throughout the school year. Keep the pool of possible spelling pattern cards at a workable level so that children have enough cards to support the problem-solving process and not so many cards that they become overwhelmed. When teaching does not go well, step back and think about the level of your instruction.

From whole class minilessons on making words, children can move into regular practice in small developmentally different groups for the ten to fifteen minutes of exclusive practice under your guidance. Word making practice concludes with sentence writing. Thus, the idea that reading is meaningful is kept intact. The question "Does this sentence make sense?" should be a frequent refrain in teachers' and children's talk.

VARY WORD RECOGNITION PRACTICE.   Learners of all ages are drawn to the unique. Children take special delight in learning new and playful ways to work with words. Part of the teacher's job is to carefully select and make available a variety of high-quality materials that change from time to time. An interesting supply of materials and access to activities also provides children what they need for good decision making when they self-select. A word of caution about change: Young children need consistency, so introduce new activities and materials carefully.

WORD HUNTS.   Word hunts help children make a connection between spelling words and reading them. This is important because some children do not automatically make the spelling/reading connection (Ehri, 1997). Word hunts also incorporate children's literature, poetry, or other whole texts. Word hunts work just as well in third, fourth, or fifth grade with the right materials and teacher guidance. This strategy is also helpful in content area reading. The following second-grade sample lesson is an example of a word hunt based on a poem.

Sample Lesson:

In the fifth week of school, student teacher Breanna demonstrates a word hunt for her first-grade children. She works with eight to ten children at a time, and she teaches and assesses along the way.

Breanna reads the poem "Books, Books" by Ritsa Tassopoulos (personal communication, April 10, 2002) to the children from a large chart and then says, "Now, let's read it together."

BOOKS, BOOKS

Books, books fun to read
Books, books just what I need
Books, books fill my head
Books, books in my bed
Books, books morning noon and night
Books, books make me feel just right

The children follow along well. After reading, the children reread together in partner groups. Breanna says, "What do you notice about some of these words?"

*Children talk. They voice their observations and volunteer to read rhyming words (*times *and* rhymes*).*

Breanna says, "Now I'm going on a word hunt. I want to find two words that don't rhyme."

*Thinking out loud about rhyming and nonrhyming words and how they sound and look, she lists two words—*head *and* need*—in separate columns. Breanna organizes the group into pairs and asks them to work together. She says, "Copy these two words onto your papers, and make them look like this (pointing to the columns). Find rhyming words to match the one in each column. The words can be new ones you think of, words from our word walls, and words in this poem. Get ready to talk about what you've found. This is just practice. No one has to get everything right; it's practice. Don't worry, we'll have fun talking about what makes words rhyme."*

SPEED SORTS.   After children become accurate with word sorts, they can extend their expertise by seeing how quickly they can sort. This activity supports fluency and healthy competition in a gamelike task. (Sixth to eighth graders really like them.) Like so many developmentally appropriate activities, speed sorts build intrinsic motivation and provide that all-important sense of satisfaction!

A speed sort is done as follows:

- Use a timer of some type. Egg timers really help and are quiet!
- Children sort as fast and as accurately as they can.
- Children self-assess the sorts with a rubric alone or with another child. If they encounter any uncertainty, they skip the word and later get help with it.
- Children may chart the number of words sorted correctly in N minutes. Once the activity has been taught well, a teacher-made charting sheet aids children's independent charting. Learners thrive on healthy competition with themselves.

TEACH IT!

7

Word walls are just one way students can organize new words they learn.

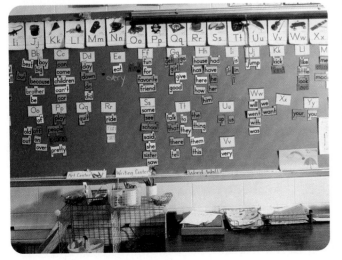

WORD WALLS.   Word walls can provide strong support in children's learning and teachers' systematic instruction. Word walls consist of words that children are learning arranged alphabetically on the walls of the classroom in ways that allow the words to be easily seen and accessed. Cunningham (1995) has extensive information on word walls. Word walls should be interactive, made and used by the teacher and the children. Unfortunately, teachers who do not fully understand the value of this activity often wind up with words on a wall that children cannot use because they cannot even read them and there is no interactive and purposeful instruction on what to do with these words. Word walls, like any other teaching technique, are helpful only in the hands of a knowledgeable teacher.

Much good instruction can spring from various kinds of words on walls, including serving children's self-assessment needs. Here is a brief description of two types of word walls and how they be might be used (see also Pinnell & Fountas, 1998; Bear et al., 2000; McGee & Richgels, 2000):

- *A picture-word wall:* Post the words from favorite books, inquiry units of study, words and pictures with the letters of the alphabet. It is nearly always best if words are put on the wall *during* the teaching process.

- *A literature-based picture-word wall:* This example can be applied with young children and older children. Add the critical literacy component discussed in Chapter 4 and a more mature presentation, and older children will work well with a rich and meaningful picture book. Picture having read *Lilly's Purple Plastic Purse* (Henkes, 1996). You introduce the word wall by showing an enlarged picture or colorful sketch of Lilly on the wall with Lilly's name under it. Next you ask for suggestions about other words children want to add from the book. You write their words in full view, leaving space for the pictures that will come. The children are asked to remember their favorite word. Next, they are asked to draw a picture that depicts or explains their word and write the word and explanation. The teacher talks the children through some examples of what they might write.

As children's development progresses, word walls change from picture-word walls to word-only walls. Word hunts and word sorts expand the word study. Books are reread to keep a focus on meaningful reading and for enjoyment. Imagine the word walls on science and other inquiry work you can have with middle and upper grades.

SIGHT WORDS.   Sight words are learned primarily through sheer exposure. Repeated readings are key. Children should reread their favorite books while they also select challenging books from several the teacher recommends.

Sight word walls contain high-frequency words that are posted as the children encounter them in their reading and in lessons. The teacher should engage children in doing sight word walls regularly (Cunningham, Hall, & Sigmon, 1999). When word walls are used daily in the course of reading, writing, and spelling, they are embedded in authentic literacy practice. This is how a teacher can create and use a sight word wall:

- Adding words gradually (about five per week).
- Make words highly accessible by putting them where all students can see them, writing them in large print with big black letters, and using colors for words that are often confused, such as *for, from, that, they,* and *this.*
- Select only the words children encounter most frequently in their reading and the words they use most frequently in their writing. Do not overwhelm them or yourself with too many words. Nothing succeeds like success!
- Practice the words by saying, spelling, and writing them ("do the wall").

Word Recognition in Kindergarten, First, and Second Grades

During the first three years of school, children need to learn basic phonics, focusing on consonants, vowels, and two- to three-syllable words. Because of the range of development in classrooms, the teacher should provide for a wide range of learning oppor-

TEACH IT!

★ ★ ★ ★

Minilesson: Phonemic Awareness

The class is made up of children who are not yet at the late beginning or early transitional stage of reading. The teacher has decided to have the children practice rhyming words and letter patterns to improve their phonemic awareness.

Plan: Engage the children in rich oral language; students should be able to read, write, and say rhyming words.

Observe and make notes on children during and after the lesson.

Materials: A well-known book such as *So Many Bunnies* (Walton & Miglio, 1998). Chart paper and markers

After rereading *So Many Bunnies,* the teacher states, "I notice some interesting words on the second page. It says

(*pointing to the words*) 'One was named Able. He slept on the table. Two was named Blair. She slept on a chair.' What do you notice?"

The class spends some time discussing the reading, likely indicating the rhyming pattern. The teacher then says, "Ah yes, some of you say the words rhyme. Do all of you notice that? Which words rhyme?"

After allowing the children the opportunity to identify the rhyming pairs of words, the teacher says, "Let's look at what makes them rhyme."

The teacher focuses on letter/sound spelling patterns, in T <u>able</u>/<u>Able</u> and <u>chair</u>/Bl <u>air</u> and talks with the children about beginning letters. The children interact by going to the chart paper and pointing to the rhyming words and the parts that rhyme as they work through the lesson.

Refer to your **Teach It!** booklet for further activities you can use to reinforce concepts discussed in this chapter.

tunities. One good way to help students develop understanding is through writing and spelling, since the children have to attend carefully to all sounds and writing patterns. The Teach It! box provides an example of a minilesson for second graders who need more support in phonemic awareness.

Effective teachers need to assess their students' progress on a regular basis and can do so by asking two simple questions: (1) Are the children experiencing success and enjoying themselves, or are they frustrated (acting out, playing around, avoiding engagement)? (2) At what points are individual children or a small group trying but not quite succeeding? The answers to these two questions help teachers decide what to do next.

**Family &
Community
Literacy**

Technology

FAMILY AND COMMUNITY.   Home support by families or caregivers can be built from nearly any lesson that is taught at school. For example, easy word sorts can go home for five- to seven-minute practice sessions; word sort games can be especially fun when played with a loved one. Simple turn-taking and charting progress or keeping score (with little ones winning!) create a game. Include for the adults one page of simple and limited suggestions for conversations about words with take-home sorts. Ask for a "read around the house" adventure. Adults help children read any and every word they find in the kitchen, bathroom, or elsewhere. Groups of parents, caregivers, and children who play together or attend community functions will benefit from getting together to support their children in literacy play. Some thoughtful adult structure and guidance can help regular play groups move into literacy games and activities.

TECHNOLOGY.   For home and school technology materials, look into word recognition software programs. A good program that is very popular with young children is Wiggle Works from Scholastic Publishing and the Center for Applied Special Technology. Wiggle Works focuses on emergent, early, and fluent language development using reading, writing, speaking and listening. It contains a variety of creative activities that entertain while also building skills. Additional programs can be found online at Superkids.com (www.superkids.com), where teachers and parents can check out various programs and read reviews of their efficacy. For an up close look at how two second-grade teachers have used technology in their classrooms, visit http://buckman.pps.k12.or.us/room100/room100.html.

Word Recognition in Grades Three to Five

Intermediate-grade learners know many words. They continue to build their word knowledge and learn to decode longer words. Literature and inquiry units (science, social studies) provide good opportunities for word walls. As words with specialized meanings are encountered, discussed, and included in writing, they become more readily recognized in use. Transitional and early to middle intermediate learners' exclusive word study should take place for about fifteen to twenty minutes a day. Follow the whole/part/whole rule of thumb, and use the studied words in sentences. A focus on meaning is critical in all that children do with words. Effective teachers systematically incorporate highly contextualized word study and vocabulary instruction in students' reading and writing throughout the curriculum. They often read aloud high-quality children's fiction and information books and take advantage of opportunities to teach new words.

WORD LEARNING.   Intermediate learners must learn much about syllables and how syllables work in spelling (where syllables meet inside words). Among the spelling concepts to be learned and practiced at this level are when to double the consonant (*run – ing = running*) and when not to (*sing – ing = singing*). Compound words, base word affixes, syllables, and accents on words are among the intermediate learners' challenges.

Multisyllable words can be learned through sorting practice. Demonstrate sorts with words such as *act, con, help,* and *loud.* These cards are combined with cards for *-tion, -test, -ful,* and *-est.* Following sorting practice and self-assessments with a rubric, you and the children work with two- to four-syllable words in sentences. **Vertical listing** serves as a wonderful way to help children work with multisyllable words (Tattershaw, personal communication, June 15, 2002). Teachers and children take whole words, list their syllables vertically and put them back together, and end with using the words in sentences. Here is an example of vertically listed syllables:

	Easier			More challenging	
ac	con	rep	ad	um	a
tion	test	tiles	ver	brel	maze
			tise	la	ment

Children read the syllables vertically and then write the whole word. For additional attention to detail, children may underline syllables with colored markers. Syllable cards may also be made by children (or adults) and used to make vertical lists. The cards are then pushed together to make whole words that can be used in sentences.

SPELLING. Transitional learners benefit from spelling instruction on long vowel words, blends, and digraphs (three-letter words such as *spr – spring, scr - scream*). As you saw in Chapter 3, long vowel learning is challenging because it does not exhibit the pattern of one letter to one sound. Children must think abstractly to master long vowel spelling patterns, and they must segment words and think about silent letters (*su i t*). Complexity increases as they move to diphthongs and R-controlled words.

Work with homophones (such as *meet* and *meat*) and homographs (such as *tear in the jeans* or *tear in the eye*). Depending on children's strengths and needs, vocabulary teaching may be included in the exclusively fifteen to twenty minutes of word study or given its own fifteen minutes at another time. Beck and her colleagues (2002) caution that grade-level word lists are not always the best source of vocabulary words. Select carefully and rely on the books children read (literature and content area) and the words that are in the culture at large and in the classroom. Work on plurals (*hats* /s/ and *beds* /z/), and make clear that letters do not consistently convey distinct pronunciations (Strauss, 2001).

Teachers can ask students to keep vocabulary notebooks in which they list words and the children's views of the words' meanings. You can also supply key words for students, and help them to distinguish meanings that vary by context. By using the vocabulary notebook, children use words they like in their writing.

Teachers can also introduce words taken from popular media and appropriate movies to add variety and develop children's interest in words. Sorting words by categories is a challenge for all elementary children. Provide a lot of practice discussion, and make the task easier with two categories or more challenging with several categories.

Often at the intermediate level, especially with instruction that includes self-selection and self-assessment, children have a sense of what they need to read. Trust children to select words they want to learn as you implement the vocabulary curriculum.

**Family &
Community
Literacy**

FAMILY AND COMMUNITY. It is important to continue home/school connections. Often, once children move from the primary grades, home/school interactions and support fade. You can help to keep this important connection by showing parents and caregivers activities that are enjoyable as well as good for word learning. For example, children and adults can read the newspaper and then brainstorm and list all the plural words, or words with affixes on a particular page, and so on. These literacy activities are easily extended into the community. Parents, caregivers, and teachers can serve a great need through proactive efforts to get literacy activities into after-school centers, where students sometimes do their homework or wander aimlessly.

TECHNOLOGY. There are computer programs that read aloud to children as they watch the words on the screen. For some children, this additional time of being read to is an asset. As children mature and keyboarding is no longer difficult, writing workshop pieces can be done on the computer. This takes specific computer hardware so that all

Technology

children have adequate access, but it is worth it. Many schools have this technology and a teacher expert. Writing on the computer relieves children of the stress of handwriting and aids them in revision. But the teacher needs to monitor the spell checker. It is good for publishing but not for learning how to spell. Spell checkers do not *teach* spelling. With proper child-safe controls, surfing the web provides lots of reading and vocabulary breadth. Children need computer literacy to learn to access information accurately and use multiple sources of data. These skills are part of living in an information age, and they can promote higher-level thinking. Companies such as the Scholastic Software Club (http://teacher.scholastic.com/clubs/) and Sundance (www.sundancepub.com) offer hundreds of books and audiovisual materials (CD-ROMs and videos) for the classroom.

Word Recognition and Vocabulary in Grades Six to Eight

At the upper levels, students encounter an increasingly large number of informational words and words with specific content definitions. Cunningham and Stanovich (1997) reported that vocabulary knowledge accounted for more than 30 percent of eleventh graders' reading comprehension. Without meaning-based understandings and rich vocabulary, older students' school success is at risk. Therefore, teachers need to continue to use word walls, hunts, and word sorts. Challenge children by adding about six new words a week in alphabetical order and with rich discussions and the use of the words in sentences. Use tricky spelling patterns and derivation words. You can have children plan and create their own concept sorts, for example, science-related words, math-related words, and sports-related words. Remember to step back if the children get frustrated.

Word knowledge instruction with older students focuses more on understanding things such as derivations and word analysis.

STRUCTURAL ANALYSIS. Teach students to analyze words and identify the roots, segments, and affixes. As you have learned, children at this level learn how new words are derived from others; for example, *photograph* is derived from *photo* and *graph*. This

way of thinking about words provides for **structural analysis**. You should teach structure patterns (e.g., *affect/affection, introduce/introduction, pronounce/pronunciation*) and spelling changes (e.g., *permit* and *permission, determine* and *determination*). Teach children when to drop the *e* (e.g., *educate/education*), which words get -*able* and which get -*ible* added, and so on. This is a good time to teach students that many content words come from Latin and Greek origins. Fifteen to twenty minutes of word study for children at this level should be meaning-driven. These lessons are critical, as they provide authentic reading and writing word use.

WORD ORGANIZATION. Help students to keep words organized in ways that makes sense to them. You can keep students actively involved by helping them to demonstrate a deep personal interest in words, by letting them make their own decisions, and by using self-assessment techniques. Have children read every day, and have them read with others and discuss their books. Prompt children, and remind them to focus on interesting words, words they did not know before reading the book, and words they cannot figure out in the contexts of their reading.

DEVELOPING AWARENESS WITH NEW WORDS. Vocabulary instruction includes many of the suggestions that already have been introduced but made more challenging. Other teaching strategies include a suggestion box to which children add words and from which the teacher draws daily. The words are discussed and used in various contexts (e.g., sentences, paragraphs). Older children can bring in words they have heard on TV or in movies, read in the newspaper, or seen on signs. The words are shared and can be posted to encourage some healthy competition (girls against boys, taller versus shorter students, or those who prefer fiction versus those who prefer nonfiction). Go on timed word scavenger hunts in the classroom or library. Have children select words that have a relationship in spelling or in meaning with a word they know (Beck et al., 2002). Bear and colleagues (2000, p. 197) suggest the following options for study of high-frequency words and spelling:

- When new words are introduced, engage in instructional conversations that ask children why a part of the word might be hard to remember. Have the children copy the word onto their paper, talk together, and analyze it before responding.
- Self-corrected test: After the new words have been introduced, written, and discussed, children fold their papers over and cover the list; a student in each small group calls out the words, and the children write them and self-check.
- Self-study activity: Look at the word and say it, cover the word and write it, check the word, see what is correct, and write it again if some of it is wrong. (This activity is well known; it supports visual memory and attention to detail.)
- Practice and final test: Words are called out, and students write them and self-check against the word wall or chart; they may work again in pairs or independently. Importantly, they engage in word analysis, having been taught specific techniques.
- With about six new words a week, the spelling success rate is high, and problem word patterns are easily identified.

Regular spelling checks can help students monitor their learning. The wall or chart is covered, students spell words again, and the teacher asks several students to be checkers. With word lists in hand, they check papers, and each student with 100 percent joins the teacher and classmates in checking others (Gaskins et al., 1988). Checking is completed in a matter of minutes, and there is time for a structural analysis discussion. There are times at which the teacher will want to test spelling (this is different from teaching spelling). This is when the teacher collects and grades papers. Daily instruction is teaching, not testing, so the grading of every paper becomes a nonissue.

However, careful review of children's written work for evidence of progress or problems is vital. These are data that inform teaching and keep the teacher accountable. The effective teacher talks with children daily, pointing out areas in which they are improving and one or two problems that need work. In group and individual talks, learners are given explicit feedback on what they do well and what they should be doing better.

**Family &
Community
Literacy**

FAMILY AND COMMUNITY.   As was stated earlier, the importance of family or care-giver involvement in children's word learning does not decrease with the child's age. An easy and interesting mall walk creates a discovery game for older students. It involves giving the child a list of Greek root words: *aero* (means *air*), *bio* (means *life*), *geo* (means *earth*), *log* (means *word*), *meter* (means *measuring*), *phone* (means *sound*), *therm* (means *heat*), *photo* (means *light*), *hydra/hydro* (means *water*), and so on. The child and adult(s) identify words in the mall signs that have a Greek root and do a structural analysis of the word. For example, a father spots "log" in a word on a store sign, the child reads "logo," and the father and child read the sign: "T-Shirt Logos in One Hour." Many word games are created once adults and older children begin to play them. For example, consider the derived, multisyllable, and plural words that are seen on driving trips. Work in the community might well be part of the (middle and) upper elementary student. Volunteer work provides many opportunities for literacy and its authentic use.

A brochure from the International Reading Association (IRA) on family literacy is available at http://bookstore.reading.org, and the Public Broadcasting Service (PBS) offers educational television programs for children ages nine to twelve. Online, the Corporation for Public Broadcasting offers information about new, safe, engaging, and educational programming on television and the Internet for this age group (www.cpb.org/ed/5).

Technology

TECHNOLOGY.   Upper elementary children often keyboard well and are quite computer literate. At school, they create their own vocabulary word files. In addition, the computer's thesaurus can be useful for vocabulary learning. Older children can use it to explore synonyms, antonyms, and word roots and derived words. A small group might work on a thesaurus project and present and teach it to the class. Creating a multimedia presentation requires hard thinking and group cooperation. Desktop publishing opens a world of opportunities as well. Importantly, words are in play and are used as tools in getting written language and communication done.

Certainly, computer searches are quite useful for children in their inquiry or research projects. Such projects extend to the content areas with ease. Software from the National Geographic Atlas (www.nationalgeographic.com) or the World of Encarta African Book Club (www.africana.com/kbookclub) helps children to interact with texts. A word study component of this software is that when an unknown word appears, the child can access its meaning and its pronunciation. As helpful as this might be, however, it precludes the child's application of any problem-solving strategies in analyzing this word. This is an important point and is something to be considered carefully in evaluating many interactive programs that "give" correct responses. In these instances, the child is not doing the thinking.

Not all technology in the classroom is without issue. For example, Donald Leu notes in his chapter in the 2000 edition of the *Handbook of Reading Research*, that it is difficult to conduct research on software uses in schools because the software changes so quickly. Teachers are deluged with software advertisements and might find it difficult to pick out high-quality programs. Leu presents a well-constructed and positive discussion on technology in the classroom. He recommends the following web sites to learn from teachers who are making good use of technology in their classrooms:

- Classrooms at Loogootee Elementary West in Indiana: www.siec.k12.in.us
- One or more of thousands of schools located at Web66: International School Web Site Registry: web66.coed.umn.edu/schools.html
- BreadNet at the Breadloaf School of English, Middlebury College: www.middlebury.edu/blse/breadnet/

Teaching English Language Learners and Struggling Readers

Language & Diversity

There is a difference between English language learners and struggling readers. The majority of English language learners would not have a problem learning to read in their mother tongue. In contrast, the English-speaking struggling reader has no second language burden to overcome. At times, however, some children are both English language learners and struggling readers. The teacher must keep these distinctions clear when working with both populations.

Fortunately, most of the instruction that English language learners and struggling readers need is quite similar. For example, these children thrive on more frequent and meaningful interactions with words. If an average reader needs ten to twenty exposures to learn a vocabulary word in several contexts, the struggling child might need forty, seventy, or more. These children respond to patience, teacher expertise, and carefully designed time in the school day for the experiences that are needed to succeed. Teachers should also involve families as much as possible and take full advantage of the specialists' support available in the school.

Struggling Reader

A hallmark of struggling readers across grade levels is inconsistency. In one day or in twenty minutes, a child will appear to know a word and then seem not to know it even in the same context. Effective teachers in every grade understand this and make the difference in struggling readers' lives. With understanding, you will be able to avoid frustration *(She knew this word ten minutes ago!)* and dig in to teach and teach until the children are able to retain word recognition. Several strategies have been found to be very successful with helping English language learners or struggling readers build word knowledge.

Tutoring

One-on-one tutoring is extremely helpful for these children. In fact, this kind of tutoring is sometimes the only way they can develop full literacy, have an opportunity to finish high school, and go on to higher education. It is vital that the tutor be a literacy expert. Only the highest level of expertise is worthy of these children. The education of struggling readers should not be placed in the hands of well-intended volunteers or paraprofessionals. They do not have the knowledge and skills needed to teach struggling children. Clearly, the problems of struggling readers take the teacher's very best instruction and effort; your professional development journey will help you become the reading specialist struggling readers must have.

Some positive benefits of expert tutoring are the following:

- Tutoring provides for closer observation, immediate feedback, and more opportunities to match instruction to the child's needs (to be in the child's zone of proximal development).

- Tutoring helps to build trust and respect between learner and teacher.

- Tutoring provides ways of building a disposition for learning: persistence and stamina along with concepts, skills, and strategies.

- Tutoring provides greater use of intensive instruction, an increase in rereading with highly predictable books, and optional word-building routines suggested by Ehri (1997).

Tutors can use more supportive materials that are custom-made for the individual child. Tutors and all teachers must be extremely careful in using books with controlled vocabulary. The value of these books is not supported by research (NRP, 2000), but the teacher should not dismiss a very brief use of these texts if there are ample additional high-quality reading materials and time to read them. Frequent language experience lessons can eliminate the need for any use of controlled vocabulary. The language experience approach is preferred, as it provides its own vocabulary control with words generated by the children.

Using a technique such as repetition of favorite things, the Language Experience Approach can be a meaningful way to teach all young children to read, particularly ESL children.

The Language Experience Approach

The **language experience approach (LEA)** assumes that children have enough word knowledge and emergent concepts to engage in talk about a topic of interest (Crawford, Allen, & Hall, 1995). Children can also dictate individual words and phrases, the complexity of dictations increasing as their proficiency with language increases. For example, young children might dictate the components of their favorite meal at a takeout restaurant. For older children, other high-interest topics include sports words, and music words, and shopping words. Across grade levels, most children will have good beginning reading and writing skills after 100–300 hours of participation with key words and the LEA.

This approach to reading constitutes a very clear example of a whole/part/whole approach to reading instruction. The whole is represented by the authentic text dictated by the children. We move to the parts when the children begin to recognize which sentences provide which information about their dictated text and when the children are beginning to recognize words and letters in the words. As the text is reassembled, the children read it as a whole again. Because there is a great deal of interaction between the teacher and the children in LEA, the teacher's role is an important one. Some key characteristics of the teacher in this role are as follows:

- Be a good listener.
- Be supportive.
- Be positive.
- Use the children's words and ideas. It is their story.
- Keep the length of dictations brief—five or six sentences for beginning readers.
- Praise the children's efforts.
- Always read *to* the children first.

TEACH IT!
1, 35

The language experience approach is an ideal methodology for helping children see the relationship between language and print, between sound and letter, especially children whose experiences with print are minimal. They are literally deconstructing and reconstructing the entire process, using language from their own experiences and backgrounds.

The approach can be used as an introduction to a more formal reading program or as a supplement, perhaps used one or two days each week. An example of an adapted language experience approach for struggling readers or English language learners is provided in the Teach It! box on pages 196–199 at the end of this chapter (Crawford et al., 1995).

Key Vocabulary Approach

Another helpful strategy that can be used for English language learners and struggling readers is the **key vocabulary approach** (Veatch et al., 1979). In the key vocabulary approach, a teacher might sit with a small group of students and have each child select a word of personal importance that the teacher has written on a card. Then the child traces the word with a finger as the teacher records the word in a key word book. The child then dictates a sentence using the key word, and the teacher records that sentence in the key word book as well. The child reads the dictation back to the teacher and illustrates it. Finally, each student copies the word and the sentence.

To extend this lesson, the teacher could meet with the children in groups of two—and later three—to read and interact with one another's words and sentences. These meetings combine rich discussion among the children, each word being loaded with personal meaning. The activity strongly encourages children's talk and dictation and reading of more than one sentence.

Both the LEA and the key vocabulary approach are highly scaffolded and make it possible for children to reach beyond what they can do on their own. Thus, the teacher helps them to work in their zone of proximal development. Each provides for authentic, meaningful, literacy experiences.

⭐ Assessment

Good teachers use a variety of **informal assessment** strategies that are systematic and provide evidence-based information on children's learning. These assessments are not produced for thousands or millions of children, as are standardized, formal assessments; they are not created to yield a comparison of one child to all other children at the same grade level. Rather, most informal assessments are carried out daily in teaching. Informal assessments are important to your demonstrating accountability. This is one reason why you need to watch children closely and make frequent notes on their development. For example, you can use a special rubric to track and record the developmental patterns in children's spelling, such as the one shown in Figure 5.8 on page 192. This allows you to review the kinds of errors children make at various developmental levels. Your analysis and what you know about the child provide information on what to teach.

Children's vocabulary should show growth over time and a growing understanding about meanings of words in various contexts (Beck, McKeown, & Omanson, 1987). Beck and her colleagues do not recommend formal (normed and standardized tests) for young children. Instead, they provide examples of the kinds of teacher-made assessments that are used in accord with the words children and you are reading. For example, the words *fiction, adventures,* and *rhymes* appear in Hopkins's *Good Books Good Times* (1990). After rereading the poem and after talking about word meanings, an assessment such as the following can be useful, either orally or in writing.

> *My dog had an* _____ *(rhyme or adventure).*
> *The three little bears story is* _____ *(fiction or rhyme).*

Giving a developmental word list to children in the emergent stage is not appropriate. Examples of emergent spellings are more evident and useful in these children's writing.

Early emergent: Lclo (I like animals); late emergent: I llke the zoo (I like the zoo)

The following examples reveal children's spelling knowledge (on one test) once they are in the early beginning stage and beyond (transitional, intermediate, and advanced).

Correct spellings	Examples of *letter name* and *within word* spellings	
Bed	bed	spells all but one
Ship	sep	word correctly
When	wan	
Lump	lop	
Float	flot	
Train	tran	
Place	plas	
Drive	driv	
Bright	brit	
Shopping	shopn	shoping

Correct spellings	Samples of *syllable affixes* and *derivational spellings*
Confusion	confusetion
Pleasure	plesour
Resident	resedent
Puncture	punchure
Confidence	confedense
Fortunate	fopchininte

Correct spellings		
Succession	sucession	successtion
Propellant	propelent	propellent
Commotion	cumotion	comotion
Criticize	critasize	criticise
Reversible	reversable	reversable
Except	ecsert	exsert

FIGURE 5.8

Developmental Spelling Rubric.

Source: From *Words Their Way: Word Study for Phonics, Vocabulary, and Spelling Instruction,* 2nd ed. by Donald R. Bear, Marcia Invernizzi, Shane R. Templeton, and Francine Johnson. Copyright © 2000. Reprinted by permission of Pearson Education Inc., Upper Saddle River, NJ.

Children can also write or dictate their own sentences using new vocabulary words. Beck, McKeown, and Omanson (1987) provide word association assessments for older children, such as the following:

> *Having discussed the words,* accomplice *and* novice, *children associate the words with the following question.*
> *Which word goes with crook?* _____ *(accomplice, buddy)*

Increase the number of words and questions to challenge children. For the average child, a weekly writing/word sample taken during word study activities and a monthly developmental spelling test (see Bear et al., 2000, pp. 288–301) are usually sufficient for assessment purposes. For children you worry about, collect a writing sample twice a week, write more notes, and give these children a developmental spelling test more often. Keep checking, comparing, and contrasting different kinds of data (spelling, vocabulary) at the developmental level that most accurately represents the child. Then engage in the teach/assess cycle until improvement is shown.

Successful Tools

Running records (Clay, 1985) and miscue analysis (Goodman, Watson, & Burke, 1987) are among the most useful tools available for capturing and understanding reading accomplishments and problems.

RUNNING RECORD.   A running record codes and records a child's oral reading performance, which is recorded on paper (or on a formal running record form, as shown in Figure 5.9 on page 194). As the child reads orally, the teacher marks and codes correctly read words and errors. Here is an example of coding a running record:

A child sees the sentence "A desert snake lives under rocks" and reads the sentence as "A desert snake long under rocks." In capturing oral reading, the teacher makes checks or slashes for each correct word and identifies errors

A	desert	snake	lives	under	rocks.
/	/	/	long	/	/

This example shows that the child is using syntax, semantics, and graphophonemic information correctly and has an error on one word, saying *long* for *lives*. The teacher can then see that the child is using letter/sound relationships *(both words begin with the letter L)* and determines what the child knows about snakes *(they are long)*. However, the teacher sees a problem, since "A desert snake long under rocks" is not a sensible sentence. The teacher also notices that the child is not analyzing the whole word; for example, the child saw *l* (in *lives*) and guessed, using prior knowledge. A young child must be taught to analyze the entire word. If the child stops and tries to self-correct his or her reading, this is a very good sign. The teacher marks the error but also marks the child's attempt at self-correction (or successful self-correction). Once a large oral reading sample (about 100 words) has been collected, the teacher scores it. With 95 percent of the words correct, the child is reading at the instructional level. The running record score helps the teacher determine what to do next. The teacher knows how to intervene (stay at this level book for a while, step up a level, or step back a level), recognizes which cueing systems need to be taught, and decides to emphasize the use of all cueing systems.

All primary teachers should learn and use the running records assessment; however, note that Clay (1985) designed running records for first grade *only* when fully correct reading supports attention to details, fluency, and word and text meaning. Also, because running records focus on errors and correctness, some teachers prefer to use miscue analysis, which focuses on the quality of miscues (rather than correct word reading). Both assessments are valuable.

SUMMARY OF RUNNING RECORD

Name:_____ Date:_____ D. of B._____ Age:_____yrs _____mths
School:_____ Recorder:_____

SUMMARY OF RUNNING RECORD

Text Titles	Running Words Error	Error Rate	Accuracy	Self-Correction Rate
1. Easy:_____	_____	1:_____	_____ %	1:_____
2. Instructional:_____	_____	1:_____	_____ %	1:_____
3. Hard:_____	_____	1:_____	_____ %	1:_____

Directional Movement:_____

ANALYSIS OF ERRORS   Cues used and cues neglected
Easy:_____
Instructional:_____
_____
Hard:_____
_____

CROSS-CHECKING ON CUES

Page	E	SC	Cues Used*	
			E	SC

FIGURE 5.9

A Running Record.

Teacher Self-Assessment

Within the assessment cycle, teachers use various methods of teaching to keep instruction interesting for children. Gradually expand your teaching to more challenging words. However, keep in mind that if children are pushed to their frustration level, they will not succeed. (Nothing succeeds like success.) Following is an example of a second-grade teacher's observation/assessment discussion with her team teachers:

> *I worked with Michele today. She is putting extra vowels in some words and leaving needed vowels out in others. Today, she spelled chin chian and cream crem; this is a pattern for her. I looked it up in a textbook, and this means that she is using but confusing vowel and consonant patterned words. Easy to see, but now what? She is on the verge of getting it but needs help. Here is what I am thinking. First of all, I don't think she can read the words she is trying to spell—chin and cream are not known words for her. I need to step back to a point at which she can succeed. What do you think? Give me some feedback.*

This teacher received suggestions from the team on increasing Michele's writing, an increase in teaching spelling patterns and vocabulary, and a strong teach/assess cycle. Effective assessment is every bit as critical as effective teaching. Teachers benefit from comparing and contrasting their ideas with those of others and through using multiple assessment measures. If the opportunity for collaboration does not exist in your building, create it with at least one other teacher. With teachers in your building, create regular meetings to talk shop before or after school, at planning times, or during working lunches.

Because of their many variables, teaching and learning are always in flux. Assessment helps to make order and sense of teaching and learning. For direction and planning, you will learn what children know on a daily basis. When physicians prescribe medication, they are following a routine that is grounded in research on groups of people. In addition, however, physicians tell patients, "Get back to me if this doesn't help within three days, and call me if you have any serious side effects." Modern medicine is wonderful, and much of its success depends on knowing what generally works and on the individual's responses. There is no silver bullet in the practice of medicine or the practice of education. However, we have good evidence on more successful medical and teaching practice that we must use to improve.

TEACH IT!

★ ★ ★ ★

The Language Experience Approach for English Language Learners and Struggling Readers

The Language Experience Approach (Crawford et al., 1995) works for people of all ages who are learning to read and need additional support. This approach is a cumulative process of several steps. There are many variations in how the steps may be presented, but the following approach is consistent with the whole/part/whole philosophy and is effective with English language learners.

First Lesson: In the first twenty- to thirty-minute lesson with children, the teacher should complete the three steps.

Step 1: Talking about experiences

- Explain the procedure you are going to use and that together you will create something that will help them read (first few lessons only).

- Talk with the children about something they are interested in and enjoy. Ask questions, and as they respond, praise their ideas, and let them know that these will make a good story.

Step 2: Dictation

- Ask the children, "What shall I write about your ideas? Tell me what you want to say."

- During the first lessons, ask a child to point to the place on the chart where you should begin writing. If the child is not sure, guide his or her hand to the upper left corner.

- Write their words on the chart or chalkboard as they watch.

- Read each idea or sentence to the children and ask them to read it back to you. Read it with them and then have them read it without you. Do this with each idea or sentence before going on.

Step 3: Reading the Text

- Tell the children that now it is time to read their text.

- Read the text *to* them, and ask them to watch, explaining that your hand will be under the part you are reading.

- Next, ask them to read along *with* you. If this seems difficult, read it to them again. You might want to do this several times.

If at all possible, give the children copies of their text after the lesson. After several sessions, they can begin to copy their own. They should not copy their stories until they can read them alone. At the beginning, have them copy only one or two sentences.

In this initial two-day cycle of LEA, the first lesson consists of motivation and discussion, dictation and reading, and shared reading, as described above. On the following day, there are several additional steps.

Second Lesson
Step 1: Reading the Text

- Tell the children that they are going to read their text again.

- Read the text *to* them, and ask them to watch, explaining that your hand will be under the part you are reading.

- Then, ask them to read along *with* you. If this seems difficult, read it to them again.

Step 2: Reassembling the Text

- Before the lesson, copy each sentence from the dictated text of the previous day onto a sentence strip.

- Have the children look at the original complete text and then look for the first idea or sentence among the sentence strips.

- When it has been located, encourage a child to try to read it.

- Then ask the child to place it at the top of a sentence strip holder that is standing next to the chart rack holding the original text.

- Ask all of the children to read the sentence or idea together.

- Line by line, the children search for the other corresponding sentences, read them, and arrange them in descending order according to the original dictated text.

- As each sentence strip is placed, the children read it and then read the entire text from the reassembled text up to that point. The teacher can also ask the children to point at the sentence that tells ....

This two-day cycle is repeated once or twice every week with a new theme for each set of lessons.

Keep in mind that children will not learn all of the words in the initial language experience charts they work with. Nonetheless, continue to develop new charts with new themes to maintain their interest. They will have many opportunities for rereading previous charts and learning those other words later.

After a period of time, usually several weeks, you will likely notice that many children are beginning to recognize individual words in new dictations that they have used in previous lessons, even without help from the teacher. At that point, the teacher can add a third lesson on sight vocabulary development and establish a three-day cycle instead of two.

Third Lesson

Step 1: Reassembling the Words into Sentences

- Before the third day in the cycle, the teacher should cut each sentence strip from the second day into individual words.

- On the chalk rail or in the sentence strip holder, the teacher can place the word cards for the first sentence from the original text in random order and ask the children to reassemble the words into sentences on the basis of their recognition of many of those words. They can refer to the original story if necessary.

- As they complete each sentence, they should read it aloud.

- As they add sentences, they should read each one and then the entire text up to that point.

(continued on next page)

TEACH IT!

★ ★ ★ ★

Continued

- Other word activities to use in the lesson are as follows:

- Give word cards from the sentences to the children, and ask them to find the words in the text.

- Say, "Here is the word _____. Find the same word in the text. Put the paper under where you see the same word in the text."

- Make a copy of a text with some words left out. The copy should be just like the original except that there will be empty spaces where a word is missing. Tell the children that some words are missing and ask whether they can figure out what the missing words are. Read the text with the children. Pause briefly when you come to a missing word. Write in the missing words when the children tell you what belongs in the empty space. You might want to have the missing words written at the bottom of the page before starting this activity.

- Ask the children keep a collection of the words they learn. These collections will be their personal word files. At the beginning, they will just collect the words. After they have fifteen or twenty words, they can do practice activities and play games with their word files.

- Ask children to point to a word they know or to put their hands around it. Ask them to tell you what the word is. Praise them if they are correct. If they are not correct, tell them what the word is, or find the word they said. Read it to them, and then ask them to read it.

- Write some of the words from the text on pieces of paper. Have the children find the words in the text. You can say, "Here is the word _____. Find the same word in the text. Put the paper under where you see the same word in the text." They can also read the sentence in which the word appears.

- Ask the children to find words that are names of people or places, words that are the names of animals or colors or foods or clothing, words that are things in the out-of-doors, words that are important to them, and words that show an action.

These cards can then be used as an individual or pair activity after the lesson by placing them in envelopes, one envelope for each sentence and labeled by the colors on the reverse of the cards. Before cutting the sentence strips into words, however, draw a straight and centered crayon line the long way down the middle of the reverse of each sentence strip, using a yardstick to make it straight. Each sentence strip should have a unique color. When there are no remaining unused colors, two crayons of different colors can be used simultaneously so that the cards from each sentence strip have a different color or colors on the reverse.

The vocabulary cards from different sentence strips are inevitably mixed up as children reassemble them into sentences at their desks or tables, and they are easily sorted back into groups of words for each original sentences according to the colors on the reverse side. If you draw a curved line on the reverse, the very bright children will quickly discover that they can reassemble the curved line like a puzzle without reading the words on the other side, resulting in the correct sentence when they are reversed back. A straight colored line on the reverse ensures that the children will read the words to reassemble the sentences.

Several weeks or a few months after the sight vocabulary phase is introduced, many children will likely begin to attack new words using knowledge they have intuited about phoneme-grapheme correspondences in words they already recognize. This is a sign to add a fourth day to the cycle, a day for word analysis using the context of words the children now recognize at sight.

Fourth Lesson

Step 1: Word Recognition Study

- Ask the children to read the story.

- Ask them to find words that begin alike. Finding words that start with the same letter and sound is a way in which some children learn to associate letters and sounds. They will learn most effectively about letters and sounds from words they already know.

Using an inductive questioning strategy, you can lead the children to draw conclusions, that is, phonic generalizations, out of their observations of letters and corresponding sounds that appear in words they know. They will also begin to apply those generalizations to new words they have not seen before. Word recognition instructional activities that you might otherwise use in direct instruction lessons can be used with words from the children's sight vocabularies and from their dictations. This makes powerful use of their background knowledge and helps them to extend their knowledge of sounds and letters in known words to new words. You can also bring out old language experience charts from time to time for review lessons and practice. Repeated readings develop automaticity, the stage at which students recognize words without paying attention to them, permitting their attention to focus instead on comprehension (Samuels, 1979).

Refer to your **Teach It!** booklet for further activities you can use to reinforce concepts discussed in this chapter.

FOR REVIEW

Throughout the elementary grades, children need systematic, frequent, and flexible opportunities to learn words. They must have word recognition instruction that is grounded in reading as a sense-making and meaningful activity. Many word-learning activities may be used successfully from grades one to eight in exclusive practice time periods of about ten to fifteen minutes. About thirty minutes of word work in context and in exclusive teaching and practice usually works for most children. Use a whole/part/whole approach in highly contextualized word instruction, especially in exclusive word study. That is, always return to word, sentence, and text meaning.

This chapter focused on word recognition, what it contributes to the reading process, and why it is important. Vocabulary teaching is a critical part of word learning across all grade levels; the chapter provided background and specifics on vocabulary development. Specifics included aspects of synthetic phonics, aspects of reading, and how to teach vocabulary from kindergarten to eighth grade. This chapter highlighted phonics and how to handle phonics and teaching word recognition, how much phonics to teach and for how long, and how to conduct word and phonics assessments. The graphophonemic (phonics) cueing system was included. Children's word learning development was described from emergent to advanced stages, along with teaching strategies for each stage from kindergarten to eighth grade. Ongoing assessment, an inseparable part of instruction, was emphasized. English language learners and struggling readers were given specific attention.

For Your Journal

1. Imagine a grade level you wish to teach or are teaching. Make a list of things you think you need to know about teaching words. Jot down any related concerns or frustrations you have at this point or anticipate.
2. Try this on your own, or work with a partner. Review the "Eeensy Weensy Spider" lesson described in the chapter opening vignette, and make a list of instances when Ms. Gupta engaged the children in demonstration and immersion. Then search for an instance or two of her helping the children engage in attention to detail.

★ Taking It to the World

Interview two friends or family members. Ask them to tell you about learning to spell in school. Find out whether they think they are good spellers, and ask them what spelling strategies their teachers used and whether these strategies were successful. Compare these strategies with those you read about in this chapter. Have your interviewees spell some words from an advanced spelling list. Engage with them in an analysis of their spellings with the list and the kinds of correct and incorrect spelling people have at the syllable juncture and derivational relation stages. Have a conversation about your findings and the spelling process. Share some of the strategies you are learning to teach.

⭐ Being a Professional Reading Teacher

There is great controversy about how children learn to recognize words as they read. What are some of the key elements of this controversy, and how are they supported in research and applied in best practice?

Fluency

- How can you recognize when a child has reached the level of fluency in oral reading? What aspects of fluency, above and beyond the use of graphophonic cues, indicate that children understand what they are reading aloud?
- What is meant by the term *synergistic* when it is applied to the roles of cueing systems in fluency?

Word Recognition and Vocabulary

- According to recent research, what is the optimum amount of phonemic awareness instruction for children? What are some possible outcomes of not providing this instruction? What are some possible outcomes of exceeding it by a wide margin?
- What are some arguments to support the desirability of children learning some very common words by sight or memory?
- What is the relationship between knowledge of vocabulary and reading? How can vocabulary be increased without drill and memorization activities?

Spelling

- What are the implications of stages of spelling in a developmental view of learning?
- What are some positive effects of using word sorts for improving word recognition and spelling?

Your Portfolio

Including a statement of your philosophy about teaching beginning reading in your portfolio provides evidence of how you view children and reading. It also provides a window on your writing abilities. Think about including a reflection about why you incorporated such a statement into your portfolio. Supporting your views with scientific research evidence strengthens your statement. Among many possible sources of evidence are the following refereed professional journals: *Reading Research Quarterly, The Journal of Literacy Research, The Reading Teacher,* and the *Journal of Adolescent and Adult Literacy.* Additional sources are cited in the chapter.

Teaching Resources

Word sorts are very useful activities for strengthening children's abilities in word recognition and spelling. Now is a good time to begin accumulating different kinds of prompts to use in word sorts at many levels and for a variety of purposes.

Technology Connections

1. The International Reading Association holds that it is the responsibility of teachers to prepare students for a future that will require new literacies. These include becoming users of computers, high-quality software, and word processing. Visit the association's special Focus on Technology web site at www.reading.org/focus/tech.html, and investigate what IRA is doing to help reading teachers incorporate technology into their classes.

2. Visit Learning Media at www.learningmedia.com, and click on the "Literacy and Media" button to learn more about key areas of literacy. Investigate the menu options at the left of the page. What can you find out about guided reading? What are the steps to guided reading? What other key topics in literacy education does this web site cover?

3. Many useful articles are available online through the International Reading Association. The following web sites offer additional information on some of the major topics in this chapter:

    *   Using think-alouds to analyze word sorts: www.readingonline.org/articles/fresch

    *   Teaching vocabulary to adolescents to improve comprehension: www.readingonline.org/articles/curtis

    *   Effects of traditional versus extended word study spelling instruction on students' orthographic knowledge: www.readingonline.org/articles/abbott

4. Visit the Scholastic Software Club web site (http://teacher.scholastic.com/clubs/) to investigate some of the various software options you can use in the classroom. Conduct your own review of materials you think might be helpful when you teach.

Connect with Research

Research Navigator.com

Review the following key words from the chapter, and then connect to Research Navigator (http://www.researchnavigator.com) through this book's companion web site to conduct a search into research on each of the various topics as they relate to reading and literacy education today.

analytic phonics	phonogram patterns	synthetic phonics
decoding	phonological recoding	vertical listing
fluency	semantic web	whole/part/whole approach
informal assessment	sight word	whole-word approach
key vocabulary approach	structured analysis	word recognition

Further Readings

Baer, B., Invernizzi, M., Templeton, S., & Johnston, F. (2003). *Words Their Way*. New York: Prentice-Hall.

An activity-based text that presents theory about word recognition and spelling and provides numerous spelling and phonics activities.

Beck, I. L., McKeown, M. G., & Kucan, L. (2002). *Bringing Words to Life: Robust Vocabulary Instruction.* New York, NY: Guilford Press.

A rich discussion on vocabulary development that also provides practical examples and advice on teaching vocabulary across the grade levels.

Meyer, R. (2002). Killing Us Softly with Phonics. *The Reading Teacher, 79,* 2–27.

This article contains a good discussion of a mandated phonics program and a teacher who learned how to work with it.

Strickland, D. S., Ganske, K., Monroe, J. K. (2002). *Supporting Struggling Readers and Writers: Strategies for Classroom. Intervention 3–6.* Portland, ME: Stenhouse Publishers for IRA.

Provides a thoughtful discussion of factors that contribute to success and failure in literacy and offers best-practice tips for helping low-achieving students and English language learners, including successful intervention strategies.

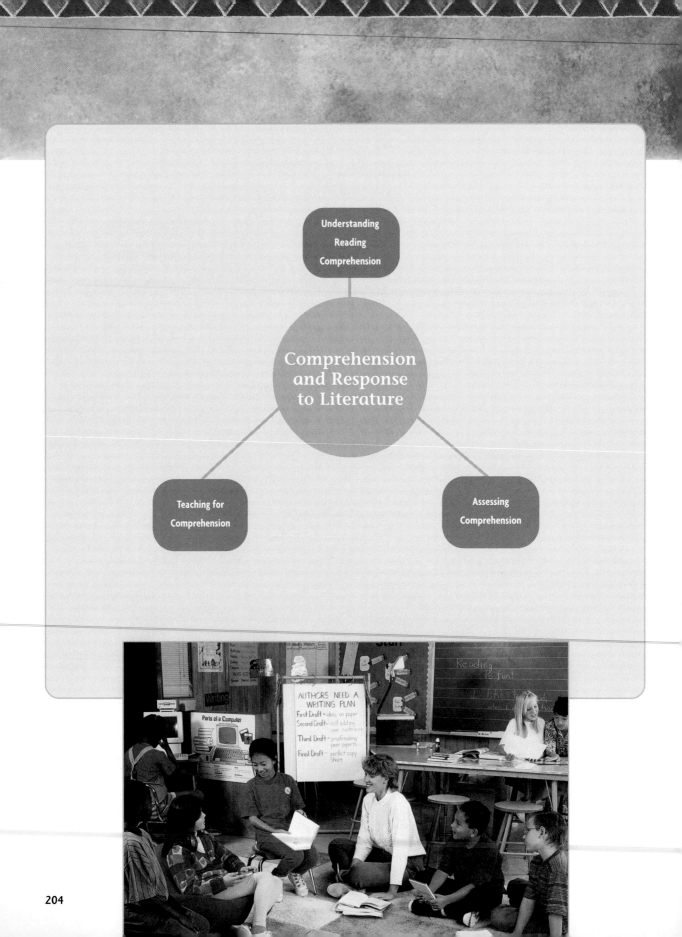

Comprehension and Response to Literature

T he following questions will help get you thinking about the topics of this chapter. Answer true or false in response to each statement. As you read and learn more about the topics in these statements, double-check your answers. See what interests you and what prompts your curiosity toward more understanding.

Anticipation Guide

_____ **1.** Comprehension, or understanding what you read, is mostly a process of memorizing the details of the author's message.

_____ **2.** Schema theory holds that readers understand what they read by using what they already knew to interpret the new information.

_____ **3.** Readers vary considerably from one another in what they understand and take away from a text.

_____ **4.** Comprehension is the aspect of reading that has traditionally gotten the most attention in classrooms.

_____ **5.** Good teachers show how readers read with comprehension, by "demonstrating their own thought processes when they read."

_____ **6.** Good comprehension lessons have three parts: _Consolidation, Building Knowledge,_ and _Anticipation,_ in that order.

_____ **7.** The structure of the text helps the reader make sense of what is written.

_____ **8.** Struggling readers need an entirely different kind of instruction in comprehension from more able learners.

_____ **9.** Drama has no place in the teaching of reading comprehension.

Reading Activity in a Fourth Grade Classroom

The students in Hank da Silva's fourth grade at North Street Elementary School can predict the day's events in broad outline but not completely. They know that after the morning class meeting, they will talk about their topics in social studies. They have been reading about the settlement of the Great Plains in their social studies text. At the same time, they have been reading Patricia McLachlan's *Sarah, Plain and Tall* and Laura Ingalls Wilder's *The Little House on the Prairie.* Mr. da Silva reads to them from *Letters from a Woman Homesteader,* a work of nonfiction told in the form of letters home from a feisty single woman in the 1880s. He has also bookmarked and assigned three Internet sites where students will find information about the settlement of the Great Plains by European Americans.

The class has written dual-entry diaries every day about their readings. They have also created a Venn diagram comparing what skills people have to have if they move to a new place now compared to what skills people needed in the days of the homesteaders. Figure 6.1 shows what the class has come up with.

This morning, Mr. da Silva is conducting a discussion of a couple of pages of the social studies book. He begins by pointing out that sometimes textbooks do not make their meanings very clear.

"Take right here, for instance," he points out. "The text says, 'Westward expansion gave the new country a constant sense of excitement, of new possibilities.' What do you suppose the author means by that sentence? Let's start with 'Westward expansion.' What do you suppose he means by *expansion*? If the author were here, what do you think he would say about that?"

After lunch, Mr. da Silva has reading workshop. According to the rotation chart on the wall, some students read independently. Today those students are doing something special: They are writing self-assessments about their reading comprehension, which they will later give to Mr. da Silva. A group of six students who are reading Phyllis Reynolds Naylor's

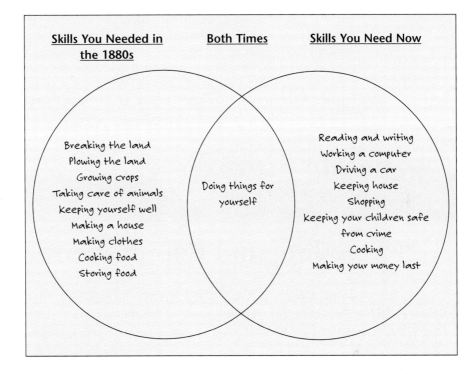

Skills You Needed in the 1880s

Breaking the land
Plowing the land
Growing crops
Taking care of animals
Keeping yourself well
Making a house
Making clothes
Cooking food
Storing food

Both Times

Doing things for yourself

Skills You Need Now

Reading and writing
Working a computer
Driving a car
Keeping house
Shopping
Keeping your children safe from crime
Cooking
Making your money last

FIGURE 6.1

What You Need to Live in a New Place.

Shiloh meet with Mr. da Silva for a literature circle; each of the six students is conducting a part of the discussion, according to a role she or he has been assigned. Mr. da Silva takes part in the discussion, but he also is taking occasional notes. He writes about how the discussion is going. He writes a note to remind himself to ask the students to ask more questions of each other in the literature circle rather than just reporting on what they think. He also makes a note that four of the students do not seem to make the connection between the boy's asking the shopkeeper for stale bread to feed the dog he has hidden away and the food that people in the community begin leaving for his father, a mail carrier. In other words, they are not making inferences. In the course of the next week, Mr. da Silva will make a point of reading with each one of these students to see what they know about reading comprehension. He will also teach a minilesson on making inferences during reading workshop tomorrow.

The goal of reading instruction is for all students to read with comprehension — understanding what they read. Comprehension in reading is also a sort of thermometer measuring the intellectual life of a classroom. True, teaching children to read with comprehension is partly a matter of teaching them a special set of reading skills. But it is also a matter of exposing students to literature, cultivating their knowledge about a range of subjects, stimulating their habits of inquiry, helping them make connections between ideas, and inspiring in them a broad range of interests. Students' reading comprehension has too often been left to chance, as if it would follow naturally from their learning to read the words. Indeed, surveys of reading instruction in elementary schools, from twenty years ago (Durkin, 1978–79) and more recently (Pressley, 1999),

STANDARDS & LITERACY

Reading and Comprehension

It has been noted that many schools have not given students as much explicit instruction in reading comprehension as they need (Durkin, 1978–79; Pressley et al., 1996). Such will not be the case in Texas as the state learning standards take hold there. The Texas standards for reading in elementary schools (Texas Education Agency, 1998) call for students to learn essentially the same subskills of comprehension and response that were discussed in this chapter:

Reading/comprehension. The student uses a variety of strategies to comprehend selections read aloud and selections read independently. The student is expected to:

(a) use prior knowledge to anticipate meaning and make sense of texts (K–3);

(b) establish purposes for reading and listening such as to be informed, to follow directions, and to be entertained (K–3);

(c) retell or act out the order of important events in stories (K–3);

(d) monitor his/her own comprehension and act purposefully when comprehension breaks down such as rereading, searching for clues, and asking for help (1–3);

(e) draw and discuss visual images based on text descriptions (1–3);

(f) make and explain inferences from texts such as determining important ideas and causes and effects, making predictions, and drawing conclusions (1–3);

(g) identify similarities and differences across texts such as in topics, characters, and problems (1–2);

(h) produce summaries of text selections (2–3); and

(i) represent text information in different ways, including story maps, graphs, and charts (2–3).

Reading/literary response. The student responds to various texts. The student is expected to:

(a) respond to stories and poems in ways that reflect understanding and interpretation in discussion (speculating, questioning) in writing, and through movement, music, art, and drama (2–3);

(b) demonstrate understanding of informational text in various ways such as through writing, illustrating, developing demonstrations, and using available technology (2–3);

(c) support interpretations or conclusions with examples drawn from text (2–3); and

(d) connect ideas and themes across texts (1–3).

have found that word recognition instruction is very common, but it is less common to find teachers explicitly trying to develop their students' comprehension.

Developing reading comprehension is prominently featured in a set of twelve standards for literacy that were issued jointly by the International Reading Association and the National Council of Teachers of English in 1996 (see Table 6.1) The standards emphasize using explicit strategies for comprehending materials written in a variety of genres.

TABLE 6.1

Literacy Standards of the International Reading Association and the National Council of Teachers of English

1. Students read a wide range of print and nonprint texts to build an understanding of texts, of themselves, and of the cultures of the United States and the world; to acquire new information; to respond to the needs and demands of society and the workplace; and for personal fulfillment. Among these texts are fiction and nonfiction, classic and contemporary works.
2. Students read a wide range of literature from many periods in many genres to build an understanding of the many dimensions (e.g., philosophical, ethical, aesthetic) of human experience.
3. Students apply a wide range of strategies to comprehend, interpret, evaluate, and appreciate texts. They draw on their prior experience, their interactions with other readers and writers, their knowledge of word meaning and of other texts, their word identification strategies, and their understanding of textual features (e.g., sound-letter correspondence, sentence structure, context, graphics).
4. Students adjust their use of spoken, written, and visual language (e.g., conventions, style, vocabulary) to communicate effectively with a variety of audiences and for different purposes.
5. Students employ a wide range of strategies as they write and use different writing process elements appropriately to communicate with different audiences for a variety of purposes.
6. Students apply knowledge of language structure, language conventions (e.g., spelling and punctuation), media techniques, figurative language, and genre to create, critique, and discuss print and nonprint texts.
7. Students conduct research on issues and interests by generating ideas and questions, and by posing problems. They gather, evaluate, and synthesize data from a variety of sources (e.g., print and nonprint texts, artifacts, people) to communicate their discoveries in ways that suit their purpose and audience.
8. Students use a variety of technological and information resources (e.g., libraries, databases, computer networks, video) to gather and synthesize information and to create and communicate knowledge.
9. Students develop an understanding of and respect for diversity in language use, patterns, and dialects across cultures, ethnic groups, geographic regions, and social roles.
10. Students whose first language is not English make use of their first language to develop competency in the English language arts and to develop understanding of content across the curriculum.
11. Students participate as knowledgeable, reflective, creative, and critical members of a variety of literacy communities.
12. Students use spoken, written, and visual language to accomplish their own purposes (e.g., for learning, enjoyment, persuasion, and the exchange of information).

Source: From *Standards for the English Language Arts* by International Reading Association, Newark, DE, and National Council of Teachers of English, Urbana, IL. Copyright © 1996. Reprinted by permission of the International Reading Association.

Understanding Reading Comprehension

Our understanding of reading comprehension and literary response, as well as our expertise in teaching them, has grown tremendously over the last twenty years. With advances in cognitive psychology came the recognition of the reader's active role in comprehending. The reader is a sense-maker, one who works to construct meaning. What do people do when they understand something that they read? Many reading specialists' favorite explanation of the act of comprehension is *schema theory*, articulated by Richard Anderson and David Pearson (Anderson & Pearson, 1984). As we seek to understand how individual readers make different meanings from texts, another theory comes into play: *reader response theory*.

Schema Theory

Schema theory (Anderson & Pearson, 1984) holds that readers understand what they read by finding clues in it that lead them to summon up frameworks of stored knowledge that they have in their memories. Then they use those frameworks, or *schemas*, to make sense of the details in the text. Once readers have a schema in mind, they use it to make sense of the other details. There is a complementary relationship between readers' schemas and the details on the page: Reading the details tells them what schemas to evoke, and evoking the schemas helps them to make sense of the details. Consider the following example:

> Shawn's footsteps slowed as he approached the door to Belinda's apartment. Two children were ahead of him, already knocking on the door. They were dressed in the proper clothing. But Shawn had on his old jeans. Shawn was also embarrassed because he was empty-handed. His mother had been at work when he got home from school, and he hadn't any money of his own.
>
> The door swung open, and there was Belinda in a nice dress and a party hat.
>
> "Hi," she said. "Come on in."
>
> "Hi," he said as he sidled into the apartment, his hands behind his back. Inside, the table was set for the celebration and piled high with the things other children had brought. Shawn avoided the table and slid into a corner.
>
> Just then, Belinda's mother shouted from the kitchen, "Get ready to sing, everybody. Here it comes!" She marched ceremoniously in from the kitchen holding forth her beautiful creation, her face brightened by the nine tiny flames.

You probably worked out that the passage recounts a birthday party. Once you realized that, you evoked a cognitive scheme that helped you understand Shawn's embarrassment because he hadn't worn party clothes or brought what the other guests had piled on the table—a birthday present. You also knew what song would be sung ("Happy birthday to you . . ."), and what it was the mother proudly carried in from the kitchen (a birthday cake with nine candles). How much of what you understood about the passage was actually supplied by the text? And how much information did you yourself supply?

Schema theory is a powerful way of understanding comprehension. It shows us that students' prior knowledge (or their schemas) is very important to their reading comprehension. Furthermore, understanding is real activity. Readers do not passively absorb meaning from the page; they construct meaning by making sense of details according to the schemas they already possess in their memories. Understanding depends in part on the reader's will. Hence schema theory is often said to support a constructivist approach to reading comprehension.

Reader Response Theory

Different readers understand different things from the same text. The **reader response theory** provides some understanding of what happens when individual readers make meaning from texts (Bleich, 1978; Iser, 1978; Rosenblatt, 1978). As formulated by Louise Rosenblatt, reader response theory suggests that three considerations are involved whenever a fictional text is read meaningfully: the reader, the text, and the poem.

THE READER. The reader brings to the reading her or his knowledge of vocabulary; associations for words; experiences in the world with certain people, places, and things; and experiences in literature with certain authors, genres, plots, symbols, and themes. In the case of a birthday party, for example, the knowledge and associations would include the reader's experiences with birthdays, both as a member of a cultural group and as an individual.

THE TEXT. The text offers marks on the page put there by the author. Usually, the author is trying to orchestrate understandings and emotions in the reader. But the author's intended meaning might never be identical with the meaning that readers make for themselves. The author's words are suggestions only. It is up to the readers to bring the words to life in their own way.

THE POEM. From the reader's construction of the author's words is created *the poem*: a sort of virtual reality that comes into being in the reader's imagination as he or she reads and stays in memory after the reading is done. (Rosenblatt is using the historical sense of the word *poem*, meaning a "created thing," not necessarily something that rhymes!) The poem is what comes to mind when you think back on a book you have read. It is not just the author's exact words. It is not just your memories from your own life and your knowledge of word meanings and literary devices that you called to mind as you read. It is a construction that is made of both.

During the act of reading, the reader and the text transact as the poem is created, and the poem colors what the reader makes of the text. Once the reader has decided that a book is "about X," that interpretation will color what the reader selects for response from the author's words, from the text.

Rosenblatt made a distinction between what happens when readers respond to fictional texts and what happens when they respond to informational texts. When we read fiction, we take what Rosenblatt (1978) called an **aesthetic stance**—that is, we respond to the work with our feelings and thoughts as we create the poem. Most fictional works have meaning for us and tell us some kind of truth, but we take away the total or thematic meaning of the work and do not expect its parts to be literally true. In the real world, frogs and toads do not carry around picnic baskets, and hippopotamuses do not have loafers to pour pea soup into; but both Arnold Lobel's Frog and Toad books and James Marshall's George and Martha books tell children things about friendship that are arguably true in the real world.

When we read informational works such as an account of the geography of Ireland, we take a different stance and expect every detail in the work to correspond

Taking notes while reading can help the reader identify the details of information content and organize them for understanding.

truthfully to details in the real world. Because we can carry away facts and knowledge from the work, Rosenblatt calls the typical stance to nonfiction the **efferent stance**.

Even within a single work, readers might move back and forth between the aesthetic and efferent stances. For example, readers of Katherine Paterson's historical novel *Lyddie* (1994) take an aesthetic stance as they construct the character of a brave young woman who tries to make a life for herself in oppressive circumstances; but they also take an efferent stance as they learn details about life in a nineteenth century New England textile mill.

Based on observational studies of students reading and discussing literature, Judith Langer (1995) teased out a pattern of stances that describes what happens when readers create and work with the poems that Louise Rosenblatt brought to our attention. Langer's **envisionment** is a virtual stage-set constructed, with the help of the author's words, in the reader's imagination. Readers move in and out of several stances of the envisionment at different points in their reading. Langer's stances of envisionment are:

- *Being out and stepping into an envisionment.* From the author's clues about setting, characters, and dramatic situation, the reader begins to create in the mind's eye the virtual stage set. The reader tentatively picks up and tries out more and more clues as to what this virtual world is like, until he or she is able to leave something from the literal world behind and step into the envisionment.

- *Being in and moving through the envisionment.* Having created or co-created a mental image of the setting, characters, and dramatic situation, the reader now follows the logic of the plot forward while asking questions and seeking answers. At this point, the reader may feel completely absorbed in the moment-to-moment living of the fictional world of the text.

- *Stepping out and rethinking what is known.* Occasionally, the reader may pause to consider the text, wondering what will happen next or thinking about what the text means to the reader's own life.

- *Stepping out and objectifying the experience.* This fourth stance normally is taken after the reader has read the whole book. Reading through a text is a linear event, in which one thing leads to another; but when readers look back on the finished text the experience of it becomes whole and rounded. The reader objectifies the experience after reading the story.

Langer's concept of envisionments and the stances we take them toward is a helpful way of looking at the experiences of reading literature. This idea leads us to think of understanding literature as something different from understanding informational text. As other writers have pointed out, we understand literature not simply by comprehending and remembering the details. Rather, we use the details in a fictional text to create an imaginative whole and to comprehend and learn from fiction by relating that fictional whole to what we know about life.

THE WORLD OF READING

Reader Response in Action

Diane Barone (1992) reports on a second- and third-grade class in which the teacher was having her students record their reactions to each chapter of Roald Dahl's *Danny the Champion of the World* (1998) in a kind of response journal called a *dual-entry diary* (see page 227). An early chapter in the book describes the cozy days enjoyed by Dahl's protagonist, living in a gypsy wagon with his father. After reading this chapter, a student in the class wrote that he was expecting the woman to come into the story at any time. The teacher was puzzled, because the only woman that had been mentioned in the book was the boy's late mother, who had died before he was born. But in entry after entry, her student registered his worry that the woman might come into the story on the very next page. As it turned out, this young reader had lived a cozy existence for some time alone with *his* own father—until the father found a female companion. For the little boy, the woman really did come along, and the boy no longer had an exclusive claim to his father's attention.

The boy created a poem out of *Danny the Champion of the World* that was about the almost-too-good-to-be-true bliss of a boy's living alone with his father and his feeling of dread at its loss. The boy's concerns had led him to write responses that seemed bizarre at first.

Yet it serves as a good example of how stories can evoke different responses from different people, children included. Teachers need to be aware of this critical piece of information.

As the boy's reading of *Danny the Champion of the World* suggests, there can be striking variations in the interpretations or poems created by different readers. That is why David Bleich (1970) urges teachers to think of literature discussion groups as interpretive communities. *Interpretive communities* are places where readers share their responses to works of literature so that communities of understanding can be formed. The sharing of individual responses not only contributes to a larger understanding of a work, but also promotes students' awareness of each other's thinking. Becoming aware of others' thinking is of particular value when the students come from different social and cultural backgrounds.

It takes special approaches on the teacher's part to set up an interpretive community. Merely asking students to answer literal questions will not do it. What is needed is to create a risk-free environment and to conduct—or let students conduct—discussions that invite personal responses to questions such as, "What did you notice in the text? What did it make you think of? How did it make you feel?"

Critical Literacy

If schema theory and reader response theory were the only relevant accounts of how texts have meaning, newspapers would not print editorial pages, politicians would not make speeches, and television and radio programs would not be interrupted by advertisements. The fact is that texts (including storyboards for advertisements) are written by someone for a purpose, and that purpose is usually to have an effect on the reader (or viewer). Especially because the purpose is not always transparent, readers need to exercise their critical faculties to filter what they understand and are asked to believe from texts. **Critical literacy** is an approach to reading that stresses the reader's exercise of constructive skepticism in the face of a text. Often it is the unquestionable text that passes on messages we might want to challenge. When reading a persuasive text or even an informational text that we have reason to doubt, readers might ask questions like the following (modified from Browne & Keeley, 2000):

- What is the question this text is answering?
- What answer does it offer?
- Does it give good reasons for that answer?
- What has the text left unsaid?
- What other answer might I give to that question? Which seems stronger: my answer or the one offered by the text?
- Are there "facts" in the text that I might have reason to doubt?
- Does the text use loaded language (terms such as *trouble-maker* or *good citizen*) that smears or exalts what it is talking about without making a real argument against it or for it?
- Who wants me to believe this text? Why do they want me to believe it?

With the case of fiction, stories, as William Doty (1986) points out, usually pass on some attitude toward the social order—the rights, privileges, and relative worth of male and female, young and old, beautiful and unbeautiful, rich and poor, upper class and lower class, and so on. The story might do the following:

- *Challenge the social order* (as do Robert Munsch's *The Paper Bag Princess* (1992) and Jane Yolen's *Sleeping Ugly* (1997) with respect to sex roles)
- *Affirm the social order* (as do Frances Hodgson Burnett's *Little Lord Fauntleroy* (1906, 1996) and the early *Babar* stories with respect to the stratification of social classes)
- *Pass on assumptions about the social order without criticizing them* (as do so many fairy tales, such as "Cinderella" and "Snow White" with respect to sex roles)

When reading a fictional text, readers can ask questions such as the following:

- Who "won" in this story? What did he or she do to win? Who lost? Why? What lessons might be drawn from the winning and the losing?
- What difference would it make to the outcome of the story if the sex of the characters were changed (or the income group, race, or physical characteristics)? Why?
- With whom does the author of this work seem to want the reader to identify? That is, who is the reader supposed to be "for" and "against"? How can the reader tell?
- How would this story sound if it were told from the point of view of a different character?

Asking questions like this often brings to light prejudices in works that children might not agree with if these prejudices were stated clearly. Children might wonder, for example, why it is usually the female character (as in "Beauty and the Beast") who must be selfless in order to gain a reward, whereas the males get to go after what they want, or they might wonder what would have happened if the ugly duckling had remained ugly (Biklen, 1981). Would his ugliness have been grounds for others to shun him?

Acts of Comprehension

What are key strategies and skills that children and other readers use to comprehend text? Researchers have agreed on several. This list, derived from Pressley and Afflerbach (1995), captures the issue nicely. Comprehending a passage well involves the following:

Engaging prior knowledge

Knowing vocabulary

Visualizing details and events

Following the patterns of texts

Asking questions and pursuing answers

Making inferences

Monitoring comprehension

Noting main ideas from supporting details

Summarizing and rehearsing main ideas

TEACH IT!
11

**Family &
Community
Literacy**

ENGAGING PRIOR KNOWLEDGE.   When they begin to read, good readers focus on the topic of the text, decide what they already know about it, and make predictions about what they are likely to learn. As they read, they go back and forth between what they knew about the topic and what they are finding out. When they are finished reading, they might reexamine what they knew or thought they knew and take note of how their knowledge has changed on account of the reading they have done. Not all readers do this fully developed version of engaging prior knowledge and checking new information against it, but readers should at least sense the topic of the reading and be reminded of what they already know about it.

Families can support children's development of comprehension by keeping up their contributions to children's background knowledge and supporting children's voluntary reading. Teachers can remind parents of the importance of taking their children to the library and museums and of putting informative children's magazines on their children's gift lists. *Ranger Rick* (www.nwf.org/rangerrick/index.html), the nature magazine, features enticing photographs of animals in the wild and articles on wildlife that fascinate children ages seven and up. *Cobblestone* (www.cobblestonepub.com) magazine features interesting articles on historical topics that appeal to children ages nine and up. *National Geographic World* (www.nationalgeographic.com) features highly illustrated articles on everything from undersea exploration to mountain climbing, and *Sports Illustrated for Kids* (www.sikids.com) follows teams and players and talks about the basics of the sports.

For general reading, including stories to read, *Cricket* magazine (www.cricketmag.com) for children ages eight and up and *Ladybug* for slightly younger children feature work that makes good reading by well-known and aspiring children's authors. *Highlights for Children* (www.highlights.com) also features stories and interesting informational articles, as well as riddles and games.

VISUALIZING DETAILS AND EVENTS.   In creating works of fiction, authors take pains to describe events so the reader can visualize them and be drawn into the scene, or in Langer's term, "step into the envisionment." Frances Temple begins *The Beduin's Gazelle,*

> *Halima sat with her chin resting on her knees, close enough to touch her kinspeople, yet with her mind far away. The singsong of the storyteller's voice lulled her. The lanterns threw a soft glow on the dark wall of the tent, on the red and brown embroidered cushions, on the familiar faces of the listening women and children. Halima played with her bangles, her mind drifting with the story.* (Temple, 1996, p. 1)

The author's appeal to sights, sounds, and touch leads a competent reader to create an image of the scene in a beduin's tent in North Africa, where the events of the novel will soon unfold.

KNOWING VOCABULARY.   Knowing the words in a text is an issue both in word recognition and in comprehension. As an aspect of comprehension, vocabulary items can be considered building blocks of understanding. It is possible to understand a text without knowing all the words, by making inferences from the context surrounding the unknown word. But making such inferences ties up concentration that might otherwise be used to comprehend the larger meaning of the text. Whether by making important information unavailable or by distracting attention, a shortage of vocabulary makes comprehension harder. A good reader has a vocabulary available that is nearly equal to the vocabulary she or he encounters in reading.

FOLLOWING THE PATTERNS OF TEXTS.   Texts come to us in **genres**. Genres are a combination of purpose and pattern. The narrative or story genre, for instance, has the purpose of relating fictional events in an entertaining or edifying way that usually evokes an emotional response. Stories follow structures or patterns called *story grammars*. A story usually introduces a main character and other characters in a setting, and engages that character in an initiating event that leads the character to set a goal; then there might follow a series of episodes in which the character makes attempts to reach the goal. Each attempt has an outcome, then follows a consequence, the state of affairs at the end of the story (Stein & Glenn, 1979). As we discussed in Chapter 3, research and experience have shown that even by the time they are in first grade, listeners and readers use their knowledge of story grammar both to understand and to produce their own stories (Temple et al., 1992).

Of course, texts have other kinds of structures, too. Patterns such as lists, **taxonomies** (hierarchical lists), descriptions, comparisons, and cause-and-effect and problem-and-solution explanations have been shown to guide readers' understanding. Persuasive essays use the structure of claims, reasons for the claims, and evidence to support the reasons.

Technology

Text on the Internet has a sort of **concatenated** structure; that is, items are linked to other items, as in a chain or a web. Readers can click on a term within an entry and be taken at once to a new entry that explains the term. While reading the new entry, readers might be invited to click on another term within that entry and be taken to a new entry explaining that term. So an entry on mammals might allow readers to click and go to an explanatory entry about elephants. There they might be invited to click and go to another entry or even a whole new web site on Tanzania, since that country is home to many elephants. The challenge to the reader, of course, is to keep in mind the topic of the original search and the questions that guided that search.

Reading by the pattern can help to guide the reader's understanding below surface events toward the deeper logical structure of the text. Readers who know how to follow the patterns of text when they read learn to raise questions and search for answers according to the way the text reveals its contents. When they are reading a story, readers can identify the problem that the character has and try to anticipate the solution to the problem. When they are reading a problem-and-solution explanation, readers can identify the problem and look for solutions.

ASKING QUESTIONS AND PURSUING ANSWERS.   As they summon up ideas related to the topic of the text, good readers make predictions about what they will find out. Then they monitor what they are learning from the text to see whether those predictions are being confirmed. When good readers read a story, they can follow the outlines of the plot to generate predictions and experience satisfaction or surprise as those predictions are confirmed or not by what happens. In fact, authors count on readers' acts of prediction to evoke readers' emotional experiences of suspense, surprise, and completion as patterns of events raise expectations and sometimes thwart and sometimes satisfy them.

MAKING INFERENCES.   When readers have to piece together information themselves that is not directly supplied by the text, they are making **inferences**. Fiction writers often leave gaps in the text (Iser, 1974) that must be filled in by the reader's inferences, and readers experience the activity of filling those gaps as engagement. Even young readers make inferences. For example, kindergarten children enjoy listening to Harry Allard and James Marshall's popular picture book *Miss Nelson Is Missing* (1977)**,** about a too-sweet school teacher who is replaced by a very mean substitute teacher. Most young children, but not all, can infer the substitute teacher's identity from the next-to-the-last page of the book. There, the illustration shows (but the text does not mention) an ugly black dress hanging in the sweet teacher's closet underneath a box with the word *WIG* written in upside-down letters.

MONITORING COMPREHENSION.   Good readers are aware when a text is making sense, and they are alerted when it does not. Perhaps they misread a word, or they assumed that the text was going to say something that it does not. Then the breakdown in their comprehension leads them to go back and make a "repair." They reread the misinterpreted word or reconsider where the argument is going so that they again have the feeling that they are understanding the text. Comprehension monitoring, then, assumes that readers think on two planes: They think about what the text means, and they are also aware of their own understanding or lack of it.

In the case of fictional or poetic texts, in which there is figurative language or symbols, or irony to be navigated, the reader has more interpreting to do.

NOTING MAIN IDEAS AND SUPPORTING DETAILS.   Readers who are aware of the argument of the text can distinguish main ideas from small details. Consider, for example, a child reading this passage from *Charlotte's Web:*

> *On foggy mornings, Charlotte's web was truly a thing of beauty. This morning each strand was decorated with dozens of tiny beads of water. The web glistened in the light and made a pattern of loveliness and mystery, like a delicate veil. Even Lurvy, who wasn't particularly interested in beauty, noticed the web when he came with the pig's breakfast. He noted how clearly it showed up and he noted how big and carefully built it was. And then he took another look and saw something that made him set his pail down. There in the center of the web, neatly woven in block letters, was a message. It said:*
>
> SOME PIG!
>
> *Lurvy felt weak. He brushed his hand across his eyes and stared harder at Charlotte's web.* (White, 1952, p. 77).

There are many details in this passage about the way the spider's web looked. But a reader who gets the main idea will focus on the fact that the spider has written words, and they describe her friend Wilbur the pig, and they have been noticed with great surprise by Lurvy the farmhand. The child who has been following the plot of the story will realize that Charlotte's writing is a possible solution to the main problem of the book because they are meant to impress Wilbur's human owners so that they will spare the little pig's life.

Readers who distinguish main ideas do so by following the argument of the text. They understand the problems the text is setting out to solve, and they are aware when information is significant as answers to questions or solutions to problems posed by the text: Such information is a main idea.

SUMMARIZING AND REHEARSING MAIN IDEAS.   Once they identify main ideas, good readers might slow down, reread the passage that contained them, and rehearse the ideas so that they will remember them later (Pressley & Afflerbach, 1995). Following the reading, the readers might retell the main ideas to themselves, or they might reread important passages aloud to a friend. Good readers might reread the key passages in the text to make sure the main ideas were stated the way they remembered them. In this way, good readers hope to store the main ideas in memory and learn from the reading.

Scaffolding: From Strategies to Skill

Once you are aware of the component abilities that make for reading comprehension, you can deliberately and overtly teach readers to use those strategies until they become internalized, that is, until they become skills (Duffy & Roehler, 1989). You can teach reading strategies to children by using the four-part model introduced in Chapter 1:

- **Demonstration and immersion:** Reading and thinking aloud in front of the children to show them how you use the strategy.
- **Attention to detail:** Describing exactly how you use the strategy and getting children to verbalize how it is done;
- **Guided practice:** Getting students to practice the strategy while you observe them and give them corrective feedback;
- **Application and extension:** Reminding the children to use the strategy when they read independently so that they will internalize the strategy and make it a skill.

Skilled and struggling readers use the same processes to read with comprehension that we described above. But struggling readers might need more support to make sure they use all of these strategies and orchestrate them into fluent reading with comprehension. Kameenui (1998) recommends that teachers of struggling readers employ these steps:

Struggling Reader

1. *Make strategies explicit.* Through modeling, think-alouds, and regular reminding, show the students how to carry out each of the comprehension strategies we described in the previous sections.
2. *Supply scaffolding.* Scaffolding is temporary support for students as they learn to do a task or apply a skill. Scaffolding may be used temporarily and be withdrawn when students can function independently. An example of scaffolding is a story map, in which students are asked to identify the character, setting, problem, and solution in a story they are reading.

3. *Connect ideas.* Remind students of ideas they find in a text that they have seen on a field trip or in a lesson in another subject. Struggling readers might be so preoccupied by the act of making sense of what they read that they do not think about the larger ideas. They need the teacher to point out to them the relatedness of ideas.

4. *Provide background knowledge.* Struggling readers might not have the background knowledge they need to make sense of what they read. A story about an early twentieth century immigrant's journey from Europe to America will make little sense to a student who does not realize that Europe is a continent that lies thousands of miles across the ocean from America or that until a few years ago, travel from Europe was so difficult and expensive that people who made the trip could not go back.

5. *Review skills and ideas often.* Struggling readers need to be reminded of both the skills they have learned and the ideas they have gained. They need to be reminded of both, and they need to apply the tasks and ideas in new settings.

Teaching for Comprehension

Teaching for comprehension and response is not just a matter of teaching skills. Although it is important to develop children's reading strategies and support the strategies until they become skills, it is also important to develop children's familiarity with literature as well as their knowledge and interests.

Organizing Instruction for Comprehension and Response: The ABC Model

Children should have many opportunities to read for meaning and for pleasure in personally chosen books that are not used for instruction by the teacher (Block, 2000). Children should also have lessons in which the teacher guides them through aspects of comprehension so that the students will internalize those aspects and practice them when they are reading independently. Teaching comprehension successfully requires that teachers engage students' thinking and invite students to keep their minds appropriately active throughout the reading process. The ABC model offers instructional choices for guiding comprehension—for activities to be used before reading *(in the anticipation phase)*, during *(in the phase of building knowledge)*, and after reading (in the phase of *consolidation*) after Vaughn and Estes, 1986 and Steele and Meredith, 1997. The ABC model is flexible. Within its three parts or phases, the teacher can make many choices. So, eventually, can the students, since they need to internalize the pattern of thinking that is captured by this model and use it when they read independently.

TEACH IT!
11, 12

ANTICIPATION.   Before they read, readers should think about the topic, then recall their prior knowledge about it. If they don't have very much prior knowledge about the subject or if their thoughts about it are disorganized, the teacher might want to spend some time telling the students more about the topic and organizing their thinking about it. Readers should wonder how their present knowledge about the topic might relate to the text they are about to read. If they are to read an informational text, what do they still want to know about the topic that they might learn from this text? If it is a fictional text, what other works do they know by this author or in this genre? What does their prior knowledge lead them to expect from this reading? This preliminary phase of the lesson is called ***anticipation***.

Teaching goals in the anticipation phase are to prepare the students to read with comprehension. We want them to do the following:

- Connect the topic (or the genre, or the author) of the text they are about to read with their prior knowledge

- Raise questions about the text they are about to read and set purposes for reading

- Know the vocabulary they will need to make sense of the text

Several teaching approaches can be used to achieve these goals.

Focusing Questions.   Questions that make a connection between what the students already know and what the reading will cover are valuable ways to prepare for a reading. In keeping with the goal of encouraging principled knowledge, it is advisable to steer questions toward the main ideas of the passage.

For example, a group of fifth graders are reading Pam Conrad's *Pedro's Journal* (1992), a fictional account of Columbus's historic voyage. Before the students begin reading the first chapter, the teacher asks, "If you were about to sail three ships across the Atlantic Ocean in 1492, at a time when nobody knew for sure what was on the other side of the ocean, what three pieces of advice would you give yourself?"

How does the Think/Pair/Share activity encourage anticipatory reading?

The students might discuss the question as a whole group, or using the think/pair/share procedure (see below). Doing so activates thoughts and ideas that will help them make sense of and appreciate what they will encounter as they read the book.

Think/Pair/Share.   Focusing questions can be still more effective when a mechanism has been provided for all students to consider and answer them. Think/pair/share (Kagan, 1997) is a cooperative learning activity in which the teacher puts an open-ended question to the class, preferably by writing it on the chalkboard. Children are given two minutes to respond to the question individually. (Often they are asked to do this in writing.) Next, each child turns to a partner, and they share their answers with each other. Finally, the teacher calls on two or three pairs to share their answers with the class. Then the class begins reading the text. In a think/pair/share activity, every student—even in a class of thirty or more students—is motivated to think about the topic and to discuss it with someone else.

Anticipation Guide.   Anticipation guides are used with fiction or with informational text. In using an anticipation guide (Vaughn & Estes, 1986), the teacher prepares a set of questions with short answers (usually true/false answers) that tap important aspects of the topic of the text. The questions are distributed to children on a worksheet, and the children are asked, individually or in pairs, to answer the questions as best they can before reading the assigned text. After reading the text, they return to the questions at the end of the class to see how their thinking has changed. An example of an anticipation guide is found in Figure 6.2.

Paired Brainstorming. When factual information will be shared, older students can be asked to make personal lists of the facts they know or think they know about the topic of the reading (Vacca & Vacca, 1986). After two minutes, they turn to a classmate and combine their lists. The teacher can make a master list of the class's ideas and leave their ideas on the chalkboard or on a piece of newsprint so that the students can compare them to the ideas they have after they have read the text.

Terms in Advance. A teacher may display a set of key terms that will be found in a reading and ask students to ponder their meanings as well as the relationships between the terms. The students are asked to predict how this particular set of terms might be used in the passage they are about to read. For example, if the book they are about to read is *Miss Nelson Is Missing,* the terms might be as follows:

TEACH IT!
13

kind teacher	mean substitute	police inspector	return
misbehave	make faces	homework	disguise

Instructions: Before reading <u>Pedro's Journal</u>, answer these questions *true* or *false* on the left-hand side. After reading the book, enter new answers on the right-hand side.

<u>Answer Before</u>   <u>Answer After</u>

_____ 1. Columbus was well-liked by his crew.   _____

_____ 2. Columbus prepared his ships to sail in front of the wind.   _____

_____ 3. Columbus's captains were very loyal to him.   _____

_____ 4. The first people Columbus met lived in a city.   _____

_____ 5. Columbus was very respectful of the people he met.   _____

_____ 6. Columbus seemed very interested in finding gold.   _____

FIGURE 6.2

Anticipation Guide for *Pedro's Journal.*

BUILDING KNOWLEDGE. Once students have had their expectations raised for what they are about to read, they are ready for activities that will help them construct meaning from the text or build their knowledge. As they read, students need to compare their expectations with what they are learning from the text. They should be able to revise their expectations or raise new ones as the text reveals more information, raises more questions, or plants more clues. They also need to think about what they are reading and be able to identify the main points. They will need to reflect on what the text is meaning to them personally and fill in any blanks in the text—that is, to make inferences about what the text says. Finally, they should be able to question the text—to argue with it. This phase of the lesson while children read is called **_building knowledge_**. Several strategies for helping students to build knowledge are described below.

Talking Through a Text.   If reading with comprehension is a process, it makes sense for the teacher to demonstrate that process to learners. Talking Through a Text is an open-ended technique for demonstrating reading comprehension strategies students can use as they work their way through a text. In talking through a text, the teacher reads the text aloud, calls attention to particular features, suggests a strategy

TABLE 6.2

Strategies for Building Knowledge

COMPONENTS OF COMPREHENSION	STRATEGY	DEMONSTRATION OF THE STRATEGY	SUGGESTION FOR INDEPENDENT USE
Engaging Prior Knowledge	Identify the topic and remind yourself what you already know about it	"On page 7, we see mention of the Depression, and learn that the story was set around 1932. I know from my prior reading that the depression was a time when many people lacked jobs. What else do you know about the Depression?"	"When you read, ask yourself what the topic of the work is, and what you already know about it."
Knowing Vocabulary	Understanding vocabulary items from context	"On page 7 it says '. . . but there's a *depression* going on all over this country.' The next sentence says, 'People can't find jobs and these are very, very difficult times for everybody.' After listening to the second sentence, what kind of a period of time do you suppose a depression is?"	"When you come across a word you don't know when you are reading, read the sentence before and after the word. Often you will find a clue to the word's meaning."
Visualizing Details and Events	Activating "the mind's eye"	"The social worker is telling Bud that the new home is going to be just fine, although Bud knows it won't be and maybe she does, too. How does her face look when she is talking to him? How does her voice sound? How does this make you feel about her? How would you be feeling, and what would you be thinking, if you were in her position?"	"When you read, stop and ask yourselves how the character looks. Say his or her words to yourself and try to sound like the character's voice sounds. Take note of the feelings you get when you hear the sounds spoken that way."
Following the Patterns of Texts	Making predictions from the plot	"Things look pretty bad for Bud in Chapter 1. He's about to leave an orphanage to stay with another foster family who may not really want him. Now he's found this flyer about a jazz musician and he says, 'I've never met him, but I have a pretty good feeling this guy must be my father.' You know, novels like this often give us a big question in the first chapter that we want to learn the answer to. Right now, I'm wondering if the guy on the flyer is really Bud's father. Do you think he is? How do you think we'll find out?"	"The next time you're reading a story, look toward the beginning for a question the author raises. Then get ready to find out the answer."

for responding to each feature, engages students in talking about the features and applying the strategies, and reminds the students to use the strategies in their own reading. Table 6.2 identifies some strategies that can be used. Focus on two or three components of comprehension each time you talk through a text, but be sure to address each component at some point.

COMPONENTS OF COMPREHENSION	STRATEGY	DEMONSTRATION OF THE STRATEGY	SUGGESTION FOR INDEPENDENT USE
Asking Questions and Pursuing Answers	Following questions the author plants in a text	"In Chapter 1 we read that Bud's mother got upset when she brought home the flyer that said the jazz band was playing in Flint, Michigan. Why would that upset his mother? What do you think we'll find out about that?"	"When you read a story, look for questions the author asks, and read to find the answers to them."
Making Inferences	Figure out an idea the author suggests, but doesn't quite say	"Here in Chapter 6, Bud has gotten to the food line, but they're closed. Then a man grabs him by the neck and says, 'Clarence, what took you so long?' and the man's wife calls Bud "Clarence," too, and tells him to get in line with them and get some lunch. Do we have any idea why they did that?"	"Sometimes authors suggest things and leave us the fun of figuring out the meaning for ourselves."
Monitoring Comprehension	Asking yourself if your idea of what the text means is making sense	"You know, in Chapter 8 when Bud kissed Deza Malone, I felt sure she would do something important in the book after that. But now we're in Chapter 11 and he's met Lefty Lewis, and I think I was wrong about Deza Malone. Does anyone think she will be part of the story after this?"	"When you read a story, ask yourself from time to time what it means to you, and what you think is going on. Check you understanding against what the text says from time to time, and be prepared to change your ideas if it turns out they weren't correct."
Noting Main Ideas and Supporting Details	Judging what will be significant ideas in the text	"When Bud is walking along the highway at 2:30 in the morning, a man stops his car and tries to coax Bud inside. Should Bud go? What signs do you have that Bud should trust him, or that he shouldn't trust him?"	"When you read a story, look for big ideas, and look for the small details that support those big ideas."
Summarizing and Rehearsing Main Ideas		"Here in Chapter 12, Bud finally meets Herman E. Calloway, but the old man denies he is Bud's father. Let's think over the reasons Bud had for believing Mr. Calloway was his father in the first place. They could still prove to be important . . ."	"As you read through a story, stop and think back from time to time on what you know."

Questioning the Author.   The Questioning-the-Author technique, designed by Isabel Beck and her colleagues (Beck et al., 1997), rests on the realization that readers sometimes fail to understand what they read, not because they are incompetent, but because the authors haven't made their meaning sufficiently clear. When students listen to their peers reading their works aloud in a writing workshop, they don't hesitate to say, "I don't know what you mean right there. Help me understand." Yet when young readers come across unclear passages in a published text, they often assume that the problem is theirs for not understanding, rather than the author's. This focused reading techinque encourages students to question what they don't understand in a text.

To prepare to conduct the Questioning-the-Author procedure, choose a portion of texts that will support an engaged discussion of 20 to 30 minutes. Read through the text in advance and identify the major concepts that the students should gain from the text. Plan frequent stopping points in the text to devote attention to the important ideas and inferences in the passage. Write some probing questions to be asked at each stopping point to motivate discussion.

Conducting the Questioning-the-Author lesson then proceeds in two stages:

Stage 1. Preparing the Students' Attitudes. Begin the discussion by reminding students that comprehension often breaks down because authors don't tell readers everything they need to know. Things may be unclear. Ideas may have been omitted or hinted at but not stated. A good way to comprehend is to think of questions you would ask the author if she or he were present and imagine what the answers might be. Since the author is not present in the classroom, the class will attempt to answer for the author.

Stage 2. Raising Questions about the Text. Now have the students read a small portion of the text. At a preselected stopping point, pose a question or query about what the students have just read. Early in the text, initiating queries might be:

- What is the author trying to say here?
- What is the author's message?
- What is the author talking about?

Later in the text, follow-up queries might include:

- So what does the author mean right here?
- Did the author explain that clearly?
- Does that make sense with what the author told us before?
- How does that connect with what the author has told us here?
- But does the author tell us why?
- Why do you think the author tells us that now?
  (From Beck et al., 1997)

As you ask these questions, ask several students to contribute ideas. Prod the students to clarify their thoughts, to elaborate their ideas, to debate each other's ideas, and to reach a consensus opinion.

TEACH IT!

14

The Directed Reading-Thinking Activity.   The Directed Reading-Thinking Activity (Stauffer, 1975), or DRTA, uses the dynamic of prediction and confirmation to create interest and excitement around a reading assignment, provided that the text is

TEACH IT!

★ ★ ★ ★

Conducting a DRTA

The directed reading-thinking activity is a sound strategy for helping students build knowledge as it helps create interest and excitement around a reading assignment. Following are the steps in a DRTA:

1. *Tell the students that you are about to read a story together, using the method of prediction. The activity should be enjoyable, but it is necessary that they follow your instructions closely. You will tell them to make predictions about what they are going to read. Then you will have them read short passages of the text and stop. It is very important that they stop reading where you tell them to and not read ahead until asked.*

2. *Tell the students the genre of the story: realistic fiction, tall tale, folk tale, etc. After naming the genre, ask them what kinds of characters they expect to meet. Ask what kinds of events they expect to happen.*

3. *Read the title, and show the students the accompanying picture, if there is one. Ask them what they think will happen. Remind them that it will not be possible to know for sure, but ask them to stretch their imaginations and take a guess. Press for the most specific answers you can get. Write some of these on the chalkboard. (Remember to leave room to write three more rounds of comments.)*

4. *Before the students read on, ask them to consider the predictions they have heard and silently choose the one they think is most likely to happen. Then ask them to keep their predictions in mind as they read to the next stopping place.*

5. *Now they should read (silently) to the stopping place and turn their books over when they have finished.*

6. *At the stopping place, review several of the predictions and ask the class whether the predictions are seeming to be borne out by the text or contradicted. Ask for proof from the text: Which predictions are coming true? What evidence do the students find in the text that makes them think so? You can put check marks on the board next to the predictions that are coming true, minuses next to those that are not, and question marks beside those that are uncertain. Ask the students how things look now in the story.*

7. *After some discussion, ask the students to make more predictions, choose the most likely ones, and read ahead as in step 4.*

8. *When the students have reached the end of the story, review the predictions, and ask the students what it was that made them guess what turned out to be the correct predictions. What was it about the characters, the plot, or the genre of the story that helped to guide their predictions?*

Refer to your **Teach It!** booklet for further activities you can use to reinforce concepts discussed in this chapter.

a work of fiction with something of a predictable structure. The DRTA is normally done with a group of six to ten students; this size is large enough to yield a range of predictions but small enough for everyone to participate. It is advisable that the students be roughly matched for reading ability, since all students must wait for the slowest one to finish reading each section.

The DRTA can be used by itself, or it can follow one of the activities we introduced above in the anticipation phase. Some teachers precede the DRTA with the *terms-in-advance* procedure or with the *anticipation guide.*

The teacher prepares for a DRTA by choosing four or five stopping places in the text, yielding more or less same-sized chunks of text. The stops should be placed right at points of suspense, places where the reader has been given some information and is wondering what is going to happen next (in other words, where the commercial break would be placed in a television thriller). One of these is normally right after the title. The Teach It! box demonstrates the DRTA process.

Note that in a DRTA, the questions are worded in a very open way. The teacher asks, "What do you think will happen? Why do you think so?" More specific questions from the teacher would take some of the initiative for making predictions away from the children, and the point here is for children to learn to ask their own questions about what they are reading.

There are a number of ways to scaffold a DRTA to make it more accessible to students. One is to read the text aloud instead of having the students read it. This variation of the method goes by a different name: the *directed listening-thinking activity*. Another is to think aloud yourself. If the predictions are slow in coming or seem to be going too wide of the mark, the teacher can offer a choice. For *Miss Nelson Is Missing,* the teacher might say, "I'm wondering if Miss Nelson has gone away to teach in another school where the kids are better behaved, or if she'll come back to her same class. Which one do you all think will happen?" Finally, in third grade and above, instead of a teacher-directed activity, a directed reading-thinking activity can be done by individual students or pairs of students.

CONSOLIDATION.   By the **consolidation** phase, the students have gone through the text and have at least begun to comprehend it. They need to go further, though, and do something with the meaning. They need to summarize it and be able to interpret and debate the meaning while applying it to new situations and creating new examples of it.

Students need to practice higher-order thinking with the issues from the text. After they read, students should be able to think back over the material and *summarize* the main ideas. They should *compare* what they found out with what they thought about the subject when they first approached the reading. If the ideas are not transparent, students should be able to *interpret* them. If the text is evocative in some way, students might be able to make personal responses to the ideas, such as *applying* them to the way they normally think or to the realities of their own lives. Students should also be able to test out the ideas—using them to *solve problems* or think up other solutions to the problems posed in the text.

Several teaching approaches are available to assist teachers with guiding students to consolidate and extend their ideas about what they have read. For fictional texts, teachers can use activities that allow students fairly free responses, some techniques that guide their attention to different aspects of the text, or for more analytic approaches that help to guide students in taking a close look at some aspect

---

TABLE 6.3

Activities for Consolidation

TEACHING APPROACHES

Open Response	Focused Approach	Analytic Approach
"Save the Last Word for Me"	Shared inquiry	Story maps
Literature circles	Discussion web	Character clusters
Value line	Debate	Character maps
Sketch-to-stretch		Dramatic roles
Dual-entry diary		Structured opposites

---

or aspects of the text. Table 6.3 identifies various activities with the appropriate approaches.

TEACH IT!
15

Dual-Entry Diary.   The dual-entry diary (Berthoff, 1981) is a kind of journal students use to record responses to readings. To make a dual-entry diary, the students draw a vertical line down the middle of a blank sheet of paper. On the left-hand side, they write a passage or image from the text that affected them strongly. Perhaps it reminded them of something from their own experience. Perhaps it puzzled them. Perhaps they disagreed with it. Perhaps it made them aware of the author's style or technique.

On the right-hand side of the page, they should write a comment about that passage: What was it about the quote that made them write it down? What did it make them think of? What question did they have about it?

There are a number of ways in which these journals may be treated next. Students can exchange them and comment on each other's quotes. The teacher can take them up (a few each day) and comment on them. Or the children can bring them to a discussion group in which the students are reading a common book and offer their comments to the discussion.

TEACH IT!
16

Save the Last Word for Me.   "Save the Last Word for Me" (Short, Harste, & Burke, 1996) provides a framework for a small group or whole-class discussion of a text. The procedure is especially good for encouraging children to take the lead in discussing their reading. The steps of the strategy are as follows:

1. After being assigned a reading to do independently, students are given note cards and are asked to find three or four quotations that they consider particularly interesting or worthy of comment.
2. The students write the quotations they have found on the note cards.
3. On the other sides of the cards, the students write comments about their chosen quotations. That is, they say what the quotations made them think of, what is surprising about the quotations, and why they chose them.
4. The students bring their quotation cards to discussion groups. The teacher calls on someone to read a card aloud.
5. After reading the quotation on his or her card, the student invites *other* students to comment on that quotation. (The teacher might need to help keep

comments on the subject of the quotation.) The teacher also may comment on the quotation.

6. Once others have had their say about the quotation, the student who chose it reads his or her comments aloud. Then there can be no further discussion. The student who chose it gets to have the last word.

7. That student can now call on another student to share his or her quotation and begin the process all over again. Not all students will be able to share their quotation if the whole class takes part in the activity, so the teacher will need to keep track of who shared quotes and make sure other children get chances to share their quotes the next time.

Literature Circles.   *Literature circles* (Short & Kauffman, 1995), *grand conversations* (Eeds & Wells, 1989), and *book clubs* (Raphael et al., 1995) are all terms for literary discussions in which students' curiosity about the text is allowed to play a directing role.

Typically, students in such discussions have read the same work; that work might be a short text they have already read or heard, or it might be a longer work. That is discussed while students are still in the middle of it. The choice of texts for literature circles is critical, since not all works are equally successful in evoking interested responses. Those that do often have a core mystery, elements that invite more than one interpretation, and a clear connection to issues that matter to the students.

These discussion groups may at first be conducted with the whole class at once until students have grown familiar and comfortable with the procedure. Then they may be conducted in smaller groups of four or five students meeting simultaneously. Literature circles are conducted several times a week. Early in the year, they might last no more than twenty minutes, but as students gain experience and confidence talking about literature, they might run for up to forty minutes, not counting the time it takes to read the text. Everyone is free to offer comments and questions in literature circles, and students are reminded that they are free to address their comments and questions to other students and not always to the teacher.

The role of the teacher in a literature circle is mainly to be a spirited participant; however, Martinez (in Temple et al., 2002) points to four additional roles teachers play:

1. *The teacher is a model.* The teacher might venture her or his own questions or responses to get a discussion going. The teacher is careful to speak as one seeking insights and not as a lecturer. The teacher's statements might begin, "I wonder about . . . . "

2. *The teacher helps students learn new roles in a literature circle.* Although all students know how to have conversations, they might need reminding of ways to participate in conversations in a classroom. These include rules such as these:

    - Sit in a circle so that everyone can see each other.
    - Only one person speaks at a time.
    - Listen to each other.
    - Stay on the topic.

3. *The teacher moves the conversation forward.* Without dominating the discussion, the teacher might invite other students to comment on something one student has said. The teacher might ask a student to clarify an idea. Or the teacher might pose an interesting open-ended question that she or he has

TEACH IT!
17

thought about in advance. (Such interpretive questions are discussed in the section on shared inquiry below).

4. *The teacher supports literary learning.* Lecturing about literature is not an adequate substitute for having students think and talk about it; nonetheless, it helps if teachers supply students with concepts and terms they can use to give form to ideas they are trying to express or insights they are struggling to reach. A student might notice that there is a point in a story where tension is highest because the main question in the story is about to be answered. The teacher tells the student that this is a *climax*. Researchers have noted that students' discussions go deeper when they have literary terms available to them (Hickman, 1979, 1981).

When conducting cooperative learning activities, the teacher might need to assign students particular roles to play in a group. Over time, when individual students learn to play the many roles of *encourager, timekeeper, facilitator, recorder,* and *summarizer,* they eventually learn all of the aspects of a good participant in a group because a good participant may practice most of these roles at once.

Literature circles often function better when students have particular roles to play. Also, by performing designated roles, students may exercise the many tasks that are carried out by an effective reader and discussant of literature. Table 6.4 outlines roles that students may play in a literary discussion (Daniels, 1994, 2001). Five suggestions will make the use of these roles more successful:

1. Teach the roles to the whole class, one at a time. The teacher might read or tell a story, then introduce one of the roles—for example, the connector. The teacher might then call attention to a connection between something in the text and something in real life. Then the teacher will invite several students to

---

TABLE 6.4

Roles in a Literary Discussion Group

- *Quotation finder:* This student's job is to pick a few special sections of the text that the group would like to hear read aloud.
- *Investigator:* This student's job is to provide background information on any topic related to the text.
- *Travel tracer:* When characters move from place to place in a text, this student's job is to keep track of their movements.
- *Connector:* This student's job is to find connections between the text and the world outside.
- *Question asker:* This student's job is to write down (in advance of the discussion) questions for the group to talk about—questions he or she would like to discuss with the others.
- *Word finder:* This student's job is to find interesting, puzzling, important, or new words to bring to the group's attention and discuss.
- *Checker:* This student's job is to help people in the group do their work well by staying on the topic, taking turns, participating happily, and working within time limits.
- *Character interpreter:* This student's job is to think carefully about the characters and to discuss what they are like with the other students.
- *Illustrator:* This student's job is to draw pictures of important characters, settings, or actions so that the other students may discuss the pictures.
- *Recorder:* This student's job is to take brief notes on the main points raised in the discussion.
- *Reporter:* This student's job is to report on the group's discussion to the teacher or to the whole class.

do likewise. Over several days, many of the roles can be introduced in this way before students use them in an extended discussion.

2. Encourage students to ask questions from their roles rather than to say what they know. For example, the *character interpreter* might invite the other students to construct a character map or a character web about a character and venture his or her own ideas only after the other students have shared their own.

3. Choose only the most useful roles for a particular discussion. Sometimes four or five roles are sufficient.

4. Rotate students through the roles. Each student should play many roles over the course of several discussions. The accumulated experience of playing many of these roles adds dimensions to each student's awareness of literature.

5. Be careful not to stress the roles more than the rich discussion of the literary work. Having students carry out the roles is a means to the end of sharing their insights about a work. Once the conversation is under way, the teacher should feel free to suspend the roles and let the conversation proceed.

Sketch-to-Stretch.   An ingenious device for having students of all ages respond together to a literary work is "Sketch to Stretch," from Short, Harste, and Burke (1996). After the students have read and thought about a poem or a story, they are invited to draw pictures that symbolize what they believe are the main ideas or central themes of the piece. One student shows his or her drawing to a group of students, and they interpret the picture, saying what they think it means and how its images relate to the literary work. After the other students have had their say, the student who drew the picture is invited to give his or her own interpretation of the picture.

Shared Inquiry Discussion.   The Great Books Foundation developed the *shared inquiry* method to accompany their literature discussion program (see Plecha, 1992), which has been conducted in thousands of schools and libraries for more than thirty years. Shared inquiry is a procedure by which the teacher leads a deep discussion into a work of literature. It is best done with a group of eight to ten students, to maximize participation but allow for a diversity of ideas. The procedure follows these steps:

1. Before the discussion takes place, choose a work or part of a work that encourages discussion. Such a work should lend itself to more than one interpretation (not all works do this well) and raise interesting issues. Folk tales often meet these criteria surprisingly well.

2. Make sure that all of the students have read the material carefully. (The Great Books Foundation insists that students read material twice before discussing it. But in our experience, a reading using some of the comprehension methods described above can make the students very aware of the contents of the reading selection.)

3. Prepare four or five discussion questions. These should be what the Great Books Foundation calls *interpretive questions*, and they have three criteria:

   a. They are real questions, the sort of question you might ask a friend as you walk together out of a provocative film.

   b. They have more than one defensible answer. (This criterion guarantees a debate. If it is not met, the discussion won't be a discussion but a "read my mind" exercise.)

   c. They must lead the discussion into the text. (A question such as, "Why was the giant's wife kinder to Jack than his own mother was?"

leads the children to talk about what is in the text first, even though they might then comment on what they know from experience. A question such as, "Have you ever done anything as brave as Jack?" leads the discussion away from the text and out into twenty-five different directions.)

4. Write the first question on the chalkboard, and ask the students to think about the question and then briefly write down their answers. (If the children are so young that writing answers is laborious, allow plenty of time before calling on anyone. This allows them time to think about their answers.) As you invite students to answer, be sure to invite reluctant speakers to read what they wrote as well. Encourage debate between students, pointing out differences in what they say and asking those and other students to expand on the differences. Press children to support their ideas with references to the text or to restate ideas more clearly. However, avoid correcting a child or in any way suggesting that any one answer is right or wrong. Finally, do not offer your own answer to the question. Keep a seating chart of the students' names with a brief record of what each one has contributed. When the discussion of a question seems to have run its course, read aloud your summaries of the students' comments and then ask whether anyone has anything to add.

5. Once the discussion gets going, follow the children's lead and continue to discuss the issues and questions they raise.

Even when they don't use the whole approach, many teachers use aspects of the shared inquiry procedure in conducting book discussions. For example, they might ask students to write down ideas to bring to a discussion, or they might take notes during the discussion, or they take care to draw out the students' ideas and not dominate the discussion themselves.

The Discussion Web.   The discussion web is a cooperative learning activity that involves all students in deep discussions of readings. The discussion web proceeds with the following steps:

1. The teacher prepares a thoughtful *binary* question—a question that can be answered "yes" or "no" with support. For example, in discussing "Jack and the Beanstalk," a binary discussion question might be "Was Jack right to steal from the giant?" For Louis Sachar's book *Holes* (1998), the question might be "Did Stanley succeed in the end because of his personal qualities, such as being strong and good, or was it because the luck of his family finally changed?"

2. The teacher asks pairs of students to prepare a discussion web chart that looks like the one in Figure 6.3 on page 232. Those pairs of students take four or five minutes to think up and list three reasons each that support both sides of the argument.

3. Next each pair of students joins another pair. They review the answers they had on both sides of the issue and add to each other's list. Then they argue the issue through until they reach a conclusion, that is, a position they agree on, with a list of reasons that support it.

4. At the conclusion of the lesson, the teacher calls on several groups of four to give brief reports of their position and the reasons that support it. The teacher can invite groups to debate each other if they took different sides of the argument.

TEACH IT!
18

YES   Was it wrong for Jack to steal from the giant?   NO

CONCLUSION

FIGURE 6.3

A Discussion Web.

Debates.   With students in third grade and up, it is often useful to follow the discussion web activity with a debate. The purpose of the debate is not to declare winners and losers, but to help the students practice making claims and defending them with reasons, even when others defend different claims. Working with claims, reasons, and arguments and debating ideas without attacking people—these are key elements in critical thinking.

To have a debate, you need a *binary question*—that is, a question that has a yes/no answer (since the discussion web we saw above also uses binary questions, you can follow the discussion web with a debate). Here are the steps:

1. Think of a question you think will truly divide the students' opinions, and put the question on the chalkboard for all to see. If you are not sure the question will divide the students roughly equally, ask for a show of hands on each side of the issue before going forward.
2. Give students an opportunity to think about the question and discuss it freely.
3. Ask students to divide up: Those who believe one answer to the question is right should go stand along the wall on one side of the room; and those who think the other is right should stand along the wall on the other side. Those who are truly undecided (that is, after thinking about it, they believe that both sides are partially right or neither side is right) should stand along the middle wall.
4. Explain or review the two ground rules:
    a. Don't be rude to each other. (You might have to explain and demonstrate what this means.)
    b. If you hear an argument that makes you want to change your mind, walk to the other side (or to the middle). Here is a hint to the teacher: As the debate proceeds, you can model the behavior of changing sides with a pantomime, by looking thoughtful for a moment after someone offers a good argument and moving to that student's side.
5. Give the students on each side three or four minutes to put their heads together and decide *why* they are on that side. Ask them to come up with a sentence that states their position. Then ask them to appoint someone to say that sentence.
6. Begin the debate by asking one person from each side (including the undecided group) to state that group's position.

7. Invite anyone on any team to say things (counterarguments or rebuttals) in response to what the other team has said or give more reasons in support of their own side.

8. Monitor the activity to make sure the tone stays away from negative attacks. Ask for clarification. Offer an idea or two as necessary from the devil's advocate position. Change sides. Encourage the students to change sides if they are persuaded to.

9. When the debate has proceeded for ten or fifteen minutes, ask each side to summarize what they have said.

10. You may follow the debate with a writing activity: Ask each student to write down what he or she believes about the issue and why. (See Chapter 8 for suggestions of ways to structure this writing activity.)

Value Line.   A cooperative learning activity that is an extension of the debate procedure is the value line (Kagan, 1991). The value line is well suited for questions that have more than two good answers and students might have a range of answers along a continuum. Here are the steps:

1. Pose a question to the students on which answers may vary along a continuum. For example, after reading *Ramona and Her Father* (Cleary, 1997), you might ask the children, "Do you think Ramona's parents really understand her?"

2. Give the students three minutes to consider the question alone and write down their answers.

3. Now stand on one side of the room and announce that you represent one pole, or extreme position, on the argument. You might say, "Yes, I think Ramona's parents understand her perfectly, 100 percent of the time." Invite a student to stand at the other end of the room to represent the other pole of the argument. The student might say, "No, I don't think Ramona's parents understand her. Not at all. Never."

4. Now invite the students to line up between the two of you in places along the imaginary value line between the two poles of the argument. Each stands at a point in the line that reflects his or her position on the question. Remind the students to compare their views with those of the students immediately around them to make sure they are all standing in the right spots. After hearing others' answers, some students might elect to move one way or another along the value line.

5. Students may continue to discuss their responses with the students on either side of them.

6. Identify three or four clusters of students who seem to represent different views on the question. Invite them to prepare a statement of their position and to share it with the whole group.

7. As an option, the formed line may be folded in the middle so that students with more divergent views may debate their responses.

8. You might want to follow this exercise with a writing opportunity in which students write down what they think about the issue and why. In this way, the value line serves as a rehearsal for writing an argumentative or persuasive essay.

What can students learn by acting out a story? What does it mean to "unpack" the meaning of a story?

Drama in Response to Stories. James Moffett (1976), a brilliant teacher of the language arts, pointed out many years ago that forms of literature differ in the degree to which they move closer to or farther away from actual events. An essay about human nature is abstract (the word comes from two Latin roots that mean "drawn away from"), far removed from actual events. A story is more concrete, getting closer to events. Still, by putting events into story form, an author summarizes them, compresses actions, and leaves out much of what might really have happened. Drama, however, is live action: it is about as close to the real events as we can get because it plays the events out in real time for us so that we can see, hear, and feel them as they unfold. Here is Moffett's shorthand way of stating these points:

- Drama shows what is happening.
- A story tells what happened.
- An essay tells what happens.

Dramatizing a story, or a part of a story, can be a very effective way for children to unpack its meaning. Dramatization should be done after the children have read or heard a story and have had a chance to air their first thoughts about it. The Teach It! box demonstrates a procedure for dramatizing a story.

The teaching approaches that we have considered up to now encourage discussions of stories or enactments of them. It is also useful to lead students in activities that teach them particular aspects of stories.

Story Maps.   As a rule, students read with better comprehension when they are asked questions that conform to the main arguments or developments of a text. When it comes to reading fiction, it helps if students are encouraged to raise questions along the lines that the stories are organized, and that usually means following the plot. The plot is a structured way in which authors organize places, people, actions, and consequences to make all of those things meaningful for the reader. The elements of a plot are as follows:

TEACH IT!
19

- *The setting:* the time and place the story happened
- *The main characters:* the persons the story is about
- *The problem:* the challenge the main character faces, which it is his or her goal to solve
- *The attempts:* the effort or series of efforts the character makes to solve the problem, along with their *outcomes*
- *The solution:* the attempt that finally pays off in solving the problem or the event that otherwise puts an end to the action
- *The consequence:* how things are for the characters at the end, including what the events of the story meant for them

TEACH IT!

★ ★ ★ ★

Dramatizing a Story

Dramatizing a story allows children to take a closer look at a story by getting a real feel for the action. The procedure for dramatizing a story is adapted from the works of Spolin (1986) and Heathcote (Wagner, 1999).

Immerse students in the story. You need to make sure the students get the story on a literal level—that they know what happened. This might mean reading the story to them or asking them to reread the part you are going to dramatize.

Warm them up to do drama. There are many warm-up activities that work well to prepare students to act with more expression:

1. *Stretches: Have the students stand in a circle. Now tell them to stretch their arms as high as they can as they spread their feet apart and make very wide faces. Now tell them to shrink up into tiny balls. Then stretch out big again. Have them do the same with their faces: Lion face! (expansive expression). Prune face! (shrunken expression).*

2. *Mirrors: Have students stand opposite each other. One is the person, and the other is the person reflected in the mirror. Have the person move (slowly) as the other mirrors the person's movements. Then switch roles.*

3. *Portraits: Have students get into groups of four or five. Have them think of something to depict that uses all of them as parts. For example, to*

depict a skier, children can act as poles, skis, and the person.

4. *Superactions: This activity is more complex. Explain to the students that when we do things with other people, we often act on two levels: what we are doing and what we mean by what we are doing. For example, when we pass somebody we know in the hallway, having just seen the person a short time before, we might nod and say, "Hi." But when we see a friend in the hallway who has just come back to school after a long illness, we might say "HI!" with more exuberance. In both cases, the action is the same: to greet the friend. But the superaction is different. In the first case, it is just to show the person that we know he or she is there; in the second case, it is to show that we are surprised and delighted to see the person. Now practice dramatizing superactions by setting up brief situations, such as a waiter taking a customer's order. Write superactions on small pieces of paper, and give one privately to each actor. Have different pairs of students act out the same scene, with the same actions but with different superactions, leaving time for the other students to guess what they thought the superaction was and say why they thought so.*

Choose critical moments. It can be particularly useful to dramatize just a few choice scenes from a story, especially the turning points when the most is at stake. In "Jack and the Beanstalk," such a scene might be when Jack first approaches the Giant's castle, knocks on the door, and is greeted by the Giant's wife.

(continued on next page)

TEACH IT!

★ ★ ★ ★

Continued

Segment the Situation. Now assign students to take each of these roles. Invite other students to join them as they think about the situation from each character's point of view. What must be on Jack's mind when he approaches the huge door? What do the door and the walls of the castle look like? How large are they in proportion to Jack? What does Jack hear around the place? What does he smell? How does the place make him feel? What makes him pound his fist on the door? What is at stake for him? What are his choices? What will he do if he *doesn't* knock on the door? Why does he decide to do it?

Do the same for the Giant's wife. How does the knocking sound to her—thunderous or puny? What does she think when she sees the small but plucky boy at her door? What thoughts go through her mind, knowing what she knows about her husband? What are her feelings as she looks down at Jack?

Ask the actors to focus their minds on a few of these considerations as they prepare to act out the scene.

Dramatize the scene. Use minimal props and minimal costumes to help students think their way into their roles. Ask the other students to watch carefully and see what the actors make them think of.

Side coach. As the director, don't be passive, but take opportunities to make suggestions from the sidelines that will help children act more expressively. You might ask, "Jack, do you feel scared now or brave? How can you show us how you're feeling?"

Invite reflection. Ask the other students what they saw. What did they think was on the characters' minds? It is worthwhile to invite several groups of students to dramatize the same scene and have the class discuss the aspects of the situation that each performance brings to light.

Refer to your **Teach It!** booklet for further activities you can use to reinforce concepts discussed in this chapter.

For many years, researchers have noted that students down to age five and even younger use something like a plot or a story grammar to understand and tell stories (Stein & Glenn, 1978; Sutton-Smith et al., 1999). You can help students use the plot consciously in understanding a story by using a **story map**, a chart that invites them to identify the keys parts of a story (see Figure 6.4) The process builds their responsiveness to the structures of story plots. For students younger than second grade, it might be preferable to use a simpler version of a story map consisting of only the *setting*, the *characters*, the *problem*, and the *solution*.

Character Clusters.   Not only are stories developed through plots, but characters come to life in them, too. Literary critic Roland Barthes (1994) suggested that characters

Setting	Characters	Problem	Attempts	Solution	Conclusion
In . . .	there was	who wanted	so she . . . , but . . . And she . . . but . . .	Finally, she . . . and . . .	In the end . . .

FIGURE 6.4

A Story Map.

are mostly just bundles of attributes that authors put into situations and play off against each other to show us what happens. In essence, writers ask themselves, "What would happen if a person like X got stuck in a situation like Y with people like Z?" Children's comprehension and appreciation of stories can be enhanced by showing them some ways to think about characters.

One way is the **character cluster**, which is a kind of graphic organizer: a semantic web with the character's name written in the middle, main features of the character written as satellites around the character's name, and examples of those features written as satellites around the features. Figure 6.5 on page 238 contains an example of a character cluster.

TEACH IT!
20

As when using other graphic organizers, you need to teach the whole class how to create a character cluster first. Then they can use it on their own as a guide to thinking more deeply about characters.

Character Maps.   When characters in stories interact with other characters (which is most of the time), students might need some way of keeping track of characters and the relationships between them. **Character maps** are a way to guide students' thinking about relationships between characters. In a character map, you would write the names of two or more characters in their respective circles. The circles should be spaced widely apart on the page. Then draw arrows between the characters. Along the arrow that points from Character A to Character B, write about how Character A feels about Character B. Along the arrow that points from Character B to Character A, write about how Character B feels about Character A. An example of a character map for two characters in Mildred Taylor's *Roll of Thunder, Hear My Cry* (1997) is found in Figure 6.6 on page 239.

Following Dramatic Roles.   As French drama critic Etienne Souriau (1955) pointed out many years ago, a large part of the way we understand characters in stories is by the symbolic roles they play in the plot. That is because, whether we are

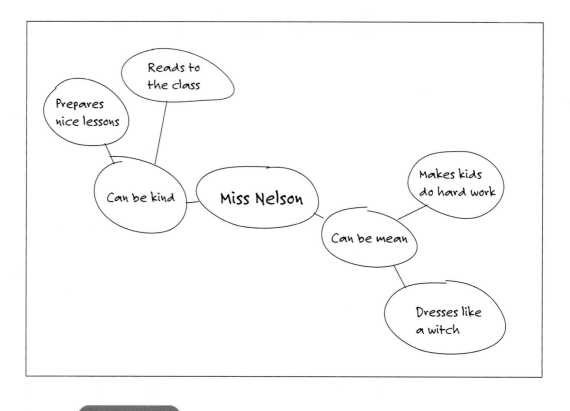

A Character Cluster.

watching sports or reading fiction, it is normal for us to cheer the hero, boo the rival, and have a warm place in our hearts for the trusty helper. Authors of stories wittingly or unwittingly use these propensities to shape the reader's reactions to characters: assigning one the role of protagonist or main character, another the role of helper, and another the role of rival or enemy.

Making children aware of the roles characters play in stories can help them interpret the stories and, eventually, to better understand how stories work. Following are common roles that occur in stories:

- *The hero* is the person whose desires and needs drive the story forward. In "Jack and the Beanstalk," to use that story as an example, the hero is Jack.
- *The goal* is the hero's main need or desire. In "Jack and the Beanstalk," Jack's goal seems to be to get money or to get some independence and not be thought of as a dolt.
- *The rival* is the person who stands between the hero and her or his goal. The rival in "Jack and the Beanstalk" is certainly the giant.
- *The helper* is a person or persons in a story who helps the hero achieve his or her goal. In "Jack and the Beanstalk," there are a couple of candidates for the helper: the mysterious old man who sells him the beans and the giant's own wife.

Feels loyal to him but doesn't really trust him

```
          > ------------------------------------------------------------>

          <-------------------------------------------------------- <
```

Cassie   T.J.

Hangs out with her and her brothers sometimes;
wants to prove himself better than them; but he
will betray them if it's to his advantage

FIGURE 6.6

A Character Map for *Roll of Thunder, Hear My Cry.*

The teacher can use dramatic roles in several ways to think about stories. One way is to have students nominate candidates for each of the roles and discuss their choices in small groups or as a class. These discussions can become lively, because not all role assignments are obvious. Is the *helper* in "Jack and the Beanstalk" the mysterious old man or the giant's wife? If it is the giant's wife (and the giant is the *rival*), why should she help the person who is striving against her husband? Is Jack's *goal* to obey his mother, to get money, to satisfy his curiosity, or to prove himself? Or is it all of these things? Discussing these issues takes students deep into the story.

Another way of using dramatic roles is to help students take different perspectives on a story. The teacher does this by asking students to take a character who seems to be playing one role and ask how the story would seem if we imagined that character playing a different role. For example, in "Jack and the Beanstalk," suppose the giant's wife were the hero; that is, suppose we saw things from her perspective. What is her goal? Who is her rival? Exploring these questions can lead to some very interesting discussions of stories and exercises the comprehension strategies of inferring and interpreting.

Reading for Structured Opposites.   People often find it most natural to think of extreme contrasts first, and then to think of things in the middle. For example, we learn hot and cold, huge and tiny, before we learn tepid and middle-sized. Storytellers tend to use extreme contrasts, as well. As Bruno Bettelheim (1975) observed, characters in fairy tales are very good or very bad; few are mixtures of the two. Stories tend to deal with the same great problems and urges again and again, as the folklorist Joseph Campbell (1968) brilliantly showed us. Thus, we can see similarities in those things that are most starkly contrasted in stories, and then begin to ask what those contrasts remind us of in our own experiences. Claude Levi Strauss (1970) argued that a useful way of interpreting stories is to look for their contrasts, ask what things are similarly contrasted in other stories, and then find parallel contrasts and tensions in our own lives. This method is called **reading for structured**

Jack	The Giant
Small	Huge
Young	Old
Poor	Rich
Uses wits and courage	Uses brute strength
On his way up	"Over the hill" and on his way

FIGURE 6.7

Looking for Contrasts between Characters.

opposites. A folktale works very well for introducing this method and could be taught like this:

1. Ask the students to think of the two characters in the story they are reading who are most unlike each other or most opposed to each other. For example, if the story is "Jack and the Beanstalk," the two characters might be Jack and the giant.
2. Write the names of those two characters at the heads of two columns (see Figure 6.7). Ask the students to come up with contrasting descriptive words about those two characters. That is, ask for a word that describes one character; then ask for an opposite word that describes the other character.
3. Now create two new columns beside each of the original two. Use one pair of these columns to list other characters in literature or movies or on television who are contrasted much as the original characters are. Use the other pair of columns to list people in the real world—in history, current events, or in our personal experience—who are similarly contrasted (see Figure 6.8).

Shared Reading

Shared reading (Holdaway, 1979) provides a flexible framework for guiding younger students' reading with comprehension. The method combines *immersing children in a reading experience, demonstrating comprehension strategies,* and *providing practice* using those strategies. Shared reading is flexible because the teacher designs a lesson according to the skills that the students need to develop.

BEFORE READING. Think of the skills and concepts you want to teach. These will come from your observation of the children's needs and from the curriculum you are following, and they might include phonics and word recognition strategies; vocabulary; the parts of a book (title, author's name, table of contents, glossary, etc.); and the

In life?	In books and movies?	JACK	THE GIANT	In books and movies?	In life?
Serfs . . .	David Tweety R. Runner Harry Potter Frodo The Logans	Small Young Poor Uses wits & courage On his way up	Huge Old Rich Uses brute strength On his way down	Goliath Sylvester W. Coyote Valdemoort Saran Harlan Granger	Medieval Barons . . .

FIGURE 6.8

Looking for Contrasts between Characters—Detail.

genre of a book (pattern book, tall tale, concept book, etc.). These skills should also include comprehension strategies, such as the following:

- Summoning and using background knowledge
- Raising questions about the topic of the book and looking for answers
- Making predictions and confirming them from the reading
- Making inferences about ideas that are not directly stated
- Monitoring comprehension
- Deriving word meanings from the context
- Visualizing what is described
- Finding main ideas
- Summarizing

Choose a text that will serve as a vehicle for teaching these skills. With younger children, the lesson can be taught by means of a big book. Lessons that build comprehension can be done even when the teacher has the sole copy of a book that is read aloud, however.

DURING READING.   Explain to the children the main skills you will be addressing. Then preview the book, discussing the title and the cover illustration. Ask students what they already know about the topic. Ask them to predict what they think they will read or hear in this book. Do a "picture walk" through the book, discussing what the children see happening and what they think will happen.

Begin the first reading, using an interesting voice. Think aloud as you go: Raise questions, make predictions, wonder about word meanings, sense the pattern of the text. Invite the children to join you in commenting on the text. Pause and invite the children to fill in blanks. Ask them to repeat phrases, and if you are reading a big book, point to the phrases as the children repeat them. Keep up the pace enough that children can follow the thread.

Read the book again, asking the children to join in more and more.

AFTER READING. Ask the children to shut their eyes and think of one thing to say. Ask them what the book made them think of and how it made them feel. Ask one or more open-ended questions about the story. Invite the children to ask questions about the book for the class to discuss. Display the book prominently, and encourage the children to reread it on their own. Also consider using a language chart.

THE LANGUAGE CHART. As a way to motivate children to think more deeply about themes and other features of the book, you might choose three or more books that share similarities, and construct a **language chart** as a means of comparing them. A language chart (Roser & Hoffman, 1995) asks the same question about all of the books, as shown in Figure 6.9. Children discuss these and other questions at the time they read each book. Then the teacher records a summary of their answers in the space provided on the chart. After they have read two books, they compare them according to the questions. Using a language chart has been shown to lead even young children into more analytical thinking about what they have read.

Books by William Steig	What Was the Problem?	What Was the Solution?	How Were Things Different at the End?
Sylvester and the Magic Pebble	Sylvester got turned into a rock.	His parents found the magic pebble and wished him back to his old self.	Sylvester was happy to be normal.
Caleb and Kate	Caleb got turned into a dog.	Kate said the magic words and changed him back.	Caleb and Kate were glad to be together.
The Amazing Bone	Pearl was going to be killed by a fox.	The bone said a charm and shrunk the fox.	Pearl was glad to be home with her family.

FIGURE 6.9

A Language Chart.

Assessing Comprehension

Children's comprehension can be observed on an ongoing basis to make the teacher and the children aware of the children's use of comprehension processes. Assessment can also be done periodically to gauge students' progress and achievements in comprehension. Techniques for assessing comprehension include the following:

- *Observational assessments*: Here you observe and assess students' comprehension behaviors as students demonstrate them in real reading tasks.
- *Self-assessments*: Here you ask students to observe and critique their own use of comprehension strategies. Self-assessments have the advantage of teaching students to be mindful of reading strategies and deliberate about in their use when they read.
- *Quantitative assessments*: Periodically, you might gather data that allow you to compare students' performance against some standard, such as grade-level expectations.

Observational Assessments

One kind of observational assessment is simply to keep a folder for each student into which the teacher places observations about each student that he writes down every few days. The observations consist of whatever strikes the teacher as being worthy of note.

A more systematic way of making observational assessments is to keep a checklist of reading behaviors—in this case, comprehension behaviors. The teacher schedules an eight-to-ten minute period every week to read with each child, individually or in a group of no more than four, and record observations on a checklist such as the one shown in Figure 6.10 on page 244.

Student Self-Assessments

Self-assessments (see Figure 6.11 on page 246) are recommended because they not only give the teacher some information about how the child is reading, but also make the child aware of what she or he should be doing while reading. In other words, self-assessments teach at the same time that they assess reading behaviors.

Students will need to be taught what each of the questions on the self-assessment instrument mean. Each question can be presented in a minilesson and added to the self-assessment instrument after it has been taught. This means that the self-assessment instrument will get longer and more elaborate as the year goes on and as more component strategies of comprehension are taught and then added to the instrument.

Students can be given self-assessments to complete every two or three weeks. It is helpful to review the assessment instrument with the students just before they complete a reading assignment and have them fill out the assessment afterwards. Discuss with the students how the strategies they indicate they are using help them to understand what they read. Talk over the strategies they still need to learn to use, and teach those strategies if necessary.

Student's name: _____ Date: _____ Observer: _____

Material read: _____ Level: _____

1. Before reading

a) The reader demonstrated familiarity with the topic (or the author or the genre) of the text before reading.

No prior knowledge shown	*Some prior knowledge shown*	*Much prior knowledge shown*

b) The reader raised questions about the content of the text before reading.

No questions offered even when asked	*Vague questions raised when asked to by teacher*	*Precise and informed questions offered*

c) The reader was able to make predictions about what was coming in the text.

No predictions offered even when asked	*Imprecise or illogical predictions made when asked for by teacher*	*Made logical predictions spontaneously*

2. During reading

a) The reader read aloud with animation that honored the meaning of the text.

Expressionless reading	*Sometimes showed emphasis and drama*	*Consistently showed proper emphasis and reflected the dramatic contours of the text*

b) The reader knew the vocabulary in the text.

Did not know many key words	*Knew most key words; used context for some but not all others*	*Knew almost all key words and was able to use context to figure out others*

FIGURE 6.10

Observational Checklist for Assessing Comprehension.

c) The reader continued to ask questions and make predictions.

No questions or predictions even when asked	Some questions and predictions when asked by the teacher	Asked insightful questions and made reasonable predictions

d) The reader found answers to questions or confirmed predictions.

Seldom	Sometimes, when asked	Consistently

e) The reader was able to make inferences.

Unable to, even when asked	Occasionally, when asked	Consistently, and picked up on subtle nuances

f) The reader monitored comprehension.

Frequently misread text without self-correction	Occasionally misread text and made some self-corrections	Rarely misread text or always self-corrected

3. After reading

a) The reader could retell or summarize the text.

The retelling had major gaps	The retelling was fairly complete	The retelling was complete, and the reader summarized the main points

b) The reader could interpret the text.

Offered limited response or interpretation when asked	Offered responses to aspects of the text	Offered personal response to or interpretation of the main point of the text

Your name: _____ Today's date: _____

What you read: _____ Pages: _____

	Not at all	A little bit	A lot
Before Reading			
I thought about what I knew about the topic of the reading.			
I thought of things I wanted to find out.			
It was a story. I tried to predict what would happen.			
While Reading			
I read with expression to make it sound real.			
I thought about what I was finding out.			
It was a story. I predicted what would happen next.			
I was able to figure out words I didn't know from the words around them.			
I was able to tell what was going on, even when the author didn't come right out and say it.			
After Reading			
I thought back over what I had found out so I would remember it later.			
I thought about what it meant to me.			
I thought about why the author wrote this text and what he or she was trying to say.			

FIGURE 6.11

Student Self-Assessment.

Quantitative Assessments

Teachers and students also need to know how well students are reading in comparison with their grade-level group. As we noted in Chapter 1, teachers and grade-level teams can focus attention on aspects of teaching that need improving—but only if they have evidence that tells them where the strengths of their instructional program are as well as the areas in which they need improvement.

Several kinds of assessment devices are available. For the purpose of getting a close look at readers' strengths and areas of need, the most informative are informal reading inventories. Several of these are published commercially. Informal reading inventories must be administered one at a time, so they are time consuming. But the fact that they yield both quantitative results (in terms of reading levels) and detailed portraits of most areas of students' reading abilities makes them worth the investment of time.

Informal reading inventories are thoroughly discussed in Gillet, Temple, and Crawford's *Understanding Reading Problems* (2004).

Some recommended informal reading inventories include:

Lauren Leslie and JoAnne Caldwell. (2000). *Qualitative Reading Inventory–3*. New York: Pearson Education.

Paul C. Burns and Betty D. Roe. (2001). *Informal Reading Inventory: Preprimer to Grade Twelve*. Boston: Houghton Mifflin.

Nicholas Silvaroli and Warren Wheelock. (2000). *Classroom Reading Inventory*. New York: McGraw Hill.

Mary D. Applegate, Kathleen B. Quinn, and Anthony J. Applegate. (2003). *The Critical Reading Inventory*. New York: Pearson Education.

FOR REVIEW

Reading comprehension is using the knowledge we already have to understand the new information we find in the text. It is an active process in which we quest after new knowledge and make meaning in the process. Responding to literature, too, is an active process in which we bring our own expectations and associations to the words the author has strung along the pages of the text.

Comprehension has several components: knowing the vocabulary of a text and being able to follow the text's structure, visualizing it, making predictions about it, summarizing its meaning, getting the main ideas in it, making inferences within it, interpreting it, arguing with it, and monitoring one's comprehension of it.

To encourage students to carry out that activity, there are teaching techniques we can use before, during, and after the reading or during the phases of a lesson we have called *anticipation*, *building knowledge*, and *consolidation*. In the anticipation phase, we remind students to think of what they already know about a topic, raise questions about what they are about to read, and otherwise prepare for reading. In the building knowledge phase, we guide students in using strategies to set expectations and meet them and to clarify meanings. In the consolidation stage, we have a host of methods for having students think back over what they have gained from the reading, respond to it, interpret it, critique it, apply it, and debate it.

In this chapter, we also stressed the importance of assessing students' comprehension. The three general approaches that we discussed were observations, self-assessments, and quantitative assessments.

For Your Journal

1. Return to your answers to the anticipation guide that opened this chapter. Look at the items for which your answers remained the same. In your journal, explain how you came to know the answers. Look at the items to which your answers changed, and explain how your thinking has changed.

2. This chapter explained how reading comprehension of fiction and response to literature work. The next chapter focuses on teaching students to comprehend and learn from informational text. What do you think the main differences are between teaching students to comprehend and respond to fiction and teaching them to do this for informational text?

3. Recall the vignette of Hank da Silva's classroom that began this chapter. He used a combination of strategies for teaching students to read with comprehension. Think of a class you have taught or might teach. Describe the combination you might choose from the reading comprehension strategies you have seen in this chapter. How would you make them work together?

★ Taking It to the World

1. When they observed skilled teachers teaching reading comprehension, Michael Pressley and his colleagues (1996) found that they usually taught their students to do the following:

- Make predictions of what was to come in the text based on their prior knowledge
- Generate questions about issues in the text
- Seek clarification about confusing parts
- Form mental images of what they read
- Relate what they already knew to what they are reading in the text
- Make summaries of what they have read

Alone or with a group of your fellow students, observe three reading lessons in a primary grade school. Do these six activities capture what the teachers are doing by way of helping the children read with comprehension? Do they do other things as well, such as encouraging students to make inferences or debate about what they read?

2. Go to a school, and practice a shared inquiry lesson. Make sure you use a text that has core of mystery to it (many folktales work fine), and prepare your questions carefully according to the criteria given on page 230. Before you put the questions to the children, though, write out your own best answers to your questions. How do the students' answers compare to yours? Are you surprised? If so, what surprises you and why?

3. Using the text you used with your shared inquiry lesson, try the dramatic activities described on pages 234–236 with your classmates. Then try the activity out in an elementary school. What different insights about the text come to light when you dramatize it rather than discuss it?

★ Being a Professional Reading Teacher

Reflecting on the Chapter

Reading comprehension is a process that takes students from their prior knowledge—the schema they already have—and leads them to construct new meaning from the new knowledge they gain by reading.

The Role of Questioning in Reading Comprehension

What kind of question do teachers ask most frequently? What kind should they ask? Provide an example of each type.

Schema Theory and Background Knowledge

We know that background knowledge is an important component of reading comprehension. Can you think of instances in the past year in which your background knowledge has helped you to understand something you were reading? Do you have an example where a lack of background knowledge about a topic made it difficult to understand what you were reading?

Story Grammar and Reading Comprehension

You have learned that knowledge of story grammar supports reading comprehension. How could knowledge of the story grammar of a fairy tale help a student write her or his own fairy tale?

Critical Literacy

We often think of critical literacy as a skill for upper-grade and secondary students and adults. How early can children be involved in critical literacy lessons? How would you make a case for beginning in kindergarten or first grade?

Your Portfolio

Be sure to include a lesson plan for reading comprehension in your portfolio. It should include higher-order questions that lead students to activate background knowledge and use it to assimilate and then apply new knowledge from their reading. Are your only classroom experiences with kindergarten or first grade? If so, use a listening comprehension lesson, in which, instead of reading themselves, the children listen to the teacher read aloud.

Teaching Resources

You have learned about many very useful comprehension strategies in this chapter. You might want to reread the chapter, making a list of strategies and how they are used most effectively in lessons—as anticipation activities, for building knowledge, or as consolidation activities. As you begin teaching, refer to the list, and make an effort to use each item. Your students will appreciate the variety of approaches, since they can become bored after encountering the same strategy on many occasions.

Technology Connections

1. In 2001, the International Reading Association (IRA) issued a position statement on the use of information and communication technology (ICT). Visit the International Reading Association online (www.reading.org) and locate this position statement, entitled "Integrating Literacy and Technology into the Curriculum." Summarize the context of the statement. What are the six "rights" the IRA believes students have with regard to ICT? What will be teachers' primary challenges in addressing these rights?

2. The Great Books Foundation offers training in their methods, including the shared inquiry method, in many places in North America. Visit the foundation's web site (www.greatbooks.org) to find further information. What materials or trainings are available through the organization?

Connect with Research

**Research
Navigator.com**

Review the following key words from the chapter, and then connect to Research Navigator (www.researchnavigator.com) through this book's companion web site to conduct a search into research on each of the various topics as they relate to reading and literacy education today.

aesthetic stance	consolidation	language chart
anticipation	critical literacy	reader response theory
building	directed reading-	reading for structured
knowledge	thinking activity	opposites
character cluster	efferent stance	schema theory
character maps	genres	story map
concatenated	inferences	taxonomies

Further Readings

Alexander, P. A. (2001). "Learning from Text: A Multidimensional and Developmental Perspective." In M. Kamil, P. B. Mosenthal, P. D. Pearson, and R. Barr (Eds.), *Handbook of Reading Research* (Vol. III). Hillsdale, NJ: Erlbaum.

Schema theory stresses that prior knowledge is important in comprehension—but what kind of comprehension? This article reviews research that suggests that it is worth the time to help students to develop a more structured understanding about topics before asking them to read about them.

Book Talk and Beyond.

A useful collection of articles on ways to stimulate discussions of literature in classrooms.

Daniels, H. (2001). *Literature Circles: Voice and Choice in Book Clubs and Reading Groups.* Augusta, ME: Stenhouse.

Daniels lays out in great detail ways of using cooperative learning techniques to enhance discussions of literature.

Langer, J. (1995). *Envisioning Literacy: Understanding and Literature Instruction.* New York: Teachers College, Press.

In this seamless blend of theory and practice, Langer develops her theory of envisionments and shows how it plays out in teaching children to respond to literature.

Pearson, P. D., & Anderson, R. C. (1984). "A Schema Theoretic View of the Learning to Read Process." In P. D. Pearson, R. Barr, M. Kamil, and P. Mosenthal (Eds.), *Handbook of Reading Research.* New York: Longman.

An authoritative, readable, and thorough account of the schema theory of reading comprehension.

Peterson, R., & Eeds, M. (1999). *Grand Conversations (Grades 2–6).* New York: Scholastic.

A seminal book on ways to conduct book discussions with children.

Rosenblatt, L. (1978). *The Reader, the Text, and the Poem.* Carbondale, IL: Southern Illinois University Press.

Rosenblatt was the first literary scholar to credit the reader's activity in making meaning. This work lays out her theory very nicely.

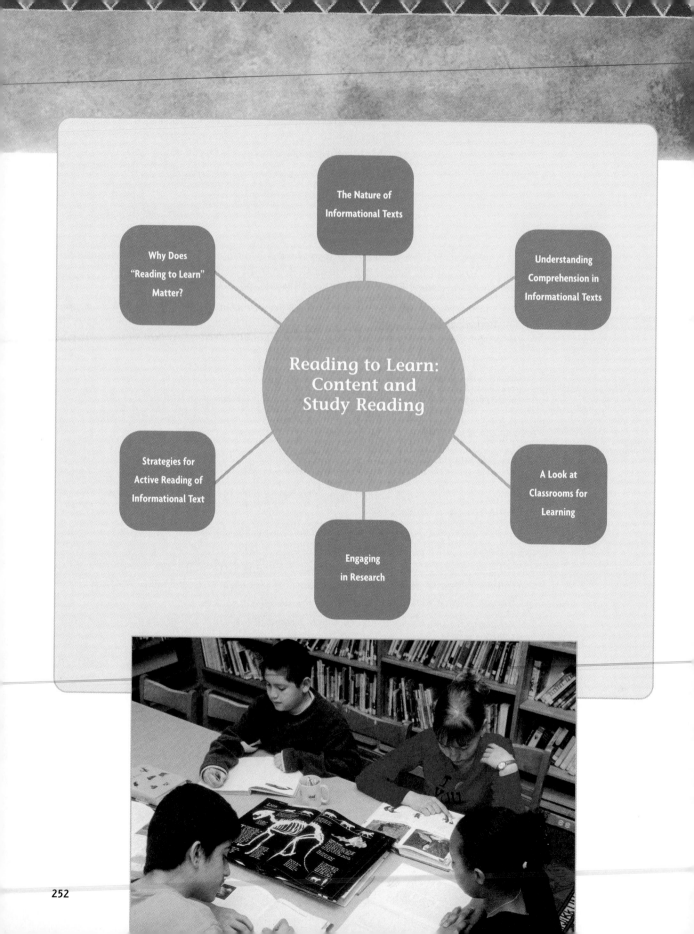

The Nature of
Informational Texts

Why Does
"Reading to Learn"
Matter?

Understanding
Comprehension in
Informational Texts

Reading to Learn:
Content and
Study Reading

Strategies for
Active Reading of
Informational Text

A Look at
Classrooms for
Learning

Engaging
in Research

Reading to Learn: Content and Study Reading

The following statements will get you thinking about the topics of this chapter. Answer true or false in response to each statement. As you read and learn more about the topics in these statements, double-check your answers. See what interests you and prompts your curiosity toward more understanding.

Anticipation Guide

_____ 1. There has been a big shift from fiction reading to informational reading by adult readers in the United States.

_____ 2. Primary children get too confused with the different formats of nonfiction texts. Instruction in using nonfiction should wait for third grade and above.

_____ 3. Teachers in the United States have changed their teaching practices to show students how to comprehend informational material.

_____ 4. One of the best ways to show students how to read informational text with comprehension is to read informational text yourself and discuss it with your students.

_____ 5. Having prior knowledge helps students to comprehend, but one kind of prior knowledge is about as useful as another.

_____ 6. Students who have had an extensive introduction to a topic are likely to be more motivated to learn about it than are those with only superficial knowledge.

_____ 7. Just as stories have a "grammar" that readers can follow to understand the story, informational texts have recognizable structures.

_____ 8. Reading strategies for informational texts are the same as those for fiction.

_____ 9. Informational texts have so many different structures that there is little point in teaching students the parts of an informational text.

_____ 10. When it comes to teaching vocabulary, teachers should stress only the words the authors of the text prioritize.

Reading to Learn in a Primary Classroom

Teacher Debbie Gurvitz likes to introduce her first- and second-grade students to informational reading through integrated units of study. In the spring, she develops an expanded science unit that involves real problem-based inquiry. It serves as a way of expanding students' reading skills in nonfiction and of teaching some science standards. Last year, Ms. Gurvitz focused the unit on pond life and the relationship between the quality of the water for animals and the human community. To introduce the unit, she invites a naturalist from the local nature preserve to speak to the students. This year, when the naturalist showed the students some of the animals from the pond, they became fascinated with the mutant frog he included. "Wow, that's weird!" "That doesn't look like the frog I have at home. Who did that to it?" "What happened?" The children's questions came naturally and quickly. Garth, one of the first graders, expressed the feelings of the whole group when he said, "Ms. Gurvitz, we really have a problem!"

Ms. Gurvitz took her lead from the children and helped them to focus their study of the natural environment on the frog problem. They began by framing the problem—exploring what facts and information they already knew and iden-tifying the questions they had. They made a list of what they knew about frogs on a large piece of chart paper. She helped them write questions for research; these also filled a sheet of chart paper and were hung on the wall. As a result of these discussions, she divided the class into smaller groups that searched for information to help solve the problem. In this case, it was a very real problem. Scientists do not understand why so many frogs in the area are being born with strange looking body parts. This created an authentic study full of the kinds of ambiguities that are found in most scientific research.

Ms. Gurvitz was careful to make sure she could locate the kinds of reading texts the children could read. She wanted some that would be at an independent level for all the children and some that would be good instructional level texts for her guided reading groups. After collecting the books, she leveled them to ensure that she could accommodate the whole class with appropriate materials.

In considering the language arts and reading objectives she wanted to address, Ms. Gurvitz focused instruction on helping students find answers to questions they posed. She wanted them to learn to use the table of contents and the index in books to locate the information they needed. She knew this would be a good opportunity for them to learn to make decisions about what sections of a text they would read and gain control over information searching as contrasted with fictional reading. She also wanted the children to learn to make notes about what information they were collecting so that those notes could guide their reporting. To do this, she made copies of the Amazing Fact Sheet (see Figure 7.1) and put them in a shoebox on the inquiry table so students could take one whenever they wanted to save some interesting or important information.

AMAZING FACT SHEET

An amazing fact about frogs is that

_____

_____

Found in (provide the source of your information)

_____

Written by _____ p. _____

Reporter _____

FIGURE 7.1

Amazing Fact Sheet.

As she introduced this way of making notes, Ms. Gurvitz used one child as a model. Side by side at the overhead transparency, Ms. Gurvitz and Andrew made a note card of the information he wanted to remember.

"Andrew, what do you want to write?" Ms. Gurvitz asked.

"It says that frogs lay lots of eggs in water," Andrew replied.

Ms. Gurvitz encouraged him, "So, can you write that on your Amazing Fact Sheet?"

As Andrew began to write on a transparency, the other children watched. When he tried to write "water," he hesitated.

"What is giving you trouble with that word?" Ms. Gurvitz asked. "Can you find it written somewhere?"

With that nudge, Andrew turned to the book again and located the word; without any further help, he finished his writing. Ms. Gurvitz reminded him to list the book title, the author, and the page that contains the fact on his note. Finished, he then signed the note on the Reporter line.

Ms. Gurvitz praised his efforts, "Good work, Andrew."

She concluded the minilesson by reminding the children that when they found interesting information, they should write that on an Amazing Fact Sheet and put it in the Amazing Facts Box on the counter. Each morning, Andrew and other children read their cards during the morning share time and used them to build their knowledge.

When parents volunteered, Ms. Gurvitz gave them specific guidelines on how to work with the children. Some helped children to record information on their Amazing Fact Sheets. Ms. Gurvitz also asked parents to involve their children in talking about what they learned when they were at home. Some Home Links letters included specific questions parents were to ask their children and space for them to record what the children told them. These letters were sent home regularly to inform parents of what the children were doing and help them become part of the learning activities. The children would then return these links the next day to be shared in class.

The children got very involved in this unit of research, and so did several of the families. One family created a frog pond in their own yard, and the children loved hearing of its progress. By the conclusion of the unit, each student had a report prepared by himself or herself and their research team report. Large murals the children created gave a focus for their presentations of results to the class and to visiting classes that came to learn from their study.

Assessment is an integral part of good instructional planning. In her work as a primary teacher, Ms. Gurvitz is always assessing her students' development as

Family & Community Literacy

learners. She finds the integrated units a natural place to teach (*attend to details of reading*), provide *guided practice,* and then have opportunities to observe how the children *apply* her teaching of strategies in their individual work and in the group projects. During guided reading using the frog and pond texts, she monitored each child and periodically did a running record of the child's performance with attention to his or her strategy use. She had no problem in checking to see whether the students monitored their own reading for meaning. She knew that they were full of questions, and their Amazing Fact Sheets provided records of the information they gained.

When they read their own fact sheets during the class share, she got another chance to watch them read their own writing and then explain what they knew in response to other students' questions.

Ms. Gurvitz noted that some children actually moved to higher levels of books as a result of their increased familiarity with the words in the unit that occurred regularly. She monitored their reading carefully, since she did not want to push students too quickly and knew that as they read in other materials, they might not have the same level of knowledge to support their reading. Yet the students gained real confidence in their reading as they explored many books and articles about frogs. As students worked in groups, Ms. Gurvitz was by their side, observing how they used the information they gathered to think about their aspect of the problem. Some children became good at locating facts in the books they read, while others relied on the clear visual diagrams and photographs in the texts. All the children had their own responsibilities and also completed Home Links periodically, so she had ways of monitoring their independent work, too. At the end of the unit, as the groups presented the findings of their research, Ms. Gurvitz carefully recorded notes on each child's performance. When parents came in for conferences, she had a rich set of notes on what the children had read, their growth in reading and writing, and their part in the class learning experiences that she could share with the parents.

To be human is to be a learner. Young children are full of questions—so many that parents and teachers are sometimes amazed by the depth and breadth of children's curiosity. As we grow, we continue to be curious about the world around us and ask questions. To find answers to these questions, we read informational materials—from textbooks like this one to cookbooks, travel guides, biographies, self-help and diet books, and newspapers and magazines. To be successful learners in school, students must also learn to read and study about concepts that society considers important. These are generally elaborated on in textbooks and other reference materials. Therefore, it is important for teachers to prioritize helping young readers develop the joy in and ability to read a wide range of materials. They need guidance so that they can become confident and flexible readers empowered by the variety of strategies they have developed to navigate the wide range of materials and formats in the informational materials they encounter daily. They also need to learn to study new material and find strategies that will help them retain that material.

Why Does Reading to Learn Matter?

Much of the reading we do is to learn. Schools require that students use textbooks and a wide variety of other resource materials throughout the grades. Unfortunately, too often we just assume that students will develop good strategies for using informational materials and knowing how to prioritize what they need to remember. Most schools also spend little time teaching students how to use informational materials effectively for answering their own questions and for creating reports. Yet this kind of reading becomes increasingly important as students progress through the grades. Most content courses still depend heavily on textbooks, but no one seems to take the responsibility to teach students to use these resources effectively. Most middle and secondary school teachers also expect students to engage in independent research and write informational essays and reports. The skills needed to be successful learners can be introduced in the primary grades and developed throughout the grades.

What we read outside of school also underscores the importance of knowing how to read and use informational materials. Recent research studies on the reading habits of adults reflect the shift away from fiction to informational reading and nonfiction sources (Smith, 2000). We read newspapers and magazines to find out about the world around us and our favorite activities. We browse the World Wide Web to gain in-depth information and alternative points of view. We read self-help books and books on health and fitness because we want to improve our health and lifestyle. We read spiritual and religious books to reflect on our beliefs and deepen our quality of living.

As a society, we are shifting from a nation of fiction readers to a people who read a preponderance of **informational texts**. We want to know as much as possible—about ourselves as well as the rest of the world. Publishers recognize this shift in interests and are publishing more and more informational texts, both printed and electronic. The wide range of magazines being published reflects the wide range of reader interests. Just check a magazine stand for the hundreds of specific topics that are available to address particular interests and tastes of readers. The best-seller lists generally have one section for fiction, another for nonfiction and often a third for self-help books. One of the real transformations in the last decade has been the explosion of materials available for us to read on an enormous range of topics on the World Wide Web as well as in more traditional publishing venues.

Knowledge Standards and High-Stakes Assessment

The current focus on knowledge standards and measuring what students learn each year puts pressure on teachers to cover more content. This means that students are asked to read more and remember what they are taught. In this climate of rising expectations,

STANDARDS & LITERACY

★ ★ Content Area Standards ★ ★

The standards of many states now include expectations that students be able to read and learn from informational texts. Although traditional reading instruction has focused on story reading, a real shift is occurring, and both fiction and informational reading are being highlighted. Standards such as the following are frequently found:

- Use information to form questions.
- Summarize content using text organization.
- Use table of contents.
- Use information presented in simple tables, pictures, and charts.

Standards for teachers also may specifically address the importance of teaching content reading. For example, Illinois now has a reading strategy standard for all content area teachers. Check to see what you will be expected to know and be able to do as a teacher helping students with reading to learn. Then examine the instruction provided elementary students in your schools. Do students have regular opportunities to engage with informational texts and build their confidence by reading a wide range of materials?

students who have read widely possess the background knowledge that enables them to remember new material and deepen their knowledge schemata. (See Chapter 6 for a discussion of the role of schemata in reading and comprehending.) Instead of diminishing, the demands on learners as readers are increasing.

Another implication of the current accountability climate for teachers is that even the assessments of students' reading abilities are now much more balanced between reading for literary purposes and reading to learn. These newer assessments reflect the fact that for students to be successful as readers throughout schooling and life, they need to read for a variety of purposes from a variety of materials. Reading fiction for pleasure is only one of many forms reading takes. More important for school success across the curriculum is the ability to read informational texts and learn from them (Ogle & Blachowicz, 2001). Standardized tests, state performance assessments and the current international tests (Donahue (2001), Organization for Cooperation & Development, 2000; Sainsbury, 2001) all incorporate a variety of materials and purposes. Reading for information is as important as reading for literary purposes. Many state standards tests balance fiction with informational passages. Standardized tests also include a range of reading passages and expect students to be able to read for literary purposes, for information, and to perform tasks.

Instructional Priorities

Despite the priority being placed on informational reading in society and in tests, the data collected recently in studies of classrooms (Duke, 2000; Taylor et al., 2000; Pressley et al., 2001) indicate that primary teachers have not shifted their teaching to reflect these higher expectations of students. Most primary teachers are still using fiction almost exclusively in their teaching. This is not adequate preparation for children who will live most of their literate lives in a culture of nonfiction with responsibility to learn from their engagements with texts of many types. Studies in intermediate classrooms replicating Durkin's early work (1978) also indicate that little instruction is given to students on how to read informational texts (Pressley et al., 1998). Responsible teachers need to provide a broad range of instruction in reading strategies and purposes and make students comfortable negotiating a variety of text types. Students deserve this help so that they can be successful learners for life.

Because purpose has such a powerful effect on individual reading habits, it is important to provide opportunities for many purposes, from learning new information to performing tasks to recreating experiences and representing them in new ways. Teachers need to prioritize the importance of learning to read and remembering information in textbooks and the reference materials that are used heavily in schools. This kind of reading ability often determines whether students will be successful throughout their schooling. Informational reading does not develop automatically and deserves concerted attention by teachers. In addition, teachers need to help students use a variety of materials as they engage in inquiry and report writing. Reading across texts, comparing authors and ideas, and evaluating materials are important priorities in many assessments. Students' abilities to read, write, and think critically will become even more important in the future, especially with the range of unedited ideas available on the Internet. Today's classrooms need to reflect the kinds of experiences that will help students develop these skills throughout their elementary and middle school years.

Teachers as Role Models

One of the most important things teachers can do to help students become engaged readers of informational materials is to model such reading themselves. Teachers can use their own insights as a starting point in helping students; they can provide immersion in and demonstrations of a variety of informational texts. By sharing widely ranging forms of reading—from newspapers to professional books and articles, to biographies and autobiographies, and other materials—teachers can help students appreciate the breadth of what reading is and set the stage to help students develop the different strategies they can use in reading.

A natural starting place is to share some personal reading interests with students. You can talk about what you read, share some materials with them, and then read aloud from these materials and from good informational texts at the students' level. A good guideline is to read daily from a variety of informational materials. For example, read interesting pieces from the newspaper, perhaps about how to raise special flowering plants, about current music or entertainment, or something about the foods we eat. You and your students can learn together. This is often one of the gifts of reading to learn: With the changing nature of our world, we all can learn together. Later in the day, read aloud something related to a topic the class is studying, from a more difficult text than the students would be able to handle themselves—perhaps a biography or magazine article. This can be valuable in helping the students understand that their curriculum relates to what others know and care about and can help them develop a broader vocabulary and sense of how content is structured by adults.

Understanding Comprehension in Informational Texts

Learning from reading is an active, ongoing process that can be described by what we do before, during, and after engagement with a text. Just as we do with reading literature (see Chapter 6), we follow the simple ABCs of reading to learn. We begin by *anticipating* what we want and need to learn. Then we *build knowledge* as we read and engage with authors. Finally, we *consolidate* the ideas with what we previously knew, sometimes modifying those ideas and sometimes expanding on them. This ongoing process is also a recursive one. That is, with each new set of ideas we read, we rethink what we knew, ask new questions and set new purposes, and build on the ideas that are freshly ours. Some essential aspects that undergird active reading to learn include the following:

- Assessing schemata or prior knowledge
- Assuming a metacognitive orientation
- Setting ones own purposes and asking questions
- Actively seeking information and making notes so that it can be retained for connecting and organizing ideas
- Forming interpretations of what is read
- Consolidating new information and ideas
- Analyzing and evaluating the sources and adequacy of information
- Creating a synthesis and representation of the learning that can be shared
- Reaching conclusions about and finding applications of what has been learned

As students develop their own control over reading to learn, all of these aspects of the process need attention. How teachers introduce learning tasks to students and give students instructional tools to use as they learn will determine to a great degree students' success at becoming learners. Planning carefully across each year, beginning with initial assessment of what students already know and can do and then structuring good teaching and guided practice activities, will lead both teachers and students to success.

The Importance of Background Knowledge

Reading is always an active, constructive process during which students need to activate what they know to make sense of text. As was noted in Chapter 6, readers comprehend by having the details in the material they are reading lead them to evoke relevant knowledge schemata. Then they use these schemes to give meaning to the details and, ideally, to understand the meaning of the whole passage. There are at least four kinds of background knowledge that readers need in order to comprehend well. The first is knowledge of the *vocabulary*. The second is knowledge of *text structure*. The third and fourth deal with *content knowledge*, both *topical* and *principled*.

VOCABULARY.   One of the most important tools to understanding content is having a grasp of how the key terms are used in a specific content. Vocabulary represents the knowledge of words and their meanings. In reading, the issue of vocabulary knowledge ranges between word recognition and comprehension. In word recognition, children

The layout of a book or magazine can either encourage or impede the understanding of the content. What would the design of a textbook need to look like in order to be attractive to middle school students?

may labor to recognize a word in print, but once they recognize it, they know the spoken word and its meaning. On the meaning end, students might be able to recognize or sound out a word but not comprehend its meaning, or they might recognize a word and know some but not all of its meanings. Obviously, a reader must know the meanings of most of the words in a text to read it successfully.

KNOWLEDGE OF TEXT STRUCTURE.   The structure of a text is a little like the grammar of a sentence. Because you understand the grammar of a sentence such as "The man bit the dog," you know who was bitten and who did the biting. In the same fashion, if you understand the structures of stories, you know how to follow a plot. If you can understand the structure of explanations, you know how to find the questions and get the answers to them. If you understand the structure of persuasive writing, you know how to spot the claim and weigh the support for it (Goldman & Rakestraw, 2000). The more you know about the way informational articles and texts are generally organized, the more you will be able to predict and read actively. This knowledge of structure also helps you retain what you read, since you can organize the ideas into major categories for memory.

TOPICAL CONTENT KNOWLEDGE.   This term **topical content knowledge** represents a fairly shallow level of knowledge, consisting of little more than some passing familiarity with the subject of the reading. For example, assume that while reading, a little girl is faced with a scientific passage about ducks. If she has seen a Donald Duck cartoon (and realizes that the character of Donald is based loosely on a real duck), she will have some topical knowledge about ducks. She will realize that ducks have beaks, two wings, and two webbed feet and that they make quacking sounds. This amount of knowledge will not help much when reading a scientific text about ducks, but at least it will help the child picture what is being talked about.

PRINCIPLED CONTENT KNOWLEDGE.   In contrast to topical content knowledge, **principled content knowledge** is knowledge of a deeper kind. It consists of familiarity with the topic as well as an understanding of its parts, its causes and effects, and other issues related to it (Gelman & Greeno, 1989). For example, readers who have studied the lives of geese and know something of the lives of migratory aquatic birds will have principled knowledge with which to understand a scientific passage about ducks.

Readers with principled knowledge are better prepared to understand challenging passages than are readers with only topical knowledge. Their curiosity is likely to be deeper, and their expectations will conform more closely to the unfolding presentation of information in the text. The reader with topical knowledge, by contrast, might recognize isolated parts of the information in the text but will be less prepared to make sense of the flow of information or the more important ideas in the text.

The Teacher's Role in Guiding Instruction

The choices teachers make in determining instructional focus and the kind of guidance they provide greatly influence how students think as they read and make a difference in the kinds of knowledge students gain about the subject matter in the curriculum. Too often, content reading becomes frustrating for both students and teachers. To prevent this, teachers need to take care to focus instructional time on the most important aspects of comprehension development. As has already been noted, a key is to ensure that students have an understanding of how the content or text they are reading is organized. This framework provides a structure within which students can distinguish key ideas from those of lesser importance. During instruction, teachers have several important tasks. These include modeling and guiding engagement with text, teaching skills and strategies, eliciting students' own interests and motivation and providing adequate time for students to explore ideas and concepts in depth.

DEVELOPING PRINCIPLED KNOWLEDGE.   The kinds of knowledge students gain about the subject matter in the curriculum is very important. In reading to learn, the content-specific information needs attention, something that is not a priority when reading fiction. A key to comprehending a text is linking ideas presented within and across sentences to create a sense of a whole text. Teachers influence students' knowledge formation in two important ways: by the questions they ask and by the depth of study they encourage with their students.

The Questions Teachers Ask.   The ideas to which you call children's attention, by means of your questions or comments, influence the course of the children's thinking about what they read and study. You can direct students' attention toward important ideas or trivial ones. When reading a story, it makes a difference whether you dwell on minor details or ask questions that call attention to the deep structural elements of the story: the character's problem, goal, conflicts, and solutions to problems or the author's message or theme in the story. When reading informational text, it matters whether you call attention to minor details or to important ideas such as chronological development, cause and effect, or hierarchical relationships between ideas.

The Depth to Which Teachers Lead Children to Study a Topic.   You can encourage children to gain deeper knowledge about topics by staying with subjects for more than brief periods. You also can enhance children's understanding by looking at topics through many different disciplines. For example, look at a historical phenomenon such as immigration through fictional works in addition to the social studies text. By seeing phenomena through the eyes of fictional participants, students have more possibility of connecting with, visualizing, and interpreting the concept. Lengthy discussions, especially those that make connections between the subject of study and the children's own experience, also make it more likely that children will form deep, principled knowledge about a subject (see Allington & Johnston, 2002).

SKILLS AND STRATEGIES.   In addition to some background knowledge with which to understand text, readers need skills and strategies. **Skills** are processes that readers use habitually. **Strategies** are the processes by which they use their skills under conscious control. Teachers need to know what skills and strategies students possess and consciously develop a strong repertoire in all students.

When children first learn to read, they may be taught to perform comprehension activities consciously as reading strategies. For example, when they come across a word they do not know, the teacher might urge them to read to the end of the line to get a sense of the meaning of the sentence, then go back and guess the unknown word. This strategy is known as the *reading ahead/reread activity*. Later on—possibly much later on and after continued support from the teacher—when the readers habitually use the context to figure out unknown words, the behavior has become a skill.

When readers are working with difficult material, however, or when they want to be especially careful in their reading, skilled readers often employ some reading strategies consciously (Pressley & Afflerbach, 1995). For example, even when their reading skills are adequate for comprehending a reading in a social studies text, readers might choose to consciously apply the strategy of summarizing and rehearsing main ideas in order to remember them for a discussion the next day.

INTEREST AND MOTIVATION.   Performing acts of comprehension takes some effort, and exerting effort takes will. No wonder children are more likely to take the trouble to do what they need to do to understand what they read when the topic is interesting to them. This fact, while not always honored in school curriculum, has been recognized for the better part of a century (Dewey, 1913; Beane, 2002; Guthrie, 2002). But readers may be interested in a topic in different ways, and these differences have consequences. In the chapter-opening vignette, as Ms. Gurvitz began her unit on the pond, she had a naturalist speak with the children and show them samples of the frogs that were deformed. This piqued their interest. Readers might be interested in a topic because it has been presented in an engaging way—with exciting illustrations or dramatically written and with explanation points. Or they might be interested because they have some reason to find out more about a topic and they want to know more about the line of inquiry the text is following. For example, because you want to know how to help your present or future students read with comprehension, you might find this textbook of particular interest. You likely don't need movie poster–like illustrations to draw you into the ideas presented here. If you pick up the Sunday magazine in your newspaper, however, it might take an interesting picture with a curiosity-provoking caption to get you interested in reading about something that is new to you.

These motives for interest correspond to the kind of prior knowledge readers have about a topic. Readers who have principled knowledge about a topic tend to be interested in adding to and deepening that knowledge, whereas readers with the shallower, topical knowledge might not be motivated automatically to learn more about something through reading. Research has shown (Alexander, 1998) that readers with these different kinds of background knowledge will notice different things in a text. Readers with only topical knowledge might focus on flashy or exotic details to the exclusion of main ideas and arguments, while those with principled knowledge might do just the opposite.

THE "MATTHEW EFFECT": ASPECTS OF COMPREHENSION ARE INTERRELATED.
What we have just considered as separate aspects of comprehension—prior knowledge, strategies and skills, and interest—are in fact interrelated. Although it is true, as Duffy and Roehler (1992) and others have shown, that children can profit from being taught to carry out comprehension strategies, it is also true that reading comprehension develops as a conglomerate of achievements (Alexander et al., 1994). For example, engaging

prior knowledge can be helped along by teaching; however, for this teaching to be successful, children must have some prior knowledge of the topic to call on. Moreover, children are more likely to have deep enough interests in the topic to use the strategies of applying prior knowledge, making predictions, arguing with the text, or finding main ideas—unless their prior knowledge is deep and principled. To carry this point further, if their prior knowledge about a topic is deep and principled, then their interest in the topic will also extend below the surface to main ideas and structures of argument.

The process is cyclic and is an example of what researcher Keith Stanovich (1986) called the "Matthew effects" in reading (see Chapter 2). If young readers have deep and principled knowledge, they will have deep interest; if they have deep interest, they will use thoroughgoing strategies of comprehension; and if they use thoroughgoing strategies, they will gain more principled knowledge (see Figure 7.2). The cycle works the other way, too. A reader might lack deep knowledge, not habitually use thoroughgoing reading strategies, or have only superficial interest in the topics being read. These factors may interact to prevent satisfactory comprehension. The best teaching for comprehension, then, will include attention to all these aspects:

- Creating a learning environment in which students can become immersed in a topic over time and explore it deeply

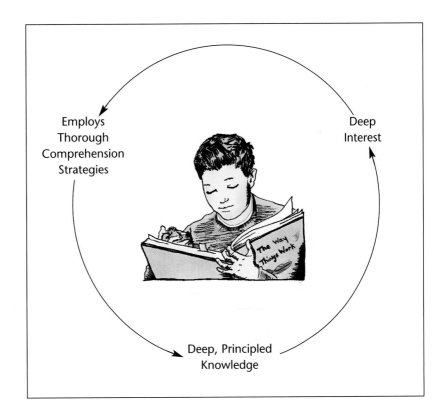

FIGURE 7.2

The Matthew Effect in Reading Comprehension.

- Guiding students' attention to the way the texts they read are organized
- Helping students develop principled knowledge by encouraging children to consider ideas deeply, and pointing them toward the main ideas and the underlying structures and issues
- Teaching thoroughgoing, powerful strategies for comprehending and remembering and then supporting and reinforcing these strategies until they become habituated into skills
- Engaging children in deep discussions of what they read and getting them to think about, write about, and respond to what they read so that they will understand issues deeply and extend their curiosity about things in the world
- Focusing their attention on the vocabulary of the topic or area so that they will develop a more precise way of thinking and differentiating ideas
- Encouraging students' questions and taking their inquiry seriously, weaving their deep-seated interests into the very fabric of the school day

Student Engagement

Although the teacher's role in developing a thoughtful classroom is critical, students play equally important roles as learners. Right from the beginning of the school year, teachers need to take time to observe how students approach learning. How involved and aware are students of what learning entails? They need to be active—and interactive—if they are going to be successful learners. People learn best when they do so strategically. That means taking charge of their own reading with a clear purpose. Just as in reading fiction (see Chapter 6), students need to be actively engaged while reading and learning from nonfiction and other content materials. Because content material is usually dense with ideas to be learned, the following strategies are especially important.

ANTICIPATING.   Students need to *anticipate*—to ask what they want to learn from the reading. They do this by first assessing what they know and what the task demands are and what needs to be accomplished. For young students, this initial orientation is modeled in the K-W-L framework discussed later in this chapter (see pp. 278–282). As students begin their engagement with a new topic, watch them and discuss with them how they begin. Do they skim through the material and activate what they know and make connections with the text? Do they look closely at diagrams or pictures and think about their meaning?

Once students have assessed their starting point in learning, they then need to develop a plan for how to proceed to accomplish their goals. That means knowing that there are options for how to proceed. Students too often think that all they can do is read and then reread. Rather, they need to know that they can use a variety of tools to guide their acquisition of knowledge. They are going to want to make notes when they encounter new information that is important or use some form of marginal notation if they can keep the materials. Post-it notes serve wonderful purposes in helping students keep track of what they want to learn. These notes can then be grouped later by the student to chunk information in a way that will give the student a more coherent sense of what is to be learned. Some students learn best when they can create a graphic network of ideas or draw diagrams of what they learn. Being active during the process of learning is essential. It takes little time to check whether students have some active strategies they use when reading informational material that is full of important concepts and main ideas. (Several strategies that support students' active engagement are discussed later in the chapter.)

BUILDING KNOWLEDGE. Students build knowledge as they deal with the ideas they are reading about. That means monitoring what they are thinking and learning, asking questions as they go, and creating summaries of ideas for themselves. Some students like to think aloud, others make notes in the margin or on sheets of paper, some prefer drawing key ideas to represent the text's main ideas, and some like to share with another person what they are getting out of a text as they read. Teachers need to model each of these approaches to building new learning. Asking students to put Post-it notes in their text material as they read is an easy diagnostic of how they attend to important elements of these texts. As you expand their options for engaged reading and help them practice these strategies frequently, your students will become better equipped to make decisions about which work best for them in particular situations.

CONSOLIDATING WHAT THEY LEARN. As students continue to build their knowledge and understanding as a result of reading, they also consolidate what they are learning. That means going back and thinking again about how the ideas fit together and what they mean. Students can create a new graphic representation of what they have learned. They might write an outline and then elaborate on it in a summary, or they might want to talk to someone about the ideas they have gained. If students are using a textbook or a guide from a teacher, they can return to the questions or talk about the main objectives. If students are going to retain important ideas, they need to actively do something with them—by summarizing or extending on what the authors have presented. Most elementary students need sustained teacher guidance and support to develop the habit of rehearsing what they are learning. Several graphic organizers discussed later in this chapter can help students to organize their thinking and provide good visual reviews of content. If they transform the ideas into a new form, students have a greater chance of remembering ideas. Simply asking the question "What did that mean to me?" helps students to stay active metacognitively. Strategies for working together to read, question, and reflect can be used with even the youngest students, who can learn to pair and ask each other what they have learned (Pressley, 2002).

Finally, good readers engage in evaluation of both the materials they read and their accomplishment. If the text seems unclear or lacking in information, they might decide to read other material to clarify ideas or to confirm accuracy and currency. Good readers also assess the achievement of their own purposes. Returning to their questions or categories that were unclear, good readers make sure they understand and have met their own purposes. They know that learning takes effort. Those who are not confident learners often feel disadvantaged when there are intense content expectations. You can help them to realize that they can learn new material but that it is a process that takes time and active involvement on their parts. Giving insecure learners and second language learners models of process learning and time to rehearse and clarify ideas is essential. They need to understand that reading a text once is never enough if the material is new and important. Studies of effective fourth-grade teachers (Allington & Johnston, 2002) revealed that they often help students to engage in rehearsing the same materials many times as a tool to their learning. Regularly modeling and reinforcing a process of anticipating, building knowledge, and consolidating learning will create active, confident readers (Pressley et al., 1992).

The Nature of Informational Texts

Reading to learn is linked generally to reading informational materials, not pieces of fiction or poetry. Successful reading for the sake of learning requires readers to develop specific strategies to use magazines, trade books, newspapers, primary documents, and Internet sites. For example, readers of informational texts will notice that they don't have to start on the first page and read to the end of the material. Rather, by using the table of contents and index, they can find a pertinent section without reading the whole text. Or they might be able to skip parts that are less essential to their purposes. The first thing they might observe about informational material is that it is organized differently from fiction both internally and externally.

Developing Familiarity with External Features of Informational Texts

One of the first things we notice when we pick up nonfiction or informational materials is that they generally have a format different from fiction, with many external aids to help readers negotiate them. These aids include the following:

Table of contents

Chapters

Headings and subheadings

Illustrations (maps, graphs, diagrams, pictures, cartoons, etc.)

Captions

Index

Vocabulary noted in italics or other graphic ways

Glossary of terms

References

In surveying the features of books, we note that in addition to a table of contents, these books generally include a glossary and index. The chapter titles are worth some attention, since they are often important indicators of how the author has organized the information. Within each chapter, there is likely to be a further breakdown of information with headings and subheadings designed to guide our reading to important content or main ideas. Many books and articles also highlight key vocabulary with italic or boldface type, or in marginal notes that provide explanations of the terms. A well-organized informational piece includes several of these external features that help us locate the part of the text we want to read when we have particular questions we want answered. In addition, because timely, accurate information is important, readers need to be aware of both the copyright date and the author's qualifications.

Books for very young readers are just now becoming more complete, so looking for chapter divisions is important before books are selected for primary students. Check to see whether the pages are numbered, since it is hard to locate and return to information without some pagination. As you help children use informational books, be sure you have high-quality books available for them. Sometimes the color photographs are stunning, but the rest of the important book features are inadequate or missing.

Some books now display graphics in a wide variety of places on the pages and often on a two-page spread. The captions are often placed variously, too. Sometimes the captions are beneath the picture; at other times, they are beside or even above the illustrated material. Only by carefully studying the individual pages and mapping the positions of text, graphics, and captions can their relationships be determined. Then it is important to share with the children that process of exploration and what is learned about the text layout. Without support from teachers, young readers can overlook much of the richness of these new informational texts. When you introduce a new informational text or textbook, it is useful to do a picture and visual walk through the text. Each new text deserves attention because there are so many different formats and organization is highlighted in so many ways.

FOCUS STUDENTS' ATTENTION ON FEATURES.   As a way to reinforce the special nature of informational books, you could have students complete a nonfiction book report using the checklist shown in Figure 7.3. The book report might ask for what

Title   ———————————————

Author   ———————————————

Nonfiction Book Checklist

———— 1. Table of Contents
———— 2. Index
———— 3. Photographs
———— 4. Realistic, accurate illustrations
———— 5. Maps
———— 6. Diagrams
———— 7. Captions – bold lettering
———— 8. Glossary – words and definitions
———— 9. Page numbers
———— 10. Other

Something I liked about this book:

Something I learned from this book:

FIGURE 7.3

Nonfiction Book Checklist.

they liked, what they learned, and what would make the book better. When their attention is drawn to these features of the text, students begin to use them more regularly and think of them as resources (adapted from D. Gurvitz).

Intermediate-grade teachers also can have children preview expository texts they are using both as textbooks and as other resource materials. At the beginning of the year, it is always good to refresh students' use of all the ways information is available. Reading aloud to students from magazines and books and consciously thinking aloud provides further opportunity to focus attention on illustrations, captions, and other presentations of information. Making a transparency of the first one or two pages in a chapter or arti-

TEACH IT!

★ ★ ★ ★

Using the Table of Contents to Predict

There are many ways to help students become familiar with the structure and organization of informational materials. One of the easiest is to predict what content a book might contain and then check the table of contents to see how the authors have organized the text. For example, before beginning an oral reading of a book on polar bears, a first-grade teacher asked her students what they thought they might learn as they listened to her read this interesting book. One eager boy blurted out, "How they fish for their food!" Soon other children volunteered their ideas: why they are white, how they take care of their babies, and more. The teacher praised the children for their ideas and then turned to the table of contents of the book. She ran her finger down the list of chapters or sections and said, "Um, yes, the book begins with 'An Arctic Home'—that must tell about where they live. 'A Fight for Food'—that must tell us about how they get their food." In this way she modeled for the students the way they can begin to think like experts—and build the foundation for principled knowledge of polar bears.

With older students, skimming through the headings of an article or chapter can provide an overview of the organization the authors' have indicated. When these reader aids do not indicate the text structure, students can do a quick read and use Post-it notes to label the text parts as they occur. Then students can create a graphic organizer to guide their reading of the material. Many teachers have found that having students learn to create graphic organizers of informational texts (articles, chapters or books) provides a good road map for reading materials that might seem so dense that readers are in danger of getting get lost in details otherwise.

Refer to your **Teach It!** booklet for further activities you can use to reinforce concepts discussed in this chapter.

cle lets you talk with the students about what they do when they navigate a page of informational text. In fact, informational texts are similar to the computer screens at which many students spend a great deal of leisure time. They can have fun exploring the similarities and differences in materials presented in these two formats. After such a comparison, encourage students to add diagrams and other visuals or links from their textbooks to other sources. They can become active in making materials more accessible to them. Rather than feeling overwhelmed by texts, students need to develop confidence in using texts and in going beyond single texts when these are not clear.

Predict Tables of Contents.   Intermediate students should begin to anticipate how informative expository material is organized. By third grade, most students should be able to predict what might be in the table of contents of an animal book (description, habitat, food, family, etc.). Before studying regions of the earth in fourth grade, some students should be able to identify some possible topics that will reoccur with each region studied (plants, animals, geography, human life, etc.). Fifth graders need to know that biographies have some common topics that are used to organize information (early life, education, hardships, accomplishments). One way to assess students' awareness of these expert ways of organizing content information and then using it to prepare for reading and learning is to have them create a possible table of contents alone or with a partner. In this way, teachers can help students begin to think more deeply and begin to develop principled knowledge.

Create Chapter Graphic Organizers.   At the middle grade level, some teachers have students identify and use the external structure of chapters in textbooks and magazines to make notes. They skim through the chapter and create a graphic organizer or map of the chapter with the title in the center and each of the main headings on one spoke of their spider map (see Figure 7.4 on page 272). This graphic organizer is then used while students read to help them understand how the information is related. This mapping of the text can also be used as an interactive guide for reading. The students can brainstorm what they know about each section before reading; write those ideas on the map; highlight the areas that are least familiar and that will require slower reading, note making, and possible rereading; and then make notes on their map of new information as they read. This active engagement helps students to focus and retain information as they read.

Jigsaw Text Sections.   Another strategy teachers use to help students utilize the external structure of articles and chapters is to have a chapter read in cooperative fashion using a type of "jigsaw" cooperative learning strategy. The class first previews the text by identifying the major sections, and the teacher writes these on the board. Then the class is divided into teams, one team per major section. Each team of students reads and creates a visual report of the key ideas of their one section of the text. Because many of the informational chapters and articles have such a heavy load of information, asking students to learn just one section from reading makes it manageable. Each group then reports on their section. Serving as "teachers" for the rest of the class both enhances the students' engagement in reading and creates a shared environment for learning.

USE VISUAL AND GRAPHIC INFORMATION.   Information that is presented visually in pictures, diagrams, and graphics is also critical in many informational texts. Think of an informational book you have recently read or a children's book such as

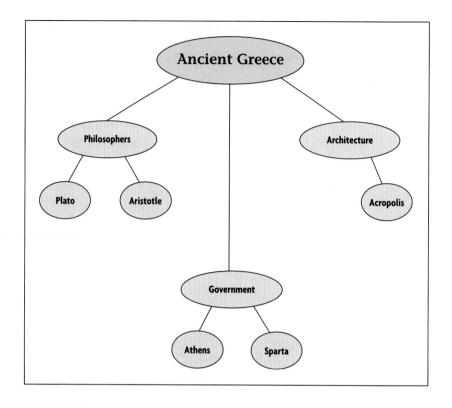

A Chapter Graphic Organizer.

My Season with Penguins (Webb, 2000) with its maps, drawings, and journal format. Today, good informational books, textbooks, and magazines use more pictures and visuals to enhance engagement and help readers understand the concepts than ever before. Much of the information is, in fact, often presented in the pictures, graphs, diagrams, maps, cartoons, and their captions. This visual information is often essential to understanding the content. Teachers need to help students read this information and integrate it into the rest of the narrative textual content.

There are several ways in which you can guide students' use of these texts to learn. First, you need to assess how students attend to pages of busy text. Informally ask students individually to describe how they read a two-page spread in a book or magazine. As they do, make notes of their approaches. Where do they start? Do they read the visually presented information? When do they read it? Do they integrate the visuals and the running text? Do they read captions on graphs and pictures? Are they aware of how they approach reading when the materials are presented in a variety of formats? Do they integrate these different sources in notes they make or in summaries they create? Questions such as these can help you to assess students' engagements with text materials.

From this assessment, you can develop your instructional focus. A good starting point is modeling how to approach busy text by doing think-alouds, such as the following, with groups of students. Make a transparency of one or two pages of text and, using an overhead projector, demonstrate how you survey the page, noting the different layout of information and graphics and raising questions that are stimulated by the text. Start by looking at the title of the chapter or section, note the way the sections are marked—with boldface print or words in capital letters, for example. Then focus on the visuals, such as pictures, diagrams, or notes in the margins. You might ask, "Why did the author/s use this cartoon? What is its role in this section? Let's see, the caption says . . . . Oh, yes, I bet it is an example of . . . ." You can also cover the text on the transparency and ask students to survey the graphic information. From this survey, ask them to predict what content they think is being highlighted and what questions they think will be answered on the next page or two. In this way, the importance of using the visually presented material may become clearer to them. In fact, sometimes this kind of preview can reduce the actual reading time considerably.

When a teacher takes time to think aloud about how to approach informational texts, students begin to think metacognitively about their own approaches to texts. Adults use many of these strategies automatically when appropriate. Students, by contrast, often need to hear another person's thinking before they understand how active they need to be as readers.

Developing Understanding of Internal Organization

Another key to reading and learning from materials written to inform is becoming familiar with the way the writer has organized the ideas. As readers of narrative stories, we have learned—often first by listening to stories our parents read to us—that there is a predictable pattern to fiction. We read to find out who the characters are, what problem they encounter, and how they go about resolving it; and then we savor their victory at the end. No similar single pattern characterizes informational texts. They are written with different internal organization patterns. The most common ways of organizing ideas include the following:

Description (main ideas and details)

Compare/contrast

Problem/solution

Cause/effect

Sequence of events

TEACH IT!

22

These varying patterns can make predicting and organizing ideas more difficult for novice readers; therefore, it is all the more important that teachers provide guidance so that students can learn to identify these internal structures. As they do, their ability to write informational pieces and reports more effectively also will improve. Here again, graphic organizers can help students recognize the underlying organization of texts. Some simple models are shown in Figure 7.5 on page 274.

COMPARE TEXTS.   One way to introduce students to internal patterns is by collecting several books on the same topic and guiding students to compare their internal structures. By introducing the reading of the book in this way, you engage the students in thinking of the big picture of what an author is trying to accomplish in a text. An easy way to create varieties of texts is to download articles from online encyclopedias and Internet articles and compare their organization. This can be a starting place for contrasting and comparing longer articles and books.

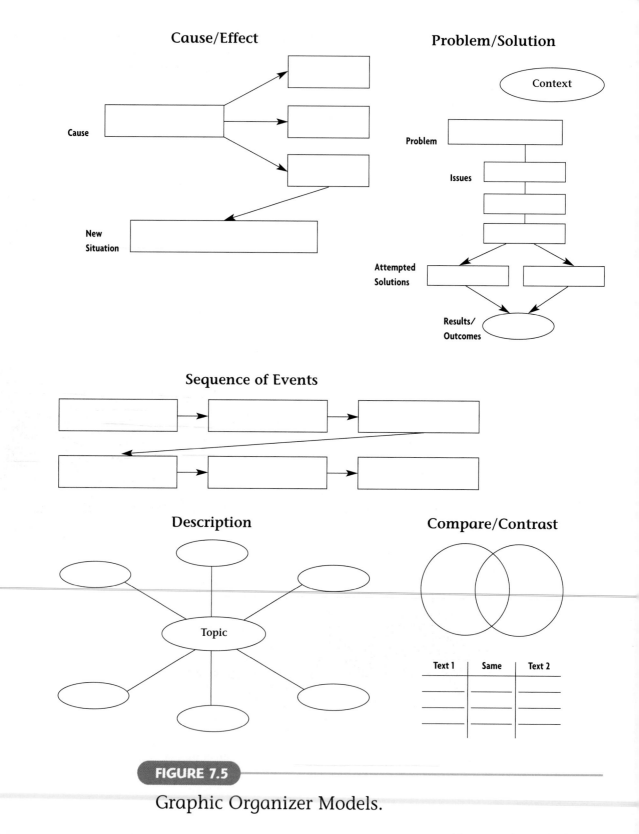

Cause/Effect

Cause

New
Situation

Problem/Solution

Context

Problem

Issues

Attempted
Solutions

Results/
Outcomes

Sequence of Events

Description

Topic

Compare/Contrast

Text 1   Same   Text 2

FIGURE 7.5

Graphic Organizer Models.

WRITE TEXTS.   A good way to help students apply their knowledge of text organization is to have them write their own books using the structure of one they have studied. For example, during a unit on insects, third-grade students used Brown's (1949) *The Important Book* as a model for their writing. Each student wrote about his or her chosen insect and used the book structure as a guide. Figure 7.6 shows examples of how two students used this structure for their reporting. One wrote the text, and the other used the computer for the content; both created special illustrations of their insects.

ATTEND TO VOCABULARY AND CONTENT-SPECIFIC TERMINOLOGY.   A key to learning content material is attention to vocabulary that conveys key concepts. Again, the differences between reading for one's own purposes and reading to learn are dramatic. When one reads for oneself, unfamiliar vocabulary can be ignored. In fact, good readers attend only to information that they know is helpful in comprehending.

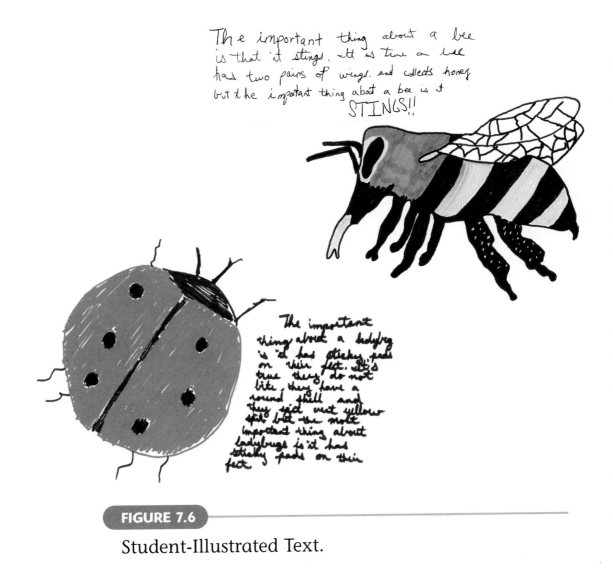

FIGURE 7.6

Student-Illustrated Text.

Therefore, unfamiliar terms are skipped. In reading to learn, however, this practice can hinder comprehension. The unfamiliar terms are often exactly what the reader needs to attend to. Therefore, the teacher needs to help students develop the habit of attending to key terms that are content carriers. There are three important components to vocabulary learning in content materials:

- Words the authors prioritize (e.g., with boldface, italics, marginal definitions, or illustrations)
- Teacher-highlighted key new terms
- Students' own monitoring of what words are new and need to be learned

The first place to start in attending to vocabulary is by noting what the authors have already indicated as important. Students often overlook these aids without teacher guidance. Because authors often help readers by highlighting these terms, helping students to preview material to find these indicated words can be a great help to later reading and learning.

Teachers can help students note key words, too, by creating a list of key terms and then giving students some activities to focus their attention on these terms. One easy way to do this is to ask students to connect two (or three) of the terms and create new sentences using them (see Figure 7.7). Even if the students do not know much about the words, they can have fun anticipating what they mean. Working with partners to create new sentences gives children a chance to use the words orally, too, thus increasing their awareness of the words both visually and orally. A more sophisticated activ-

---

CONNECT TWO

Look over these words that are important in the chapter we will read on glaciers. Choose two and use them in a single sentence. Then try to connect another pair in a new sentence. You don't know much about what these words mean yet, but try to guess their meanings and possible uses.

Words   Meaning
Glacier
Moraine
Debris
Epoch
Pleistocene
Ice
retreat

_____

Sentence:

_____

Sentence:

FIGURE 7.7

Connect Two.

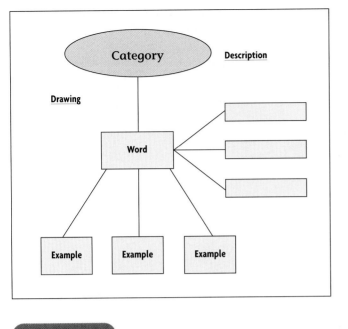

Concept of Definition Map.

ity is to ask students to chunk new words into categories and then label the groups and justify them to the class. The children now are attuned to these words and will definitely notice them as they read.

Students need to follow their initial search for terms with some active ways of retaining them. You can model this process by keeping a list of key terms on the board or on a word wall. This list can include both the words you introduced and ones the students identify as important. Then students can find more examples of these words being used in other places in their reading and listening and build a more elaborate meaning for the words. Asking students to draw their own images of the terms also helps to lock new words in place. Elaborating associations with new words through drawings and personal examples will help students to retain the words. Concept maps for the terms can also be used (see Figure 7.8). In this way, students learn that terms have meanings, associated examples, and attributes.

Specific terms are critical in content learning. Students need to move from dependence on textbook and trade book highlights to their own metacognitive control over what words are new to them, and they need to develop ways to retain those particular terms. Making new vocabulary a part of the oral talk of the classroom is an essential component in this process. Some teachers use a reward system to encourage usage, such as giving students points when they hear and note a new word being used by a fellow student. This highlights oral as well as written vocabulary recognition and provides an internal incentive as well.

Strategies for Active Reading of Informational Text

As students become familiar with the structure of informational text, it is important that they develop ways to actively engage with the authors of those texts and think about the content. There are some basic strategies worth practicing to the extent that students can use them on their own. They have been developed independently but often work well when used together.

Prereading Preparation

Until students are able to take control of their learning by finding their own questions and level of knowledge, it is unlikely that they will retain much of what is studied. Therefore, the time spent activating personal and class interest is important.

K-W-L Charts provide a good strategy for motivating students' interest in new topics.

TEACH IT!
24

K-W-L.   Students become much more engaged in reading when they and their interests are the starting point for new inquiry and learning. K-W-L (Ogle, 1986, 1991) is a group process in which the teacher models and guides active engagement with informational texts. It uses the knowledge and information students bring to help each other build a better starting place for learning and for sharing the results of their reading. The adept teacher weaves together what some class members know (either topical or principled knowledge) and stimulates questions for all to pursue as they read to learn. The process also helps students who lack confidence in both reading and writing, since the teacher is the first one to write on the board. This permits children to see the written forms of key terms they will encounter later in the text. It also models what the students will write on their own guidesheets (see Figure 7.9) or in their learning logs.

What We *Know.*   The teacher and students begin the process of reading and learning by brainstorming together what they *know* (the K in K-W-L) about the topic. The teacher guides students to probe their knowledge statements and find conflicting or partial statements of what they know. For example, as a group brainstorms what they *know* about the desert, one student says, "Nothing much lives there." Another volunteers, "That's not true! I know lots of insects live there. I just read a book about tarantulas."

The teacher can encourage more student engagement by continuing the thinking: "Does anyone else know something about what lives in the dry, barren lands of the desert? Can anyone frame a question that may help us find out more?"

Another student chimes in, "We'd better find out what animals can survive there with little water or food."

The teacher writes on the blackboard, overhead, or computer what the students ask as their own questions, and what they volunteer they think they know, writing

1. K – What We Know	W – What We Want to Learn	L – What We Learned and Still Need to Know

2. Categories of Information We Expect to Use:	3. Where We Will Find Information:
A. E.	1.
B. F.	2.
C. G.	3.
D. H.	4.

FIGURE 7.9

K-W-L Guide.

Source: From "K-W-L: A Teaching Model That Develops Active Reading of Expository Text,"
by D. Ogle, *The Reading Teacher* (1986), 36(6), pp. 564–570.

WHAT WE KNOW

Lots of snakes
Sand and windy
Cactus
Road Runners
Tarantulas
Hot weather
No water
No rain
Gila monster
Lizards
Bats
Phoenix
Sun City
Oil under the ground
Utah and Arizona

FIGURE 7.10

What We Know
about Deserts.

down their ideas just as the students volunteer them (see Figure 7.10). The teacher does not correct or evaluate but encourages and stimulates students to think broadly about what they bring to the study. Through this brainstorming process, some questions or uncertainties generally surface.

The teacher's role is to help students activate their knowledge and develop interest in the topic. Some basic rules are established at the beginning:

- All ideas are acceptable.
- Say what first comes into your mind. These ideas will be later checked and edited or revised later.
- Listen to each other, but do not judge the quality of ideas.
- The goal is to get as many different ideas out as possible in the time allotted.

As ideas are voiced and written down, they might seem random and unconnected. At this point, the teacher needs to make a decision. If the group is engaged and ready to think a little more deeply, the teacher will ask the students to think of ways in which the experts organize information on this topic. This move to a deeper level of thinking (to principled knowledge) can begin by first focusing on categories of information about which the children already have some intuitive knowledge. The teacher can initiate reflection: "Look at what we listed in the 'Know' column. Are any of these items connected? For example, I see three items about animals that live on the desert. I also see some plants. Can you find other items that go together in a category? What are the basic categories of information we are likely to need to use?" In this case, the categories might be those shown in Figure 7.11.

The teacher might also begin simply by asking students to step back and think about the topic generally: "If you were going to write a table of contents on this topic, the desert, what would you include?" The ideas students volunteer can be listed on the bottom of the "Know" column.

What We *Want* to Know.   With a variety of ideas being shared the teacher can easily ask what the students *want* (the W in K-W-L) to know. Again, it is the students' responsibility to think of real questions as the teacher writes down what they say.

Categories of Information:

A. animals   C. location   E. physical features
B. climate   D. plants

FIGURE 7.11

Categories of Information.

These questions form the second column on the worksheet or blackboard. If students are not familiar with the process of generating their own questions, the teacher might need to model some questioning at the beginning. The teacher might be able to extend comments made by class members into questions.

For example, if the class is beginning a unit on the desert region and someone has listed cactus as a plant in the desert, the teacher can extend this by suggesting, "I wonder whether there are any uses people make of cactus in the desert?"

The teacher can write this in the "We Want to Know" column and continue to guide students to find questions, suggesting, "Is there anything else we might want to learn about the animals that live on the desert? Do we have to be careful of any of them? If we were hiking, should we watch out?"

This process puts the students right in the center of any new study. Rather than beginning with a text and previewing it, the students and the teacher become active listeners and recorders. This group-focusing effort helps students think about the range of ideas that they and others already have on the topic. It should also help them make new connections and become intrigued by what they don't know. Listening to each other can stimulate new vocabulary and associations; the writing done by the teacher often helps more reluctant readers begin to make associations between oral language and the written forms of words they will encounter as they read.

Once the students have discussed the topic, they are more ready to begin their own reading. It might be useful to have students individually write down on their own worksheets or learning logs the pieces of information they individually think they *know* and the questions they *want* to know more about. In this way, both the group and the individual are respected. You could have students work in pairs to do both the writing and reading, as this is more stimulating and supportive of some children who lack confidence in writing and taking risks.

What We *Learned*.   Teachers can diagnose from this discussion what texts will be most useful to the students. It might be that what the teacher thought would be adequate turns out to be inappropriate. Rather than reading the planned text, the class can collect other materials and even write some of their own materials as needed. This is where the Internet can come in handy as a resource. Look up a few sites, and bookmark them for the class. If the text or texts in the classroom and school library are appropriate, students can read and make notes on their own of what they *learn* (the L in K-W-L)—both answers to their questions and unexpected information that they think is interesting and/or important. Many teachers create large bulletin boards with sections for the "What We Know," "What We Want to Learn," and "What We Learned" sections of the K-W-L. Students can keep adding information and questions to the class chart as they study. Small index cards work well for this kind of class activity. You can also make photocopies of material or graphics that students find and want to have shared.

K-W-L+.   After years of working with students in content areas, teachers know that even with motivation and engagement, students will not remember much of the new information the first time they encounter it. Therefore, the "plus" in K-W-L+ (Carr & Ogle, 1987) extends this learning process by asking students to do more reorganizing of what they have learned by making a semantic map or graphic organizer of the key information (see Figure 7.12 on page 282). Students select the major categories and list facts under those categories, thus rethinking what they are learning.

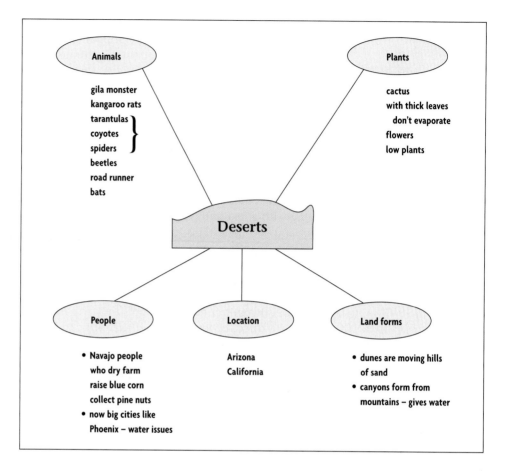

FIGURE 7.12

K-W-L+ Semantic Map.

Finally, they write what they have learned in an essay, summary, or more personal form (see the example in Figure 7.13). The cognitive activity needed to use ideas they have been learning in a new written format deepens memory and provides an additional opportunity to consolidate their learning. Engaging actively in this variety of learning gives the students a sense of how they can become active learners on their own, even when the teacher is not present. Reorganizing and rehearsing new knowledge and connecting it with what was previously known establishes for students the effort needed in learning and reinforces their personal self-esteem, since they possess a productive process for school tasks.

I-CHART.   Using multiple sources of information is an important way to help students find texts that meet their own levels of knowledge and interest, find answers to their own questions, and compare and contrast authors' points of view. It encourages the critical thinking that is so needed in the world today. Yet many students have a difficult time using more than one source effectively. Hoffman (1992) has developed

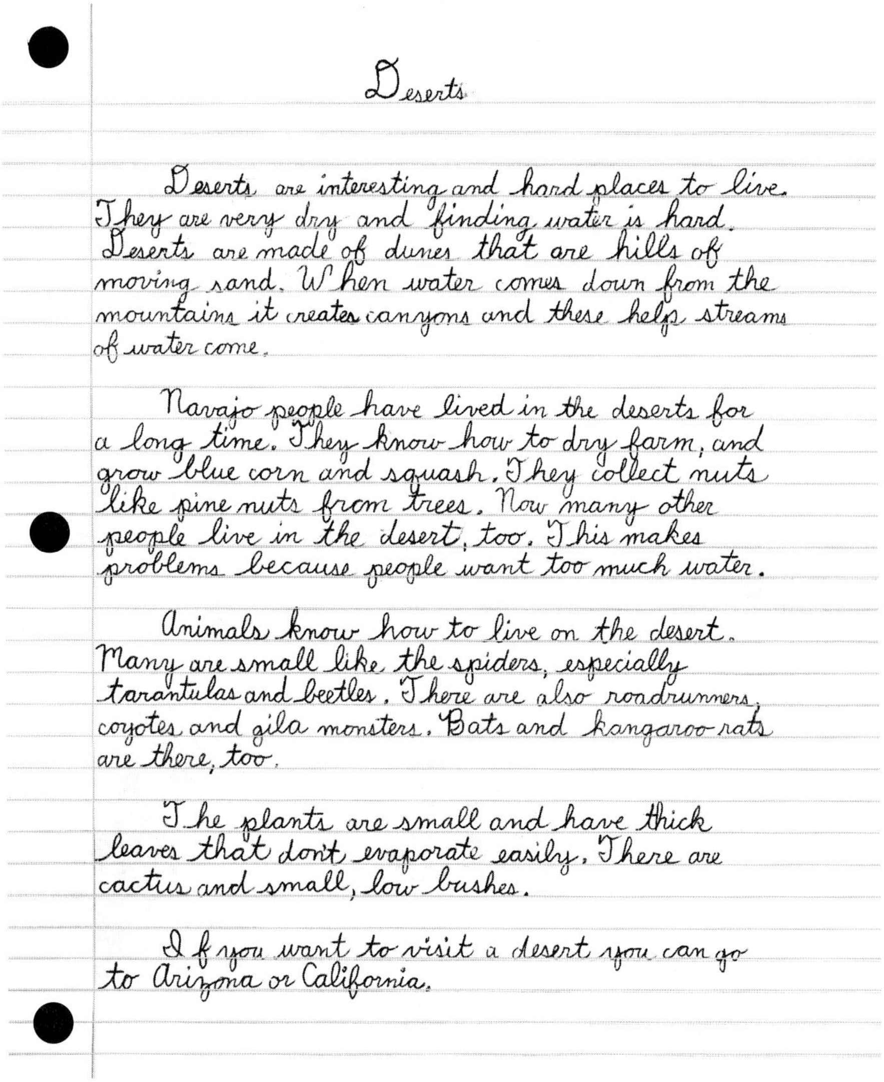

Deserts

Deserts are interesting and hard places to live. They are very dry and finding water is hard. Deserts are made of dunes that are hills of moving sand. When water comes down from the mountains it creates canyons and these help streams of water come.

Navajo people have lived in the deserts for a long time. They know how to dry farm, and grow blue corn and squash. They collect nuts like pine nuts from trees. Now many other people live in the desert, too. This makes problems because people want too much water.

Animals know how to live on the desert. Many are small like the spiders, especially tarantulas and beetles. There are also roadrunners, coyotes and gila monsters. Bats and kangaroo rats are there, too.

The plants are small and have thick leaves that don't evaporate easily. There are cactus and small, low bushes.

If you want to visit a desert you can go to Arizona or California.

FIGURE 7.13

K-W-L+ Essay.

a very useful tool in the **I-Chart** (see Figure 7.14 on page 284), which helps students take important questions, select three to four sources of information they want to use to explore those questions, and then come to their own conclusion about the questions they framed initially.

Once students have used the K-W-L process to activate their knowledge and interest, they select some key questions for more in-depth research they can do together. The class or small groups can decide on the questions they want to concentrate on and write these on the chart. Then the best sources of information for the questions are

Questions	What We Know	Text 1	Text 2	Text 3	Summary
1.					
2.					
3.					
Interesting new info./ New questions					

FIGURE 7.14

I-Chart.

selected, usually with teacher help and guidance, and are also listed across the top of the chart. This simple framework establishes that in seeking answers to questions multiple sources are needed. The practice of summarizing the information and answering their own questions scaffolds the process of inquiry well. Using the I-Chart establishes a simple framework for a systematic search for information. The chart also includes a column for interesting information, pieces that do not fit the basic questions but still are relevant to the students' inquiry. This often becomes an important way to take notes on ideas that can be shared with the class later—ideas that are full of potential for more reading.

Reading Strategies

K-W-L and the I-Chart are frameworks through which teachers can engage students personally and cooperatively in thinking about their relationship to a content to be studied and in setting a course for learning. The frameworks do not, however, show students how to actually engage with the text as they read it. That is where one of the following strategies is most useful.

Struggling Reader

RECIPROCAL TEACHING.   One of the most researched strategies for engaged reading of informational text is **reciprocal teaching**. Developed by Palincsar and Brown (1984, 1986) to help less able readers handle the demands of expository texts, reciprocal teaching includes four different strategies that students learn to use. The teacher first models each of the strategies and then turns the teacher's role over to the students. The students apply what they are learning by becoming teachers for their classmates and guiding the continued reading of small portions of text. The four basic strategies are as follows:

TEACH IT!

25

- Summarize what has just been read.
- Think of two or three good questions about the passage.
- Clarify any ideas or information that was not clear.
- Predict what you think will be in the next part of the text.

In conducting a reciprocal teaching exercise, decide in advance how large the chunks of text will be that the students will read before you engage them in thinking about that portion. The text units should be short enough that the students can discuss each in five to seven minutes. Tell the students that you will be the first discussion leader and that the students should pay attention to *how* you conduct the discussion, not just focus on answering the questions.

Model reading a short section of text and creating a summary of the main ideas. Depending on the group and the amount of time needed to teach each of the four strategies, you might spend several sessions on a single strategy, or you might model more than one at a time until all four strategies become part of the readers' response to each paragraph or segment. Students learn to ask good questions of the text through this process. They also learn to identify problems that hinder comprehension —vocabulary items that are unclear or unfamiliar, for example, or references that are confusing or other unclear aspects—and ask questions to clarify these problems posed by the text. Finally, they learn to make predictions of where the text is leading. Students then assume the teacher role for each segment of text so that during a class period, many students have had the opportunity to lead their fellow students in considering the meaning of a common text. You could create a visible chart of the four strategies to help students understand the process. This becomes a guide for students when they lead the discussions.

This form of guided and shared reading has been effective in helping less-able readers make sense of dense text material. The combination of good interactive strategies with group-oriented teaching and a shared learning approach helps students to maintain interest and focus on the material they are studying. The Teach It! box provides an example of how one teacher used reciprocal teaching in his classroom.

Increasing interest and giving students a sense of power when dealing with difficult and dense reading material are not easy. Both reciprocal teaching and the next teaching strategy—questioning the author—give teachers and students supportive alternatives to round robin reading, a still too often used way to have students read content texts.

QUESTIONING THE AUTHOR.   Rather than having to memorize text content, with the questioning-the-author teaching strategy (Beck, McKeown, & Kucan, 1997) students learn to think more about who has written a text and how successful the writer was in conveying the message to the reader. Students develop a dialogue with the author, just as they would with a person talking with them face to face. In classrooms where students write a lot, the analogy of having the textbook or text author in the "author's chair" helps the students to visualize the writer as a person. Students

TEACH IT!

Reciprocal Teaching

George Mead and five of his fifth-grade students are reading a short informative text on crocodiles and alligators. Mr. Mead is still modeling the reciprocal teaching process with these troubled readers, since they have had only a few experiences with the process. He has decided in advance that this text is best read in units of paragraphs, since the students are very unconfident of their abilities as readers and the text is dense.

Mr. Mead announces that he will be the discussion leader for the first paragraph. He advises students not only to pay attention to the paragraph and participate in the discussion, but also to observe carefully how he conducts the discussion. They know that each of them will play the role of the discussion leader when the next paragraphs are read. Mr. Mead has prepared a chart that lists the steps that are taken after each paragraph is read. He refers the students to the chart to help them follow the procedure he is using as he leads the discussion.

Mr. Mead asks everyone to read the first paragraph silently. When they are finished, he gives a verbal summary of the paragraph and looks around at the students to ask if they would summarize the passage the same way or have something to add. Next, Mr. Mead formulates a question. He takes care with the question, because as well as eliciting their ideas, he is demonstrating the art of questioning for the students. He asks, "What are the easiest ways to tell the differences between alligators and crocodiles?" He draws out the students' ideas on this question and affirms their sugges-

tions. When Matt volunteers that the shape of the mouths might be easier to notice than either how their teeth fit together or whether the animal has sensory pits, especially if one were coming at you, he gets a nod.

Next, Mr. Mead attempts to clarify parts of the paragraph that are unclear to the students. He notes that the word *crocodilian* is used for the whole group of reptiles that includes crocodiles, alligators, and caimans. He asks whether someone can clarify when to use *crocodilian* and when to use *crocodile*. As the students try to differentiate the uses of the terms orally Mr. Mead knows that they are becoming more familiar with these words in both their reading and their speaking. To help them as they clarify, he writes the words on the chalkboard as one student explains that *crocodilian* should be above the other three words, *crocodile, caiman,* and *alligator*, since they are all examples of this group of reptiles. Then Mr. Mead goes on to make a prediction, suggesting that the text will probably tell how these different reptiles survive. Finally, he assigns the next section of the text.

After that paragraph is read Mr. Mead takes another turn as discussion director to make sure the students fully understand how to carry out the steps in conducting a discussion before it becomes their turn. Mr. Mead often refers to the chart as he conducts each step in the discussion. He knows that if the students do not clearly understand how to conduct the procedure, he will have to intervene later, which will undermine the students' autonomy and confidence. Before the third passage is read, Mr. Mead points to the student on his left and asks her to lead the next discussion. After that student has had her turn, the role of discussion leader passes to the student on her left, and so on.

Refer to your **Teach It!** booklet for further activities you can use to reinforce concepts discussed in this chapter.

are encouraged to "query" the absent author, asking questions that explore the writer's decisions. It can be difficult initially to engage students in such an activity, so introducing it by having a small group model the process with the rest of the class observing can be useful. Teachers can also work with students in small groups, as they do with literature discussion, to develop this habit of thinking. Following are some basic questions students might ask:

- What is the author trying to say?
- Why is the author saying this?
- What could the author have said instead?
- What was the intent of the author?
- What is the point of view?
- How could something be stated more clearly?

Students are led by their teacher in discussion of short segments of text, just as they are in reciprocal teaching, but this time, they focus on the author, thinking about how the author has written for them as readers or learners. After reading a paragraph in a sixth-grade history text, students might begin by asking one or some of the following questions:

- Why do you think the author spent a paragraph explaining the religious beliefs of the Egyptians?
- What do you think it represents to the author?
- What else about the society might have been more important?
- Was it clearly written?
- Could something have been added to make it easier to understand?
- How would you have written this?
- Would a diagram or chart have helped you understand?

By questioning or querying the author, students take a different stance in relation to the text and begin to feel more active as participants in the process of communication about content topics. In classrooms where teachers use this approach, they have reported that the students seem to engage more deeply with the material they are asked to read and are more willing to read content textbooks.

METACOGNITIVE GRAPHIC ORGANIZER. Although several variations have emerged in the recent years (Caverly, Mandeville, & Nicholson, 1995), the key to the metacognitive graphic organizer strategy is that students create their own *graphic organizer* as they preview a chapter of text and use this visual as a guide for their reading. The term *metacognitive* refers to the process in which the learner is self-aware of his or her own learning needs and can monitor and adjust to the demands of the text. Students place the title of the chapter or article in the center of a sheet of paper and then add the major headings from the chapter as they survey the material. After doing this, they return to the text and look at the visual information in charts, diagrams, and the like. They put key ideas from these visuals on the graphic where appropriate under the headings. They can add subheads if necessary to make the flow of the text clear. Once the author's structure and visuals are clearly framed, the student returns and does the metacognitive check by asking himself or herself which sections are familiar (✓), which are unknown or unfamiliar (?), and which seem interesting (+). Sections that seem most necessary for the course, if that is the purpose of reading, can be highlighted with an asterisk (*). In this way the reader creates a personal guide for reading and study. Then while reading, the student can make additional notes on the outline or on Post-it notes.

When finished reading, the student reviews the graphic and the notes made and decides whether to revise the graphic, add to it, or write some extended notes to rehearse the important ideas. The final step of note making is one that is designed to encourage student reflection and learning. What an individual student does depends on how much detail needs to be absorbed to achieve the learning goal. It might be that the actual organization of the text is different from what the student initially drew and requires creating a revised text graphic. It might be that there are many new ideas, and the student needs to write a summary explaining the meaning of the ideas. Students monitoring their own learning can adjust this final stage of learning to their own needs to retain the content.

Personal graphic guides are very helpful to many students. They combine attention to the text and to the learner at the same time. In longer chapters, they help students maintain their focus on how all the ideas and sections fit together. They also provide a great tool for review and rehearsal later.

Questioning

Before we close this section on learning, it is valuable to address the role of *questioning* for both teachers and students. Asking and answering questions are major parts of the life of schools. Each of the active strategies described here requires both teachers and students to become good at asking important and thoughtful questions. Questioning is an important active thinking activity that learners use while reading and trying to make sense of text. It is a central part of comprehension for students and teachers. Therefore, it is valuable to spend time both in analyzing the questions you ask and in developing students' sensitivity to what constitutes good questions and good questioning. A starting place is to discuss with students what role questioning plays in learning and what they think good questions are. Direct the discussion to include the realization that some questions ask for very specific and direct information (e.g., "What was the pharaoh's role in religion?"), some for more abstract interpretations or conjectures (e.g., "What effect did the caste system have on how people treated each other or, "What similar situation have we had in our country?"), and some are very personal (e.g., "What do you think or how do you feel?").

You also need to analyze periodically how you use questioning and audiotape yourself during class discussions. Traditionally, and continuing into today, many teachers have used questions to find out how well students have comprehended what they read. The teacher asks the student a question, the student answers, and the teacher gives some evaluative feedback. Researchers (Mehan, 1979) refer to this form of school dialog as I-R-E (initiation, response, evaluation) and conclude that the process helps teachers test students more than it aids student comprehension. To encourage students to ask good questions and engage in metacognitive self-monitoring, you need to model good thinking when sharing ideas out loud and questioning students.

You can use questioning to model the process of thinking before and during reading. Begin a lesson or introduce a story by asking students what they already know about a topic. This kind of questioning activates students' own thinking. Most teachers use questions to help students connect ideas, consolidate what they have read, and reflect on ideas. However, you can ask much more thoughtful and reflective questions by first considering how you want to focus students' reflections about what they have read. Think about how you can involve students in reflecting together to deepen their responses to questions you or texts pose.

Reading specialist, Marge Harter (2000), who has worked with teachers in her school to develop better questioning, suggests making the process of questioning very explicit with teachers. In her teacher workshops, she has helped them to focus on a nd identify good questions and has developed a chart (see Figure 7.15) based on the

<table>
<tr>
<td>

PREDICTING

What is your prediction for this passage?

What strategies will you use to help your students predict?

</td>
<td>

CLARIFYING

What words, phrases, or ideas do you need clarified?

What words, phrases, or ideas do you think your students may need clarified?

What strategies and responses will you use to help clarify those parts of the text?

</td>
</tr>
<tr>
<td>

SUMMARIZING

Write your summary for this passage.

How will you help your students summarize?

</td>
<td>

QUESTIONING

What "Quality Questions" are you asking your students?

1.

2.

3.

Why are these questions "Quality"?

Answer these questions on the back of this sheet.

</td>
</tr>
</table>

FIGURE 7.15

Content Questions.

Source: Harter (2000).

reciprocal teaching strategies for teachers to use in planning lessons. One group of teachers developed their own guide called "Questions Teachers May Ask to Help Students Clarify Text." In the guide, they suggest these options:

- Does anyone need anything clarified?
- Please share words or phrases you're uncertain of.
- What do you think this means? Can anyone add to what has been given?
- What other resources might we use to help us clarify and answer our questions?
- Where did this information come from? If you used the textbook, what part was most helpful?

As Harter worked with the teachers, they also discussed ways to help their students become more aware of their questions. She encouraged the teachers to discuss with their students the role of questioning in thinking and learning. The students in one middle level classroom made a chart of what they thought constitutes good questions.

A Good Question:
1. *Cannot be answered "yes," "no," or ask for a one-word answer*
2. *Requires a researcher to give more information that is focused or directed to a concept*
3. *Possible beginnings — Describe, How, Why, Compare, Explain*

What can a teacher do to activate students' interest in a new topic and promote involvement by all students?

The teacher then put this chart on the board so that the class could refer to it regularly. Both students and teacher became much more conscious of their questions as a result of this activity.

Some teachers extended their attention to questioning by engaging students in discussing what kinds of questions are most interesting to have answered and how much elaboration is needed in answering well. From an initial discussion of questions, teachers expanded students' understanding of kinds of questions and appropriate responses. Writing questions on the board and making them visible led to good discussion of the significance of the questions and helped students to understand the value of voicing their own uncertainties.

Many educators focus on the nature of the process of constructing meaning and argue that questions should ask students, "What do you predict will happen?," "What else could have been done?," and "What does this remind you of?" They argue that the reader-text interaction should be the focus of attention and that questions should derive from those interactions. Do readers connect and respond personally to what they read? Can they establish a purpose and fulfill their own purpose? This focus leads to another range of questions about text construction or engagement. Some students never seem to connect text to their own lives or to the reality around them. Thinking of this dimension of questioning can be helpful in planning for activities so that students see school learning as part of their own world.

THE WORLD OF READING

Using Taxonomies in Questioning

As we take time to consider the role of questioning in learning, we need ways to categorize and analyze the nature of our questions. There are some commonly used frameworks that can be used to help us in this activity. The most widely used is probably one developed by Benjamin Bloom and his colleagues in the 1950s. Bloom's taxonomy was not really developed for use by teachers but was developed as a taxonomy of educational objectives to measure school goals and assessment. However, teachers saw its value and have used it as a tool to help us reflect on our classroom questioning patterns. The taxonomy has seven levels of questions: memory, translation, interpretation, application, analysis, synthesis, and evaluation.

In research studies of classroom talk, it is not uncommon to see analyses of the "levels" of teacher questions. In some descriptions of reading comprehension and reading assessment, Bloom's seven levels have been chunked into three or four levels. For example, one common way of describing reading is by thinking of *literal, interpretive, applied,* and *critical* levels of comprehension to define kinds of questions in relation to text.

Raphael (1986) has helped students to think about sources of information for questions they are to answer by creating four categories:

Right there: Questions that can be answered directly from the text

Think and search: Questions that require more than one piece of information from the text

Author and you: Questions that go beyond the text

On your own: Questions that rely on the reader

The whole strategy is named Question-Answer-Relationships and provides very practical definitions that make it easy for students to become more involved in both planning their strategies for responding and becoming metacognitively aware of the range of responses they need to be able to make to the text.

Taxonomies provide a helpful language to think about questioning and the kinds of thinking we want to help stimulate in students. Some teachers keep the levels of questions in their teacher manuals or put them on the bulletin boards so that both they and students are more aware of the need to go beyond the literal or memory level. Other teachers do not like to use taxonomies to evaluate comprehension. Rather than conceiving of them as a hierarchy, these teachers see taxonomies as an array of options that are available to use as appropriate.

Because the process of asking and answering questions is a critical part of teaching and evaluation, some focused attention to questions is necessary. By considering the nature of the questions they ask and the questions in the materials they give students, teachers can make the questions as valuable as possible. Modeling and attending to questioning provides the context for students to become more aware of their own questioning and encourages them to develop questioning skills that are useful to their own learning. Two strategies to use while students are reading that help them apply their knowledge of good questions are ReQuest and paired reading/paired summarizing.

REQUEST PROCEDURE.   The ReQuest procedure (Manzo, 1969) is best suited for use with informational texts. In this procedure, two students read through a text, stop after each paragraph, and take turns asking each other questions about it, which the other student must try to answer. It helps if the teacher serves as a partner when the technique is first introduced. Because one goal for teaching comprehension is to develop principled knowledge of the topic, the teacher's questions serve as valuable models of ways to inquire about the important ideas in a text.

For an example of the ReQuest Procedure in action, assume that the teacher has assigned the students in the class to pairs. Amalia and David are reading a text together. After they both read the first paragraph silently, Amalia asks David three good questions about that paragraph. She asks questions about main ideas. She asks questions that probe beneath the surface. She asks what importance some item in this paragraph might come to have later in the text. David answers those questions as well as he can. After David has finished answering Amalia's questions, they both read the next paragraph. Now it is David's turn to ask Amalia questions about the new paragraph, and Amalia has to answer them. When both students have brought to light the information in that paragraph, they read the next one, and Amalia gets the first turn at asking David several good questions about that paragraph, and so on.

The ReQuest procedure can be used well with a whole class, too. One way is for the class to read one or two paragraphs from the text. Then the students pause and close their books, and students take turns asking the teacher all the questions that come to mind. Following that, they read a new paragraph and the roles are reversed: The teacher asks the students several good questions, taking care to model not just factual questions but also those that probe concepts and implications. After several such exchanges, the teacher might shift the activity to ask students to predict what the rest of the assignment will be about and state why they think so (Vacca & Vacca, 1996). Another variation for a whole class use of the ReQuest procedure is to assign students to teams of three and have them take turns asking and answering questions.

PAIRED READING/PAIRED SUMMARIZING.   Paired reading/paired summarizing is an elaboration on the ReQuest procedure that introduces more comprehension processes into the mix. In paired reading/paired summarizing, students pair up and read a text together and then divide the text into "chunks" of one or two paragraphs. The first student reads a chunk aloud as the other student reads along silently. Then the first student summarizes what the passage said. The second student then asks questions about the passage to probe its meaning. Both students attempt to answer the questions. The students exchange roles for the next passage. Like the ReQuest procedure and reciprocal teaching, students will play their roles more effectively if the first teacher demonstrates what is meant by making an effective summary and by asking good questions.

Engaging in Research

An important part of study reading is learning to conduct research and write reports. This skill is often left for the middle grades, where teachers teach a semiformal approach to research. However, when primary-grade teachers engage students in content reading and study, the process can be scaffolded so that by the time students reach the middle grades they are already confident in the skills that permit them to conduct good research. Think back to the activities that have been described already. Research requires the following:

- *Asking good researchable questions.* Learning to narrow one's topic is a basic skill that needs to be developed. When children use K-W-L and I-Charts, they become experienced in finding good questions.

- *Locating good sources of information.* Integrated units that are framed around students' questions develop students' abilities to find the materials they need and to locate within the texts the sections that will answer their questions.

- *Making notes of important ideas.* Children who get in the habit of writing Amazing Fact Sheets have already learned how to make good notes. The use of graphic organizers and journals also helps students build good note-making skills.

- *Critically evaluating information.* Students who have regularly read several texts on the same topic know the importance of evaluating the sources of information they use and cross-checking them for accuracy and currency. They learn to check the authors of web sites for their expertise and biases. They also know that textbooks and encyclopedias are good, reliable backup sources for their use.

- *Organizing information.* When students learn to chunk ideas as part of the K-W-L process, when they cluster new vocabulary, and when they learn to look for and use internal text organization in their reading and writing they develop skills in organizing ideas into interesting and coherent texts. The more writing they do throughout the elementary grades the more confident they become in creating interesting and meaningful texts.

- *Presenting information visually and graphically.* Students who have studied how authors and illustrators present visual information and weave it together with the connected texts are more able to create their own. The computer tools and digital cameras that schools now possess make this task an exciting one for young students.

Look back over the different strategies that help to engage students actively as learners across the content areas. All of these taken together prepare students to be active, thoughtful learners. With this foundation, doing research and writing reports and even creating a more formal research papers is not difficult.

Writing & Reading

As we think of learning new material and conducting research, writing becomes an essential part of the ongoing literacy curriculum. When children write regularly, they develop their skills and fluency as writers. An example of how Anne, a sixth grader, has developed as a writer should make this point apparent. In her writing portfolio, she includes the persuasive essay "Energy Is Electrifying!," which she wrote when she wanted to be selected to attend an energy workshop that would take her out of school for a few days (see Figure 7.16 on page 294). Anne has learned to argue for a particular point of view and to provide detail and reasons to support her choices. She knows how to invite readers into her piece and hold their attention with great life and detail in her writing. Other pieces she has written for her class—a story about her great-great-grandfather who fought in the Civil War, an essay explaining why she has selected Stacy Dragila as her favorite Olympian, an essay on the importance of the DARE program in her school, and a report on West Indian Manatees—illustrate the range of writing that Anne has been encouraged to do. She possesses the skills necessary for good report writing, including conducting research, and could easily complete these tasks. Regular writing, just like regular reading in a variety of genres for a variety of audiences and purposes, creates confident and capable learners.

Energy Is Electrifying!

"Turn that light on! Turn off the television! Plug in the CD player!" We use energy so much in our everyday lives that sometimes we forget just how important and amazing it really is to us! There is so much to learn about energy. It's almost impossible not to be interested. I would be the best choice to go to the energy workshop. I am a responsible student, a great teacher, and as a member of generation 9-11 my future depends on it.

First, I am a very responsible student. I will be able to get the assignments I miss on the day of the workshop finished, and turned in on time. I have always been a straight A student and have had a clean pass sheet the whole time I have attended Nagel. Being a responsible student, I can listen well and be able to remember what I learned.

Secondly, I am a great teacher. I am not afraid to talk in front of large groups of people. I understand that after attending the workshop we will be helping you teach our classmates about what we've learned. I love to teach people just as much as I love to learn new things. It will be fun for students to teach students. I will be able to take the material and teach it to others well.

Lastly, as a member of generation 9-11 it is very important for me to learn as much as possible about energy. We are at war with Afghanistan and the Middle East supplies 40 percent of the world's oil. We may need new sources of energy. Also, we need smart people with good ideas involving energy, to help fight terrorism. With my new knowledge of energy I could be one of these people. The energy team needs someone like me who thinks about the future.

In conclusion, with my responsibility for my schoolwork I will be able to finish the assignments I miss. Since I am good at explaining things to others, I will be able to take what I learn and help my classmates to understand it. As a member of generation 9-11, I will be able to convince others to solve the problems of our future since we may need to find new sources of energy. These are excellent and electrifying reasons why I would be the best choice to attend the energy workshop.

FIGURE 7.16

Research Essay.

A Look at Classrooms for Learning

As teachers take seriously the importance of helping children become confident readers and learners with informational materials, the greatest challenges are finding the time and structuring the learning experiences properly. Two general approaches are often used. The first is to think of teaching reading as finding a balance between the reading of fictional literature (for literary purposes) and the reading of informational material (to learn). The second approach is to create integrated units of instruction and combine standards and strategies for both literacy and content learning.

Balancing Fiction and Informational Texts

Planning for instruction needs to include attention to both types of reading equally. In fact, some educators and researchers argue that because children have a much better foundation in reading fiction, even more teaching attention needs to be given to the development of reading informational materials (Ogle & Blachowicz, 2001; Duke, 2000). With the great variety of informational materials available now and the increasing attention by basal publishers to informational materials, it is not hard for teachers to find good materials to use. Selecting materials also means finding both kinds of materials that are appropriate for the students and are at their instructional levels. In setting learning goals, students' ability to read informational materials successfully becomes as important as their ability to read fiction. Direct instruction and guided practice in the skills of reading to learn need to be prioritized and monitored.

Integrating Instruction

A second way to approach instruction is to develop integrated content units. In fact, the recent study of outstanding fourth-grade teachers provides examples of how they integrate reading into content learning (Allington & Johnston, 2002). Earlier studies (Knapp, 1995; Pressley, 1998) also indicated that meaning-oriented and content-rich classrooms promote higher achievement than do classrooms that teach with a skill focus and provide less content-rich instruction. Some teachers alternate between social studies and science in their integrated units. First, the teacher might develop a rich social studies unit around both the content and the reading skills and strategies students need to learn. Then the next unit is developed as a combination of science content and reading skills and strategies, as Ms. Gurvitz did in the unit on frogs described in the chapter-opening vignette. The use of integrated units of instruction takes time; most teachers begin with one unit and then add others year by year. When teams of teachers work together, the development of such units is much easier and more enjoyable. Librarians serve as great resources to teachers, since librarians often have a working knowledge of the resources available to students. They also can guide teachers to many additional sources of information and support.

Involving English Language Learners

Language & Diversity

Integrated units provide an open framework in which teachers can involve students at all levels of language competence in the same classroom learning focus. Because the unit model provides for a range of materials and activities, students with little English can participate using resources in their own language and can begin their learning in their first language. Helping English language learners to create vocabulary lists with words in both English and their first language makes their participation in the general classroom activities more possible.

Teachers and English language students can often gain from the students' knowledge about the topics of study. Often, their experiences have been rich in the content of focus. For example, students from South America might have personal experiences with some varieties of frogs we consider exotic and might have a sense of their value that is different from the sense that urban dwellers in North America have. Children from North Africa can contribute much to the study of civilizations that have derived from ancient Egypt or of studies of deserts. All children bring with them their experiences, language, and folktales and stories that can enrich any unit of study. Think of the potential resources represented by diversity in the classroom, and seek out what your students and their families can bring to each other.

During the development of the units, English language learners also can participate in ways that go beyond verbal learning. They can take major roles in creating the visual displays and the graphic representations of the topics, as in the development of the murals of the frog issue. If some dramatic presentation of content is part of the unit, these students can build their English skills by memorizing parts and participating in group presentations.

Using Computer Resources

Technology

Units of instruction provide an ideal place to introduce the use of computer resources. A number of excellent web sites exist that can be resources to learning. With the help of the instructional media or technical support team in a school, specific and appropriate Web resources can be bookmarked for a class, and students can participate in learning from these resources. Many also contain great visual content, so students with limited English proficiency can learn in easy ways.

The computer also makes the development of reports easier for all. Digital cameras make it possible to dress up reports—for example, by importing pictures of direct explorations during science units. The ease with which corrections can be made on the computer gives students more freedom to compose their own reports and not fear misspelled words or poor handwriting. Students take great pride in producing reports with great graphics and print quality that reflect their best work. Knowing that their work can be turned into high-quality products serves as incentive to many students. For primary students, the support of parent helpers or older-grade aides in the classroom can make the computer accessible and not consume all of the teacher's time.

Encouraging Shared Learning

Many of the strategies that have been introduced in this chapter work well in cooperative learning settings. Integrated units of study, in particular, have an added advantage because they provide a framework in which students of a variety of levels of competence can work together. Multiple skills are needed, and multiple materials are used to learn. Therefore, even students with little reading ability can use the highly visual materials and electronic information for learning. They can represent what they are learning through icons, drawings, and physical and artistic means. They can become engaged in active learning using multiple sources of material and lose some of their fear of print materials. As they learn more, they can even find more meaning in print. We have noted many students begin units ignoring the printed texts and later go to them with a sense of confidence, since they have a grounding in the content and realize that there is much they know in the texts. In this way, the unit experiences and the time spent developing the content has provided a scaffold for the students' entry into print.

Planning Instruction: A Reflection

Teachers can build a strong reading to learn curriculum in both of these ways—with a balance between fiction and informational material in the reading block of the day or by integrating reading to learn instruction with content units. Our experience has been that for new teachers, it is easier not to do all the instruction through integrated blocks initially but to be sure there are resources for the range of reading and learning needs of students in your class first. What is critical is that teachers pay attention to what students bring with them in skills and strategies for reading informational texts and provide instruction so students develop increasingly sophisticated knowledge of how to read to learn in a variety of materials and for a variety of purposes. Reading to learn science content is different from reading to learn from social studies materials. Both are different from reading that is taught as if a selection of text were sufficient just to be read and enjoyed.

FOR REVIEW

Students are eager to learn about the world around them. The teacher's job is to provide the scaffolds so they can do so successfully. This chapter began with an explanation of why teaching students to use informational texts is so important. Then the ABC model of active reading was applied to reading for information. Four kinds of background knowledge were identified: vocabulary, text structure, and content knowledge, both topical and principled knowledge.

Many children have little experience with informational materials. Therefore, specific features were explained that teachers need to introduce to students. These include external features like chapter headings and sub-headings, captions, illustrations, the glossary and index and even the Table of Contents.

The internal structures of informational texts are also important for students to identify so they can determine what is important information and retain it. The use of graphic organizers, having students jigsaw the reading of sections of texts, and having them write using the pattern of the authors were suggested as ways to highlight text organization.

This chapter introduced two frameworks and several instructional strategies that help students become aware of and utilize these features and become active questioners and thinkers. K-W-L and I-Charts help frame students' inquiry. Reciprocal teaching, Questioning the Author, Metacognitive graphic organizers and ways to develop good questioning through Paired Reading/Paired Summarizing and ReQuest help students build their knowledge as they engage actively with text ideas.

Finally, the chapter concluded by highlighting the importance of helping students develop their abilities to engage in research and establishing a rich classroom environment where students' inquiry can be nurtured with print and technological resources.

For Your Journal

Keep a record for one or two days of all the reading you do. Note the material you read, the time you spent, and how you engaged yourself in the materials, including what you thought and felt as you read. Try to remember your school experiences, and write about what kinds of materials you were taught to read. What tips did you learn for reading and comprehending informational material?

★ Taking It to the World

1. Most children are curious about the world around them. Yet sometimes teachers get very busy meeting all the curricular demands and overlook students' interests as a natural connection point to content. Visit a school library or a public library and become familiar with some of the excellent magazines available for young readers. Sit down and talk with some children about which of the magazines they enjoy most. Then see whether the library has a service that permits you to search the magazines by topic so that you can use articles in the future as you develop your own teaching units and extend readings on key topics in the curriculum.

2. Try out your skills in eliciting from students what they know about a topic and helping them articulate good questions to extend their knowledge. The K-W-L process is an easy way to start. Ask a teacher to allow you to teach a lesson with a small group of students around some topic of current interest—an item in the news or some community event. Have two or three short texts with you so that you can read to the students to help them answer their questions after the first two steps in the K-W-L are complete. Keep a copy of the chart you create so that you can reflect on thee students' knowledge and interests after the session.

⭐ Being a Professional Reading Teacher

As children develop their abilities to process information through reading, expository text becomes a very important source. What are the major differences between processing expository text and processing narrative text? What strategies are most effective?

Reading Comprehension in Expository Text

- Why is background knowledge such an important factor when students are reading informational text? How can we tap that knowledge before and during reading?
- How are vocabulary and text structure factors in understanding expository text?
- Name some effective strategies for reading informational text. Compare and contrast them with strategies for reading narrative text.

Text Features

What text features do authors of expository text use? How can they be useful to students reading this textbook? How would the appearance of this textbook change without them?

Your Portfolio

To document a well-rounded reading program, it is helpful to include evidence of the capability to teach expository text effectively. A K-W-L chart from a lesson planned and taught during field experiences is an effective and graphic way of showing this side of your teaching.

Teaching Resources

Consider preparing a list of expository text processing strategies for use in your classroom. You might divide them into three categories: anticipation strategies, knowledge-building strategies, and consolidation strategies. When you are teaching a social studies lesson, for example, you can examine the text to be read and then review your list, which will remind you of all of the possibilities. You can then select strategies that will accommodate the text well and also interest the students.

Technology Connections

Visit the National Geographic Kids web site (`www.nationalgeographic.com/kids/`), and investigate what it has to offer young children. How does it utilize graphics to enhance the information? Is the layout organized in a way that is easy to follow? What options are available to help students search for more information about specific topics?

Research
Navigator.com

Connect with Research

Review the following key words from the chapter and then connect to Research Navigator (`www.researchnavigator.com`) through this book's companion web site to conduct a search into research on each of the various topics as they relate to reading and literacy education today.

I-chart	principled content knowledge	strategies
informational texts	reciprocal teaching	topical content
metacognition	schema	knowledge
motivation to learn	skills	

Further Readings

Allington, R. L., & Johnson, P. H. (2002). *Reading to Learn: Lessons From Exemplary Fourth-Grade Classrooms*. New York: Guilford.

This collection of portraits of excellent teachers in action provides a good vision of classrooms alive with literacy learning.

Barton, M. L., & Heidema, C. (2002). *Teaching Reading in Mathematics*. A supplement to *Teaching Reading in the Content Areas Teacher's Manual* (2nd Ed.). Aurora, CO: Mid-continent Research for Education and Learning.

Many teachers find developing reading in mathematics challenging. This book is full of concrete ways in which teachers can scaffold literacy skills and strategies while teaching math.

Barton, M. L., & Jordan, D. L. (2001). *Teaching Reading in Science*. A supplement to *Teaching Reading in the Content Areas Teacher's Manual* (2nd Ed.). Aurora, CO: Mid-continent Research for Education and Learning,.

Like its companion on teaching mathematics, this is a valuable collection of concrete ways to make reading and learning in science more accessible to all readers.

Burniske, R. W. (2000). *Literacy in the Cyberage: Composing Ourselves Online*. Arlington Heights, IL: Skylight.

Burniske raises some basic issues about how students use the Internet and the ethics of cybercommunication. He goes on to share exciting ways in which students and classes around the world are utilizing this new resource for learning and sharing.

McLaughlin, M., & Vogt, M. E. (Eds.). (2000). *Creativity and Innovation in Content Area Teaching*. Norwood, MA: Christopher-Gordon.

Chapters in this book highlight ways in which teachers can make content learning enjoyable by including a variety of arts, active engagement, and fun.

November, A. (2001). *Empowering Students with Technology.* Arlington Heights, IL: Skylight.

Practical ways to use technology in classrooms so that students develop a sense of the power of the Internet and other electronic resources.

Rasinski, T. V., Padak, N. D., Church, B. W., Fawcett, G., Hendershop, J., Henry, J. M., Moss, B. G., Peck, J. K., Pryor, E., & Roskos, K. A. (Eds.). (2000). *Teaching Comprehension and Exploring Multiple Literacies: Strategies from* The Reading Teacher. Newark, DE: International Reading Association.

Many short articles written by practitioners giving practical strategies for enhancing students' learning.

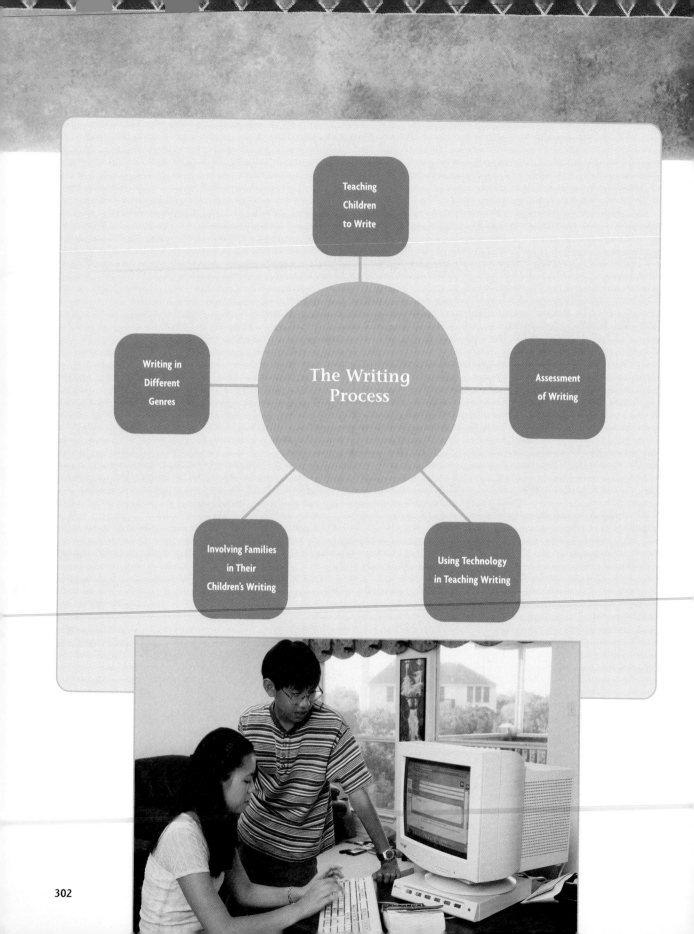

Teaching
Children
to Write

Writing in
Different
Genres

The Writing
Process

Assessment
of Writing

Involving Families
in Their
Children's Writing

Using Technology
in Teaching Writing

The Writing Process

The following statements will get you thinking about the topics of this chapter. Answer true or false in response to each statement. As you read and learn more about the topics in these statements, double-check your answers. See what interests you and prompts your curiosity toward more understanding.

Anticipation Guide

_____ 1. In general, children never write until they have been carefully taught how.

_____ 2. When we speak of a *writing process*, we mean a process by which many successful adult writers as well as schoolchildren produce written compositions.

_____ 3. The goal of writing instruction is to teach children to write everything once and write it correctly.

_____ 4. Children can help each other learn to write.

_____ 5. It is generally better for teachers to assign writing topics than to let children choose their own.

_____ 6. Children need different levels of support as they learn to write. Some children flourish in the open atmosphere of the writing workshop, but others need more explicit guidance.

_____ 7. It is important for teachers to write in front of children and demonstrate writing as a studio craft.

_____ 8. The difference between editing and revising is that editing is done only by professional writers.

_____ 9. There is no such thing as different levels of support teachers give to writers at different ages. Writing is a sink-or-swim affair.

_____ 10. Reading helps children learn to be writers because it shows them the choices that writers make in crafting language into print.

The Writing Process in a
Third-Grade Classroom

A t West Street School in Geneva, New York, Anne Bergstrom is trying a new approach to her third graders' study of African geography. The school's experience has corroborated what the National Assessment of Educational Progress has found: Not only do elementary students need to know more geography, but they also need to know how to think with geographical information. So this spring, since their student teacher from last fall, Sarah Barry, is studying in Dakar, the capital of Senegal, Ms. Bergstrom has arranged to conduct an inquiry lesson on Senegal via the Internet.

In the fall, the students located Senegal on a map and discussed its tropical climate and its history as a slave state and as a colony of France, and they read material about Senegal from the National Geographic web site. They also did their best to make sense of the U.S. State Department's web-based information. In December, the students thought of questions they wanted Sarah to investigate, wrote them on a piece of chart paper as part of a K-W-L chart (see Figure 8.1), and sent them to Sarah in an e-mail.

Sarah wrote the students an e-mail from Senegal and asked them how they wanted her to find answers to their questions: "Who do you want me to talk to? What do you want me to ask?" The students took turns writing e-mails to Sarah on the classroom computer.

But Sarah realized that there are fascinating things about Senegal that the students did not know to ask about. So she sent them occasional transmissions that she called "mysteries," intriguing photographs with questions attached. The students took turns writing to Sarah about the mystery; they sent guesses or questions they wanted to ask her. In a way, Sarah became an extension of the class, their remote-control anthropologist.

In the spring, Ms. Bergstrom had the students prepare write-ups of what they had learned. The students used the writing workshop to

The First Questions We Have

1. Do they go swimming?
2. What is the population?
3. Do they know about King's fight for freedom?
4. How do they talk?
5. What do they eat?
6. How hot does it get?
7. What are their houses made of?
8. What do they do in their spare time?
9. Was it a slave trading place?
10. What do they celebrate?
11. What games do they play?
12. What kinds of animals do they have?
13. What are their religions?
14. How do people treat each other?
15. What kind of jewelry do they wear?
16. Does anyone have piercings or tattoos?
17. Do they trade? What do they trade with other countries?
18. Does everyone have a job?
19. Are there homeless people?
20. How do they dispose of trash?
21. Do they brush their teeth, and if so, with what?

FIGURE 8.1

The First Questions We Have.

focus on their topics, write a first draft, revise their drafts, edit them, and prepare them for publication. Later, the class collaborated on a joint composition: the script for a class play about aspects of life in the West African country of Senegal, which they performed for an audience of the whole school.

As you can see from the vignette, in Ms. Bergstrom's class, writing provided the third graders a valuable tool for finding out about their topic of West Africa. Because the students eventually had an audience for their findings—when they performed their class play for the school—having to write about Senegal gave the students a feeling of authority over their information and helped them to think about it all the harder. The tools of writing and reading worked together nicely in this project. The students needed to *read* about Senegal so that they would have a better idea what to ask, and they had to *write* out their questions, *read* the student teacher's responses, and *write* more questions. Because they had become inquirers about Senegal, they read material about that country with more interest.

Humans are the most communicative animals. Remembering, imagining, and communicating in words come naturally to us. If you take a stroll down the street or look around in the waiting area of any shop or business, you will see that we find it natural to communicate in print.

Even young children share the human fascination with print. By the age of two, children are making marks on things with pencils and crayons—and jelly and gravy and anything else they can lay their hands on! By age four or five, especially if they have a parent in the house who is also a writer or a student, children will imitate that parent and produce page after page of script (see Figure 8.2), show it to the parent, and ask, "What did I write? What does this say?"

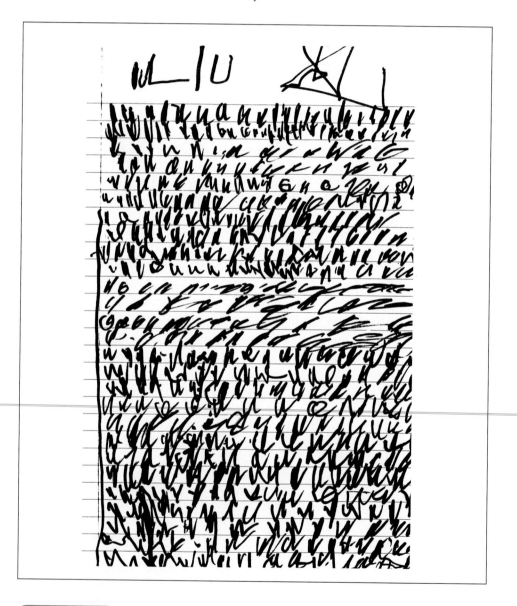

Iuliu's Script at age 4.

No Geting
To eat turcky.
No Pillgrims.
No indeins
No inething.
Like I say
if you Dont thank
that's Not Boring Whdt
IS

FIGURE 8.3

Early Writing.

Source: Temple, Nathan, Burris, and Temple,
The Beginnings of Writing. Copyright © 1992.
Allyn & Bacon Publishers, Inc.

With a little encouragement in kindergarten and first grade, children write inventively and sometimes voluminously. Children go through a golden age of creativity between the ages of four and seven that is manifested in their spontaneous poetry (Heath, 1984), in their play-acting (Pellegrini & Galda, 2000), and most especially in their artwork (Gardner, 1980). The exuberance of young children's writing can be a joy to read (see Figure 8.3) (Temple et al., 1993). When teachers structure environments for writing and give the proper kinds of instruction and encouragement, children's native creativity as writers can mature and be nurtured into a disciplined skill.

Releasing children's writing creativity, however, is not always a simple matter of "just letting them write." For one thing, enthusiasm for writing differs among children. Because children differ in the amount and kinds of literacy encouragement that they receive at home (Heath, 1984), some will find writing—even the laborious efforts of writing by sounding out words and spelling them inventively—natural and even fun, while others will be puzzled by the whole business of writing and will expect the teacher to tell them exactly what to do (Delpit, 1996). Also, children might find writing natural at one age but difficult later. That might be because the cognitive changes that children undergo beginning at the age of eight or nine make them more self-conscious and less spontaneously creative (Winner, 1982; Calkins, 1996). Thus, children who with little prompting produced dazzling artwork and daring verbal creations with ingeniously original spelling at age six might worry about their lack of correctness by age nine and need careful instruction and a lot of encouragement to write more than a few safe but bland sentences. Moreover, schools escalate their expectations of children's writing as children progress through the grades, so by fourth grade, children must demonstrate correct spelling and grammar, stick to the point, and answer the assignment in addition to showing enthusiasm.

The task of kindergarten and first-grade teachers is to show children how to record thoughts on paper and then give the children many opportunities to write and share what they write. But the tasks of teachers of second grade and above are to teach writing in such a way that they keep alive children's enthusiasm and creativity while teaching them to use writing deliberately for many purposes and to honor the conventions of correctness and propriety.

Teaching Children to Write

Not that long ago, if you asked most teachers about writing, they assumed that you meant handwriting or possibly the format of a friendly letter. The idea had not yet dawned that young people had important things to say, that they could get their ideas elegantly onto paper, or that they would enjoy sharing their ideas with a wide and interested audience. Since the early 1980s, an outpouring of research—much of it based on studies of what competent writers do when they write and what happens when students are shown how to do those same things—has changed the thinking about young people's writing and has developed a framework for teaching young people

Writing & Reading

to write using a process approach. The advantages of promoting writing among students turn out to be many:

- Writing makes students more observant, both of their own experience and of the outside world.
- Being writers makes students closer readers of other writers. It makes them more appreciative of words and builds their vocabulary and their skill at choosing just the right word.
- Writing makes students more reflective, as they record an idea, examine that idea in print, and have a further idea in response to it.
- Writing builds community. As students work hard to capture and communicate their thoughts and experiences and as they listen to their classmates' efforts to do the same, students reveal themselves to each other and come to understand each other.
- Applied to literature and to other subjects in the curriculum, writing responses and other kinds of inquiry also serve as a powerful learning tool.

Those who have developed the *process approach* to teaching writing to children and young people have themselves had two main groups of teachers: professional writers and young people themselves. They studied what writers do when they write and the conditions they need. Then they have tried to set up circumstances for young people to carry out the same processes under similar conditions.

What Writers Need

If you were to study the work habits of professional writers, you would learn many secrets of the trade that help them work successfully. Young writers can use these secrets to write well too.

AUTHENTIC REASONS TO WRITE.   Some writers write because readers love their stories. Others write because they know about something other people will want to read. Children may also write for these reasons. Or they may write because they want to compare their predictions about a story with those of their classmates. Or they may write because they want to compare their impressions of a book they have read with those of the teacher or a classmate. All of these are authentic reasons to write. As such, they are more motivating than random assignments by the teacher would be.

REGULAR CHANCES TO WRITE.   Writers need to know that they will be expected to sit down and write something out. If they know that, they begin to think up ideas even when they are not writing. Regular chances to write are important for another reason. Because many of people's best ideas come while they are writing, writing regularly gives writers more time in which they are most open to new ideas—even ideas they never suspected they had.

TOPICS THAT ARE INTERESTING TO THEM.   Professional writers choose their own topics, and they decide what is most interesting about those topics and how to make readers interested, too. Unlike children who are given narrow assignments in school, professional writers usually write about things they know about and care about. Sometimes they write about things they want to know more about, and they enjoy using writing as a kind of inquiry.

COLLABORATION. Many professional writers collaborate to present research results or to tell different parts of a story. Children enjoy writing with other children, too. They can help each other find the most effective ways of expressing something. They enjoy having each other for an audience.

MODELS AND DEMONSTRATIONS. Most professional writers are intensely tuned into the writings of others. They pounce with delight on a phrase, a word, a technique, or a form that another writer uses successfully, and they frequently borrow the best ideas of others. The already-written serves as **static models** for what others might write.

Writers also need **active models** who demonstrate writing while explaining that even adults' writing often begins with brainstorms and doodles, includes false starts and reverses on itself, and is marked up many times and corrected before some fraction of the writer's output turns into the flawless flow of print seen in published books. Without this sort of modeling, where published writing came from would be mysterious. Donald Graves (1982) describes writing as a "studio craft"—one that is best taught by example. The teacher must provide the model of what a writer does. The teacher must go first and provide direct teaching. Children need to be *shown* how to write—from thinking up ideas, to verbalizing sentences, to sounding out words and spelling their sounds, to composing in different genres.

PUTTING CONVENTIONS IN THEIR PLACE. People who agonize over handwriting, spelling, and neatness on their first draft soon suffer from self-doubts and writer's block. The most confident writers are those who can write out a draft of an idea in the full knowledge that they will be able to come back later to make it neater, more grammatical,

STANDARDS & LITERACY

★ ★ Writing Process Requirements ★ ★

The writing process is promoted in classrooms that follow what is called the *writing process approach* (Graves, 1982; Calkins, 1996). Not many years ago, this approach was used by the more innovative and adventurous teachers. Now the approach is widely accepted as a best practice of English language arts instruction. Indeed, many states are requiring that teachers instruct children in the writing process. For example, in Texas, the TEKS, or Texas Essential Knowledge and Skills (Texas Education Agency, 1998), calls for students in grades one through three to be able to do the following:

Writing/writing processes. The student selects and uses writing processes to compose original text. The student is expected to:

(A) generate ideas before writing on self-selected topics (K–1);

(B) generate ideas before writing on assigned tasks (K–1);

(C) develop drafts (1–3);

(D) revise selected drafts for varied purposes, including to achieve a sense of audience, precise word choices, and vivid images (1–3); and

(E) use available technology to compose text (K–3).

better organized, and correctly spelled. This is not to say that conventions are not important, but writers should consider conventions only *after* they have gotten out what they want to say.

The Writing Process

The model of the **writing process** used here was put forward several years ago by Pulitzer Prize-winning journalist and writing teacher Donald Murray (1985) and language arts specialist and researcher Donald Graves (1982). According to their writing process model, thoughtful writers may go through five steps or phases as they produce their works: rehearsing, drafting, revising, editing, and publishing.

REHEARSING.   Rehearsing is the act of preparing to write by gathering information and collecting one's thoughts. Student writers think of what they might like to write about, the teacher surveys what they know about the topic, and then they begin to plan a way to write about it. There are several strategies available that can teach students to rehearse their ideas before writing:

- *Brainstorming and clustering.* Children can jot down in list form their ideas about a topic before embarking on writing about it. As a more elaborate version of the brainstorm, you can have them create a graphic organizer, such as a cluster or semantic web, with the topic listed in the center connected to "satellites" around it (see Figure 8.4).

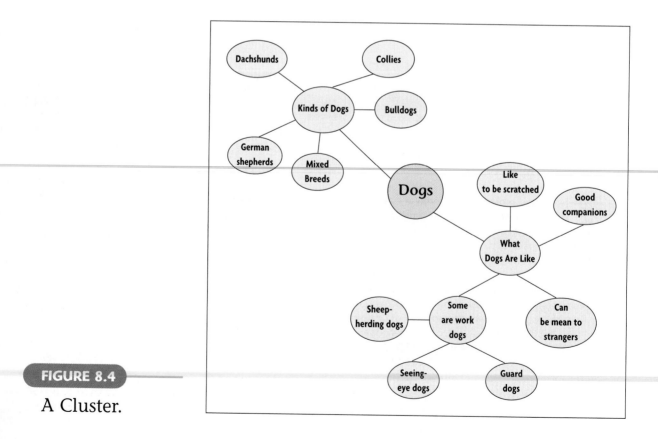

FIGURE 8.4

A Cluster.

- *Interviewing each other to find the story.* Students can interview a partner. Whether or not a writer has already prepared a cluster, it often helps if another student asks the writer questions about the topic to help the writer "find the story." The student asks questions such as the following:

   "Why did you choose this topic?"

   "What most interests you about the topic?"

   The student also asks questions about details, things that the writer might not realize readers will want to know.

- *Making class collaborations.* In introducing a new kind of writing, such as a poem or a fairy tale, it might be best to ask the students to compose one work together before writing on their own. This is especially helpful for younger students. The teacher can contribute as well to help steer the work in positive directions. If the students have difficulty beginning, offer them a series of choices:

   Where does the story take place? In a big city or a small village?

   Who should be the main character? A young girl or an old magician?

   A young girl? Okay. Then who can describe her? And what is her problem?

- *Researching the topic.* Students might be able to write stories or papers about personal experiences off the tops of their heads, but when they are writing about the world outside of themselves, they usually need to collect information about their topics. They might need to read up on it or interview experts about it, or they might observe carefully and collect details about it. Lucy Calkins and her colleagues in the New York City Writing Project (1992) suggest having students keep notebooks for gathering observations.

DRAFTING.   Drafting involves setting ideas out on paper. Drafting is tentative and experimental. Students write down their ideas so that they can see more of what they have to say about their topic; often their best ideas do not occur to them until they begin committing thoughts to paper. The phase of drafting is not the time to be critical about spelling and handwriting. Such mechanical concerns are better dealt with later; this is the time for students to focus on getting their ideas onto the page.

Most young writers do not have the habit of writing more than one version of a paper. Proficient writers, however, believe that good writing is rewriting. You can encourage students to think of writing as drafting in a number of ways:

- Stamp the papers "DRAFT" or use recycled office paper. Both means make it clear to everyone that these versions of their papers are not final.

- Have the students write on every other line. This leaves room for them to add material they think of later on.

- Show students how to use arrows, carets (^), and stapled-on sections to indicate on a draft how it should be rewritten. Unless they are shown, students will not know how physically to mark up and modify a draft and use it to plan the next version of the paper.

- Remind students not to worry too much about spelling, handwriting, and mechanics at the drafting stage. A large advantage to writing more than one draft of a paper is that it frees writers to concentrate on their ideas at first and worry about form and correctness later. This should be explained to students at the start, and the treatment of their early and later drafts should be consistent with it. Be careful, however, that you do not encourage students to be messy. Bromley (1999) advises against calling an early draft of a paper a "sloppy copy."

REVISING.   After their thoughts have been written out in draft form, students need to consider how the ideas can be stated more clearly. Most students need to be shown ways in which writing can be improved: by having clear beginnings, middles, and ends; by finding a topic and sticking to it; by showing and not telling; and the like. You can teach these points through focused lessons (discussed on pages 315–316) and help young writers internalize them by means of conferences. There are two main kinds of conferences in teaching writing.

Teacher-Led Conferences.   Conferences allow you to help students clarify their writing and also to model for the student ways to ask helpful questions that will help encourage other struggling writers—peers. You need to ask questions that teach, pulling solutions from the students themselves and always respecting the students' ownership of their writing. Ask students questions to help them focus on areas to improve their writing, and provide checklists of things to watch out for.

Peer Conferences.   Once you have modeled the process, students can hold conferences with each other. Because many conferences will be going on in the room at one time, it helps if students understand their tasks clearly. You might put together a checklist of good questions to ask as they review with each other, such as the following:

- Did my opening lines interest you? How might I improve it?
- Do I need more information anywhere? That is, where could I be more specific?
- Do you ever get lost while reading my draft?
- Do I stay on topic?
- Do I come to a good conclusion?

EDITING OR PROOFREADING.   Once a paper has been drafted and revised, it needs to be reviewed for mistakes. Of course proofreading is held off for last because paragraphs or even pages might be cut or added in the revising stage. The habit of proofreading must be taught; it consists of three things:

- Caring that the paper be correct
- Being aware of particular errors
- Knowing how to set them straight

A caring attitude toward their writing is probably best developed by publishing what students write. Students are most likely to care about correctness once they realize that writing is not simply done for a grade, but that their works must pass the scrutiny of others, who will be distracted from their ideas if the papers are marred by flaws in spelling, grammar, and handwriting.

Children should be made aware of errors through focused lessons that demonstrate one or two errors of writing at a time. Focused lessons treat errors that one or more students are actually making in their writing. Areas in which children make errors might include the following:

- Beginning each sentence with a capital letter and ending it with terminal punctuation (a period, a question mark, or an exclamation point)
- Making each sentence express a complete thought, avoiding sentence fragments and run-on sentences
- Spelling correctly

After clearly teaching students to be aware of different kinds of errors and how to repair them, the next step is to get the students to proofread their own work. Give them a checklist to guide their proofreading, such as the one shown in Figure 8.5. Each point on the checklist should be carefully introduced, explained, and practiced before students are sent off to use it on their own. Several versions of the checklist might be

---

_____ 1. Did I spell all words correctly?
(Underline words you are unsure of. Try looking some of them up.)

_____ 2. Did I write each sentence as a complete thought?
(This is an incomplete thought: "On the street." This is a complete thought: "The little puppy stood all alone on the street." Note: Sometimes writers use an incomplete sentence on purpose—to create a certain effect. For example: "Not me!")

_____ 3. Do I have any run-on sentences?
(Here is a run-on sentence: "The little puppy stood all alone on the street and he couldn't find his mother and he was so, so frightened that he thought he would die and so he looked around to find a friend and he didn't find one so he walked on and on." This is a run-on sentence, too: "I don't have a pet at home do you?")

_____ 4. Did I end each sentence with the correct punctuation?
(Here is a sentence that has the wrong punctuation at the end: "Could the puppy find his mother." The sentence needs a question mark, not a period.)

_____ 5. Did I begin each sentence with a capital letter?

_____ 6. Did I use capital letters correctly in other places?
(Names, days of the week, months, titles, etc.)

_____ 7. Did I use commas, apostrophes, and other punctuation correctly?
(Commas are used between words in lists, before a conjunction introducing an independent clause, after salutations, etc. Apostrophes are used with possessive forms [Jimmy's shoes, the boys' lockers] and in contractions [can't, it's—for "it is"].)

_____ 8. Did I indent each paragraph?
(Whenever you start a new idea, you need a new paragraph. Dialogue [talk between two or more people] also requires a new paragraph each time a different speaker talks.)

FIGURE 8.5

Proofreading Checklist.

Source: Reprinted with permission from *Classroom Strategies That Work: An Elementary Teacher's Guide to Process Writing* by Ruth Nathan, Frances Temple, Kathleen Juntunen, and Charles Temple. Copyright © 1989 by Heinemann Educational Books, Inc. Published by Heinemann, a division of Reed Elsevier, Inc., Portsmouth, NH. All rights reserved.

introduced during the year as new points for correction are added to the students' repertoires. Once the checklist has been introduced, students should practice using it with a partner to go over each other's papers before they are ready to use the checklists by themselves.

PUBLISHING.   Publishing is the final stage of the writing process and actually drives the whole endeavor. The prospect of sharing what they have to say with an audience makes many students want to write, rewrite, and smooth out and refine—especially if they have seen other students' work received with appreciation and delight. Publishing also lets students see what others are doing. A good idea is contagious; and anything from an interesting topic, to a plot structure, to a way to use dialogue, to the habit of taking risks with spelling may be shared from one student to another through the process of publishing.

How to Organize and Manage a Writing Workshop

A popular approach to teaching children to write is the **writing workshop**, in which students are taught to use the writing process and are given regular opportunities to use it in order to produce many different kinds of writing. Teachers who teach writing successfully work three elements into their teaching:

- *Time.* Writing workshops should be scheduled at regular intervals so that students know when they will have opportunities to write. When students know that they will have these opportunities, they are more likely to collect ideas during their daily lives that they can write about during writing workshop.

- *Emphasis on Communication.* There is an important difference between writing for the teacher (to demonstrate skill or to get a grade) and writing because you want to say something to people who will be interested in hearing it. When writing is real communication, students engage their full powers of expression. Therefore, students should have opportunities to choose their own topics or—when the topic is assigned—to decide on their own approach to the topic. When conferences are conducted to help students improve writing, their ownership of the work—that is, their communicative intent—must still be respected, with freedom left for them to choose the advice they will follow.

- *Demonstration and Direct Instruction.* Teaching writing is a studio craft, with attention to the process of creating. The teacher should demonstrate every phase of the process so that students will know how writing is done. The teacher should also teach skills of writing, from organization to correct punctuation, but teach them in the context of writing for communication so that students will actually come to use them.

The length and frequency of writing workshops will often vary from one teacher to another, but having a consistent plan will help each teacher to encourage student writing. Figure 8.6 shows one plan for managing the time in a writing workshop. This writing workshop lasts an entire 60-minute class meeting, perhaps three days a week, with time set aside for five distinctive activities.

SENSE-OF-THE-CLASS MEETING.   Assuming that the students are already engaged in writing tasks, the period begins with a brief sense-of-the-class meeting (Atwell, 1986) to find out who is working on what writing topic. Students keep a list of writing topics

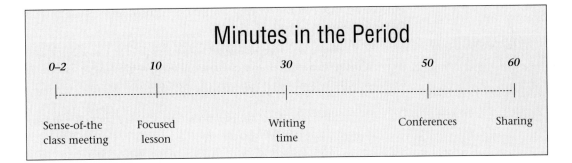

FIGURE 8.6

Daily Schedule of a Writing Workshop.

in a journal or a writing folder; if they do not have a work in progress, they should already have a topic ready to be written about. By finding out and recording several interesting things about each child at the beginning of the year, the teacher can have a lively suggestion ready if a student comes up empty.

FOCUSED LESSONS.   The goals of writing workshops is to encourage students to write about things they care about to real audiences and to improve their writing so that it communicates more and more effectively. It is essential to give students time, models, and opportunities to write. But students also need careful instruction on all aspects of writing—from how one carries out the writing process to proper punctuation. Focused instruction helps children in the rehearsal and drafting stages by showing them strategies for writing, and it helps them in the revising and editing stages by giving them criteria or working standards for making their writing better. In the past, focused lessons were called *minilessons*, and teachers tried to hold their length to five to seven minutes; now the preferred term is *focused lessons*, to give due attention to the importance of writing instruction (Routman, 1996; Bromley, 1999).

Focused lessons may relate to any aspect of writing, from mechanical issues such as spelling and punctuation; to word-choice issues such as showing, not telling, in order to write vividly and clearly; to composition-related issues such as ways to write strong introductions and closings. Focused lessons also may highlight the writing process itself, showing students how writers get ideas and narrow them, how writers put ideas into words, how writers go back and make the work better, and how writers share their work and learn from their peers' comments.

The goal of all focused lessons is for children to internalize the main points and observe them while critiquing their peers' paper and their own. In other words, the writing teacher tries to work himself or herself out of a job. It is important to conceive of focused lessons not as teaching writing skills in the abstract, but rather as ways of adding information and guidance to the children's own writing and editing processes.

Focused lessons follow the same four-part model used throughout this book to teach skills in context: demonstration and immersion, attention to detail, guided practice, and independent use. In the writing workshop, focused lessons use those four parts in the following ways.

(1) *Finding a text that demonstrates a point or skill you want to teach.* For example, if you want to show children how to write vivid beginnings to stories by jumping right into the action, read the beginning of *Charlotte's Web:*

> *"Where's Papa going with that axe?" said Fern to her mother as they were setting the table for breakfast.*
>
> *"Out to the hoghouse," replied Mrs. Arable. "Some pigs were born last night."*
>
> *"I don't see why he needs an axe," continued Fern, who was only eight.*
>
> *"Well," said her mother, "one of the pigs is a runt. It's very small and weak, and it will never amount to anything. So your father has decided to do away with it."*
>
> *"Do away with it," shrieked Fern. "You mean kill it, just because it's smaller than the others?" (White, 1952, p. 1)*

(2) *Sharing the example and calling students' attention to the skill it demonstrates.* E. B. White could have begun his story by describing the setting and the characters, but he didn't. He started right in with the action. He decided to have Fern ask that question, hear that terrible answer, and get upset. After just these few lines, it is evident that the main problem of the story will be saving the little pig's life, and readers will want to know what can be done to solve this problem.

You might ask the students how the beginning made them feel and what it led them to expect. What advice do they suppose E. B. White gave himself that made him begin the story that way? Discuss this example until the point is clear that a good way of beginning a story is to start right in with action that shows readers a problem and makes them care what will happen in the story.

(3) *Providing the students with guided practice using the skill.* Ask the students to take out a draft of a story they are writing. Have them rewrite the beginning of the story so that it starts right in with action or dialogue that leads the reader right into the main problem of the story. Have the students pair up and take turns explaining to a partner the changes they made to their paper.

(4) *Encouraging students to use the skill in their independent writing.* So that the points taught in the focused lessons enter students' repertoire of writing skills, you might add each point to a writing rubric or editing checklist or to your guidelines for good writing. You can also add that point into rubrics used to evaluate students' writing or into the checklists they use to edit their own and each other's drafts.

WRITING TIME.   During much of the writing workshop, all of the students are writing. This is quiet time. The teacher writes for the first five minutes as well, to help establish an atmosphere for quiet independent work. For the next ten minutes, the teacher might move around to individual students, to encourage them as they write. Nathan and colleagues (1988) advise that the teacher go first to those who appear to be having trouble writing.

CONFERENCES.   After the students have written, a period of conferences begins. The teacher can conduct a conference for the whole class, with one student, or with a small group. Students may confer with a partner or with a small group. Conferences were discussed in detail on page 312. Students who wish to continue writing during this time may do so.

SHARING.   The last ten minutes of the workshop are reserved for sharing. The teacher should choose students to share who are far along in a draft or whose work displays an interesting issue. Different students should share each time, since only one or two can normally share in a ten-minute period. Some teachers extend sharing time to get in three students a day; that way, every student gets to share every other week.

Different Levels of Support for Writing

The writing workshop model assumes that students are capable of a fair amount of self-direction and that they understand at least the rudiments of how ideas are put down on paper. It is true that children as young as kindergarten age can participate in writing workshops in some fashion. But teachers find that many young writers—and not just the youngest—sometimes need more explicit support as they learn to write. Fountas and Pinnell (1996) and Tompkins (2000) suggest that teachers prepare to give different levels of support for young writers and provide a range of activities for doing so. Those that give higher levels of support put the teacher in the role of demonstrator and explainer. Those that give lower levels of support maximize the children's initiative and put the teacher more in the role of coach and guide. Five kinds or levels of writing support are *modeled writing, shared writing, interactive writing, guided writing,* and *independent writing.* Figure 8.7 on page 318 shows examples of the kinds of activities that are conducted at each level of writing support. Although some of the activities at the more highly supported end of the scale are intended for young children, it is not the case that only younger writers need more support and only older writers need less. At one time or another, writers of all ages can use both support and freedom to create.

MODELED WRITING.   In **modeled writing,** when students need to be shown some aspect of the writing process, the teacher models it for the class. For example, if you wish to introduce the writing process to young students for the first time, you might proceed as follows:

> *Gathering the children in front of you, announce that you are going to write about something important. Explain that you are first going to draw your ideas as you talk about them and that you will then write in a space below the picture. Take a piece of chart paper, and fold it horizontally so that the crease is about a third of the way from the bottom. When the paper is flattened out, the crease will mark off the space for writing.*
>
> *Now think aloud by naming and talking about your topic: your aging family dog. Using a page of chart paper, draw a picture as you talk, and demonstrate how you can use drawing as a way of rehearsing or thinking out your ideas. Then think of one line you want to write about the dog in the space you left for writing underneath the picture.*

My dog is old.

		Teacher Input and Support		

<table>
<tr><td colspan="6">**High** ←------------------ Teacher Input and Support ------------------→ **Low**</td></tr>
<tr>
<th>*Kind of Support*</th>
<th>**Modeled Writing**</th>
<th>**Shared Writing**</th>
<th>**Interactive Writing**</th>
<th>**Guided Writing**</th>
<th>**Independent Writing**</th>
</tr>
<tr>
<td>**How many?**</td>
<td>*Group*</td>
<td>*Group*</td>
<td>*Group*</td>
<td>*Group*</td>
<td>*Solo or buddy activity*</td>
</tr>
<tr>
<td>**Whose ideas?**</td>
<td>*Teacher composes*</td>
<td>*Teacher and students compose*</td>
<td>*Teacher and students compose*</td>
<td>*Students compose*</td>
<td>*Student composes*</td>
</tr>
<tr>
<td>**Who writes?**</td>
<td>*Teacher writes*</td>
<td>*Teacher writes*</td>
<td>*Teacher and students write*</td>
<td>*Students write*</td>
<td>*Student writes*</td>
</tr>
<tr>
<td>**Sample activities**</td>
<td>*Demon- strations*</td>
<td>*K-W-L charts; dictations*</td>
<td>*Daily news; songs, poems*</td>
<td>*Class collaborations form poems; formula books; (concept books; riddles, etc.)*</td>
<td>*Writing workshop; journals; plays; free compositions*</td>
</tr>
</table>

FIGURE 8.7

Writing Instruction with Different Levels of Support.

(*Source:* Adapted from Tompkins, 2000.)

> *You say the sentence to yourself several times and then announce that you're going to write the first word, "My," which you pronounce slowly.*
> *"What sound does it begin with?" you ask.*
> *"Muh," you say, "and what letter makes that sound?"*
> *"M," you say and write M on the board.*
> *You then pronounce the next sound and spell it, and you write the other words in the same way. When you are finished, you have the children read the sentence with you and discuss the picture. Ask the children to identify one thing that interests them about the picture and writing and to ask one question. Post the composition on the wall for the children to look at later, and remind the children that they can write down their ideas in the same way.*

SHARED WRITING.   In **shared writing**, the teacher not only models acts of writing, but also engages students in composing the writing. When shared writing is used, the topic needs to be one that both the teacher and students know about and are excited about. Such a topic might be a shared experience such as a field trip, a story that all are reading, or a topic that is under investigation by the class. Completion of a K-W-L chart offers a natural occasion for shared writing. Another kind of shared writing activity is group dictation. Here the writing activity is preceded by some kind of activity that excites the students and stimulates talk about it. The teacher leads a discussion and helps students find things to say, then asks the students to offer comments about the topic and writes these down on a piece of chart paper. The teacher might lead the students to sound out some of the words and to offer spellings for them.

**Phonics &
Phonemic
Awareness**

INTERACTIVE WRITING.   **Interactive writing** is a procedure developed to help emergent and beginning readers and writers explore the writing system in its details. Developed in London by Moira McKenzie, the method has been incorporated into Fountas and Pinnell's Guided Reading program because "Interactive writing provides an authentic setting within which the teacher can explicitly demonstrate how written language works." (Fountas & Pinnell, 1996, p. 33).

Interactive writing works very much like taking a dictated account except that the teacher and the children "share the pen." The procedures follow these steps:

1. The teacher and a medium-size group of students share an experience and agree on a topic. The topic might be a retelling of a story or a poem or a song, the daily news, or an idea that the class is studying.
2. The children offer a sentence about the topic. The teacher has the children repeat the sentence many times and even count the words to fix them firmly in their minds.
3. The teacher asks the children for the first word, then pronounces that word slowly, writing its letters.
4. The teacher now asks for the next word and invites a child up to write the whole word, a few letters, or a single letter. The teacher fills in letters the children miss. Each time a word is added, the whole text is read back by the children, with the teacher pointing to the words.
5. To help the children orient themselves to the text and add letters, the teacher might write blanks where the letters should go.
6. The teacher uses correction tape to paste over letters that are poorly formed.
7. The teacher teaches about words and print as the lesson progresses, reminding children of words they know or almost know, reminding them of spelling patterns they have seen before, reminding them to leave spaces between words, and to add punctuation.

Enthusiasm for writing differs among children, but it's an important part of literacy that goes beyond just learning how to put words on a page.

GUIDED WRITING.   When teachers teach students to create a particular pattern of writing or use a particular strategy, compose a sample piece as a group, and then ask individuals or pairs of students to produce their own writings according to the form or the strategy, they are guiding student writing. **Guided writing** is used when students can handle the rudiments of writing—making letters and spelling words—but still need to know some strategies for organizing their ideas on the page.

Many kinds of the writing lessons described in the next section on writing in the genres lend themselves to guided writing. For example, the form poems of *cinquains* and list poems can be done as class collaborations and then individually by students as guided writing activities.

THE WORLD OF READING

Helping Struggling Writers

The writing workshop is a wonderful forum for many children's creativity, but it has not always served all children well. There are some students for whom the self-direction afforded by the writing workshop seems almost tantamount to neglect—particularly children whose home culture and language differ significantly from those of the school (Delpit, 1996). One explanation of the difficulty is offered by Collins (1998), who points out that writing is a *secondary* form of discourse that is normally based on speech, which is the *primary* form of discourse. If the kind of discourse a child sees in books and is expected to produce with a pencil fairly closely resembles the kind of discourse that is spoken, then the task of learning to write is largely one of discovering or *acquiring* the relations between speech and writing—that is, to figure out the strategies that enable us to put down on paper what we say in speech. The kind of writing workshop described earlier should serve this child well, for as Collins tells us,

> When literacy activities involve language forms and functions that are close to one's primary discourse, they can be achieved through a balance between acquisition and learning which favors acquisition. The typical writing workshop shows this balance in favor of acquisition, owing to its pronounced student-centered methods, including student-generated topics and genres for writing, multiple drafts to gradually improve writing, and supportive feedback from teachers and peers. When literacy activities involve ways of using language substantially different from one's primary discourse, the balance shifts in favor of learning. (Collins, 1998, p. 6, emphasis added)

As you might recall from the discussion of language acquisition and language learning in Chapter 3, *learning* refers to formal, teacher-directed, explicit instruction. *Acquisition* means learning by discovery and inference from being immersed in writing activities. Moving the balance toward learning means explicitly teaching students what they need to know to carry out the processes of writing. Struggling writers do not need to be taken out of writing workshops and given skill sheets to fill out. It is still possible for teachers to teach students *strategies* for writing that they can use to express themselves to an audience of their peers (Harris & Graham, 1996).

Strategies are explicit procedures. Strategies relate to every aspect of writing, from choosing a topic, to deciding which parts of the topic to include and which to leave out, to organizing ideas on paper. Strategies may be taught in two ways. One is by means of focused lessons. In a focused lesson, the teacher makes it very clear to the students when and how to use a particular technique in writing, whether it be a beginning + middle + ending organization for a paper or the way to punctuate dialogue. Another means of teaching a strategy is using writing guides or *graphic organizers*. For struggling writers, having a graphic organizer to follow, such as a story map or an outline for a persuasive essay, helps to make the writing strategy explicit. After the students understand the steps to the strategy, the teacher gives them guided practice using the strategy and provides feedback on their use of it. After they have learned to use the strategy, they will no longer need to use the graphic organizer.

INDEPENDENT WRITING.   **Independent writing** includes writing in journals, self-initiated writing of all kinds, and writing done in writing workshops. It is important that children of all ages have regular chances to write independently. Doing so allows children to exercise many of their ideas and strategies for writing—from letter formation, to the direction of print on a page, to spelling, to the use of illustrations, to the arrangement of ideas in a composition. Good writing ideas are contagious. If you observe children who have spent extended time in writing workshops, you will see that many more ideas emerge from the children and are passed from child to child than the teacher would have time to think up and teach them during more structured writing time.

Some children will produce writing on their own, but many will not. That is why the writing workshop is so useful—because it uses a combination of teacher example and direction with encouragement of children's peers to get them writing.

Writing in Different Genres

A writing **genre** is a form of writing related to a purpose. Writing expert Lucy Calkins (1994) suggests that teachers immerse students in genre study, in which they read several published works written in a particular genre and then try their hands at writing in that genre. The format for teaching lessons of genre study is similar to that of focused lessons and is demonstrated in the Teach It! box. Different kinds or genres of writing pose different challenges to writers. The main genres of writing include the following:

TEACH IT!
26

- *Journals.* These are personal accounts of events or ideas whose purpose is to record experiences and help writers remember them and think about them deeply.

- *Stories.* These are fictional accounts of characters in settings who attempt to overcome problems. The purpose of stories is to be outlets for writers' inventiveness and to entertain others.

- *Poems.* These are compositions that capture and convey emotions and insights while taking liberties with sentence and paragraph construction.

- *Expository accounts.* These are intended to be careful descriptions or explanations of things in the world.

- *Persuasive essays.* These convey writers' views of real issues in their lives and try to influence their readers' views.

These genres include important subtopics: A play is a kind of story; a song is a kind of poem; an observation report in science is a kind of expository account, as are biographies and autobiographies; and an advertisement is a kind of persuasive essay. They may also be mixed with each other; sometimes writers describe or explain in order to persuade readers or to tell them a story. Fictitious journals can be a form of storytelling, as Pam Conrad ably demonstrated in her novel *Pedro's Journal* (1992), a fictional day-by day account of the voyage of Christopher Columbus.

Journals and Other Personal Writing

Journal writing consists of writing down thoughts, feelings, and impressions that are close to the writer and that are addressed to the writer herself as audience. Such writing usually comes fairly naturally to young writers because it has few formal demands. Nonetheless, the kind of personal expressive writing that is used in journals is important for students to use, because it serves as a sort of playground or laboratory for the imagination (Britton, 1970). Students may begin ideas in journals that they later turn into more formal pieces.

TEACH IT!

✦ ✦ ✦ ✦

Teaching Students to Write in Genres: Descriptive Writing

Writing expert Lucy Calkins (1994) suggests that teachers immerse students in genre study, in which they read several published works written in a particular genre and then try their hands at writing in that genre. The format for teaching lessons of genre study is basically the same as that for focused lessons.

In the following sample lesson, teacher Paul Darion has decided to immerse his students in descriptive writing.

- *Sharing a Sample of the Writing Form.* To demonstrate descriptive writing, Mr. Darion selects the opening paragraphs from Frances Temple's *Tonight, By Sea* (1995) and makes copies of them for his students. He plans to call the students' attention to the author's skill at writing vividly. In this case, the writer has carefully observed a process and shown it to the reader, step by step, and has put the reader in the picture by naming sights, sounds, smells, and tactile sensations.

- *Calling Attention to the Features of the Writing Form.* Mr. Darion reads the passage aloud as the students read along. Then he invites the students to say aloud what they experienced in reading the passage. He invites one student to retell the

process of lighting a fire. Then he invites several more students, one at a time, to name a detail the writer has given and say whether that detail is a sight, a sound, a smell, or a feeling. Mr. Darion has also decided to pass out different colored pencils and ask students to use different colors for words that appeal to different senses. This part of the lesson ends with the students saying aloud how the writer achieved vivid descriptive writing: "Descriptive writing names things exactly, and uses words for sights, sounds, smells, tastes, and feelings."

- *Providing Guided Practice in Using the Writing Form.* Sometimes, the next thing Mr. Darion does is to have the students observe something carefully in the classroom and describe it in writing. Today, however, he pulls out a mystery bag he created beforehand. It is nothing more than a paper bag containing an object (such as a chess piece, a spark plug, a sewing thimble, or a Christmas tree light bulb.) Mr. Darion invites the students, one at a time, to reach into the bag and touch the object. The students then describe it *on paper*—with the understanding that they must thoroughly describe the object before they name it.

- *Make a Poster Explaining How to Write in That Genre.* Mr. Darion has the students create a poster that names the kind of writing, provides an example of it, and includes a graphic organizer that makes clear the instructions for writing in that form or genre. The students will now be

Refer to your **Teach It!** booklet for further activities you can use to reinforce concepts discussed in this chapter.

Kneeling in the sand, Paulie shredded dry seaweed and fluffed it into heap between the three black cooking stones, half forgetting that she had no food to cook. She broke palm fronds over the seaweed, then propped two pieces of driftwood with their tips just above the palm. Raking the sand together with her fingers, she built up a ring around the outside of the stones, careful to make room for the air to blow in and give life to the fire, a little and not too much.

Paulie leaned back, still kneeling, circling her upper arms in her hands to warm them. Night had come. The tree frogs stopped singing all at once.

"You got matches, Uncle?"

Paulie's uncle was washing in seawater from a bucket, pouring it down his back to get off the sweat and the sawdust, rinsing his arms.

"All the matches gone, Paulie."

"Go see if you can borrow a coal," her grandmother said. Sitting on the steps of her house, a cloth around her thin shoulders, Grann Adeline leaned toward the fire as if it were already lit. She frowned, slapped at a mosquito on her ankle. "Go on, girl. Ask sweetly and somebody bound to give you an ember."

Paulie wandered down the sand path. The small houses clustered under the trees were mostly dark. She could hear voices talking softly, a baby crying. A thin dog came out and sniffed at the backs of her knees. Paulie looked for the glow of a cook fire, smelled the breeze for one. She could feel the sea air, and hear the waves coming in, but it seemed like nobody was cooking.

Source: Frances Temple, *Tonight, By Sea,* pp. 1, 2. Copyright 1952, renewed 1980 by Frances Temple. Reprinted by permission of Scholastic, Inc.

able to refer to the poster as they complete their own writing.

- *Encourage the Students to Write in That Genre during Their Independent Writing.* Mr. Darion reminds the students of what they know about descriptive writing and encourages them to describe things

carefully with words that appeal to the senses. The term *descriptive writing* enters the students' vocabulary, and the reminder to "use words that name sights, sounds, smells, tastes, and feelings" is commonly heard among the students themselves.

DUAL-ENTRY DIARY. Journals have other important pedagogical uses, too. Response journals are used to encourage students to reflect on their reading and their learning. A simple but powerful approach to response journals is the dual-entry diary (Berthoff, 1981; Barone, 1992). In a dual-entry diary (DED), the students are asked to divide the page down the middle with a vertical line. Then on the left-hand side, they record phrases that they found striking, important, or puzzling. On the right-hand side, they write comments on the passages. DEDs can be used to respond to literature or a host of other topics. After the students have written their DEDs, the teacher may write comments in them or may ask the students to share their entries in a discussion group.

DIALOGUE JOURNALS. In this form of response writing in journals, students are assigned to pairs by the teacher. After they have read a part of a book or participated in some other learning event, they write their impressions of it in their journals. Later, they have written conversations with each other. One makes a comment in writing and ends with a question for the other. The other answers the question, makes a comment as well, and writes another question for the partner, and so on.

Stories

Most students enjoy writing stories, and because they are surrounded by stories, they find it natural to do so. Yet the structure of stories is fairly complicated, so some instruction in writing stories is helpful. There are many ways to show students how to write stories.

IMITATING AN AUTHOR. In the genre study approach, you might read the children several stories by the same author and then ask them to write a similar story. For example, second- and third-grade children delight in writing their own episodes about *Amelia Bedelia* (Parrish, 1992), James Marshall's character *Fox* (Marshall, 1994), or Russell Hoban's character *Frances* (Hoban, 1995).

USING STORY MAPS. Story maps are outlines that give shape to stories. In Chapter 6, story maps were used as devices for calling children's attention to the parts of a plot. In writing, story maps can be used as frameworks like the one shown in Figure 8.8. In using a story map as a way of planning to write a simple story, students fill in the blanks on the right-hand side of the chart. The parts in parentheses are filled in when a story has more than one episode. After the students have filled in the chart, they write the story out, adding details and whatever other twists occur to them. No one would maintain that a story written to a formula will be interesting to read, but children can use story maps during the rehearsal stage of writing as they think and talk through—individually or with a partner—where their story might go.

DIALOGUE STORIES. A simple but effective pattern for structuring stories is the dialogue story. Students can be shown an example of a dialogue story, such as John Archambault and Bill Martin, Jr.'s *White Dynamite and the Curly Kid* (Archambault & Martin, 1989). Then ask the students to write their own story in dialogue form. As a rehearsal step, have two students make up an oral story together and each write their own version of it later.

There was a person . . .	
who wanted . . .	
So she . . .	
but . . .	
(and she . . .)	
(but . . .)	
And then she . . .	
And finally, . . .	
So . . .	

FIGURE 8.8

A Story Map.

Poems

Styles of poems range from those that put an emphasis on form to those that stress ideas and let form take care of itself. Below are three different approaches to writing structured poems. Even though the form is tightly prescribed, children write poems that are lively and surprising with these frameworks to support them. To teach children to write a form poem, follow these steps:

1. Show the students an example of a well-written poem that follows the form. (You might need to write this yourself or save it from a previous class.)
2. Have the students help you create a poem as a group. Discuss each choice they make so that they understand the process well.
3. Have individuals or pairs write their own poems.
4. Share several of the poems, and discuss their qualities. Also call attention to the ways in which the poems followed the structure.
5. Make a wall chart in which you feature several of the students' poems; also outline the procedures for writing a poem with the structure in question.

ACROSTICS.   These are probably the simplest form poems to use. Students write their names in capitals vertically down the left side of a page and then go back and insert a word that begins with each letter. For example,

Persistent

Energetic

Never dull

Native of the mountains—

Yes, you will like this person.

CINQUAINS.   Christmas tree–shaped poems that look like the following are called *cinquains*:

> *Harry*
> *Young, charmed*
> *Studying, flying, surviving*
> *Ron Weasley's best friend*
> *Wizard*

Cinquains are surprisingly useful means of encouraging students to think about a concept and follow a simple pattern:

- The first line names the topic.
- The second line contains two describing words.
- The third line has three action words ending in *-ing.*
- The fourth line is four feeling words, which may be written as a phrase.
- The fifth line is a one-word synonym for the name in the first line.

LIST POEMS.   Throughout the ages, many fine poems have been developed around the idea of lists. Take this medieval prayer, for example:

> *From Ghoulies*
> *And Ghosties*
> *And long-legged Beasties*
> *And Things that go bump in the night:*
> *Good Lord, deliver us.*

Writers can use the idea by listing all of the things that are:

—dark

—lonely

—round

—scarce

The effect is heightened when writers include in their list both concrete and abstract things. For example,

> *A pebble in the pond*
> *a policeman's beat*
> *the moon's halo*
> *subway tokens*
> *surprised eyes*
> *a ghost's mouth*
> *and the world—*
> *are round.*

Expository Writing

This genre includes writings that describe or explain. Young writers can be helped to write expository works by focused lessons that share good examples from literature and encourage their imitation. Graphic organizers serve as valuable tools for helping to write descriptive and explanatory prose. A number of graphic organizers are popular with children from second grade up and have been discussed at various points in the book. As you might recall, graphic organizers are important learning aids in comprehension (Chapters 6 and 7) as well. This reinforces an important theme of this book about the close connection between the teaching/learning of reading and writing.

CLUSTERS.   Clusters, also called *semantic webs*, are linked circles that show relationships between ideas. The writer starts by naming the topic of the writing in a circle in the center of the page and then writes subordinate topics in satellite circles around the main circle. Aspects of each subordinate circle are written in still more satellites (see Figure 8.4 on page 310).

VENN DIAGRAMS.   Venn diagrams are helpful planning aids when writers want to compare and contrast two items and consist of two interlocking circles (see Figure 8.9). In the outer left-hand circle is listed everything that is true about Topic X but not Topic Y. In the outer right-hand circle is written everything that is true about Topic Y but not Topic X. In the overlapping part in the middle is written everything that is true about both Topic X and Topic Y.

CAUSE-AND-EFFECT CHARTS.   When students plan to write about cause-and-effect chains, they may organize their ideas before writing using a cause-and-effect chart. A cause-and-effect chart (Figure 8.10 on page 328) may have few or many boxes. Causes are listed in separate boxes on the left-hand side of the chart with effects listed on the right. Several causes may contribute to a single effect, which may simultaneously be the cause of several other effects. The chart in Figure 8.10 shows how many causes may result in air pollution, which cause a great many other effects.

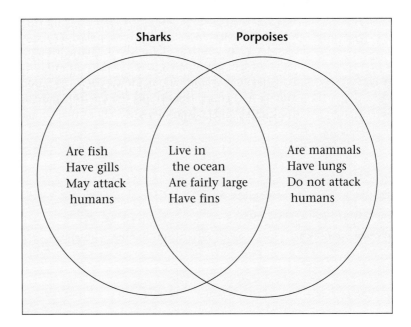

FIGURE 8.9

A Venn Diagram.

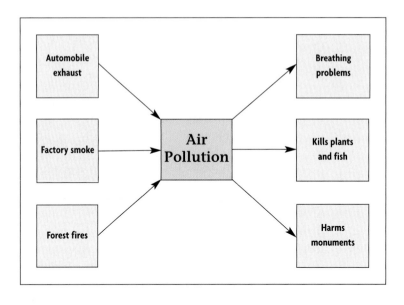

FIGURE 8.10

A Cause-and-Effect Chart.

Persuasive Essays

There are many ways to help students produce arguments, and shape them on paper into persuasive essays. A popular procedure for helping students formulate their ideas for a persuasive essay is the K-W-L strategy (Ogle, 1984), which was discussed in Chapter 7. By constructing a K-W-L chart, students consider what they already *know* about a topic, formulate questions that say what they *want to know* about it, and later list what they *learned* about the topic. Having done this activity, you can then construct a new chart, labeled like the one in Figure 8.11, that will guide the students to think about and take positions on actions that should follow from those findings.

TEACH IT!
28

What?	So What?	Now What?
Pollution from automobiles and industrial pollution cause global warming.	Global warming is bad for plants and animals, including humans.	We should reduce automobile pollution by driving less and reduce industrial pollution by using less fossil fuel.

FIGURE 8.11

What? So What? Now What?

What do you believe should be done about _____?	We should reduce automobile pollution by driving less and reduce industrial pollution by using less fossil fuel.
What is one reason why that should be done?	Pollution from automobiles and industrial pollution cause global warming.
(What is a second reason why that should be done?)	Global warming is bad for plants and animals, including humans.
(What is a third reason why that should be done?)	We are ruining our environment by warming the whole planet's climate.
So, say again what you believe should be done about _____.	Therefore, we should reduce automobile pollution by driving less and reduce industrial pollution by using less fossil fuel.

FIGURE 8.12

Framework for a Persuasive Essay.

After the students have completed the chart, they might think about ways to use their entries in an argumentative essay. One way in which the essay can be structured is to enter the information into another kind of format, like the one shown in Figure 8.12.

Assessment of Writing

Various parts of this chapter have focused on teaching children to revise and edit their own work. Revising and editing are basic forms of assessment of children's writing. Assessing students' writing and providing ongoing feedback are critical in encouraging students to write. However, in assessing students' writing, keep in mind some valuable principles:

- Not everything should be assessed. Most of children's writing should be for communication and should not be graded.
- Assessment should teach; that is, children should learn about writing from the assessment.
- The criteria for assessment should be explicit and clear.
- Children should be involved in their own assessment.
- Assessment should show strengths and progress as well as needed improvements.

Six Traits Writing Evaluation

The Six Traits model for writing assessment meets all of the principles just identified. Developed by Vicki Spandel and her associates (1996, 2000) at the Northwest Regional Education Laboratory, the Six Traits model seeks to direct teachers' and students' attention to six aspects of writing: *ideas and content, organization, voice, word choice, sentence fluency,* and *conventions*.

1. **Ideas and content** are the quality of having something to say and saying it clearly to the reader. It includes having found out something about the topic before writing about it and having an original point of view. It can include providing details that lend an eyewitness feel to the paper.
2. **Organization** refers to the paper's having a beginning, a middle, and an end. It may include supporting main ideas with details, sticking to the topic, and making clear transitions from one point to another.
3. **Voice** describes the quality of reaching for words that express ideas well, even when this means writing words one has not been taught to use or taught to spell. A paper with a well-developed voice approaches the writer's oral fluency and expressiveness.
4. **Word choice** is the quality of showing the writer's meaning with precise words and specific details, and using fresh ways of expressing ideas, avoiding clichés.
5. **Sentence fluency** means a reader can easily read the work aloud. There are sufficient numbers of sentences to convey the meaning, and the sentences are varied in their length and form.
6. **Conventions** include spelling, capitalization and punctuation, and grammatical correctness. In later grades, conventions may refer to allocating separate ideas to separate paragraphs.

Naturally, children of different ages and levels of development will be more or less advanced in their performance within each trait. Spandel and her associates have listed behavioral descriptors at four levels of development:

- *Exploring writers* are young writers who are experimenting with the whole enterprise of making meaning with graphic communication. Thus, within the trait of ideas and content, exploring writers might use pictures and scribbles to express ideas.

- *Emerging writers* are still young writers, but they have advanced to the point at which they are starting to work the features of conventional writing into their graphic productions. Thus, within the trait of ideas and content, emerging writers may use pictures or both pictures and mock writing in such a way that a reader might be able to guess an approximate meaning.

- *Developing writers,* through a mix of their own inventions and discoveries and overt teaching, can produce written messages that convey clear meaning, with the beginnings of formal organization and attention to some of the conventions of spelling and capitalization. Thus, within the trait of ideas and content, developing writers create stand-alone messages that are more readily decipherable. Their works show some attention to detail.

- *Fluent/experienced writers* express meanings more eloquently in print and take advantage of many features of fluent writing within all six traits. Thus, within the trait of ideas and content, fluent writers create works that show advancing mastery of qualities of writing, including the ability to say things clearly and in fresh and interesting ways, honoring more and more of the conventions of writing.

Six Traits writing evaluation can guide you in evaluating and grading children's written works. But it has another, equally valuable purpose, which is to call children's attention to the things they are doing well and point the way toward improvement. One highly effective way of showing children what they are doing well and what they can do to improve is to use rubrics.

Using Rubrics

Rubrics are detailed presentations of quality criteria. Rubrics address several aspects of writing at once, and they explain clearly what constitutes a good job. Rubrics may be constructed by the teacher or by the teacher and the students together. Rubrics should be closely connected to the qualities of writing that have been stressed in the focused lessons and any checklists that have been used to guide the students' revising and editing. Students should be fully aware of the meaning of each criterion (aspect of quality) on the rubric before they produce the work that will be assessed. A sample rubric for middle elementary grades, which was adapted from the Six Traits writing evaluation, is found in Figure 8.13 on page 332.

Following are the steps for using rubrics:

- Choose four to eight qualities of writing to assess. (Consider having the children suggest qualities of good writing.)
- Make sure the qualities of writing you assess have been carefully explained.
- Describe good work according to each quality. You may also describe fair and poor work.
- Share the rubrics with the students before they write the works that will be assessed.
- Use the rubrics often so that students learn what they mean and are able to use their criteria to guide them when they write.

Work Sampling

Another effective approach to evaluating writing is work sampling. One way to sample work is to choose representative pieces of each child's writings at intervals during the year but at least once per month. Sit down with the child, and discuss the improvements you both see. Ask the child to take the lead in pointing out the improvements. If the child needs help, you might comment on the following:

- The length of each piece
- Organization—sticking to a topic and saying interesting things about it
- The appearance of new features, such as description or dialogue
- Attempts to write in new genre, such as persuasion or description
- Attention to mechanics, such as spelling, punctuation, and handwriting

Before ending the conversation, ask the child to set goals—writing improvements to make in the next month. Write these down, or have the child write them, with a copy for yourself and a copy for the child. Provide regular reminders of the goals.

Ideas and Content:

Clear ideas. It makes sense. _____

The writer has narrowed the idea to a manageable topic. _____

Good information—from experience, imagination, or research. _____

Original and fresh perspective. _____

Details that capture a reader's interest. Makes ideas understandable. _____

Organization:

A snappy lead that gets the reader's attention. _____

Starts somewhere and goes somewhere. _____

The writer continually makes connections within the work. _____

Writing builds to a conclusion. _____

The writer creates a memorable resolution and conclusion. _____

Voice:

Sounds like a person wrote it. _____

Sounds like this particular writer. _____

Brings topic to life. _____

Makes the reader respond and care what happens. _____

The writer has energy and is involved. _____

Word Choice:

Words and phrases have power. _____

Word pictures are created. _____

Thought is crystal clear and precise. _____

Strong verbs and precise nouns. _____

Sentence Fluency:

Easy to read aloud. _____

Well-built sentences. _____

Varied sentence length. Some long sentences, some short. _____

Conventions:

Looks clean, edited and proofread. _____

Free of distracting errors. _____

Easy to read. _____

No errors in spelling, punctuation, grammar and usage, capitalization, and indentation. _____

FIGURE 8.13

A Rubric for Assessing Writing: Six Traits Writing Evaluation Sheet.

Involving Families in Their Children's Writing

Family & Community Literacy

Families can be partners in all stages of children's growth as writers. Research has shown that children who are drawn into family literacy activities, and especially into letter writing activities make more progress as readers and writers (Clay, 1987).

Family Writing for Young Children

When children in kindergarten and first grade begin to explore the writing system, it helps if parents give them reasons and opportunities to practice their early writing, even when it bears only a slight resemblance to adult writing. As was discussed in earlier chapters, children make progress both as readers and as writers if they are allowed to produce pretend versions of writing. Indeed, with a little training, it is possible to ensure that important concepts about print are discovered and practiced through early writing experiences, even scribbling and invented spelling. Families of younger children can invite children to write some of the following:

Greeting cards to relatives

Grocery lists

Captions on their drawings

Refrigerator notes to the rest of the family.

You might need to explain to parents the importance of encouraging young children to write even before they have learned to do so conventionally. Many parents may worry that early untutored writing could reinforce incorrect habits. Assure them that this is not the case. However, you must then observe some safeguards in your classroom, such as making sure that the materials displayed for children to practice reading is written conventionally.

Family Writing for Older Children

When children are able to spell words and write sentences, they should be encouraged to do meaningful writing at home. Writing at home might include the following:

- Writing up family stories to share on special occasions, as in family letters to relatives
- Letters to friends and relatives
- Writing to a safe circle of friends via a computer-based instant messaging service

Children will be inspired to write if they see family members writing. Some families make a custom of compiling and writing down family stories that occur during the year—the most outrageous camping trip, the funniest family event, and so on. These can be a fine addition to a family photograph album, and can be written by all—children included.

Using Technology in Teaching Writing

It is in the area of children's writing that technology plays one of its most useful roles in children's education. Technology—computers, email, and the Internet—are a powerful invitation for children to write. Anyone who is a regular user of email knows

Children feel encouraged to write more when they receive letters . . . in one way or the other.

Technology

how much more writing is done when you can communicate with friends online. The same is true for children of all ages. But as Larry Cuban (2001) warns, in most cases, children use computers more frequently and more imaginatively at home than they do at school. This raises the specter of a technology gap, or **digital divide**, between families that can afford computers and the monthly fees levied by Internet service providers and the many families who cannot or do not spend the money on these things.

Communicating via Computers

Because communication via computers is still mostly done by typing on a keyboard, computers elicit a great deal of writing from children when they write to others via email or instant messaging or in chat rooms. Children can communicate via computers in four main ways.

INDIVIDUAL EMAIL ACCOUNTS.   Conventional email allows users to read and send messages from and to people all over the world. Email systems save the messages that one receives and sends, and they enable the user—at the click of the mouse—to reply to messages, send messages to many people at once, and even to block senders of messages. Regular email is not well suited for carrying on a conversation, however, since there may be delays of many minutes between the time a note is sent by one person and when it is received by another, and the reply might not come for hours or days.

INSTANT MESSAGING.   Instant messaging software is supplied by AOL, Microsoft, and others. It enables people to have nearly instantaneous conversations with a limited group of "buddies." Users typically sign up using a fictitious name—a fact that can, in some cases, invite people to write to others without the sensitivity they would normally maintain if their identities were known to each other. It is worthwhile to talk to students about the etiquette of chatting by instant messaging and in chat rooms (see Figure 8.14).

1. Let your parents know each time you go online. Tell them where you are going and with whom you are communicating. Let your parents participate in the conversations.

2. If anyone says something offensive to you online, log off and alert an adult—don't answer the message.

3. Don't write something online that you would not say to someone in person—in short, be polite.

4. Don't say unkind things about others online. Once they leave your computer, messages may "stay alive" and circulate to people other than those to whom you sent them.

5. Don't reveal personal contact information—not your last name, or your home address, or your telephone number. The person you are talking to might not be who you think that person is.

6. Limit the amount of time you spend in computer-based chats. Other people in your house may need to use the computer or the telephone line.

FIGURE 8.14

Etiquette for Electronic Conversations.

CHAT ROOMS.   Similar to instant messaging are Internet-based chat rooms, in which people may log in and exchange messages with many parties at once. Like instant messaging, chat rooms usually offer the option of signing in under a pseudonym. Chat rooms are sometimes moderated by someone whose job it is to screen out offensive messages. Children should be warned to avoid chat rooms that are not especially moderated to keep them safe for children.

LIST-SERVS.   List-servs are networks of users who sign up to receive messages from each other, usually focusing on a certain topic. There are list-servs for stamp collectors, kite flyers, fans of sports teams, fans of entertainers, and devotees of an infinite host of other topics. List-servs can link students to communities of others who share unique interests.

PEN PALS AND OTHER EXCHANGES.   In the 1920s, an inspired French educator named Celestin Freinet (Temple, 1994) devised ways of having his elementary-grade students study geography and climate by corresponding with other students from around Europe and the world. Freinet's students asked about other children's surroundings, their weather, and their climate and how these affected their activities. Freinet's lessons were very popular with his students because investigating distant places by talking to the children who lived there was far more concrete, vivid, and engaging than reading dry facts from a book. Yet to pull off this innovative style of inquiry, Freinet's students used what computer savants today contemptuously call "snail mail." Their exchanges took weeks. With the use of e-mail and the Internet, pen pal networks have a global reach, and exchanges can be completed in a matter of days or even hours.

Today, many pen pal networks are available to students. Some central sources link individual children as well as whole classrooms in many countries around the world. Most of the sites have safety procedures, including moderators, to keep children out of contact with unseemly sorts, although caution is still in order. Two such sites are the following:

- Kids on the Web at www.zen.org/~brendan/kids-pen.html
- ESD 105 at www.esd105.wednet.edu/kp.html

Protecting Children from Harmful Material Online

Web sites, mailing lists, and chat rooms enable children to virtually leave their own neighborhoods and communicate with others around the world who share the same interests. But this infinite mobility has a negative side. As psychologist James Garbarino (2000) points out, in some mailing lists and chat rooms, young people may find communities of a harmful sort. In an actual community, for example, a young person who has violent fantasies is not likely to find like-minded companions for encouragement, but in the virtual community of a chat room or a mailing list, this young person might find the support of others like himself or herself.

Parents should be reminded to monitor their children's email and Internet use, just as teachers and librarians do when children are in school. Online services and software companies such as Norton and McAfee market programs that give families the ability to screen out whole categories of web sites, such as those with prurient or violent content. Most email software can be set to block undesirable email messages, but only if the exact name or email address of the sender is known.

Using Computers for Writing Reports

Computers show their greatest strength as learning aids when it comes to children writing papers. The ease with which young writers can add, delete, and move their words around makes computers the ideal support for the writing process that was described earlier in this chapter. Computers give children control over design capabilities that only layout artists could manage just a few years ago. Now they can arrange their writing in columns, experiment with different typefaces and even colors of fonts, and add artwork from software archives. All of this adds great appeal to the whole enterprise of writing.

With access to the Internet, children can download and paste into their papers photographs as well as text from a nearly infinite array of sources. Having control over so many variables expands children's creative potential, but it also sets them up to be scavengers of the fruits of other people's creativity unless teachers set clear guidelines for what constitutes original work. Strategies such as the I-Chart (see Chapter 7) are recommended when children are writing reports, because the I-Chart format invites children to write a narrative of their investigation and then report their findings.

Several online services are available to children for their review and to inform their research:

- Scholastic, Inc., has a web site at www.scholastic.com that includes a *Research Starters* section. There, students will find illustrated presentations on a growing list of topics (e.g., Pilgrims, dinosaurs, Native American cultures) that are designed to whet their curiosity and give them enough information to begin inquiries that will take them beyond what is presented there.

- The Public Broadcasting Service offers a children's page (www.pbskids.org) (grades four and up) with links to interesting online articles.

- The National Geographic Society operates a web site for children that is accessible through their main site at www.nationalgeographic.com

- Classics for Young Children (www.ucalgary.ca/~dkbrown/storclas.html) is a large set of links to scores of complete works for children, many of them illustrated, that are in the public domain. The works include the E. Nesbit books (e.g., *The Treasure Seekers*), Frank Baum's *Wizard of Oz* books, Frances Hodgson Burnett's *The Secret Garden*, works by Mark Twain, and many others.

FOR REVIEW

This chapter focused on both the process and products of writing. The process was described as one of interlocking, usually sequential activities: rehearsing, drafting, revising, editing, and publishing. Students as young as kindergarten age can learn to use some version of the writing process. They are helped to do so by a writing workshop, a regular period of class time set aside for students to receive focused lessons on one aspect of writing, do some writing, have conferences with the teacher and with each other, and share their works.

The products of writing are arranged into genres. Genres include expressive writing such as journals, stories, poems, expository writing, and persuasive essays. Suggestions were given for helping students write in each genre.

Children sometimes need more explicit support than the writing workshop gives them. Different levels of support for children's writing include modeled writing, shared writing, interactive writing, guided writing, and independent writing. The special problems of struggling writers were also addressed, and it was suggested that strategies for writing be introduced to them through focused lessons and graphic organizers and be regularly practiced.

Assessment is an important part of teaching children to write. Assessment should teach, by employing means that communicate clearly what the children are doing well and what needs work and by involving the children in assessing their own work.

Families have a role to play in supporting students' writing, and suggestions were given for families of younger children and older children. Instructional technology can play a valuable role in children's writing. More and more children in later elementary grades find it natural to communicate via email or in chat rooms. Once the difficulty of keyboarding has been overcome, using the writing process to compose papers is ultimately easier on a computer than with a pencil. The variety of formatting possibilities on a computer is also a draw. That said, there are concerns about children's use of computers. There is plenty of material available on the Internet that is not suitable for children, and although schools have screening software, not all homes do. Also, while the Internet (and electronic encyclopedias) give report-writing students ready access to a wealth of material on virtually any subject, the challenge for teachers is to help students past merely downloading other people's material and teach them to use this information to inform their own reports.

For Your Journal

1. Try out the writing process for yourself with the assistance of a partner, although you can do this activity alone.

   - Make a list of five topics you might write about. These should be topics you might share with children in grades one though five.
   - Ask yourself or have a partner ask you what interests you about each topic. Find your story!

- Choose the topic that you most want to write about. Write it in the middle of a cluster. Brainstorm subtopics, and add them as satellites in the cluster.
- Look over your cluster, and circle the details that seem most interesting to write about.
- Write a draft of your paper. Write for eight minutes without stopping.
- Read back over your paper, or have a partner read it, and consider areas you need to revise.
- Write another draft of the paper, and incorporate the changes.
- Now use the proofreading checklist to look over your paper.
- Write your finished copy in your journal.

Once you have completed this process, reflect on what happened as you wrote. Did new ideas occur to you as you made your cluster? As you wrote your first draft, were you surprised at some of the ideas you came up with? Did the revision review lead you to helpful changes?

2. In helping children learn to write, where do you think the proper balance can be found between the need to encourage children to feel ownership for their writing and take initiative for their learning and the need to teach them to write better—that is, more coherently and correctly?

⭐ Taking It to the World

1. The writing process described in this chapter—rehearsing, drafting, revising, editing, and publishing—is often described as the way professional writers create. But is it? Find and interview at least two writers. If possible, look for writers of fiction and poetry as well as writers of nonfiction. Ask them what they do when they write. (*Hint:* Don't mention the writing process or talk about the steps. See whether they mention those themselves.) Compare your notes with those of your classmates. Do the writers do similar things as they write? Does the process they use seem to depend on whether they are writing fiction or nonfiction? Do their processes resemble the process described in this chapter?

2. The writing workshop that was described in this chapter is widely described in the educational literature as a valuable development. There are many teachers who use the workshop approach successfully and many children who seem to have internalized the steps of the writing process—but maybe not as many as reading the literature might suggest. Visit an elementary school, and ask the teachers whether they use writing workshops with their children. If so, how often? What do you like about it? Does it work for all students? If not, what modifications must they use for the children who struggle? If they don't use the writing workshop, why don't they? What approach to writing instruction do they use?

⭐ Being a Professional Reading Teacher

Reflecting on the Chapter

We have learned that writing should be integrated into the reading program early and that children should write every day. How can we accomplish those two goals?

Creating a Supportive Atmosphere for Teaching Writing

- Why is it so important for students to have an audience in mind when they write? Why is it not so useful for that audience to be only the teacher?
- Describe how you might use an author's chair in your classroom to emphasize the importance of writing.
- How can teachers develop a community of writers? Why is the community aspect so important?

The Developmental Nature of Writing

- In a developmental view of children's writing, why is error correction such an important issue?
- Why is it important for a teacher to consider so carefully the issue of correct spelling at different points of a writing cycle?
- How can skills development be integrated into children's writing lessons in such a way that grammar or mechanics doesn't become the main focus?

Your Portfolio

Of course, it is always useful to include writing samples of your students in your portfolio. Sometimes, it is difficult to convince students to part with their best work, but you might be able to photocopy pieces of writing that they want to keep in their own portfolios.

In addition, think about including samples of your own writing. Here are some examples that you might consider: a letter to the editor of your local paper or a magazine, a poem submitted for publication, or a short piece of work submitted for a university class. Your reflections about artifacts in your portfolio and your statement of philosophy of education are also examples of your own writing that might be included in your portfolio.

Finally, think about including a photograph of your author's chair. The more it looks like a throne, the more importance children will attach to it.

Teaching Resources

You have learned about many very useful writing strategies in this chapter. You might want to reread the chapter, making a list of strategies and where they are used most effectively in lessons—as anticipation activities, such as quick-writes; as knowledge-building activities, such as constructing a story grammar while reading; or as consolidation activities, such as the written retelling. Of course, some writing activities are just that—opportunities to write using different styles and conventions. As you begin teaching, refer to the list and make an effort to use each strategy. Your students will appreciate the variety of approaches, and they will not grow weary of the same tired strategy used over and over.

Technology Connections

1. Visit the web sites of Cyber Patrol (www.cyberpatrol.com) and Net Nanny (www.netnanny.com), and compare the services each company has to offer parents for protecting their children from gaining access to offensive sites.

Which site would you recommend to parents? Why? Does either service offer the option of blocking undesirable email messages?

2. Check out the online magazine for writing for and by children called *Cyberkids* (www.cyberkids.com). Investigate the Creative Works gallery. How might you be able to use this site to help you teach children to write?

Connect with Research

Research
Navigator.c✦m

Review the following key words from the chapter, and then connect to Research Navigator (www.researchnavigator.com) through this book's companion web site to conduct a search into research on each of the various topics as they relate to reading and literacy education today.

active models	independent writing	shared writing
digital divide	interactive writing	static models
genre	modeled writing	writing process
guided writing	rubrics	writing workshop

Further Reading

Atwell, N. (1986). *In the Middle*, Portsmouth, NH: Heinemann Educational Books.

Atwell, a middle-school reading teacher from Maine, wrote one of the most popular books about teaching with a writing workshop and a reading workshop (using response journals).

Calkins, L. (1996). *The Art of Teaching Writing*. Portsmouth, NH: Heinemann Educational Books.

Lucy Calkins has been instrumental for many years in the writing process movement. This very thorough guide to teaching children to write is highly recommended to teachers of grades kindergarten through the elementary grades.

Gillet, J. W., & Beverly, L. (2002). *Directing the Writing Workshop*. New York: Guilford Press.

Two veteran teachers describe in great detail how to set up and manage a writing workshop, and how to teach every aspect of writing.

Harris, K., & Graham, S. (1996). *Making the Writing Process Work: Strategies for Composition and Self-Regulation*. Cambridge, MA: Brookline Books.

Directed at teachers of elementary school children, this book is full of helpful ideas for explicitly teaching strategies that will enable struggling writers to succeed in writing, even in a workshop environment.

Leu, D., & Leu, D. D. (2000). *Teaching with the Internet: Lessons from the Classroom*. Norwood, MA: Christopher-Gordon.

This is a very thorough guide to teaching with the Internet, from e-mail to chat rooms to web pages. It is full of classroom vignettes and includes a great many useful links to educational sites.

Classroom management is so hard. Have a plan on how to manage the classroom and let the students know the rules you expect. I had a set of rules that I shared with the class, then we discussed them together, and the rules were so reasonable that the students saw their value, and we adjusted them a little bit.
— ELIZABETH. FIRST-YEAR EIGHTH-GRADE TEACHER
CHICAGO

I've found that the hardest thing about teaching reading is incorporating strategies beyond the very structured reading program that they require me to use. Another is finding time to meet all of the standards while looking beyond reading and mathematics. My students know nothing about history and science.
— MARY. FIRST-YEAR TEACHER, GRADES 4–5
LOS ANGELES

The road to literacy isn't just about learning to read. It involves using techniques that involve fostering communication skills, creativity, and problem-solving. The bond I've formed with my kids is great. To see their trust in me manifest itself in day-to-day events is wonderful.
— BRYAN. HEAD START TEACHER
WASHINGTON, D.C.

Organizing and Managing the Literacy Program

PART

3

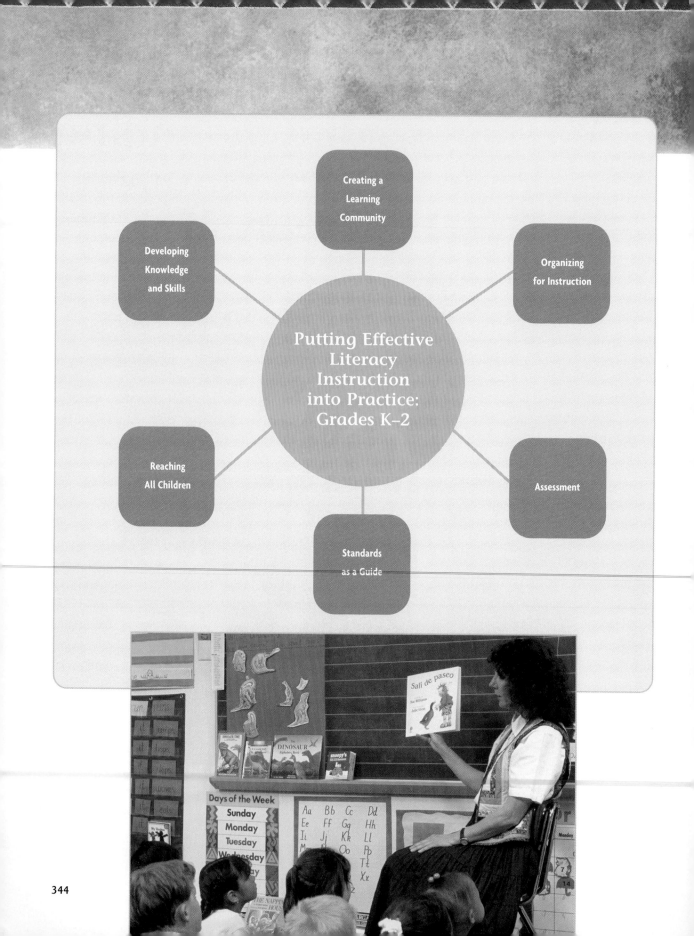

Creating a
Learning
Community

Developing
Knowledge
and Skills

Organizing
for Instruction

Putting Effective
Literacy
Instruction
into Practice:
Grades K–2

Reaching
All Children

Assessment

Standards
as a Guide

Putting Effective Literacy Instruction into Practice: Grades K–2

The following statements will get you thinking about the topics of this chapter. Answer true or false in response to each statement. As you read and learn more about the topics in these statements, double-check your answers. See what interests you and prompts your curiosity toward more understanding.

Anticipation Guide

_____ 1. Establishing a friendly and supportive psychological/social climate in the classroom should be a teacher's first concern in teaching early literacy.

_____ 2. It is more important for children to learn to follow the teacher's rules than to manage their own behavior.

_____ 3. Young children should be encouraged to develop intrinsic motivation; stickers and other rewards should never be used.

_____ 4. The single most important way teachers can help children learn to read is to read to them.

_____ 5. "Synthetic phonics" is so called because this teaching method is stilted and artificial and almost completely unrelated to real reading.

_____ 6. Researchers comparing and contrasting skills-based and literature-based instruction have found dramatic differences in children's learning to read.

_____ 7. The "five-finger test" is a way of telling if a book is too difficult for children to read: If children miss five words on a page, the book is probably too hard.

_____ 8. Children who are English language learners will not profit from reading instruction until they reach an _advanced_ level of proficiency in English.

_____ 9. Elkonin boxes are useful devices for teaching children phonemic segmentation.

_____ 10. The only kind of assessment that is truly useful in classrooms is formal testing, using devices whose validity and reliability have been established by scientific means.

Vignette of Literacy Activities in a First-Grade Classroom

It is an early September morning, and nineteen first-grade children are reading and looking at books as their teacher, Ana Lopes, sets up for a lesson with a book entitled *Bread, Bread, Bread* (Morris, 1998). She read the book with the children twice the day before. This picture book has photos of people and their bread from all over the world, including Mexican tortillas, Indian nan, and French baguettes. Ms. Lopes stops to review her notes from the day before and rechecks a list of children who will not be participating in this particular lesson. She calls these children together and discusses two things they have been working on: the posters they are making for a science project and the new interest center the class created the week before. She tells the students that while she works with the other students in the class, they can work part of the time on their posters and part of the time in the interest center; or they can spend their entire time either in the center or working on their posters. She allows each of the children to select his or her own activity.

Ms. Lopes then calls the remaining students into the group area and sets the big book on a stand. She says to the group, "You know we really enjoyed this book yesterday, so I thought we'd read it again. But first let's look at the pictures." The children look at the illustrations.

Ms. Lopes says, "Now, whisper something about this book to your neighbor. What did you like? Did you ever eat one of these breads?"

Ms. Lopes likes to use the whispering technique to provide varied and frequent opportunities for children to talk and interact. It ensures that everyone gets involved and prevents children from having to sit with their hands in the air waiting for the teacher to call on them.

After the students have shared with each other for a minute, Ms. Lopes reads the big book to the children, pointing to each word as she reads and explaining that for each word spoken there is a letter or unit of letters that make the word. She is teaching the concept of "word." As reading proceeds, she stops a few times to spark discussions about the story or aspects of the writing. By doing this, she makes sure an instructional conversation takes place. She is teaching good reader behaviors and encouraging the readers to think and relate personally to books. She also shows the children that she is interested in what they think.

Ms. Lopes points out that some words in the story repeat again and again, such as "bread, bread, bread." She asks the students to find other words that repeat.

A child responds, "I see the word *eat*."

"Excellent word watching!" Ms. Lopes responds. "Now let's see if we can spot the word *eat* repeated again."

As the literature responses proceed, Ms. Lopes explicitly draws the children into more focused reading by asking them to think about the book's words. As she points to various words, she wonders aloud, "I notice something about this word. [Pointing to the word *bread*]. What is the word?" The children say "bread," and Ms. Lopes points out other words beginning with *br-* and about blends and beginning letter sounds and then asks the children to pretend that they are making bread and eating it.

As the pretend play unfolds Ms. Lopes quickly makes a list of words on the board, then passes out marker boards, erasers, and markers. She covers the board words with a sheet of paper and says, "When I say the word, you try to write its beginning letter on your marker boards and say the sound that the letter makes."

She encourages the children by telling them to take risks and reminding them that the exercise is just for practice. "It's okay if some letters are not quite right. If you can't make the letters, look at the alphabet on the wall. Let me know if you need help."

As the children write and whisper to one another, Ms. Lopes prompts them as necessary and observes and makes notes. Some begin to work independently, saying words, writing letters, and saying letter sounds. Ms. Lopes can see who is taking a chance, who seems able to work on her own, who seems very dependent, who seems to have a grasp of letter/sound relationships, and who seems lost. This segment ends with removing the paper covering the words on the board and helping the children check their writing; children rewrite as needed.

She extends the lesson by showing the students a word wall containing some sight words from the bread book. "Do you see any words that have the same letter and sound as those you just worked with?" she asks.

The children point out some matches. Ms. Lopes then says and writes the words and letters under discussion on the board for all to see. She says, "There are some words that have a good letter/sound match and some that don't. We call the words with a good match 'easy decode' words. For example, in the word *pot*, we can see and say /p/ for the sound *p* makes and the /ot/ for the sound that the letters *ot* make. We can match each letter or chunk of letters to the sounds we say and hear. If we can't see *and* hear a good letter/sound match we call the words 'tricky.' The word *float* is a "tricky" word. We see the *fl* and hear and say /fl/; we see the letter *o* and hear and say /o/; and we can see the letter *t* and hear and say the /t/ sound. But we can't match all the letters in *float* to the sounds we hear and say because we see the letter *a* and don't hear the /a/ sound in *float*, do we? So that makes it a 'tricky' word."

Ms. Lopes then asks them to find some "easy decode" words in the book.

The children work and talk with one another about words. Ms. Lopes then consolidates the lesson by reading the bread book once more, with the children taking the lead. She prompts, guides, and redirects as needed.

As Ms. Lopes teaches this lesson, she makes mental notes and jots down ideas about some children on a notepad. Her ongoing assessments are quick and valuable. She checks children's concept of word, word recognition, and competence with beginning letters and blends among other things. Later, she will take a few moments at her desk to write more notes about each child's progress and put the notes into the children's files.

N ow is truly the time for literacy for all. Becoming a global community and serving the rapidly changing student population necessitate changes in teaching practices and teachers' thinking. Students are diverse people with different and deeply rich cultures and languages. Because beginnings are so important, teachers of young children must provide the opportunities, explicit teaching, materials, and classroom communities in which children learn to read and write. In the act of gaining meaning from written language, children engage in a complex act of human cognition.

In the making of a reader, cognition transacts with affective pr_
(interest, persistence, curiosity, and courage) and results in the so_
ing alive with meaning. It is the teacher's responsibility to assi_

The goal of early-grade instruction is to nurture children emo_
and to ensure their exposure to print, concepts about print, and the joy u_
writing (NAEYC, 1998). Teachers need to support children's literacy skills a_
belief in themselves as learners. Effective teachers carefully craft their teaching so u_
children experience success. To be an effective teacher, you need to understand literacy development and instruction and assessment techniques. The more you study
development, how children learn, and fundamentals about becoming a learner, the
more you can improve your instruction. The purpose of this chapter is to further connect what you know about children's literature with effective instruction and information about organizing and managing the literacy program.

Creating a Learning Community

Young children come to school believing that they will learn to read and write. With
eyes wide and minds open, children enter school trusting in the teacher's expertise.
Some will be more anxious than others. In organizing and managing your classroom
as a learning community, you manifest your respect for children. The effective and caring teacher in the early grades can make a tremendous difference in their lives. Bill
Ayers (1993) notes that teaching requires sustained energy and dedication, which
becomes self-sustaining when it is supported by certain attributes:

To create a literacy-rich classroom, it's important to include an array of books that appeal to all children's needs and interests.

- Strong principles
- A strong sense of responsibility for student learning and motivation
- A desire to search for personal strengths
- An enjoyment of interactions with students and an abiding compassion for them

How is a learning community created? Reading instruction is no more effective
than the classroom organization in which it occurs and how it is managed. A healthy
classroom culture is steeped in mutual respect
and responsibility. This kind of classroom
uses an approach to children that engages
them productively and happily and makes
true instruction possible. Without a respectful, well-managed classroom, school becomes
a place in which children and teachers fail to
thrive. It is important, however, to draw distinctions between discipline and controlling
children and managing and building a learning place. At the most fundamental level, the
teacher's understanding of learning itself and
knowledge of children's development generate and sustain the organization and management of literacy-rich classrooms and effective
reading instruction.

Establish Structure

Before children come to school, you need to have in mind ways in which you will help them learn to manage their own behaviors. Generate a few simple rules or guidelines for your classroom, but be aware that for some children, it might be the first time they have experienced such structure. Teach the children what is and is not appropriate behavior at a given time in the classroom. Eventually, they will learn to monitor their own behavior. This places appropriate responsibility on the child while you provide feedback, guidance, and support.

Talk with the children about what will happen during the day. You might want to write this out on a chart and post it for the class to see. Repeating the day's routine again and again, providing special attention as needed and drawing the children into play activities will help calm anxiety, particularly for younger primary students. By second grade, students will be used to school routines. You might want to include children in your planning as a way of encouraging them to take responsibility for their own time.

Walking children through even the simplest of routines, such as moving around the room, going to the bathroom, lining up for lunch, and entering and exiting the classroom provides them with reassurance. Young children need repeated discussion about what will happen next until everyday acts happen smoothly and children feel confident.

Providing special learning centers, such as reading areas or writing centers, is important in teaching small groups. But centers can be a problem if children are not taught to use them well. Two ways of teaching children proper behavior in the centers are as follows:

- Role-play good center behavior and unacceptable center behavior. Provide plenty of practice and be open to repeating these roles as needed.
- Have children help in formulating rules for center behavior. Change, review, and improve center rules as needed.

Understand Misbehavior

Classroom structure is necessary to establish routines and teach children self-discipline, but you will still experience behavioral problems. Just remember that authoritarian control does not work. Misbehavior is frequently rooted in children's anxiety or frustration about the work they have to do. They might feel inadequate and not know how to handle it. In some cases, children might be bored with the work. If the work is not meaningful, efforts to teach it are bound to fail. If misbehavior occurs, step back and get to a level of instruction that guarantees success. Talk about taking on challenges, and make it clear that the children can come to you when they feel the need. Some children are simply hard to reach or have extensive personal problems. Find help in the system for these children. Work with parents, call on your grade-level team for help, and collaborate with your colleagues. Be innovative in finding solutions that will work for *your* classroom. For example, primary teacher, Lisa Campbell teaches in an inner-city school where her children come from a variety of backgrounds. Lisa has established a "time-out" area in her classroom where children can put themselves until they are ready to participate properly in the classroom. The time-out area contains selected books. Lisa watches the time-out place and works individually with the children who select it. She came up with a creative way to help children learn to manage their own behavior.

Provide Motivation

Effective teachers understand the primacy of intrinsic motivation (Oldfather & McLaughlin, 1993; Guthrie & Wigfield, 2002). Although extrinsic motivation (tangible rewards such as stickers and treats) can help at times, they should be used sparingly. Prepare for a honeymoon period at the beginning of each new year, and use external rewards as needed, but keep in sight the goal of eliminating them. Much more can be accomplished with children if their motivation for learning comes from within themselves. Your teaching skills, personal responses, and deep respect are most important in building children's internal satisfaction. Children recognize genuine responses and respond well to them. Provide encouragement, and integrate some fun. Children also appreciate a sense of humor and find it liberating. *"A second grader writes a note to his teacher. 'Why is a tree worse than a dog?' The teacher writes back, 'Because it has more bark!'"* (Wharton-McDonald, 2001, p. 129).

Still, regardless of your teaching skills, children will have problems. A strategy that helps deal with conflicts is to establish an "I have a problem" writing place where children can write and draw about their problems. Set up a small table and chair in a part of the room that offers some privacy, and put up a sign marked "Private." Provide writing materials and a "problems basket" where students can submit their writings and drawings to you. Assure the children that you will read all the messages in the basket and help them solve their problems. After you read the messages, you can help each child calmly engage in discussing his or her problem. Figure 9.1 shows an example of the kind of message that might be written in an "I have a problem" note.

The literacy-rich classroom itself is a critical component of literacy success. The research of Hickman (1979), Morrow and Weinstein (1982), and Neuman and Rosko (1991) has shown that an abundance of high-quality books, classroom libraries, self-selection and ownership, the physical arrangements of the room, and children's construction of personal meanings contribute to a love of books. These things also support appreciation and preferences about genre, the habit of choosing to read more often, higher reading achievement, and intrinsic motivation.

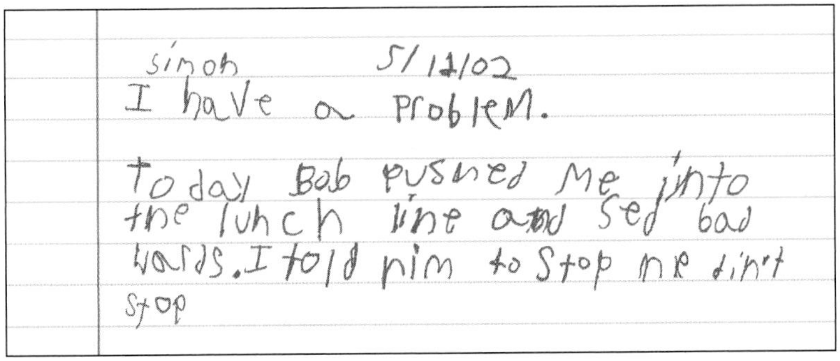
simon 5/14/02
I have a Problem.
today Bob pushed me into
the lunch line and sed bad
words. I told him to stop he din't
stop

FIGURE 9.1

I Have a Problem Note.

THE WORLD OF READING

Quality Questioning

Good questioning on the part of a teacher promotes critical thinking in children and provides high-quality oral language teaching and practice. Open-ended questions require children to infer, reason, use language to express thought, and think deeply. Open-ended questions call forth more thinking and expressive oral language. Open-ended questions might include: Why do you think that? Why did the author of our story write about _____? What do you think will happen? What would you do? Can you tell me more about that? What is your prediction? Show how you can confirm that. Show us why you make that prediction. How do you think this problem can be resolved? Consider the following examples of open-ended questions and the child's answers:

Teacher	*Child*
What did the princess do to help?	She went off on her own to take care of the dragon.
Why did she do that?	She just did. Cause the prince wouldn't.
How could she do that?	She was brave, and she wasn't afraid.
How did the princess and prince dress?	Well, the prince was in nice prince clothes, but all the princess had was a dirty paper bag.
Why?	Because of the dragon. He burned up everything even her clothes.

Teacher	*Child*
What did the prince do?	He just stayed in the cave and said her clothes were a mess. And her hair too. That wasn't very nice.

Notice the vocabulary and textlike phrasing use: *brave, nice, prince, clothes.* Notice the length of the sentences and the clarity of thought, and consider the critical analysis that occurs in the child's last sentence. "That wasn't very nice." This child's responses demonstrate the use of inference.

Now consider this same discussion but with the teacher employing constrained, or closed, questions:

Teacher	*Child*
What happened to the princess?	She ran away
The prince was no_____?	Help
Who was the prince afraid of?	The dragon
What did the princess do to the dragon?	Made him tired

Children can respond "correctly" to constrained/closed questions, yet totally miss the real meaning in the book. With practice, teachers learn open questioning. Some examples of open questions should be kept by your side as you teach. It is important to preread and know the children's literature you will use.

Developing Knowledge and Skills

As a primary teacher, you might ask, "What is the most important learning in the first years of school?" The answer is twofold. First, children need to learn the basic skills of reading, writing, and spelling in the early grades. Second, the teacher must understand the developmental changes new readers experience. K–2 instruction needs to focus

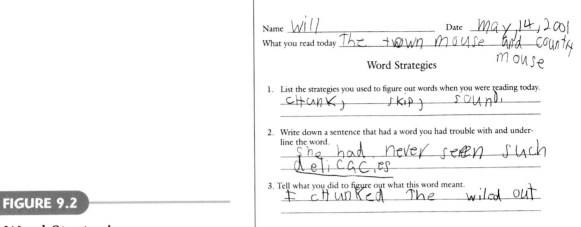

Name Will   Date May 14, 2001
What you read today The town mouse and county
                                                    mouse
                    Word Strategies

1. List the strategies you used to figure out words when you were reading today.
   chunk,   skip,   sound,

2. Write down a sentence that had a word you had trouble with and underline the word.
   She had never seen such
   delicacies

3. Tell what you did to figure out what this word meant.
   I chunked the wiled out

FIGURE 9.2

Word Strategies.

Writing &
Reading

on helping children to develop oral language, word recognition, fluency, and com-prehension. By third grade, most children should achieve the ability of silent read-ing (with good comprehension) of texts at their independent/easy level. Typically, children subvocalize, moving their lips slightly and speaking words very softly, before moving into true silent reading, which is a critical process in their devel-opment, allowing them to become more fluent readers and better able to learn from texts.

As they achieve silent reading, children become better readers by reading more challenging books, becoming more aware of their own understanding and strategies, learning more from books, and taking more action based on their learning, research-ing, and writing in inquiry studies. Helping children to understand what they know about good strategies provides them with metacognition, which supports the skill of self-monitored reading (see Figures 9.2 and 9.3). Developing these skills extends to all areas of their education as well as their personal life. These skills open up the world to children.

Why Does Reading Aloud Help?

What is the most important thing *you* can do to help young children learn to read? Read to them (Adams, 1990). Through an analysis of the oral and written language of well-read-to young children, Victoria Purcell-Gates (1991) found that those children under-stood the vocabulary and structures of written language even before they learned to read. Thus, children who have had extensive read-aloud experiences before starting school have an important advantage.

In another study with low-income children who had not been well read to before starting school but then received extensive reading in kindergarten and first grade from their teachers, Purcell-Gates, McIntyre, and Freppon (1995) found that by the end of first grade, these children's knowledge of written language was comparable to that of upper-middle-class, well-read-to children. It is reasonable to infer that class-room read-alouds compensated for the children's limited reading experiences prior to

> A good reader needs to now how to read. They need to pratis to be a grat reader. They need to skip it if they don't no it. They neen to make a gassand go bake and see if ther gas is rite. You shud read with a parint to see if you are nite with a wrde.
>
> I am Kathleen and I am a prity good reader

FIGURE 9.3A

I am a good reader—Kathleen.

> A good reader sawhds out the welds. and per tends it is gess the coverd word. a good reader never geves up. a good reader read day and nite.

FIGURE 9.3B

I am a good reader—Katie.

school. Reading to young children is one of the most important things teachers can do. You make the difference.

Phonics Knowledge and Skills

Phonics & Phonemic Awareness

As you know, phonics knowledge is necessary, but not solely sufficient, for learning to read. Effective reading instruction and assessment are based on well-established developmental stages of word recognition, writing, spelling, and vocabulary (Ganske, 2000). Phonics, however, plays an important role in balanced literacy instruction.

PHONICS IN CONTEXT.   As much as a total of thirty minutes a day in the early grades may be spent on various kinds of phonics instruction. As was noted in earlier chapters, instruction within the context of reading or writing provides effective phonics learning opportunities. Children's writing and use of invented spelling is extremely important to phonics learning. A helpful view of phonics in context comes from Dahl, Scharer, Lawson, and Gorgan: "Phonics in context means: in the context of children's needs, in the context of children's developing language knowledge, (and) in the context of classroom reading and writing activities" (2001, p. ix). The Teach It! box demonstrates phonics in context.

TEACH IT!

★ ★ ★ ★

Phonics in the Context of Children's Needs

Daniel Woo is teaching a group of eighteen children in a transitional first grade. They have completed kindergarten, but are not yet ready for first grade. Most of the children struggled in kindergarten, and some are English language learners. Mr. Woo's school and its teachers recognize the need for an additional year of expert teaching before first grade to prevent later failure.

In the following lesson, Mr. Woo engages the children in explicit word study that is highly interactive and appealing to them. He has arranged for half of his class to go to music in the morning and half in the afternoon. In this way, Mr. Woo can provide more focused attention to specific children with similar needs in a smaller group. His needs-based lesson follows:

Mr. Woo asks the children to raise their left thumb if they are ready for word play. The children love word play and eagerly help one another find their left thumb.

He then asks the children to give him their "important" word, cautioning them that it must be a real word. This activity is similar to the key vocabulary teaching discussed in Chapter 5. Mr. Woo says, "Tell us your word and new letters you want to try."

Taking turns, the children say their word and letter(s) they want to substitute as the begin-

ning letter. A child volunteers the word Lex *(his dog's name) and the letters* D *and* B.

Mr. Woo writes the word Lex *on the board; then the children spell* Dex *and* Bex*. Mr. Woo then writes these words on the board.*

Next, he asks the children to work with the two words bat *and* big*, and he writes the words on the board. He and the class change the beginning letters to make new, real words, with the children leading the conversation.*

Mr. Woo guides the instructional conversation, but makes every effort to "lead from behind." He employs scaffolding actions—warmth and responsiveness, coming to shared understandings with children, staying in their zone of proximal development—as he teaches.

For consolidation, he guides the children's participation in word learning practice. He chants, "If I know pig, I know jig." The children read this refrain with him from chart paper. The teacher and the children continue: "If I know day, I know play. If I know . . . ."

As an application and extension of the lesson, Mr. Woo distributes word cards that have the letter/sound patterns just taught and has the children engage in exclusive word learning practice in partner groups and individually.

As part of his ongoing assessment, Mr. Woo takes notes on several children after he has observed and interacted with them as they sort through the word cards. He makes a note to do a formal phonemic awareness test with three children he is worried about.

Refer to your **Teach It!** booklet for further activities you can use to reinforce concepts discussed in this chapter.

TEACHING PHONICS.   *Synthetic* and *analytic* are two approaches to teaching children to read words by paying attention to the relations between their letters and their sounds. The two terms roughly mean part-to-whole and whole-to-part. When they use the synthetic approach, teachers teach children the sounds represented by individual letters, and children combine and substitute the letters to construct words. When they use the analytic approach, teachers have children examine whole words, identify the letter-to-sound combinations that make them up, and extend this knowledge to reading and writing new words.

Let's look first at the synthetic approach. To teach phonics synthetically, teachers typically introduce the letters and their most common sounds one at a time. They may teach both consonants and vowels fairly quickly, even covering the most common letter to sound combinations between September or October and January of the first grade year. As they learn to associate sounds with letters, children assemble letter combinations for beginning, medial (middle), and final sounds. They can begin building and reading words after just a few combinations are introduced. This is true because even a few letters can be combined to make different words. For instance, the letter-sounds *p, i, t, n, s,* and *a* yield dozens of words when arranged in different orders, so these letters are often the first to be introduced (Johnson and Watson, 1997). Children working with letters on plastic chips can make words like *pin, tip, pit, tap, sat, pat,* and dozens of other words by combining those six letters. Children can be taught to combine individual consonants into **blends** (like *sp, bl*), but must be taught consonant and vowel **digraphs** (like *th, ch, au, and ai*) as units.

Teaching phonics analytically is done by comparing words that share spelling patterns to identify the common patterns, and then using knowledge of those patterns to read and write new words. Imagine, for example, that from reading a whole text such as a dictated experience account, students learn to read *pat* and *fat*. The teacher points out that these words share the *rime* or phonogram pattern *–at,* and have different onsets *p* and *f.* The teacher then shows children the words *sat, cat,* and *mat* and leads the students to read and spell these, too, by adding the onsets *s,c,* and *m* to the rime *–at.* In Chapter 5, as you will recall, activities were demonstrated that teach phonics analytically. Two prominent ones were **word sorting** and **word walls**.

Even when phonics are taught analytically, children still need to know not only the rimes or phonogram patterns like *–at, -ike,* and *–igh,* but also the initial consonants or onsets like *h* and *s* that join with those rimes to make up words. At the same time it helps if they realize that *tap* can be turned into *tag* by changing the final consonant, and that *tap* can be turned into *tip* by changing the medial vowel. In other words, children should be taught the sounds of individual letters, too, and not just onsets or phonogram patterns. Teachers commonly use both the synthetic and analytic approach to phonics at the same time.

We recommend that the approach to teaching phonics in grades one through three be a balance of synthetic and analytic phonics that includes these principles:

- Children should learn all of the consonants and vowels and their most common corresponding sounds.

- Children should be taught to blend consonants to make combinations like *bl-, nt,* and *st-;* but consonant and vowel digraphs (such as *ch, sh, th;* and *ai, ea,* and *–igh*) should be taught as units.

- Children should also be taught to read and write common rimes or phonogram patterns *such –ant, -art, -ip*, and *–ut*, and they should be shown how to read words **by analogy**: that is, if they can read *part* and they know the common sound of initial *c*, they should be able to figure out how to read *cart*.

- Children should constantly read and write extended and meaningful text, so that they understand that reading and writing are communicative acts, that they depend on words, and that phonics is the work of reading and writing words by their parts.

Organizing for Instruction

Nearly all young children benefit from and enjoy learning literacy with their peers. Young children approximate literate behaviors and reading and writing behaviors for some time before the behaviors become part of their repertoire. But not all children enter school with the same abilities. Some children have been in preschool for three or four years, while others may be experiencing school for the first time (Riley, 1996). Some might have disabilities, some might read independently, others might have literacy skills typical of a three-year-old, and for some, English might be a second language. Therefore, instruction must have breadth and great flexibility. In the early years in particular, teachers need to know what to expect in children's development, recognize differences, and find strategies that work.

Grouping and Planning

Grouping children and planning for instruction are major strategies in teaching that are designed to address differences in children's abilities to learn. **Traditional grouping,** which identified students as *high, medium,* or *low* in ability, nearly guaranteed underachievement for many children and teachers. How could a teacher be effective and still have the same children in the same low-ability group for nine months? For years? This concept is based on an invalid deficit learning model, and it invites a "blame the kid" attitude (Pressley et al., 2001, p. 233).

Research shows that once a child has been assigned to the low reading group, it is highly unlikely that the child will ever be moved to a higher group (Hiebert, 1983; Good & Marshall, 1984). Children in low groups receive instruction with fewer opportunities to think and work with meaning (Allington, 1983; Allington & McGill-Franzen, 1989). Traditional ability grouping also can be damaging to children's self-esteem, and more language-diverse children are likely be placed in low ability groups (Eder, 1983). Two programs, however, offer grouping ideas that are designed to help avoid the pitfalls of traditional grouping. Each approach makes a distinction between the organizational structures and the kind of instruction that goes on in them. Grouping strategies and other organizations for literacy instruction (e.g., writing time, word time, reading group time) are not prescriptions for effective teaching. Rather, what teachers do with children in specific blocks of time is what really matters.

DYNAMIC GROUPING. Fountas and Pinnell (2001) developed the concept of dynamic grouping as a way of providing targeted guided reading opportunities. **Dynamic grouping** involves the creation of several kinds of reading/writing groups that work together and receive instruction over the course of a school day. For example, dynamic groups provide for non-ability-based interest groups, peer tutoring and cooperative learning pairs, cross-grade buddies, and needs-based small groups (flexible and ability-based). In needs-based groups, children are moved regularly so that no child is stuck in any one group. Chapter 10 provides further discussion on dynamic grouping and reading and writing instruction in guided reading.

FOUR BLOCKS.   Another alternative is **four blocks**, which describes four specialized reading periods that address some of teachers' most challenging issues. No matter what reading program is used, all teachers are faced with the challenges of managing to teach a class of twenty to thirty students in ways that meet their needs *and* avoid having some children labeled and taught as "low ability." Additionally, the question of how to manage grading young children looms large. Cunningham, Hall, and Sigmon (1999) and Cunningham, Hall, and Defree (1991) created a framework to address these questions and issues and to provide guidelines for organization, planning, teaching and grading. The four blocks provide varied ample opportunities for primary grade children to learn and teachers to teach reading and writing.

The framework of four reading periods occurs during the school day and includes (a) guided reading, (b) self-selected reading, (c) writing, and (d) working with words. Within each block, specific structured activities take place. A major goal of four blocks is to give children a balance of reading, writing, and word instruction. Four blocks planning provides what it takes for teachers to make each block as multileveled as possible. **Multileveled groups** include children with different needs and strengths (Cunningham et al., 1999). These four blocks contain key elements of instruction for all classrooms with dynamic or multileveled groups:

- *Guided Reading:* For thirty to forty minutes, the teacher helps children to learn children's literature and reading comprehension. The lesson focuses on developing prior knowledge, oral language, meaningful vocabulary, self-confidence, and motivation. Guided readings are periods in which the teacher works with small groups teaching reading concepts and skills. Within guided reading periods, children often engage in shared reading—with the teacher reading to the children, the children reading with the teacher in unison, or the children taking turns reading. They read a big book or sets of the same little books. Following instruction, children read with their partners (often two children who read at somewhat different levels but who are compatible enough to read together). Next, the group comes together again to discuss major points in the book. The children or the teacher and the children usually write something about their reading.

- *Self-Selected Reading.* The goal is to share different kinds of literature. The teacher leads read-alouds, encourages reading interests, provides instructional-level materials, and helps to build intrinsic motivation. Besides read-alouds, children read the books *they* select and then conference with teacher individually to talk about books. This block lasts about thirty minutes.

- *Working with Words.* For about thirty minutes, the teacher and the children engage in various word-related activities, such as reading familiar words on the word walls and reading the new words added weekly (about five). The teacher asks the children to review the wall words and talks with them about the importance of these words (sight words, high-frequency words, and words in units of study such as science and social studies or literature studies). Children write the words, say the words, look for patterns in words, and discuss and practice the words' spelling patterns. The teacher writes the words, showing how the letters and words are formed and pointing out word patterns (rhyming, blends, diagraphs, short/long vowel words, and so on, according to children's needs and strengths). The children practice making words and sorting words in a variety of ways.

- *Writing.* A minilesson, also occurring in a *writing workshop*, begins each writing period, which lasts forty-five to sixty minutes depending on how young children get along in an extended time period (see Chapter 8). Goals of this period focus on having every sentence making sense and using capital letters and other punctuation to end a sentence. In addition, the writing block focuses on spelling. Children write during the minilesson on their own and with partners. This is an easy block to teach on multiple levels. Children engage in writing books, stories, and information pieces; illustrate their writing; and have conferences with the teacher for individual instruction. The word wall helps children to find words they need and work on spelling. Writing time concludes with sharing writing in the author's chair. Be aware that different teachers use different formats and structures for writing workshops. What is important is that all writing workshops include the basic essentials, such as time to write, writing/spelling instruction, strong support, a warm and inviting work environment, and specific roles for teachers.

Cunningham, Hall, and Sigmon (1999) provide some basic guidelines to consider in using four blocks teaching:

- Long-term planning for four blocks teaching is organized around units of study (inquiry units) and the curriculum (literature, math, etc.). Short-term planning is laid out in weekly and daily descriptions.
- Oral language is not a specific part of the four blocks but rather is integrated into all four blocks.
- Four blocks teaching is not an add-on. Even in basal-based classrooms, the basal text can be used in the guided reading block with multileveled small groups.
- Four blocks teaching does not eliminate the need for interventions such as reading recovery.
- Use volunteers and paraprofessionals to help support four blocks teaching.
- Use four blocks in any order that works in your classroom.

Lesson Structures

Because children need many and varied learning opportunities, teachers use various types of lessons to accomplish the desired outcomes in their classrooms. In all lessons, the teacher uses a before, during, and after structure. There is an introduction to the lesson, a period in which the heart of the lesson is conducted, and a conclusion, usually followed by an extension and application of what has been taught. Each type of lesson has structural aspects that help teachers to meet their specific instructional needs. For example, some lessons are more comprehensive and include a strong focus on word study, while reading or writing is also taught. Such lessons include the four-point model introduced in Chapter 1 that includes demonstration and immersion, guided practice, attention to detail, and application and extension. Other types of lessons that have been discussed in the book include minilessons, teachable moments, and think-alouds. All include some, but not necessarily all, elements of the four-point model.

MINILESSONS. Minilessons require fewer materials and are planned and taught fairly quickly. A minilesson is often taught at the beginning and focuses on one or two teaching points, such as self-monitoring one's comprehension and metacognition, providing the anticipation and focus of the lesson. The following is an example of a writing minilesson conducted by teacher Dr. Jill Dillard:

> *Recess is over and the second graders are either reading or sitting at tables playing word games. Dr. Dillard asks the children to get ready for writing workshop.*
>
> *They gather around her and she talks with the children about yesterday's topic lesson,* "I'm an expert." *Several children generated new topics after that minilesson: Jarad selected a pet story; Sammie Ann selected a learning-to-swim story; and Kyle selected a story about his baseball team (see Figure 9.4).*
>
> *Dr. Dillard invites the children to talk to a neighbor about their writing topic. During this time, she circulates among the children prompting and encouraging.*

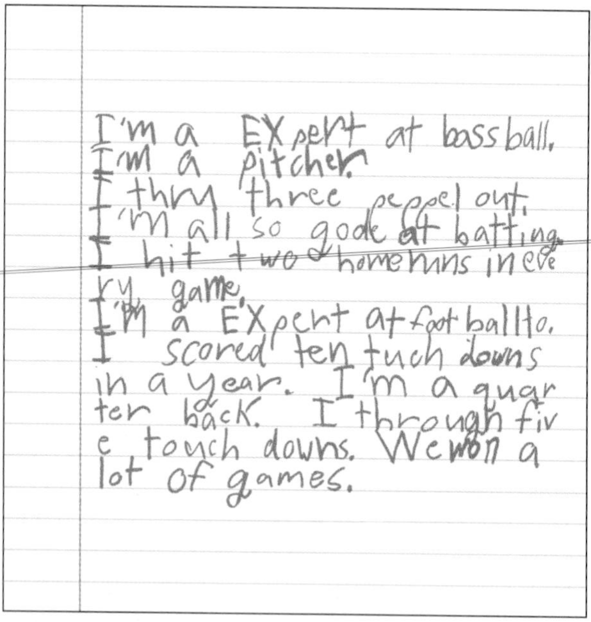
I'm a EXpert at bassball.
I'm a pitcher.
I thry three pepel out.
I'm all so gode at batting.
I hit two homeruns in eve
ry game.
I'm a EXpert at foot ballto.
I scored ten tuch downs
in a year. I'm a quar
ter back. I through fiv
e touch downs. We won a
lot of games.

FIGURE 9.4A

I am an expert—Kyle.

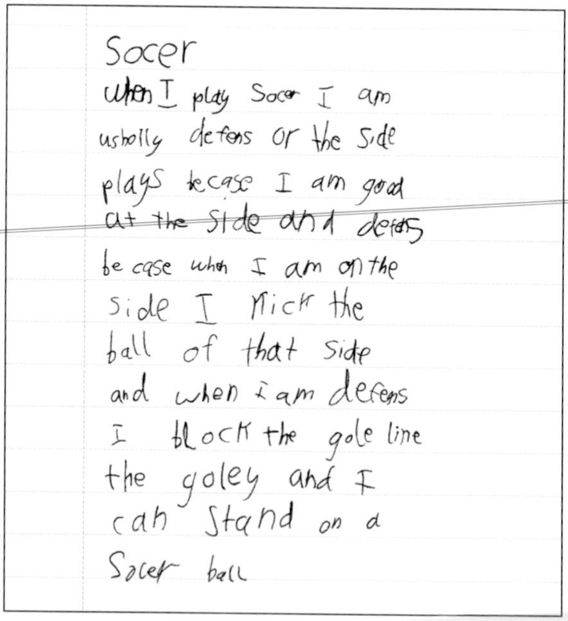
Socer
when I play Socer I am
usholly defens or the side
plays becase I am good
at the side and defens
be case when I am on the
side I kick the
ball of that side
and when i am defens
I block the gole line
the goley and I
can stand on a
Socer ball

FIGURE 9.4B

I am an expert—Allyson.

Dr. Dillard confirms the children's good ideas for stories and information writing and then asks the class whether they are ready to begin.

With the children's consensus, she calls Monday's small writing group to meet with her to talk about their tall tales before Annie, the high school volunteer, arrives.

TEACHABLE MOMENTS.   Teachable moments are lessons where the teacher seizes on an incident or observation of something to reinforce a concept. For busy teachers, teaching moments are golden opportunities for providing individual instruction in the context of a child's need. The next example demonstrates how much a teacher can do in a very short time:

First-grader Ransika is working in the writing center. As Mr. López walks by to check on him, he notices that Ransika is putting capital letters in the middle of some of his words. Mr. López intervenes immediately, asking Ransika whether he is using capital letters.

Ransika nods yes, and Mr. López reviews the morning talk about when to use capital letters.

With a sheepish grin, Ransika realizes his errors and begins to erase. Mr. López nods approval and turns to help another child.

With that brief check, Mr. López was able to reinforce the morning's lesson quickly and positively.

THINK-ALOUDS.   Think-alouds are lessons that demonstrate and model. They often show children how to think like a reader, writer, or speller. The following is an example of a reading comprehension think aloud.

Ms. Novacek rereads Sheila Rae, The Brave *(Henkes, 1987) to her first and second graders in a multiage classroom. This book is a favorite, as is* Lilly's Purple Plastic Purse, *also by Henkes (1996). The children and Ms. Novacek discuss the topic of bravery, which the children think is the book's theme. For discussion among the children, Ms. Novacek has paired a slightly less experienced reader with a somewhat more experienced reader.*

Ms. Novacek's goal is to help the children work toward understanding a deeper meaning, one that has to be inferred. Henkes's books provide opportunities to teach children to infer meaning, and the implied meaning in Sheila the Brave *is about sibling relationships.*

Ms. Novacek engages in the following think-aloud: "Class I've been thinking about this book and what Sheila Rae is like. I'm going to read a bit and keep thinking." *Ms. Novacek reads and says,* "I make a connection with Sheila Rae. When I was a child, I had a little brother, and I wasn't always nice to him. Sometimes I'd say mean things. What do you think about this?"

The children discuss the idea, and Ms. Novacek picks up on their levels of understanding and carefully guides them to make inferences. She repeatedly talks about her own thinking and inferences.

School-Day Script Questionnaire

Child's name: _____ Date: _____
Teacher's name: _____

Ask the whole class to complete the questionnaire (or administer as an individual interview with a child). Tell the students that when a new student transfers into your class, some of them will be asked to use their questionnaires to help that new student learn about the class. Ask the students the questions and write their responses.

1. Tell me what happens when you come to school each day. What happens first . . . second . . . and so on?
2. Where do I usually stand when I want everyone to pay attention?
3. What do I say or do to get everyone's attention?
4. How do you know when I am changing to a different subject or activity? (For example, how can you tell that I am finished reviewing yesterday's work and will begin explaining something new?)
5. What are the rules in this class? What are the reasons for each rule?
6. What happens if someone breaks a rule?
7. How do you know what your homework will be each day? Do I write the assignment on the board or simply tell you what to do?
8. How do you remember what books or papers to take home so that you can do your homework?
9. Tell me about your homework time at home. Where do you do your homework? What do you do first, second, and so on?
10. How do you remember to bring your homework back to school?

FIGURE 9.5

School Script Questionnaire.

Routines That Teach

As was mentioned earlier, well-balanced daily schedules help young children to adapt more quickly and happily to the school day. Teachers incorporate a variety of strategies for implementing classroom routines. One strategy is to use a school script questionnaire and a teacher observation form, like those shown in Figures 9.5 and 9.6 (see page 364), with children to help them adjust to classroom routines and take owner-

Script List

Child's name: _____   Date: _____

Teacher's name: _____

Please list the student's activities in the order that they occur on a typical school day. Write day-to-day variations, such as gym or library class, on the right side. This list will be used to assess and teach the child's knowledge of school activities and to select appropriate activity scripts for use in language assessment and intervention.

Typical School Day   Regular Variations

_____   _____
_____   _____
_____   _____
_____   _____
_____   _____
_____   _____
_____   _____
_____   _____
_____   _____
_____   _____
_____   _____
_____   _____
_____   _____
_____   _____
_____   _____
_____   _____

ship of them (Tattershaw & Prendeville, 1995). This strategy is particularly helpful with students who have difficulty adjusting or have learning difficulties. Students' completed questionnaires also can be used to teach classroom routines to new students who might enroll later in the year.

The following routines and lessons serve as examples of systematic routines that provide opportunities to work on important skills, such as word recognition and reading comprehension, in highly authentic situations.

Teacher Observations

Student's name: _____ Date: _____
Teacher's name: _____

Please use the following statements to guide your observations of the child on a typical school day. Write your comments after each statement.

1. The child seems to know the order of events in a typical class day.
    Yes   No   Comments: _____
    ❏   ❏   _____

2. The child looks in your direction when you are standing in your usual teaching spot.
    Yes   No   Comments: _____
    ❏   ❏   _____

3. The child responds appropriately and in a timely manner to your signals for attention.
    Yes   No   Comments: _____
    ❏   ❏   _____

4. The child can usually restate directions that you have given in his or her own words when asked to do so.
    Yes   No   Comments: _____
    ❏   ❏   _____

5. The child restates only the first part of directions.
    Yes   No   Comments: _____
    ❏   ❏   _____

6. The child restates only the last part of directions.
    Yes   No   Comments: _____
    ❏   ❏   _____

7. The child responds appropriately to your signals for transitions. (For example, the child puts away materials used for prior tasks, gets out materials for the new activity, or looks at you with apparent readiness for the new information or activity.)
    Yes   No   Comments: _____
    ❏   ❏   _____

FIGURE 9.6

Teacher Observation Form.

8. The child seems to have diffculity leaving a project or task when you signal a transition.

    Yes   No   Comments: _____
    ❏   ❏   _____

9. The child seems to look at and follow peers' actions rather than respond independently to your signal for transitions.

    Yes   No   Comments: _____
    ❏   ❏   _____

10. The child's comments are appropriate for the topic under discussion.

    Yes   No   Comments: _____
    ❏   ❏   _____

11. The child seems able to understand and follow the rules and procedures of a game or classroom activity.

    Yes   No   Comments: _____
    ❏   ❏   _____

12. The child follows the class rules for behavior without reminders.

    Yes   No   Comments: _____
    ❏   ❏   _____

FIGURE 9.6 ─────────────────────────

Continued

Source: From *Using Familiar Routines in Language Assessment and Intervention* by S. Tattershaw and J. Prendeville. Copyright © 1995. Reprinted by permission of The Psychological Corporation.

Daily Routines in K–2 Classrooms

TEACH IT!
30

KINDERGARTEN ROUTINES.   A typical day in a kindergarten class would include many, if not all, of the following elements (Vukelich, Christie, & Enz, 2002, pages 45, 54–57):

- *Morning Greeting.* Engage in one-on-one conversations with the children, and use this time to observe how children talk with each other and which centers they self-select (e.g., reading center, writing center). This allows you to check for interest and avoidance.

- *Taking Attendance.* Use a creative technique to take attendance, such as singing a song that includes the children's names. Children sing along and learn one another's names. Use large name tags that children read and hang up on the attendance chart during the singing.

- *Shared Reading.* Read aloud to the children predictable books with repeated phrases. As the children become familiar with the words and phrases, have them join in. Read-alouds should occur several times in the course of a day. Figure 9.7 provides a typical read aloud lesson plan. This structure provides scaffolding.

- *Shared Writing*. Model aspects of writing, such as letter formation, thinking about what to say, or using conventions such as periods and capital letters. Then have the children take turns writing letters and words. This provides high scaffolding.

- *Writing Center*. Encourage use of the writing center where children can self-select and write on their own about topics of special interest to them (see Figure 9.8).

- *Group Time*. Use group time to emphasize purposeful oral language. Demonstrate purposeful speaking, good listening, taking turns, and idea sharing. Use group time to discuss the daily schedule and center assignments. After center assignments have been made, a group of about six children are assigned to sharing time.

- *Sharing Time*. In smaller groups, children can be more at ease and engaged than they are when in larger groups. You also have opportunities to ask natural questions, such as "What happened next, Mark?" or "Does anyone have a question for Michael?" (Moffett & Wagner, 1983).

Objectives: Engage children (through a shared reading).

Goals: Provide rich oral and written language experiences. Demonstrate the joy of reading. Increase intrinsic motivation. (Guthrie & Wigfield, 2000)

Materials: Big book copy of <u>The Wheels on The Bus</u> (Kovalski, 1987), drawing paper, and crayons.

Demonstrate what is going to happen.

Immerse children in the literacy event by discussing illustrations.

Provide Attention to Detail, and Guided Practice, by reading the book, rereading children's favorite parts, building knowledge by singing and rereading.

Apply and Extend by having children draw their favorite part of the story.

Share several new little <u>Wheels on the Bus</u> books, invite children to read them as much as they wish.

Ongoing assessments: Write and file notes on level of participation, enjoyment, skills, and interest on the three to five children you select as focal for the week.

FIGURE 9.7

Reading Aloud Lesson Plan.

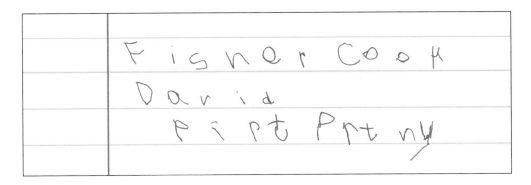

Translation:
Fisher	Cook
David	
Pirate	Party

The theme of Fisher David Cook's birthday party is Pirates!

(middle name is David)

FIGURE 9.8

Topics of Interest.

Beginnings are important, and good teachers teach children many things on the first day of school. The Teach It! box provides a model of how one teacher organizes her first day of kindergarten.

The use of wall charts for things such as attendance and lunch schedules help students learn to establish routines. How does this carry over to benefit children's learning?

FIRST-GRADE ROUTINES.   Routines that incorporated authentic reading and writing in kindergarten also work well with first and second graders. For example, taking attendance, lunch count, and accounting for jobs for the day require children to read and think. Wall charts that are used as tools in everyday teaching also serve children well. In early first grade, children need the support of illustrations and pictures to comprehend the reading they need to do. Later, these supports are removed as children become better able to read without them.

First Day of Kindergarten

The following schedule was contributed by Linda Headings, M.Ed., a highly effective kindergarten and first-grade teacher.

HALF-DAY KINDERGARTEN SCHEDULE

Before the first day of school with all the children together, the children come to school in groups of about seven for one or two days until all have been transitioned into classroom life. Teacher Linda Headings welcomes the children and teaches them about centers and the number of children allowed in a center, how to work with the materials, and so on. She introduces a teacher-made attendance chart with all the children's names. Pictures of children taken on the transition days are mounted on the "Our Class" poster. Ms. Headings has used the first partial days to gather some personal information about each child from parents or from children's conversations in class.

Goals: Begin (a) relationship building with children, (b) establishing daily routines, and (c) gathering data by observing children's interactions with environmental and class-created print and with read-alouds.

FIRST DAY OF KINDERGARTEN WITH ALL THE CHILDREN

Greeting: Greet children by name at eye level with a smile as they come in.

Refer to your **Teach It!** booklet for further activities you can use to reinforce concepts discussed in this chapter.

Remind children to put their belongings away in their cubby, to hang up their name on attendance chart, and to sit on the group rug (use warmth, caring, and support).

Demonstrate and Immerse

Review the Daily Schedule: Tell children what is going to happen; be descriptive and lively while discussing group time, story time, taking a school tour, recess, center time, and time to go home. *[Use a schedule chart at children's eye level, and point to the words as you talk.]* After reviewing the schedule, put it at the children's eye level for review. *[Going over the schedule often comforts an anxious child. The chart demonstrates that print carries meaning and that it carries important information.]*

Attention to Details

Attendance and Reading: Hold up each child's name written on a large sentence strip. Have the child wave when his or her name is read so that the children can start to put the name with the face. As their name is called, children wave, and you make a personal connection— for example "Hi, Billy Jack. I hear you like animals."

Apply and Extend

- Do sorting activities with children's names. Use a magnetic board on an easel. Sort name strips by *boys* and *girls*. Note beginning letters in names.

- Read *Dogger* by Shirley Hughes (1977). Introduce the main character Alfie, and share that we will be reading other stories about Alfie the rest of the week. *[first author study]*

- In small groups, invite sharing from the children of their favorite "lovey" brought from home. *[warmth and caring]*

School tour: Review the locations of restrooms and the principal's office; talk about walking in line and using appropriate voices. Take children out to play on the playground for about fifteen minutes. If someone is having separation problems, delay playing outside. Work in a little recess when all the children are calm.

Center time: After returning to the classroom, review the names of the centers and their rules: (1) Only five children can be in a center at one time, and (2) children put their names on a waiting list so that everyone can have a turn. Demonstrate using waiting lists, role-play. *[Shows children the function and power of print.]* Review options if the waiting list is long. Role-play frequently. Dismiss the children from the group rug to the centers.

Centers and materials:

- Writing Center: Pencils, markers, note cards, name word cards, a variety of paper, etc.

- Reading Center: Big books, manipulative charts, books on tape, bookshelf, magnetic letters, flannel board story

- Dramatic play center: Shoe store (correlation with buying new shoes for school), shoes, rulers, boxes, calculators, chairs, storage shelf, paper and pencil, receipts, a mirror (for looking at shoes).

- Math sorting activity with shoes children are wearing (color or number of shoes $\times$ number of people or shoe type: buckles, slip-ons, ties, sandals, gym shoes)

- Math center: Blocks, Unifix cubes™, puzzles, sorting items, counting games

- Science center: Magnets, materials to experiment with, magnets, a scale, paper and pencils

As children use centers, monitor and observe who works well together, who engages, who likes to work by themselves, group dynamics, problem solving, who uses the waiting lists, and so on. Intervene as needed.

Transitions:

- Signify a transition by a bell or singing softly; ring the bell twice to signify clean-up.

End of day: In the whole-group meeting area, review the day, and explain something interesting that will be happening tomorrow. Close with the song *The More We Get Together* (Raffi, 1996), which has been written on a chart in advance. Point to the words as you sing. *[Demonstrates meaning and enjoyment of print.]*

Dismiss:

- Tell children to gather their gear and line up at the door when you call their names.

- Make a quick trip to the teachers' lounge, coffee break, and prepare for the afternoon group.

Teacher Linda Headings conducts a journal writing exercise with her students.

Each day, at some point during the day, all children engage in the following: Guided reading, being read to, self-selected reading, peer or buddy reading, and writing.

Read-alouds might begin to introduce some reading from information books such as topics on science or social studies. Far too often, the primary grade curriculum is strongly based on storybooks (fiction). Providing some reading of information books early helps to prepare children for comprehension studies in later grades (Duke, 2000).

Establish learning centers where children can focus on particular reading and writing skills. Centers might include a writing area, an inquiry study area, a listening area with audiotaped books, a computer area with options for self-selecting from two or three activities posted on the computers, a word work center, and perhaps an interest center. These centers, along with the teacher's guidance, provide vital reading experiences. Children should be rotated through the learning centers, and these assignments should be charted for the children to see. They can check the chart for center assignments and go to work in them while you teach blocks of reading and writing.

The Teach It! box provides a model of how one teacher organizes her first day of first grade.

SECOND-GRADE ROUTINES.   On the first day of second grade, you and the children might follow a schedule that is highly similar to the one used in first grade but with more advanced materials and activities. Just as in first grade, each day should include guided reading, being read to, self-selected reading, peer or buddy reading, writing, and word study/spelling. Table 9.1 models part of a weekly schedule for second

TABLE 9.1

Daily Schedule

OCTOBER	WEEK 1	GUIDED READING	BUDDY READING	INQUIRY CENTER
	Monday			
Daily read-alouds		Ben, Shealee, Sam, Tessa, Mark, Jenny	Books of choice (oral language practice)	Book research: work with frog facts (write findings)
	Tuesday			
Reading and writing		Joe, Michael, Dan, Angela	Listening center and read together	Report writing: science
Literature study		Janet, Nicki, Don		
		Helen, Jane, Chris, Mickey	Oral language practice	Author study (write and share)

Source: Adapted from Fountas and Pinnell (1996).

TEACH IT!

★ ★ ★ ★

First Day of First Grade

Goals: Begin relationship building with children. Begin establishing daily routines. Begin gathering data by observing children's interaction with environmental and class-created print and with read-alouds.

Greeting: Greet children at the door at eye level; invite them to put their personal items on any table and come to sit on the gathering rug. Take attendance and lunch count. Children stand and point to their names on attendance chart and point to wording on lunch chart.

Opening: Introduce myself by sharing objects that tell the children about myself. Pull individual items out of a pillowcase, and share what they mean to me. Draw a web or graphic organizer of the pillowcase contents. *[This provides a visual introduction to webbing, organizing ideas, and storytelling and building relationships.]*
Tell the children that one of my favorite things to do on Saturday mornings is to go out to garage sales to find books for our classroom and to hunt for other treasures we can use at bargain prices.

Welcome: Welcome children as a group by doing some sorting activities and writing them down on large pieces of white construction paper in front of the children *[Introduction to making a class big book.]* Use one page for each pair of children. *[Collaboration begins.]*
Sorting examples that create the first class-made book are:

- Number of children in classroom enrolled along with number of boys and girls
  - Number of children who walk, who ride the bus, who are dropped off
    - Types and number of pets children own
  - Favorite foods
  - Favorite holiday

After selection of the sorting topics, the pairs of children dictate pages. After each page is written, read it together, pointing at each word. Observe who is attending and participating.

School tour of locations: bathrooms, lunchroom, office, nurse, music, gym, and art room.

Read aloud: *A Porcupine Named Fluffy* (Lester, 1986) *[The focus is on adjusting to a different place and making friends.]*

Work on book illustrations: Hand out the class book pages from earlier in the morning for each pair of children to illustrate. *[collaboration in action]* Talk about the size of illustrations and filling up the page so that the pictures can be seen from far away. Demonstrate by comparing the size of illustrations in a standard text to a big book's illustrations.

Classroom explorations: Following the book illustrations, allow children free exploration of the classroom. Items in the room for their explorations include puzzles, a variety of books, books on tape, Unifix cubes, magnets, pattern blocks, magnetic letters, checkers, art supplies, flannel board with story props, and some simple games.

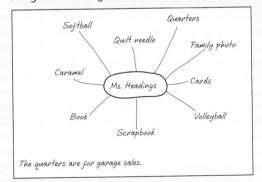

The quarters are for garage sales.

Graphic Organizer: Pillowcase

(continued on next page)

Continued

After children's exploration, clean up and line up for lunch by holding up the last name of each child. Observe and record impressions. Read as needed.

Lunch time.

After lunch read aloud *Tacky the Penguin* (Lester, 1993) *[Expands on the theme in* A Porcupine Named Fluffy.]

Journals: Introduce journal writing using the overhead projector. Illustrate a think aloud writing of an idea. Write a bit on the topic idea. Tell the children that they will write in their journals. Encourage inventive spelling: "Spell words the way they sound to you. Don't worry about spelling, this is just practice." Ask all children to add an illustration to their writing until you are familiar with their spelling proficiency. (Collect written artifacts to check for writing, sketching, and illustration.)

Before children begin journal writing, divide them into two groups. Group 1 works on journals, and group 2 engages in buddy reading in the gathering rug area. Use leveled books, kindergarten to late first grade, from the Wright Group or Rigby Books. Circulate among the two groups, observe, and talk with children about their work.

There are always lots of hesitations and questions when children start journals. Working with half the class helps keep order. Work in blocks of about twenty minutes and then have the children switch. Observe and record students who worked quickly but shabbily, who procrastinated, who struggled, who went to the bathroom, and who seemed to love the writing process. As children finish their journals, they must check in with me to read their writing aloud. Observe and teach voice/print matching. Keep journal writing and reading to a time limit to regulate and work on pacing.

Science: The sink and float experiment.

Students sit in circle on group rug with a large shallow tub of water. Ask the children what types of objects sink or float in water? *[Taps prior experiences, supports oral language.]* Pull out objects individually from a container.

Help the children hypothesize by predicting with thumbs up or down on what will happen when an object is placed in water. Assess. *[Watch for interactions. Who is in the lesson and who is out?]* Have small groups of children search the classroom to find one item they would like to test. Engage in the hypothesize/test cycle. Write group conclusions on chart paper. *[first inquiry study]*

Closing: Review the teacher-made attendance and lunch charts. Request that they hang up their names on attendance chart and make their lunch request on the lunch chart before coming to the rug area the next morning.

Homework: Instructions to the children: To share their interests, bring some personal items to school tomorrow in a labeled bag. Six children will share each day. Two children share in the morning, two after lunch, and two at the end of the school day. *[Introduction to sharing with the classroom community.]* Put the homework paper describing the project in the home/school correspondence folders.

Introduce correspondence folders: Discuss the folders with the children, and show them the basket where the folders are kept. The children are to bring their folders to school every day and place them in the basket first thing in the morning. Ask the children where they will put their folders at home. *[role-play]*

Dismiss: Children line up to go home by responding to a riddle: "I'm holding the folder of a boy whose name begins with the sound of /ch/." Observe and record their responses.

The ideas and procedures in the first day of first grade are easily modified for second or third graders. Revise this first-grade summary after reviewing the developmental levels at which you find your children. For example, older children can collaborate on making the class-made book by doing some or most of the writing and illustrating. Children might also write and illustrate their own little books.

Contributed by Linda Headings, M.Ed.

> Refer to your **Teach It!** booklet for further activities you can use to reinforce concepts discussed in this chapter.

grade that might be helpful. Creating such schedules helps to ensure that many varied learning opportunities are included daily.

Second-grade planning proceeds until all children are scheduled for a week of varied learning opportunities. The teacher's long-range plans need to be open to change and should include daily read-alouds, small group reading, children's self-selected reading, spelling and word work, and at least twice-weekly comprehensive writing workshops with daily writing activities. You might also want to incorporate a block of pleasure reading, perhaps every Monday, Wednesday, and Friday for twenty minutes right before the end of the day.

Providing Appropriate Materials

Before the children come through the door on the first day of school, teachers have prepared the classroom for learning. They have also thought about the materials they will need to assist with that learning.

CLASSROOM LIBRARIES.   Classroom libraries are essential in a literacy-rich classroom. Teachers and children use the book collection for lessons, pleasure reading, and inquiry work. Work with your school librarian to build your collection. In addition, join book clubs that offer good children's literature at reduced prices; leave no garage, yard sale, or library sale unexamined; find used bookstores; and contact the local public library to see if they have a program for obtaining children's books on a regular basis. Involve parents in helping to find ways to obtain books. A good source for identifying books nominated as children's choices is *The Reading Teacher*, which can be accessed at http://www.reading.org/choices/. When selecting books, provide a wide variety of reading materials, including informational materials such as brochures from stores, automobile sales offices, community information centers, and the local police and fire departments. Add children's own works as they write and publish their books.

Leveled Books.   When you teach, review the leveled books your school has to offer. **Leveled books** are rated by a child's reading development stage, not by age or grade. Basal readers and other texts are often leveled only by grade. Often grade level ratings are not sufficiently helpful. It is essential that texts be subjected to fine-grained leveling. Features that distinguish leveled books are level of syntax complexity (simple to more complex), number of words in sentences or on a page, accumulating vocabulary (number of high-frequency words and new words introduced), placement of words and sentences on a page, and level of support from illustrations. Fountas and Pinnell (1999) provide some criteria for book selection for reading recovery:

- Sentence complexity (length of sentence)
- Vocabulary (number of high-frequency words)
- Print features (length of book, illustrations, format of the book)
- Language features (similar to oral language, high-level written language)
- Content (children's special interest, universal themes are a good idea)

Reading recovery leveled books are rated from A to Z, with levels A–C for kindergarten, D–E and F–H for first grade, and F–H and I–K for grade 2. Many children will be able to read above these levels, but the system provides a place to begin in selecting books. Here are some examples of books at each of these levels (Fountas & Pinnell, 1996).

A–C: *Wake up Dad* (Randell, 1996c), *At the Zoo* (Peters, 1995), *The Animals Went to Bed* (Theodorou, 1996)

D–E: *Mrs. Wishy-Washy* (Cowley, 1990), *Baby Bear Goes Fishing* (Randell, 1996a)

F–H: *The Hungry Giant* (Cowley, 1998), *Cookie's Week* (Ward, 1997), *The Carrot Seed* (Krauss, 1989), *Ben's Tooth* (1996b), *Rosie at the Zoo* (Cowley, 1985)

I–K: *Happy Birthday Sam* (Hutchins, 1978), *Henny Penny* (Galdone, 1968), *Leo the Late Bloomer* (Krauss, 1987), *Tidy Titch* (Hutchins, 1994), *Danny and the Dinosaur* (Hoff, 1999), *Henry and Mudge* (Rylant, 1987), *Nate the Great and the Pillowcase* (Sharmat, 1972), *Keep the Lights Burning, Abbie* (Roop & Roop, 1985)

Assessing Book Levels.   Some children need guidance when self-selecting books. The teacher might offer an array of books and ask the children to look them over and select from this array. The "five-finger test" offers one simple method: The child holds up fingers and thumb, reads the book, and turns down one finger for each word missed on a page. If the child gets to the thumb, the book is probably too difficult. At times, however, children should read books they self-select regardless of level of difficulty. Children use such books to practice known words and to engage with a book they find interesting. Children should not continue to read a book they do not like. There are far too many wonderful books available for that to happen. Be aware of easy books that might hold high appeal for struggling readers and diverse language learners so that they can experience success.

Technology

TECHNOLOGY.   Technology is necessary material in your classroom as today's students are comfortable with it. A number of programs can assist in the learning of basic literacy skills. Because of the fast-breaking changes in the Internet and products online, the new and improved programs become available very quickly. But many products are not as good as their hype. Use caution when selecting technology programs for your classroom. Here are some helpful resources to get you started:

- Australian Storytelling Guide (NSW) Inc. (www.home.aone.net.au/stories/) Purposeful practice in storytelling and oral language is critical for K–2 children when they are learning to read (Roth, Speece, & Cooper, 2002). This storytelling site provides wonderful opportunities.

- Crayola.com (www.crayola.com) offers online stories, songs, and craft activities.

- Teacher Created Materials (www.teachercreated.com) offers a variety of word work activities and games.

Reaching All Children

Language & Diversity

There is little doubt that you will have English language learners and struggling readers during your teaching career. Teaching English language learners and struggling readers is one of your primary responsibilities in making sure all children can read.

English Language Learners

The listening comprehension of English Language Learners (ELL) of any age is ahead of their ability to speak the new language, let alone read and write it. Much of the focus in the early years needs to be on oral literacy and providing helpful teaching at every step. Helpful teaching includes the following:

- Warmth and acceptance of differences
- Reading the same book(s) in the ELL children's language and English
- Using parents and paraprofessionals, community volunteers, and anyone available in the school (all other support staff) to read and write with the children in their mother tongue
- Playing naming games of classroom objects in both languages
- Singing songs in two languages
- Making many positive and comforting experiences with cultural differences

Use snacks, dramatic play with culturally appropriate clothing, holiday and birthday celebrations, and units of study with home and family, friends, and visitors to demonstrate culturally interesting facts about the children's homelands. If you do not speak a child's particular language, call on parent volunteers, paraprofessionals, or a bilingual teacher in your school for assistance. Work with these people and watch, pick up as much of the language as possible, and study it if you can.

ENGLISH LANGUAGE LEARNERS IN KINDERGARTEN.   For learners who come to school with some English literacy, learning will move more rapidly than it will for those with little exposure to English. A few might be ready for phonemic awareness activities in English by late kindergarten but probably not before—and certainly not before they reach an intermediate level in spoken English. One strategy for identifying young children at the intermediate level is to read a predictable storybook in English to a small group of children. Intermediate English speakers should be able to respond to most comprehension questions fairly well.

Few English language learners will reach the intermediate level at a young age unless they speak English (as well as their mother tongue) at home. At the intermediate level, children are able to benefit from instruction in English syntax. Such instruction is done most effectively through modeling in ESL lessons. For teachers with children who are not yet at the intermediate level, oral language instruction is essential. However, the results of a study by McCafferty and Iddings (2001) indicate that children's naturally occurring play in learning centers sometimes yields more and higher-quality practice in oral English than any teacher assignments can. Provide meaningful and frequent oral practice.

Picture two Hispanic kindergarten children, one more advanced in English than the other, seated in the housekeeping center. Nicole (the more experienced English language learner) is reading a very well-known storybook in English to Jorge (as assigned by the teacher). Nicole knows the story by heart, and in spite of the fact that this lesson is appropriate for these children, they soon become less and less engaged in the reading until the book is tossed aside. Nicole stands up and begins to pretend that she is preparing food for Jorge. She speaks in English as she makes a sandwich, and Jorge responds. He immediately joins in the pretend play. The two children engage in an extended English conversation in which Jorge actually speaks more English than Nicole!

Productive play episodes such as this are exactly what Jorge needs to gain the oral proficiency necessary for moving into written language instruction. This is an example of what can happen when children have opportunities to use English in their pretend play and how being off task can sometimes be beneficial. Productive play is most likely to occur when the teacher has made sure the children have sufficient English vocabulary and some focused English as a second language (ESL) instruction. This instruction is oral and is often structured via the language experience approach (LEA) strategy described in Chapter 5 (Crawford, Allen, & Hall, 1995). A simple discussion about favorite foods or places to go creates a fine opportunity for vocabulary instruction in English. Children respond well to vocabulary words of personal significance to them, and book reading is a perfect place to teach vocabulary. Provide personal dictionaries (for home and school) in which children's favorite words may be kept. When your English language learners are ready for reading instruction, use **voice/print matching** with small groups and plenty of instructional conversations.

Voice/print matching is the action of a child matching his or her voice (speaking the word) to each written word. Pointing to the words while saying them, or tracking, helps children focus on each word individually. When children do this correctly, they demonstrate an understanding of a critical concept in early reading—words in written language. They recognize that words consist of letters, spaces between words represent something, and that letter patterns are put together to make separate words that convey meaning.

For children with little or no significant exposure to English before kindergarten, ESL instruction will be necessary. Delay phonemic awareness activities in English to focus solely on oral literacy. Children are ready for phonemic awareness activities in their mother tongue but not yet in English. (See Chapter 12 for a discussion on sheltered English.) Here is an example of an ESL lesson for intermediate English language learners who speak Spanish.

Read a storybook in English that the children already know in their mother tongue (someone else might read the Spanish version). For example, *The Very Hungry Caterpillar* (Carle, 1987) is also available in a Spanish-language version entitled *La Oruga Muy Hambrienta* (Carle, 1994).

Engage the children in an enjoyable conversation, and then reread the book using children's suggestions for their favorite parts and using rich, scaffolded discussion. With an English big book version or text on large chart paper, use voice/print matching and more discussion. Demonstrate how to identify a word, and help children identify words. To teach the concept of *word,* put your fingers and then their fingers at the beginning and end of a word. Make both book editions available for children's use in other explicit lessons and for self-selected use in pleasure reading and partner reading. The shared reading techniques described throughout this book help to extend this lesson. Use shared writing as well.

Using children's "favorites" in a LEA activity is a meaningful way to provide guided reading instruction to young children at the emergent or beginning phase of reading.

ENGLISH LANGUAGE LEARNERS IN FIRST AND SECOND GRADES.

Remember that some English language learners might enter your first-grade classroom having had no preschool or kindergarten experiences. When they begin first grade as their first formal school experience, these children are many months away from being ready for phonemic awareness activities in English. Their greatest need is for a strong emphasis on ESL lessons. As children who must learn to read only in English begin the first grade, they will probably have developed English only at the level of basic interpersonal communication skills, a nonconversational level (Cummins, 1986, 1989). Pronunciation difficulties often complicate letter/sound relationship or phonics learning.

Many English language learners must learn to read first in English because there are too few speakers of their language to offer a program of bilingual education or because state law or district policy does not permit such a program. Unfortunately,

TEACH IT!
35

Making a book available in your ESL students' mother tongue as well in English can help them make the connection between the languages.

TEACH IT!
7, 10

they have probably not mastered English at an oral level sufficient to support academic instruction in English. The primary focus of your instruction therefore needs to be on word recognition and comprehension.

Phonics will be the English language learners' weakest modality for learning to read, even after they have learned to communicate orally in English. A phonetic approach is based on knowledge of the sound system, and ELL students probably speak English with a heavy accent, a very strong indicator that they have not yet mastered the sound system of English. Does this mean that you cannot teach these children to read until they master the purely phonetic approach? Not at all. Lessons discussed throughout this book provide varied and sound instruction.

From the children's dictated texts (in the mother tongue for preintermediate children, in the mother tongue and English as children move into the intermediate stage), you and the children can select sight words and high-frequency words for vocabulary practice. Focus on meaning, and support children's additions to the list; make word walls, word sorting cards, word hunts and games. Involve the children as much as possible. When they help to create word walls and cards for sorting, a great deal of purposeful and authentic discussion about words occurs.

The second dimension, reading comprehension, depends to a large degree on background knowledge and vocabulary. English language learners have background knowledge, but it might not correspond to what is assumed by the authors of the reading instructional materials used in most classrooms in the United States. Another significant factor is their limited vocabulary. English language learners might be able to understand and use the word *big* but not the words *huge, gigantic, enormous*, and so on. Authors of children's literature give precision to their writing by using such wonderfully descriptive words that might be unfamiliar to most beginning English speakers.

Scaffolding is especially necessary for these children. Keep a list of scaffolding tips and strategies close at hand for reference. The habit of providing scaffolding is not learned overnight; however, once learned well, it is an invaluable habit of mind and action that you will use every time you teach.

Children who do not show steady literacy growth in kindergarten, first grade, and second grade need careful consideration. Additional support or intervention steps taken in kindergarten may prevent greater struggles. Vukelich, Christie, and Enz (2002) note that congenital language disorders are uncommon, but they do occur. Usually, such a disorder is shown in disfluent oral language (stuttering, speaking very rapidly, speech that is incomprehensible and unclearly articulated). Use your own expertise and that of school experts to distinguish between a child who is coming along but is behind and a child who has language problems.

Often, children making the transition from their mother tongue to English have periods of stuttering or other issues such as pronunciation and articulation. However, these periods do not necessarily signal a language disorder. In time, most of these children will improve. It is important to keep in mind that English language learners are no different than any other populations of children; and just as with English speakers, a few may have problems with literacy learning (even in their mother tongue).

However, the vast majority simply speak a language other than English and have many challenges to overcome.

Struggling Readers

**Struggling
Reader**

Young children who do not show steady reading, writing, and spelling growth need careful evaluation and immediate intervention. The causes of delayed development may include a lack of early literacy experience or true lags in neurophysiological, psychological, and cognitive development.

Interventions such as reading recovery (discussed in Chapter 4) and the Elkonin Box (Clay, 1985) provide support for struggling first graders. High-quality summer programs are also recommended. The **Elkonin box** strategy focuses children's attention on letter/sound relationships. The routine goes as follows: The teacher might begin by asking a child to identify the problem word. When the child points to the word, the teacher writes the word.

got

Then, together, they segment the word in chunks of letters and draw boxes around each letter chunk:

integrating a good deal of discussion about the letter/sound relationship along the way. A variation on this would be for the teacher to draw the boxes first and then coach the child to write the letter (chunks) in the boxes as they work through the letter/sound relationships.

If the child cannot pronounce the word, the teacher provides support by saying the word first. To consolidate the lesson, the student and teacher write the word in a sentence and use it orally in a sentence.

The Elkonin box strategy fills several needs for children. For older children who still need help, the strategy clarifies segmenting and manipulating letter/sound relationships. The Elkonin box can also be used as a visual aid in working with multiple syllable words. A more typical use of this strategy is to help young children who do not fully grasp phonemic awareness and who struggle in perceiving letter/sound relationships. Figure 9.9 provides an example of an accomplished teacher using an Elkonin box strategy with a struggling first-grader.

A fundamental concept for young children to understand is that the twenty-six letters in our alphabet provide us with the ability to write and read an infinite number of words just by combining the various letters. This is known as the *generative principle* and is described in the context of emergent literacy in Chapter 4. Most children grasp the generative principle as they acquire phonemic awareness, work with units of letters in word study, and write. Generally, children's knowledge of the generative power of the alphabet remains tacit (unspoken). You need to watch for children who lack this fundamental concept. When they do, demonstrate and discuss it early and often with struggling readers until they understand. Although knowing or being aware that letters combine to make words is not the same thing as being able to manipulate them to make words, having this understanding will make it easier.

Elkonin Box Teacher and Child Conversation

Teacher: That was a wonderful job retelling that story. What would you like to write about that story?

Child: I want to say, "The crocodile got on."

T: That will be a fun sentence to write. [Here is where the teacher can encourage a more complex or a simpler sentence, depending on the needs of the child.] How would you begin the sentence, "The crocodile got on."?

C: With 'the.' I know 'the.'

T: I know you do! Write it on our book writing page. [The book writing page is the page where everything appears correct.]

Child writes the word 'The'.

T: I noticed you put a capital 'T'. Why did you do that?

C: 'Cause it starts the sentence.

T: You are just learning so much about writing! OK, say your sentence again.

C: The crocodile got on. I need crocodile.

T: Yes, let's see if we can work on that one together. What sounds do you hear in 'crocodile'?

C: Is it a 'c' or a 'k'?

T: What do you think?

C: 'c'

T: You got it! What else do you hear?

C: [*child stretches word*] 'r' and another 'c'

T: There is an 'r' and a 'c'; put the 'r' down and listen as I say the word. What do you hear before that other 'c'? [*Teacher stretches word*]

C: Oh! I hear an 'ah'. Ah, ah, octopus! 'O'!

T: You are really listening carefully for those sounds. OK, write o and the 'c' you heard. What does that much say?

C: The croc

T: Yes, let's finish this word together [Teacher and student sound word together and collaborate on writing letters—student supplies all but the silent e, which the teacher adds] So now we have The crocodile; we need to finish the sentence. What did you want to say?

C: The crocodile got on. I need got.

T: I want you to work out got by yourself. I know you can do it! I'll tell you that 'got' has 3 sounds. [Teacher draws 3 lines on the try page; some teachers use boxes]

C: I know it starts with 'g'

T: Yes, sir! What do you hear next?

C: [*Stretches word*] A 't'!

T: 'T' is in that word! But where do you hear it? Say it again and listen.

C: 'Got'—it's at the end. 'Got'. Oh, I know! It's 'o' again! G-o-t

T: Wonderful work! I could just see your brain in action! Now, what do we need to finish your sentence?

C: The crocodile got on. We need on. a –n, right?

T: Let's think about it. You just told me crocodile had an 'o' for the 'ah' sound; and got had an 'o' for the 'ah' sound. So what do you think makes the first sound in ah-ah on?

C: 'o'!

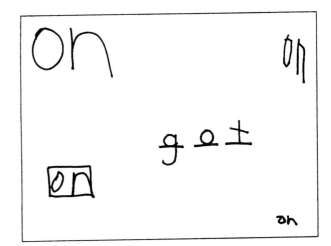

FIGURE 9.9

Elkonin Box.

Interventions

The earlier the intervention begins, the better the potential outcome. However, children in intervention programs are rarely able to function at grade level after the intervention stops (Bronfenbrenner, 1974; Spache, 1981). Gaskins (1998, p. 534) states that there is "more to [helping] delayed readers than good instruction." Here is a list of insights and recommendations that Gaskins and the teachers at Benchmark School in Media, Pennsylvania provide:

- Engage in extensive reading instruction.
- Show respect and teach the children self-monitoring and self-directing.
- Hold the idea that all teachers can change is their own approach to children and that children change as a result of teacher and teaching change.
- Focus on academic and nonacademic roadblocks (issues with engagement, having a disposition for learning, self-esteem).
- Work with other teachers and school experts, outside services, and parents to plan goals and plot the most efficient route to achieve the goals.
- Realize that long-term intervention is critical; most delayed readers need help from kindergarten through middle school.

Using sound reading instruction with young at-risk readers can result in tremendous benefits years later.

At Benchmark, the teachers work with children's dispositions or characteristics, such as attentiveness, organization, and conscientiousness. Research indicates that accelerating reading ability was not sufficient for at-risk learners. They must also acquire a disposition for learning and other affective or cognitive abilities (Dahl & Freppon, 1995; Freppon, 1995).

Among the many instructional focuses used at Benchmark, one of the most important is teaching the active search for meaning. Graphic organizers, rich discussion, and other techniques need to be used intensively over time with struggling readers.

If a child receives intervention, the specialist's instruction and the teacher's instruction must be in accord (Gaskins, 1998). Children are often put even more at risk when the specialist teaches in one way and the classroom teacher in another. In addition, teachers can learn a great deal by communicating with school specialists.

Cunningham and Allington (1999) suggest the following strategies for providing struggling readers with extra practice:

- Organize an after-lunch bunch in which you work with these children for ten or fifteen minutes reading easy books just for fun.
- Organize an easy reading time for ten or fifteen minutes after school using the strategies for an after-lunch bunch.
- Create a classroom learning center and have at least thirty minutes, perhaps two fifteen-minute periods of the day set aside for struggling readers to work in this center.
- Include in the learning center materials such as Legos™, puzzles, computer games, word board games, math and science manipulatives, Play-Doh™, chalk (slates),

markers, pencils, stickers and stamps, children's magazines, and a TV connection for watching *Reading Rainbow* or other educational videos.

Another way to increase reading practice and build confidence and self-esteem is to provide opportunities for first and second graders to read to kindergartners or to read to the school staff and the principal. Children will practice long and hard for the privilege of being a "visiting reader." With teacher arrangements made behind the scenes, children may call on the people they wish to read to and record the day and time for the readings on a sign-up sheet. Extend this in varied ways; for example, children may begin to take requests for the next reading by taking some additional books they want to read to the "audience" and inviting them to select the next book. Readings build fluency and are often popular with younger children. This kind of purposeful practice is exactly what struggling readers need.

Nearly all children want to learn and enjoy learning. Most children begin school excited about learning, thinking that they can do everything. However, children who struggle can become defensive and appear to lose interest in learning. This stance can be well established even by first grade. Sometimes fear of failure can be traced to instruction that focused on right answers at the expense of making sense and using errors to increase learning. Some children engage in negative behaviors, such as refusing to turn in their homework, because of a deep fear that it will be incorrect or because of a family problem. Children who are troubled might engage in behaviors that are self-destructive. These children need help, not blame.

Children with struggles need the entire school system working for them. Beyond the risk of reading failure for the child, children's failures deeply hurt teachers, parents, and families (Dudley-Marling, 1990, 2000). Failure is suffering that no child, family, or teacher should have to experience.

Standards as a Guide

Despite the controversies surrounding standards-based education, standards can provide good guidance for schools and teachers. However, most standards call for an overwhelming number of student performances and can result in frustration. You might feel that you are expected to do everything but you know you cannot, and you might feel as if you have no idea where to begin. Here are some recommendations for teaching in accord with standards (Caldwell, 2002):

- Don't agonize. Talk with colleagues, attend workshops and conferences, and take graduate classes that will help you find the insights you need. Let your administrator know that you need support. If you are interviewing for your first position, ask the administrator with whom you are interviewing about the support the school or district provides for teaching in accord with standards. Be proactive.

- Hold onto what you know is true and right. Keep your teaching in line with children's development. Find ways of consolidating standards and focusing on those that are most important for your children.

- Keep looking at the big picture and see what your standards really mean. Although stated in discrete pieces, standards cover overarching concepts that are critical to learning to read and learning from reading. Work with colleagues, and find ways to consolidate and group standards according to categories you relate to, add subcategories as you move along, and reread to consolidate.

STANDARDS & LITERACY

★ ★ Reading Applications ★ ★

The standard addressed in this lesson was selected by the creator and writer of this lesson, classroom teacher, Heidi Varner, M.Ed. The overview of the lesson; its purposes, structure, and time; and how it address benchmark and indicators follows.

The Standard: *Reading Applications: Informational, Technical, and Persuasive Text*
Benchmarks: By the end of the K–3 program, the child will:

- Use text features and structures to make predictions, organize content, draw conclusions and build text knowledge.

- Identify the central ideas and supporting details of informational text.

- Use visual aids as sources to gain additional information from text.

- Read and follow multiple-step written directions.

This lesson is designed as an introduction to a "Fall Outdoors" thematic unit in kindergarten. It weaves together good instruction and required standards. Use an information text for using pictures to aid comprehension. Focus on the main ideas of the text, and probe children's background knowledge about fall outdoors. Share the book *Fall* (Hirschi, 1991) with the class, discussing the content and pictures throughout. This thirty- to forty-minute lesson culminates with students illustrating, talking, and writing about what they learned from the book. The benchmark indicators addressed in the lesson are as follows:

Indicator 1: Use pictures and illustrations to aid comprehension
Indicator 3: Identify the main idea of a selection that has been read aloud.

Resources/Materials:

Hirschi, R. (1991). *Fall.* New York: Cobblehill Books.

Blank paper or journals for students
Large chart paper for word wall
Markers and crayons

Before the Lesson: Demonstration and Immersion

Informally assesses students' background knowledge through a brief discussion of what students already know about fall.

T: *"We are going to be talking about fall today. Who can tell me what fall makes you think about?" (Value all reasonable answers.)*

T: *"What kinds of things happen outdoors in nature during the fall? I will add some of your fall words to our chart."(large chart paper for word wall) Accept all reasonable answers, making sure to direct children back to nature and the outdoors as needed. Write in full view of the children on a word wall individual fall words, grouping them according to plants, animals, and descriptive words/action words.*

T: *Before reading a book, discuss what good readers think about and what the book might be about. Children also look through the book for any pictures to see if they can find even more clues about what the book will be about. These things help good readers think about what they will find out in the book.*

Introduce *Fall* by Ron Hirschi by previewing the book by sharing the photos, discussing them, and pointing out how some photos have words next to them to tell what they are.

T: *"Is there anything else we can add to our word wall after looking at these photos?"*

During Reading: Attention to Detail and Guided Practice

Read the title, the author's name, and the photographer's name, from the cover. Then read the title page and the dedication page.

> T: *"As we read the book, you will see the photos for a second time. Try to take a picture in your mind of what you see in order to help you remember the words you hear me read. Thinking about those pictures in your mind later will help you remember what the story is about."*

The teacher guides the students:

> T: *"I wonder what this page will be about?"* Ask for predictions from students. (trees, yellow leaves, etc.). Read the page to see whether the predictions are confirmed. Acknowledge responses, and praise correct predictions and effort.

> T: Read the next pages with the moon and spider web. *"What do you think lilies, larkspurs and shooting stars are?"* Reread the first part of the sentence to show how the author gives us a clue: *"The last flower petals fall . . . ."*

> T: Read the pages with the squirrel and turkey. *"Why do you think the author uses the word treasure?"* (It is important for squirrels and other animals and their survival during the winter.)

Continue this format of reading and discussing throughout the rest of the book.

After Reading: Application and Extension

> T: *"Are there any other words we can add to our word wall now?"*

> T: *"One helpful way to remember what happens in a book is by thinking about the main idea of the book. The main idea is the big idea that can explain all about the whole book. We know that this book talks about plants."* Show photo examples from the book. *"We know that this book also describes animals."* Show photo examples from the book. *"These events take place during the fall. How could we say all of that in one sentence?"* (Accept any reasonable responses, e.g., *"This book is about what happens to plants and animals during the fall. This book is about the changes plants go through and the jobs that animals do during the fall."*)

Assessment

> T: *" I will give each of you a piece of paper. I would like you to draw a picture that tells about something important from this book. Write a sentence that tells about this story as best you can. I will come around to ask you about your illustration and writing as you work."*

Teacher action: Take a class chart for notes to keep a record of what children say about their illustrations. You will be able to determine whether or not children got the ideas in the text through analysis of their verbal description of their illustrations. Note children's writing, —clarity of ideas, letter-sound relationships, spacing, and so on.

Student action: The students should use paper and markers or crayons to develop an illustration about the book. They should use inventive spelling to write about their illustration.

Reflection

After the lesson, take a few minutes to reflect on the lesson and write about it. What worked for you? What did not go well? How did students respond to various parts of the lesson? What parts of the lesson should you keep the same? What parts of the lesson could you change to improve?

- If the school or district mandates a basal or other reading program that you are expected to follow, work backward from the lesson you must teach to the skills and knowledge in the standards. You will find that you can match your lesson objectives with standards' benchmarks and grade-level indicators. When the instructional focus and materials are the teacher's decision, it might work well to read a group of consolidated benchmarks and indicators you have categorized and plan accordingly.

Caldwell (2002) advises connecting instruction and assessment according to standards. Each state and each school district provides a list of standards and benchmarks that outline the phonics and literacy instruction that is required. Look at these benchmarks and indicators, and think about how you want teach them. Because you know how to teach and assess, you can link your instruction with standards benchmarks or indicators and the matches will make sense. For example, the Standards and Literacy box illustrates a kindergarten lesson plan designed to teach to the following standard: *Young children need to be able to identify an information text's central ideas and supporting details, be able to use visual aids, and follow multiple-step written directions.*

Assessment

Without assessment, instruction is powerless. Imagine teaching with little knowledge of what children already know and what they have learned. For a long time, teachers depended on a yearly assessment, usually a normed test, that showed how children perform in comparison to others at the same grade level. Such mandated tests and some teachers' records informed instruction. Tests were focused on right or wrong answers written by test makers or on children obtaining specific skills by a specific time—period. Of course, throughout history, good teachers have learned from their children and have used their knowledge to assess the children, but not every teacher reached this level of competence. Today, however, change exists in the form of evidence-based assessment based on what children actually do in the classroom and our knowledge of literacy development.

Formal and Informal Assessments

Formal assessments are those developed on the basis of their reliability and validity and are commercially produced to test large numbers of children (such as normed tests). **Informal assessments** are those effective teachers use in everyday classroom life, such as quick checks on comprehension with open-ended questions or a check on the kinds of miscues or errors children make as they read.

NORMED TESTS.   Generally, normed tests should not be given to kindergartners or first graders. Normed tests are designed to achieve a rank order for each child in a classroom. Vito Perrone, Director of Teacher Education Programs at Harvard University (1990, p. 1), says of normed tests,

> While these tests have come to affect Americans of all ages, in all fields, (normed/standardized) intelligence and achievement tests come down most heavily on the young . . . they are particularly deleterious for children in preschools and primary grades. For it is in these early years that children's growth is so uneven, so idiosyncratic, that large numbers of skills needed for success in school are in such fluid acquisitional stages.

Normed tests simply cannot evaluate what young children know because the tests are constructed to yield scores that place about half of all children in the average to above-average ranges and about half of all children in the average to below-average ranges (Harman, 1990).

Having said this, however, there are times when normed test results are useful. For example, low scores can help to initiate action for getting help and special financial assistance requires documentation. Nearly all school districts require some level of standards-based testing, regardless of age. In such cases, the tests should be criterion referenced. **Criterion tests** are structured to measure performance according to clearly defined skills (spelling a word) and knowledge (knowing that proper names begin with a capital letter).

Although measures of children's performances against a standard benchmark are an improvement over normed testing, these tests are not more valuable than the records of effective teachers who know the children in their classrooms better than anyone. However, if criterion tests are used in combination with teachers' assessments, they contribute greatly to the assessment process.

GRADING.   Because grading is a challenge and a trial, Cunningham and her colleagues note that the concept of grading young children in the typical sense is simply not realistic. Putting a number or letter grade on young children is not informative or helpful because children vary so much. In traditional grading, the struggling reader or English language learner will always receive lower grades (marking them as "not as good as others"), and the more experienced and fortunate children will always receive higher grades (marking them as "better than others"). Teachers work hard to communicate to parents and school administrators that grades should reflect effort and growth. What matters most in teaching is that children are developing and making progress. Avoid marking any child as a learner with static ability.

In *Classrooms That Work* (1999), Cunningham and Allington argue that education must change the way grades are determined. They too recommend that grades be based on effort and growth. The typical grading system tells children who struggle: "You are a failure." Many schools throughout the country do not assign letter grades to young primary children, focusing instead on their development. Even if you must work with a mandated traditional grading or report card system, you can maintain an encouraging attitude that is explicitly conveyed to children. Donald Graves (1983, p. 93) states, "Grading is a fact of life. It's the most difficult responsibility placed on teachers." He advises teachers to use grades to encourage children and to document well what children do in class.

Caldwell (2002) cites the limited format of report cards and suggests that teachers add to the report card in ways that show the children's growth and hard work. For example, add a list of good comprehension strategies the child is working on and uses, and do the same for word learning. To keep grading records such as these, divide the grade book into sections labeled with your teaching emphasis, for example, predicts in reading, connects self and the world to stories and information books, is doing well in learning word families. If you have a narrative report card, divide the report into categories, and keep information on all children in the same categories (reading comprehension, letter/sound relationships or phonics, spelling, etc.). In this way, you provide continuity in your report cards and even-handedness for all the children (Afflerbach, 1993).

ANECDOTAL NOTES.   Another assessment that is vital for evaluating children's progress is teachers' anecdotal notes. Anecdotal notes are narrative notes written when observing a child or children (McIntyre, Personal Communication, September 10, 2001). They are descriptive (avoid a rush to judgment.) They may pose questions ("Why is he doing that?") and hunches ("I wonder if he understands the flexibility of writing?"). Anecdotal notes are based on what is actually seen and heard. Taking anecdotal notes helps teachers ask good questions such as: Where is the child on meeting the first-grade standard benchmark indicator ____? Is the child engrossed in reading? Is she attending to print or dependent on pictures? Is the child anxious, distracted and, if so, by what? Does the child ask for help and, if so, from whom? Is the child benefiting from help? Can she successfully accomplish her work with help? What do I need to do?

Teachers take anecdotal notes to understand children's development and plan instruction and to demonstrate accountability when called upon. Teachers write about observable behaviors and insights and about what happens when they intervene, reteach, and provide high scaffolding. It is hard to imagine effective instruction without data gathered and analyzed through daily, informal notes. With knowledge of children's development in mind and the support of written developmental guidelines right beside them, effective teachers analyze anecdotal notes to gauge their students' progress or lack of it. In addition, anecdotal notes can be written in ways that closely link to state standards (benchmarks and indicators). For example, a typical state benchmark states that young children must have alphabetic awareness. Teachers who write a portion of their anecdotal notes explicitly on children's demonstrations of this knowledge and skill will have very important information at their fingertips for report cards, parent meetings, and meetings with other school experts. Best of all, teachers have the information needed for planning and conducting future lessons. Build the habit of attending to standards and children's progress in daily note making. For example, a child might meet the criteria *regularly, sometimes,* or *rarely.* This, with a line or two of description about what the child is doing, creates reliable data when carried out consistently. A note might be something as brief as the following example:

> Date _____
> Focus Fred on the difference between blends and digraphs.

Or a note might be as long as the following example:

> Date _____
>
> Today Shealee manipulated letter cards to make sp words. She was correct some of the time, she was interested and engaged (no worry there), and she stuck with her work in spite of some struggle. This child has really grown in her capacities to engage and stay with challenging work.
>
> Alphabetic awareness is about 50% there or better. To meet the standard (standard number or benchmark indicator may go here), she needs to keep moving.
>
> Keep working with familiar word families and add some partner work with Cody all next week, reassess and add new words. Shea is a quick learner, this should really help.

In the beginning it is often difficult to know what to write down in anecdotal records or to know what to do with the information. Carry a clipboard or pack of sticky notes with you so that you can write anecdotal notes throughout the day. Use your notes to look for patterns. For example, identify a child who never seems to know short or long vowel words, who wanders around the room, or who is consistently left out of social activities. Recognizing patterns is the first step in intervention.

Assessment Strategies

Assessment informs and guides instruction every day all year long. Effective teachers use their daily classroom assessments and informed insights about the child and compare them to more structured assessments. This process of comparison and contrast of assessments helps to form a rich body of data that goes into each child's file. When children are not making good progress, the assessment evidence and descriptive narratives written by the classroom teachers, information from other teachers who have contact with the child, and information from parents and other experts make a significant contribution toward decisions that might need to be made for a child.

Children need to be assessed on the literacy processes and, at intervals, reading and writing products in order for you to monitor their development and your plan. Assess the use of multiple cueing systems in oral reading, comprehension strategies, word recognition, and writing. Comprehensive reading assessments must be made on all children over the course of the school year. This is usually at the transitional stage (usually first and second grade). Ongoing assessments of some of your children's development needs to be done daily. In addition to the assessments provided throughout this book, the following strategies may be of help:

- *Intentionality.* To learn to read and write, children must have the concept of **intentionality**, knowing that written language is a symbol system with linguistic meaning. Children who possess this concept know that written language provides understandable communication (Purcell-Gates, 1991). Without it, the child is lost in learning to read and write (Harste, Woodward & Burke, 1984). This critical concept is easily taught once the teacher understands the children's needs. Assessment of intentionality should be done by using a combination of formal observations and anecdotal notes. A child may demonstrate by responses in the classroom that she or he realizes that written language carries meaning via the squiggles on the page, yet not exhibit this knowledge in an assessment situation. To determine children's concepts of intentionality, the following assessment might be helpful. You will need a tape recorder for this assessment.

  As with all assessments, ensure that the child is comfortable before you begin. Begin by explaining that the assessment will not be graded, nor will what the child does be on his or her report card. Assure the child that you are trying to learn how to be a better teacher and need the child's help. Playing with the tape recorder for a minute before and after assessing usually gets the interaction off to a good start and ensures comfort.

  Give the child a piece of paper on which appears this sentence (or any similar sentence): "A long time ago there was an old man." Note what the child says in response to the following questions:

1. Is there something on this paper?
2. What do you think it is?
3. What do you think it could be for?
4. Why do you think it could be here?

If the child answers with "writing," "words," or "letters" but does not answer the other questions, probe with "Have you ever seen writing (or words or letters) before? What do you think it was for? Why do you think we have writing?" You will likely need to ask only one or two questions to find out whether the child is grasping the concept of intentionality.

- *Comprehension.* To assess reading comprehension, Beaver's (2000) Developmental Reading Assessment is very teacher friendly and provides a way to continuously monitor progress.

- *Word Identification.* For a quick look at word identification, you might ask a child to read a list of grade-level words. Explain to the child how reading the word list is to help you, the teacher. Acknowledge that you both know that words all by themselves are not much use. You might need to help clarify this point, since children can become quite confused when teachers say one thing and do another, such as emphasizing word meaning and then requesting a reading of a list of mere words. For a more comprehensive look at word recognition, the Woodcock Reading Masters, Revised (Woodcock, 1987) is helpful. For additional assessments, see http://sedl.org/reading/rad for 160 early reading assessments.

- *Prereading.* For kindergarten and first-grade children who are not yet reading, the Test of Early Reading Ability is helpful (Reid, Hresko, & Hammill, 1989).

A helpful tool when assessing your students is to create a simple assessment checklist of small groups of children like the one in Figure 9.10. On a sheet of paper, write what you are assessing and a scale at the top—for example, Reading Comprehension: *often, sometimes,* and *rarely.* State the comprehension skills you are looking for (*uses prediction, connects book information with own life or the world*), and leave spaces on the paper for checkmarks in the appropriate block. As you observe the children, check the appropriate places on your list. Collect three or more sheets on children, and look for patterns. Identified patterns will show you where to focus instruction.

Regular use of assessments and checksheets is essential not only for good teaching, but also for accountability. Make checksheets for all the most important things you are teaching—for example, specific word families, vocabulary words, or words used in units of inquiry. You can create the same kinds of assessment checksheets to assess children's affective behaviors (Caldwell, 2002). For example, to assess personal involvement, your checksheet might state, "The child demonstrates it *often, sometimes,* or *rarely.*" On learning disposition, "the child wants to learn, seems confident, or persists in the face of difficulty *often, sometimes,* or *rarely.*" Affective checklists will help you to glean patterns that can guide your teaching. You can identify who avoids tasks, who is growing in their independence, or who may have emotional problems that need more professional help. With the assessments recommended in this book and good records, you will be able to demonstrate your accountability with ease.

READING COMPREHENSION

Without prompting, the child demonstrates: RC (reading comprehension by predictions that indicate good understanding), PC (personal connections and connections to other books, or the world)

NAMES / DATES	Often RC / PC		Sometimes RC / PC		Rarely RC / PC	
Simon						
Fisher						
Shea						
Cody						
Tessa						

FIGURE 9.10

Assessment Check Sheet.

Finally, remember that no teacher should assess all the children alone. Teams of primary-grade teachers and other school experts can and should help you with assessing struggling readers and English language learners. Caldwell (2002) offers these suggestions for assessment management:

- Keep it *manageable*. Do not try to assess all children all the time.
- Assess children who struggle more often than you assess others (select a few focus children to concentrate on each week).
- Teach and support children's self-assessment and self-correction.
- Don't assess everything; assess important things.

FOR REVIEW

This chapter connects research-based information on children's learning with effective instruction and assessment from kindergarten through the second grade. It provides practical information for new and practicing teachers with discussions on grouping children, planning, balanced instruction and materials. Included are grading, four blocks (Cunningham et al., 1999), and guided reading and dynamic grouping (Fountas & Pinnell, 1996).

The use of standards as a guide in your teaching and assessing is presented with discussion on how you can work with standards. English language learners and struggling readers are focal topics. This discussion provides information on language diversity, recommendations, and insights into teaching and assessing these young children.

A significant portion of this chapter is devoted to practice that develops the knowledge and skills of young children and your own! Here phonics, context, analytic and synthetic phonics, whole-part-whole instruction, and various lesson structures and plans provide concrete guidance. With routines that teach, you have opportunities to learn even more about the implementation of effective instruction. Organization and management of the classroom learning community include discipline and family and community. A discussion of materials, leveled books, and technology extensions help to complete this chapter.

For Your Journal

1. Review Ana Lopes' lesson in the chapter-opening vignette. Identify specific instances or examples of Ana's teaching that provide a specific scaffold or scaffolds.

2. Look at the following notes, and write each in your journal. Then analyze each for its value as an anecdotal note. Indicate what valuable information about the child is provided, what makes it a good or poor anecdotal note, and how you might write it to make it a more informative note.

   a. Larry seemed miserable all day. He drew pictures and didn't attempt any scribbling, writing letters, or reading. I've seen this response for days and days. What's up? I need to talk with his parents and ask the school psychologists and my literacy specialists to sit in on some classes.

   b. Victoria is driving me crazy. I think her mother is at the root of this. Mom works and is never home!

   c. Breanna is so smart. She always knows the answers! If only I had more like her in my class. I remember her sister Donna, who was just as smart as Breanna. That was a good year; I had a bunch of Donnas and Breannas!

   d. Cody pretend-read *Frog and Toad* to me today; he uses a lot of textlike phrases and his own mix of oral language. This little guy maintains a story formation with a beginning, middle and end. He even connected the real frog he had with Frog in the story!

★ Taking It to the World

Develop a home literacy project that will help make school life more authentic and draw families into the school community. For such a project, it is wise to connect homework activities with inquiry projects and to have culminating activities in the classroom to which parents and caregivers are invited. Identify an inquiry project that would provide an excellent forum for family member/caregiver involvement. Create questions the children could use for interviews, and plan for how they might be able to supplement the information with photos, toys, or perhaps a articles of clothing. How would the children be able to tell their stories?

★ Being a Professional Reading Teacher

Reflecting on the Chapter

A purpose of this chapter is to organize the reading program for children in kindergarten through second grade. How can we assemble the important elements needed for this program in such a way that the diverse needs of all of the children are met?

Grouping

- How can you group children for instruction without creating a sense of low group and high group among your students?
- Why is the four blocks system of organizing for instruction so effective at these early grade levels?

Assessment

- How can you use standards as a basis for organizing your reading program without surrendering creativity and spontaneity in your teaching?

Interventions with Young Children

- Using what you have learned, write up an intervention for a small group of struggling learners following the use of the Figure 9.6, teacher observation form on pages 364–365. Focus on three to four teaching points you find important.

Your Portfolio

- Including a statement of your philosophy about teaching beginning reading in your portfolio provides evidence of how you view children and reading and also provides a window on your writing abilities. Think about including a reflection about why you incorporated such a statement into your portfolio.
- Even if you intend to teach at a higher grade level, your portfolio will be greatly strengthened if you can incorporate some experiences in the levels from kindergarten to second grade. Because some older children are preliterate or not literate in English, providing evidence of your knowledge of emergent

literacy and early reading can be important for any grade level. Lesson plans, thematic literature units, and lists of high-interest, low-vocabulary children's literature are among the artifacts you might think about including.

Teaching Resources

If you are interested in teaching in the primary grades, a list of wordless books will be a very valuable resource. Children's librarians, sales staff in children's bookstores, other primary teachers, and even a search at google.com can help you locate these resources. The next step is to begin collecting the actual books. Try swap meets, thrift shops, friends whose children are older now, garage sales, and bookstore remainder tables. If you find two of the same title, buy both; trade with a friend later. Keep your receipts for these kinds of purchases; they are usually deductible for teachers when they file their income tax returns.

Technology Connections

1. Children in grades K–2 nearly always go through a period of intense interest in dinosaurs. Build on children's natural interest in dinosaurs and increase your teaching opportunities by using the following web sites and books to enhance pleasure reading:
   - www.enchantedlearning.com/subjects/dinosaurs (an interactive child-friendly site with basic information about dinosaurs and extinction.
   - www.fmnh.org/sue1 (a site dedicated to Sue, the largest tyrannosaurus rex yet discovered)
   - *Allosaurus! The life and death of big Al* (2001) by Stephen Cole (information book)
   - *Dinosaurs Forever* (2002) by William Wise (poetry)
   - *Dinosaurs of Waterhouse Hawkins* (2001) by Barbara Kerley (picture book)
   - *The Shy Stegosaurus of Cricket Creek* (2001) by Evelyn Sibley Lampman
   - *Outside and Inside Dinosaurs* (2002) by Sandra Markle (nonfiction with fossils photographs)

   Read two or more of these children's books, and access the web site that relates most closely to the books you read. Write up notes for two primary-grade lesson plans working through the whole-part-whole framework for your lessons and design one lesson to connect with home and caregivers. For example, extend that lesson with homework that children and their families/caregivers will find enjoyable.

2. Nearly all teachers are concerned with motivation, and some experts believe that technology has motivational advantages over conventional teaching methods. Jill Mizell recommends electronic mentoring as a way to support struggling readers and/or children who are English language learners. E-mentoring is a system that combines traditional mentoring and the technology of email. Moreover, most children can benefit through carefully selected mentors and well-developed programs such as Youth Trust in learning the language arts. Many mentoring web sites provide ways in which mentors and children talk about writing and engage in editing and feedback in revising writing. Explore the following web sites, and identify two or three that might work well with younger children (K–2). Add your views on why you think they would be useful.

- `www.youthtrust.org` —then need to click on "e-mentoring"
- `www.itown.com/athens/mentor`
- `www.gifted.uconn.edu/mentoruc.html`
- `www.leahremini.net/HELP.html`

Research
Navigator.com

Connect with Research

Review the following key words from the chapter and then connect to Research Navigator (`www.researchnavigator.com`) through this book's companion web site to conduct a search into research on each of the various topics as they relate to reading and literacy education today.

analogy	formal assessments	multileveled groups
balanced instruction	four blocks	productive play
criterion tests	informal assessments	traditional grouping
dynamic grouping	intentionality	voice/print matching
Elkonin box	leveled books	whole-part-whole instruction

Further Readings

Dahl, K., Scharer, L., Lawson, L., and Grogan, P. (2001). *Rethinking Phonics: Making the Best Teaching Decisions*. Portsmouth, NH: Heinemann.

The authors provide a classroom-lived experience of excellent phonics teachers, how they think about children's development and make teaching decisions.

Fountas, I. C., and Pinnell, G. S. (1999). *Matching Books to Readers: Using Leveled Books in Guided Reading*. Portsmouth, NH: Heinemann.

A valuable resource for new and experienced teachers. This resource book guides teachers to a wide selection of leveled books appropriate for reading levels and with enough breadth to offer books of varied genre and topic interest for individual children.

Freppon, P. A. (2001). *What It Takes to Be a Teacher: The Role of Personal and Professional Development*. Portsmouth, NH: Heinemann.

Told through first-hand accounts of six outstanding teachers, this lively book offers interpersonal connections to readers as well as many "how-to-teach" suggestions.

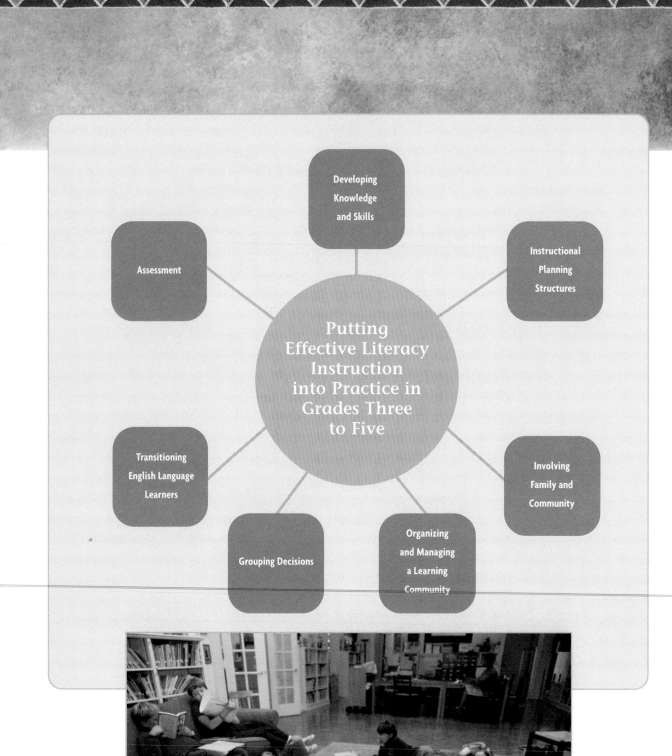

Developing
Knowledge
and Skills

Instructional
Planning
Structures

Assessment

Putting
Effective Literacy
Instruction
into Practice in
Grades Three
to Five

Transitioning
English Language
Learners

Involving
Family and
Community

Grouping Decisions

Organizing
and Managing
a Learning
Community

Putting Effective Literacy Instruction into Practice in Grades Three to Five

T he following statements will get you thinking about the topics of this chapter. Answer true or false in response to each statement. As you read and learn more about the topics in these statements, double-check your answers. See what interests you and prompts your curiosity toward more understanding.

Anticipation Guide

_____ 1. When children enter the third grade, there is little change from the first grade in the use of literature, in word recognition instruction, in reading in the content areas, and in writing.

_____ 2. Teachers in grades three to five devote much less attention to phonemic awareness and phonics than those in grades K–2.

_____ 3. When children move from grades K–2 to grades 3–5, the balance between oral reading and silent reading is about the same.

_____ 4. As children reach higher grades, there is a greater range between their achievement levels, resulting in the need for careful grouping for instruction.

_____ 5. The child's home can be the source of many family literacy activities.

_____ 6. When children are reading orally for fluency, it is not possible to judge their comprehension.

_____ 7. Formal assessment processes such as standardized testing do not provide information that is valuable in diagnosing the needs of individual students.

_____ 8. Teaching English phonics to English language learners is the same as teaching it to native English speakers.

_____ 9. Most children go through similar stages of spelling development.

_____ 10. Computer technology is more useful in writing instruction than in reading instruction.

Vignette of Literacy Activities in a Third-Grade Classroom

hantell DeLaney is a third-grade teacher in a suburban classroom. Her twenty-seven students represent many different cultures and ethnic groups, but all are proficient in English. Today she has organized her students into three groups according to their levels of reading comprehension. One group reads slightly below grade level, another group reads at grade level, and some children read at fourth- and fifth-grade levels. Ms. DeLaney's children come together in these groups from time to time, but her overall approach to grouping for instruction is flexible, according to the children's needs and to the goals and standards she is addressing.

In today's lesson with a group of twelve children who are reading at grade level, Ms. DeLaney's plan reflects a three-stage structure: anticipatory reading, building knowledge, and consolidation. She begins with two anticipatory reading strategies. She first conducts a read-aloud of the story title and the first page of the story, asking the students questions about the illustration on the page, which she shows them from her copy of the book. She asks, "Based on the title and the illustration on this page, what prediction can you make about the story?"

Vinh says, "It's about a big animal. What is it?"

"Who knows?" asks Ms. DeLaney.

Theodore responds, "A hippopotamus!"

"How large is a hippopotamus?" asks Ms. DeLaney.

"Really big!" they shout.

She then introduces two new vocabulary words from the story, "huge" and "gigantic," with a t-graph, a graphic organizer.

For the part of the lesson in which the children build knowledge through reading, Ms. DeLaney uses two strategies that are often used in tandem: guided reading and chunking. She focuses the children's reading by asking a higher-order (comprehension-level) question before they read and by chunking the amount of reading they do after she asks the question, usually a single page, occasionally more than one page, or sometimes only a paragraph or two in difficult or lengthy material. After she poses the purpose-setting question, the children read silently to find the answer and then discuss what they have found out. Ms. DeLaney then proceeds to the next question and the next chunk. She uses the questions as a scaffolding strategy in a Directed Reading Activity (DRA). Placing the focus on the children's reading comprehension of what they read silently instead of only on accurate pronunciation and speed strengthens the children's abilities to understand what they are reading.

Ms. DeLaney's procedure is as follows: "Boys and girls, we are going to read a story about a girl who tries to hide the pet hippopotamus she found from her mother. Look in the table of contents for the story, turn to the first page, and close your book with your finger in the place. I am going to ask you a question before you read, and I want you to read to find the answer. How does Kamesha solve the problem of feeding her new pet so that her mother doesn't find out about it? Please read silently to find the answer." The children read silently and, one by one, raise their hands as they find the answer. Ms. DeLaney repeats the question and calls on Theodore, who responds correctly. She says, "That's correct, Theodore. Now, please read us the sentence that proves your answer." She asks another question about the same page or chunk that they have just read, and they then move on to the next page, repeating this procedure for several pages.

In a consolidation activity after the children have read about half of the story, Ms. DeLaney asks them to retell the story so far in their own words, each child contributing part of the retelling. She asks, "How did our story begin?"

Tran contributes, "Kamesha found a huge hippopotamus at the park."

Nestor adds, "Her mother will be angry if she sees it."

"Why?" asks Ms. DeLaney.

"Because it will eat a lot of food," responds Nestor.

The children continue, negotiating with each other when there are disagreements or something is left out. Ms. DeLaney then asks the children to write two or three sentences predicting what Kamesha's mother will do when she discovers the hippopotamus. They can choose to read a library book or play one of the many reading games available to them as independent activities after they finish their writing. They will finish the story the next day but with only a brief review activity before the children continue reading.

A s children move into grades three through five, most have acquired a concept of print, can decode most of the words they encounter, especially when they are contextualized in connected text, are reading silently, are understanding what they read, and are expressing themselves in writing. The purpose of Chapter 10 is to weave together the major elements of a comprehensive and balanced reading program for implementation in self-contained classrooms in grades three through five.

Developing Knowledge and Skills

As you saw in earlier chapters, there is much variation in beginning reading programs for kindergarten and first and second grades. The range extends from scripted, direct instruction, one-size-fits-all programs of explicit phonics to literature-based programs in which shared reading of authentic connected text is a major activity, with phonemic awareness and phonics taught in the context of words the children have already learned to recognize. A basal reading program is also frequently employed; such programs are less scripted than formal code-emphasis programs, but have more connected text for the children to read. Phonics elements and skills are systematically sequenced and presented explicitly. The text they read might be authentic in the case of anthologies of original versions of children's literature, but less so in the case of traditional basal readers, in which text is often manipulated to conform to various criteria.

Consolidating Primary-Grade Gains in Grade Three

Teachers in grades three to five must organize according to the experiences the children had in kindergarten and first and second grades and according to their degree of success there. Several very basic changes from children's initial reading experiences begin to appear in their reading instruction in the late second grade, continuing into the third grade. Individual differences among children not only continue to exist, but also grow into even greater differences as some children have not been successful in kindergarten through second grade, most have been moderately successful, and others are leaping ahead in their abilities to process and benefit from both narrative and expository text. The result is an increased need for flexible grouping according to different needs, an increased need for a variety of instructional materials on several levels, and a need for more sensitive instructional strategies, especially for children who are not meeting standards for the grade level. Although this process might not always be under the control of the individual classroom teacher, the teacher should have the knowledge and skill necessary to develop such a program where that opportunity does exist or to adapt and augment the adopted program where possible.

USING CODE-EMPHASIS PRIMARY-GRADE PROGRAMS. A trend in some school districts is a reading program through which all children proceed at the same pace, regardless of differences in home language, proficiency in English, previous experiences or lack of experiences with print, knowledge of the sound system of English, availability of print in the home and community, and parent roles in providing emergent literacy experiences. Typically, these programs focus on phonemic awareness and explicit decoding skills, with text reading occurring in decodable text or fragments of text that are written specifically to provide regular practice in decoding. The major goal of such programs is for the children to achieve **automaticity**, which involves rapid and accurate pronunciation of words that follow phonic generalizations. Children may be discouraged from using cueing systems other than the graphophonic system. The obvious strength of such a program is seen in the formidable decoding skills of successful students when they attack regular words. But there are also problems with such a methodology:

- The focus of instruction is on accurate and rapid pronunciation not on comprehension.
- Motivation is a frequent problem in that decodable text tends to be less interesting than authentic literature.
- Because of the systematic and sequential nature of instruction, children who fail to master some skills and elements have difficulty learning subsequent skills and elements that are based on previous teaching. Similarly, some children are already able to decode virtually any unknown words through skilled use of all cueing systems, but they are required to follow the program nonetheless.
- Many children have difficulty in the application of phonics generalizations to words that are not regular, especially if they lack experience in using other cueing systems as tools in the decoding of unknown words.
- Many English language learners must try to learn to decode in a language they do not understand and in which they have not mastered the sound system.

These children will benefit from additional emphases in their later reading instructional experiences:

- Extensive reading of authentic children's literature and expository text
- Instruction in the use of strategies from other cueing systems for when the children encounter new words that do not yield to analysis with regular phonics generalizations, such as using context clues, ignoring unknown words and reading on, using structural analysis skills, and questioning whether or not a word makes sense in the passage
- An increasing focus on silent reading as children gain proficiency in the middle grades, with questions to scaffold or guide that silent reading, followed by discussion

This situation was very much on Ms. DeLaney's mind when she planned her third-grade reading program. In grades one and two, her children's teachers used a code-emphasis reading program that was characterized by explicit and systematic phonics in a very scripted, direct instruction approach.

To meet their comprehension needs, Ms. DeLaney selected a basal program that has particularly attractive and interesting literature. She continued to build their phonics and related word recognition skills from the program, but she drew those brief

Whether you use a basal program or a literature-based program in your class-room, what is most important is making sure sound reading principles and instruc-tional techniques are incorporated to meet the needs of your particular students.

lessons out of the literature that the children were reading in the program in a process called "breaking the lockstep." She taught the components in the program but not always in the order in which they occurred in the teacher's manual.

USING BASAL PRIMARY-GRADE PROGRAMS.   Basal reading programs tend to be broad and eclectic. Basal programs provide detailed teachers' manuals, often to the point of being scripted. Attention to phonemic awareness and phonics is usually ample. Instruction in the use of reading strategies, such as decoding, comprehension, and content reading skills, is provided in a sequence linked with the text to be read. Teachers often need to break the sequence by providing additional instruction related to a skill that is presented with a given story; this instruction might take several days. In the meantime, the children continue their reading of stories apart from this instruction, sometimes falling behind with respect to the skills presented with each story. On the other hand, a teacher might wisely decide to skip some direct skill development for children who have already demonstrated these abilities.

As children move into the middle grades from a basal reading program, you might choose the following options:

- Augment with multiple copies of trade books, apart from the basal reader or anthology

- Provide scaffolding activities beyond those recommended in the basal reader when the children lack background knowledge about a story theme

- Supplement skill development in decoding when gaps are encountered in the children's knowledge and skills, sometimes by reviewing word recognition lessons from previous levels of the program and sometimes by preparing new brief focused lessons.

USING LITERATURE-BASED PRIMARY-GRADE PROGRAMS.   Some children might have had a less structured experience in the primary grades, such as those who have been in a language experience approach or a literature-based program. Children who were in a literature-based program have often had extensive experiences with shared reading in the primary grades. Their texts are often group sets of authentic literature, for example, multiple copies of *The Very Hungry Caterpillar* (Carle, 1983), that a group of children works with for a week or two before moving on to another piece of literature. These books are often leveled, their difficulty being assessed and taken into account before they are selected for use (Pinnell, Bridges, & Fountas, 1999).

Decoding skills are sometimes taught opportunistically rather than systematically. For example, teachers using this approach might notice that there are several words in a piece of text that begin with the same sound/letter correspondence. It might be an element that the children have not examined formally, such as the consonant blend *spl*. The teacher develops a lesson on this sound/letter correspondence that has emerged from words the children have encountered in the story.

When you teach a group of children who have such an experiential background, there might be a need for a more systematic approach to word recognition to augment their earlier instruction and exposure to many types of comprehension scaffolding strategies.

Moving toward Independence in Grades Four and Five

As children move further into the middle and upper grades, the same elements of the reading framework are in place, but there are changes in the emphasis in each area and in the content. First, there is much more independent work now that the children can read and write on their own. They still need support from the teacher, but they are much more self-sufficient.

Second, there is a diminished focus on skill development, since the children have now mastered most of the word recognition skills that they need to acquire. The focus on details is now more on vocabulary study than on letters and sounds, although occasional lessons are taught on letter/sound correspondences that are less regular or less frequently encountered, such as the silent consonants in *knee, write, pneumonia,* and *psychology* or prefixes of Greek origin, such as *poly-* and *biblio-*.

A third major change is that more instruction focuses on reading in the content areas of the curriculum, with some lessons focusing as much on science or social studies as on reading. Writing activities are also broadening out from early narrative efforts into various aspects of expository writing, including persuasion and argumentation.

Building Fluency in Reading

Phonics & Phonemic Awareness

Although the reading fluency of many children is well established by the end of second grade, some children will benefit from continuing emphasis in this area. According to Cunningham (2000), **fluency** is fast, expressive reading that results from extensive easy reading and writing. Zutell and Raskinski (1991) provide an expanded definition of fluency that includes rate, accuracy, and automaticity with phrasing, smoothness, and expressiveness. According to the report of the National Reading Panel (2000), children should read orally with appropriate timing, expressiveness, stress, and intonation. When necessary, fluency can be promoted through the following:

- Providing daily self-selected reading of easy books at the children's independent levels
- Asking children to rehearse by reading to themselves before reading aloud
- Discouraging children from interrupting each other's oral reading with corrections
- Not being concerned about errors that do not change the meaning of the text and providing time for self-correction
- When correction is needed, focusing on comprehension by asking whether what was read incorrectly made sense
- Incorporating daily writing and encouraging invented spelling

Helping struggling readers to develop fluency in the middle grades is always a challenge because they already might be discouraged and they do not want to be perceived as needing to read easy books. Fielding and Roller (1992) suggest that the teacher can sometimes make more difficult books accessible to such children by doing the following:

- Having the children read to themselves first before reading aloud
- Providing paired reading opportunities in which a stronger reader supports a weaker reader (Caution: This can be overdone to the detriment of the more able reader.)
- Building background knowledge with easier books

- Having older children read easy books to younger children, which provides a good rationale for using less challenging materials at their independent reading levels
- Having children read the text in the mother tongue before reading orally in English (Crawford, 1993)

Finally, older children need extensive time for free-choice **sustained silent reading**. Worthy and Broaddus (2002) suggest beginning with about ten minutes each day, increasing to about thirty-five minutes each day as the children become capable of maintaining their attention and motivation for more time. Of course, the students need large numbers of high-interest books in a wide variety of genres.

Instructional Planning Structures

Throughout the book, you have seen and will see numerous strategies that support various aspects of reading instruction. Teachers must make decisions daily, and sometimes by the hour and minute, as to which strategies to use, when to use them, how to sequence them, why to use them, and even how many to use.

A major factor in planning reading instruction relates to the type of program being implemented. A highly scripted program requires little planning in the sense of organizing instruction, but it might be necessary to prepare charts and other materials to be used in the lesson from the manual. Basal programs are also highly organized with many activities, usually more activities than could be done during a typical lesson.

The task, then, is to plan the comprehensive reading program, assuming that you have the latitude to combine elements and strategies from many sources to provide instruction that addresses the needs and interests of your students and the standards established for the school. When that latitude is limited or does not exist at all, the opportunity to precisely address children's individual needs is diminished.

Planning at the Daily Level

When planning daily reading lessons, consider the framework elements recommended in Chapter 1:

1. Demonstration of the acts of reading and writing in meaningful literacy activities
2. Attention to detail and developing students' knowledge of the structure of written language
3. Guided practice in meaningful reading and writing so that the children internalize effective strategies
4. Carrying out independent activities in which they apply and extend their reading and writing abilities and develop lifelong habits of literacy.

State-adopted standards should also be reflected in lesson elements.

In grades three through five, there will likely be more than one reading group in the classroom, sometimes three or four. Furthermore, one or more of those groups might be learning to read in Spanish or another language before moving into reading English later. The amount of needed planning can be daunting for a beginning teacher, but a year of teaching experience leads to efficiencies that facilitate the planning process.

THE LESSON PLAN.   Most lesson plans will contain several common elements:

- One or more student objectives that emerge from student needs and standards
- Needed text and instructional materials
- An estimated amount of time planned for the lesson
- The body of the lesson:
  - Anticipatory reading activities to motivate and to activate or introduce needed background knowledge and vocabulary
  - Reading activities to build knowledge for guiding and scaffolding the students' reading and comprehension of the text
  - Consolidation reading activities, in which students apply new knowledge
  - A brief focused word study lesson, usually an element that is related to or emerging from the text to be read
- Assessment, often incorporated into a consolidation activity after reading, and also part of an ongoing process of observation and recordkeeping described in Chapter 9.

The Standards and Literacy box illustrates a lesson plan that might be designed to address some version of Little Red Riding Hood, a story that is familiar to most children. There are three objectives in the lesson, each emerging from one or more state standards—from the state of Massachusetts in this case. A description of materials that the teacher will need is provided along with an estimated amount of time scheduled for the lesson.

The body of the lesson contains the three elements that make up most reading lessons. The prereading *anticipatory activities* are brief and simple because the story is well known to most children. The *activities to build knowledge* during reading are focused on higher-order questions. The children read silently to find information needed to answer the teacher's questions, and they occasionally read evidence aloud to support their responses. The postreading *consolidation activities* allow them to negotiate the story during the oral retelling. They enjoy the authentic writing activity at the end. They are writing to a real audience—the judge (their teacher)—and they have an authentic purpose for writing. They will enjoy reading the teacher's *judgments* about the culpability of the wolf. The assessment of the children's achievement during the lesson is also authentic, as the teacher is observing their actual listening, reading, thinking, and writing behaviors.

**Phonics &
Phonemic
Awareness**

This teacher has incorporated a brief, focused lesson on phonics that reflects a need of the children and that uses vocabulary from the story as a base for the phonics minilesson. In this case, the unvoiced final sound of /*th*/ is the focus of the lesson, and the teacher will check phonemic awareness, even though the children will undoubtedly have no problem with this aspect in the third grade. Then the teacher moves from the sound to words the children already know that end in the element, some of which come from the story they have read. Finally, the children combine their background knowledge about the sound and the letter and draw a conclusion about the sound in that position in new and unknown words. The focused lesson on phonics is brief and explicit, only about five minutes, but it is related to and emerging from the literature they have read. It is in the analytic or whole-part-whole mode.

As this lesson plan is examined in terms of the four block multimethod, multilevel approach described in Chapter 9 (Cunningham, Hall, & Sigmon, 1999), each of the four blocks—guided or directed reading, writing, self-selected reading, and working

STANDARDS & LITERACY

★ ★ Sample Lesson Plan ★ ★

Daily Lesson Plan:
Third-Grade Level

Little Red Riding Hood

Prepared to align with standards from the Massachusetts Language Arts Curriculum Framework, 2000.

Reading and Literature Strand

Standard 12: Students will identify, analyze, and apply knowledge of the structure, elements, and theme of a work of fiction and provide evidence from the text to support their understanding.

Objective: Students read silently and respond to inferential questions about the text.

Reading and Literature Strand

Standard 7: Students will understand the conventions of print and the relationship of letters and spelling patterns to the sounds of speech.

Objective: Students correctly pronounce the unvoiced consonant digraph /th/ in final position in new words (brief focused lesson).

Composition Strands

Standard 19: Writing. Students will write compositions, such as narratives, summaries, essays, letters, or directions, with a clear focus supported by logically related ideas and sufficient detail.

Standard 20: Consideration of Audience and Purpose: Students will write for different audiences and purposes.

Objective: Students write letters that present a coherent argument and in which writing conventions of spelling, punctuation, and grammar are grade-level appropriate.

Materials: Twelve copies of the story text—*Little Red Riding Hood;* easel and chart paper, markers

Time: Forty minutes

BODY OF LESSON PLAN

Anticipatory reading activities: The teacher shows the book cover, and the children immediately recognize a familiar story. The teacher asks one or two students to share the beginning of the story before they begin reading. The teacher introduces two vocabulary words using the context of the sentences in which they occur: *hood* and *forest.*

Building knowledge through reading activities: guided silent reading, chunking, and discussion

Read the first two pages to find out how the author told you that Little Red Riding Hood was a disobedient girl.

How did you know that the wolf was hungry? Please read the sentence that proves your answer.

Let's read the next page to find out the effect on the wolf of his great hunger.

with words—is found. What is not readily seen in this example is the multilevel aspect of the four block approach. This could be accomplished by teaching the lesson to the entire class, making the text accessible to all students with multiple readings involving read-aloud, paired reading, and small flexible groups. There would be no problem in incorporating the writing and self-selected reading blocks of the approach, but the word study block might be less successfully applied in this example for grades three to five. Some lower-achieving students might still not be comfortable with the unvoiced /*th*/ in initial position, which they should probably know before moving on to that phoneme in final position. And some children would have learned the sound/symbol correspondence of the final unvoiced /*th*/ years before.

When Little Red Riding Hood returns home, what will her mother say to her? Why?

Read the next page to find out what kind of man the hunter was. How do you know that?

How do you know that this is a fantasy story?

BRIEF FOCUSED LESSON ON PHONICS ELEMENT

Step One: Students listen to words that contain the final unvoiced consonant /th/, such as *teeth* (the wolf's teeth from the story), *both*, and *bath*. The teacher asks how the words sound alike, as well as other questions that focus the children on the target sound.

Step Two: The teacher shows known words that contain the sound, asking how the words look alike. The teacher asks the students to focus on the letters that make up the sound and where they are.

Step Three: The teacher shows new words that contain the same element in the final position and asks the children to pronounce them. The teacher then asks the children to make a rule about the letters and the sound they have pronounced.

CONSOLIDATING READING ACTIVITIES

Oral retelling of the story: The children retell the story in their own words.

Writing activity: The teacher appoints each child to be an attorney for the wolf, who is in jail. Each child is to write a letter to the judge, asking for the release of the wolf. The teacher is the judge who will decide the wolf's fate in response to each letter. RAFT: Role is attorney; Audience is judge; Format is formal letter; Theme is getting the wolf out of jail (Buehl, 1995).

Read another fairy tale of your choice. Find two story elements that are similar to *Little Red Riding Hood* and two that are different and make notes about them. Be ready to talk about them tomorrow.

ASSESSMENT

Reading comprehension during reading: Success of the children in responding to inferential questions about the story and giving evidence for their answers.

Writing assignment: Coherence and persuasiveness of the argument to release the wolf; attention to the conventions of spelling, punctuation, and syntax.

Focused lesson on phonic element: Success of the children in decoding new words and correctly pronouncing the final sound of /th/ in them.

Strategies to Integrate into Daily Lessons

A rich variety of instructional strategies that were introduced in earlier chapters can be used as scaffolding strategies to support children's reading comprehension for use in reading lessons (see Table 10.1 on page 406). Scaffolding is the temporary support provided by teachers when children are engaged in a task within Vygotsky's zone of proximal development. Bruner (1978) has described scaffolding as a temporary launching platform designed to support and encourage children's language development to higher levels of complexity. Pearson (1985) later described the temporary nature of scaffolding as the gradual release of responsibility. Good teachers intuitively use such scaffolding strategies to help children maintain their participation in learning activities (Crawford, 1994a).

TABLE 10.1

Examples of Scaffolding Strategies to Support Reading Comprehension

ANTICIPATORY ACTIVITIES BEFORE READING

Teacher read-aloud of beginning or selected parts of text

Discussion and predictions from book cover, title page, illustrations

Motivation by relating text to students' previous experiences

Think-pair-share

Quick-Write

Introduction of new vocabulary with semantic map, contextualized discussion

Activation or installation of background knowledge with semantic map, semantic feature analysis, advance organizer, shared discussion

ACTIVITIES TO BUILD KNOWLEDGE DURING READING

Guided or directed silent reading

Oral reading (generally limited to plays, dramatic activities, puppet shows, reading for expression, providing evidence)

Silent sustained reading

Think-aloud

Specific strategies, such as K-W-L, reader response, literature circles, the ReQuest procedure, reciprocal teaching, and questioning the author

CONSOLIDATION ACTIVITIES AFTER READING

Oral retelling

Written retelling

Review and elaboration of semantic map, semantic feature analysis from anticipatory activities before reading

Writing workshop

Role-audience-format-theme (RAFT)

Reader's theater

Paired reading

Silent sustained reading

And more reading

And yet more reading

Some strategies are appropriate as anticipatory activities to prepare children for the reading they will do. Others might be helpful for building knowledge during their reading, supporting their comprehension, engaging them in the ideas they will encounter, and providing them with a structure to share their ideas with other students and the teacher. Others are most appropriate as consolidation activities to be completed at the conclusion of a lesson or even as homework. Some anticipation strategies, such as semantic mapping and semantic feature analysis, can be revisited as consolidation activities at the end of lessons for additions and revisions of initial predictions.

As you think about how these many strategies can be used in lessons, you should first consider that, as in choosing a meal in a cafeteria, you will take from each category the strategies that support your instruction but not so many that the lesson becomes confused. Over the period of a year, you will likely use most or all of these strategies, but there is no need to use each one every week or even every month. As in all things, moderation is important. The most important activity in every lesson is the reading of connected text.

The recommended strategies that follow are those that will provide the underlying support or scaffolding needed for reading comprehension. It is the isolated skills development that you should consider carefully. Skill development should be viewed as an outcome of learning to read, not as its cause (Samuels, 1971; Smith, 1985). When a child's needs suggest that a directed skill lesson is needed, you can seek out an appropriate one in the teacher's editions and workbooks of traditional reading and language arts programs.

Finally, the structure of the following strategies has been applied to the narrative text in the vignette, but it can also be applied to expository text in science and social studies textbooks and related readings. Reading can be taught in many other subject areas of the curriculum.

Anticipatory Strategies before Reading.   An examination of Ms. DeLaney's lesson in the opening vignette makes it clear that she has given deep thought to organizing her instructional program in reading. She has identified the children's needs and has planned a program that addresses them carefully. She includes anticipatory activities before the part of her lesson during which children read so that they can activate background knowledge about the story and become familiar with the meanings of any new vocabulary words that might be needed. There are many strategies that she could use for these two purposes, but she uses only two in order to move the lesson along to the most important part: the reading.

Many strategies can be used to prepare children to read the text selected for a reading lesson. Two important factors affecting their readiness for reading are the background knowledge they bring to the task and vocabulary. Literature or expository text can be grouped into three levels of challenge with respect to these factors (see Table 10.2 on page 408). The first category of text is not challenging because the background knowledge and vocabulary needed to understand are present in the culture and language of the children who will read it. In addition, the story might be in their oral tradition, or they might have been exposed to the story in a read-aloud or story-telling activity before their reading. In this case, you might elect to skip unneeded preparation activities that are provided in the teacher's manual of the typical basal reading program. When English language learners have read a story in the mother tongue in a parallel version of their reading program, the story might fall into this category.

The second category of text requires some activation of background knowledge and introduction of new vocabulary, and those anticipatory activities are usually provided for in the teacher's manual. If not, you should develop the needed activities, as Ms. DeLaney did.

The third category of text is very difficult because the children have little background knowledge about it, and new vocabulary is extensive and challenging. Although anticipatory activities are provided in the teacher's manual, you might decide that they are insufficient or inadequate. One option is to skip the story or text and move on to the next one. Another is to augment the anticipatory activities before reading, especially in areas of need for the children. How do you know in which of the three categories the text falls? That decision requires a professional judgment based on your knowledge of the children's strengths and needs and on analysis of the text before they begin reading.

TABLE 10.2

Choosing Reading Texts Based on Readiness

READINESS CRITERIA

Text Level	Vocabulary	Background Knowledge	Teacher Action
easy ↑ 1	Present in daily culture	Present in daily culture	Preparatory activities may not be necessary
2	Part of oral traditions	Part of oral traditions	
difficult ↓ 3	Introduces some new vocabulary	Some activation of background knowledge	Some activities necessary to introduce new vocabulary
	Extensive new vocabulary	Little activation of background knowledge	Augment anticipatory activities as necessary
	Very difficult		

All children have acquired background knowledge, but there is often a discontinuity between the background knowledge a child has and that assumed by the authors of instructional materials or literature used in the classroom. Crawford (1994) indicates that the discontinuity between the assumption and the reality is deeper when the child comes from a language or culture different from that of the children for whom the materials are designed or intended—usually middle class native English-speakers. A story about a birthday leads a Mexican child to activate background knowledge about a piñata, while most children in the United States activate background knowledge about a party, a cake with candles, pin-the-tail-on-the-donkey, and gifts. Children from Senegal and Morocco do not think about birthdays at all because birthdays are not celebrated in their cultures. If children lack a schema or background knowledge for a birthday tradition presented in a literature selection representing a culture they do not know, then background knowledge must be activated or developed as a prereading activity. A very effective anticipation strategy for activating and developing background knowledge is **semantic feature analysis** (Pittelman et al., 1991). This strategy involves helping students build knowledge about a new topic by comparing it to knowledge about related topics about which students do have background knowledge. The Teach It! box illustrates this effective anticipation strategy.

TEACH IT!

32

Reading Strategies for Building Knowledge during Reading.   According to Smith (1985), children learn to read by reading. This fundamental idea should underlie your thinking about how children's time is best spent during reading instruction. Rather than having children study about reading by mastering skills, maximize the amount of reading they do. Some obvious counterproductive strategies are pencil-and-paper exercises. Another is the still-common practice of round-robin oral reading, in which each child takes a turn reading aloud to the group or class. This usually consists of having a child laboriously reading aloud a passage she or he has never before read, even silently, while the rest of the children in the group pretend to listen or read along. You might have memories of counting the children ahead of you in the first grade so that you could determine which paragraph you would read, although some wise teachers skipped around to prevent that strategy.

The child reading aloud focuses on pronunciation, not on understanding what is being read, and the other children are either bored or preparing to read when their

TEACH IT!

★ ★ ★ ★

Semantic Feature Analysis

Students in a suburban school may have limited background knowledge about the *falcon*, the topic of expository text from a science book. Related areas about which students in a suburban school would already likely have background knowledge might be *parrot*, *chicken*, and *crow*. These topics are listed on the *x*-axis of a chart (the top) and generic elements that relate to parrots, chickens, crows, and falcons are listed on the *y*-axis (the left) (see the figure). The teacher prepares the chart before the lesson and presents it on the chalkboard, a transparency, or a large piece of paper. Information about the falcon should be available in the text to be read. In a prereading group activity led by the teacher, the students discuss, marking a plus (+) where they know that a relationship is true, a minus (–) where they know that it is not true, and a question mark (?) where they do not have information or do not agree.

On the sample chart, the prereading predictions of a student group are listed and marked accordingly. The students then read the text on falcons, looking for information about elements from the chart.

At the conclusion of the reading, the students discuss the text and return to the semantic feature analysis chart as a consolidation activity. They discuss again, change incorrect predictions, providing evidence they have found in the text, and fill in areas where question marks were indicated.

Unlike some other text-based strategies, semantic feature analysis lends itself well to reading expository text in mathematics and the sciences. For example, a mathematics teacher might list the following elements in the left column: triangle, isosceles triangle, parallelogram, trapezoid, square, rectangle, right triangle, equilateral triangle, and circle. Across the top, the teacher might list such elements as parallel lines, nonparallel lines, straight lines, no straight lines, equal lines, pairs of equal lines, angles, equal angles, pairs of equal angles, and right angles.

Refer to your **Teach It!** booklet for further activities you can use to reinforce concepts discussed in this chapter.

Semantic Feature Analysis Chart
The Falcon

	parrot	chicken	crow	falcon
What color are they?				
Brilliant colors	+	–	–	?
Brown	–	+	–	?
Blue	–	–	–	–
Black	–	–	+	?
What do they eat?				
Meat	–	–	+	?
Fruit	+	–	+	?
Seeds	–	+	–	+
Where do they live?				
In the jungle	+	–	–	?
In the mountains	–	–	–	?
On the farm	–	+	+	–
In the desert	–	–	–	?
In the city	–	–	+	?

turn comes. This practice is especially deceiving in regard to children who read in Spanish, for example. They can read orally with confidence in English, albeit with a Spanish accent and no comprehension. They are, in fact, pronouncing and not reading. Table 10.3 identifies various reasons why round-robin reading should be kept to a minimum.

There are, however, some excellent uses for oral reading: reading a sentence aloud to provide evidence for a response to a question; reading poetry; reading roles in puppet shows and readers' theater; assessment; sharing writing; buddy reading or paired reading as a practice activity; read-aloud to parents, grandparents, or siblings; and improvement of fluency. Otherwise, valuable instructional time in grades three to five should be used for guided silent reading and skill development.

It is more difficult for teachers to provide extra support to English language learners, because their need for it might be less obvious during the largely independent activity of reading silently. The need should be based on children's abilities to interact with the teacher and each other about what they have been reading—that is, their comprehension of what they have been reading.

Guiding children's reading with questions, a variation on DRA, provides valuable support in maintaining comprehension (Crawford, 1993). The teacher needs to precede the children's reading of a page or passage of a piece of literature by asking a higher-order question, that is, an open-ended question whose answer requires the child to use background knowledge and combine it with information from the selection to be read. An example of such a question is "Please read page 71 to find out why the main character is worried." Students will read page 71 to find the answer to the question; it focuses them on comprehension, not on production and accurate oral reading.

This questioning strategy brings key story concepts to children's attention as they read, and, perhaps more important, it provides moral support, interest, and motivation from someone who cares about them: the teacher. Children who cannot or will not read a lengthy selection alone might do so in chunks of a paragraph, or a page or two at a time within the security of a supportive teacher-directed group. These chunks are manageable and comprehensible sections, and questions can be used very effectively and naturally to accomplish this chunking. You can structure children's reading

TABLE 10.3

Reasons for Minimizing Round-Robin Oral Reading

- It diminishes the amount of actual reading that children do.
- The focus is on pronunciation, not comprehension.
- Strong readers love to perform by reading orally, but they could read more, and faster, by reading silently.
- Poor readers hate to read aloud, disclosing their reading problems for the whole class to hear.
- Both children and teachers dislike listening to the agonizing efforts of poor readers.
- Although teachers can informally assess student outcomes during oral reading, a more systematic approach is needed (see the informal reading inventory discussed in this chapter).
- Teachers sometimes convert an oral reading lesson into a phonics lesson that interferes with comprehension.

with questions that elicit predictions, with timely resolution of those predictions through discussion and any needed mediation.

Although there is considerable debate about the value of teaching reading comprehension skills through direct instruction, there are enough other reasons to guide silent reading with higher-order or comprehension-level questions. Table 10.4 provides some examples of poor low-level questions and strong higher-order questions. It takes no longer to formulate and ask a higher-order comprehension question than a low-level recall question before asking children to read to find the answer. Guided silent reading provides an opportunity for children to make inferences and predictions, identify cause-and-effect relationships, and apply other higher-order critical thinking skills when their comprehension is supported (Crawford, 1993). This is seen in Ms. DeLaney's lesson in the chapter-opening vignette. Her students are now in the third grade, and they need to read silently with a focus on comprehension. But their abilities in this area are still limited, and she therefore scaffolded their comprehension by guiding their silent reading with carefully formulated higher-order questions. She also limited how much they read after each question to an amount they could understand and remember for the discussion that followed each chunk. Ms. DeLaney provided occasional opportunities for oral reading, as described in her lesson. She often asked children to read the sentence or sentences aloud that provided evidence for their responses to her higher-order questions.

Consolidation Strategies after Reading.   Ms. DeLaney concluded her lesson with two consolidation activities. She integrated an **oral retelling** and a small, authentic writing assignment into the closing part of the lesson—part to be done while she was

---

TABLE 10.4

Examples of Different Levels of Questions from *Little Red Riding Hood*

LOW-LEVEL RECALL QUESTIONS

Tell what happened on the first page of the story.

Where did the wolf first see Little Red Riding Hood?

What color is Little Red Riding Hood's cape?

Where is Little Red Riding Hood taking the food basket?

HIGHER-ORDER COMPREHENSION QUESTIONS

How did the author tell you that Little Red Riding Hood was a disobedient girl?

How did you know that the wolf was hungry?

What was the effect on the wolf of his great hunger?

When Little Red Riding Hood returns home, what do you think her mother will say to her? Why?

Why did Little Red Riding Hood go to Grandmother's house by the forest road?

What kind of man was the hunter? How do you know that?

What advice would you give to Little Red Riding Hood for the future? Why?

with the group and the rest to be done after she left them. She collected the children's written predictions and later responded briefly in writing to the content of each one. If she noted a spelling error in a child's prediction, she used the word correctly in her response to that child. She also reviewed their papers for common problems, such as the correct use of the comma in a series. Instead of correcting that error, she would plan a minilesson on the element or detail for the next day. The children could then examine their own work and make needed changes or corrections.

Retelling is an excellent consolidation activity after reading. An oral retelling provides children with the opportunity to negotiate with each other about the meaning of the selection and requires them to listen very attentively to each other (Brown & Cambourne, 1990). Often, through this process, children can incorporate new information gained through reading into existing background knowledge. They also observe that retelling promotes multiple readings of text as a part of the negotiation process. Koskinen, Gambrell, Kapinus, and Heathington (1988) found that the verbal rehearsal that occurs in the retelling process also serves to improve the reading comprehension of less proficient readers. English language learners might elect to retell in their mother tongue what they read or heard in their second language (Crawford, 1993).

Retelling also provides a means for integrating writing into the program. Either through a cooperative learning process or through individual or paired writing, children can prepare a written retelling (Strickland & Feeley, 1985). As a result of their earlier discussion, the knowledge they gained through reading, and such prereading activities as semantic mapping and the examination of story grammar, children are better prepared to write a well-structured retelling. Like the demonstration that they provide during read-alouds, teachers should also model retelling with an actual example.

The most obvious consolidation activity after reading should not be overlooked: more reading. If you are successful in providing high-quality literature that children will choose to read and in supporting their comprehension, then you can expect gains in all areas of the language arts. Reading is more powerful than direct instruction in developing vocabulary, grammar, spelling, and reading comprehension, especially for English language learners. Provide extensive free voluntary reading with messages that are understood in low-anxiety situations. Good writing is promoted more by extensive reading than by writing (Krashen, 1985, 1993).

Writing &
Reading

Long-Term Planning Using Thematic Literature Units

The **thematic literature unit** is a very useful structure for organizing reading instruction around a topic that is of interest to children. It consists of a framework for organizing the work of several days or weeks (Zarrillo, 1994). This structure often parallels social studies units, such as *The Westward Movement*, or science units, such as *Growing Up*, and usually includes goals and objectives, activities, instructional materials, and assessment. The thematic literature unit provides an opportunity for you to integrate reading and writing across the curriculum, since a part of the unit can incorporate expository text from social science, science, or other subject areas. You can augment the text in the classroom and library with text on the theme from the Internet as well.

A typical integrated thematic literature unit can be seen in Table 10.5. The teacher has assembled expository text, authentic literature, film, and other resources that reflect the theme of the unit, *Endangered Dolphins*; it therefore fits into the genre of critical literacy as well. There are two videos to initiate the unit and motivate students, one of news accounts of dolphin kills and another about dolphins in general. The unit

TEACH IT!
34

TABLE 10.5

A Thematic Literature Unit on **Endangered Dolphins**

GOALS/OBJECTIVES*	ACTIVITIES	ASSESSMENT	TEXT SOURCES	INTERVAL†
Formulate questions about dolphins and their endangered status	View video	Quality of student questions generated	National Geographic's *Dolphins: The Wild Side* (VHS); news videos; cans of tuna	One day
Read with fluency	Paired reading	Accuracy of oral reading in primary level book	*In Dolphin Time* by Kathleen Dudzinski	Periodic over four weeks
Read silently with comprehension	Guided reading in small groups; discuss findings in literature circles	Observation; quality of discussion	*See and Explore Library: Whales, Dolphins, and Porpoises* by Mark Carwardine; other sources	Four days
Read silently with comprehension	Guided reading during science lesson	Observation; quality of discussion	Science textbook	Two days
Locate information on the Internet or in newspapers; interest groups formed to work together	Select theme to research: Poem about dolphins Miami Dolphins football team Greek myth about dolphins Other themes of interest	Criteria: use of descriptors, refinement of descriptors, appropriateness of selected text	Google.com	Periodic over four weeks
Write informational and persuasive text about protecting endangered dolphins	RAFT (Role/Audience/Format/ Theme) Word processing	Rubrics	*Dolphins: What They Can Teach Us* by Mary M. Cerullo	Three days following research activities
Illustrate informational writing accurately	Illustrate informational and persuasive writings	Relationship of illustrations to text written by students	*Drawing Whales and Dolphins* by Books Watermill	One day following writing activities
Read silently with comprehension	Silent sustained reading of self-selected narrative and expository books about dolphins and related ocean mammals	Motivation, conferences	*Island of the Blue Dolphins* by Scott O'Dell, *Dolphins at Daybreak* by Mary Pope Osborne, and other leveled books	Periodic over four weeks

*Goals and objectives reflect school district/state standards.
†Note: Days do not have to be consecutive.

includes expository text about dolphins and other sea mammals; multiple copies of trade books, including the Newbery Award-winning book *Island of the Blue Dolphins*; symbolic text to read on the sides of cans of tuna; related selections of text from the science textbook used in the classroom; and a book on drawing dolphins so that students can illustrate their written work. Over a period of about four weeks, the children will read the texts, building background knowledge and vocabulary related to the theme. Word attack skills and vocabulary will be developed in the context of their reading. Writing activities will also emerge from them, resulting in social action: student posters urging shoppers to buy only dolphin-safe tuna.

Critical literacy provides many opportunities for integrating across the curriculum within thematic units, involving not only literature, but also science, social studies, mathematics, and technology. It is also an excellent place to incorporate the writing process, especially persuasive writing. Powell, Cantrell, and Adams (2001) provide several assumptions that underlie critical literacy:

- Literacy instruction can never be neutral because of the decisions teachers make in planning every lesson.
- Critical literacy is a major element of a strong democratic system, requiring shared decision making in society.
- Literacy instruction can lead to transformative action.

Standards as a Guide

Most states and several professional organizations, including the International Reading Association and the National Council of Teachers of English, have developed standards for reading/language arts and other curriculum areas. These are most often expressed as expectations or minimal competencies to be attained by children, and they are sometimes tied quite specifically to grade levels. Recall that the Standards and Literacy box on page 404 demonstrated how standards can be used to develop specific lesson objectives and a lesson plan.

Standards provide valuable focus on important elements of the reading/language arts curriculum. One unfortunate outcome of overreliance on standards for planning instruction, however, is a narrowing of and rigidity in the curriculum and a focus on teaching to the assessment tools that states, school districts, and schools use to assess the extent to which students have met those standards (Nolan, Haladyna, & Haas, 1992; Herman & Golan, 1993). There should always be room for the teacher's creativity and for taking advantage of the teachable moment that occurs when, for example, a child brings an injured bird into the classroom or when a tragedy such as September 11, 2001, occurs. The reading/language arts activities that emerge from such a moment will almost always address one or more important standards.

⭐ Assessment

Although there are already differences in achievement among children at each level from kindergarten to second grade, there is a much broader range of levels of proficiency in reading and writing in grades three through five. Most states and school districts now conduct an annual or biannual assessment of children's reading achievement at several grade levels, but the data that those standardized tests yield are not designed for use in planning instruction for individual children. Teachers need to gather information about the individual strengths and needs of each child in order to plan instruction, select appropriate instructional materials, and group children.

Informal Assessment

In the chapter-opening vignette, Ms. DeLaney had divided her students into ability groups for that part of her instruction. According to results from the informal assessment she administered during the first week of school, the twenty-seven students in her classroom were reading at grade levels from second to fifth, with one group reading slightly below grade level, one group reading at grade level, and some children reading at the fourth- and fifth-grade levels. How did she assess to form those groups?

INFORMAL READING INVENTORY. Perhaps the most widely used authentic assessment for reading is the **informal reading inventory (IRI)**, which is used to evaluate students' reading ability. The IRI allows the teacher to determine children's individual needs. It consists of a series of graded passages, generally 100–200 words in length, with one or two passages for each grade level from one through ten. The levels of the passages are often determined by the level of the text from which they are taken, but these levels can be verified according to their levels on a gradient of leveled text (see later in this chapter). In addition, each passage is accompanied by four or more questions at the level of comprehension.

Administering the Informal Reading Inventory. The IRI should be administered at the beginning of the school year, when the teacher is planning instruction, selecting textbooks and trade books for the class, and grouping children with similar needs. Because children are often grouped for instruction on the basis of the outcomes of the IRI, it is desirable to administer an IRI once or twice during the school year. Children have spurts of achievement gain, and groups that are formed at the beginning of the school year should not be so rigid that children never move from one to another. It might not be necessary to systematically administer an IRI to every child at the same time later in the year, as is done at the beginning of the year, but children should be reassessed when the teacher observes a change in achievement, whether positive or negative.

Reading assessments can help identify a child's reading level as well as comprehension. How can a teacher use this information to plan for instruction?

An IRI is an individual test, and a substantial investment of classroom time must be dedicated to the process of assessing each child, but it is time well spent. A skilled teacher can administer an IRI to an entire class within several hours, and the process goes faster with experience. Each child needs ten to fifteen minutes of uninterrupted time with the teacher. It is tempting to begin assessing the first day of school, but classes are often reorganized because of rapid changes in enrollment during the first week. Therefore, it might be wise to delay this process until enrollments in the school settle down late in the first week. You need to provide

activities for the children who are waiting their turn for assessment and for those who are already finished. It is also important that children not be able to hear the assessment of their peers on this oral procedure. A paraprofessional or a parent volunteer can be invaluable in supporting the quiet environment needed during each child's IRI.

On the basis of widely accepted percentages of accuracy and comprehension, the teacher needs to decide what levels to administer, and the answer will be different for each child. Most teachers administer a grade level below their estimate for the child that is based on test scores and information on the cumulative record from the teacher of the previous year. For example, a third grader who was reading at grade level the year before would usually begin with an IRI passage on the second-grade level. The child should feel successful on the first passage. Children know when they have failed, and they are often reluctant to continue to another level, even if that level is lower—perhaps especially if that level is lower.

Explain to the child that he or she will be reading some passages out loud to you and will then respond to some questions about what has been read. The child then reads a passage aloud to you as you record the oral reading errors made by the child. Then take the passage back from the child and ask the questions that accompany it. On the basis of the child's performance, another passage will be administered, as described below.

Interpreting the Outcomes.   The IRI yields four levels: frustration level, instructional level, independent level, and capacity level. The most important are the instructional and frustration levels. The instructional level is the level at which the teacher should target instruction and for which instructional materials should be selected. It corresponds to Vygotsky's zone of proximal development (Vygotsky, 1978).

In determining the instructional level of a child, the frustration level is determined at the same time. Children are asked to read and respond to questions from passages at various levels until they fail to meet criteria for **instructional level,** which are 90–95 percent accuracy in oral reading and 75 percent in comprehension. They should not have seen or read the passages before the assessment. The level at which the child fails to reach the criteria is the **frustration level**; the next level down—that is, the highest level where the criteria are met—is the instructional level. The percentages for accuracy are focused on a base score of 100 percent, each oral reading error resulting in the loss of one percentage point. The types of errors are as follows:

Mispronunciation: The student mispronounces a word, even if it is self-corrected.

Substitution: The student substitutes another word that makes sense in the passage.

Omission: The student leaves out a word.

Insertion: The student adds a word that is not in the original passage.

Reversal: The student reverses the order of letters, words, or clauses.

Repetition (regression): The student repeats words already read, sometimes an entire sentence.

Punctuation ignored: The student ignores punctuation.

Hesitation: The student hesitates for two seconds or more.

Teacher support: After five seconds, the teacher supplies the word.

The 75 percent criterion for comprehension is based on answering three of four comprehension questions—25 percent for each correct response.

Age of student 9 Gender M Grade level 4 Home language English		
Level administered	Accuracy	Comprehension
2	99%	100%
3	97%	75%
4	94%	75%
5	89%	25%
Frustration level***	4	
Instructional level*	3	
Independent level**	2	

*Highest grade level with 95% accuracy, 75% comprehension
**Highest grade level with 99% accuracy, 100% comprehension
***Next level more difficult than instructional level

FIGURE 10.1

Informal Reading Inventory (IRI) Results.

This complex process is best understood with an example. The teacher assessed a fourth-grade student who, according to the previous teacher and cumulative records, was reading at grade level last year. The teacher therefore administered a third-grade passage to begin, using the form shown in Figure 10.1 to record results. The child was successful in reaching at least 90–95 percent accuracy and 75 percent comprehension, indicating that his instructional level was at least third grade. On the fourth-grade passage, he also met the criteria, but not at the fifth-grade level. The frustration level was at fifth grade, indicating that the instructional level was fourth grade because it was the highest level at which criteria were reached.

Figure 10.2 on page 418 shows how the teacher evaluated the accuracy of oral reading on the third-grade passage. The accuracy percentage from Figure 10.1 was 97 percent, indicating the three oral reading errors that were subtracted from 100 percent. When a student commits a series of errors that are related, only a single error is counted. For example, if a student hesitates, mispronounces a word, then repeats the words that preceded it, and finally gives up on the word, only a single error is counted. This student, for example, was unable to pronounce *gift*, although he produced the sound of /j/, ordinarily a correct pronunciation of the /g/ followed by short /i/. He anticipated

Once upon a time there was a hunter and his wife who lived very well. Then a son was

born to them. One day the hunter caught a baby fox and brought it home *A* to his son as a *j* gift.

The little fox was very quick and smart. The boy like him very much. His mother often left the

boy and the fox together and went to help her husband *punctuation ignored* When she returned, the little fox

would run to meet her.

One day she returned home at noon. She was surprised because the little fox did not come

meet
to greet her.

C 1. Describe the family in the story.

(The hunter, his wife, and his son)

C 2. Why did the little boy like the fox?

(He was quick and smart)

√ 3. What was the effect on the little boy's mother when the little fox didn't greet her?

(She was surprised)

C 4. What did the mother do with the little boy when she went to help her husband?

(She left him with the little fox)

FIGURE 10.2

Example of Accuracy Scoring of IRI Passage.

the problem with the word *gift* and repeated the phrase "to his son as a" preceding it and then hesitated before mispronouncing the sound of /j/. But the teacher counted only a single error because all were related to the problem with the word *gift*. The child ignored the period after *husband* and substituted *meet* for *greet*, a logical substitution that did not change the meaning of the sentence and that was consistent with the /ee/ in both words. In a process called *reading miscue inventory,* a skilled, experienced teacher can interpret children's errors and make valuable inferences about the children's strengths and needs (Goodman & Burke, 1972; Goodman, Watson, & Burke, 1987).

It is often possible to determine through observation that a student is reading at frustration level. The student exhibits some or all of the following behaviors: laborious word-for-word, or even letter-by-letter, reading with flat intonation; pointing behavior, especially when that is not observed in easier passages; squinting or moving the text very close to the eyes; and rocking back and forth, kicking the chair or table. Think about what your own physical behaviors would be if you were asked to read aloud from a quantitative chemistry text that you did not understand at all.

The **independent reading level** is the level at which the child can read without support. It is generally one to three years lower than the instructional level. It is the highest level at which the child reads with 99 percent accuracy and 90–100 percent comprehension. In the example in Figure 10.1, the teacher had to drop to the second-grade level to determine the independent level. If the student had achieved less than 99 percent accuracy and 100 percent comprehension on the second-grade passage, the teacher would have dropped to a first-grade-level passage.

Determining the independent level can dramatically increase the time it takes to administer and interpret an IRI, and the extra information might not be useful enough to warrant the additional time required. Essentially, it is important to know that children who select a library book to read independently will probably select an easier book than the one that is used in their reading group. This is the way it should be, because the teacher is providing extra scaffolding and support to children during the lessons that is not available during independent reading. Children with strong interests in a theme or topic might select books for independent reading at higher levels, but the extra motivation of a child reading about the butterflies he or she collects will compensate for the added difficulty.

This is also good information to convey to parents: When they help their children select books at the library or the bookstore, they should not steer the children to books at the same level as the textbooks they are using in the classroom. Children's independent reading should be done at a level at which they are very comfortable, reading for enjoyment and not struggling with decoding tasks or difficult vocabulary and concepts. Your own recreational reading as an adult is similar: you are likely to read more John Grisham than Marcel Proust.

Language & Diversity

Interpreting IRI Results for Linguistically Diverse Students.   Most assessment strategies used with English speakers will function well in other languages and also in English with English language learners. Some adaptations are indicated, however. For example, one element of evaluating oral reading accuracy in the informal reading inventory is the mispronunciation, each occurrence of which is counted as an oral reading error or miscue. When a mispronunciation error can be attributed to a conflict point with the mother tongue or dialect of English, and when it does not interfere with comprehension, a short *i* pronounced as a long *e*, for example, then an error would not be counted.

Kenneth Johnson (personal communication, 1977) provides a test sentence to illustrate this principle for the African-American child whose mother tongue is African American Vernacular English. The sentence often elicits a mispronunciation that has the potential to interfere with comprehension. The child is asked to read the following sentence aloud: *"As I passed the sign, I read it."* In conformance with African American Vernacular English, the African-American child sometimes pronounces *passed* as *pass*, dropping the -*ed* suffix that is also a past tense marker. If the child comprehends the marker, that is, understands that *passed* is in the past tense even though pronounced as in the present tense, then the child will pronounce *read* in the past tense. If not, the child will pronounce *read* in the present tense. According to Johnson, these children invariably correctly pronounce *read* in the past tense. In a study of teachers who administered IRIs to Spanish-speaking children, Lamberg, Rodriguez, and Tomas (1978) concluded that to avoid such problems, teachers need special training to use them with English language learners.

THE WORLD OF READING

Using the IRI Capacity Level as a Measure of English Language Proficiency

Many commercial instruments for assessing English language proficiency exist. Most examine pronunciation, knowledge of syntax, vocabulary knowledge, and other discrete skills. Because state and federal funds are often involved for qualifying students, English language learners are usually assessed for redesignation as fluent English speakers in a very formalistic and legalistic process. The information gained from this type of assessment is less useful for instructional planning. To teach English language learners to read in English, teachers need to know how well the students comprehend English.

According to Crawford (1982, 2000), teachers can use the reading capacity level, another level that is yielded by informal reading inventory, as a measure of listening comprehension that is a useful reflection of English language proficiency. They can use the IRI to make an informed decision about readiness for English language reading instruction in given materials by reading a selected passage aloud to the child. Crawford reported that children who read in the mother tongue and also respond correctly to 75 percent of comprehension-level questions about the material read to them in English usually have sufficient

second language proficiency to begin learning to read at the highest level at which they successfully respond to those questions.

For example, a second-grade teacher who believes that an English language learner might be ready for formal English reading instruction would read a passage of 100–200 words aloud to the child from the second grade text used for teaching English reading in the classroom. Children who can respond correctly to three of four comprehension level (not recall) questions about the text in English when it is read to them are providing evidence that they are ready to begin formal reading instruction in English at the second grade level. This level is described as one of Cognitive Academic Language Proficiency (CALP), which is explained further in Chapter 12. For those children learning to read in their mother tongue in a bilingual program, this is often at or near the grade level at which they are reading in that mother tongue. They will need all of the scaffolding support that is described in this chapter. The levels of their English vocabulary and syntax will in no way correspond to those of children who have been communicating in English since birth.

Sources of IRIs. Many major publishers of reading textbooks provide IRIs that are designed to accompany their programs. Schools generally purchase only one set of IRIs for each grade level when they contract for a new reading program, and you might have to ask around among other teachers on your grade level to find out who has them. In other schools, they might be in one of the administrative offices.

There are also commercial IRIs—including those of Burns (1999), Silvaroli and Wheelock (2000), and Stieglitz (2001)—available from a number of publishers. Finally, many teachers prepare their own IRIs, a process described for Spanish in Chapter 12 that can also be used in English. All of these are appropriate sources of IRIs to use in the classroom. It is important to ensure that the IRI that is selected has not been so overused in the school that the children have read the passages on many previous occasions and therefore can read them from memory and answer the questions even before they are asked.

OTHER INFORMAL MEASURES OF READING AND WRITING. As you saw in Chapter 9, there are many informal measures that teachers can use to assess their students' progress through the developmental processes of learning to read and write. Chantell DeLaney, the teacher in the chapter-opening vignette, uses many of these measures daily. Although she makes effective use of the informal reading inventory on a periodic basis for all students, and when needed for individual students, she can observe the frustration level in her students' physical behaviors, as described above. She might note that some children rarely participate in discussion activities after silent reading, even with the support of the many scaffolding activities she provides. She takes careful notes about these observations and uses them in planning future instruction.

Each student in Ms. DeLaney's classroom has a portfolio of writing products. She urges them to add a sample of writing to their portfolios from their work each week. This can be used as a motivation tool when students are able to observe their progress as they page through the portfolio, week after week. It is also a valuable tool for use in parent conferences to document for parents their children's progress.

Formal Assessment

In most schools, one of the rites of spring is annual achievement testing. In these days of high-stakes testing, the results of these tests often have consequences in terms of children's academic prospects, school budgets, future curriculum planning, and even personnel changes within schools or districts. In short, they have become very, very important. In some schools, the curriculum has become focused on raising test scores at all costs; all instruction is directed at this end. Aspects of the curriculum that are not directly related to testing outcomes, such as science, social studies, art, and music are sometimes eliminated from the curriculum.

Normed referenced achievement tests permit schools and school districts to make comparisons of the reading performance of their children to those on a national level. Children often spend weeks practicing exercises presented in the format of these tests, usually multiple-choice items of word meaning and paragraph meaning. Unfortunately, the results of such tests are not very useful in making instructional decisions about individual students. They are designed for assessing groups of students, not individual students. Possible test items might be as follows:

Word meaning (Circle the best answer):

After winning the grand prize of one thousand dollars, Emily was

a. sad   X **b.** ecstatic   **c.** pleased   **d.** bored

Paragraph meaning (Read the paragraph and select the best answer to the question):

Once upon a time there was a hunter and his wife who lived very well. Then a son was born to them. One day the hunter caught a baby fox and brought it home to his son as a gift. The little fox was very quick and smart. The boy liked him very much. His mother often left the boy and the fox together and went to help her husband. When she returned, the little fox would run to meet her. One day she returned home at noon. She was surprised because the little fox did not come to greet her.

What problem did the hunter's wife have?
    a. The little boy was quick and smart.
    b. The little boy didn't like the fox.
  X **c.** The fox didn't greet the hunter's wife.
    d. The woman helped her husband

Many states have developed their own competency tests, usually reflecting state standards. These tests enable states to determine whether or not students have met those standards, but not how their students are faring in comparison with comparable students in other states.

Transitioning English Language Learners

Language & Diversity

It is often during grade three that English language learners who have been in a mother tongue bilingual education reading program begin a process of transition to English language reading instruction. This may occur earlier or later for some children, depending on their age when they arrived. When children speak and understand English at an intermediate level and when they are reading confidently in the mother tongue at least at second or third grade level, they are ready to begin a formal transition to English, although they will have had many English language reading experiences before the formal transition. How can teachers help English language learners begin to make the transition into English language reading instruction?

Using the Language Experience Approach in English

In past years, it was commonly held that second language learners should not begin learning to read and write at all in the second language until they had reached an intermediate level of fluency in speaking it. Teachers now recognize that informal processes of reading and writing in the second language can begin early in the English language acquisition process, especially for children who have developed literacy skills in the mother tongue. This early reading instruction is informal and incidental; it is not a formal English reading program. In addition, this incidental instruction should not be substituted for mother tongue instruction when it is possible to provide it.

Bilingual teachers who teach reading in the mother tongue recognize that children's motivation to begin reading and writing in the English language is strong. Although it has already been noted that, where possible, it is most beneficial for children to learn to read and write first in the mother tongue, teachers can begin a cautious, early introduction to literacy in a second language to take advantage of that motivation. Although used mostly with young children, the language experience approach (LEA) can also be used in grades beyond second grade when children are just beginning to learn to read in English or when older preliterate children need more time at the earliest stages of English reading, especially if they are unable to read in the mother tongue. Some migrant children or the children of refugees might never have been in school, even though they are ten or twelve years of age or older.

As was noted in Chapter 5, the language experience approach (Crawford, Allen, & Hall, 1995) for teaching reading and writing is an approach in which a small group of children or an individual child and a teacher talk about an idea or topic, such as a favorite story or another topic of interest. Children express their own ideas to the teacher, who writes them down sentence by sentence to use as reading text. With support from the teacher in a shared reading process, the children read the text many times. After many exposures to the text, children begin to recognize words that are used over and over in the dictated material; soon, they are able to read those words in other materials, as well. Children also begin learning to write early in this approach. The level of language is controlled by the students, who dictate text to be written down by the teacher; the teacher is merely the children's "pencil."

TEACH IT!
35

ROOTED IN WHAT IS REAL.   The language experience approach to reading works well because it is based on the children's oral language, because children understand what they are reading, and because the ideas and language are their own. It is more interesting because they read about real ideas, not artificial syllables, leading English language learners to quick and early success in reading with this approach. One way to reinforce for English language learners the concept that we read for meaning, not only for correct pronunciation, is to have them read aloud from LEA charts in different voices. Ask one child to read the chart in an angry voice, another in a happy voice, and another in a questioning voice.

As children dictate text for the teacher to record, some will use incorrect syntactical structures and inappropriate vocabulary. There is some controversy about whether or not teachers should record exactly what the children dictate. Children will most easily learn to read the type of oral language they use. When you correct the language of children as they dictate, it often signifies to the children that you lack respect for them. It is best to write exactly what the children say, especially at the beginning. Again, the teacher is the children's "pencil." But words that are not pronounced correctly should be spelled correctly.

The language experience approach is best captured in an old Chinese proverb, which can be paraphrased as follows:

- What I can think about, I can say.
- What I can say can be written by me or someone else.
- I can read what I can write.
- I can read what other people write for me to read. They can also read what I write.

HELPFUL ACTIVITIES.   There are many LEA activities that can be adapted for English language learners. For example, multiple readings of the text are helpful to them (Crawford et al., 1995). Using a copy of the text with some words left out and with empty spaces where words are missing, children can practice reading the text. This practice is known as an **oral cloze procedure**. Tell the children that some words are missing and ask whether they can predict what should be in the space. Reading the text with the children, the teacher pauses briefly when encountering a missing word, writing in the missing words as the children identify them.

Children may accumulate new words they learn, with these collections serving as their personal word files. After they have fifteen or twenty words, they can do sorting activities with their word files (Bear et al., 2000). Finding words that start with the same letter and sound is a way in which some children learn to associate letters and sounds, allowing them to learn best about letters and sounds from words they already know. They can look for words that are names of people, places, animals, colors, foods, and clothing.

If children are collecting the words they can read, they can try to build sentences with them. You might need to demonstrate before asking them to try it. Read their sentences to them if they cannot read them independently. Children can also try to reconstruct the same sentences they have used in their dictated texts.

One nonthreatening way to elicit text that reflects more mature syntax and vocabulary is an adaptation called the *collaborative chart story*. When children are dictating and beginning to read with confidence later in the process, ask them to negotiate their suggested text with the group. You can invite questions from other children about a suggested sentence, for example, by asking how they feel about the way it is stated and how effectively the vocabulary provided expresses what the group wants to say. When children who have dictated sentences with grammatical errors hear suggestions from

TEACH IT!

1

other children about how it might be said in another way, they invariably agree to the change. The children do not view this collaboration as correction, but rather as reflecting the contributions they all make together in communicating with the audience that will read their text later. It is probably better to accept exactly what is dictated at the beginning of the LEA process so that children can see the direct links among what they say, what you write down, and what the group reads back later.

The language experience approach can be used with students who are learning to read in English as their second language as a way to initiate students into print of interest and relevance to them (Nessel & Jones, 1981; Dixon & Nessel, 1983; Moustafa & Penrose, 1985). According to Crawford (1993), the language experience approach also provides a means through which students can experience authentic literature in English that is above their ability to read and comprehend for themselves. After you tell or read a story aloud, the students can then dictate the story back, that is, retell it for you to record, although probably in a less complicated version than the original.

What can you do to help your ESL students to make the transition to English-language reading instruction?

Beginning a language experience approach activity with a piece of authentic literature will often result in a better structured dictation than the random list of sentences that often results from LEA dictations stimulated by an illustration, a manipulative, or other prompts. Peck (1989) suggests that listening to read-aloud stories helps children to develop a sense of story structure, which should be reflected in their dictated version, and it enhances their abilities to predict in this and other stories. The dictated text allows children to think, talk, read, and write about the piece of literature and to be exposed to its valuable cultural content. At the same time, they are actively interacting with it at a level of comprehension and of second language proficiency appropriate for their stage of development.

Vocabulary Development

Reading is also a major factor in the vocabulary development of English language learners. Second language acquisition and literacy in English can contribute mutually to each other's development for intermediate English language learners. In keeping with a meaning-based approach to teaching English language learners, Harmon (1998) provides an excellent contextualized strategy for vocabulary development. She provides two examples of how a teacher uses a new term and then elaborates and expands its meaning immediately:

> "Let's start <u>recounting</u> the events of the story. <u>Let's tell about the beginning, middle, and end.</u>"

> "This is an <u>excerpt—a small part.</u>"

In another strategy described by Nagy and colleagues (1993) and by Cummins and Corson (1997), Spanish-speaking students can use cognates they recognize from

Spanish and English to support their reading comprehension in English. Words such as *general* are the same in spelling and meaning in both languages, and many other cognates are the same in meaning and similar in spelling, such as an example provided by Nagy and colleagues: *transform* in English and *transformar* in Spanish. But looking beyond their study, children must also be taught to be wary of such false cognates as *actual*, which means *nowadays* in Spanish, and *dime*, which means *give me*.

When children read, their lack of vocabulary knowledge is often an obstacle to comprehension. Because they may have insufficient academically related background knowledge and vocabulary development in the mother tongue that would accompany it, this can be an even greater problem for children who must read in their second language. Vocabulary is an aspect of background knowledge in prereading, but it is treated separately here to examine several concepts that relate more specifically to vocabulary.

One aspect of vocabulary development relates to the richness of language that surrounds children. It is well recognized that children become familiar with the meanings of words when those meanings are highly contextualized, not when they are studied in isolation as new vocabulary words. It follows, then, that a richer language environment should result in increased exposure to contextualized vocabulary and therefore to understanding of their meanings (Crawford, 1994b).

Schools often postpone or even eliminate instruction for at-risk children, however, in the very areas of the curriculum where new vocabulary words will be offered in the most highly contextualized ways—in science, social studies, art, music, health, and other areas of the curriculum. This is even more common for children who are learning in their second language. According to Crawford (1993), teachers must ensure that these areas of the curriculum are provided for all children, including English language learners, and that they are presented so that contextualized exposure to a rich vocabulary is promoted.

Another aspect of vocabulary is the issue of direct instruction. Although many vocabulary words will be acquired incidentally, some literature or content selections will contain a few vocabulary words that must be clearly grasped if the text is to be understood. There will be other words not known to the children that need not be addressed through direct instruction because they are not critical to understanding the selection or because they can be quickly analyzed through the context in which they appear.

Many of the strategies recommended for the activation or development of background knowledge constitute direct approaches to vocabulary instruction. Semantic mapping is one of these strategies, but its application should be limited to those key and conceptually difficult vocabulary terms that are more in the realm of background knowledge. Otherwise, there will be little time left for reading following the completion of anticipatory activities before reading.

Adapting Phonics and Decoding Strategies for English Language Learners

English language learners bring to the classroom phonemic awareness of sounds in the mother tongue. They should first learn phonics in the mother tongue out of the context of words they already recognize on sight, probably learned from their print environment and from language experience charts and big books. English language learners who learn phonics in the mother tongue generally have a much easier time learning phonics in English than do children who must learn phonics first in English.

**Phonics &
Phonemic
Awareness**

Some languages, such as Spanish and Korean, are very regular in their sound/letter relationships. Not only is phonics easier to learn, but children have more confidence in the process than do children who are learning to read in a language in which sound/letter relationships are not regular, such as English.

The language experience approach and shared reading are holistic strategies for teaching reading. In these strategies, teachers do not begin with phonics. But learning about letters and sounds (phonics) is a part of learning to read in all methods, including these. In a developmental approach to teaching about letters and sounds, children should learn about reading first. They should dictate many LEA charts and read them, learning to read some 100–200 words on sight. They should have many shared book reading experiences, and then they are ready to learn about letters and sounds using words they already know in English.

The real dilemma for English language learners is when they must learn phonics in English first. Although they might have learned to speak and understand English, they still lack the phonemic awareness skills in English of a native speaker. For example, a native Spanish-speaking child will speak the forty-three sounds of English using the twenty-five sounds of Spanish. There are only five vowel sounds in Spanish, but fifteen in English. This accounts for the difficulty that Spanish-speaking children have in pronouncing short vowels in English, especially the schwa; they have similar difficulty in "reading" (correctly pronouncing) these sounds in a phonetic approach to reading. Although there are variations in the differences between other languages and English, similar difficulties arise for children who speak those languages. However, for children who learn phonics in their mother tongue, the process of learning English phonics is much easier because they have already figured out how the process works. The process transfers from the mother tongue, even if many of the sounds do not.

Finally, Sleeter and Grant (1999) remind teachers that they need to distinguish between mechanics and meaning when teaching students whose mother tongue is not English or standard American English. They concluded that teachers should not be bogged down in remediation whenever they encounter gaps in student learning that relate more to mechanics than to understanding.

Writing and Spelling

Writing &
Reading

A major principle of a developmental view of literacy is the interdependence of listening, speaking, reading, and writing. Hudelson (1984) observed that English language learners address the four language processes as a totality, not as separate entities. According to Fitzgerald (1993), writing begins when children can draw, and there is no need to wait for reading. These ideas can be extended to English language learners, who should be encouraged to write in the second language early, especially if they have writing skills in their mother tongue. The errors they make should be viewed in the same way that errors in oral production are viewed: as a part of the natural processes of approximation and acquisition (Crawford, 1994).

For English language learners, writing can flow out of a variety of language acquisition activities, including the key vocabulary and language experience approaches to reading and the consolidation strategy of written retellings after reading text. The structuring of their writing or their selection of vocabulary may be further supported through the use of semantic maps.

Spelling is another area in which instructional strategies must be adapted for English language learners. Consistent with the communicative approach principle of minimizing error correction and with the developmental nature of second language acquisition and literacy, described in Chapter 12, teachers of English language learners, like teachers of English speakers, should accept the invented spellings of their children as a very natural aspect of their developmental growth in writing. There are differences, however, in how English language learners will progress through some of the developmental stages of invented spelling.

In the letter name–alphabetic spelling stage of Bear et al. (2000), English language learners begin to approximate an alphabetic orthography and to conceptualize the alphabetic principle (see Chapter 3). They begin to demonstrate the relationship between sound and letter, and they sometimes use letter names as words. They begin to understand the left-to-right convention, and they may begin to segment words. Differences in the nature of invented spelling between languages will appear. The use of consonants tends to predominate over the use of vowels when children write in English as a mother tongue, for example, but vowels predominate over consonants when children write in Spanish as a mother tongue (Ferreiro & Rodríguez, 1994).

In the within-word pattern spelling stage of Bear and colleagues (2000), children have learned most basic rules of the orthographic system. They are aware of such word structures as prefixes, suffixes, contractions, compound words, and homonyms, and they continue to learn some less common spelling patterns and rules. It is at this stage that they begin to recognize when a word *looks* correct, a phenomenon that corresponds to the natural approach characteristic in which second language learners begin to recognize when something *sounds* right or *feels* right. They are able to spell a large number of words automatically.

English language learners who are literate in another language will tend to move much more rapidly through developmental stages of spelling in their new second language of English than they did in their primary language. Nathenson-Mejia (1989) found that in their English writing, Spanish-speaking children in the beginning stages of English spelling made extensive use of Spanish pronunciation in their invented spellings in English. Edelsky (1982) made the same observation in a more generic sense. She adopted the positive point of view that children are applying some mother tongue writing skills to the second language rather than the negative point of view that it reflected interference from the first language on the second.

Scaffolding Strategies for Improving Reading Comprehension

Your own experiences in learning another language might remind you of the importance of reading for comprehension as opposed to word calling. Remember that comprehension and communication are the focus of reading and writing. There are many reading strategies that will help to ensure that children focus on comprehension instead of only on correct pronunciation.

The use of scaffolding strategies to support the comprehension of children in general is of great importance; but for English language learners, it is the difference between success and failure (Crawford, 1994a). Some English language learners have tended to be placed in perpetual compensatory or remedial programs in which teachers expect them to learn to read and write by acquiring isolated skills through interaction with incomplete fragments of language. These children rarely move successfully into the mainstream curriculum; more frequently, they leave these programs only when they complete their schooling—all too often as dropouts. Scaffolding strategies sometimes resemble most closely the enrichment activities that teachers of English language learners sometimes never have time for because they are busy teaching the isolated skills that the children seem to lack. Variations of two common comprehension strategies are especially effective in working with English language learners.

THE CUMULATIVE SEMANTIC MAP.   Ordinarily, a semantic map is used for activating background knowledge or introducing vocabulary as an anticipatory activity before reading. It is developed and completed for one or two related lessons and is not referred to subsequently. Teachers often find, however, that they are dealing with some language topics on repeated occasions. Therefore, it can be useful to return to a semantic map on such a topic, to add to it, and to contrast new additions with earlier ones. Crawford has identified this semantic mapping strategy as the **cumulative semantic map** (Crawford, 1994a).

    Figure 10.3 shows a cumulative semantic map on the theme of feelings and emotions that has been augmented periodically during the first few weeks of school (Crawford, 2000). A teacher might introduce the new word *furious* from a piece of literature they are about to read and ask children where it should be added to the existing cumulative semantic map for words about feelings and emotions. At that point,

TEACH IT!

36

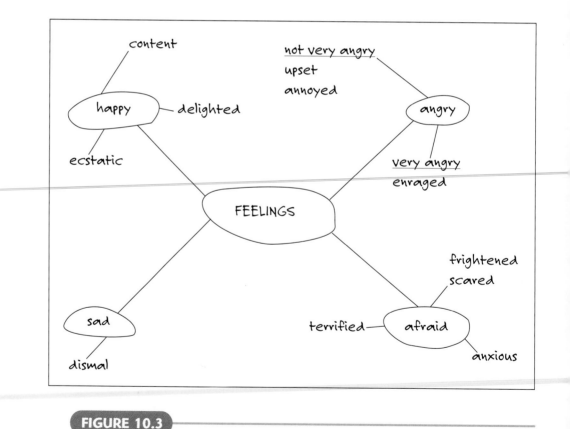

FIGURE 10.3

A Cumulative Semantic Map.

the children can discuss how much anger the word *furious* implies, as compared to *miffed, enraged,* and *upset,* which had been added to the semantic map on earlier occasions. They add the new word *furious* to their cumulative semantic map. Many weeks later, the map has been elaborated, as seen in Figure 10.4, and, of course, this process continues through the school year.

When written on self-stick notes, the various words in a cumulative semantic map can be arranged and rearranged in ascending order of increasing anger as children negotiate the meanings with each other. Moustafa (1997) suggests placing words on cards for charts with cellophane tape across the top. The teacher can use the same piece of tape over and over by affixing the cards to a large wall chart made of plastic shower curtain material. This strategy can be adapted to the cumulative semantic map, which facilitates the moving of words from one place to another on the chart or in making room for a new word to be added.

In a writing assignment perhaps several months later, English language learners might refer back to the cumulative semantic map on the wall when they want to select just the right word to convey the degree of anger they have in mind (Crawford, 1994). Discussing the choice of word with the teacher or with other children will be particularly helpful. When children are ready to add yet another synonym for *angry* a week or a month later, they will have the opportunity to review other words or expressions for

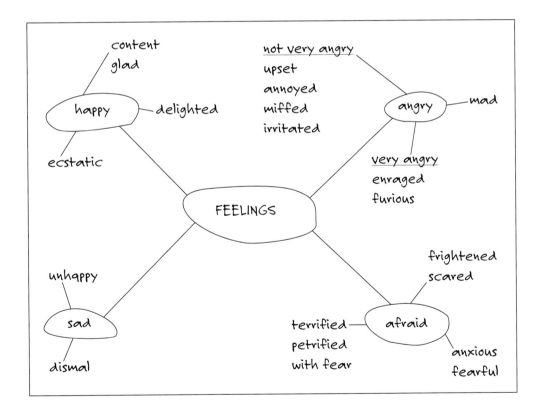

FIGURE 10.4

An Elaborated Cumulative Semantic Map.

the same feeling but within a context of known or somewhat familiar vocabulary. Teachers can view a well-developed cumulative semantic map as a "graphic thesaurus." Other suitable topics for cumulative semantic maps might include *see* (stare, peek, glare, etc.), *motion* (crawl, creep, dawdle, dash, poke along, lope, etc.), and *touch* (poke, tap, jab, stroke, etc.). Only the topics come from the teacher; the source of vocabulary is the literature the children are reading.

If your classroom has a word wall, this might be the place to attach several cumulative semantic maps that are used frequently. If there are so many that they do not all fit, several might be mounted on top of each other on the wall or an easel with a way of folding them up so that the one in use during a lesson is visible. At the end of the school year, you might consider passing the cumulative semantic maps on to the children's teacher for the next grade, especially if most of the class will move to the new classroom intact as a group. Many teachers also save the children's portfolios for the children to pick up when they start the next school year. The children can take their portfolios to their new classroom and use them to introduce themselves to the new teacher.

READ-ALOUD ACTIVITIES.   English language learners often benefit from read-aloud activities by the teacher, followed by discussion. Vocabulary is presented in context, and someone in the group will likely have some knowledge of most words. Other words may be analyzed by reviewing the illustrations in a story or an appropriate illustration, manipulative, or visual aid provided by the teacher. Because illustrations provide important visual information, paging through a selection and discussing the illustrations before reading provides an opportunity for presenting new vocabulary and for making predictions about the text.

Occasionally, you might find that presenting the entire selection as a read-aloud is needed before English language learners read themselves, especially in a particularly challenging piece. When a parallel version of a text is available in the children's mother tongue, you might choose to read it aloud before the children read later in the second language. Children in school are not bored or disturbed by several exposures to the same literature selection. The familiarity of a story that is an old friend becomes a real comfort. Familiarity with the background knowledge and structure of a story permits children to read with better comprehension and with fewer time-consuming visual cues, especially for children's early literacy experiences in English. The read-aloud activity also provides the teacher with the opportunity to demonstrate and model predicting, thinking about context, and other metacognitive strategies in a think-aloud during the teacher's oral reading.

Grouping Decisions

Grouping children for instruction is a tricky proposition. Some advocate for teaching the entire class at one time, a strategy that is very effective in some areas of the curriculum. For example, placing students in small groups according to individual needs is not a common practice in the areas of science, social science, art, and music.

Whole-Class Instruction

When instruction in reading is consistently conducted with the whole class, it is often characteristic of highly scripted and sequenced direct instruction reading programs. This use of this type of approach implies that all children are the same and that a one-size-fits-all program is adequate for all. In reality, this means that every time a lesson is taught, it is just right for some children, too difficult for children who were unsuccessful in earlier lessons and did not attain prerequisite skills, and repetitious and boring for children who mastered the material weeks, months, or years before. Instruction should be planned to meet individual needs. This does not imply a separate lesson for each individual child, but it does permit children with similar strengths or needs to be grouped together for appropriate instruction. There are some reading activities that can be conducted with the entire class, such as a review of how to avoid run-on sentences in writing when almost all children show the need, teacher read-aloud activities, library visits, using a video of a story, conducting a poetry hour, and readers' theater (Burns, Roe, & Ross, 1999).

Grouping: Why and Why Not?

Schools are sometimes tempted to group students homogeneously by reading ability on a classroom basis across an entire school. If there are five fourth grade classes, why not place the students who are nonreaders in one classroom, those reading at grade level in another, those above grade level in yet another, and so on? The assumption is that each teacher will need to plan only a single reading lesson for the entire class. Teachers need to recognize that one result will often be racial, linguistic, and gender isolation. Another outcome is the classroom at each grade level with the lowest achieving children—twenty-five of thirty children are likely to be boys, and many of them will display behavior problems. English language learners often end up in the same class, despite their need to associate with native English speakers.

When all of these children with important needs are placed in the same classroom, the challenges for the teacher are extreme. The management of behavior in this classroom requires the most able and experienced teacher in the school, but all too often, this class is assigned to the newest teacher. The results can be negative attitudes, low self-esteem, and continuing low achievement. The classroom with the highest achievers will tend to have a preponderance of girls, along with much of the student leadership potential on the grade level. Although this classroom might seem to be an attractive assignment for most teachers, it is also a challenge.

There is really no such thing as a homogeneous group. Even children who have similar levels of achievement at the beginning of the school year will be very different from each other after a few months of instruction in which some gain more than others. In addition, teaching a reading lesson to a classroom-size group might not be the most effective way to provide effective instruction to them. If twenty children in a classroom are really reading at the same level and have similar strengths and needs, most experienced teachers would divide them into two groups and teach similar lessons to each smaller group in order to maximize individual attention.

In many countries, children are promoted from one grade to the next on the basis of their achievement, not their age. The tradition in the United States has been to promote on the basis of age because of research that indicates that children do not benefit from being held back (Wheelock & Dorman, 1988). According to the Texas Education Agency (1996), being older than other students in your grade is a better predictor of future dropping out than underachievement is. In some states, there have been attempts to hold children back who do not reach a standard for their grade level, but most of these efforts are quickly abandoned when the numbers of children

What are the potential benefits of grouping students for instruction?

retained are much larger than was expected. The result is that children are usually grouped for instruction in reading in order to better address their different needs.

Grouping is most common in reading and mathematics. The higher the grade level, the greater is the need for grouping children as some fall behind and others forge ahead. In a first-grade classroom, as you have seen, most children are not reading, they are reading some, or they are reading well at a first-grade level. But in a fifth-grade classroom, the children might range from those not reading at all to some reading at a college level. Those who are not reading at all will tend to be children with severe reading disabilities or occasionally immigrant children without school experience or with very limited school experience.

Grouping children within the classroom can also have negative consequences. It does not matter what names the groups have; the children recognize that there are high groups and low groups, and they know which group they are in. This sends an unmistakable message to children in the "low" group. These expectations often become a self-fulfilling prophecy. Children in the "low" group in the first grade are all too often still there in the fifth grade.

Grouping Students without Tracking

The dilemma is how to meet individual cognitive and affective needs while avoiding the negative effects that can result from grouping by ability. Children need to receive reading instruction at their instructional levels, and so teachers must form groups that permit children to read at levels where they will be successful, interested, and engaged. Some fifth graders will be learning beginning reading concepts in the language experience approach, and some in the same classroom will be reading and enjoying Shakespeare. It is difficult to put children from these two levels together when they are in guided reading lessons. There are two possible solutions to the dilemma, and they can be used at the same time: non-ability-based groups and dynamic groups.

GROUPS NOT BASED ON ABILITY AND ACHIEVEMENT.   The interest group is a grouping structure that is not based on ability and achievement—perhaps a group of children who are interested in fairy tales. They can all read fairy tales, even the same fairy tale in the same lesson, but from books written at different levels or from the same book but with different levels of teacher support. This allows students who are working at a lower level to work with students reading at higher levels from time to time so that they are able to say, "Sometimes I am in the same reading group as Janie." Interest groups might meet one day a week instead of every day, and they might meet for a month before dissolving so that students can form new and different interest groups. Fountas and Pinnell (1996) add other structures in order to introduce flexibility, including peer tutoring, cooperative learning pairs, and cross-grade buddies. In literature circles, children who have decided to read the same book, poem, or other text compare and share ideas about what they have read (Daniels, 1994).

Struggling Reader

DYNAMIC GROUPING.   One other accommodation serves to loosen up the rigidity of grouping by achievement. Occasionally, the teacher should recognize that certain students need to work with a reading group other than their own for specific reasons. A bright but troubled and struggling reader might advance to a higher ability group to read a story for three days because the story will be of great interest to the student and because the student has much background knowledge about it. An otherwise high-achieving reader who has trouble decoding words with prefixes might join a lower-achieving group that happens to be working on that specific skill for a few days.

The ability grouping in Chantell DeLaney's third-grade classroom is what Fountas and Pinnell (1996, 2001) refer to as dynamic grouping, bringing students together for a period of time when, and for as long as, they have abilities and needs in common. The most capable readers, reading at fourth- and fifth-grade levels in Ms. DeLaney's classroom, occasionally joined the group working at the third-grade level, perhaps to learn or practice a needed word recognition skill or comprehension strategy. Often, however, they are working in individualized reading and on projects of interest, periodically meeting with Ms. DeLaney as a small group or conferencing with her.

Organizing and Managing a Learning Community

The lesson in the chapter-opening vignette seemed relatively simple and straightforward, but, of course, Ms. DeLaney doesn't just come in each morning and begin teaching. She has planned activities for students who are not working directly with her as she teaches small groups, she has arranged the furniture in the classroom, she has carefully selected instructional materials, she has scheduled precious instructional time, and she has made decisions about how to assess the outcomes of her teaching for the day.

Children's Identity and Motivation

In Ms. DeLaney's lesson on *Little Red Riding Hood*, the focus was only on the group of children she was teaching. Over the period of a week, an observer in Ms. DeLaney's classroom sees a very complicated structure. She is usually working with one of several groups while the other two groups complete independent work, read trade books from the classroom library, write letters for the classroom postal system, work on projects in which reading and writing activities are integrated across the curriculum, use the classroom computers, and work in learning centers. There is much movement of students between groups, orchestrated by Ms. DeLaney as she assesses needs and asks students to join groups for a single lesson, a week, or even a month for activities to meet those needs.

A very important part of her planning involved the other two groups that were working independently while she was teaching the lesson to this group. The other large group that reads slightly below grade level needed much guidance and supervision. They had an independent assignment from the previous day's lesson to complete, but she also had learning centers that they could work in and a large variety of trade books at many levels for them to read. The group that was reading above the third-grade level required less direct supervision. Many of them were working on independent projects from social studies and science, and they were also deeply engrossed in library books that they were reading independently.

During Ms. DeLaney's guided reading lesson, there were intervals in which the children read silently for a few minutes. Ms. DeLaney took advantage of their focus and walked around the classroom to help children with questions. They knew that she would come around during the lesson and that they should not interrupt the group's work. In addition, she used her walks as a preventive classroom behavior management strategy, settling down children who were noisy or off task. But she always did this with a touch on the shoulder, a gentle tug on a pigtail, or a smile that said, "I caught you—back to work now." By the time the lesson group had finished the chunk they were reading, after just a minute or two, Ms. DeLaney was back with the group and seated, ready to continue with them until they read the next chunk of text.

On alternate Fridays, the children participate in an individualized reading program based on the many books Ms. DeLaney has accumulated for her extensive classroom library. They range from large-format picture books and simple stories to novels and nonfiction materials at upper grade and secondary levels. Self-selected silent sustained reading (SSR) characterizes the Friday program. As a good model for the children, Ms. DeLaney demonstrates how she reads for her own pleasure during part of the reading period, but she also spends much of her time conferencing with individual children about what they have been reading and encouraging them.

Managing Students and the Classroom for Learning

One important set of decisions for teachers in grades three through five concerns how to set up the classroom for instruction in reading and other subject areas. There are some elements that are inflexible, such as the positions of doors, windows, chalkboards, fixed cabinets, computer network connections, and the sink. But other elements will indicate much about the philosophy of the program. Think about the difference between two university classrooms: one with chairs set up in straight rows facing the front, where a podium has been placed for the instructor, and another where there are round tables with chairs around them and no podium or front to the classroom.

One possible middle-grade classroom arrangement for reading/language arts instruction and also instruction in other areas of the curriculum would include the following:

- A U-shaped or kidney-shaped table for small-group lessons, with the teacher seated with back to the wall to be able to observe the entire classroom while teaching
- Movable individual children's desks that can be quickly and quietly rearranged when groups or activities change (two-student desks are only slightly less convenient)
- A library center with numerous trade books at many levels and places to sit, such as cushions on the floor, pillows in an old bathtub (for reading only), or a sofa (check the fire regulations.)
- A computer center with at least two or three computers in the classroom
- The author's chair (Hanson & Graves, 1983), a very special chair in which children sit only when sharing their writing with others

- Other learning centers for individual or paired work, such as science, writing, or mathematics, with task cards that require children to read, write, and discuss
- A word wall above the writing center
- A listening center with earphones and a player for audiotapes, videotapes, and/or CD-ROMs
- Easels that can be moved from place to place, even for grades three to five

Most teachers find it necessary to control or limit access to learning centers, which can often disrupt lessons. This can be done by doing the following:

- Limiting the number of students who can work in a center at the same time
- Limiting the amount of time each student can work in each center
- Assigning centers every day, with children rotating each day to a different one.
- Occasionally informing children who misbehave when together that they cannot work in a center at the same time until they demonstrate more maturity

All of these controls have negative effects on children's spontaneity and their interests. Most teachers find that they can relax and even eliminate these controls over time, but they are very helpful early in the school year.

Selecting Appropriate Materials

There is a big difference between text used to teach reading at the primary-grade levels and at the fifth-grade level. It is partly in the quantity; fifth-grade students will be able to read more text during a reading lesson than primary-grade students will, but the difficulty of the material is also a major factor. It is easy to observe that text in basal readers at the third-grade level has fewer difficult words and complex sentences than text has at the fifth-grade level. There is a difference between text included in basal readers and that in authentic literature. The biggest difference between authentic literature and basal reader stories or so-called decodable text is the variety of vocabulary that skilled authors use when they select the precise word needed to best express an idea. This increases the difficulty of the text but also the interest levels of the students (Crawford, 2000).

LEVELED BOOKS.   After the teacher determines student reading levels using an informal reading inventory, it is then helpful to be able to identify the levels of textbooks and especially of trade books so that they can be matched to the children's levels. Many thousands of children's trade books have been leveled for the text gradient, a measure of text difficulty developed as a part of the reading recovery program (Fountas & Pinnell, 2001).

According to Fountas and Pinnell (2001), text difficulty is a function of the following factors:

- Book and print features, such as length, print, layout, illustrations, graphic features, and organizational aids
- Themes and ideas, such as interest, sophistication, and maturity
- Language and literary features, such as literary and figurative language and dialogue

- Vocabulary, such as multisyllabic words and content-related words
- Sentence complexity, including length, embedded clauses, and punctuation
- Content, including topics, organization, and special graphic features
- Text structure, including fiction (narrative, literary devices such as flashbacks) and nonfiction (compare and contrast, cause and effect, description, temporal sequence, and problem/solution)

The resulting text gradient ranges from A (kindergarten) through Z (grades seven and eight). Grade-level ranges for typical children are assigned to each letter, which allows teachers to select books that are in the so-called Goldilocks range—not too difficult, not too easy, but just right. They are also within Vygotsky's zone of proximal development. Fountas and Pinnell provide lists of thousands of leveled books in their many publications (Fountas & Pinnell, 1996, 1999, 2001; Pinnell & Fountas, 2001).

Technology

USING TECHNOLOGY IN GRADES THREE TO FIVE. Technology has the potential for creating many changes in the teaching of reading and language arts, some positive and some perhaps negative. You need to keep in mind, however, that the promise of instructional television and language laboratories to transform teaching never was realized (Griffith & Lynch-Brown, 2002). Possible roles for technology in grades three to five will be examined in two dimensions: reading and writing.

In Reading. In the area of web text reading, as contrasted to print text reading, Sutherland-Smith (2002) reported that students needed to use different reading strategies to acquire meaning from the two sources. She based this on student comments about the need to work fast on the Internet, in contrast to a more leisurely style of reading from books. She found that web text reading was less linear, less hierarchical, and less sequential than print text reading. It was more interactive, allowing the reader to add, change, or move text, blurring the relationship between reader and writer. She described several strategies to help students in their web text reading, all of which support the inquiry-based technology strategies already offered in Chapter 6:

- Encourage "snatch-and-grab" reading, scanning or reading superficially to find pertinent information and returning to it later if it survived the culling needed when large quantities of information are found
- Help students to focus on finding key words for searches as an important skill
- Encourage students to refine or delimit their problem or question so that they are not overwhelmed with the amount of information they encounter
- Provide "sure-thing" links to students for their initial forays into the Internet
- Help students to differentiate between informative text and impressive visual images that might offer little information

In Writing. A very effective use of technology in teaching writing in grades three to five is in the area of word processing. There are several word processors that are designed for children, including *The Amazing Writing Machine* from

Computers can serve a number of purposes in the classroom. What do you think is the most common use of technology in the literacy classroom?

Writing & Reading

Broderbund and *The Student Writing Center for Windows* and the *Children's Publishing Center* from the Learning Company. In addition, *Bank Street Writer III* is a program that has been available in various versions for both Windows and Apple platforms for many years. Many teachers find that they can use Microsoft *Word* or the more simple word-processing program included in Microsoft *Works* with children, teaching only the aspects of these complex programs that are needed for their writing. The appearance of the screen can be simplified by suppressing some of the toolbars and reducing the numbers of functions in those that remain to what is necessary for that grade level.

Finally, Wood (2000) has developed many interesting activities that incorporate the use of technology into the writing process:

- Use the web to publish student work; it is very exciting for children to see the results of their writing published on the Internet, perhaps with digital photos they have taken
- Initiate email exchanges between children in which they write to each other about topics of common interest; Wood provides an example of two boys comparing Quidditch teams (from the Harry Potter books) they have organized (in their imaginations), whose members are well-known American professional basketball players
- Help children to establish their writing portfolios on their personal or class web page
- Encourage children to develop their own writer's voice. They might even want to pretend to be someone else in order to write in a new voice

Involving Family and Community

Adults other than teachers play major roles at home and at school in supporting literacy instruction, even in the middle grades.

At Home

Authentic environmental print is a valuable resource that teachers can exploit in the home. Purcell-Gates, L'Allier, and Smith (1995) provide valuable print-embedded family literacy activities that are especially useful for children in grades three to five because they are authentic. Among them are the following:

- Daily living routines, such as shopping lists, reading recipes, and cooking together
- Entertainment, such as reading novels, storybooks, or television program descriptions
- School-related activity, such as homework or school assignments
- Interpersonal communication, such as notes on the refrigerator, email
- Religion, including reading stories from the Bible, the Torah, the Koran, and other religious books treasured by the family
- Participating in information networks, such as sharing scores of sporting events, news of interest, and reactions to new films
- Work-related tasks, such as reading instructions, pay stub information, and catalogues

Teachers often give students a consolidation or application activity to complete at home after their daily reading lesson. This activity often involves reading aloud to parents, siblings, or others who live in the home. When students are asked to read aloud, they should read something they have already read and practiced in the classroom. If they are to read something new, it should ordinarily be at their independent level, not at the instructional level. When children struggle with reading aloud, potentially a very positive experience and one the teacher wants the child to have, it can turn into a negative experience with a well-meaning parent who tries to help by criticizing or by teaching a phonics lesson.

Similarly, the teacher might send the parents a note asking them to listen to the child read for ten minutes from an assigned book. The parent wants to do more and asks the child to read for thirty minutes from a more difficult book. Again, the well-meaning parent is trying to help the child, but fails to understand the importance of following the teacher's directions carefully.

Parents also often ask teachers for advice about buying books for their children. It is most helpful if teachers can recommend specific books, but be careful to recommend books at the child's independent level; the child will seldom have someone at home to provide the scaffolding that is needed to maintain comprehension and motivation. If motivation is high, then a child might struggle and read successfully at a higher level—for example, the child who receives a computer and a book about how to use it.

At School

The presence of other adults in the classroom can be an important asset. Teacher assistants or instructional aides are paid paraprofessionals who may work all day or part of a day to support the teacher. They might range from a minimally educated community resident to a university student who is ready for student teaching. Paraprofessionals are particularly important in working with English language learners.

Another source of adult support in the classroom is the parent volunteer, who might also be a grandparent or other extended family member or caregiver. Tinajero and Nagel (1975) suggest that you need only invite participation. They recommend that you ensure in advance that parents have the needed skills to accomplish assigned tasks and that the activities you request are culturally appropriate. You might find it helpful to demonstrate for adult volunteers so that their roles are clear. Adult volunteers can make many important contributions, including sharing information in oral discussions; tutoring; participating in journal activities by responding to children's entries; reading aloud to students, including in the mother tongue other than English, where appropriate; helping with homework assignments in after-school study; storytelling; and sharing life events, personal oral histories, and job experiences.

FOR REVIEW

The reading program for most children changes as they proceed through the grades, with more emphasis on reading comprehension, silent reading, reading in the content areas of the curriculum, and writing in grades three through five. There is still attention to phonics and other aspects of word recognition, but it occupies less time than it does in the primary grades. Developing fluency and automaticity may still receive some attention in the third grade.

The organizational structures for teaching reading are based on the framework from Chapter 1 that includes demonstration and immersion, attention to details, guided practice, and application and extension. Teachers can use three typical stages of reading lessons for planning that reflects this framework: anticipatory reading activities to build interest and connect students to background knowledge, reading activities to build knowledge through scaffolding students' reading and comprehension of text, and consolidation reading activities where students apply new knowledge and have opportunities for writing. These stages are supplemented with minilessons focused on word study or another specific skill that usually have emerged from the text to be read in the lesson. Long-term planning can be systematized with thematic literature units that are often integrated with science and social studies instruction, even including critical literacy.

There is more variation in the reading levels of students in the middle grades than in the primary grades, and the need for grouping for instruction arises. Most useful is dynamic grouping that is flexible and that includes multiple structures for instruction, including small ability groups, interest groups, buddy reading and cooperative learning pairs, peer tutoring, occasional whole-class instruction, and the frequent formation of temporary focused groups to address common weaknesses of students from all ability levels.

The informal reading inventory (IRI) is an important informal assessment tool for identifying students' reading levels. It should ordinarily be administered during the first week or two of school and then, as needed for individual students whose achievement changes, periodically through the school year. Formal assessment usually takes the form of standardized or normed reading achievement tests, whose results are interesting for school and district level decision-making, although less so for instructional decisions about individual students.

Most English language learners who have learned to read in the mother tongue are by now able to understand and speak English at an intermediate level. They are also often ready to begin a transition to English language reading in the third grade. Many scaffolding and support activities are particularly important for these students as they begin reading in their new second language, English.

You have now seen those students' abilities to understand text vary widely and that students are grouped accordingly for some important comprehension instruction. Teachers must then be able to find textbooks, literature, and trade books that reflect those levels. Many thousands of books have been leveled on a gradient of difficulty, and teachers can quite accurately select books for students for whom they have assessment data. There is a growing role for the effective use of technology in the classroom in the middle grades. Children can do extensive reading on the

Internet, but they must be prepared to deal with the immense amounts of information returned in the typical search. The introduction of new reading skills, such as identifying descriptors and criteria, scanning titles of returned references, and delimiting problems or assignments done on the Internet, will assist in their effectiveness. Children can make effective use of various types of word processors in the writing process at these grade levels.

Adults other than the teacher can make important contributions to students' progress in literacy. There are many activities that parents and caregivers can provide at home to complement efforts in the classroom. Teachers also need to take advantage of the services that other adults can provide in the classroom as paraprofessionals and volunteers.

For Your Journal

1. Using the lesson plan and the strategies illustrated in the chapter and the strategies you would like to incorporate from throughout this book, plan a similar lesson for the Three Little Pigs, another story that most children know. Working with a partner should enrich your thinking as well as speed up completion of the task.
2. Identify a theme you could introduce to a class, such as "change." Visit the children's section of your local bookstore or public library, or look on a search engine for books, such as that at amazon.com. Try to find three trade books at about the same grade level that fit into the theme of your unit. Develop activities and assessment tools for integrating these books into the unit.

★ Taking It to the World

Now that you have moved into grades three to five, you have found that most children have acquired a concept of print, that they are able to decode many words they encounter, especially when they are contextualized in connected text, that they are beginning to read silently, that they are understanding what they read, and that they are beginning to express themselves in writing. What changes from a second grade reading program do you now expect to find in the use of literature, in word recognition instruction, in reading in the content areas, and in writing as children enter the third grade?

Write down one or two thoughts with respect to each of these elements of literacy, and compare notes with another student. Try to agree on a single list of how the focus on these elements might be different from grades K–2.

★ Being a Professional Reading Teacher

Reflecting on the Chapter

You have now seen the balanced literacy approach that is reflected in this book. How can your choices reflect balanced reading instruction in grades three to five as you address the problems that follow?

Grades Three to Five

- How can you accommodate your reading program for the third-grade student who reads word by word without expression, unable to answer higher-order questions about the text read?
- Suppose that writing has not been the focus of instruction for your fifth-grade students in grades one to four. How do you begin to incorporate it as an element of your fifth-grade program?

Assessment

- If you were reviewing the writing portfolio of a fourth grader, what criteria would you be using?

English Language Learners

- You have seen how some sounds in English are difficult for Spanish speakers. How would you go about determining which sounds in English are difficult for speakers of Korean?
- How do you decide when an English language learner is ready to begin formal instruction in English reading? What are the factors that you consider?

Your Portfolio

If you are interviewed for a middle-grade teaching position, you will likely be asked to describe how you would organize a reading/language arts program for the level. Your portfolio should include examples that you can show in response to that question: lesson plans that focus on reading comprehension; a thematic literature unit; student writing samples; and sample assessment tools, such as rubrics, observation criteria.

Teaching Resources

Children greatly increase their abilities to read with comprehension in grades three to five. Their interest in reading authentic literature grows, as well. This is a good time to begin identifying literature for them. Look at lists of books such as Children's Choices from the International Reading Association (www.reading.org). Search on "children's book lists" at Amazon (www.amazon.com) for other examples. Then search for the books in the usual places.

Technology Connections

1. Teachers can find reviews of software and books appropriate for the classroom by visiting The Kids Domain section of the The Kaboose Network at www.kidsdomain.com. Check out the latest review of a Broderbund's Amazing Writing Machine word processing program for children on the Internet at www.kidsdomain.com/review/kdr/awmachine.html.
2. Using a search engine, such as Google (www.google.com), complete an internet search for reviews on Kid Pix, Reading Blasters, Bank Street Writer III, and Mattel Interactive Student Writing. What do the reviews say about these technology products for children? How could they be used in grades three to five?

3. Visit Education World's "Technology in the Classroom Center" online at www.educationworld.com/a_tech. Identify at least three technology products recommended by Education World's tech experts as appropriate for students in grades three to five. What do the experts say about these products?

Connect with Research

Review the following key words from the chapter and then connect to Research Navigator (www.researchnavigator.com) through this book's companion web site to conduct a search into research on each of the various topics as they relate to reading and literacy education today.

automaticity	independent reading level	oral retelling
cumulative semantic map	informal reading	semantic feature analysis
fluency	inventory (IRI)	sustained silent reading
frustration level	instructional level	thematic literature unit

Further Readings

Brown, H., & Cambourne, B. (1990). *Read and Retell*. Portsmouth, NH: Heinemann.

Prominent Australian educators Brown and Cambourne offer a very thorough treatment of important reading consolidation activity, retelling. Dozens of examples are provided.

Gillet, J. W., Temple, C., & Crawford, A. N. (2003). *Understanding Reading Problems: Assessment and Instruction* (6th edition). Boston: Allyn & Bacon.

These three authors provide a detailed overview of working with children who are struggling with reading, including a major focus on English language learners.

Gunning, T. G. (1998). *Assessing and Correcting Reading and Writing Difficulties*. Boston: Allyn and Bacon.

Gunning's treatment of corrective reading is thorough and comprehensive.

Johnson, T. D., & Louis, D. R. (1990). *Bringing It All Together: A Program for Literacy*. Portsmouth, NH: Heinemann.

Johnson and Louis describe how the various elements of literacy should be assembled into a comprehensive program.

Kohn, A. (1996). *Beyond Discipline: From Compliance to Community*. Upper Saddle River, NJ: Merrill Prentice Hall.

Kohn focuses on the creation of a learning community.

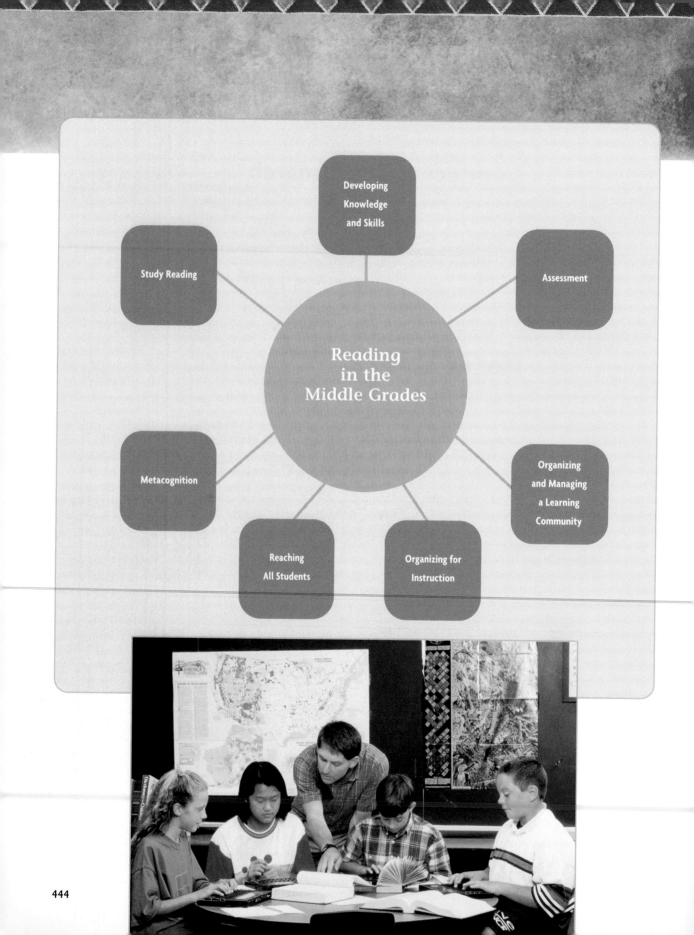

Developing
Knowledge
and Skills

Study Reading

Assessment

Reading
in the
Middle Grades

Metacognition

Organizing
and Managing
a Learning
Community

Reaching
All Students

Organizing for
Instruction

Reading in the Middle Grades

The following statements will get you thinking about the topics of this chapter. Answer true or false in response to each statement. As you read and learn more about the topics in these statements, double-check your answers. See what interests you and prompts your curiosity toward more understanding.

Anticipation Guide

_____ **1.** Schools can safely stop teaching reading by the time students reach the middle grades. Virtually all students will have learned to read adequately by then.

_____ **2.** Middle grade students should be assured daily opportunities to read because reading ability grows with practice.

_____ **3.** Having students post new words they have learned on a vocabulary bulletin board is effective because it helps for students to take ownership of their learning.

_____ **4.** "Possible Sentences" is a method of fitting punishments to crimes, and "Personal Clues" is a means of locating criminals.

_____ **5.** Reading aloud to students, and encouraging them to listen to audio-tapes is important because it provides an internal model of fluent reading.

_____ **6.** An Informal Reading Inventory reports students' reading ability on four levels.

_____ **7.** An important form of assessment is for the teacher to learn to look and listen carefully as students read.

_____ **8.** Part of a teacher's responsibility is to help students organize their time to afford more time for reading and studying.

_____ **9.** It is pointless to ask students to reflect on their strategies when they read because fluent readers are simply unaware of what they are doing.

_____ **10.** Teachers should be sure to give English language learners extra mini-lessons on reading materials before that material is discussed in class.

Vignette of Integrated Reading Instruction in a Sixth-Grade Classroom

As part of an integrated unit on the Middle Ages, Rasheed Graham's sixth-grade students had the choice of reading *The Midwife's Apprentice* or *Catherine, Called Birdy*. Mr. Graham was concerned that some of the students might encounter difficulty with the setting and wanted to revisit a scene to emphasize its meaning and check for their understanding early on in the reading of one of the books. During Friday story share, Mr. Graham has students sit in a circle on the floor while he reads from what he considers a pivotal chapter in the book *The Midwife's Apprentice* about the adventures of the main character shopping at a medieval market. The students follow along with the text as he reads aloud. Mr. Graham's goal is to make sure the students reflect on the significance of this section. While reading aloud, he stops to comment and ask the students for their thoughts on the content and then he asks them to make predictions: "I thought you'd like to revisit this chapter since it seems like such a big moment for the main character. Let's see how we all interpreted this section. What do you all think about it? Let me read this part again while you follow along. The set-up, as you recall, is that Beetle, the main character, has been directed by the midwife to buy some items at the market. Beetle has never been there before, and she is overwhelmed by all the new sights, smells and sounds."

Mr. Graham reads from Chapter 5, then stops after reading, "She sniffed all the spices for free before buying nutmeg and pepper. The hangman was doing a brisk trade in murderer's wash water." To help the students develop the skill of reading for understanding, Mr. Graham has the students think critically about a sentence that might otherwise go unnoticed because of lack of understanding. He asks, "What do you think that means? It's not a beheading, but a hanging, so what do you think is going on?"

Jason speaks up, "Murderers' wash water? Isn't that just dirty bathing water? Why would anyone want that?"

"Does anyone have any ideas?"

"I guess it's like collecting things, you know, like stamps or rabbits feet," offers Tran.

Next, Mr. Graham reads a section in which the main character sees an ivory comb at a merchant's table. She loves the comb but has no money to buy it. Mr. Graham asks, "What do you think will happen? Will she use the money given her by the midwife to buy the comb or will something else transpire?"

Kayleigh states, " I hope she doesn't do that. If she does, the midwife will fire her, and she'll be worse off than she was before."

"I think she gonna steal it," calls out Deanna.

Mr. Graham continues to prod the students' thinking: "What makes you think that she would do that? Is there anything in her character that makes her out to be either a thief or irresponsible? Can you show that to me in the text?"

Here, Mr. Graham has asked students to match their predictions with the character's actual behavior so that they learn that predictions need to be linked to previous knowledge of events and actions. Then he continues reading and stops to help students focus on the key to this section: the development of the main character.

As for vocabulary, Mr. Graham checks to see how the students have dealt with some of the descriptive words and phrases the author had used in creating this scene. He first asks the students whether there are any particularly memorable descriptive phrases they liked. Then he focuses their attention on one that he found rich, asking them to turn to page 29 and read the paragraph silently looking for the phrase he wrote on the board: "charming solemnity." Mr. Graham asks them what image that phrase evokes for them. Once they locate the phrase in the sentence "Although, or perhaps because, she was new at the bargaining game, Beetle handled it with such charming solemnity that the merchant took a fancy to the skinny young thing and, with a broad wink, threw the comb with the cat into the pack with the flasks."

When there is no response, he asks them to try to define the meaning of the word *solemnity* as a reference to the way in which the main character bargained for spices: "Can anyone figure out what *solemnity* means? You might want to see if you can figure it out by reading it in the context of the paragraph."

One student offers, "Does it mean that she was nice to the merchant, maybe nicer than most people, especially the midwife?"

"That's a good guess," Mr. Graham says, "but what do you think the word actually means? Can we find the root word and work from there?"

He writes the word on the board as the students agree that the root word was *solemn,* but nobody seems able to define it. At that point, Mr. Graham suggests that a synonym is "serious, in a dignified manner." "Sometimes we think of the memorial services for those who died on 9-11 as very solemn," he says.

He then asks what the phrase would mean if we read "charming seriousness." "Why do you think this might be an appropriate way to describe Beetle?"

Jason responds, "Well, she probably was pretty scared doing this bargaining for the first time, and she knew she had to do well for the midwife, so she would probably have been pretty serious. Charming—well, the guy really seemed to like her—so she must have had some special way about her that he liked."

Jamaal adds, "Yes, and on page 31 it says that 'Beetle stood perfectly still. What a day. She had been winked at, complimented, given a gift, and now mistaken for the mysterious Alyce who could read.' So she must have been pretty interesting—and attractive to others even though she didn't think so. 'Charming!'"

"Maybe she won't be so solemn the next time she goes to town!" pipes up Kara.

Mr. Graham is pleased that the discussion has returned to the word *solemn* and that it is attracting attention so it can become part of the words they would attend to later. He decides to keep *solemn* on the board and return to it later to build a larger set of associations for it with the students.

He also decides to take this phrase a step further and asks whether anyone can stand up and adopt a pose that would reflect "charming solemnity." Amid giggles, some hands come up, and Mr. Graham asks one student to mime the phrase. "It worked!" Mr. Graham thinks to himself.

Mr. Graham had decided to do this lesson after careful consideration of the students' responses to the initial chapters of the story. He observed the students' responses in their journals and through his one-to-one discussions with three of the students. He quickly diagnosed their weaknesses in attending to and being able to use the descriptions of the setting and of Beetle. An initial check of students' vocabulary knowledge also had reinforced his need to guide students to the key terms, as they were generally unfamiliar with much of the language used by the author. Mr. Graham, therefore, planned this lesson (attending to details) with his students' learning needs in mind. As he guided their responses in this lesson, he made mental notes to himself, which he wrote in his student observation notebook later, about their participation during the lesson. For example, he noted the responses of both students who had elaborated on the meaning of "charming solemnity" by finding added information in the text. These were the kinds of uses of the text he was trying to scaffold.

Reading instruction is just as important in the middle grades as it is in the first grade. However, in recent years, there has been a declining emphasis on middle-level reading. Many schools have dropped the teaching of reading by the middle grades. This may be due to the great attention paid to content standards, and also, many schools want more elective options for students. However, not teaching reading is shortsighted, since reading is part of learning across the curriculum and specific reading skills and strategies are needed in many different subject areas. Middle-level readers have increasing demands placed on them to become flexible and competent in reading a much broader range of materials than they had to read in earlier grades.

As students mature, the range of reading strategies they need expands as well. Both national and state standards include a range of areas of reading expected during the middle-school years. Most state standards specify levels of work that indicate that students are able to read in these ways. Some show examples of the levels of response that can be expected from competent students. Some states also include lists of the books that students should know and be able to discuss for each grade level. State web sites often have examples of proficient student work. If you are unsure of what middle-grade students are capable of doing, these sources are good to use—and also to show students so that they can develop a realistic assessment of their own work in relation to what others are doing.

Adding to the complexity of reading instruction in the middle grades is the changing structure of this level of schooling. Many schools are organized into content departments, so students move from teacher to teacher, creating challenges in efforts to provide flexibility in time and integration of reading and writing with content-area learning. When students have multiple teachers and the curriculum becomes very content intense, aspects of good reading instruction often get overlooked. This chapter provides a framework for thinking about what needs to be taught and examines how different classrooms are organized so students have the opportunities to learn that they deserve. Recognizing the importance of reading for older students, the International Reading Association's Commission on Adolescent Reading (Moore, Bean, Berdyshaw, & Lycis, 1999) has published a document that lists seven reading rights of adolescents, as shown in Table 11.1 on page 450.

TABLE 11.1

Reading Rights for Adolescents

1. Adolescents deserve access to a wide variety of reading materials that they can and want to read.
2. Adolescents deserve instruction that builds both the skill and desire to read increasingly complex materials.
3. Adolescents deserve assessments that show them their strengths as well as their needs and that guide their teachers to design instruction that will best help them grow as readers.
4. Adolescents deserve expert teachers who model and practice explicit instruction in reading comprehension and study strategies across the curriculum.
5. Adolescents deserve reading specialists who assist individual students having difficulty learning to read.
6. Adolescents deserve teachers who understand the complexities of individual adolescent readers, respect their differences, and respond to their characteristics.
7. Adolescents deserve homes, communities, and a nation that will support their efforts to achieve advance levels and provide the support necessary for them to succeed.

Developing Knowledge and Skills

Given the wide range of reading development needed during the middle years, classroom instruction needs to be carefully structured so that all aspects of reading can be included. As a teacher, you need to ensure that you attend to each of these through the programs you develop. The following nine components provide an overview of what to include in your program.

Daily Opportunities to Read

Reading is not a single activity, but one that is complex and changes according to the situation, purpose, and type of text. For students to develop as flexible readers, they should be given a variety of purposeful reading opportunities each day. Each new type of text requires special attention, and the classroom teacher must supply assistance to students in approaching new materials. Teachers can remind students to adapt their reading strategies to their purposes and materials. Skimming headings and skipping from one chapter or section to another can be an appropriate strategy to use when reading for specific information. Reading and rereading may be the tactic to adopt when trying to understand and appreciate a poem. Some of the various purposes that students have for reading different texts include the following:

- Self-selected texts for personal enjoyment
- Texts for group discussions and sharing with others
- Content-area learning from textbook and resource materials, news magazines, newspapers, and electronic texts
- Experiences with poetry, humorous word plays, and cartoons
- Texts that enable students to perform tasks and follow directions
- Texts for specific problem solving and learning

One of the most important kinds of reading is self-selected, independent reading. It is clear that students who read widely have a great advantage over students who do not read much or who never engage in self-selected reading. Cunningham and Stanovich's (1999) article "What Reading Does for the Mind" makes a strong case for wide reading. The article summarizes data from various studies that shows that relying on oral input to learn is just not adequate. An analysis of the vocabulary load of various books and television programs demonstrates that even preschool children's books have a more sophisticated range of vocabulary than adult television shows. Students will never encounter the words and concepts they need to succeed in a professional world if they do not read. When middle-level students read this information, many become convinced of the importance of their continued independent reading. It is through engagement in a great deal of reading that we encounter the concepts and forms of written discourse needed for life. We must keep reading!

Daily Reading at the Appropriate Instructional Level

Finding a balance between appropriately challenging reading materials and those that students can handle independently is part of each teacher's task. Students will improve in their reading when they have instructional-level materials that both challenge and reward them. If reading materials are too difficult, students cannot apply their skills to extend their proficiency. If materials are too easy, they do not need to apply their skills, so finding the instructional middle is essential. This is the zone in which students can develop as readers. Even so, situations in which the student must deal with materials that are too easy or too hard will still occur. Students need some easy materials so that they can gain pleasure from reading and move comfortably through texts.

In whole-class instruction, many students also will be faced with materials that are above their instructional level. In spite of these situations, support mechanisms are available and should be used to assist students. Some of these support mechanisms include the following:

- Prereading activation of knowledge and vocabulary under teacher or adult guidance; this might involve seeing videos to set the context and build knowledge
- Audiotapes of texts
- Use of buddy or partner reading
- Assistance from older or adult readers
- Adapted, easier texts on the same topic

Integrating Reading and Writing

Both reading and writing develop better when they are taught as companion tools for learning about and expressing ideas. Integrating units of content instruction with language arts skill development provides a rich context in which to help students learn. With more extensive units, teachers have time to develop students' background knowledge and to help them find their own questions and interests. Thus, the instruction can be personal and focused. Reading more deeply on a particular topic helps students to gain control of the ideas and learn the vocabulary and concepts more fully than a quick covering of curriculum often provides. As student knowledge of a topic increases, the student becomes more able to write about it with a sense of confidence and perspective. Examples of situations that encourage integration of curriculum and reading and writing together are included in this chapter, both in the opening vignette and later as we explore organizational options for teachers. Additional options include the following:

- Science fairs and history fairs, family history projects, and other events put on by a class, school, or larger organization that encourage projects for which students working as individuals, pairs, or small groups choose topics, conduct research, and create exhibits. All language arts are integrated when students engage in these types of inquiry and sharing.

- Addressing broad questions as in the Great Books Program (Plecha, 1992) and the Paidea program (Adler, 1982), with groups coming together after reading to discuss key issues and topics raised. After rich discussions, students can write their own point of view on one of the questions raised. They might begin by using a graphic organizer to help them compare and contrast ideas raised or to identify a theme statement and then list examples and details that support their perspective.

- Inquiry projects in which students frame their own areas of inquiry around current problems and questions in the students' world and then go about answering their questions. Sharing the results of their inquiry becomes a shared, community event so students need to present their findings in visual, written, and oral formats.

Strategies for Independent Reading

Various types of texts and tasks can provide models with which to teach specific strategic behaviors. To help students develop these strategies, you need to incorporate them in your planning for each part of the text lesson: before, during and after the instruction as they Anticipate, Build knowledge, and Consolidate what they learn. You need to explain how to use the strategies and the benefits that come from them. Then students can apply the specific strategies or make modifications that fit their own styles and preferences within the general ABC framework as they learn.

ANTICIPATING.   Students need to learn some simple strategies that they can use before reading that will assist their learning. First, they need to learn the importance of establishing purposes for reading. Remind students repeatedly that they can read texts in different ways and that the manner in which they read a text should grow out of their purpose for reading. Review several purposes for reading:

- Wanting to skim a text or scan some kind of reading material to see what it contains
- Reading for enjoyment
- Reading to learn how to do something
- Reading to remember facts and ideas.

Second, show students how to survey or preview the materials to determine both the external and internal features of the text. Explain to students that visual clues and signal words are features provided as aids to easier comprehension. External features include visual clues such as chapter and section headings, changes in typeface and font size, and illustrations and charts. Internal features include signal words that point to the text's structure. "Once upon a time," for example, signals the beginning of a fictional

THE WORLD OF READING

The Nation's Report Card

Since 1969, the National Center for Education Statistics (NCES) has assessed the educational progress of our nation's children in a variety of subjects, including reading, mathematics, science, writing, history, civics, geography, and the arts. Known officially as the National Assessment of Educational Progress (NAEP), and unofficially called "the Nation's Report Card," these periodic assessments have two major goals:

To measure student achievement in the context of instructional experiences and to track change in achievement of fourth-, eighth-, and twelfth-graders over time in selected content domains.

The degree of interest in education today is unparalleled in American history. More than ever before, parents, educators, and policymakers are concerned with whether America's children will have the knowledge and skills necessary to be productive members of our global society. NCES points out, however, that we can only know if our schools are succeeding in this task if the nation has impartial information about what students know and can do, whether their performance has improved or declined, and the ways they study and learn. The Nation's Report Card is intended to provide a common yardstick across all states and districts for evaluating student performance objectively and to monitor whether that performance changes over time.

Although the NAEP has been conducted at some level since 1969, the fall of 2003 marked a significant step in the assessment. While participation in NAEP is voluntary, the No Child Left Behind Act provides strong incentives for school districts and states to participate. Beginning with the fall 2003 assessment, any state receiving Title 1 grants from the federal government must participate in national and state assessments at least once every two years in reading and mathematics in grades 4 and 8. Therefore, 2003 marked the first year all 50 states participated, which included approximately 187,000 fourth-graders and 155,000 eighth-graders. For the reading assessment, students answered a combination of multiple-choice and constructed-response questions after reading three types of texts from typical grade-appropriate sources, representing different contexts for reading:

- Reading for literary experience
- Reading for information
- Reading to perform a task (grade 8)

Achievement is reported in two ways—scale scores and achievement levels. Scale score results report the distribution of achievement for groups and subgroups. Achievement levels categorize student achievement as *Basic, Proficient,* and *Advanced* and are used to report results in terms of a set of standards for what students should know and be able to do. Under the No Child Left Behind Act, the goal is for all students to score as proficient in math and reading by 2014 or face sanctions.

Results from the 2003 NAEP for Reading indicate reading achievement remained relatively flat with little change from 1992 or 2002 in the average score for fourth-graders and the score for eighth-graders decreasing one point from 2002. Eighth-graders did show improvement over 1992 scores. However, although 63 percent of fourth-graders and 74 percent of eighth-graders read *at or above basic level,* 37 percent of fourth-graders and 26 percent of eighth-graders read at a *below basic* level.

In addition to the national test, part of the NAEP testing in 2003 was the second step in the Trial Urban District Assessment (TUDA) of Educational Progress, funded as part of the No Child Left Behind Act. The first TUDA, conducted by NAEP in 2002, examined reading and writing in five urban districts. In 2003, nine public urban districts (including the original five) participated in the TUDA in reading and mathematics at grades 4 and 8. Scores showed continued differences between ethnic groups and males and females, although these gaps indicated some narrowing. Results of the TUDA portion of the NAEP indicate all but one of the participating urban districts scored lower than the national average at both grades 4 and 8, with more students reading at a *below basic* level than the national average.

NAEP is not without its critics as some see what was once considered a relatively neutral assessment now being used to assess individual state testing as well. Critics worry that linking results to federal funds will ultimately lead to a national curriculum and remove individualism from states. Some educators also feel that such a *national* assessment could be an "indictment" in some cases and put added pressure on individuals and school systems. Secretary of Education Rod Paige, however, feels "we are moving in the right direction; but we are nowhere near satisfied with what we are trying to accomplish. We will not be satisfied until the achievement gap is completely closed and all students are reading at very high levels, at proficient levels."

For a complete review of the findings and to examine sample questions and evaluations, visit the Nation's Report Card online at http://nces.ed.gov/nationsreportcard.

Source: National Center for Education Statistics, National Assessment of Educational Progress (NAEP), 2003 Reading Assessment.

narrative. Words such as *consequently, therefore, because of, as a result of,* and *therefore* indicate the use of a cause-and-effect pattern.

Finally, students need to learn how to activate what is already known about the topic. Remind them that they will better understand what they read if they can connect it to what they already know both about the topic and about the way in which it is presented. Some ways to activate prior knowledge are the following:

- Brainstorming (Students can individually, in pairs, or in groups make lists of what they already know and then group these items into categories.)
- Writing out a list of questions they want answered
- Predicting what they expect will be in the text.

BUILDING KNOWLEDGE. While reading, students add to what they know and deepen understanding as they construct meaning from the text ideas by doing the following:

- Making and confirming predictions
- Visualizing
- Summarizing and drawing inferences
- Generating questions
- Making connections
- Self-monitoring their progress
- Reflecting on an author's purposes and voice
- Checking accuracy of sources
- Comparing various texts on the same theme or topic.

Ways of saving the ideas and images encountered in reading include using journals, bookmark notes, Post-its, and graphic organizers. Writing and drawing require active thinking and processing and help to encode information in long-term memory as well as to create memory aids to help retrieve information later.

CONSOLIDATING NEW UNDERSTANDING. After students complete a text, they can review the whole and create a summary for themselves, generalize from the ideas, consider the text in relation to its purposes and content, make connections to other texts and their own experiences, participate in group sharing or writing experiences, identify themes and create interpretations of literary pieces, essential to the enjoyment and appreciation of literature, and reconstruct the major ideas of informational texts.

Engaging in Inquiry

Students also learn how to engage in inquiry projects and research. As they use their language skills in exploring new ideas, they have a real opportunity to make use of a wide variety of resources. Students engage their own thinking in both real and important pursuits. These applications of research and thinking abilities are not only made in language arts classes but across the curriculum. They need to develop their abilities to do the following:

- Ask good questions
- Seek appropriate sources of materials and evaluating their quality

- Synthesize ideas from multiple sources of information
- Use electronic media as a resource in learning, both in seeking information, organizing it, and in presenting ideas to others
- Create written, visual, or oral presentations to share findings

By the middle grades, instruction focuses on content area reading and helping students to develop a structured approach that will help them with formal school work.

At some point in the middle grades, schools introduce the more formal aspects of writing research papers and reports. This is where the teacher can provide a great deal of structure and guidance, since it is usually the first time such formal work has been required in which students need to show footnotes or references and develop a bibliography. Establish explicit guides for students and clear timetables for the work. You might have the students track their research and turn in weekly journal entries indicating what has been done during the time allocated so that you and the student ensure that things move forward. When there are questions or issues, conduct conferences with the students on their progress. This process of developing students' research skills is an example of where teachers can carefully scaffold the initial two components of good instruction: demonstration and immersion and attention to detail. Because the research takes so long to complete, you are preparing students for work they will be expected to do more independently in high school. Middle schools can help students to become more familiar with the research and writing process by giving added research opportunities with guided practice.

Strategies for Building Vocabulary

In the middle grades, students regularly encounter words in texts that they never hear in oral communication. Therefore, they must learn to attend to these new terms and have strategies to remember them. Vocabulary plays a crucial role in content learning, since terms convey key concepts, and even familiar words often take on different and specific meanings. For example, consider the word *angle;* it means one thing in mathematics, in social studies it has another meaning, as in "what was the government's angle on the incident," and in general use it can be either a noun or verb (e.g., "the stream angled through the woods" or "he loved angling in the stream").

There are many ways in which teachers help students develop their language facility. A key to students' continuing vocabulary development in the middle grades is increasing their understanding of the ways in which words are formed and also how words enter English. When students become sensitive to identifying new words that they perceive as important, the chances of their being interested in words and retaining the ones they select are higher (Blachowicz and Fisher, 1996). Encouraging students to look for words outside of the classroom also is an important component in their developing sensitivity to words. Beck and McKeown (1983) found that the most significant component of their rich vocabulary instruction program was the word wall. Almost incidentally at first, one of the teachers made bulletin board space and encouraged students to post examples of the new words they were learning in class. This factor alone significantly improved the

TABLE 11.2

Basic Elements of a Good Vocabulary Program

- The teacher models interest in language.
- Students engage in enjoyable word play.
- Students become attentive to new words and self-select words to learn.
- Students learn about the history and growth of English including the nature of words — affixes, combining forms, base words, and derivatives.
- Students develop basic strategies for learning and retaining new content specific words.
- Students are involved in a great deal of reading that extends their knowledge.

students' learning. Making vocabulary learning interesting and giving students ownership are two key ingredients of successful activities. As you plan your approach to vocabulary development, keep in mind several important components. Just playing games with words, for instance, is not enough. Nor is doing spelling and vocabulary worksheets. Table 11.2 identifies six basic elements of a good vocabulary program.

TEACHER MODELING OF INTEREST IN LANGUAGE.   By keeping a small set of books about language growth and development on your desk and reading about words periodically, you help to build students' inquisitiveness about language. Books by Richard Lederer and Bill Bryson are great sources for read-aloud pieces on language. The *Readers Digest's* regular vocabulary quiz is another easy resource that students (and teachers) enjoy taking and then exploring the definitions and uses of the terms. Jokes, too, often involve play with words and can be great starters for talk about language. Table 11.3 identifies some books to keep as resources.

STUDENTS ENGAGE IN ENJOYABLE WORD PLAY.   Middle-level students love to play with words and language. Music, clean rap word games, and jokes are wonderful ways they explore language. Even joke books should be considered for the classroom library. Comics are another favorite source of a very expansive vocabulary. The teacher can have great fun by introducing strange and unusual forms of words and together enjoying sesquipedalian words, portmanteau words, other palindromes and other

TABLE 11.3

Valuable Language Resources

Bryson, B. *The Mother Tongue: English and How It Got That Way.* New York: Avon Books, 1990.

Bryson, B. *Made in America: An informal history of the English language in the United States.*
    New York: Avon, 1994.

Lederer, R. *Crazy English: The Ultimate Joy Ride Through Our Language.* New York: Simon & Schuster, 1998.

Lederer, R. *The Miracle of Language.* New York: Pocket Books, 1999.

Rheingold, H. *They Have a Word for It: A Lighthearted Lexicon of Untranslatable Words and Phrases.* Louisville, KY:
    Saraband Books, 2000.

strange word forms. Two great resources are *Superdupers: Really funny real words* (Terban, 1989) and *A cache of jewels and other collective nouns* (Heller, 1991).

SELF-SELECTION.   Students do better in learning language when they have some control over and choice in what they learn. Studies of students' ability to self-select words they want and need to learn have shown that students are quite good at determining key terms when they are given practice and opportunities to discuss their selections with others (Blachowicz & Fisher, 1996). By first modeling how to notice unfamiliar words, the teacher helps students to realize that this is part of what good readers do regularly. The teacher should then provide opportunities for students to build vocabulary by recording words they find interesting and new, trying to determine meaning from context and word parts, confirming hunches with dictionary or glossary checks, and then sharing their choices with others.

HISTORICAL DEVELOPMENT OF ENGLISH.   The way our language has grown and changed is fascinating. William and Mary Morris's (1962) *Dictionary of Word and Phrase Origins* still is a great source of information about our language, as is Bartletts's (2003) *Dictionary of Americanisms*. Small sets of paperback books on language history give students the opportunity to read and discuss the English language together. The talk about words and language also reinforces the use of new words and words used in new ways.

Students in the middle grades need to have some structured study of words and language, too. At this stage, they should be learning how affixes work, how to use Greek and Latin combining forms, and how to connect derivations with base words. Content-area learning involves a great many specialized terms, so knowing how to look for specialized meanings of common words is also valuable. Table 11.4 on page 458 provides a list of affixes of which students should become aware. Two useful books are *Techniques of Teaching Vocabulary* (1971) by Bamman and O'Rourke and the more recent *Words Their Way* by Bear, Invernizzi, Templeton, and Johnston (2004).

Figurative language is also important to highlight and teach, especially for second language learners in need of help in understanding the many expressions of English. The elementary *Amelia Bedelia* books (Parish, 1966) and *The King who Rained* (Gwynne, 1989) offer good strategies for introducing figurative language and helping students become aware of the challenge of our language for English second language learners.

LEARNING AND RETAINING CONTENT-SPECIFIC VOCABULARY.   Students' self-selection of words they want to learn is an important component of language growth. However, in content learning teachers don't want to leave to chance key terms that students need to make sense of the content. Therefore, some good strategies are needed to draw students' attention to specific words and their meanings in the particular context being studied. A few of these are listed below:

- *Chunking and categorizing words.* Students are given a list of key terms and asked to chunk them together in groups that fit. Once the groups are made, students are to give each chunk a label or category. In preparing for the activity, the first step is to create a list of the most important terms that students will encounter in their reading. Next the teacher ensures that there are at least two or three words that can be chunked together. If there are not, the teacher adds some words from the content that will help students build categories of related words.

- *Possible sentences.* Students are given a list of the key terms to be learned and, working with a partner or individually, try to connect two or three of the words into a

TEACH IT!
37

TABLE 11.4

Affixes

PREFIXES	MEANING	EXAMPLE
Un	not	*un*happy
In	not	*in*correct
Re	again	*re*pair, *re*move
Dis	not or away	*dis*agree, *dis*miss
Pre	before	*pre*school, *pre*pare
Ex	out	*ex*hale, *ex*port
Anti	against	*anti*freeze, *anti*war
Sub	under, below	*sub*way, *sub*marine
Super	over, more than	*super*sonic, *super*man
Com	together, with	*com*plete, *com*munity
Con		*con*nect
Col		*col*lection
Co		*co*operate
Cor		*cor*respond
Mid	in the middle	*mid*day, *mid*summer
Mis	wrong	*mis*behave, *mis*understand

NUMBER SUFFIXES		
Mono	one	*mono*tone
Uni	one	*uni*corn
Bi	two	*bi*cycle
Di	two	*di*alogue
Tri	three	*tri*cycle
Deca	ten	*deca*de
Centi	hundreth	*centi*pede
Cent	hundreth	*cent*ury

SUFFIXES	MEANING	EXAMPLE
s-es	plural	clock*s*
s-ing-ed	verb, time	sing, sin
er, est	comparison	late, lat*er*, lat*est*
ly	how done	quick, quick*ly*
ful	full of	peace*ful*
out	full of	fam*ous*
less	without	use*less*, sleep*less*
its, ian	one skilled in	scient*ist*, physic*ian*
ness	state of being, having	sad*ness*, sick*ness*
ify, fy	to become, make	magn*ify*, de*ify*
en	make, cause, made of	soft*en*, wool*en*
able	can, able to, deserving	cap*able*, lov*able*
ible		poss*ible*, vis*ible*
tion	action, process	comple*tion*
ion		rebell*ion*
ish	have, quality of	fool*ish*, child*ish*
ment	state of, action	fulfill*ment*
ry, ery, ary	product or action of, place where	bak*ery*, pott*ery*
ize	make, made into	dramat*ize*
ism	practice of, act of	hero*ism*, vandal*ism*, patriot*ism*

Sources: From Dole, O'Rourke, & Curtis, *Vocabulary Building: A Process Approach.*
Copyright © 1986. Reprinted by permission of Zaner-Bloser, Inc.

sentence. They write these sentences and later share their possible sentences, even though they might be unsure of the real meanings of the words. The activity raises students' awareness of words they will need to attend to as they read.

- *Exclusion brainstorming.* The teacher gives students a list of words that includes both words they will need for the content being studied and some that do not relate to the topic. The teacher asks the students to predict which words do not fit the content. This activity is fun, since it shifts the purpose of task from what students normally get while highlighting new words.

- *Predict-o-gram.* The teacher presents students with a list of words that come from the story they will read. The teacher asks the students to predict which words relate to the characters, setting, problem, or resolution. The teacher can use a graphic organizer with four blocks and space for students to write a prediction they make about the story content after completing the activity of categorizing the terms.

- *Vocabulary word cards.* Vocabulary word cards can be a fun and powerful way for students to build their vocabularies. They select the ten most important words from the unit of study and then create a 3 × 5 word card for each. On the front side of the card, they draw a picture to illustrate the meaning of the term. On the back side of the card, they write the word, the central definition, and added information to help them understand how to use the word. This might mean a sentence, some synonyms, or phrases in which the word might be found.

- *Personal clues.* The personal clue approach (Carr, 1985) is also an effective way to learn words in content areas. Words are grouped by the concept they are associated with or by the element or character in a piece of literature. Then students list attributes of the target words and think of one personal association that is the clue they will use to store the terms. For example, when learning *laconic*, one student wrote *terse* and *miserly* and associated them with Scrooge before Christmas. Then, on the second day, the student decided that from his study of American history, Calvin Coolidge was a better choice. On the third day, he added another clue: his New England uncle who hardly ever said more than three words. He had fun finding the right clue for *laconic* — but certainly wasn't laconic in his efforts (see the example in Figure 11.1).

TEACH IT!
23

  - *Connect two.* Using the list of words to be learned, students practice them by creating new and sometimes zany sentences that use either two or three of the new words. Doing this with a partner makes it more enjoyable for students, since the sentences that must respect the definitions of the words can still be fun.

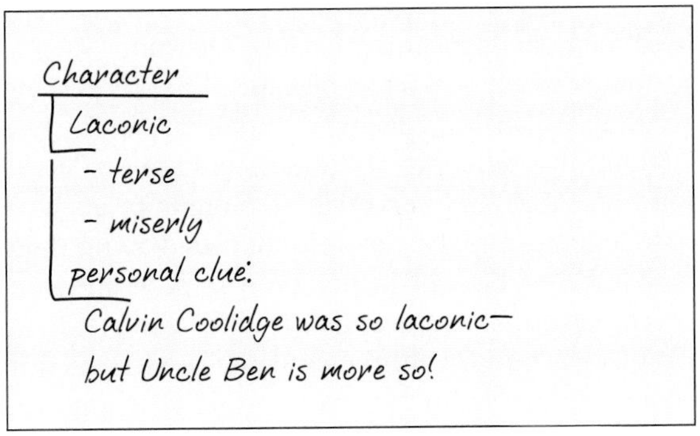

Students also can use graphic organizers such as concept maps to help them learn new words. The organizer contains boxes or cells in which a question or concept is to be filled in. For example, a concept of definition map could include questions such as "What is it?" "What is it like?" "What are some examples?" and "What are some attributes?" After creating the web, students can keep expanding their webs — some

```
Character
  Laconic
    - terse
    - miserly
  personal clue:
    Calvin Coolidge was so laconic—
    but Uncle Ben is more so!
```

FIGURE 11.1

Personal Clue.

draw pictures of the concept, some add antonyms, and others collect sentences in which the term is used—to help deepen their understanding of the term. (See Chapter 7 for examples of various graphic organizers.)

WIDE READING.   Doing a great deal of reading is a critical way in which students build their recognition of vocabulary and learn the specific contexts in which words are appropriate. There is no substitute for reading. Studies have shown that direct teaching of specific words can account for only part of the growth in word knowledge needed to develop an adequate vocabulary (Beck & McKeown, 1983; Anderson & Nagy, 1991). When students enjoy reading and are attentive to language and vocabulary, they continue to build their awareness and ability to use an increasingly wide range of vocabulary terms.

In summary, you can guide students in their development of vocabulary sensitivity and curiosity by having them do the following:

- Keep personal records of words new to them or new uses of known words
- Develop strategies for building meanings for these words
- Use appropriate visual or graphic organizers to build and retain meanings
- Practice using new terms in speaking and writing
- Use resources, especially dictionaries, thesauruses, and glossaries
- Engage in word play by creating and enjoying jokes, word puzzles, poetry, and games such as *Scrabble*™ and *Pictionary*™
- Understand how our language is evolving and how vocabulary grows and changes
- Keep examples of new words and new usages (sports, pop music, and fashion are areas that keep inventing new words and usage that middle-grade students are interested in following.

Student Self-Reflection

In addition to self-monitoring, which refers to the active checking of one's own thinking while reading, students also become more confident readers when they learn to engage in reflection after the text has been completed. They learn to think about what they have just read and what is new or different. They also can reflect on their own active thinking processes and how well they have used their energies during reading. Questions such as "What did I learn?" "Was I using my energy wisely so I made best use of my time?" and "Did I use the best approach to the reading: visualizing, making a mental map of the test, outlining, or rephrasing as I read?" Adopting a reflective attitude encourages readers to take responsibility for their reading and to realize they can often do more to be effective readers. The teacher can encourage students to improve self-reflection by having them make marginal notes while reading and learning, discuss the process with peers and himself or herself, and keep a journal for self-reflections at the end of reading activities.

Another aspect of self-monitoring is learning to think about the process used in conducting research. Some teachers create guides for students to follow in forming and answering questions about their research: How did you begin your research process? How did you use your prior knowledge as a frame for deciding on what you would need to research? How did you compare and contrast different sources of information? Others have students keep journals of their research process and make notes of what they have done as they go. Another good way to increase students' self-reflection is to use the I-Search Paper model (Macrorie, 1988). In this model, students choose a topic and conduct research on it but focus most directly on how they go about the process rather than just focusing on the final paper. They reflect on how they went about their research, what caused problems for them, and what they would do the next time. The strategy creates a more reflective and powerful response to extended learning activities.

Opportunities to Model Fluent and Reflective Reading

The teacher can do a great deal to help students develop an internal model of what fluent reading is like by reading aloud to them on a regular basis. Selecting a variety of material to read helps students understand the beauty and depth of what can be communicated by writers. Contemporary students do not have many opportunities to engage in reflection about reading. Bringing in good audiotapes of texts being read can also help students begin to appreciate the sounds of writing language read orally. For example, listening to books on tape such as James Joyce's *Dubliners* (1993) and Tony Hillerman reading his own mysteries helps students to gain an appreciation for the varieties of oral readers. This strategy can also help students to think of using their Walkmans and time spent in the car as potential time for listening to good books and poetry.

Reading aloud from interesting material also can be used to model critical thinking engaged in while reading. When reading to students, pay particular attention to reading with expression, asking questions as you read, and responding to the ideas in the text. Comments such as, "That was beautifully described—I can almost see it!," "Did I understand what the author just said?," "That doesn't sound possible to me," and "That reminds me of something else I just learned" are the kinds of reflections students need to use in their independent reading. Modeling such thinking encourages students to evaluate their own habits and can build new habits if they do not already use them. You can enhance the power of this thinking aloud by putting some of these thinking asides on the board or on strips hanging from the ceiling so that students are regularly reminded of them. Listening to you read aloud in this manner from a wide selection of texts provides students with many benefits, not the least of which are increased interest in print and sensitivity to vocabulary and language use. Think of the power of reading aloud in providing the following:

- A model of fluent reading
- A model of active and reflective reading
- A way to increase their store of knowledge about the world as well as their vocabulary

Fluency through Repetition

Rereading texts improves students' word knowledge, reading speed, and accuracy and deepens their understanding of that particular text. Effective methods for incorporating rereading and guided oral reading in the middle level classroom and thus promoting fluency include the following:

- Rereading poems and short passages using techniques such as choral reading, two-part reading, and echo reading
- Readers' theater, a technique that involves students in rehearsing and reading aloud their interpretation of a character's lines in a passages from a short story

- Self-timing drills, a procedure in which students time themselves or partners in reading and rereading short passages to increase their speed
- An introduction to a variety of new books and genres, giving students short amounts of time to skim through a variety to see which they like best

Assessment

Assessment is the starting point for good instruction. Students in the middle grades vary significantly in their reading abilities and interests, and with the increasing range of reading genre and purposes that students this age must handle successfully, there is much teachers need to attend to. Throughout the year, the teacher's job is to monitor what all the students know and can do and to provide supportive instruction. Because this is a challenging task, it is also good to remember that the students themselves also can be good assistants in the task of monitoring their knowledge and abilities. In fact, they should be made aware of their strengths and should participate in setting and monitoring their goals throughout the year.

Determining Reading Levels

As a result of the daily reading by students of materials in the classroom, the teacher should have a good idea of their development as readers and can guide them into reading appropriate materials. Determining students' instructional and independent reading levels can be done in a few ways.

INFORMAL READING INVENTORIES.   If a reading series is available for use, one of the easiest ways is to use an informal reading inventory (IRI) provided for the reading program. As you read in Chapter 10, the IRI contains a series of increasingly difficult reading passages; students are asked to read the passages and then to demonstrate their comprehension by answering a series of questions. If the IRI asks for oral reading of the passages, the guideline is generally that oral reading with 99 percent accuracy and 90 percent comprehension indicates *independence* with the material. The range for *instruction* (where your guidance as a teacher supports the reading) is 95 percent word accuracy and 75 percent comprehension. Less success with passages indicates that the material is really too difficult for students to be asked to read. In the language of reading assessment, those texts are at a *frustration* level for students. If the IRI involves only silent reading, then the students' comprehension responses are the focus. Usually, the kinds of questions that are included on the inventory try to tap some basic recall of main ideas of the text, some inferences that can be drawn, and some vocabulary knowledge. Be sure to look at the questions in advance. If you are not satisfied that they give you the information you need about particular students, go back and talk over the answers students gave with them and find out why the students responded as they did. Asking students to write a summary of a text is another good way to get information on how well students can follow the main structure and ideas of a passage they read. Then, with students for whom there are questions, some individual discussion about their reading and thinking can be useful. You will not need to have an individual diagnostic discussion with all the students but can focus on those about whom you have some concerns.

ADVANCED INFORMAL INVENTORY.   As students mature, teachers also need to find out how well they can read information from more than one source, combine ideas, and learn to think critically about what they read. Teachers need to ask students to compare and contrast two different texts on some appropriate topic. A contemporary news story, two pieces of student writing with different perspectives, editorials in newspapers, and personal letters to the editor all make good content for student thinking. This will provide you with good data as you plan for having students do research (and use the Internet) and engage in extended projects. You can copy two short articles and create a few questions that require contrasting the pieces or ask students to write their opinion about the question addressed in the articles, citing references they find useful in the texts.

Another form of an advanced IRA is one that is specific for a content course. The teacher selects passages from the textbook or instructional materials that students read. Questions need to tap the range of reading comprehension tasks—from identifying key ideas, inferring relationships, understanding specific vocabulary meanings to reading visual information contained in charts, maps and graphs. This inventory can be completed in a group setting, so it saves much time for teachers.

LEVELED BOOKS.   Many districts now have leveled the books they have available according to difficulty taking into account a variety of features, including vocabulary and concept load, complexity of sentences and redundancy, and layout of the materials. If you have this resource available, you can select a representative set of books at a range of levels and ask students to read short sections. Then summarize what they have read or have them answer a few of your questions and find their instructional levels this way.

Classroom Fluency Measure

One of the easiest ways to begin to get information on your students' reading is to use the **classroom fluency measure** (see Blachowicz, Sullivan, & Ciply, 2001). For this quick assessment, select a passage from the reading anthology you will be using or from other material that you will be asking students to read. Type the passage for your use, and number each line in the margin. Set up a time when you can work with each student individually, either when the class is doing silent reading or individual tasks or before and after school. Then, as you work with each student, ask the student to read orally for one minute while you follow the reading and then ask the student to recall what he or she can from the passage. While the student reads, you record any deviations the student makes from the text and subtract the errors from the total number of words read during the minute. By marking the student's location at the end of one minute, you can do this calculation easily after the student tells what he or she recalls from the text. When you have done the fluency check on each of the student's, you can create a class grid, arranging the students' scores from lowest to highest. This gives you a clear sense of the range within a class and will help you to determine which students you need to do more assessment with immediately and which you can observe in other ways to plan for future instruction.

Strategy Knowledge

A third important component of students' reading that needs to be assessed early in the year is their awareness of the strategies they use to read successfully in different kinds of materials and for different purposes. One middle-grade teacher begins her year by asking students to fill out a survey of what their strategies are for reading (see

WHAT DO YOU KNOW ABOUT YOUR
STRATEGIES FOR READING TO LEARN?

Your language arts teacher has set up a unit in which you will read novels in groups. Each
night you will read one chapter. What strategies work best for you to help you enjoy and
understand novels? What will you do?

_____

_____

_____

_____

Your social studies teacher has assigned you a 25-page chapter on Monday. On Friday you will
have a test on the material. You are on your own to read and learn. There are lots of headings
and boldfaced vocabulary in the text. At the end of the chapter, there are many questions and
activities. What will you do this week with this chapter? What is your plan?

_____

_____

_____

_____

_____

FIGURE 11.2

Reading Strategies.

Figure 11.2. On it are examples of the kinds of reading tasks teachers in this departmentalized school expect of students. What the teacher and students learned by doing
this survey one year was that the students were very "teacher and parent" dependent.
Several students responded to the query about how to prepare for a social studies test
that would be given on Friday by indicating that they would read over the chapter,
maybe more than once, and then ask their mothers to quiz them using the end of
chapter questions. When asked how to figure out a difficult mathematics problem,
again the response was to ask Mom. To develop students' awareness of what good readers do, discussing responses to this kind of survey can be a starting place.

Another approach is to ask students to indicate what they are aware of doing as they
read a challenging short article. Inform students that they can use Post-it notes if they want
to, while reading so that they do not forget their thinking or strategies. When finished
reading, each student should write a reflection on what he or she did before starting to
read, what he or she was conscious of doing while reading, and what he or she did afterward. If students are frustrated by this task, it means that they are not yet fully conscious
of what reading is as a strategic behavior and there is much for the teacher to do with them
during the year to develop a vocabulary for and awareness of reading strategies.

Content Reading

Another area that is important for students who are developing reading abilities is
their flexibility in reading a variety of different informational texts and in developing
strategies for using that information. The teacher needs to know whether students can

use the features of informational textbooks as well as glossaries and thesauruses and whether they can read and weave information from graphs, charts, tables, and pictures (with their captioned information) together with information in the narrative content. Do students use the physical layout of material they read to learn (see Chapter 7)?

Vocabulary and Concept Learning

As you listen to students read and respond to what they read, attend to their use of the language of the text materials. Ask them to define some of the key terms. You might want to be more formal initially and prepare a short vocabulary assessment for one of the first articles or stories you have students read with you in a guided reading setting. Vocabulary knowledge is so important to reading comprehension that you do not want to leave it to chance. You want an idea of students' vocabulary, and then you want to know whether they have learned and use any self-conscious strategies for adding words to their use vocabularies.

A quick way to find out how well students know the vocabulary of a particular novel, story, or informational text is to have them complete a Rate Your Knowledge chart (Blachowicz, 1987). Select eight to twelve key words that will be important for students to understand, and list them on a chart like the one shown in Figure 11.3 on page 466. Give students choices to indicate their level of familiarity with the terms. Have students rate their own level of knowledge for each word. Asking students to define the words they mark as familiar can help to keep students from overestimating their knowledge.

You also want to know whether students have any self-conscious strategies for learning new words and phrases and whether they are interested in vocabulary. Asking a few questions (orally or in written form) about how students note new terms that they think are important and how they then go about learning the terms can stimulate some new ideas and help make some more focused on this aspect of reading and learning. For others, you might find out a lot about how your students learn language and what rehearsal tools they have found useful (making cards, drawing pictures of terms, writing and using the terms orally, etc.). Some English language learners can provide good ideas for all students, growing out of their high need for vocabulary. Highlight their experiences if they are willing to share how they learn language. This is a good place for you to be a model and share your own vocabulary-learning strategies as a way of stimulating students' reflection and realization of the importance of being self-conscious learners.

Understanding Students' Interests

If students are going to develop as readers, they need to be reading regularly both in school and beyond. Therefore, you will be able to encourage students most effectively if you have some idea of what they are interested in reading and have an idea of their particular interests. This will allow you to help them combine these interests with new kinds of reading. For example, a student who is interested in snowboarding might find a magazine on the sport fascinating and develop an interest in deeper reading on this topic from articles in magazines. You can find out about student interests by observing students as they interact with others, by engaging them in conversations, and by doing some journal writing with them about their own lives and what they read and do. At the beginning of the school year, simply asking your students to write about

Put a check by the level of knowledge you have of each word. If you think you really
know a term then either write a few words to define it or draw what it means.

Key Words	Unfamiliar	Have Seen	Know and Use	Definition/Drawing
Scavenge				
Scrawny				
Dung heap				
Midwife				
Apprentice				
Risk-taking				
Haggle				
Ointment				
Merchant				
Herbs				
Self-awareness				

FIGURE 11.3

Rate Your Knowledge.

their two favorite books can help you get a feel for them as readers. There are several
commercially available Interest Inventories that can also help you and the students
identify areas for more reading and for ways you can involve librarians in helping
locate appropriate and new materials for the class.

Developing a Diagnostic Eye and Ear

One of the most important forms of assessment is what you observe students doing
during your ongoing classroom reading activities. During these activities, you will see
students engaged with texts and responding to them in a variety of ways. Use all of
these typical situations to observe carefully and make notes of what students show
about their developing reading abilities. Experiment with ways to can record information from these classroom events so that you will build a profile of your students
as readers. Many teachers keep a clipboard nearby and focus on two or three students
a day, making notes about their engagement in discussions, their response to specific
questions, or their thinking aloud as they read with a group. Other teachers prefer
looking at the whole class and recording evidence of students' thinking, no matter

who seems to be revealing their strategies and understanding. Writing short Post-it notes of these occurrences and noting the students' names on the notes permits you to add these Post-its to a student folder where a variety of performance indicators are collected along with samples of their written work. Another approach is to shadow a particular student for a day, a form of observation that helps a teacher to create a more complete sense of how the student reads across a variety of situations.

Study Reading

As students enter the middle-school years, many find the shift in expectations quite startling. Instead of having teachers guide them through their assigned work, students are expected to know how to read and learn from assigned materials, to organize their own study time and come to class prepared, and to be able to study and learn a vast amount of knowledge. There are several areas in which teachers need to guide students so they can be successful.

Scheduling Time to Study

Allocating time for study is an important aspect of learning for middle-school students. This is a good time to provide students with weekly schedules and talk through ways to find regular study periods on weeknights and weekends. However, students often are not inclined to listen well to a teacher's recommendations. You can stress the need to study by calling on older peer models. Invite former students from high schools and universities to talk with your students about their study habits. Some students in class might have older siblings who can speak with authority about their strategies for learning. When middle-level students hear from older teens they respect, it becomes easier to guide them into more attentive reading and reflecting.

Students need to learn to keep a schedule for their study. You might ask visitors to bring their study plan books with them and show how important it is to develop a study schedule and keep records of assignments and time. Some of your own students might already have some form of study plan book or have parents who have given them planners. This can be a stimulus to help students review each week what they need to be working on and the time they will need to be prepared for all their assignments and projects.

Test Taking

Learning how to study for tests is important—and generally unknown to middle-level students. Take time to make a grid for different kinds of study and discuss with students strategies that are effective, particularly the advantages of spaced study and repeated rehearsal of new concepts and terms. Practice tests are something that is becoming very familiar—almost too familiar—in states with high-stakes testing. However, making students aware of the nature of those experiences is important. Talk through with the students how they went about answering questions. How did the format of the test influence their strategy for taking the test? When did they read the questions—before or after reading the story or passage? Did they skim through the text if it was fairly long? How did they finally make the decision to answer the question as they did?

Introducing the **Question Answer Relation (QAR) strategy** (Raphael, 1986) at this point is a good way to help students understand the difference between typical classroom questions that are often of a higher thinking nature and those asked on standardized tests. The QAR approach divides questions into four types: those that can be answered by finding one piece of information (right there), those that require searching the text (think and search), those that require drawing on background knowledge to add to the text (author and you), and those that go beyond information in the text itself (on your own). Standardized tests given to thousands of students must include answers that are available in the text passages themselves. Therefore, according to the QAR terminology, there are no "on your own" questions. All questions have answers that can be found either in a specific location in the text (right there) or by combining bits of information from sections of the text (think and search).

Teacher Modeling

Another way to raise interest and awareness of the cognitive choices readers need to make as they read is to describe your own reading behaviors when you are learning. For example, you might describe how you study for a graduate course you are taking. Show students how you study, and get them to compare and contrast their own habits with yours. A key habit you can reinforce is the need to read the same text sections several times and make notes about what you consider to be important. Show students your own text markings or the Post-it notes you insert at important points in a text.

Metacognition

Middle-level students are very pragmatic and seem to always want to know "Why do we need to do this?" They often lack the knowledge of what reading really involves and are unable to describe what they do. Middle-school students need to be better informed about what happens when they read and how they can become better readers. They need to develop **metacognition** about their learning, this is, an awareness of how they think. It involves three basic strategies: connecting new information to former knowledge; developing strategies for thinking; and planning, monitoring, and evaluating how they think (Dirkes, 1985). Activating metacognition can be done in a number of ways.

Active Reading

Students' metacognitive awareness of what good readers do while reading should be developed at this level. Teachers often begin this process by engaging in thinking aloud when they read orally. Using books that have margin notations on them is also a good way to stimulate students' attention to the thinking that goes on when good readers interact with pieces of text. You might create your own examples by having older students mark up a story or essay that your class is going to read. Go over the notations, and discuss them with the students: Why do you think this note was made? What would have stimulated this comment? How would you have responded? Comparing two or three different people's responses to the same article gives students a clearer idea of the wide variety of ways in which people engage with text. Then you can build a list of the kinds of engagements that others have made and begin to think of these as thinking

STANDARDS & LITERACY

★ ★ Creating Visual Images
While Reading ★ ★

Having noticed that many of her students rushed through their reading of fiction, the teacher questioned three students about what images were being created in their heads when they read. She got blank stares in response. Knowing that this was one of the objectives of the state standards, she decided that it was time to provide a focus on visualizing and imaging while reading.

A State Standards Literacy Plan

From Texas state standards: **Describe mental images that text descriptions evoke.**

TEACHER DECISION MAKING ABOUT THE LESSON.

Focus of Instruction: Modeling imaging through a think-aloud process followed by students creating their own images as they read a short section of text.

Materials: The teacher creates an overhead transparency of a short paragraph that evokes images. The teacher makes copies of two paragraphs from a short story students can easily read that has good images.

Before the lesson: The teacher explains to the students that an important part of active reading is the creation of our own personal images—or seeing a movie in our mind. Some readers think of having a mind's eye that creates pictures from words on print.

Albert Einstein once said, "If I can't picture it, I can't understand it." A good way to ensure that you are comprehending when you read is to check to see whether you are creating mental pictures of what you red.

During the lesson: The teacher models the process by putting the paragraph on the transparency and uncovers the sentences one at a time. She thinks aloud about her own images as she reads each sentence. Then the teacher involves students in sharing any images they have. She writes down her own ideas on the transparency and does the same with the students' as they share.

> The woman slowly emerged from the hollow.
> In one hand she carried her good shoes.
> She carefully protected the large,
>   bulging bag she carried over her shoulder.

After this introduction to imaging, the teacher asks students to take the copies of the two paragraphs she had copied for them and read them silently, drawing or writing the images that were created as they read. She then asks them to share these images with their partner. When this is completed, the class comes back together to reflect on their imaging.

After the lesson: The teacher asks that as the students read their novels that evening, they make notes in their journals of images that came to them as they read. They will share their own images the next day in class. She suggests that if students prefer, they can find pictures in magazines that reflect their images and create a collage of ideas from the reading.

TEACH IT!
38

strategies for your class, that is, visualizing, connecting to another text or author, marking it as providing an answer to a question, arguing with the text, etc.

Many good teachers use Post-it notes as a way of helping students monitor and develop their thinking as they read. They pose the question "What kinds of thinking do we do as we read?" To explore their own minds during engaged reading, each student can be given several Post-it notes and instructed to use them when ideas, images and questions come to them while reading. When the group (either the whole class or a small group) is finished reading, the students can compare their notes and begin to understand how different students think about the same text. These different responses can then be categorized, and students can talk about how they think. Extending this activity to explore how the same students read a different kind of text helps the group also extend their understanding of the impact of the text on reading and thinking.

Self-Assessment

Once you have developed students' awareness of how to read and learn from text, they can then regularly include their own self-evaluation of the strategies they use in the work they do. You can do this by asking students at the end of class periods to fill out 3 × 5 cards on their class participation and work. You can alter the questions each day you hand out the cards with stems like these:

- What did you learn today?
- How did you learn best today?
- How was your class participation?
- What could you do better to help the class learn?
- What bothers you, or is still unclear?
- What was most interesting to you today?
- What would you like to learn more about? What question do you have?

Begin the next class session by reviewing what the students had written the day before. This simple process gives students a regular way to think about their learning and to know that the teacher is serious about taking advantage of class time to ensure learning. It also provides the teacher with important feedback on the success of the class sessions.

Learning Logs

Learning logs also give students a vehicle for ongoing self-reflection on their learning. At least weekly, students should be encouraged to review what they have learned that week, what questions they have, and how they have contributed to the class accomplishments. Key concepts and new vocabulary are also important to record in a learning log so that students stay focused on their primary purposes in school. This is serious business, yet it is very enjoyable when each student can keep a record of growth. Too often, students shift attention from learning to social acceptance at this age, and all the ways teachers can use to involve students in knowing and evaluating their own successes help to balance the intense peer focus these students feel.

Extended Unit Assessment

Units of instruction are another place where student self-reflection is important. Right from the start, students should have a record of what they know and the questions they want to have answered from their study. Keeping this record in the form

A teacher's feedback and guidance can help students learn to assess their own development.

of a K-W-L chart in students' notebooks means that it will be available when students have completed their units. One teacher had students also generate a possible table of contents for the insect report they knew they would write as a culmination to their integrated language arts/science insect study and make a semantic map of how those topics might be related. All of these pieces were kept in the students' notebooks throughout the unit. At the end of the unit, the teacher again asked students to look at their actual table of contents and compare it with the first one they had predicted would work. The teacher also had the students create a new semantic map and make a comparison with their first one. The teacher asked that the students respond in writing to some questions:

- What surprised you most about your learning?
- How did your first table of contents compare to your final one?
- What did you notice about your semantic maps?
- How do you feel about your learning?

One student responded, *"I can't believe how much I learned! I even thought spiders were insects when we started. I learned what that crunchy sound is when you step on an insect — it is the eco-skeleton. I also learned how to create a semantic map and show the relation of body parts and what insects can do."*

Students also can use personal notes like the "Post-it" notes I-Chart (see Chapter 7) to evaluate their typical responses and thoughts while reading. When they compare their patterns with those of others in their class, they can begin to develop a broader sense of what reading can be and may consciously try to enhance their own thinking.

Portfolio Evaluation

Portfolios are great tools for student and teacher assessment at this level. These consist of personal collections of illustrative student work annotated to explain how they demonstrate learning or accomplishments. Students can collect examples of their own work that illustrate their best achievements and that also show the points they still need to take as goals. When you have students annotate or add note cards to the pieces in the portfolios, the students' self-reflection is deepened. Be careful in giving guidelines and setting parameters for portfolios, however, because they can easily get out of hand. Students love to sort and annotate their work and can spend hours creating covers for the portfolios. Space to save the portfolios is also an ongoing concern. So some clear guidelines about selecting a few pieces each quarter that illustrate both best work and work in progress can make the portfolio process integral to students' learning. Keeping a list of books and articles students have read with a short summary and evaluation can also become a lifetime habit. Students need visual records of what they are learning and reading and the portfolio is a natural aid in helping them to celebrate the results of their efforts.

Reaching all Students

Each year that students grow and learn, they become more individual in their knowledge, skills, learning styles, and strengths and interests. Good teaching encourages and nurtures the particular talents and differences in students' learning, so we all must celebrate these increasing variations! Research on multiple intelligences has helped us to understand that variations are natural and need to be considered in organizing for instruction.

Your students will bring with them a wide range of cultural and linguistic abilities. Many students know more than one language and have had experiences in diverse cultural settings. You can enrich your own learning and provide great resources to the whole class by using these opportunities sensitively and well. Therefore, as a teacher, you have real challenges in creating classroom experiences that meet students where they are and challenge them as literacy learners.

Identify Strengths

A key to reaching all of your students is being careful observers, or, to use the term coined by Yetta Goodman (1985), becoming a good *kid-watcher*. Each day you observe how your students come into your classroom, you can observe how they interact with their peers; you can listen to what they share; you can watch them as they read; and you can engage them in conversation. It takes just a few moments each day to become attuned to students. The effort is most valuable. Keeping a notebook page with bits of information gained from informal observations can help you to build a profile of each student that can be useful over time. Then, at an opportune moment, the particular strengths of a student can be called forth. For example, who is good with music and can help to plan the background pieces to accompany the presentations by the novel groups? Who is good at drawing and can illustrate the class book or movie reviews? Who is great at organizing on the computer and can catalogue the independent reading records? Who is a good oral reader or actor to help others visualize texts they are reading? Some of the less-adept readers and writers may have other strengths that will help them to learn more effectively and also contribute to the group in ways that can enhance their identity with literacy.

Recognize Students' Cultures

Language & Diversity

Teachers can help to make all students feel a part of the classroom by ensuring that materials about their cultures and situations are available and by reading from some of these materials. Teachers can also sensitize students to the plights of immigrants and minority students by reading aloud from some stories that represent situations similar to those of students in the school. It is often from ignorance that young teens can seem callous and not caring. When they hear the stories of what others have had to experience, their sense of fairness and empathy can be expanded. Table 11.5 identifies some books that can be good for such read-alouds.

English language learners bring with them a wealth of knowledge about their own languages and often have the ability to contrast languages in ways that can be helpful to monolingual students in your classroom. Having bilingual or trilingual students in

TABLE 11.5

Often Un-represented Voices of Youth

Allison, A. *Hear these voices: Youth at the edge of the millenium.* New York: Dutton Children's Books, 1999.

Bode, J. *New Kids in Town.* New York: Scholastic, 1989.

Na, A. *A Step from Heaven.* Asheville, NC: Front Street, 2001.

Rice, D. *Crazy Loco: Stories by David Rice.* New York: Dial Books, 2001.

Soto, G. *Baseball in April and Other Stories.* New York: Odyssey Books, 1990.

Walker, R. *Black, White and Jewish.* New York: Penguin, 2001.

class can be a real asset. Help them to become comfortable talking about these differences in language and culture:

- When you are discussing characters in stories, ask them to reflect on how the same character's actions would be perceived in their culture of origin. Discuss how characters would have handled the same situations.

- Have them act out the behaviors of a character in a story as if the character were from their culture. Compare these with how the same character's actions are depicted by some other students.

- Analyze the language used. Would it be different if from another culture? For example, would characters express their emotions as they do in the story you are reading? How would they interact with strangers?

- When reading classic stories, ask whether students from other cultures have stories similar to those you are reading. Do they have the same story in translated form or is the story from their culture (e.g., Arabian Nights, Aesop's Fables, Cinderella, the Nutcracker)?

- Make lists of key vocabulary terms, and have students write the same words in their languages. These comparisons can often be the beginning point for discussion of where English has acquired its words.

- Graph the story structure of pieces you read with the class. Ask someone from another culture to show the structure of a typical tale from their culture. Are they the same? (For example, Athabaskan and Japanese tales often have a less defined beginning and ending than Eurocentric tales do and can go on and on, leaving more to the reader to determine.)

- Read orally from news that reflects the world as represented by students in your school. Use maps so that the areas they come from become familiar to everyone. Use current events as the texts for some of the reading strategies you model. Often, students coming from abroad have a better sense of world events than do U.S. students, and their knowledge can be used to expand everyone's perspectives.

Adjusting Teaching for English Language Learners

When students are functioning in a second or third language, they need more time to process what they read and hear and more time to compose their own responses. Even when students have exited from bilingual programs, they have not had time to develop the depth of vocabulary and language usage required by middle-school literature and content texts. The more the teacher can do to support their development of English, the better they will be able to engage fully in class activities and think deeply about content.

There are a few easy ways in which the teacher can support these students' learning within each area or theme. First, brainstorm the key terms you will be using, and check the students' familiarity with them. Create a glossary of the terms that are not known, and put these on a bookmark that students can keep with them while reading and studying. Second, as a way to introduce the writing of an author to students, have some parent volunteers tape-record the first part of a text (a novel or story or a chapter of informational material) so that the students can hear the language and begin to recognize the connections between the oral and written forms.

A third way to help English language learners participate fully is to give them some pre-experiences before the class begins a new area of study. You might hear this referred to as "jump-starting" their thinking and learning. For example, if you are going to have a unit on survival tales and will read some of Gary Paulsen's books, check out a videotape showing the setting of Canada and the northlands so that students can more easily visualize as they read. You might also find some easier books or magazine stories that introduce the same concepts that you will deal with in a novel or informational unit and let students take these home and learn from them before delving into the more difficult class texts. You also might be able to find easier versions of some of the stories you will have students read and these can be used as advance organizers to prepare your English language learners for the complete version. Many readers do better with texts when they have a good idea of what the content is about; this is particularly the case for your English language learners. Help them to discover what works best for them, and then try to provide appropriate scaffolds for their learning.

⭐ Organizing for Instruction

Middle grades are just that—in the middle between self-contained elementary classrooms and high schools with their departmental structures. In some schools, grades five to eight are treated much like the earlier elementary grades, in which one teacher has a single class with some special teachers perhaps providing elective courses in foreign language and music or computers for the students. Other schools create teams of students and teachers, so between 80 and 120 students are grouped together with four or five teachers, and the teams stay together for two or three years. Many middle-school advocates have supported this model as a way to provide more guidance and create "home groups." Another variant is for students to have the same teacher for two or three subjects—usually language arts, reading, and social studies or a combined reading/language arts block. This core or combined teaching structure helps teachers to know their students more deeply, since they have fewer sections. Yet other schools are totally departmentalized with no groupings, so reading teachers teach four or five different groups of students each day. Any team teaching is done by individual teachers working together. Most new teachers have little say in how the school is organized. However, it is important that you know what kind of structure your school has in place because it provides the framework within which you have to teach.

There are several options for providing a range of reading opportunities that develop students' strategies and knowledge of reading. The following are certainly not exhaustive of how good instruction can be organized. Nor are they comprehensive.

Integrating Content Areas

As one reads about the kinds of reading strategies and skills that middle-grade students need to develop, the advantages of either teaming or having students for two or three subjects are clear. Students need to learn to read in many kinds of texts and for many purposes. They are more interested and engaged in developing these when they see the concrete and immediate use of them (Guthrie, 2003). For example, teaching students how to retain new and important vocabulary is much easier if the teacher can show students how to do it when they need to master their history or science content. Helping them learn to read dense textbooks is easier when the teacher can use the students own content textbooks. Middle graders are very pragmatic and concrete, and the more instruction is directly tied to needs, the more likely they are to attend and process the strategies.

There is so much that needs to be taught that teachers have come up with a wide variety of ways of organizing the curriculum to meet these wide-ranging aspects of reading. One of the basic issues to be faced is how to balance the reading of literature with reading in informational texts and helping students learn to use reading to learn. One good option is to divide the year into quarters and teach with fictional literature and poetry for two quarters, use a thematic focus for one quarter and involve students in reading and evaluating multiple sources, and spend another quarter on inquiry and research, linking with either science or social studies teachers so that students have both the content and process as high priorities. Within this quarter organization, there are many options for instruction.

Although there is a general organizational frame around themes and units of instruction, there needs to be a continuing focus on students' independent reading and on their developing vocabulary interest and knowledge. The teacher needs to continue to provide a central model of good reading and show students how reading can be part of daily life. The teacher also needs to attend to the community climate and encourage a positive atmosphere associated with reading and learning; without attention to the students as individuals and as a community, much good instruction can be lost.

Teaching Literature

Most elementary students have been reading fiction and can anticipate the basic structures and techniques used in this kind of text. However, in the middle grades, several new genres are introduced, and they can pose problems for readers who are on automatic pilot much of the time in independent-level materials. Science fiction, fantasy, short stories, and stream-of-consciousness pieces are often new to these students. That said, with the current rage for Harry Potter and Tolkien's Lord of the Rings books, some fantasy texts are becoming better known even among younger students. Biography is another genre that is important to teach at this level, since it provides a great link for students to the world at different periods of history and to people who have had important influences on the students' own development. Longer, narrative poetry is often given more attention in the middle grades, and students can be involved in dramatic play readings, choral reading, and readers' theater. Some teachers concentrate one unit on novel forms and a second on short stories, poetry, and drama. This is where the developmental continuum from fifth to eighth grades needs to be worked out among the reading and literature teachers so that students continue to learn more about literature each year. Teachers can develop their literature focus in at least three ways: using core novels and literature groups, literature circles, and readers' workshops.

CORE NOVEL AND LITERATURE GROUPS.   Use a core novel representing a genre you want to introduce with all students to begin the novel unit. Then have students select from four or five novels you have prearranged for their subsequent work in literature groups. By engaging all students in a single novel, you have a good context for introducing and modeling the concepts and strategies you think are important for students to be using independently later. With all students reading the same text, you can also help them develop good discussion skills and courteous behavior. Because a whole class is too large to hold engaging discussions most of the time, you can use a "fishbowl" technique and divide the class into two parts: Half the students sit in the center of the room and participate in oral discussion, and the other half sit around the outer part of the class and write their responses to the questions and flow of ideas and also monitor the participants' discussion behaviors. Use the same inner circle for the whole class period, or, if time permits, shift the roles halfway through the class period and give both groups the opportunity to participate both orally and in written form. By having the outer circle evaluate the participation of the inner circle, there is a good record of who has contributed and how the discussion proceeded. Students' written comments also serve as a good way to evaluate their own interpretation of the text and their response to the ideas discussed.

Language & Diversity

Supporting English Language Learners.   Using a single novel also helps students who are English language learners participate more fully in the class. Before the unit begins, a few students or parents can tape-record the novel or the first half of it so that English language learners can hear the sounds of the language and become familiar with the text. The teacher can also prepare special guides for these students so that they can follow the plot, know the characters, and think of questions ahead of class discussion. Some teachers have found that by giving English language learners mini-lessons before the general class sessions helps them to gain confidence in their understanding of the text so they can relax and enjoy the discussion of the text during the class periods. Finally, students gain confidence in their ability to contribute to class discussions when the teacher provides time for students to talk with partners before responding in the whole class or fishbowl. Pose a question for the group, then let students turn to their partners to think aloud about their responses, find the words and ways of expressing ideas in English, and get feedback that either modifies their ideas or confirms what they have said. Then open the conversation to the larger group. With this slight modification, many English language learners feel much more confident and comfortable participating in larger class groups. It is also a good model for all students: Think before speaking!

Connecting Writing and Reading.   While using a core novel with the whole class, you have the opportunity to model journal writing and use students' own responses to enhance the discussions. Students might need to learn how to respond to literature. Begin by showing your own journal entry for a part of the text the group is reading. Provide labels for the kinds of responses you make: connecting with the text *(this reminds me of . . .),* raising questions *(what does it matter if . . . ?),* visualizing *(I see . . . in my mind's eye),* responding emotionally *(I don't like ___ when . . .),* predicting *(I bet this problem will . . . .),* and elaborating *(I know at this time in history there were often periods of . . .).* You might need to ask students to use two or three of the kinds of responses in their own journals so that they can develop the various ways of responding and then switch to other forms in the next entry. What you think is easy and automatic might be very uncomfortable for students. Rather than presuming a great deal, it is often better to start slowly and ensure that all students understand the tasks and intent of the journal experiences.

If students have a difficult time writing journal entries, they might do well to partner with another classmate and, between talk and writing, frame their joint responses to the text. You might find it useful to give students Post-it notes to use while they are reading so that they don't lose the ideas that come to them while reading. Then they can return to those notes and elaborate on them as they write in their journals.

Journals can also serve as tools to help students focus on the features of the genre or other important elements of literature that you want to highlight. Students can keep a place in the journal where they record examples of specific literary elements, such as the setting in fantasy or futuristic elements in science fiction. They can also note special phrases or uses of language in the journal and share those later with other students. You can ask students to keep a section of their journals in which they can write new vocabulary items or new ways in which terms are used. If they record the pages on which the words occur, they can begin to see how authors often repeat the same vocabulary in different contexts. Adding drawings of the terms helps many students to enjoy this activity and remember the new words more easily.

LITERATURE CIRCLES.   Students tend to discuss books better when teachers are not leading the groups (Raphael & McMahon, 1994; Almasi, 1995; Short and Klassen, 1995; Hynds, 1997). Many teachers prefer conducting their literature units by having students self-select the books they read and work in small discussion groups rather than in teacher-led discussions of the same novel. They do their teaching in minilessons at the beginning of the class period so that all students can focus on the element the teacher highlights but in their own texts and then take on the role of active observers during book discussions led by the students. At times, teachers also serve as facilitators of the students' discussions, but do not assume the role of "expert" at these time.

The nature of the minilessons that are used should derive from observations of the students as they are involved in reading and responding and by evaluating the written work of the students. The major framework that helps teachers to develop the foci for teaching comes also from the standards students should be able to meet.

For example, in Illinois, middle-grade students are expected to learn to "compare how authors and illustrators use text and art across materials to express ideas"—for example, foreshadowing, flashback, color, strong verbs, language that inspires (Illinois State Goal 1, middle/junior high). Knowing that expectation, a team of seventh-grade teachers developed a unit around the Middle Ages using novels and art representing that time period. They selected a set of novels including *The Ramsey Scallop* (Temple, 1994), *Catherine, Called Birdy* (Cushman, 1994), and the *The Midwife's Apprentice* (Cushman, 1995). They added materials that exemplified life in medieval Europe in other artistic forms: books about life in medieval Europe, including *Anno's Journey* (Mitsumasa, 1997), and McCauley's *Castle* (1982), examples of tapestries from the collection at the Cloisters from the Metropolitan Museum for students to observe; and tapes of Gregorian chants. On the day the unit was introduced, the teachers played the music in the background, showed slides of the art, and did book talks of each of the novels. They then gave students time to look through each of the novels and make a decision about which books they wanted to read. Each student listed their first and second choices. From these lists, the teachers could help guide students to appropriate texts; some were much harder than others, and the teachers wanted all students to read somewhat challenging materials but not books they could not handle. During the unit, the teachers guided students to make comparisons about the artistic techniques used by artists in different media. Part of the journal guidelines for the students was to locate interesting examples of language used to create pictures of the times and compare that with other art. At specific points in the unit, the teachers also had students compare the plot and literary devices used by the different authors. In these and many other ways the teachers used the state standards and their own creative planning to develop a stimulating and enjoyable learning experience for the students.

Teachers varied the assignments they used to focus student learning. Because understanding point of view is another standard, some students were asked to keep a journal from the point of view of a character of their choice while reading. Students reading the same novel selected different characters so the impact of the plot and events on them could be recognized. Another group of students was asked to take particular scenes and rewrite them from a point of view different from that of the author. This proved a very interesting and challenging task. As a culmination, one group created a short readers' theater production for their novel that required students to take on the personas of the characters in the novel. In all these ways, the teachers focused the students' learning so that the maximum was gained for the time spent reading.

There are many advantages to having students in literature groups. First, the students' different reading abilities and interests can be accommodated much more easily this way, and all students can participate in the class activities. Assignments can be matched to the students' learning needs; not all able readers have developed the skills and strategies they need and can be focused through specific work. Using multiple texts permits teachers and students to make comparisons among authors and forms of art so authors' decisions and styles can be illustrated. Core vocabulary and concepts are generally repeated in various texts, so students gain a deeper understanding of the basic concepts and can develop better visual images of what they read. Students become resources for each other in very real ways when they are the authorities on particular texts. Speaking clearly, summarizing well, using good examples, and then listening to each other are very real communication skills that can be developed.

GUIDED READING AND READERS' WORKSHOPS. There is so much variety in the kinds of reading that students need to develop during the middle years that some group instruction by teachers is necessary. All students need to learn more about how textbooks are structured and the resources they contain. The differences in structures and discourse forms with which students must become familiar require teacher guidance.

The various graphic aids and formats also need explanation and some direct attention. Then there is the issue of learning to do research and study independently. The middle years are when these become very important for students, and good schools provide a significant amount of time helping them learn to do research well and to construct reports and presentations. With the availability of computers, the use of the Web for collecting and evaluating information and the use of software for creating high-quality reports with digital pictures, imported pictures, and student-created diagrams and charts also need to be taught. For teachers who prefer doing most of their classwork in fiction, this means that special segments of each week or a few weeks each quarter need to be devoted to informational reading and study.

Some teachers prefer to structure a portion of their reading program around student-selected individual reading. Atwell (1998) has developed the **reading workshop** model, during which students all read individually in books of their own choosing and then keep logs of their reading to use when they conference with the teacher. When students come together to discuss their reading, Atwell characterizes the conversations as a "dining room table" conversation about what each is reading. Although most of the time students read silently and write individual responses, the teacher brings students together periodically for minilessons in which aspects of literature or reading strategies can be explained. Later, students can apply these lesson foci when they engage in their own reading.

Depending on the amount of time the teacher has with your students each day, the two components of a rich literacy program can be developed simultaneously or on alternating days and weeks. The two aspects can also be combined if teachers want to direct students' individual reading toward a particular theme or genre. For example, if the class is working on aspects of informational textbooks and scientific articles, then students could do their individual reading in books that include scientific essays, in magazines such as *Science* and *Scientific American* (or student magazines in the areas of science), and in biography. There are great texts that students can read and use to enlarge their horizons in this more guided reading workshop.

How can students' assessments of each other's work help them to develop their comprehension and writing skills?

TEACH IT!
34

Expository Texts: Thematic Units

Most middle-level students enjoy exploring unanswered questions and making school relevant to their own lives. This is easier to do when a class is engaged in a focused group inquiry project or thematic unit of study. Because students are generally much less familiar with informational, expository texts than they are with fiction, providing a stimulating context for the study of such materials is very advantageous. By having the students read several texts on the same topic, you can more easily illustrate the various text structures that are used and can help students to determine the advantages and disadvantages of each. You can also provide activities in which students write using those same structures. Attention to the varieties of forms of informational writing is important, as is the need to make it interesting. Therefore, many teachers have found that developing units around interesting content permits better teaching and learning

THE AMERICAN DREAM UNIT OVERVIEW

Thematic Statement: Personal goals and choices are influenced by our own values.

Focus Question: Is it still possible to achieve the American Dream?

Project: Persuasive Paper: Is the American dream still achievable for me?

Selection	Genre	Perspective	Diversity	Period
The Grapes of Wrath	novel/realistic fiction	negative	Lower-class Anglo-American	1930s
The Great Gatsby	novel/realistic fiction	negative	Upper-class Anglo-American	1920s
"I Have A Dream"	speech	positive	African American	1960s
"Maya Angelou"	poem	positive	African American	1990s
"An American Dream"	magazine	positive	European	1990s
"Charlie Two Shoes & the American Dream"	magazine	positive	Asian	1950s
"Is the American Dream Still Alive"	magazine	positive	Mexican-American	1990s
"False Gold"	magazine	negative	Lower-class America	1990s

FIGURE 11.4

Thematic Unit Overview.

than other skill-focused instruction. This can be achieved either by creating units with content teachers (in departmental structures) or by integrating reading and content when you teach content and reading to the same students.

One model for integrated units developed by Michigan educators uses a key question as the focus for each unit, such as "Can the American dream be achieved?" In collecting the resources students will read, they use a planning grid to ensure that multiple perspectives on the issues are presented and that a wide variety of literature, both fiction and nonfiction, is included. See the example in Figure 11.4 of the resources for one unit.

Essays and Biography

When teachers do not feel comfortable creating more extended units around themes or content topics, they can still provide guided instruction to help students handle informational reading. Contemporary magazines for middle-school students contain

TEACH IT!

★ ★ ★ ★

A Thematic Unit

Using the theme of human rights permitted Katie Kelly, an eighth-grade teacher in Chicago, to help students learn to use their textbook more effectively and also develop skills in reading from a variety of informational texts and primary resources. The Bill of Rights of the Constitution is often seen as something very abstract and boring by students who are required to learn about it as part of their history and civics requirements. However, it is an incredibly important and contemporarily significant document. To help students understand this, Ms. Kelly began by asking some questions that students deal with in her city:

- Should there be hand gun regulation to control the numbers of guns on our streets?

- Is it right to permit such foul language in the popular music young people are listening to, singing, and repeating daily?

- Should children be able to sue their parents?

During the course of the unit, students added some of their own questions to those Ms. Kelly had raised initially, making the unit even more centered on student questions and concerns.

They began the unit using the textbook and looking at the Constitution and Bill of Rights in the glossary section of the book. Students knew that they would be responsible for taking a test on the constitution later in the year, so there was a basic level of interest in the topic. However, Ms. Kelly made the Bill of Rights come alive by posing contemporary questions that relate directly to the Bill of Rights. She

chose the issue of hand guns, since there had been several shootings in the city, and many people, including the mayor, were calling for more hand gun control. Yet the Bill of Rights ensures the right of self-protection and the right to bear arms. Ms. Kelly collected several newspapers that had articles related to this controversy in them. She then developed a guide sheet for students to use as they read about the various perspectives people were taking on the issue. She wanted them to identify the perspective taken by each writer and the arguments given. Students then were to summarize the evidence or examples provided for each argument and indicate whether they could add supporting evidence or counterevidence. Ms. Kelly wanted students to link their own prior knowledge and experience with the arguments they were encountering in the printed media. She guided them to some web pages that added information and deeper knowledge about the status of gun use in the country and about how other countries handle gun ownership. She also invited a police officer, a student's father, to speak to the class about the threat police feel with so many guns on the streets. As they developed knowledge about the issues, students were asked to define their own perspectives. As part of the unit, students developed a debate with both pro and con arguments developed by the speakers. Finally, each student had to write a persuasive essay and send it to one of the area's newspapers articulating their position on gun control with good reasons.

Ms. Kelly also had students read fiction that dealt with civil rights. She used Avi's book *Nothing but the Truth* (1994) as a whole-class read and provided

(continued on next page)

TEACH IT!

★ ★ ★ ★

Continued

several other books for student choice, including Lois Lowry's *The Giver* (2002) and *Summer Begins* (Asher, 1982). She gave students added choice by letting some read and discuss in groups and letting others read individually and keep a journal of their responses. Some students also maintained the class bulletin board of news items related to gun control and so kept the class informed about what was happening locally and beyond the city. Others maintained the class "glossary of rights" vocabulary chart. As students became aware of key terms, they would add them to the class list, someone would illustrate the term, and others would provide definitions and synonyms. Sometimes the class noted changes of uses and connotations for the words and would keep written examples of these instances and where they appeared.

Refer to your **Teach It!** booklet for further activities you can use to reinforce concepts discussed in this chapter.

This unit, rich in reading, language arts, and social studies content and strategies, was planned for three weeks but extended into more than four since the students became so involved in reading and learning. Ms. Kelly found that students became very critical readers of newspapers, magazines, and web sites. The more knowledge they acquired, the better able they were to analyze arguments and respond to them. At the end of the unit, Ms. Kelly knew that her students had learned forms of exposition and argumentation, knew how to support arguments and evaluate positions, and could write their own persuasive essays and informational pieces on the right to bear arms. They were more aware of word choice and how connotations influence meaning. Did they solve the problem of guns in the city? No, but they certainly knew a great deal more about the issue, gained confidence in having a voice in addressing controversial topics, and understood much more about the relationship of guns to Americans' sense of freedom.

much excellent writing and are good sources for reading development. *Cobblestones, Calliope, Faces, National Geographic World,* and *Boys' Life* magazines are great sources of articles. Collecting a variety of biographies, both long and short, is another way of providing texts that permit the teacher to guide students to reading more deeply in this genre. The different ways in which biography are structured provides the opportunity to focus on organization and can be linked to students' writing of a biography later. Teachers can provide a good comparative study of how biographers represent the lives and accomplishments of well-known figures by structuring assignments so that students read and compare encyclopedia-type sketches and then read more in-depth book treatments of the same person. When more than one full-length biography is available, even more critical analysis is made possible, and students find it engaging. They easily become excited (and sometimes indignant) at how people are represented. Then good questions analyzing the author's purpose, context, and perspective are natural.

Readers' Theater exercises can be incorporated into all areas of the curriculum and is a popular technique with young people.

Drama and Choral Reading

One of the most interesting aspects of written language is hearing it read and performed orally. Middle-level students also love these kinds of activities. Some teachers allocate two to three weeks during the year for production of a play or choral reading and having students perform before audiences. These dramatic events can be part of science and social studies content as much as literature units. There are web sites specifically devoted to readers' theater scripts for teacher use. This makes including this oral form of reading (and rereading for fluency) much easier for busy teachers.

For English language learners, opportunities to participate in rehearsed oral language productions or even oral reading of poetry helps to instill a sense of the sounds of English language that can last a lifetime. Regular opportunities to memorize or at least reread and rehearse language provides valuable patterns that English language learners can rely on and build from later.

Organizing and Managing a Learning Community

As you plan instruction to include all that is important for middle-grade students to learn, consider some of the options suggested in Figure 11.5 on page 484 for weekly programs. These can shift over the course of the semester; however, you need to use your time wisely, and attention to planning will always pay off. Note the allotted time for whole group activities, small groups and individual work and reflection.

Adolescents' Identity and Motivation

Reaching and teaching young adolescents takes special consideration. Students at this period in their lives are going through enormous changes; one day they might seem like they are adults and very much in control, and the next day the same students behave as if they are children, definitely in need of adult structure and guidance. Early adolescents also feel tremendous pressures from their peers. They want to be accepted and part of the peer group of those they admire. Often, this drives them away from adults and family, and teachers have to build their trust in order to create open, safe classrooms where students will engage fully.

Adding to the normal developmental changes that middle-level students go through, our current culture means that students are inundated with information and options—a sort of food court mentality. Everything students do involves choice, from what kind of milk to drink to which brand of French fries they want to eat. Even the cereals they eat in the morning might be their own selected favorites, chosen by no

Monday	Tuesday	Wednesday	Thursday	Friday
Class focusing in whole group (10 min.) Share independent reading and viewing	Class focusing in whole group (5-10 min.) Teacher shares own reading	Class focusing in whole group (5-10 min.) Reflect on goals for week	Class focusing: teacher reads orally and thinks aloud—model use of target goal	Class focusing teacher/students share vocabulary
Teacher-guided lessons: reading and writing strategies attention to detail (30 min.+) & Small group and individual reading & writing activities: guided practice and independent work	Individual silent reading and writing (15-20 min.) & Partner/small group work (5-10 min.) Teacher conferences	Small group discussions (10-15 min.) and journal reflections Teacher observation of discussion—some participation Individual reading and writing (15 min.)	Teacher guided lessons: focus reading or vocabulary strategies (10-15 min.) Individual work reading, writing and research (10-15 min.)	Small group discussions (10-15 min.) journal reflections Individual work
Reflecting/ writing/planning ahead (5-10 min.)	Reflecting/ thinking ahead (5-10 min.)	Reflecting/ thinking ahead (5-10 min.)	Reflecting/ thinking ahead	Reflecting/ writing/ thinking ahead (1-10 min.)

FIGURE 11.5

Weekly Schedule.

other family member. They become accustomed to having life tailored to their specific interests and preferences. This has real implications for their response to classroom activities. Choice needs to be a part of what is provided in terms of materials, groups, and learning activities. Children who are given choices outside of school expect them in school, too.

Young students live in a world that is ever changing and somewhat frightening to them. They look for classrooms that are safe and that respect their needs and interests. The teacher can do a great deal to make classrooms predictable and orderly simply by having clear routines and ways of engaging that students can anticipate. For instance, when students have several teachers each day, they often get confused about what kinds of participation each considers acceptable. Explaining how you want students to behave—when they have to raise their hands, when they can interrupt each other, when they can move around the room, and how they interact in small group activities helps many. Putting the rules on a chart that can be displayed regularly makes many others feel more comfortable. In addition, the clearer you make your expectations for the work students will do and how they will be evaluated, the more likely it is that students will relax and participate actively.

The humor, compassion, and idealism of young students are also wonderful attributes of this stage. They respond well to teachers who bring in humor, give them an opportunity to laugh, and encourage their fun sides. Many middle-grade students find meaning by being able to work with younger students, and some classes make it a regular practice to build buddy programs with primary classrooms so that the middle-level students serve as mentors and helpers for young children.

Finally, students at this stage need to see the relevance of the activities they are asked to do. The more learning can involve real inquiry about topics of concern to them the more likely students are to become engaged. Beane (1997) even advocates that middle-school students together at the beginning of the school year determine the units that they study. Being clear about the goals and purposes of class activities and how they relate to the students is important. Establishing a safe climate where students can ask question, engage in extended inquiry, and express their own ideas and conclusions is a foundation to their learning.

Beamon (2001) suggests that adolescents learn best when activities are interactive and purposeful and include meaningful engagement. The five circumstances that make this most likely are as follows:

- Adolescents do something that makes sense in a larger context, such as confronting real-life issues and problems.
- Their personal initiative and energy are moved into action through meaningful involvement with relevant and current content.
- Their cognitive and affective capabilities are challenged, such as when connections are made between difficult content and its application to personal experience.
- They can draw on a variety of resources in the learning environment, including personal experience, the local community and the Internet.
- Their knowledge and understanding are substantively broadened or deepened.

Selecting Appropriate Materials

Most new teachers start out the year having to use the materials that have already been selected—whether it is a reading anthology/basal series, a literature series, or a curriculum built around novels and thematic units of instruction. If there are classroom sets of novels, informational books, and magazines, these can be great resources for building a rich reading program. You want to make sure you can create a room that invites students in to reading and writing. One element of immersion is creating the right environment; the visual statement is a powerful one that all students notice. Having books and magazines is important, and ensuring that they are current and of interest is essential, as is displaying them attractively.

Assess what is available to you, and think of any holes that seem apparent. For example, check to see whether multiple levels of reading materials are available so that you can differentiate instruction for your students. Check to see whether fiction, poetry, plays, and readers' theater scripts are handy and that informational materials are in good supply. As you do your own inventory, also check with the school librarian and/or media specialist to see what resources they have for your use. And, of course, talk with the other teachers on your team or in your department so that you can be aware of all the collected materials that are available. Table 11.6 identifies some basic materials you will need to get started.

Given the current attention to state standards, a more focused curriculum is also quite likely. You will want to assess areas in which there are ample materials for your use when you want to go in-depth and do some lessons that provide attention to detail in practice materials. Some of these might be available for use on computers; make an inventory of all the resources you can locate.

Because it is important that students learn to think critically about their reading, check for ways in which you can help students read from a variety of resources on the same topic or theme. If you have an anthology to use for literature selections, can you locate two or three pieces that complement or contrast with the core text so you can go beyond a single selection? If you are linking to content areas like science and social studies, do you have both fiction and nonfiction materials that will deepen the units of study and help you guide students into more sophisticated reading of these materials?

A wealth of resources is available for use with middle-school learners. The following web sites provide resources and links to literature discussions in which students can participate:

- The National Council for Social Studies provides a list of Notable Social Studies Books for Young People at www.socialstudies.org/resources/notable/.

- The National Science Teachers Association recommends a variety of resources, including books, at www.nsta.org/recommends/.

- The International Reading Association provides lists of choice books compiled by teachers, young adults, and children at www.reading.org/choices/.

- Many books also contain book lists. Junko Yakota's book *Kaleidoscope* (2001, National Council of Teachers of English) includes a booklist for grades K–8.

- Many local libraries have web sites that provide links to online book clubs. Sometimes the libraries themselves sponsor book clubs. In many cases, libraries

---

TABLE 11.6

Materials Checklist

- Range of core text materials at varying reading levels

- Variety of types of materials (short stories, novels, informational texts, magazines, newspapers)

- Resource materials (how our language grows and changes; language usage, and vocabulary; thesaurus, dictionaries)

- Practice materials (print and electronic) including vocabulary supports

- Materials that provide contrasting points of view

- Professional materials for your use and students' use, as appropriate have partnered with the organization "Chapteraday," which has book clubs for teens as well as adults and covers a broad range of genres. Check out the following links to online book clubs: http://www.chapteraday.com, http://www.surfnetkids.com/bookclubs.htm, www.planetbookclub.com.

Assessing Reading Levels of Materials

Sometimes you have a room full of materials, but you do not know whether they are appropriate for your students' reading development. You might want to do a quick fluency check to see how many of your students can handle the material easily. Sampling a few students who scored at the middle range, a few from the lower level, and a few from the upper level as charted on your fluency scale can give you a good idea of how you can use your material. One other easy way to check the match between any particular novel, text, or other material and your students is to develop a cloze test (Bormuth, 1968) and administer it to your students.

CLOZE ASSESSMENT.   To use the **cloze test**, take a passage of about 300 words from early in the text, and retype it for your students, deleting every fifth word starting with the second sentence. Make sure that you have spaces of equal length for all the words that were left out and that the spaces are large enough that students can fill in what they think the author used. To get a more accurate indication of the difficulty of the text, sampling two or three passages will help.

Before giving the cloze test, model the procedure, since it might be unfamiliar to your students. Create a short sample from an article, leaving the first one or two sentences intact (see Figure 11.6). Then delete every fifth word until you have about five to ten spaces. Put the passage on the computer screen, on an overhead, or on the erasable board. Explain that you are going to try to fill in the exact words the author used, taking into

---

We have seen that the American colonists needed labor to build their fortunes and, in the process, build a nation. And we have seen their willingness to take that labor, by force, from Africans. But, African men and _____ did not willingly surrender _____ lives. The people who came _____ the boats were Africans, _____ by a strange tribe. _____ plantation owners did not _____ captives longing from freedom, _____ for ways to overthrow _____ who held them; they _____ slaves, people who would _____ without having to be _____ watched.

Taken from *Now Is Your Time!* By Walter Dean Myers (p. 36; HarperCollins, NY, 1991)

Exact words deleted: women, their from, captured, The, want, longing, looking, wanted, work, constantly

---

FIGURE 11.6

Cloze Passage.

account the style and total context of the piece. Let the students know that you are trying to determine whether the particular author has written in a way that matches their expectations and knowledge. Students might need another example that they can do independently or with a partner before completing the full cloze passage you have developed (see Figure 11.7). If you use this second modeling, be sure that you take time to go over the answers and explain why particular choices are better than others.

When you score the students' responses, count only the exact word the author used as correct. Although this might not seem to make sense, much research on the procedure has shown that exact word replacement leads to reliable scoring. Each student should respond to fifty items. Scores of 40 percent or fewer correct indicate that the material is at the frustration level for the students. Accuracy between 44 percent and 60 percent indicates that the material is within the students' instructional range. Scores above 60 percent correct indicate that the material is easy for the students to read and correlates to independent reading level in the IRI.

OTHER MEASURES TO DETERMINE LEVELS.   One of the most traditional ways to assess the difficulty level of materials is to use a formula that measures the difficulty of the words and the complexity of the sentences. Both the Dale-Chall (1948) Formula (for easy materials) and the Fry (1967) Readability Formula (appropriate through adult materials) use these indices of difficulty. Teachers can select a few passages from the text and determine their difficulty level; however, these formulas are general and provide only a rough estimate of difficulty for readers.

More recently, the Degrees of Reading Power (Touchstone Applied Science Associates, 1991) was developed to match readers and text difficulty. A wide range of materials was evaluated and matched to reading levels. Students' reading is measured on tests that use a cloze format. This process permits assigning readers to particular "degrees of power." Using a computer program, schools can level their textbooks and materials and match them to students' reading abilities.

Scholastic Books (MetaMetrics) has also made available a new system, called the Lexile Framework (Stenner, 2003), to determine reading levels. This system provides

---

When animal droppings and garbage and spoiled straw are piled up in a great heap, the rotting and moiling give forth heat. Usually no one gets close enough to notice because of the stench. But the girl noticed _____, on that frosty night, _____ deep into the warm, _____ muck, heedless of the _____. In any event, the _____ heap probably smelled little _____ than everything else in _____ life—the food scraps _____ from the kitchen yards, _____ stables and sties she _____ in when she could, _____ her own unwashed, unnourished, _____, and unlovely body.

Taken from *The Midwife's Apprentice* by Karen Cushman (p. 1; Clarion Books, NY, 1995)

Exact words deleted: and, burrowed, rotting, smell, dung, worse, her, scavenged, the, slept, and, unloved

FIGURE 11.7

Cloze Passage (Second Short Model).

levels for materials from kindergarten through twelfth grade. The lexile units provide a more fine-tuned range of levels than most other systems and teachers can use it to match students to the wide range of trade books Scholastic provides.

Use these tools just as rough starting places. Students' individual knowledge and interests influence how well they can understand texts they read. As students get older, the use of formulas becomes less predictive of the match between students and materials. Therefore, it is always good to check with students directly about their ability to understand materials. They can often provide clear feedback, and their ability to read and talk about what they read is the real measure we need. It is also true that the more students read on any topic, the more able they become to handle more difficult materials on the same topic. The same is true with authors; once students become familiar with an author's style, they can more easily independently handle more material by that particular author.

Involving Parents and the Community

**Family &
Community
Literacy**

Many parents of middle-school students complain that their children no longer want to share with them what happens in school. One middle school decided to create a structure that would bring students and parents together. They initiated the Generations Literature Circle as a voluntary activity and then extended it to become a full part of school life. Parents and students agreed to read the same novel and come together for a book discussion and share their responses to the book. Both groups read and made notes about favorite passages, and both groups developed questions they wanted to ask others about the book. Parents were not to ask those questions of their own children but could offer them to the whole group. The book discussion replaced part of the parent conference night. It provided a good way for parents to understand the new forms of book discussion being used by the reading and language arts department. As they experimented with the discussions, one class had fun using the inner/outer circle idea. First the students formed the inner circle and discussed some aspects of the book under teacher facilitation. Then the parents took their turn and discussed the same issues. Both groups had a great time understanding a little better the responses of the other generation.

Another exciting community reading event occurred when the mayor of Chicago declared that the whole city would read a book together. The book that was chosen was *To Kill a Mockingbird*. This book was already being used in many schools as part of the regular middle-school literature/social studies curriculum, but for the special year, the middle school teachers in one K–8 building decided to involve the local school council members (the community school board) in a discussion of the book. During the first part of the evening, the Council members sat in the inner circle and discussed their responses to the book while the eighth graders listened. Then it was the eighth graders' turn while the adults listened. What a memorable night! And what different perspectives were enabled.

FOR REVIEW

Middle-level students are at a great stage of development—moving from childhood to maturity. They are eager and impatient to find themselves in the world, especially among their peers. Books and good instruction can provide great models and stimulate their best impulses. We as teachers have a great deal we can do to ensure that they develop into their best selves.

This chapter began by laying out the wide variety of literacy skills and strategies students need to develop in the middle grades. Particularly important changes occur at this point in schooling as teachers involve students more heavily in reading informational materials. Students need to become independent in their ability to apply appropriate strategies as they anticipate, build knowledge and consolidate their learning. Vocabulary development is particularly important since students encounter so many words and concepts that are new to them. In the chapter several activities that help students develop interest in and curiosity about words and strategies to retain new words for content learning and for their own personal vocabulary enhancement were described. Examples of good references to help teachers and students learn more about the rich nature of our language were also provided.

Because students in the middle grades possess a wide range of reading abilities, the section on assessment provided many avenues through which teachers can determine what students can do and what areas need more attention. These include using informal reading inventories, leveled books, fluency measures, and assessing awareness of text features, vocabulary, interests, and strategy knowledge.

Suggestions for how teachers can help students learn strategies for studying and retaining information from reading and develop their own self-monitoring of their learning were provided. The chapter stressed the value of writing and keeping portfolios as evidence of learning.

The importance of students engaging in reading on a regular basis is a theme that continues throughout the chapter. Specific ways to reach all students including English language learners were introduced. The chapter suggested ways to organize for instruction with literature and informational texts. These include integrating content learning and reading instruction through thematic units and teaching literature by using core novels and literature groups, literature circles, and guided reading with readers' workshop.

The final section deals with ways to organize and manage a learning community by being sensitive to young adolescents and providing a rich array of materials that they can read with confidence and interest.

For Your Journal

1. What do you think is the optimal classroom environment in which to encourage and support middle-level students?

2. After reading about different ways to organize classroom instruction, take some time to reflect on which ideas and structures you think you could use most productively. What are the reasons that you selected one over another? Have you seen other ways of organizing that you prefer?

★ Taking It to the World

A pair of eighth-grade teachers added a new dimension to the study of the Bill of Rights by having their students conduct a mock court trial. The issue: A student is accused of humming during the national anthem, a violation of a rule. The teacher faces a loss of job and pension. During a month-long study of the issues, students assembled arguments and witnesses and then argued the case. Because one teacher's spouse is a lawyer, the students did get some assistance in determining exactly how they should argue both sides of the case. Class members served as lawyers, jury, clerks, and witnesses. The students got so involved in their research and legal work that the local newspaper heard about the trial and photographed the final session.

Look carefully at the U.S. Constitution's Bill of Rights. Brainstorm with a friend ways you could make a thematic study of the rights practical for your students. What issues in the community could be highlighted?

★ Being a Professional Reading Teacher

Teaching reading in grades six to eight is often accomplished in a departmentalized or semidepartmentalized structure. How does reading instruction change for young people at these grade levels?

Focuses of Reading Programs in Grades Six to Eight

- Why is knowledge of the English language such an important part of reading programs at this level?
- Describe some examples of how teacher modeling can strengthen the reading of students in the sixth- to eighth-grade classroom.
- How can the teacher scaffold reading comprehension for English language learners in grades six to eight?

Assessment

- How are standards in the middle school or junior high school different from those in the primary and middle elementary grades? What are the implications of high-stakes testing for students trying to meet these standards?

Your Portfolio

Teaching in grades six to eight requires special classroom management skills. Teaching preadolescent and adolescent young people can be a challenge. Write some reflections about how you have identified potential behavior problems related to adolescence and how you have solved them in your volunteer and/or paraprofessional experiences. These could be excerpted from entries in your daily journal.

Teacher Resources

Related to the student behavior issues mentioned above, make a list of books that you might refer to students experiencing such problems as isolation from peers, gender confusion, a divorce at home, or other critical social problems that adolescents often face. You can find many valuable sources by searching on the term "bibliotherapy" at www.google.com.

Technology Connections

1. Middle-level students love to share their ideas and find out what their peers think. Now it is possible for students to extend these discussions worldwide with some of the good sites that have been established for book discussions internationally. Search for some of the sites that help students to connect with their peers in other countries.
2. Visit the American Library Association (www.ala.org), and complete a search for materials for reluctant readers.

Connect with Research

Research
Navigator.com

Review the following key words from the chapter, and then connect to Research Navigator (www.researchnavigator.com) through this book's companion web site to conduct a search into research on each of the various topics as they relate to reading and literacy education today.

Classroom fluency measure
cloze test
metacognition
portfolios
Question Answer Relation (QAR) strategy
reading workshop

Further Readings

Beck, I. L., McKeown, M. G., & Kucan, L. (2002). *Bringing Words to Life: Robust Vocabulary Instruction*. New York, NY: Guilford.

The case for carefully orchestrated attention to vocabulary development is well articulated here. Most important are the suggestions for helping students develop their interest in words and their compentence with vocabulary.

Daniels, H. (2002). *Literature Circles: Voices and Choice in Book Clubs and Reading Groups*. Portland, ME: Stenhouse.

From years of experience with various forms of literature circles and book discussion groups, Daniels provides a much-revised set of suggestions for stimulating students' engagement with literature.

Elliot, J. B., & Dupuis, M. M. (Eds.) (2002). *Young Adult Literature in the Classroom: Reading It, Teaching It, Loving It.* Newark, DE: International Reading Association.

A key to getting students to read widely is enticing them with excellent books. Here is a good start for teachers who want to know what their students will like and what will invite them to further reading.

Hadaway, N. L., Vardell, S. M., & Young, T. A. (2002). *Literature-Based Instruction with English Language Learners*. Boston, MA: Allyn and Bacon.

Finding the right books in terms of level of reading difficulty and interest is often challenging for English language learners. Suggestions for texts and ways to teach them are well developed here.

Robb, L., Richek, M. A., & Spandel, V. (2002). *Reader's Handbook: A Student Guide for Reading and Learning*. Wilmington, MA: Great Source.

Laura Robb shares her years of experience in helping readers become competent using informational texts in this book full of practical teaching strategies.

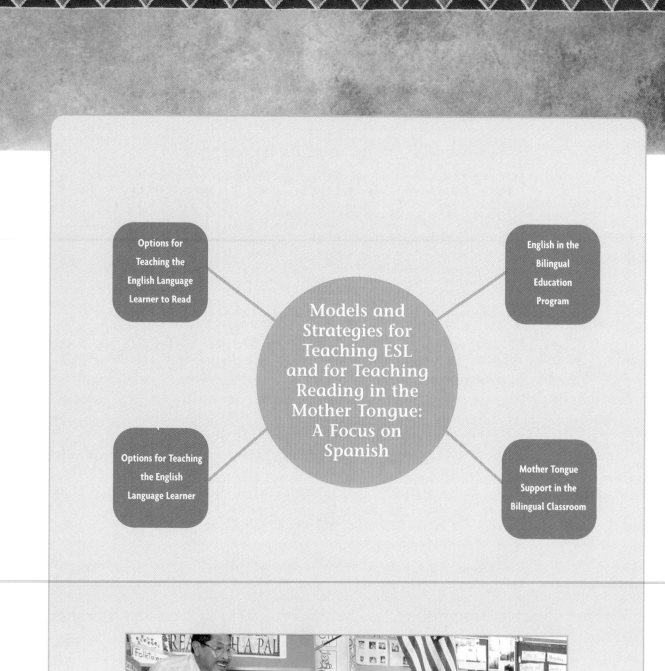

Options for Teaching the English Language Learner to Read

English in the Bilingual Education Program

Models and Strategies for Teaching ESL and for Teaching Reading in the Mother Tongue: A Focus on Spanish

Options for Teaching the English Language Learner

Mother Tongue Support in the Bilingual Classroom

Models and Strategies for Teaching ESL and for Teaching Reading in the Mother Tongue: A Focus on Spanish

The following statements will help get you thinking about the topics of this chapter. Answer true or false in response to each statement. As you read and learn more about the topics in these statements, double-check your answers. See what interests you and what prompts your curiosity toward more understanding.

Anticipation Guide

_____ 1. English language learners can learn English in one year.

_____ 2. It is a waste of instructional time to teach a child to read in the child's mother tongue.

_____ 3. Phonics is the most important component of reading for an English language learner.

_____ 4. Children should always be grouped by level of English proficiency for ESL lessons.

_____ 5. Children who learn to read in Spanish have to start over when they learn to read in English.

_____ 6. The teacher should always correct the grammatical errors of English language learners.

_____ 7. Children who have learned to read in their mother tongue have little difficulty learning to read in English.

_____ 8. English language learners should always respond in complete sentences.

_____ 9. Some adolescent English language learners are not able to read in any language.

Vignette of a Bilingual Teacher in a Bilingual Classroom

ilia Ortega is a certified bilingual first-grade teacher. Her twenty-three students speak Spanish as their first language, and their English proficiency ranges from none to a few at low-to-intermediate level. Her children are ready to learn to read in Spanish, and she is well prepared to teach them. The Spanish reading program she uses is parallel to the English language program used in other classrooms in her school, but it is not a direct translation. She also has a wealth of children's literature in Spanish.

Ms. Ortega begins her morning business in English. "Good morning, boys and girls." "Good morning, teacher," they respond, politely and respectfully addressing her by her title. After several weeks of school, the children can greet their teacher, respond to the roll and lunch count, and understand most classroom routines in English. Morning business is followed by a forty-minute English-as-a-second-language (ESL) lesson that is characterized by simple dramatized commands, questions, many gestures and smiles, and much laughter.

After recess, the children have whole class shared reading activities in Spanish with big books. In smaller groups, they dictate language experience chart stories in Spanish, read them, put the sentences in order, illustrate, read to each other, and play word games with vocabulary they have used. Independently and in pairs, they will take turns "reading" big books to each other and reading language experience stories to family members at home.

Some of the children are beginning to associate sounds with letters they recognize, and Ms. Ortega has begun to teach brief focused phonics lessons related to elements that have emerged from their language experience charts and for which they have demonstrated phonemic awareness in language play activities. They also work in the more structured Spanish reading program with anthologies of stories and some expository text. The program includes more systematic and explicit activities designed to introduce the relationships between sounds and letters in Spanish several weeks into the school year and after they have developed a basic sight vocabulary.

The children in Ms. Ortega's classroom are indeed fortunate. They are in a fully bilingual program with a highly qualified teacher and with appropriate instructional materials. She addresses them in English in the parts of her program where they are ready to understand. She consistently devotes thirty to forty minutes of instructional time each day to English-as-a-second-language (ESL), focusing on listening with nonverbal or simple responses at the beginning, with more emphasis on production later.

Her Spanish reading program is analytic or whole-part-whole, with children learning about letter/sound correspondences in the context of words they already recognize. The plentiful authentic literature in her classroom provides for a strong focus on comprehension and motivation.

The vignette also displays how Ms. Ortega presents the four elements of the framework described in Chapter 1. She demonstrates reading to her students in the shared reading activities with big books. She gives attention to details in the brief focused phonics lessons that emerge from meaningful reading and writing activities. She provides guided practice both in the shared reading of big books and in the dictation and reading back of dictated language experience charts. The children extend their reading practice in reading shared books to each other and language experience charts to family members. They will soon begin to write in Spanish as an outgrowth of their LEA activities.

The purpose of this chapter is to examine the teaching of reading in the mother tongue and also the teaching of ESL as it relates to the teaching of reading. The focus mother tongue language for the chapter is Spanish, the language that is most commonly encountered in bilingual classrooms. The audience for the chapter is threefold: bilingual teachers who will teach reading and writing in a language other than English, teachers of English language learners whose mother tongue instruction will be conducted by a paraprofessional or other staff members under the teacher's supervision, and all teachers of English language learners who teach ESL.

Options for Teaching the English Language Learner

There are two basic categories of instructional programs for teaching English language learners. These categories are presented in terms of the generic K–8 school program for them; the specific questions of second language and reading instruction are treated later in the chapter.

Teach Them in English

English-only options for teaching English language learners exist in several forms and for many reasons. In some cases, the numbers of children who have a non-English language in common at a grade level are small, and it is not feasible to offer a program of mother tongue instruction. A lack of trained teachers and mother tongue instructional materials may exacerbate this situation. Political considerations constitute another reason for providing only English-language instruction, such as in California and Arizona, where statewide ballot propositions largely discourage or make difficult the use of mother tongue instruction and mandate the use of what is characterized as structured immersion in English. But there are many limitations in teaching English language learners only in English, as you will see.

IMMERSION INSTRUCTION.   One approach to second language acquisition is immersion, sometimes called structured immersion (see Figure 12.1). Immersion instructional programs are focused on intensive English instruction during the first year, although it is well documented that children need more than one year to master enough English to learn academic subjects and reading in English (Thomas & Collier, 1997).

ESL instruction is the most important element in an immersion approach to teaching English language learners. Their academic instruction in reading, mathematics, science, and social science is also conducted in English, although English language learners gain little from this instruction. They do not understand or speak English, nor can they read in English at a sufficient level of comprehension. In some cases, support in the mother tongue is provided by a paraprofessional or parent volunteer. For example, that adult might sit down with the English language learners to assist them in understanding a teacher's lesson taught earlier in English and in completing independent work.

What is often called a *submersion* approach is a variation on structured immersion, and it is truly a sink-or-swim approach. Although most educators do not advocate its use, the submersion approach is often observed as the default methodology in working with English language learners. Non-English-speaking children are simply thrown to the mercies of a teacher, classmates, and instructional materials in English, with no concessions to their language or cultural needs. This sometimes occurs for political reasons. It is sometimes simply a reflection of the school's inability to respond to the needs of a small number of children from a less common mother tongue who do not speak English.

Lambert (1975) contrasts additive and subtractive education programs for second language learners. In an **additive program**, children add a new language and culture to the mother tongue and culture and its accompanying culture, along with a positive self-image. In a **subtractive program**, English and its accompanying culture are substituted for the mother tongue and culture, often leading to low self-esteem, leaving school, low academic achievement, and other negative consequences. Immersion programs are of the subtractive type.

There are several major principles that guide teachers' understanding of providing the best context for learning and for learning in a second language. Cummins (1986, 1989) describes two levels of language proficiency that demonstrate the need for high-level proficiency in the second language before academic instruction is provided in the second language. He describes **basic interpersonal communications skills (BICS)** as those that permit English language learners to carry on a simple conversation in the new second language, and they appear to be proficient. But a higher level

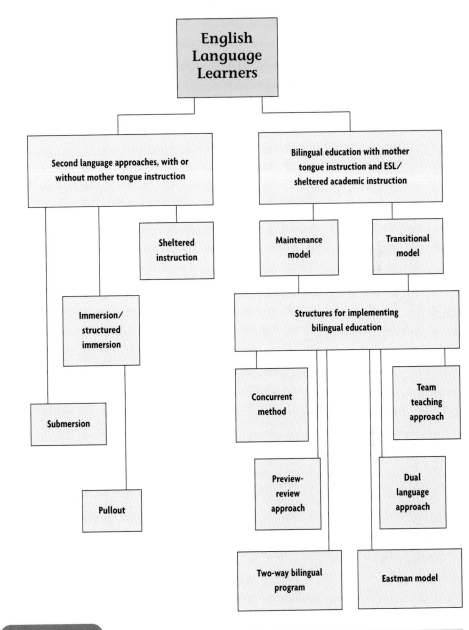

FIGURE 12.1

Model Program Structures for Meeting the Needs of English Language Learners.

of language proficiency, **cognitive-academic language proficiency (CALP),** is required for the student to learn to read in the second language or, for example, to learn the commutative principle of addition in mathematics. Cummins concludes that there is a threshold of language proficiency in the mother tongue that must be reached for the student to attain academic proficiency in the mother tongue and later in a second language. This threshold is seldom met in programs of immersion in English.

STRUCTURES FOR PROVIDING ESL INSTRUCTION.   The most common pattern for providing English language instruction is that in which the teacher in the self-contained classroom provides all instruction, including ESL. Another common pattern is the pullout program, which is usually employed in elementary schools. ESL teachers have their own classrooms, and for periods of forty to sixty minutes, they pull children out of their self-contained classrooms for ESL instruction and then send them back. In semidepartmentalized and departmentalized intermediate or junior high schools, usually at the fifth or sixth grade level and above, one teacher might have responsibility for teaching ESL to all English language learners.

Unfortunately, not every teacher is well prepared—or perhaps prepared at all—to teach ESL. An advantage of a pullout program is that a specialist can be very effective in providing this important instruction and will usually have high-quality materials for this purpose.

The pullout approach also has several disadvantages. Children miss instruction in the regular classroom, depending on the hour during which they are absent. English language learners are singled out as "special" or "different" when they leave for ESL instruction, which often has negative consequences. Pullout programs are usually organized according to homogeneous groups in that the ESL teacher will pull beginners from several classrooms for a period of instruction, then intermediate learners from several classrooms, and so on. Even in the self-contained classroom, the teacher should consider teaching the English language learners as a single group, regardless of their proficiency. As you will see later in this chapter, there are advantages to having children at several levels of English language proficiency during ESL/language development lessons, including the presence of capable English speakers.

SHELTERED ENGLISH INSTRUCTION.   **Sheltered English instruction** is a very powerful approach for working with English language learners, but it is an intermediate approach. It is designed to *follow* an initial second language acquisition program that takes students from non-English speaker status to that of intermediate speaker of English. It is therefore an important second language component of all education programs for English language learners, whether they have been in bilingual education or in an English immersion program. It constitutes, however, a submersion approach when used, or misused, with beginning speakers of English. We will examine sheltered English instruction later in this chapter.

Teach Them in the Language They Already Speak

The *Lau vs. Nichols* decision (see Chapter 2) did not mandate bilingual education as a remedy, but school districts soon found that it was one of the few ways to ensure that English language learners had equal access to education, that is, education in their mother tongue while they learned English. In most bilingual education programs, children learn to read and write and also study the other subjects of the academic curriculum—mathematics, social science, and science—in their mother tongue. Simultaneously, they learn English as a second language, a process that typically takes two to five years or more (Thomas & Collier, 1997). As the result of a transition process called **positive transfer of skills,** children can then do in English what they have learned to do in the mother tongue (Cummins, 1981). The knowledge that English language learners have in the mother tongue, they will also have in English. Furthermore, once a child is able to read in the mother tongue, learning to read in English as a second language is a relatively smooth and effortless process—the child learns to read only once. When children do not have the opportunity to learn academic subjects in the mother tongue, they obviously fall behind in those subjects during the period of time they are learning English.

The underlying principles of bilingual education are as follows:

- Teach English language learners to understand and speak English as a second language.

- Teach the academic subjects, including reading and writing, in the mother tongue while the children are in the process of learning to understand and speak English.

- Transition the children from mother tongue academic instruction to English language instruction in a sheltered mode when they have an *intermediate* level of English.

Because of the lack of instructional materials and a lack of trained bilingual teachers in many languages, non-Spanish language bilingual education programs are less common and usually limited in scope.

In *Preventing Reading Difficulties in Young Children*, Snow, Burns, and Griffin (1998) endorsed the efficacy of teaching children to read in the mother tongue wherever possible before teaching them to read in English. A major five-year developmental study conducted by Thomas and Collier (2002) provides additional evidence to support this point of view. Although many mother tongues were represented in their study of over 210,000 students in five school districts in Texas, Oregon, and Maine, most of the students were Spanish-speaking. Thomas and Collier found that one-way or dual language bilingual enrichment programs that were 90–10 or 50–50 (the ratio of mother tongue instruction to English instruction) were the only programs in which students reached the fiftieth percentile in both languages and in which there were the fewest dropouts. Children whose parents refused bilingual education programs, insisting instead on English only, had much lower achievement. The strongest predictor of English language achievement in the study was the amount of formal mother tongue instruction. Thomas and Collier found that the highest achievement in bilingual education programs was associated with those that offered a natural learning environment in school, with rich oral and written language in both the mother tongue and English, problem solving, group student activities, media-rich learning, challenging thematic units, and use of the students' bilingual and bicultural knowledge to access new knowledge.

TRANSITIONAL VERSUS MAINTENANCE MODELS OF BILINGUAL EDUCATION.
There are two underlying philosophies about how to conduct programs of bilingual education: transitional and maintenance. In the more common **transitional model,** children learn English as a second language; learn their academic subjects, including reading and writing, in the mother tongue; and make the transition to English language academic instruction in a sheltered mode when they have reached an intermediate level of English, usually between the late second grade and early fourth grade. The major goal of the transitional program is to produce a monolingual, monoliterate, and monocultural child who temporarily uses the mother tongue as a

vehicle for learning. Children in transitional bilingual programs usually continue their academic studies only in English after the onset of transition to English, although they sometimes receive continuing support in the mother tongue from a paraprofessional as needed.

In the **maintenance model**, the process is the same up to the point of transition. After the children begin academic instruction in English, they continue to receive periodic lessons in the mother tongue in all subject areas. The major outcome of the maintenance program is a bilingual, biliterate, and bicultural child who is able to function easily and comfortably in two languages and cultures.

STRUCTURES FOR ORGANIZING PROGRAMS OF BILINGUAL EDUCATION.
Within the transitional and maintenance models, there are several structures for grouping children and for assigning teachers and paraprofessionals that can be used in either model.

Concurrent Approach. One approach that is often used intuitively is called *concurrent method*. The teacher says everything twice, once in the children's mother tongue and once in English, assuming that there is only one non-English language in the classroom and that the teacher is bilingual. When the teacher is not bilingual, a bilingual paraprofessional may fill that second role, basically serving as an interpreter. It is a time-efficient approach with an uncomplicated structure. It is also very ineffective. English language learners begin to tune out the English, which they cannot understand well or perhaps at all, and they listen only to their mother tongue. If they do learn some English as a part of the process, they learn it in terms of their mother tongue. The outcome is a compound bilingual child with two interdependent language systems. The result is a lifetime of unconscious translation from one language to another, a process that takes precious time, especially on examinations such as the SAT, the GRE, or the important high-stakes tests that are now required in many states. This approach also promotes code-switching, the unconscious mixing of vocabulary and syntactical structures from two languages.

Team Teaching. The team-teaching approach is quite different. Two teachers, one bilingual, the other usually not, work together in the same classroom. They work independently; but when they teach, each teaches the entire class. The primary advantages of this approach are to provide outstanding language and cultural models to the children and to reduce the number of proficient bilingual teachers needed.

Dual Language. The dual language model resembles the team-teaching model in that there are two teachers, one bilingual, the other usually not, but in separate classrooms. The monolingual English-speaking teacher teaches English as a second language and academic instruction in English for those in the two classrooms that are ready for it. The bilingual teacher teaches the academic subjects to the English language learners in the mother tongue and also teaches the other language, usually Spanish, as a second language.

The advantages of the dual language model are that both teachers are working in a language of comfort to them and that the children are learning English and their academic subjects from teachers who are good models. Unlike the concurrent method, they are not learning English in terms of the mother tongue but rather are developing as coordinate bilinguals with two independent language systems. The major disadvantage is that the English-speaking and non-English-speaking children are rarely working together because their needs are very different. It is important for English language learners to associate with English speakers because they learn English from those children as well as from their teacher. They can avoid the fossilization or stopping-in-place that can occur when children are separated from native and capable English-speaking peers. It also important for groups of children from different languages and cultures to associate with each other to avoid ethnic, linguistic, and cultural isolation.

Preview-Review Model.   The preview-review model is very complex, but it resolves some of the shortcomings of the other models. Two teachers work together as in the team-teaching and dual language models: one bilingual, the other usually not. One teacher provides a preview of the lesson to the entire group in one language, and the other teacher then teaches the main body of the lesson to the entire group in the other language. Each teacher then reviews the main lesson with his or her language group after the main body of the lesson. The order of use of the languages is reversed in that subject area the next day. The children in whose language the main body of the lesson is not to be presented listen to a preview in their mother tongue. They also review the lesson in their mother tongue after the lesson is presented in their second language.

For example, two teachers, one bilingual and the other monolingual, teach a mathematics lesson. The bilingual teacher might conduct a ten-minute preview of the lesson in Spanish for all children. The monolingual teacher would then teach the core of the lesson to all of the children in English, probably for thirty to forty minutes. Both teachers would then review the lesson in English and Spanish, respectively, with children dominant in those languages for about ten to fifteen minutes. They would reverse the order the next day. The children always have the best possible model of both languages, and they are mixed for part of the lesson. The model also reduces the number of scarce bilingual teachers needed.

Eastman Model.   The Eastman model (Krashen & Biber, 1988) of the Los Angeles Unified School District also effectively alleviates the problem of isolating students from each other at the elementary level. Spanish-speaking students are organized for mother tongue instruction in reading, the language arts, and academic areas of the curriculum during the morning, along with a program of ESL. English-speaking students are similarly organized for reading and academic instruction in English in the morning. In the afternoon, Spanish-speaking students are mainstreamed with English-speaking students in art, music, and physical education, which are conducted in English. As Spanish-speaking students gain English proficiency after two or three years, they begin to receive sheltered academic instruction in English in the more concrete areas of the curriculum, such as mathematics and science. Social studies in English is introduced later.

Two-Way Bilingual Education.   The two-way bilingual education program has a different goal from mainstream bilingual education. It is used where two language groups of parents want their children to learn—and learn in—another language. Usually, one group of children will be native Spanish speakers learning English as a second language and academic subjects in Spanish. But another group of English-speaking students is in the classroom because their parents want them to learn Spanish and learn in Spanish. The program goal is additive in that each group learns the language and culture of the other group. The Eastman model is an effective organizational structure for conducting a two-way bilingual education program.

English in the Bilingual Education Program

Teaching English as a second language is the underlying base of programs established to meet the academic needs of English language learners. It is the major element of the full bilingual education programs in which the mother tongue is used for academic instruction while children develop sufficient proficiency in English to benefit from academic instruction in English.

Second Language Acquisition

Whether or not children learn to read and write in their mother tongue, they clearly must learn to speak and understand English. In fact, it is not possible to address literacy for English language learners without considering the close links that must exist between the teaching of reading and writing and the teaching of English as a second language. Those links are rooted in the constructivist or whole-part-whole approaches that underlie effective practice in both.

At this point, we examine the contrast between constructivist and reductionist models of instruction. A constructivist view of instruction focuses on the construction of meaning, using what the child already knows and combining it with new knowledge, concepts, and skills to be integrated. It is learner-centered and highly contextualized, important factors in working with the students from diverse backgrounds, who are often at risk of failure. The factor of background knowledge is well recognized as being a key to success in reading and writing, especially in reading comprehension. English language learners have no lack of background knowledge, but there is often a discontinuity between the background knowledge they have and that assumed by the texts they will use in learning to read and reading to learn. Within the constructivist view, language acquisition is embedded in function. Skills are taught in a meaningful context, not in a rigid, artificial, isolated, and fragmented way. There are several approaches to second language instruction that reflect the constructivist view; they are in the communicative category.

The foundation for communicative approaches to second language acquisition is based on concepts, theories, and hypotheses that have converged around the interaction of constructivist notions about making meaning, including Vygotsky's (1978) zone of proximal development as described in Chapter 2. Conversely, **reductionist models**, or skills-based models, focus on the disassembly or fragmentation of curricular elements so that isolated skills and concepts can be mastered within a linear paradigm. Traditionally, most students have studied a second language, whether English or a foreign language, using such grammar-based approaches as the grammar-translation and audiolingual methods. These are reductionist or skills-based approaches that move learners from part to whole.

Most adults have personal experience with this type of approach. Perhaps you recall the grammar-translation approach from foreign language courses you took in secondary school and college. According to Chastain (1975), vocabulary was learned in terms of English from lists in which teachers paired words in the foreign language with their English counterparts. Grammar was also a major component of instruction. English was always the window through which the new second language was viewed and contrasted. Few students became functional in speaking and understanding the new second language. At best, they passed written tests of grammar, translated with difficulty, and read with halting comprehension (Crawford, 1994a).

The audiolingual approach has its roots in structural linguistics and behavioral psychology, resulting in a methodology based on a grammatical sequence, with mimicry and the memorization of pattern drills but without the heavy grammatical analysis of the grammar-translation approach (Chastain, 1975). This approach is characterized by the unconscious mastery of sequenced grammatical forms, learning as the result of teaching patterned oral drills, and an emphasis on correct oral production of grammatical forms in response to oral stimuli (Finocchiaro, 1974).

COMMUNICATIVE-BASED APPROACHES.   The results of research have changed educators' conceptions of how a second language is acquired and how this acquisition is best promoted in the elementary and secondary classroom. There has been a major paradigm shift away from these grammar-based approaches to language learning and toward those called *communicative*, which are also consistent with meaning-based or constructivist approaches to literacy (Crawford, 1994a).

Several important hypotheses underlie current practice in most communicative approaches to second language acquisition (Krashen, 1982b). In his input hypothesis, Krashen concludes that growth in language occurs when learners receive comprehensible input, or input that contains vocabulary and structure at a slightly higher level than what they already understand. The input hypothesis reflects Vygotsky's zone of proximal development. The context of the input provides clues to maintain the integrity of the message. According to the input hypothesis, a grammatical sequence is not needed. The vocabulary and structures are provided and practiced as a natural part of the comprehensible input that the child receives, much as the process occurs with infants acquiring their mother tongue. Krashen (1981) relates the input hypothesis to the silent period, the interval before speech in either the mother tongue or second language in which the child listens to and develops an understanding of the language before beginning to produce language.

In his acquisition-learning hypothesis, Krashen highlights the difference between the infant's subconscious acquisition of the mother tongue and the conscious learning of a second language of the secondary student of French. Students *acquire* language subconsciously, with a feel for correctness. *Learning* a language, by contrast, is a conscious process that involves knowing grammatical rules. The infant, of course, is almost always successful in acquiring communicative competence, while the secondary school foreign language learner is usually not (Crawford, 1994a).

According to Krashen's (1982b) natural order hypothesis, grammatical structures are acquired in a predictable sequence, with certain elements usually acquired before others. He concludes that the orders for first and second language acquisition are similar but not identical. He does not, however, conclude that sequencing the teaching of language according to this natural order or any grammatical sequence is either necessary or desirable.

Krashen's (1982b) related monitor hypothesis describes how the child's conscious monitor or editor serves to make corrections as language is produced in speaking or writing. Several conditions are necessary for the application of the monitor:

- Time to apply it, a situation that is not present in most ordinary oral discourse, especially in classroom settings
- A focus on the form or correctness of what is said, rather than on the content of the message
- Knowledge of the grammatical rule to be applied

These conditions serve to illustrate why so few children or adults learn to understand and speak a foreign language in a grammar-translation or audiolingual foreign language course in the secondary school or university.

In his affective filter hypothesis, Krashen (1982b) concludes that several affective variables are associated with success in second language acquisition. These include high motivation, self-confidence and a positive self-image, and, most important, low anxiety in the learning environment. It is therefore important that teachers avoid high-pressure instruction and especially humiliation of students who are acquiring English.

OTHER BASIC PRINCIPLES.   Results from recent research have led to other major changes in educators' conceptions of how a second language is acquired and how this acquisition is best facilitated in the classroom, one of which is the obvious similarity between primary and second language acquisition. In both, primary and second language learners form an incomplete and incorrect interlanguage (Selinker, Swain, & Dumas, 1975), with most children moving through similar stages of development in this incomplete language.

The role of correction is also similar in both primary and second language acquisition. Approximation is a related process in which children imitate more proficient English speakers in all of dimensions of language, oral and written, and test hypotheses about it. Approximation underlies oral and written language in that children are acquiring new understandings and skills within the context of authentic wholes. Children demonstrate behaviors in which they approximate the language behavior of their English models, growing closer and closer to their levels of proficiency. In his view of successive approximation, Holdaway (1979) describes the process as one in which Vygotsky's adults and more capable peers, that is, teachers and proficient English-speaking students, use information in the output from children's responses to construct, adjust, and finally eliminate the scaffolding that facilitates progress in learning.

Terrell (1982) and Krashen and Terrell (1983) conclude that correction should viewed as a negative reinforcer that will raise the affective filter and the level of anxiety among English language learners. When errors do not interfere with comprehension, correcting them has more place in the ESL program than it does when infants acquire their mother tongue. Caregivers might expand incorrect or incomplete forms, such as "me go" or "Kitty gots four feets," and say "Yes, you go" or "Yes, Kitty has four feet." There is little evidence, however, that this expansion has any positive effect. Errors are signs of immaturity, not incorrectness; they will disappear naturally as a part of approximation in the developmental process of language acquisition (Crawford, 1994a).

These similarities between primary and second language acquisition are not consistent with either the grammar-translation or audiolingual approach. Children learning their first language do not rely on grammatical rules or on systematic acquisition of vocabulary. With its emphasis on early production instead of a silent period, on correct production instead of an acceptable though immature and incomplete interlanguage, and on grammatical sequence instead of function and communicative competence, the audiolingual approach bears little resemblance to the way primary or second languages are successfully acquired.

Finally, age is an important factor in second language acquisition. Collier (1987) examined the relationship between the age of English language learners and their acquisition of a second language. She found that those who entered the second language acquisition program at ages eight to eleven were the fastest achievers. Those who entered the program at ages five to seven were the lowest achievers, and they were one to three years behind children from eight to eleven years of age. Children who entered at twelve to fifteen years of age had the most difficulty acquiring the second language. She projected that they would need from six to eight years of classroom instruction to reach age-level norms in academic achievement.

Collier (1989) later analyzed other research on age and academic achievement in the second language and found that children who had academic instruction in the mother tongue generally required from four to seven years to reach national norms on standardized tests in reading, social studies, and science and as little as two years in mathematics and language arts, including spelling, punctuation, and grammar. She also found that children from ages eight to twelve who had at least two years of schooling in the mother tongue in their home country needed from five to seven years to reach the same levels of achievement in second language reading, social studies, and science and two years in mathematics and language arts. Young children with no schooling in the mother tongue in either the home country or the new host country needed seven to ten years of instruction in reading, social studies, and science. Adolescent children with no ESL instruction and no opportunity for continued academic work in the mother tongue were projected, for the most part, to drop out of school before reaching national norms, whether or not they had a good academic background or interrupted schooling.

Instructional Strategies for Second Language Acquisition

The implications of Krashen's hypotheses and of related similarities between first and second language acquisition are that approaches to second language acquisition should do the following:

- Provide comprehensible input
- Focus on relevant and interesting topics instead of grammatical sequences
- Provide for a silent period without forcing early production
- Avoid correction
- Maintain a low level of anxiety

There are approaches to second language acquisition that meet these criteria. The communicative approaches that are most appropriate for elementary and secondary classrooms are the **total physical response method** and the **natural approach**.

THE TOTAL PHYSICAL RESPONSE METHOD.   Asher's (1982) total physical response (TPR) method is an important communicative approach in the initial stages of second language acquisition. The TPR method provides for comprehensible input, a silent period, and a focus on relevant content rather than on grammatical form. The focus of TPR is on physical responses to verbal commands such as "Stand up" and "Put your book on the desk." Because little emphasis is put on production, the level of anxiety is low.

Lessons can be given to small groups or an entire class. In the beginning, the teacher models one-word commands. This is done first with a few children to introduce new vocabulary and structures, then with the entire group, then with small groups of children, and finally with individual children. For example, the teacher says, "Sit," and then models by sitting down. Later, the teacher issues the command without modeling. As the children's levels of language increase, the teacher begins to use two- and three-word commands, such as "Stand up" and "Bring the book."

Using physical responses as a strategy of instruction in the bilingual classroom can help to reduce the anxiety ESL students might feel about the need to "perform."

The children demonstrate their understanding by physically carrying out the commands. The order of commands is varied so that the children cannot anticipate which is next. Old commands are combined with new ones to provide for review. Whenever the children do not appear to comprehend, the teacher returns to modeling. After a silent period of approximately ten hours of listening to commands and physically responding to them, a child then typically reverses roles with the teacher and begins to give those same commands to other children. It is important for the teacher to maintain a playful mood during classroom activities.

The TPR approach can be extended to higher levels of proficiency by using the technique of nesting commands. The teacher might say the following:

> *Jamal, take the book to Svetlana, or close the door.*
> *Noriko, if Jamal took the book to Svetlana, raise your hand.*
> *If he closed the door, stand up.*

A high level of understanding is necessary to carry out such commands, but no oral production is needed. Parents of young children will recognize that their infants can understand and carry out such commands long before they begin to speak themselves.

THE NATURAL APPROACH. Terrell's (1977) original concept of the natural approach provided for three major characteristics:

- Classroom activities were focused on acquisition, that is, communication with a content focus leading to an unconscious absorption of language and a feel for correctness, but not an explicit knowledge of grammar

- Oral errors were not directly corrected

- Learners could respond in the target language, their mother tongue, or a mixture of the two.

Krashen and Terrell (1983) later added four principles that underlie the natural approach to language acquisition:

- Comprehension precedes production, which leads to several teacher behaviors: teacher use of the target language, a focus on a topic of interest to the children, and maintenance of the children's comprehension.

- Production emerges in stages ranging from nonverbal responses to complex discourse, with children able to speak when they are ready and speech errors not corrected unless they interfere with communication.

- The curriculum consists of communicative goals, with topics of interest comprising the syllabus, not a grammatical sequence.

- Activities must result in a low level of anxiety, a lowering of the children's affective filter, which the teacher accomplishes by establishing and maintaining a good rapport.

Terrell's (1981) natural approach is based on three stages of language development: preproduction (comprehension), early production, and emergence of speech.

Ms. Ortega, the teacher in the bilingual classroom in the chapter-opening vignette, uses the natural approach. The curriculum of her ESL program is made up of themes that are supported by large-format posters and charts, big books, and concrete objects in the classroom. Lilia also uses the four block approach to organizing her reading program that is described in Chapter 9 (Cunningham, Hall, & Sigmon, 1999), but her program is a five block approach. She has added ESL as an important fifth reading/language arts area of curriculum.

The Preproduction Stage.   In the preproduction stage, topical, interesting, and relevant comprehensible input is provided by the teacher in a close parallel with Asher's TPR approach. The teacher speaks slowly, maintaining comprehension with gestures. Children may respond with physical behaviors, shaking or nodding their heads, pointing at pictures or objects, and saying yes or no. It is important that input is dynamic, lively, fun, and comprehensible. Crawford (1994a) provides an example in which the teacher uses a pet turtle and says:

> *This is a turtle. It is four years old. Is it green? Who wants to hold it?*
> [Hand to child.] *Who has the turtle? Does Tran have the turtle? Yes, he does. Does Rosa have the turtle? No, she doesn't.*

This basic input can be repeated with other objects in the classroom, such as large-format posters and illustrations (Crawford, 1994a). Crawford suggests that each child in the group be given a different illustration, and the teacher provides input:

> *Who has a picture of an airplane? Yes, Olaf, you do. Is the airplane large? Olaf, give your picture to Zipour. Who has a picture of a boat? Yes, Nicole has a picture of a boat.*

These examples include three primary preproduction techniques of using TPR strategies, TPR strategies accompanied by naming objects, and pictures.

The required responses include movement, pointing, nodding or shaking the head, and using the names of other children in the group. You should remember that nodding the head for an affirmative response and shaking it for a negative one are not appropriate in all cultures; it is the converse in Albania, for example. Children might also have to learn these nonverbal behaviors. Because the emphasis at this stage is on listening comprehension, verbal responses in the mother tongue are also acceptable. This might be a problem if the teacher cannot understand the children's mother tongue, but children usually find a way to help the teacher understand.

Classroom props allow for relevant expansion of this and subsequent stages of the natural approach (Crawford, 1994a). Any manipulative or concrete object is helpful, including flannel boards and puppets. Large colorful illustrations, such as those in big books, are also very helpful. Sources of free color illustrations include calendars (outdated or otherwise), travel posters, large posters available from textbook and trade book publishers, and colorful illustrations in the annual reports of many large corporations, which are often available on request through announcements in major business magazines.

The Early Production Stage.   In the stage of early production, the child begins to produce one-word utterances, lists, and finally two-word answers, such as "big dog" and "in house." Some of the latter, such as "me want" and "no like," are grammatically incorrect or incomplete. According to Crawford (1986), teachers should view these responses as immature, not incorrect. In the presence of good models, these errors will disappear in time, just as they do among infants developing their mother tongue at home.

Several types of questions can be used to elicit one- and two-word responses that are within the reach of children as they move into the early production stage:

Question Format	Illustrative Question
Yes/no	Do you like hamburgers?
Here/there	Where is the picture of the cat?
Either/or	Is this a pen or a key?
One-word	How many dogs are there?
Two-word	What fruits are in the picture?

As in the preproduction stage, these strategies should be integrated into activities that permit a variety of responses, ranging from physical responses from those not ready for production, to brief oral responses from those who are. As the children begin production, conversations should increasingly require one-word responses. Within the same conversation, the teacher can address questions calling for longer responses to those children who are ready. Teacher questions and commands below are in *italics,* and student responses are in brackets [ ]:

> *Kjell, show us your picture. What is in Kjell's picture?* [A sandwich.] *Yes, it is a sandwich. What is on the sandwich?* [Catsup.] *Is there an apple on the sandwich?* [No. Laughter.] *What else is on the sandwich?* [Meat, mayonnaise.] *How does it taste?* [Good.] *What do you like with a sandwich?* [Cookies. Soda.] *I like chips with mine.*

The Emergence of Speech Stage.   During the emergence of speech stage, children begin to produce structures that are richer in vocabulary, longer and more complex, and more correct. This production proceeds from three-word phrases to sentences, dialogue, extended discourse, and narrative, strategies that are also helpful in teaching Standard American English to speakers of African American Vernacular English. At this stage, Terrell (1981) recommends such activities as games, group discussions, preference ranking, skits, art and music, radio, TV, pictures, filmstrips, readings, and filling out forms. An example of a chart that incorporates preference ranking is provided by Crawford (1994) (see Figure 12.2).

After surveying the children about their preferences for pizza toppings and recording them, the teacher uses the survey results in Figure 12.2 to ask questions at different levels, each directed at a particular student and designed to elicit a response that reflects that student's stage of English language development. Teacher questions below are in *italics,* and student responses in brackets [ ]:

> *Does Sofik like pizza?* [Yes.] *What kind of meat does Sofik like?* [Sausage.] *How many like tomato on their pizza?* [Three, Margarita, Nguyen, and Petra.] *How much does Abdul like pizza?* [He doesn't like it.] *Which chil-*

TEACH IT!

8

Favorite Pizzas						
<u>Name</u>	<u>Cheese</u>	<u>Sausage</u>	<u>Pepperoni</u>	<u>Tomato</u>	<u>Anchovy</u>	<u>Mushroom</u>
Margarita		X		X		X
Sofik		X				
Abdul						
Nguyen	X		X	X		
Petra		X		X		X

FIGURE 12.2

Second Language Preference Ranking Chart.

dren like the same kind of pizza? [Margarita and Petra.] *Is there a topping that no one likes?* [Yes.] *What is it?* [Anchovy.] *How do we know?* [Nobody wants anchovy.]

Not only is the chart a valuable source of comprehensible input, but the process of gathering the data for the chart is, too. In addition, children begin to read each other's names and the words for popular foods in English.

Wordless picture books can also be used as a stimulus for the production of language at the emergence of speech stage. In an article that addresses struggling upper grade readers, Ho (1999) describes strategies that will also be very effective for English language learners. After a brief book talk with the teacher, a small group of students create a short text for a wordless book. One student member of the group records the text, although a paraprofessional or parent volunteer might fill this role when the students' writing abilities make this difficult. This is of even more value when two or three groups of students independently create their own text and then share it with the other groups.

SHELTERED ENGLISH INSTRUCTION FOR INTERMEDIATE-LEVEL ENGLISH SPEAKERS.   When English language learners have reached an intermediate level of English proficiency, they are ready to move from academic instruction in the mother tongue to academic instruction in English but using **sheltered English instruction,** a mode that provides extensive support for comprehension. Sheltering strategies in the content areas of the curriculum add substantially to the knowledge and contextualized vocabulary that students need as a base for reading comprehension as they read and think in any language (Krashen, 1985). These strategies are consistent with the philosophy of communicative approaches to second language acquisition, and they additionally provide access to academic areas of the curriculum in such a way that communication is maintained. Sheltered English strategies are also very appropriate in providing support for teaching Standard American English to speakers of African American Vernacular dialect. In California, sheltered English instruction is referred to as "Specially Designed Academic Instruction in English," or SDAIE (CATESOL, 1992).

Cummins (1981) provides a set of intersecting continua that are very useful for conceptualizing the issue of balancing the complexity of curriculum content with demands on language proficiency (see Figure 12.3). The vertical continuum extends from cognitively undemanding to cognitively demanding—ranging, for example, from a conversation about what students ate for lunch on the cognitively undemanding side to a third-grade mathematics lesson about the distributive principle of multiplication on the cognitively demanding side.

Cummins's intersecting horizontal continuum extends from context embedded to context reduced, ranging, for example, from a science lesson on classification taught with concrete manipulatives on the context-embedded side to an abstract lecture/discussion about the principles of democracy on the context-reduced side. Sheltered instruction in English is most effective in subject areas of the curriculum that can be presented concretely, such as mathematics, science, art, music, and physical education. Although there are aspects of social studies that can be taught concretely, such as geography and map skills, so many abstract concepts are taught that English-language

	Cognitively undemanding	Cognitively demanding
Context enhanced	Art Lesson Playing kickball Conversation about lunch Playing a board game Singing a song	Mathematics lesson using manipulatives Conducting a science experiment about evaporation Making a map of the schoolyard Watching the news on television
Context reduced	Beginning reading skills Talking on the telephone Listening to the news on the radio Reading a set of instructions	Responding to higher-order reading comprehension questions Participating in a debate on capital punishment Taking the SAT or the GRE

FIGURE 12.3

Classifying Cognitive Level and Contextual Support of Language and Content Activities According to Cummins's Framework.

Source: Based on Cummins (1981).

instruction in this area might well be delayed until students acquire additional English proficiency, especially if expository text in English is an important source of knowledge for the children.

The purpose of a sheltered instruction approach to the core curriculum in English is to provide a focus on context-embedded activities, ensuring that comprehensible input is provided while treating increasingly cognitively demanding aspects of the core curriculum. The Los Angeles Unified School District (1985) prepared a set of English-language teaching strategies that provide the necessary scaffolding in content areas for intermediate English language learners. Among recommended strategies are that teachers do the following:

- Simplify input by speaking slowly and enunciating clearly.
- Use a controlled vocabulary within simple language structures.
- Where possible, use cognates and avoid the extensive use of idiomatic expressions.
- Use nonverbal language, including gestures, facial expressions, and dramatization.
- Use manipulatives and concrete materials, such as props, graphs, visuals, overhead transparencies, bulletin boards, maps, and realia.
- Maintain comprehension with gestures, dramatization, illustrations, and manipulatives.
- Check understanding by asking for confirmation of comprehension; by asking students to clarify, repeat, and expand; and by using a variety of questioning formats.

Teachers of English language learners can take two additional steps to ensure good communication with students as they teach: They should face the children when teaching, not the blackboard; and male teachers should ensure that moustaches are trimmed so that children can see their upper lip.

Schifini (1985) recommends a focus on student-centered activities, especially at the secondary level, where lecturing and textbook use predominate. Richard-Amato and Snow (1992) provide valuable strategies for content-area teachers of English language learners. For mainstream teachers, they recommend providing a warm learning environment, recording lectures and talks on tape for later review, rewriting some key parts of text material at lower levels, asking native-English-speaking students to share notes with English language learners, and avoiding competitive grading until students have achieved sufficient English proficiency to compete successfully with native speakers.

It is clear that many of these strategies are nothing more than effective teaching practices, but their absence is very damaging to English language learners who are struggling to learn mathematics, science, and social studies in English when they have reached an intermediate level of English proficiency.

There are several other strategies that provide scaffolding for English language learners in specially designed academic instruction activities in English. The highly contextualized interactions that take place in cooperative learning can make the difference between what Krashen (1985, 1991) describes as submersion, or *sink or swim*, and sheltered instruction, the type of scaffolded subject-matter instruction described above. Cooperative learning is most effective when, in the words of Vygotsky, more capable peers—that is, stronger speakers of English—are included in groups with English language learners at various levels.

All of these sheltered strategies build background knowledge that supports the reading comprehension of English language learners as they begin to read expository text in their new second language. When instruction in the mother tongue precedes the sheltered instruction in English, their background knowledge is much richer.

Grammar as Part of the Curriculum?

According to Crawford (1994a), teachers who would advocate teaching the first person present indicative tense to a seven-year-old English-speaking child in a primary school classroom would be incredulous at the suggestion that a parent teach the same concept to a three-year-old at home. Of course, both children can use the tense correctly, neither as the result of instruction. It is clear that the content of second language acquisition programs should be based primarily on content, not on grammatical sequence.

A communicative second language curriculum is usually organized around a set of topics to ensure the introduction of new vocabulary and concepts of interest and utility to the children. Needed language structures emerge and are acquired naturally within the context of topical lessons. Some communicative curricula include grammatical sequences as a subcategory.

Terrell (1981) suggests that the initial content should be limited to the following:

- Following commands for classroom management
- Names of objects in the classroom
- Colors and description words for those objects
- Words to describe people and family relationships
- Descriptions of children and their clothing; school areas and activities
- Names of objects in the school that are not in the classroom
- Foods, especially those eaten at school

Later in the acquisition process, topics of interest to children would include the children's families, their homes and neighborhoods, their favorite activities, and experiences they have had. They also enjoy discussing their preferences about food, colors, television programs and films, and other aspects of their lives.

Linking ESL Instruction and Literacy

There is a close link between literacy and the acquisition of second language that becomes apparent when, as a part of the natural approach, Terrell (1981) recommends that key words be written on the chalkboard in the second language, especially for older children who are literate in their mother tongue. This corresponds to the key words to reading approach (Veatch et al., 1979; Veatch, 1996). In the early production stage of his natural approach, Terrell indicates that children may express themselves quite appropriately in one- or two-word utterances as they begin to acquire a second language. According to Crawford (1994a), it is altogether appropriate that they also begin to read key vocabulary that they have expressed for their teacher to write for them. They may later produce lists of related ideas, such as foods to eat at the school cafeteria, words that describe a favorite friend, or things to do after school. These topics and this output reflect the oral language common in the early production phase of Terrell's natural approach to language acquisition, output that is well suited for children to dictate for their teachers to record and for the children to read later.

Most bilingual teachers who teach reading in the mother tongue recognize that students' motivation to begin reading and writing in English early is strong. Although it is most beneficial for students to learn to read and write in the native language (Cummins, 1986, 1989; Krashen & Biber, 1988; Snow et al., 1998), where possible, teachers can begin an early introduction to literacy in English to take advantage of that motivation. The use of the key vocabulary and language experience approaches should be done with caution to ensure that the second language acquisition program does not evolve into an English literacy program presented before the student is ready. Being able to read and write in the mother tongue is always the most desirable base from which to establish literacy in English later because of the positive transfer of literacy skills to English.

As English proficiency increases, the key word approach to reading may give way to the language experience approach described in Chapter 10. It is important that the teacher accept the language that the children use in their initial dictations. There will be incomplete sentences, missing words, and inappropriate vocabulary, but this represents the stage at which they are working in their new second language, and correction will only serve to dampen enthusiasm and diminish active participation.

As was mentioned above, big books are an excellent source of large-format illustrations for ESL lessons. Later in the process, teachers will find that many children benefit from read-alouds in their new second language, especially when these are based on the background knowledge that children have already acquired as a result of lessons using the illustrations in these big books. The big books that are of most value will be very predictable and have repetitive elements.

**Writing &
Reading**

Other early second language reading and writing activities that can emerge in the emergence of speech stage of the natural approach include the creation of vocabulary cards, with a word in English and an accompanying illustration from a magazine or by the student. These can be used for word games, including some that begin to focus on beginning sounds; this is especially productive for students who are already learning to read in the mother tongue. Children can also use their vocabulary cards for building word banks, student dictionaries, and word walls. Many children will be anxious to begin writing in their new second language. Simple poetry forms, such as the cinquain (see Chapter 7) and diamante, are useful structures for their initial attempts.

In their efforts to use the mother tongue of children in their classes, teachers sometimes provide cards with a vocabulary word in the mother tongue on one side and in English on the other. They also often provide bulletin boards in the two languages, and they often search out children's books with text in English on one side of the page and in the mother tongue on the other side. Although these efforts are laudable, such practices lead children to approach their new language of English through their mother tongue instead of directly. Vocabulary cards in English are a good practice, but a picture on the other side is a better choice than the word in the mother tongue. Teachers can and should provide bulletin boards in both languages, but not with both languages represented on the same bulletin board. For example, a science bulletin board can be provided in English on one side of the classroom, and the same bulletin board in the mother tongue can be placed on the other side of the room. Providing the same literature in English and the mother tongue has many advantages, but it is better provided in two separate books. Children will learn their new second language of English better if they do not approach it through the mother tongue.

Options for Teaching the English Language Learner to Read

There are two major options for teaching English language learners to read; these correspond to the two major categories of programs: English-only and bilingual education.

In English

In an English-only instructional program, the children will necessarily have to learn to read in English. This is not a positive approach, but it is often the only option when a mother tongue reading instruction program cannot be offered because of a very small number of children with a common non-English language, because of a lack of appropriate personnel and materials, or because of political considerations,

Assuming that an ESL program is offered beginning in kindergarten and extending into the primary grades, the English language learners should not be placed in a formal and systematic English reading program before they have any proficiency whatsoever in English. The reading program is not an appropriate place for beginning ESL instruction, which should instead focus at the beginning on understanding and speaking. When reading in English is included at the beginning stages of instruction in listening comprehension and speaking English, the ESL program all too often evolves into a phonics- and text-based reading program instead of an ESL program, with very negative results in terms of both language acquisition and reading.

As children gain vocabulary in English in their ESL program, they will be interested in writing the words they learn, and they will begin to learn to read them, too, especially if they are learning to read in the mother tongue at the same time. A complete treatment of teaching the English language learner to read in English is provided in Chapters 9 and 10 in two dimensions: (1) the very positive process of teaching the English language learner who has first learned to read in the mother tongue and who has also reached the intermediate level of proficiency in understanding and speaking English and (2) the less desirable, but sometimes necessary, process of teaching an English language learner to read in English who has not learned to read in the mother tongue and/or who has not reached the intermediate level of English language proficiency.

Finally, some families will insist that their children learn to read and write only in English, even though the children do not speak or understand that language. Often, the parents themselves can express that desire only in the mother tongue. A few parents might even believe that the purpose of using the minority language for literacy is to maintain speakers of that language in an inferior social position. In this case, teachers need to demonstrate respect for the mother tongue, and they need to assure the children and their families that they will also have the opportunity to learn to speak, read, and write English. In addition, they need to reinforce the idea that children learn to read and write only once and that learning to read and write in another language later, such as English, is a relatively simple transfer process that is well supported in research, as is seen below. Finally, teachers need to reinforce the idea that reading is *comprehension*, not just pronouncing or "reading" sounds. Nonetheless, some parents will still insist on English only, and most schools will accept that parental decision.

In the Mother Tongue

A fundamental precept of literacy for children who are English language learners is that they learn to read and write more rapidly and more effectively in their mother tongue than in a second language that they learn later. The first important and authoritative position taken on this issue was that of a UNESCO conference (UNESCO, 1953), in which it was

concluded that children learn better to read in a new second language if they first learn to read in the mother tongue. This conclusion has been corroborated by many investigators in subsequent years. Saville and Troike (1971) reported that once a child has learned to read, transferring that ability to another language is not a difficult matter. Modiano (1968) found that Mayan children in Mexico learned to read more rapidly in their mother tongue of Quiché than did Mayan children who learned to read in their second language of Spanish. Subsequently, the first group read better in Spanish than those who first learned to read in Spanish. Through succeeding years, the evidence consistently indicates that children learn to read most effectively in their second language by first learning to read in their primary lan-

How has our understanding of how English-language learners learn changed in recent years?

guage (UNESCO, 1953; Cummins, 1986, 1989; Krashen & Biber, 1988; Snow et al., 1998).

Cummins's (1986, 1989) linguistic interdependence hypothesis indicates that what students learn in two languages is interdependent. This common underlying proficiency (CUP) (Cummins, 1981) forms the basis for positive transfer of skills. Children have knowledge and skills that they have learned in the mother tongue, and they can use them in the second language. They do not have to learn this knowledge and these skills again. In fact, it is axiomatic that children learn to read only once. They can transfer reading and writing skills to their new second language, just as adults do when they study a foreign language. Cummins indicates that CUP explains why children who have attended school in their country (and language) of origin tend to demonstrate higher achievement in English later than do children who lack that experience. These principles lead to the counterintuitive, but inescapable, conclusion that success in English language proficiency is closely related to students' learning of reading, writing, and academic concepts in the mother tongue (Krashen, 1985; Hudelson, 1987; Krashen & Biber, 1988; Collier, 1989; J. Crawford, 1989; Cummins, 1989; Ramírez, 1991).

Language policy is a factor of great importance in literacy for children. Clearly, children will learn to read and write most quickly and most effectively in the mother tongue. There are many factors that must be taken into consideration, however, before that decision is made (Crawford, 1995). For example, if skilled bilingual teachers are available, if children speak a minority language for which there is a well-developed written form, and if there are instructional materials in that language, the children can be given instruction in the mother tongue. If this is not the case, then the teacher can consider using the language experience approach in English, as described in Chapter 10 and also later in this chapter.

If children speak a language for which there is not a well-developed written form, such as Hmong, then the children must be taught to speak and understand English and later to read and write in English, probably using the language experience approach and simple predictable literature in English. If bilingual teachers are not available, then even the presence of instructional materials will not be sufficient to permit mother tongue instruction. The school can also prepare a literate speaker of the minority language as a paraprofessional who works under the supervision of a fully trained teacher who is not proficient in the mother tongue of the children.

In the case of a program of bilingual education, the children will have the opportunity to learn to read in the mother tongue, usually Spanish. If a Spanish-language bilingual program is provided for that population, children who speak another non-English language instead will likely be placed in an English-only approach.

In the case of Spanish and other languages that use the Latin or Roman alphabet, there is a close correspondence between literacy skills in English and these languages and therefore much transfer of skills from reading in the mother tongue to English:

- The letters of the alphabet in Spanish are almost without exception identical to English, except for a few diacritical markings, such as the *tilde* (~) in Spanish.
- The left-to-right and top-to-bottom directionalities of the languages are the same.
- The concept of print and the alphabetic principle operate in the same way.
- Most consonant sounds and some vowel sounds are the same.
- There are significant similarities in vocabulary because of the many cognates that exist between English and Spanish, although a few are false cognates, such as *actual*, which means *real* in English and *present* or *current* in Spanish.
- Reading comprehension and organization skills are the same. When a child has learned to read in Spanish, these skills do not need to be learned a second time.

You can think of your own experiences in studying a foreign language. There were many new vocabulary words and grammatical elements to learn, but you did not have to learn to read and write again.

Teaching Children to Read in Spanish

Most English language learners in American schools speak Spanish at home, and almost all formal programs of bilingual education are conducted in Spanish (Fradd & Tikunoff, 1987). In most areas, it is only in Spanish that a wide range of instructional materials are available and that sufficient certified bilingual teachers are available to conduct such a program. Therefore, this section of the chapter will be devoted to the teaching of reading in Spanish to these children.

As you have seen, the reading and writing processes in English and Spanish have a common alphabet and similar writing conventions. A major difference between English and Spanish is in the regularity of phoneme/grapheme relationships. In English, they are very irregular and inconsistent, especially with respect to the vowels; but in Spanish, they are very regular and consistent, especially with respect to the vowels.

Given this difference, one might expect that reading methodologies in Spanish would focus on phonics to take advantage of that regularity, and many do. But Latin-American educators have found that children who learn to read using decoding as their only word recognition skill fall short in comprehension, just as occurs in English reading. Their reading is characterized as *silabeando*, that is, reading syllable by syllable. Their focus is on oral reading accuracy and speed, with little or no attention to comprehension or enjoyment. This is often observed in children who have learned to read in Spanish in Latin America.

There is a great variety of approaches for teaching reading in Spanish, just as there is in English. A summary of those approaches is provided in Table 12.1.

TABLE 12.1

Major Approaches for Teaching Reading in Spanish.

CATEGORY OF APPROACH	METHODOLOGY	CHARACTERISTICS	CITATION
Part-whole	Alphabetic (alfabético)	Letter names taught first; sequence of vowels, consonants, syllables, words, phrases, and sentences	Barbosa Heldt (1971)
	Phonetic (fonético)	Focus on sounds; sequence of vowels, consonants, syllables, words, phrases, and sentences	Barbosa Heldt (1971)
	Syllabic (silábico)	Focus on syllables; sequence of vowels, consonants, syllables, words, phrases, and sentences	Barbosa Heldt (1971)
	Onomatopoeic (onomatopéyico)	Focus on auditory associations between sounds of letters and natural sounds of the environment, such as the /s/ as the whistle of a fireworks rocket; sequence of vowels, consonants, syllables, words, phrases, and sentences	Barbosa Heldt (1971) Torres Quintero (1976)
Whole-part-whole	Everyday vocabulary (palabras normales)	An analytic approach in which words are broken into syllables, then into sounds, and then reassembled	Barbosa Heldt (1971) Rodríguez Fuenzalida (1982) Rébsamen (1949)
Global	Whole word (global)	Sequence of words and sentences, with little or no phonics	Barbosa Heldt (1971) Hendrix (1952)
	Generated words (palabras generadoras)	Sequence of sight words, syllables, and sounds; use of these elements to create new words, phrases, and sentences	Barbosa Heldt (1971)
Eclectic	Eclectic (ecléctico)	Combination of sight word development and phonics; typical of basal reader programs in English and Spanish	Barbosa Heldt (1971)
Constructivist	Whole language (lenguaje integral)	Focus on literature and authentic text; similar to whole language focus in English; phonics taught implicitly and when need demonstrated (not explicit and systematic)	Freinet (1974) Solé (1992) Goodman (1989) Arellano Osuna (1992) Salmon (1995)

These approaches range from those that are highly synthetic to those that are whole-part-whole, even including what is characterized as constructivist or whole language in English. A balanced approach in the whole-part-whole tradition provides for a strong, well-rounded program that is characterized by the following:

- Extensive read-aloud activities to build background knowledge and vocabulary in the mother tongue
- Use of the key words to reading approach, the language experience approach, and shared reading of authentic literature at the beginning stages to introduce the concept of print for children who do not have a rich print environment in the home
- Phonemic awareness activities emerging from vocabulary in children's background knowledge and from LEA charts and shared literature experiences
- An inductive whole-part-whole strategy for teaching phonics, with elements emerging from words the children have acquired in the activities above
- Use of authentic literature in Spanish to serve as a basis for teaching reading comprehension
- Extensive and early opportunities for writing

TEACH IT!

39

Application of these strategies in Spanish is similar to that in English, with the exception of phonics, which is addressed below. These key instructional activities also represent the framework presented in Chapter 1, and beyond the beginning stages of reading instruction, they should be augmented with the many highly effective strategies that are described throughout the book.

METHODOLOGIES FOR TEACHING READING IN SPANISH. "He read slowly, spelling out each syllable and murmuring it quietly, as if with great relish, and when he'd mastered the whole word, he would repeat it in one breath." In *The Old Man Who Read Love Stories*, a prize-winning novel written by a Chilean author about an elderly man who lives in the rain forest of Ecuador, Luis Sepúlveda (1989) has described very accurately the way too many Latin American children read as the result of the syllabic approach to reading instruction used in almost every country in the region. It is not uncommon to find the use of similar methodologies in the United States, often in the hands of bilingual teachers who themselves were educated in Latin America, perhaps even trained as teachers there. These approaches have many limitations when used in isolation; their best use would be as an ancillary word attack skill program to use with high quality children's literature. But as in reading English, children who read in Spanish need to employ all cueing systems in support of their word recognition efforts, the semantic, syntactic, and pragmatic systems, as well as the graphophonic. See the Teach It! box for an example of a phonics lesson in Spanish.

**Phonics &
Phonemic
Awareness**

ISSUES RELATED TO THE SOUND SYSTEMS OF SPANISH AND ENGLISH. The sequence in which Spanish phonics is introduced is different from that of English. It begins with vowel sounds because they are few in number and regular (See Table 12.2 on page 523). Consonants follow in an order that reflects their frequency and regularity. Few word attack problems appear in reading in Spanish, but there are several difficult points in Spanish, as in English, in which one letter represents several sounds. These are often observed in the invented spelling of children, as seen in Figure 12.4 on page 524. The invented spelling in the student's work presented in Figure 12.4 is very typical of children who write in Spanish, and it is also consistent with Gentry's phonetic

TEACH IT!

* * * *

Inductive Phonics Lesson

In a simple three-step inductive lesson structure, the first step of auditory discrimination serves to verify students' phonological awareness of the sound stated in the objective of the lesson (see the figure). If the students are not successful in this first step, then the teacher should substitute phonological awareness activities for the second and third steps of the lesson, such as those described in Chapters 6 and 9. If the students are successful, as they usually will be in the first grade, then the teacher should proceed to the second stage of the lesson, which is to verify that the students can already read the sight words used in the first stage of the lesson and also indicate that they recognize the letter and its position in the words.

The third stage, that of associating the sound with the letter, is the key step in the lesson. The students who can correctly pronounce the letter or syllable indicated in the objective in unknown words in the association stage should be able to use that skill to recognize and pronounce that sound in the same position in other unknown words.

Many of the children will be able to state a rule or generalization when asked how they know how to pronounce the target sound in the unknown word. A six-year-old's rule might be a statement that he or she remembered other known words with that letter in the same position, thought about how it sounded in those words, and pronounced it that way in the new word. The purpose of the extra stimulus question

("If that word is 'cola,' what is this word? 'Bala.'") is for the teacher to provide the part of the word that is not the subject of the lesson objective—only the initial syllable /*ba*/ is of interest.

This model lesson is inductive in that the teacher asks questions that lead children to think about what they already know about sounds, letters, and words. The teacher does not tell or explain. Many children will not be able to state a rule or generalization at the beginning of this type of inductive lesson, although most will be able to correctly pronounce the target element in the words. But after a number of lessons, increasing numbers of children will be able to formulate a rule. These generalizations will be remembered and applied more easily if they are derived by the children. If they are provided by the teacher in a direct instruction activity, then the child must rely on memory to recall the rule later. When children learn to derive their own rules, they can transfer this ability to new unknown words. They can also transfer this generalized ability to English.

The instructional time required for the model lesson presented in the figure should be about five minutes, certainly less than ten minutes. Most instructional activities in beginning reading in Spanish should focus on comprehension through shared reading and, later, in small group lessons in which children are reading in a directed or guided reading mode.

(continued on next page)

Continued

Spanish lesson plan	English version of Spanish lesson plan
Objetivo: pronunciar el sonido inicial de palabras nuevas que empiecen con la sílaba /ba/	Objective: pronounce the initial sound of new words that begin with the syllable /ba/
Etapa de discriminación auditiva (verificar conciencia fonémica)	**Auditory discrimination stage (confirm phonemic awareness)**
Les voy a decir tres palabras. Escuchen bien. bajo baño bate	I'm going to tell you three words. Listen to them carefully. (short) (bath) (bate [baseball of good])
¿Cómo se parecen? ¿Qué tienen en común?	How are they alike? What do they have in common?
¿En qué parte de cada palabra se encuentra este sonido?	In what part of each word do you hear this sound?
Les voy a decir tres otras palabras. ¿Cuál no pertenece a este grupo? ballena mesa barra	I'm going to tell you three more words. Which one doesn't belong with the others? (whale) (table) (bar [rod])
¿Cuál es diferente? ¿Por qué? ¿Cómo es diferente? ¿En qué parte?	Which is different? Why? How is it different? Which part is different?
¿Qué otras cosas pueden ver en el salón que empiecen con el mismo sonido?	What other things in the classroom can you see that begin with the same sound?
Etapa de discriminación visual	**Visual discrimination stage**
Vamos a leer tres palabras.	Let's read these three words.
Levanta la mano si quieres leer la primera palabra. bajo, baño, bate Muy bien, etc.	Raise your hand if you want to read the first word. (short) (bath) (bat [baseball])
¿Cómo se parecen estas tres palabras?	How do these three words look the same?
¿En qué parte de las palabras se encuentra la letra?	In what part of these words do you see that letter?
Etapa de asociación	**Association stage**

Ahora quiero que lean algunas palabras nuevas. ¿Quién quiere tratar de leer la primera palabra nueva? ¿Cómo sabías leerla?
 	
    bala   base   barra   ballena
	Now we're going to read some new words. Who wants to read the first word? How did you know how to read it?
	
	    bala base barra ballena

Si esa palabra dice "cola" ¿qué dice esta palabra? "Bala."
 	
    cola
	If that word is "cola," what is this word? "Bala."
	
	    cola

Inductive Phonics Lesson (Spanish/English)

Refer to your **Teach It!** booklet for further activities you can use to reinforce concepts discussed in this chapter.

TABLE 12.2

Sequence of Phonics Generalizations in Spanish

INITIAL SOUNDS	FINAL SOUNDS	WORD ENDINGS
a	a	os
e	e	as
i	o	diminutives
o	augmentatives	
u	d	verbs -ar
	l	verbs -er
m	n	verbs -ir
t	s	
l	r	Substitution of initial
p	z	consonants
n		
d	i	Substitution of final
s	u	elements
f		
r	**CONSONANT BLENDS**	Medial diphthongs
b		
g (soft)	br	Compound words
ll	cr	
c (hard)	dr	Verb endings
j	fr	
y	pr	Homonyms
h (mute)	tr	
ch	bl	Prefixes
z	cl	
qu	fl	Suffixes
g (hard)	gl	
c (soft)	pl	Homographs
gue, gui		
güe, güi		Grades of adjectives
x (medial)		
		Syllabication

stage (Gentry, 1981), where there is substitution of incorrect letters with similar or the same pronunciation. The word *castillo* is spelled *castio*, which yields the correct pronunciation of the word but not the correct spelling. In the words *paresio* and *isieron*, the student substituted the letter *s* for *c*, again yielding the correct pronunciation of the word but the wrong spelling. In addition, the silent *h* of *hicieron* was omitted. There is much confusion between the sounds of *b* and *v* in Spanish, both being pronounced similarly to the /b/ in English in the initial position and like /v/ in English when between vowels, resulting in the very typical substitution of *v* for *b* in *estava*.

Finally, there is a grammatical error that reflects a troublesome issue even for some adults. The conventions of Spanish require that the sequential repetition of a sound be avoided. Therefore, *y hicieron* should be written as *e hicieron* to avoid the repetition

Transcription of Text	**Normalization of Text**	**Translation of Text**
el castio se paresio y isieron una casa donde estava el castio	El castillo desaparecio, e hicieron una casa donde estaba el castillo.	The castle disappeared, and they built a house where the castle was.

FIGURE 12.4

Invented Spelling in Children's Writing in Spanish.

of the *y* (*and*) and the *hi* in *hicieron*, both of which carry the same sound (in English, *y* followed by *hi* would sound like two English long *e* sounds in succession).

Phonics lessons in Spanish should be drawn out of vocabulary from key words to reading lessons, language experience approach lessons, and the shared reading experiences of children. The words that are used in the lessons should be within the children's sight vocabulary, moving from the whole (word) to the part (element to be taught) and back to whole (word) again. Because of the nature of Spanish, elements are frequently syllables in the form of CV (consonant/vowel).

INSTRUCTIONAL MATERIALS IN SPANISH.   The variety of instructional materials for reading in Spanish is almost as rich as that in English. These include formal reading programs, authentic children's literature, and electronic resources, including the Internet.

Print Resources.   Most major publishers that provide an English reading program also offer a parallel program in Spanish. These programs would be fairly characterized as basal, although some have anthologies of original literature instead of contrived basal reader stories or decodable text. The best have children's literature from the Spanish-speaking world or children's stories written in Spanish by native Spanish-speaking authors. In both of these cases, the quality of Spanish language and the cultural appropriateness should be evaluated carefully.

Most Spanish programs also contain authentic children's literature translated from English. It is important to consider carefully the quality of translation and the cultural appropriateness. The best programs also offer selections of authentic Spanish-language literature translated to English for their English versions, a demonstration of their respect for the literary traditions of both languages and cultures. A major strength of programs with parallel literature selections in two languages is that students who read a selection in the mother tongue as part of their mother tongue reading program have a powerful source of background knowledge when they later read an English version of the same story.

There is also a wealth of children's books and big books available in Spanish. The teacher who wishes to use authentic literature for a Spanish reading program instead of anthologies or basal readers will find the constantly expanding series of books on recommended children's literature in Spanish prepared by Schon (2000) to be an invaluable resource. In addition, she has published a compendium of children's books in Spanish with themes from around the world (Schon, 2001, 2002).

Technology

Electronic Resources for English Language Learners and Their Teachers.   As was discussed in Chapter 2, access to technology is a major issue for English language learners and other children in urban and rural environments characterized by poverty. But what resources can English language learners and their teachers access when technology is available?

There are many web sites that can provide support to English language learners and their teachers, both in the areas of English language development and in Spanish. For example, an international school web site registry provides the home pages of schools around the world that are interested in establishing relationships such as pen pal arrangements with other schools (Greenlaw, 2001). These have the advantage of allowing English language learners to correspond in their developing second language of English with students in other countries who are also studying English, probably as a foreign language. In addition, they may have opportunities to correspond in their shared mother tongues. This site registry is found at http://web66.coled.umn.edu/schools.html.

The Bilingual Writing Center is a useful word-processing program for children in English and Spanish that is distributed by The Learning Company (Wepner, Valmont, & Thurlow, 2000). The teacher who conducts a search at Google.com or another search engine on the phrase "Bilingual Learning Center" will find references to many school districts that have valuable tips and information about how to use the Bilingual Writing Center on both Microsoft Windows and Macintosh computer systems.

In the area of ESL for teachers, the Internet TESLK Journal (http://www.aitech .ac.jp/~iteslj/) provides sample lessons and teaching ideas for teachers (Greenlaw, 2001). There are also articles and research papers, as well as other classroom activities.

Another valuable web site for the teacher who is searching for outstanding children's literature in Spanish is the Barahona Center for the Study of Books in Spanish for Children and Adolescents, directed by Isabel Schon, who was cited earlier for her books on this topic. The center's web site can be found at http://www.csusm.edu/csb/.

Children Who Struggle Learning to Read in the Mother Tongue

Struggling Reader

TEACH IT!

1, 3

Reading recovery has proven to be a very effective intervention strategy for children who experience reading difficulties in English (see Chapter 9). An authorized Spanish-language version of reading recovery, called *Descubriendo la Lectura*, has also been developed (Escamilla & Andrade, 1992). It follows the pattern of diagnosis and intervention of the original program, but in Spanish. Several adaptations to language and culture were necessary, including the need to locate children's literature in Spanish. The resulting program includes more than 300 books at twenty different levels of difficulty, about twenty books per level.

A Spanish diagnostic survey for the identification of students includes six observational tasks: (1) letter identification, (2) a word test, (3) concepts about print, (4) writing vocabulary, (5) dictation, and (6) running records of text reading. Procedures generally parallel those in the English language program, including the rereading of familiar books, a running record of the new book from the previous day, writing, rearranging a cut-up story, and introducing a new book. The program is designed for first-graders in the lowest 20 percent of the class after one year of reading instruction in the regular classroom.

In a national study of *Descubriendo la Lectura*, Escamilla, Loera, Ruiz, and Rodriguez (1998) found that the program had a very positive outcome with Spanish-speaking second and third graders, more than 90 percent of students at each grade level scoring above average on Spanish text reading. On the SABE, a standardized achievement test in Spanish, more than 75 percent of students at each grade level met or exceeded the average score.

Older Children Who Are Preliterate

It is not uncommon for teachers of older English language learners from other countries to observe that a few lack literacy skills. Some have been in refugee camps without educational services, others have been working to contribute to family income, and still others have lived in very rural or isolated areas where attending school was not possible because of long distances and inadequate transportation. Many indigenous children from Latin America leave school because instruction is only provided in Spanish, which they might not speak or might not speak well. There are communities of speakers of Zapotec, Mixtec, Maya, Quechua, and many other indigenous languages living in the United States. Their Spanish might be very limited.

Other English language learners have had very limited school experience and left school, either for the reasons cited above or occasionally because of the poor quality of education. According to Schifini (1996), many have large gaps in instruction in the primary grades, and they struggle as nonreaders in the higher grades. Schifini recom-

THE WORLD OF READING

My 24 First Graders Speak 14 Different Mother Tongues: What Can I Do?

An increasingly common scenario in American classrooms is the presence of children who speak many different home languages. Usually, a bilingual education program cannot be provided for most of them for the following reasons:

- The teacher is not proficient in more than one of the languages, if that.

- Reading materials are not available in the languages.

- It would not be feasible to provide reading instruction in several languages, even with a proficient teacher and adequate materials.

- There might not be enough children with a common language at a grade level to support a full bilingual education program.

When there are many children at a grade level with a common language and they are scattered among several classrooms, it might be possible to gather all of them into a single classroom. This is especially desirable if there is a teacher who can teach them in their mother tongue or if there is a paraprofessional or parent volunteer who can provide mother tongue support to lessons taught in English. Usually, these children will be taught only in English in an immersion program. Because English is the only language common to most, they acquire basic interpersonal communication skills rather quickly. Formal reading instruction is usually delayed, although children can work with key words and the language experience approach early in the process of acquiring English. Shared big books also provide excellent comprehensible input in English, as well as an early introduction to the concept of print and much valuable background knowledge.

mends several strategies for meeting the needs of these older preliterate English language learners:

- Develop a print-rich classroom environment that reflects student interests, including advertisements, brochures, bumper stickers, comics, drawings, magazines, murals, newspapers, photos, postcards, posters, and recipes, and examples of their own work.

- Include native language print in the classroom environment.

- Use reading and writing workshop strategies and shared reading and literature studies.

- Use read-aloud activities for access to the core curriculum not available through reading.

- Use writing activities such as quick-writes to connect students to background knowledge.

- Provide shared book experiences with predictable and patterned books that are of standard textbook size and that have mature story lines.

- Use collaborative chart stories, language experience charts, and other forms of shared writing.

Assessing the Oral Language Proficiency and Reading Proficiency of English Language Learners

Assessing the language and reading outcomes of English language learners is accomplished very much as is done for English speakers (Kame'enui et al., 2001). There are a number of measures of English language proficiency that are used for placement of students in bilingual education programs or programs for English language learners, depending on their levels of achievement (see Table 12.3). In general, they measure the language production of children in English, including vocabulary, syntactical complexity, and auditory discrimination/pronunciation. State and local school district authorities typically establish criteria for the reclassification or identification of children whose English proficiency has advanced sufficiently for mainstream placement in regular classroom programs of instruction, although usually with extra support from a paraprofessional or other speaker of the mother tongue at the beginning of the transition process.

There are also several widely used standardized or normed tests of Spanish reading proficiency that usually parallel similar tests in English (see Table 12.3). The results of these tests are often used to evaluate the progress of groups of children or the effectiveness of programs, but they are not very useful to teachers in identifying the levels of children for assignment to instructional groups or levels of textbooks.

On the other hand, the Informal Reading Inventory (IRI) serves the same function in Spanish as it does in English. It is an authentic measure of reading accuracy and comprehension, and the outcomes that it yields in Spanish, as in English, can be used to place children in reading groups and textbooks with some confidence (see Chapter 10 for a discussion of using the IRI in English). Some major publishers with Spanish language reading programs provide IRIs for them.

Teachers can also construct their own IRIs by selecting passages from basal readers or anthologies to represent each grade level, just as is done in English. Teachers should verify the levels of the passages by using a readability graph for Spanish (Crawford, 1995) (see Figure 12.5 on page 530). As in constructing an IRI in English, the teacher should ensure that the content of each passage in Spanish corresponds to background and cultural knowledge that the child has in Spanish. With a passage selected for each grade level and four comprehension level questions developed for each passage, the teacher can employ the same process and accuracy and comprehension criteria for Spanish as for English, as described in Chapter 10. The IRI in Spanish yields frustration, instructional, independent, and capacity levels, just as it does in English and with the same criteria.

Readability measures are often misused, and the teacher should be aware of their limitations. These measures assess only surface structure features of language, and they ignore the level of content and the background knowledge required of children. Teachers should carefully judge the content of passages they select for inclusion in IRIs for the children they will assess. Finally, teachers are often tempted to rewrite text, changing sentence length or vocabulary to raise or lower readability levels. This is a dangerous practice that should be avoided. A readability graph should be used only as a rough measure and never as a tool for writing to a level.

TABLE 12.3

Assessment Measures for Spanish-speaking English Learners

TYPE OF MEASURE	NAME OF MEASURE	SUBTESTS	ELEMENTS MEASURED	SOURCE OF MEASURE
English language Grades K–12	Basic Inventory of Natural Language (BINL)	N/A	Oral language production, language dominance, fluency, syntax, vocabulary, structural complexity	Checkpoint Systems
English language development All LEP	California English Language Development Test (CELDT)	Listening and speaking Reading Writing	Oral language (one-on-one) Reading Writing	CTB/McGraw Hill
English language Grades K–5	Language Assessment Scales (LAS)	N/A	Auditory discrimination, vocabulary, phoneme production, sentence comprehension, oral production of English and Spanish	CTB/McGraw Hill
English language Grades K–12	Bilingual Syntax Measure (BSM)	N/A	Syntax, language dominance, second language level, maintenance of first language	Psychological Corporation
English language (or other language) (observation rating scale) Grades 1–12	SOLOM	N/A	Comprehension, vocabulary, fluency, pronunciation, grammar	San Jose USD
Spanish reading (normed test) Grades 1–12	Aprenda: Prueba de Logros en Español, Second Edition	Sonidos y letras Lectura de palabras Lectura de oraciones Vocabulario Comprensión de lectura	Phoneme matching, letter identification, letter/sound correspondence Word matching with picture, word identification Sentence match with picture Synonym matching, defining words in context Reading comprehension of riddles, modified close tests, comprehension questions	Psychological Corporation
Spanish reading (normed test) Grades K–3+	La Prueba de Realización, Second Edition	Reading	Matching written words, matching spoken words with written words, picture-word matching	Riverside Publishing
Spanish reading (normed test) Grades K–8	Comprehensive Tests of Basic Skills	Reading	Word attack, vocabulary, reading comprehension	CTB/McGraw Hill
Spanish reading (normed test) Grades 1–8	Spanish Assessment of Basic Education (SABE), Second Edition, Level 1	Reading	Basic skills of reading, spelling, language skills	Hampton-Brown

Number of syllables	1.0	1.5	2.0	2.5	3.0	3.5	4.0	4.5	5.0	5.5	6.0	6.5
220												4.3
218												3.8
216												3.3
214											5.3	2.8
212									9.7	7.2	4.8	2.3
210									9.2	6.7	4.3	1.9
208									8.7	6.3	3.8	1.4
206							13.1	10.7	8.2	5.8	3.4	1.0
204							12.6	10.2	7.8	5.3	2.9	
202							12.2	9.8	7.3	4.8	2.4	
200					16.6	14.1	11.7	9.2	6.8	4.4	1.9	
198					16.1	13.6	11.2	8.8	6.3	3.9		
196					15.6	13.2	10.7	8.3	5.8	3.4		
194					15.1	12.7	10.2	7.8	5.4	2.9		
192					14.6	12.2	9.8	7.3	4.5	2.4		
190			19.0	16.6	14.2	11.7	9.3	6.8				
188			18.6	16.1	13.7	11.2	8.8	6.4				
186	23.0	20.5	18.1	15.6	13.2	10.8	8.3	5.9				
184	22.5	20.0	17.6	15.2	12.7	10.3	7.8	5.4				
182	22.0	19.6	17.1	14.7	12.2	9.8	7.4	4.9				
180	21.5	19.1	16.6	14.2	11.8	9.3	6.9	4.5				
178	21.0	18.6	16.2	13.7	11.3	8.9	6.4	4.0				
176	20.6	18.1	15.7	13.3	10.8	8.4	5.9	3.5				
174	20.1	17.7	15.2	12.8								
172	19.6	17.2	14.7	12.3								
170	19.1	16.7	14.3	11.8								
168	18.7	16.2										

Number of sentences

Permission to copy with credit to the author.

Approximate level of readability

Instructions:

1. Count the first 100 words in the sample.
2. Count the number of sentences in the 100 words, rounding to the nearest tenth of a sentence.
3. Count the number of syllables in the 100 words.
4. Look for the number of syllables in the left column of the graph. Trace to the right to find the number of sentences. The number at the foot of that column is the approximate grade level of the passage.
5. If the text consists of more than a few pages, take samples from every three pages and compute the mean for each variable.
6. If the proportion of sentences to syllables for each 100 words does not appear on the graph, then the readability of the passage cannot be determined.

FIGURE 12.5

Spanish Readability Graph.

Source: Crawford, A. N. (1985). Fórmula y gráfico para determinar la comprensibilidad de textos del nivel primario en castellano. *Lectura y Vida,* 6(4), 18–24.

Standards for English Language Learners

Some states have developed English language development standards for English language learners. These are helpful in planning curriculum, instruction, and assessment for the ESL programs that these students need. California has one of the most fully developed sets of standards for this purpose (California State Board of Education, 1999). The California standards are organized into the following categories:

- Listening and speaking
- Reading: Word analysis
  Fluency and systematic vocabulary
    development
  Reading comprehension
- Writing: Strategies and applications
  Conventions
- Reading: Literary response and analysis

Standards in these categories are provided at beginning, intermediate, and advanced levels. They are designed to be used at K–12 levels but can be used as appropriate to the developmental level of the student.

Some students may demonstrate that they have met advanced standards in the first grade, while a recent arrival may be just reaching beginning standards in the seventh grade. Examples of their standards are shown below.

Examples of English Language Development Standards in Reading

Reading comprehension

Beginning level: Respond orally to stories read to the student, using physical actions and other means of nonverbal communication (e.g., matching objects, pointing to an answer, drawing pictures).

Intermediate level: Read and orally identify the main ideas and draw inferences about written text using detailed sentences.

Advanced level: Read and orally respond to familiar stories and other texts by answering factual comprehension questions about cause and effect relationships.

Mother Tongue Support in the Bilingual Classroom

Many teachers say, "I would like to teach my children to read in Spanish, but I don't speak Spanish." Monolingual classroom teachers who are unable to teach in their students' mother tongue might be able to use the services of a paraprofessional who can. Those paraprofessionals' services can extend from follow-up mother tongue support of lessons taught in English by the teacher to instruction provided in the mother tongue under the close and careful supervision of the teacher.

Vignette of a Non-bilingual Teacher and a Bilingual Paraprofessional in a Bilingual Classroom

There are twenty-six third-grade children in Room 14. Of the twenty-six native Spanish-speaking children, eleven have made the transition into English reading. Ten continue reading instruction in Spanish while receiving ESL instruction. They will make the transition to English reading within a few weeks or months, as they become ready. Five new arrivals to the United States speak only Spanish.

Their teacher, Mr. Scott, is a certified elementary school teacher, but he does not speak Spanish. He is a very good teacher, and he provides all ESL and English reading instruction. But the Spanish reading program is conducted by Ms. Morales, a part-time paraprofessional and university student who plans to become a bilingual teacher. She is occasionally assisted by two Spanish-speaking parent volunteers who read to the children and tell stories from their childhood.

Today, Ms. Morales is teaching a reading lesson from an anthology of stories in Spanish that is part of a reading program in English and Spanish that Mr. Scott is also using with the English-speaking students. Ms. Morales begins by introducing new vocabulary that students will encounter in the guided silent reading they will do in a few minutes. In addition, she helps them to construct a semantic map so that they can share background knowledge they have about the topic of the story: a young girl who lives in the Amazon forest of South America. She guides their silent reading with higher-order questions from the teacher manual and additional questions she has formulated herself. After today's lesson, during which they read the first half of the story, the children will write predictions about how the story might end when they complete it the next day. In the meantime, Mr. Scott is teaching a word analysis lesson to the English-speaking students on the other side of the room, which will be followed by a similar literature lesson from the English version of the same anthology that Ms. Morales uses in Spanish.

TEACH IT!

9

Mr. Scott meets daily with Ms. Morales to help her plan instruction, to answer questions about how to use the teacher manual for the Spanish reading program, which is provided in both English and Spanish for his convenience, and to assess children's progress in Spanish reading. As they teach in parallel through the morning, he observes and monitors her activities. She also assists in parent conferences when needed.

Mr. Scott and Ms. Morales have molded themselves into a highly effective team, both making indispensable contributions to the language and reading development of the children in the classroom. She gains much from his long teaching experience as they plan instruction for the next day and, on a longer-term basis, for future days, weeks, and months. At the same time, he gains insights from the valuable background she has in the children's mother tongue and their culture.

Although the two are usually teaching parallel to each other, Mr. Scott is able to supervise Ms. Morales's work from his teaching station in the classroom, and he periodically walks around the classroom to encourage and reinforce the work of the children in both groups. Although he does not speak Spanish, he finds that he is able to understand much of what is occurring in her lessons.

The parallel structure of the English and Spanish anthologies from the third-grade reading program they use has many advantages. The teacher's manual for the Spanish part of the program has English and Spanish instructions on opposite sides of the teaching manual, so Mr. Scott can quickly determine the students' progress in their lessons. In addition, they will eventually read in English the stories they are now reading in Spanish. Their prior experience with the stories and the background knowledge developed will constitute an important part of scaffolding their comprehension as they move into reading in their new second language.

Supervising the Paraprofessional Who Teaches in the Mother Tongue

It is a challenging task for monolingual teachers to supervise the instructional activities of bilingual paraprofessionals. Teachers should first model for their paraprofessionals in English the teaching manner, approaches, and strategies that are to be employed in Spanish or another language. Teachers should then observe their paraprofessionals, assessing the effectiveness of their modeling. Even though teachers might not understand the paraprofessionals' words, the teachers' knowledge of what is being taught should support good communication. A major emphasis of teachers should be to impress on paraprofessionals the importance of building up the childrens' self-concepts and of avoiding harsh words, which can undo the effects of even excellent teaching.

The help of bilingual classroom aides are extremely beneficial in the ESL/ELL classroom, but it is important that the teacher and the aides carefully coordinate their instruction so the messages to the students are consistent.

At an operational level, there should be outstanding communication between the teacher and the paraprofessional. They should meet to plan before school in the morning and again before the paraprofessional leaves at the end of the day, discussing the activities of the day and planning for lessons to follow. Because the teacher and paraprofessional complement each other so well, the development of mutual respect between them is important. The teacher has skills and knowledge about teaching, and the paraprofessional contributes vital communication skills and cultural knowledge.

Many bilingual paraprofessionals are university students who are in varying stages of the teacher preparation programs. They are highly motivated to become teachers, they are proud of their abilities to manage two languages and two cultures, and they are anxious to assume leadership in their own classrooms as soon as possible. As they approach and then enter their own student teaching experience, many are able to teach parallel to the regular teacher with careful supervision.

Some paraprofessionals exhibit those same language and cultural skills, but they view their paraprofessional role as their final career goal. They are often members of the local community who might have minimal academic preparation and training as instructional aides. It is perhaps among the members of this group that teachers who do not share the language and culture with the paraprofessional must exercise their most careful judgment. Because they are not trained teachers, their strategies in interacting positively and constructively with children must be carefully monitored.

Because the supervising teacher often does not understand what the paraprofessional is saying to the children, it will be important to note the tone of the paraprofessionals' voice and the children's reactions.

Parent Volunteers

Family &
Community
Literacy

Parent volunteers can be an important support to the non-bilingual teacher in the bilingual classroom. An important aspect of preparation for literacy in the mother tongue and English later is oral language development in the mother tongue. Family resources in the form of stories from parents, grandparents, and extended family can make a major contribution to this part of the program. Teachers can invite these adults into the classroom to tell stories to the children that can be used as a source of content for language experience stories, for example.

McQuillan and Tse (1998) describe strategies for extending these storytelling experiences into the English language. The narratives that teachers, parents, grandparents, and other sources use constitute comprehensible input in the hands of an expert storyteller. The children are exposed to rich vocabulary and their background knowledge on a variety of valuable topics is enriched.

McQuillan and Tse indicate that students begin to write and tell their own stories as their own language production flourishes. When stories are related in English, the children's second language, students should be allowed to listen to stories in that target language without concerns about understanding everything. They should focus on the main ideas. Four steps then follow: (1) telling a short and simple version of the story; (2) revising the story by retelling it with different characters or settings, extending the story beyond its original ending, and narrating the story from the point of view of another character; (3) the creation of a class story, which might involve considerable negotiation among the children; and (4) individual or small group creation of stories and books.

While McQuillan and Tse are most concerned about using the process to provide comprehensible input in English, the same strategies can be used to provide a stronger base of vocabulary and background knowledge in the mother tongue. In addition, this permits parents, grandparents, and other members of the extended family to play a valued role in the classroom. Finally, it validates and reinforces the value of the mother tongue and culture.

FOR REVIEW

The purpose of this chapter was to examine the teaching of reading in languages other than English and also the teaching of English as a second language (ESL), as it relates to the teaching of reading. The focus language for the chapter was Spanish, the language that is most commonly encountered in bilingual classrooms. The chapter was designed for three audiences: bilingual teachers who are capable of teaching reading and writing in a language other than English, teachers of English language learners whose mother tongue instruction will be conducted by a paraprofessional or other staff members under the teacher's supervision, and teachers who are responsible for teaching ESL.

There are various structures and models for teaching English language learners. One major direction is English-only, that is, teaching ESL and also teaching all academic subjects, including reading, only in English. This is popularly known as immersion or structured immersion, and there is no evidence that it is an effective approach. The alternative is known as bilingual education. It consists of an ESL program as in the other approach, but academic instruction is provided in the children's mother tongue during the two to three years that are required for learning English sufficiently to support academic instruction (CALP), as opposed to a conversational level (BICS). There is substantial research support for this approach, although its application is highly political.

ESL is the major component of both immersion and bilingual education approaches. There are many approaches and methods for teaching ESL, but the natural approach is one that is well supported in the literature. It resembles most closely the language environment of the child learning the mother tongue, a process almost always successful. It is based on themes rather than on grammar. Its major features are the provision of comprehensible input, the avoidance of correction, the acceptance of immature language structures at the beginning, a silent period during which children respond with gestures instead of producing language, and maintenance of a low anxiety level in the classroom.

The natural approach consists of three stages: preproduction (comprehension), early production, and emergence of speech. During the intermediate stage that follows, children are ready to begin academic instruction in English but in a sheltered or supported mode.

Strategies for teaching English language learners to read in English are given in Chapters 9, 10, and 11. In Chapter 12, the focus was on teaching reading in the mother tongue other than English, using Spanish as the focus. Children learn to read only once. For children who learn to read in the mother tongue, there is a positive transfer of skills from mother tongue reading to the second language: English.

Learning to read in Spanish is not greatly different from learning to read in English. Word recognition skills are easier in Spanish because of the regular correspondences between sounds and letters in Spanish, but it is slightly different because Spanish is a highly syllabic language. Children tend to learn syllables instead of the sounds of individual letters.

Teachers have no difficulty finding instructional materials in Spanish for all subject areas. Spanish reading is an especially rich area; most major publishers provide Spanish language reading programs that are parallel to their English language programs. In addition, there is ample children's literature in Spanish, some originating in Spanish and some in the form of translations from English. Because of a lack of materials in most other languages, it is uncommon to find reading programs except in Spanish, especially beyond the first or second grade.

Assessment in Spanish is similar to assessment in English, and many formal measures have Spanish language versions. Instructions were provided for locating or constructing an informal reading inventory (IRI) in Spanish. A Spanish-language version of reading recovery, *Descubriendo la Lectura*, provides support to young children who are struggling.

Many teachers who do not speak their students' mother tongue find themselves in a bilingual classroom nonetheless. They are usually provided with a bilingual paraprofessional who conducts the mother tongue instruction under the teachers' supervision. It is important for them to develop a strong spirit of teamwork in which the paraprofessional benefits from the professional training and experience of the classroom teacher, who in turn benefits from the language and cultural skills of the paraprofessional.

There are also many technological resources that support the teacher who is working with ESL and mother tongue reading instruction. There are web sites that provide background information about teaching ESL and computer-based resources that children can access.

For Your Journal

Find a classmate who did not speak English on arrival at the school or spoke English as a second language but who speaks English now. Interview this person about his or her experiences in learning English and learning to read. If you have ever traveled to a foreign country and did not speak or read the language, what did you do to adjust? Discuss the feelings you might have had if you had experienced this as a child.

★ Taking It to the World

You should now have a very clear idea of the challenges facing English language learners in their new classrooms. If you were the parent of a six-year-old child and you were to move to Croatia, describe the language and reading program you would want for your child. What additional information would you need before making a final decision?

★ Being a Professional Reading Teacher

Reflecting on the Chapter
English language learners whose mother tongue is Spanish are found almost everywhere now. What is your understanding of how to teach these children to speak English and read?

English as a Second Language

- A parent insists (in Spanish) that her child be taught to read in English, although the child does not understand or speak English. What arguments could you use to persuade the parent that the child will learn to speak and read in English faster if he first learns to read in Spanish?
- Most adults believe that learning another language means learning the grammar. How could you convince a parent that communication, not grammar, plays the major role in learning English as a second language?

Beginning Reading

- Your paraprofessional insists on teaching Spanish reading with a syllabic (ma-me-mi-mo-mu) approach. How do you explain the need for delaying the introduction of syllabic phonics until the children have a concept of print?
- You have no reading materials in Spanish, although you are fluent in Spanish. What sources of text in Spanish can you tap?

Assessment

- Some of your students need to learn to read in Spanish while they learn to understand and speak English. Some are ready for English reading. How do you organize your classroom to accommodate the needs of both groups? What assessment tools do you use?

Your Portfolio

Schools value the bilingual and multicultural skills of teachers who are fluent in more than one language and knowledgeable about other cultures. Your portfolio is an excellent place to document those skills. Here are some possible additions to your portfolio:

- Lesson plans in Spanish or another language, especially if the school or district interviewer is fluent in that language (Be sure to proofread carefully.)
- A thematic literature unit with children's literature from another language or a unit with a multicultural theme
- Transcripts, certificates, and/or fluency examination scores documenting proficiency in another language or culture
- Evidence of proficiency in teaching English as a second language
- Photographs of bulletin boards in another language (Be sure to proofread carefully.)

The skills of non-bilingual teachers with volunteer or paraprofessional experience in bilingual classrooms are also valued. You document those skills and experiences in your portfolio with testimonials and letters of recommendation from teachers and school administrators and/or letters and notes of appreciation from parents and students.

Teaching Resources

High-quality and authentic children's literature is as important for reading in Spanish as it is in English. Use some of the journal and Internet resources from the chapter to identify good literature. You will probably not have as much success in finding this literature in Spanish at garage sales and swap meets as you did finding literature in English. Ask parents of Spanish-speaking children whether they have books to share in your classroom library.

Technology Connections

1. AltaVista provides a primitive translation web site where children can cut and paste text to be translated to and from English and Spanish, as well as French, Portuguese, German, and Italian. The resulting translations are only fair in quality, but it is an interesting and revealing exercise for children. Visit the site (http://babelfish.altavista.digital.com/cgi-bin/translate?), and experiment with it for yourself. How might you be able to use this site when teaching?

2. Little Explorer is a multilingual web site with a picture dictionary and graphics and multiple language translations provided. The site also includes links to other related sites. Visit Little Explore (http://www.LittleExplorers.com) and explore for yourself. Why might this site be a valuable resource in the multilingual classroom?

Connect with Research

Review the following key words from the chapter and then connect to Research Navigator (http://www.researchnavigator.com) through this book's companion web site to conduct a search into research on each of the various topics as they relate to reading and literacy education today.

additive program

basic interpersonal communications skills

cognitive-academic language proficiency

maintenance model

positive transfer of skills

reductionist models

sheltered English instruction

subtractive program

transitional model

Further Readings

Brisk, M. E., & Harrington, M. M. (2000). *Literacy and Bilingualism: A Handbook for All Teachers*. Mahwah, NJ: Erlbaum.

Brisk and Harrington provide a wide variety of reading and writing activities for English language learners.

Carrasquillo, A., & Segan, P. (Eds.) (1998). *The Teaching of Reading in Spanish to the Bilingual Student*. Mahwah, NJ: Erlbaum.

This edited volume includes chapters by various authorities in the field. Some are presented in English and others in Spanish.

Freeman, Y. S., & Freeman, D. E. (1997). *Teaching Reading and Writing in Spanish in the Bilingual Classroom*. Portsmouth, NH: Heinemann.

A comprehensive book on the teaching of reading in Spanish. It is filled with activities and practical ideas.

Freeman, Y. S., & Freeman, D.E. (2000). *Closing the Achievement Gap: How to Reach Limited-Formal Schooling and Long-Term English Learners*. Portsmouth, NH: Heinemann.

Long-time bilingual educators and authorities on reading for English language learners offer support to teachers of preliterate older English language learners.

Gonzalez, V., Brusca-Vega, R., & Yawkey, T. (1997). *Assessment and Instruction of Culturally and Linguistically Diverse Students: With or at-Risk of Learning Problems*. Boston: Allyn and Bacon.

These authors provide a focus on the assessment of English language learners, including the disabled.

Hurley, S. R., & Tinajero, J. V. (2001). *Literacy Assessment of Second Language Learners*. Boston: Allyn & Bacon.

In this edited volume, Hurley and Tinajero provide a variety of articles by national authorities on the literacy assessment of English language learners.

References

Achilles, C. M. (1999). *Let's put kids first, finally: Getting class size right.* Thousand Oaks, CA: Corwin Press.

Adams, M. J. (1990). *Beginning to read: Thinking and learning about print.* Cambridge, MA: MIT Press.

Adams, M. J. (1998). The three cuing system. In J. Osborne & F. Lehr (Eds.), *Literacy for all: Issues in teaching and learning.* New York: Guilford, 1998.

Adler, M. (1982). The Paideia proposal: Rediscovering the essence of education. *American School Board Journal, 169*(7), 17–20.

Afflerbach, P. (1993). Report cards and reading. *The Reading Teacher, 46,* 458–465.

Aitchison, J. (1987). *Words in the mind.* Oxford, England: Blackwell.

Alexander, P. (1998). The nature of disciplinary and domain learning: The knowledge, interest and strategic dimensions of learning from subject matter text. In C. Hynd (Ed.), *Learning from text across conceptual domains.* Mahwah, NJ: Erbaum.

Alexander, P., Jetton, T. L., Kulikowich, J. M., & Woehler, C. (1994). Contrasting instructional and structural importance: The seductive effect of teacher questions. *Journal of Reading Behavior, 26,* 19–45.

Allard, H. (1977). *Miss Nelson is missing!* Illustrated by J. Marshall. Boston: Houghton Mifflin.

Allington, R. L. (1983). The reading instruction provided to readers of differing reading ability. *Elementary School Journal, 83,* 549–558.

Allington, R. L. (1997). Overselling phonics. *Reading Today, 14,* 15.

Allington, R. L. (1998). *Broad claims from slender findings: Early literacy research and educational policy recommendations.* Albany, NY: National Research Center on English Learning and Achievement, University of Albany.

Allington, R. L. (2000). *What really matters for struggling readers?* New York: Longman.

Allington, R. L. (2001). *What really matters for struggling readers: Designing research-based programs.* New York: Longman.

Allington, R. L., & Johnson, P. H. (2002). *Reading to learn: Lessons from exemplary fourth-grade classrooms.* New York: Guilford.

Allington, R. L., & McGill-Franzen, A. (1989). School response to reading failure: Instruction for chapter one and special education students in grades two, four, and eight. *Elementary School Journal, 89*(5), 529–542.

Allington, R. L., & Woodside-Jiron, H. (1998). Decodable texts in beginning reading: Are mandates based on research? *ERS Spectrum,* 16, 3–11.

Almasi, J. F. (1995). The nature of fourth graders' socio-cognitive conflicts in peer-led and teacher-led discussions of literature. *Reading Research Quarterly, 30*(3), 314–351.

Anderson, R. C., & Nagy, W. E. (1991). Word meanings. In R. Barr, M.L. Kamil, P. B. Mosenthal, & P. D. Pearson (Eds.), *Handbook of reading research,* Vol. II. New York: Longman.

Anderson, R. C., & Pearson, P. D. (1984). A schema-theoretic view of basic processes in reading. In P. D. Pearson (Ed.), *Handbook of reading research.* New York: Longman.

Anderson, R. C., Wilson, P., & Fielding, L. (1988). Growth in reading and how children spend their time outside of school. *Reading Research Quarterly, 23,* 285–303.

Archambault, J., & Martin, B. Jr. (1989). *White dynamite and the curly kid.* Illustrated by Ted Rand. New York: Henry Holt.

Arellano Osuna, A. (1992). *El lenguaje integral: Una alternativa para la educación.* Mérida, Venezuela: Editorial Venezolana.

Asher, J. J. (1982). The total physical response approach. In R. W. Blair (Ed.), *Innovative approaches to language teaching* (pp. 54–66). Rowley, MA: Newbury House.

Ashton-Warner, S. (1963). *Teacher.* New York: Simon & Schuster.

Atwell, N. (1987). *In the middle.* Portsmouth, NH: Heinemann.

Atwell, N. (1998). *In the middle: Writing, reading and learning with adolescents* (2nd ed.). Portsmouth, NH: Boynton/Cook.

Austin, J. L. (1962). *How to do things with words.* Oxford, England: Oxford University Press.

Avi. (1994). *Nothing but the truth: a documentary novel.* Thorndike, ME: Thorndike Press.

Ayers, W. (1993). *To teach.* New York: Teachers College Press.

Babbitt, S., & Byrne, M. (December 1999). Finding the keys to educational progress in urban youth: Three case studies. *Journal of Adolescent & Adult Literacy, 43:4,* 368–378.

Banks, J. A., & Banks, C. A. (1996). *Teaching strategies for ethnic studies.* Boston: Allyn & Bacon.

Barbosa Heldt, A. (1971). *Cómo han aprendido a leer y a escribir los mexicanos.* Mexico City, Mexico: Editorial Pax México, Librería Carlos Cesarmán.

Barone, D. (1992). That reminds me of . . . : Using dialogue journals with young readers. In C. Temple & P. Collins (Eds.), *Stories and readers: New perspectives on literature in the elementary classroom.* Norwood, MA: Christopher-Gordon.

Barthes, R. (1974). *S/Z.* Translated by Richard Miller. New York: Hill & Wang.

Beamon, G. W. (2001). *Teaching with adolescent learning in mind.* Arlington Heights, IL: Skylight Professional Development.

Beane, J. (2002). Beyond self-interest: A democratic core curriculum. *Educational Leadership, 59,* 25–28.

Bear, D. R., Invernizzi, M., Templeton, S., & Johnston, F. (2000). *Words their way: Word study for phonics, vocabulary, and spelling instruction.* Upper Saddle River, NJ: Merrill.

Beaver, J. (2000). *Developmental reading assessment.* Parsippany, NJ: Pearson Learning Group.

Beck, I. K., McKeown, M. G., & Omanson, R. C. (1987). The effects and uses of diverse vocabulary instructional techniques. In M. G. McKeown & M. E. Curtis (Eds.), *The nature of vocabulary acquisition* (pp. 147–163). Hillsdale, NJ: Erlbaum.

Beck, I. L. (1998a). Getting at the meaning: How to help students unpack difficult text. *American Educator, 22,* 66–71, 85.

Beck, I. L. (1998b). Understanding beginning reading: A journey through teaching and research. In J. Osborn & F. Lehr (Eds.), *Literacy for all: Issues in teaching and learning* (pp. 11–31). New York: Guilford Press.

Beck, I. L., & McKeown, M. G. (1983). Learning words well—a program to enhance vocabulary and comprehension. *The Reading Teacher, 36,* 622–625.

Beck, I. L., & McKeown, M. G. (1991). Conditions of vocabulary acquisition. In R. Barr, M. Kamil, P. Mosenthal, & P. Pearson (Eds.), *Handbook of reading research* (Vol. 2, pp. 789–814). New York: Longman.

Beck, I. L., McKeown, M. G., & Kucan, L. (2002). *Bringing words to life: Robust vocabulary instruction.* New York: Guilford Publications.

Beck, I. L., McKeown, M. G., Hamilton, R.L., & Kucan, L. (1997). *Questioning the author: An approach for enhancing student engagement with text.* Newark, DE: International Reading Association.

Becker, H. J. (2000). Who's wired and who's not: Children's access to and use of computer technology. *Children and Computer Technology, 10,* 44–75.

Beers, C. (1980). *The relationship of cognitive development to spelling and reading abilities.* Unpublished doctoral dissertation. University of Virginia, Charlottesville.

Beers, G. K., & Samuels, B. G. (Eds.). (1998). *Into focus: Understanding and creating middle school readers.* Needham, MA: Christopher-Gordon.

Berthoff, A. (1981). *The making of meaning.* Upper Montclair, NJ: Boynton/Cook.

Berthoff, A. (1981). *The web of meaning.* Portsmouth, NH: Boynton/Cook.

Bettelheim, B. (1975). *The uses of enchantment.* New York: Vintage.

Biklen, D. (1981). Should "The Ugly Duckling" be banned? In D. Biklen & L. Bailey (Eds.), *Rudely stamp'd.* New York: University Press of America.

Blachowicz, C., & Ogle, D. M. (2000). *Reading comprehension: Strategies for independent learners.* New York: Guilford.

Blachowicz, C., & Fisher, P. (1996*). Teaching vocabulary in all classrooms.* Englewood Cliffs, NJ: Prentice-Hall.

Bleich, D. (1970). *Subjective criticism.* Baltimore: Johns Hopkins University Press.

Block, C. C. (1999). Comprehension: Crafting under-standing. In L. Gambrell, L. Morrow, S. Neuman, & M. Pressley (Eds.), *Best practices in literacy instruction*. New York: Guilford.

Bloom, B. (1956). *Taxonomy of educational objectives: Handbook 1. Cognitive domain*. New York: McKay.

Bond, G. L., & Dykstra, R. (1967). The cooperative research program in first-grade reading instruction. *Reading Research Quarterly, 2,* 5–142.

Boy's Life. Irving, TX, Boy Scouts of America.

Bradley, L., & Bryant, P. (1985). *Rhyme and reason in reading and spelling*. Ann Arbor, MI: University of Michigan Press.

Britton, J. (1970). *Language and learning*. Harmondsworth, England: Penguin Books.

Bromley, K. (1999). Key components of sound writing instruction. In L. Gambrell, L. Mandell Morrow, S. B. Neuman, & M. Pressley (Eds.), *Best practices in literacy instruction* (pp. 152–174). New York: Guilford.

Bronfenbrenner, U. (1974). Is early intervention effective? In M. Guttentag & E. Streuning (Eds.), *Handbook of evaluation research* (Vol. 2, pp. 519–603). Beverly Hills, CA: Sage.

Brown, H., & Cambourne, B. (1990). *Read and retell: A strategy for the whole-language/natural learning class-room*. Portsmouth, NH: Heinemann.

Brown, M. (1949). *The important book*. New York: Harper.

Brown, R. (1955). *Words and things*. Garden City, NY: Basic Books.

Brown, R. (1973). *A first language*. Cambridge, MA: MIT Press.

Browne, N., & Keeley, S. (2000). *Asking the right questions: A guide to critical thinking*. New York: Prentice Hall.

Bruner, J. (1978). The role of dialogue in language acquisition. In A. Sinclair, R. J. Jarvella, & W. M. Levelt (Eds.), *The child's conception of language* (pp. 241–256). New York: Springer-Verlag.

Buehl, D. (1995). *Classroom strategies for interactive learning*. Schofield, WI: Wisconsin State Reading Association.

Buehl, D. (2001). *Classroom strategies for interactive learning* (2nd ed.). Newark, DE: International Reading Association.

Burnett, F. H. (1906/1996). *Little Lord Fauntleroy*. New York: Puffin.

Burniske, R. W. (2000). *Literacy in the cyberage: Composing ourselves online*. Arlington Heights, IL: Skylight Professional Development.

Burns, P. C. (1999). *Informal reading inventory: Preprimer to twelfth grade*. Boston: Houghton Mifflin.

Burns, P. C., Roe, B. D., & Ross, E. P. (1999). *Teaching reading in today's elementary schools*. Boston: Houghton Mifflin.

Butler, A., & Turbill, J. (1985). *Towards a reading-writing classroom*. Portsmouth, NH: Heinemann.

Caldwell J. S. (2002). *Reading assessment: A primer for teachers and tutors*. New York: Guilford.

California Commission on Teacher Credentialing. (2001). *Standards of quality and effectiveness for profes-sional teacher preparation programs*. Sacramento, CA: California Department of Education Web site at www.ctc.ca.gov/SB2042/SB2042_info.html.

California State Board of Education. (1997). *English language arts content standards for California public schools: Kindergarten through grade twelve*. Sacramento, CA: Author.

California State Board of Education. (1999). *English language development standards*. Sacramento: Author.

Calkins, L. (1996). *The art of teaching writing*. Portsmouth, NH: Heinemann.

Calkins, L. M., & Harwayne, S. (1992). *Living between the lines*. Portsmouth, NH: Heinemann.

Campbell, J. (1968). *The hero with a thousand faces*. New Haven, CT: Bolingen Press, 1968.

Campo-Flores, A. (2001, June 4). A town's two faces. *Newsweek*, 34–35.

Carle, E. (1983). *The very hungry caterpillar*. New York: Scholastic.

Carle, E. (1987). *The very hungry caterpillar*. New York: Philomel Books.

Carle, E. (1994). *La oruga muy hambrienta*. New York: Philomel Books.

Carr, E. M. (1985). The vocabulary overview guide: A metacognitive strategy to improve vocabulary, comprehension and retention. *Journal of Reading, 28,* 684–689.

Carr, E. M., & Ogle, D. (1987). K-W-L Plus: A strategy for comprehension and summarization. *Journal of Reading, 30,* 626–631.

Carroll, L. (1992). *Alice in wonderland.* Hertfordshire, England: Wordsworth Classic. (Originally published in 1875).

Castañeda v. Pickard, 648 F.2d 989, 5th Circuit (1981).

CATESOL. (1992). *Position statement on specially-designed academic instruction in English (sheltered instruction).* Orinda: California Teachers of English to Speakers of Other Languages.

Caverly, D. C., Mandeville, T. F., & Nicholson, S. A. (1995). PLAN: A study reading strategy for informational text. *Journal of Adolescent and Adult Literacy, 39,* 190–199.

Chall, J. (1967). *Learning to read: The great debate* (updated edition). New York: McGraw-Hill.

Chastain, K. (1975). *Developing second-language skills: From theory to practice.* Chicago: Rand McNally.

Chomsky, N. (1993). On the nature, use, and acquisition of language. In A. I. Goldman (Ed.), *Readings in philosophy and cognitive science* (Vol. C, pp. 511–534). Cambridge, MA: MIT Press.

Chomsky, N., & Halle, M. (1968). *The sound pattern of English.* New York: Harper & Row.

Clark, L. K. (1988). Invented versus traditional spelling in first graders' writings: Effects on learning to spell and read. *Research in the Teaching of English, 22*(3), 281–309.

Clay, M. (1985). *The early detection of reading difficulties: A diagnostic survey with recovery procedures.* Portsmouth, NH: Heinemann.

Clay, M. M. (1975). *What did I write?* Portsmouth, NH: Heinemann.

Clay, M. M. (1987). *Writing begins at home: Preparing children for writing before they go to school.* Portsmouth, NH: Heinemann.

Clay, M. M. (1993). *Reading recovery: A guidebook for teachers in training.* Portsmouth, NH: Heinemann.

Clay, M. M. (2000). *Concepts about print.* Portsmouth, NH: Heinemann.

Cleary, B. (1997). *Ramona and her father.* New York: Harper Trophy.

Cobblestone. Peterborough, NH: Cobblestone Publishing, Inc.

Cole, S. (2001). *Allosaurus!: The life and death of Big Al.* New York: Dutton Children's Books.

Coleman, J. S., Campbell, E. Q., Hobson, C. J., McPartland, J., Mood, A. M., Weinfeld, F. D., & York, R. L. (1966). *Equality of educational opportunity.* Washington, DC: U.S. Government Printing Office.

Collier, V. P. (1987). Age and rate of acquisition of second language for academic purposes. *TESOL Quarterly, 21,* 617–641.

Collier, V. P. (1989). How long? A synthesis of research on academic achievement in a second language. *TESOL Quarterly, 23,* 509–539.

Collins, J. L. (1998). *Strategies for struggling writers.* New York: Guilford.

Conrad, P. (1992). *Pedro's journal.* New York: Scholastic.

Cowley, J. (1985). *Rosie at the zoo.* Melbourne: Nelson.

Cowley, J. (1990). *Mrs. Wishy Washy.* San Diego: Wright Group.

Cowley, J. (1998). *The hungry giant.* Othell, WA: Wright Group.

Cran, W., MacNeil, R., & McCrum, R. (1986). *The story of English.* New York: Viking.

Crawford, A. N. (1982). From Spanish reading to English reading: The transition process. In M. P. Douglass (Ed.), *Claremont reading conference yearbook* (pp. 159–165). Claremont, CA: Claremont Reading Conference.

Crawford, A. N. (1985). Fórmula y gráfico para determinar la comprensibilidad de textos del nivel primario en castellano. *Lectura y Vida, 6*(4), 18–24.

Crawford, A. N. (1986). Communicative approaches to ESL: A bridge to reading comprehension. In M. P. Douglass (Ed.), *Claremont reading conference yearbook* (pp. 292–305). Claremont, CA: Claremont Reading Conference.

Crawford, A. N. (1993). Literature, integrated language arts, and the language minority child: A focus on meaning. In A. Carrasquillo & C. Hedley (Eds.), *Whole language and the bilingual learner* (pp. 61–75). Norwood, NJ: Ablex.

Crawford, A. N. (1994a). Communicative approaches to second language acquisition: From oral language development into the core curriculum and L$_2$ literacy. In C. F. Leyba (Ed.), *Schooling and language minority students: A theoretical framework* (2nd ed., pp. 79–121). Los Angeles: California State University, Los Angeles, Evaluation, Dissemination and Assessment Center.

Crawford, A. N. (1994b). Estrategias para promover la comprensión lectora en estudiantes de alto riesgo. *Lectura y Vida, 15*(1), 21–27.

Crawford, A. N. (1995). Language policy, second language learning, and literacy. In A. N. Crawford (Ed.), *A practical guidebook for adult literacy programmes in developing nations* (pp. 9–16). Paris: UNESCO.

Crawford, A. N. (2000). Strategies for teaching reading and writing to English language learners. In J. W. Gillet, C. Temple, A. N. Crawford, S. R. Mathews, & J. P. Young (Eds.), *Understanding reading problems: Assessment and instruction* (pp. 416–453). New York: Longman.

Crawford, A. N., Allen, R. V., & Hall, M. (1995). The language experience approach In A. N. Crawford (Ed.), *A practical guidebook for adult literacy programs in developing nations* (pp. 17–46). Paris: UNESCO.

Crawford, J. (1989). *Bilingual education: History, politics, theory and practice.* Trenton, NJ: Crane.

Cuban, L. (2001). *Oversold and underused: Computers in classrooms.* Cambridge: Harvard University Press.

Cummings, D. W. (1998). *American English spelling.* Baltimore: The Johns Hopkins University Press.

Cummins, J. (1981). The role of primary language development in promoting educational success for language minority students. In California State Department of Education (Ed.), *Schooling and language minority students: A theoretical framework* (pp. 3–49). Los Angeles: California State University, Los Angeles, Evaluation, Dissemination and Assessment Center.

Cummins, J. (1986). Empowering minority students: A framework for intervention. *Harvard Educational Review, 56,* 18–36.

Cummins, J. (1989). *Empowering minority students.* Sacramento: California Association for Bilingual Education.

Cummins, J., & Corson, D. (1997). *Bilingual education.* Amsterdam: Kluwer.

Cunningham, A. E., & Stanovich, K. E. (1998). What reading does for the mind. *The American Educator* (Spring-Summer) 8–17.

Cunningham, A. E., & Stanovich, K. E. (1997). Early reading acquisition and its relation to reading experience and ability 10 years later. *Developmental Psychology, 33*(6), 934–945.

Cunningham, P. M. (1975). Investigating a synthesized theory of mediating word identification. *Reading Research Quarterly, 11*(2), 75–76, 127–143.

Cunningham, P. M. (1995). *Phonics they use: Words for reading and writing* (2nd ed.). New York: HarperCollins.

Cunningham, P. M. (2000). *Phonics they use: Words for reading and writing.* New York: Longman.

Cunningham, P. M., & Allington, R. L. (1999). *Classrooms that work: They can all read and write* (2nd ed.). Reading, MA: Addison-Wesley.

Cunningham, P. M., Hall, D. P., & Defree, M. (1991). Non-ability grouped, multileveled instruction: A year in a first-grade classroom. *The Reading Teacher, 44,* 566–571.

Cunningham, P. M., Hall, D. P., & Sigmon, C. M. (1999). *The teacher's guide to the four blocks.* Greensboro, NC: Carson-Dellosa.

Curtis, C. P. (2000). *Bud, not buddy.* New York: Yearling.

Dahl, K. L., & Freppon, P. A. (1992). *Learning to read and write in inner-city schools: A comparison of children's sense-making in skills-based and whole language classrooms.* Final report to the Office of Educational Research and Improvement. (Grant No. G008720229). Washington, DC: U.S. Department of Education.

Dahl, K. L., & Freppon, P. A. (1995). A comparison of inner-city children's interpretations of reading and writing instruction in the early grades in skills-based and whole language classrooms. *Reading Research Quarterly, 30*(1), 50–74.

Dahl, K. L., Scharer, P. L., Lawson, L. L., & Grogan, P. R. (2001). *Rethinking phonics: Making the best teaching decisions.* Portsmouth, NH: Heinemann.

Dahl, R. (1998). *Danny, the champion of the world.* Illustrated by Quentin Blake. New York: Puffin.

Damico, J. S. (1991). Descriptive assessment of communicative ability in limited English proficient students. In E. Hamayan & J. S. Damico (Eds.), *Limiting bias in the assessment of bilingual students* (pp. 157–218). Austin, TX: PRO-ED.

Daniels, H. (1994). *Literature circles: Voice and choice in one student-centered classroom.* York, ME: Stenhouse.

Daniels, H. (2001). *Literature circles: Voice and choice in book clubs and reading groups.* Augusta, ME: Stenhouse.

Daniels, H. (2002). *Literature circles: Voice and choice in book clubs & reading groups* (2nd ed.). Markham, Ontario: Pembroke Publishers.

Delpit, L. (1990). Language diversity and learning. In S. Hynds & D. Rubin (Eds.), *Perspectives on talk and learning* (pp. 247–266). Urbana, IL: NCTE.

Delpit, L. (1991). The silenced dialogue: Power and pedagogy in educating other people's children. In M. Minami and B. Kennedy (Eds.), *Language issues in literacy and bilingual/multicultural education.* Cambridge, MA: Harvard Educational Review.

Delpit, L. (1995). *Other people's children: Cultural conflict in the classroom.* New York: New York Press.

Delpit, L. (1996). Skills and other dilemmas of a progressive black educator. In L. Delpit, *Other people's children.* New York: New Press.

DeVilliers, P. A., & DeVilliers, J. G. (1979). *Early language.* Cambridge, MA: Harvard University Press.

Dewey, J. (1913). *Interest and effort in education.* Boston: Riverside.

Diana v. *State Board of Education of California,* Action No. C-7037RFP (N. D. Cal. Jan. 7, 1970 & June 18, 1973).

Dillon, D., O'Brien, D., Moje, E., & Stewart, R. (1994). Literacy learning in secondary school science classrooms: A cross-case analysis of three qualitative studies. *Journal of Research in Science Teaching, 31,* 345–362.

Dillon, D. R. (2000). *Kids InSight: Reconsidering how to meet the literacy needs of all students.* Newark, DE: International Reading Association.

Dirkes, M. A. (1985). Metacognition: Students in charge of their thinking. *Roeper Review, 8*(2), 96–100.

Dixon, C. N., & Nessel, D. (1983). *Language experience approach to reading and writing: LEA for ESL.* Hayward, CA: Alemany Press.

Donahue, P. L., Finnegan, R. J., Lutkus, A. D., Allen, N. L., & Campbell, J. R. (2001). *The nation's report card: Fourth-grade reading 2000.* (NCES 2001-499). Washington, D.C.: U.S. Department of Education, National Center for Education Statistics.

Doty, W. (1986). *Mythography: The study of myths and rituals.* Tuscaloosa, AL: University of Alabama Press.

Droop, M., & Verhoeven, L. (2003). Language proficiency and reading ability in first and second language learners. *Reading Research Quarterly, 38,* 78–103.

Dudley-Marling, C. (2000). *A family affair: When school troubles come home.* Portsmouth, NH: Heinemann.

Dudley-Marling, C. (1990). *When school is a struggle.* Richmond Hill, Ontario: Scholastic.

Duffy, G. G., Herman, G., & Roehler, L. C. (1988). Modeling and mental processes helps poor readers become strategic readers. *Reading Teacher, 41,* 762–767.

Duffy, G. G., & Roehler, L. R. (1989). Why strategy instruction is so difficult and what we need to do about it. In C. B. McCormick, G. Miller, & M. Pressley (Eds.), *Cognitive strategy research: From basic research to educational applications.* New York: Springer-Verlag.

Duffy-Hester, A. (1999). Teaching struggling readers in elementary school classrooms: A review of classroom reading programs and principles for instruction. *The Reading Teacher, 52,* 480–495.

Duke, N. K. (2000). 3–6 minutes per day: The scarcity of informational texts in first grade. *Reading Research Quarterly, 35*(2), 202–224.

Durkin, D. (1978–79). What classroom observations reveal about reading comprehension instruction. *Reading Research Quarterly, 15,* 481–433.

Durkin, D. (1983). *Teaching them to read* (4th ed.). Boston: Allyn & Bacon.

Edelsky, C. (1982). Writing in a bilingual program: The relation of L$_1$ and L$_2$ texts. *TESOL Quarterly, 16,* 211–228.

Eder, D. (1983). Ability grouping and students' academic self-concepts: A caste study. *Elementary School Journal, 84*(2), 149–161.

Eeds, M., & Wells, D. (1989). Grand conversations: An exploration of meaning construction in literature discussion groups. *Research in the Teaching of English, 23,* 4–29.

Ehrenreich, B. (2001). *Nickled and dimed: On (not) getting by in America.* New York: Owl Books.

Ehri, L. C. (1991). Development of the ability to read words. In R. Barr, M. Kamil, P. B. Mosenthal, & P. D. Pearson (Eds.), *Handbook of reading research* (Vol. II). New York: Longman.

Ehri, L. C. (1997). Learning to read and learning to spell are one and the same, almost. In C. Perfetti, L. Rieben, & M. Fayol (Eds.), *Learning to spell* (pp. 237–269). Hillsdale, NJ: Lawrence Erlbaum Associates.

Ehri, L. C. (1997). *The development of children's ability to read words.* Paper presented at the convention of the International Reading Association, Atlanta, GA.

Elbow, P. (1982). *Writing without teachers.* New York: Oxford University Press.

Eldredge, J. L. (1995). *Teaching decoding in holistic classrooms.* Englewood Cliffs, NJ: Merrill/Prentice Hall.

Elkonin, D. B. (1973). U.S.S.R. In J. Downing (Ed.), *Comparative reading.* New York: Macmillan.

Elley, W. (1992). *How in the world do students read?* The Hague: The International Association for the Evaluation of Educational Achievement.

Elley, W. (1996). *The IEA study of reading literacy.* Oxford, England: Pergamon.

Escamilla, K., & Andrade, A. (1992). Descubriendo la lectura: An application of *Reading Recovery* in Spanish. *Education and Urban Society, 24,* 212–226.

Escamilla, K., Loera, M., Ruiz, O., & Rodriguez, Y. (1998). An examination of sustaining effects in *Descubriendo la Lectura* programs. *Literacy Teaching and Learning, 3,* 59–81.

Evans, A. J. (1979). *Reading and thinking books I and II.* New York: Teachers College Press.

Feeley, J. T., Strickland, D. S., & Wepner, S. B. (Eds.). (1991). *Process reading and writing: A literature-based approach.* (Language and Literacy Series). New York: Teachers College Press.

Ferreiro, E., & Tebersoky, A. (1985). *Literacy before schooling.* Portsmouth: Heinemann.

Ferreiro, E., & Rodríguez, B. (1994). *Las condiciones de alfabetización en medio rural.* México: CINVESTAV.

Fielding, L., & Roller, C. (1992). Making difficult books accessible and easy books acceptable. *The Reading Teacher, 45,* 678–685.

Finocchiaro, M. (1974). *English as a second language: From theory to practice.* New York: Regents.

Fitzgerald, J. (1993). Literacy and students who are learning English as a second language. *The Reading Teacher, 46,* 638–647.

Fitzgerald, J. (1995). English-as-a-second-language reading instruction in the United States: A research review. *Journal of Reading Behavior, 27,* 115–152.

Flood, J., & Lapp, D. (2000). Reading comprehension for at-risk students: Research-based practices that can make a difference. (Reprinted from *Journal of Reading, 33,* 490–496, April 1990). In D. W. Moore, D. E. Alvermann, & K. S. Hinchman (Eds.), *Struggling adolescent readers: A collection of teaching strategies* (pp. 138–147). Newark, DE: International Reading Association.

Fountas, I. C., & Pinnell, G. S. (1996). *Guided reading: Good first teaching for all children.* Portsmouth, NH: Heinemann.

Fountas, I. C., & Pinnell, G. S. (1999). *Matching books to readers: Using leveled books in guided reading, K–3.* Portsmouth, NH: Heinemann.

Fountas, I. C., & Pinnell, G. S. (2001). *Guiding readers and writers: Grades 3–6.* Portsmouth, NH: Heinemann.

Fox, M., & Mullins, P. (1992). *Hattie and the fox.* Chicago, IL: Scott Foresman.

Fradd, S. H., & Tikunoff, W. J. (Eds.). (1987). *Bilingual and bilingual special education: An administrator's guide.* Boston: Little, Brown.

Freinet, C. (1974). *El método natural de lectura.* Barcelona, Spain: Editorial Laia.

Freppon, P. A. (1991). Children's concepts of the nature of reading and writing in different instructional settings. *Journal of Reading Behavior, 23*(2), 139–163.

Freppon, P. A. (1995). Low-income children's literacy interpretations in a skills-based and a whole-language classroom. *Journal of Reading Behavior, 27*(4), 505–533.

Freppon, P. A. (2001). *What it takes to be a teacher.* Portsmouth, NH: Heinemann.

Freppon, P. A., & Dahl, K. L. (1998). Balanced instruction: Insights and considerations (theory and research into practice). *Reading Research Quarterly, 33*(2) 240–251.

Fry, E., Kress, J., & Fountoukidis, D. L. (2000). *The reading teacher's book of lists* (4th ed.). Englewood Cliffs, NJ: Prentice Hall.

Galdone, P. (1968). *Henny Penny.* New York: Scholastic.

Ganske, K. (2000). *Word journeys: Assessment-guided phonics, spelling, and vocabulary instruction.* New York: Guilford.

Garbarino, J. (2000). *The lost boys: Why our sons turn violent and how we can save them.* New York: Anchor Books.

Gardner, H. (1980). *Artful scribbles.* New York: Basic Books.

Gaskins, I. W., & Elliott, T. T. (1999). *Implementing cognitive strategy instruction across the school: The benchmark manual for teachers.* Cambridge, MA: Brookline.

Gaskins, I. W. (1998). There's more to teaching at-risk and delayed readers than good reading instruction. *The Reading Teacher, 51,* 534–547.

Gaskins, I. W., Downer, M., Anderson, R. C., Cunningham, P. M., Gaskins, R. W., Schommer, J., & The Teachers of Benchmark School. (1988). A metacognitive approach to phonics: Using what you know to decode what you don't know. *RASE: Remedial and Special Education, 9,* 36–41, 66.

Gee, J. P. (1999). *An introduction to discourse analysis: Theory and method.* New York: Routledge.

Gee, J. P. (2000). Discourse and sociocultural studies in reading. In M. L. Kamil, P. B. Mosenthal, P. D. Pearson, & R. Barr (Eds.), *Handbook of reading research* (Vol. III). Mahwah, NJ: Lawrence Erlbaum.

Gee, J. P. (February 2000). Teenagers in new times: A new literacy studies perspective. *Journal of Adolescent & Adult Literacy, 43*:5, 412–420.

Gee, J. P. (2001). A sociocultural perspective on literacy development. In S. B. Neuman & D. K. Dickinson (Eds.), *Handbook of early literacy research.* New York: Guilford.

Gelman, R., & Greeno, J. G. (1989) On the nature of competence: Principles for understanding in a domain. In L. Resnick (Ed.), *Knowing, learning, and instruction: Essays in honor of Robert Glaser.* Hillsdale, NJ: Erlbaum.

Gentry, J. R. (1981). Learning to spell developmentally. *The Reading Teacher, 34,* 378–381.

Gentry, J. R. (1989). *Spel . . . is a four-letter word.* Portsmouth: Heinemann.

Gersten, R. (1998). Recent advances in instructional research for students with learning disabilities: An overview. *Learning Disabilities Research and Practice, 13*(3): 162–170.

Gersten, R., & Baker, S. (2000). What we know about effective instructional practices for English-language learners. *Exceptional Children, 66,* 454–470.

Gibson, E., & Levin, H. (1975). *The psychology of reading.* Cambridge, MA: MIT Press.

Gill, J. T. (1992). The relationship between word recognition and spelling. In S. Templeton & D. Bear (Eds.), *Development of orthographic knowledge and the foundations of literacy: A memorial fesschrift for Edmund H. Henderson.* Hillsdale, NJ: Erlbaum.

Gillet, J., & Temple, C. (1999). *Understanding reading problems, assessment and instruction* (5th ed.). New York: Longman.

Goatley, V. J., Brock, C. H., & Raphael, T. E. (1995). Diverse learners participating in regular education "book clubs." *Reading Research Quarterly, 30*(3), 352–380.

Gollnick, D. M., & Chinn, P. C. (1998). *Multicultural education in a pluralistic society.* Upper Saddle River, NJ: Merrill.

Gomi, T. (1993). *Everyone poops.* La Jolla, CA: Kane/Miller Book Publishers.

Good, T., & Marshall, S. (1984). Do students learn more in heterogeneous or homogeneous groups? In P. L. Peterson, L. C. Wilkinson, & M. Hallinan (Eds.), *The social context of instruction.* New York: Academic.

Goodman, K. S. (1967). Reading: A psycholinguistic guessing game. *Journal of the Reading Specialist, 6,* 126–135.

Goodman, K. S. (1986). *What's whole in whole language?* Portsmouth, NH: Heinemann.

Goodman, K. S. (1989). *Lenguaje integral.* Mérida, Venezuela: Editorial Venezolana.

Goodman, Y. M., & Burke, C. L. (1972). *Reading miscue inventory: Procedure for diagnosis and evaluation.* New York: Macmillan.

Goodman, Y. M., Watson, D. J., & Burke, C. L. (1987). *Reading miscue inventory: Alternative procedures.* Katonah, NY: Richard C. Owen.

Goswami, U. (2000). Phonological and lexical processes. In M. Kamil, P. Mosenthal, P. D. Pearson, & R. Barr (Eds.), *Handbook of reading research* (Vol. III). New York: Longman.

Graves, D. H. (1982). *Writing: Students and teachers at work.* Portsmouth, NH: Heinemann.

Graves, D. H. (1983). *Writing: Teachers and children at work.* Exeter, NH: Heinemann Educational Books, 1983.

Greene, J. P. (1998). *A meta-analysis of the effectiveness of bilingual education.* Austin, TX: The Tomás Rivera Policy Institute, University of Texas, Austin.

Greenlaw, W. (2001). *English language arts and reading on the Internet.* Columbus, OH: Merrill Prentice Hall.

Griffith, P. L., & Lynch-Brown, C. (2002). Owning technology. *The Reading Teacher, 55,* 614–615.

Guthrie, J. T., & Davis, M. H. (2003). Motivating struggling readers in middle school through an engagement model of classroom practice. *Reading & Writing Quarterly, 19,* 59–185.

Guthrie, J. T., & Wigfield, A. M. (2000). Engagement and motivation in reading. In M. L. Kamil, P. B. Mosenthall, P. D. Pearson, & R. Barr (Eds.), *Handbook of reading research* (Vol. III, pp. 269–284). Mahwah, NJ: Erlbaum.

Guthrie, J. T., Van Meter, P., Hancock, G. R., McCann, A., Anderson, E., & Alao, S. (1998). Does concept-oriented reading instruction increase strategy-use and conceptual learning from text? *Journal of Educational Psychology, 90*(2), 261–278.

Hall, E. T. (1966). *The hidden dimension.* New York: Doubleday.

Hall, E. T. (1983). *The dance of life.* New York: Doubleday.

Hall, R. (1984) *Singlets.* New York: Macmillan.

Hall, S. L., & Moats, L. C. (1999). *Straight talk about reading.* Lincolnwood, IL: Contemporary Books.

Halle, T., Kurtz-Costes, B., & Mahoney, J. (1997). Family influences on school achievement in low-income African American children. *Journal of Educational Psychology, 89,* 527–537.

Halliday, M. A. K. (1975). *Learning how to mean.* London: Edward Arnold.

Hanson, J., & Graves, D. (1983). The author's chair. *Language Arts, 60,* 176–183.

Harman, S. (1990). Negative effects of achievement testing in literacy development. In C. Kamii (Ed.), *Achievement testing in the early grades: The games grownups play.* Washington, DC: National Association for the Education of Young Children.

Harmon, J. M. (1998). Vocabulary teaching and learning in a seventh-grade literature-based classroom. *Journal of Adolescent & Adult Literacy, 41,* 518–529.

Harris, K., & Graham, S. (1996). *Making the writing process work: Strategies for composition and self-regulation.* Cambridge, MA: Brookline Books.

Harste, J., Woodward, J., & Burke, C. (1984). *Language stories and literacy lessons.* Portsmouth, NH: Heinemann.

Hart, B., & Risley, T. R. (1995). *Meaningful differences in the everyday experiences of young American children.* Baltimore: Brookes.

Harter, M. (2000). *A framework for reading for information.* Workshop presented at Reading Leadership Institute, National-Louis University, June 2000.

Harvey, S., & Goudvis. (2000). *Strategies that work: Teaching comprehension to enhance understanding.* Markham, Ontario: Pembroke Publishing.

Heath, S. B. (1983). *Ways with words: Language, life, and work in communities and classrooms.* Cambridge, England: Cambridge University Press.

Heath, S. B. (1986). Sociocultural contexts of language development. In *Beyond language: Social and cultural factors in schooling language minority students* (pp. 143–182). Sacramento: Bilingual Education Office, California State Department of Education.

Henderson, E. H. (1990). *Teaching spelling.* Boston: Houghton Mifflin.

Henderson, E. H., Estes, T., & Stonecash, S. (1972). An exploratory study of word acquisition among first graders at midyear in a language experience approach. *Journal of Reading Behavior, 4,* 21–30.

Hendrix, C. (1952). *Cómo enseñar a leer por el método global.* Buenos Aires, Argentina: Editorial Kapelusz.

Henkes, K. (1996). *Lilly's purple plastic purse.* New York: Greenwillow.

Henkes, K. (1987). *Sheila Rae the brave.* New York: Greenwillow.

Herman, J. L., & Golan, S. (1993). The effects of standardized testing on teaching and schools. *Educational Measurement: Issues and Practice, 12,* 20–25, 41–42.

Hickman, J. (1979). *Response to literature in a school environment.* Doctoral dissertation. Ohio State University, Columbus, OH.

Hickman, J. (1981). A new perspective on response to literature. *Research in the Teaching of English, 15,* 343–354.

Hickman, J. (1992). What comes naturally. In C. Temple & P. Collins (Eds.), *Stories and readers.* Norwood, MA: Christopher-Gordon.

Hiebert, E. H. (1983). An examination of ability grouping for reading instruction. *Reading Research Quarterly, 18,* 161–171.

Hill, R., Carjuzaa, J., Aramburo, D., & Baca, L. (1993). Culturally and linguistically diverse teachers in special education: Repairing or redesigning the leaky pipeline. *Teacher Education and Special Education, 16,* 258–269.

Hirsch, E. D. (1987). *Cultural literacy: What every American needs to know.* Boston: Houghton Mifflin.

Hirschi, R. (1991). *Fall.* New York: Cobblehill Books.

Ho, D. B. (1999). Using wordless picture books to support struggling sixth grade readers and writers. *The California Reader, 32,* 9–11.

Hoban, R. (1995). *Bedtime for Frances.* Illustrated by Garth Williams. New York: HarperTrophy.

Hoberman, M. A. (2000). *The eeensy weensy spider.* Boston: Little, Brown.

Hoff, E. (2001). *Language development.* New York: Wadsworth.

Hoff, S. (1999). *Danny and the dinosaur.* New York: HarperFestival.

Hoff-Ginsburg, E. (1998). *What explains the SES-related difference in children's vocabularies and what does that reveal about the process of word learning?* Paper presented at the Boston University Conference on Language Development, Boston, November 6–8.

Hoffman, J. V. (1991). Teacher and school effects in learning to read. In R. Barr, M. L. Kamil, P. B. Mosenthal, & P. D. Pearson (Eds.), *Handbook of reading research* (Vol. II, pp. 911–950). New York: Longman.

Hoffman, J. V. (1992). Critical reading/thinking across the curriculum: Using I-Charts to support learning. *Language Arts, 69,* 121–127.

Holaway, D. (1979). *The foundations of literacy.* Portsmouth, NH: Ashton-Scholastic.

Hopkins, L. B. (1990). *Good books, good times!* New York: HarperCollins.

Horowitz, E. (1977). *Words come in families.* New York: Hart Publishing Company, Inc.

Hudelson, S. (1984). Kan yu ret an rayt en Ingles: Children become literate in English as a second language. *TESOL Quarterly, 18,* 221–238.

Hudelson, S. (1987). The role of native language literacy in the education of language minority children. *Language Arts, 64,* 827–840.

Huey, E. B. (1908). *The psychology and pedagogy of reading.* Cambridge, MA: MIT Press.

Hughes, S. (1977). *Dogger.* London: Reds Fox.

Hutchins, P. (1976, 1995). *Don't forget the bacon!* New York: Scholastic.

Hutchins, P. (1978). *Happy birthday Sam.* New York: Greenwillow.

Hutchins, P. (1994). *Tidy tich.* New York: Mulberry Books.

Hymes, D. (1972). Models of the interaction of language and social life. In J. Gumperz & D. Hymes (Eds.), *Directions in sociolinguistics: The ethnography of communication* (pp. 35–71). New York: Holt, Rinehart, & Winston.

Hynds, S. (1997). *On the brink: Negotiating literature and life with adolescents.* New York: Teachers College Press.

Individuals with Disabilities Education Act 1997 (Reauthorization). (1997). 20 U.S.C. 1400 et seq.

International Reading Association & National Association for the Education of Young Children. (1998). Learning to read and write: Developmentally appropriate practices for young children: A joint position statement of the International Reading Association (IRA) and National Association for the Education of Young Children (NAEYC). *Young Children, 23*(4), 30–46.

International Reading Association. (2001). *Second-language literacy instruction: A position statement of the International Reading Association.* Newark, DE: Author.

Irvin, J. L. (1998). *Reading and the middle school student: Strategies to enhance literacy.* Boston: Allyn & Bacon.

Iser, W. (1974). *The implied reader.* Baltimore: Johns Hopkins University Press.

Iser, W. (1978). *The act of reading.* Baltimore: Johns Hopkins University Press.

Iverson, S., & Tunmer, W. (1993). Phonological processing skills and the Reading Recovery Program. *Journal of Educational Psychology, 85,* 112–126.

Ives, J. P., Bursuk, L. Z., & Ives, S. A. (1979). *Word identification techniques.* NY: Rand-McNally.

Johnston, R., & Watson, J. (1997). Developing reading, spelling, and phonemic awareness skills in primary school children. *Reading 31,* 37–40.

Johnson, K. R., & Simons, H. D. (1974). Teaching reading to children who speak Black English. In *MetroVoices (Teacher's Edition).* Beverly Hills, CA: Benziger.

Johnson-Coleman, L. (2001, May). *Keep on keepin' on: Motivation for the young and young at heart.* Keynote address presented at the annual conference of the International Reading Association, New Orleans, LA.

Joyce, J. (1993) *Dubliners.* Saint Paul, MN: Penguin-HighBridge Audio.

Juel, C. (1988). Learning to read and write: A longitudinal study of 54 children from first through fourth grades. *Journal of Educational Psychology, 80,* 415–447.

Kagan, S. (1997). *Cooperative learning.* San Clemente, CA: Kagan Publishers.

Kame'enui, E., Simmons, D., Cornachione, C., Thompson-Hoffman, S., Ginsburg, A., Marcy, E., Mittleman, J., Irwin, J., & Baker, M. (2001). *A practical guide to reading assessments.* Washington, DC: U.S. Department of Education.

Kameenui, E. J. (1998). The rhetoric of all, the reality of some, and the unmistakable smell of mortality. In J. Osborn & F. Lehr (Eds.), *Literacy for all: Issues in teaching and learning.* New York: Guilford.

Kerley, B. (2001). *The dinosaurs of Waterhouse Hawkins.* New York: Scholastic.

Klenk, L., & Kibby, M. W. (2000). Re-mediating reading difficulties: Appraising the past, reconciling the present, constructing the future. In M. L. Kamil, P. B. Mosenthal, P. D. Pearson, & R. Barr (Eds.), *Handbook of reading research* (Vol. III, pp. 545–562). Mahwah, NJ: Erlbaum.

Knapp, M. S. (1995). *Teaching for meaning in high-poverty classrooms.* New York: Teachers College Press.

Koskinen, P. S., Gambrell, L. B., Kapinus, B. A., & Heathington, B. S. (1988). Retelling: A strategy for enhancing students' reading comprehension. *The Reading Teacher, 41,* 892–896.

Kovalski, M. (1987). *The wheels on the bus.* Boston: Little, Brown.

Krashen, S. D. (1981). Bilingual education and second language acquisition theory. In California State Department of Education (Ed.), *Schooling and language minority students: A theoretical framework* (pp. 51–79). Sacramento: California State Department of Education, Office of Bilingual Bicultural Education.

Krashen, S. D. (1982a). Theory versus practice in language training. In R. W. Blair (Ed.), *Innovative approaches to language teaching* (pp. 15–30). Rowley, MA: Newbury House.

Krashen, S. D. (1982b). *Principles and practice in second language acquisition.* New York: Pergamon Press.

Krashen, S. D. (1985). *Inquiries and insights: Second language teaching, immersion and bilingual education, literacy.* Hayward, CA: Alemany Press.

Krashen, S. D. (1991). *Bilingual education: A focus on current research.* Washington, DC: National Clearinghouse for Bilingual Education.

Krashen, S. D. (1993). *The power of reading: Insights from the research.* Greenwood Village, CO: Libraries Unlimited.

Krashen, S. D. (1997). Conflicting claims concerning computers: A comment on Hinkson (1996). *The California Reader, 30,* 16–17.

Krashen, S. D., & Biber, D. (1988). *On course: Bilingual education's success in California.* Sacramento: California Association for Bilingual Education.

Krashen, S. D., & Terrell, T. D. (1983). *The natural approach: Language acquisition in the classroom.* New York: Pergamon/Alemany.

Kraus, R. (1987). *Leo the late bloomer.* New York: Simon & Schuster.

Kraus, R. (1989). *The carrot seed.* New York: Harper & Row.

Labov, W. (1970). *The study of non-standard English.* Champaign, IL: NCTE.

Labov, W. (1972). *Language in the inner city: Studies in Black English Vernacular.* Philadelphia: University of Pennsylvania Press.

Ladson-Billings, G. (1994). *The dreamkeepers: Successful teachers of African American children.* San Francisco: Jossey-Bass.

Lamberg, W. J., Rodríguez, L., & Tomas, D. A. (1978). Training in identifying oral reading departures from text which can be explained as Spanish-English phonological differences. *The Bilingual Review/La Revista Bilingüe, 5,* 65–75.

Lambert, W. E. (1975). Culture and language as factors in learning and education. In A. Wolfgang (Ed.), *Education of immigrant students.* Toronto: O.I.S.E.

Lampman, E. S. (2001). *The shy stegosaurus of Cricket Creek.* Keller, TX: Purple House Press.

Landrum, J. (2001). Selecting intermediate novels that feature characters with disabilities. *The Reading Teacher, 55,* 252–258.

Lau v. *Nichols,* 414 US 563 (1974).

Lederer, R. (1991). *The miracle of language.* New York: Pocket Books.

Lehr, S. (1988). Children's developing sense of theme as a response to literature. *Reading Research Quarterly, 23,* 337–357.

Lester, H. (1986). *A porcupine named fluffy.* Boston: Houghton Mifflin.

Lester, H. (1993). *Tacky the penguin.* Boston: Houghton Mifflin.

Leu, D. J. Jr. (2002). The new literacies: Research on reading instruction with the internet. In A. E. Farstrup & S. J. Samuels (Eds.), *What research has to say about reading instruction* (pp. 310–336). Newark, DE: International Reading Association.

Levi Strauss, C. (1970). *Structural anthropology.* Garden City, NY: Basic Books.

Los Angeles Unified School District. (1985). *Strategies for sheltered English instruction.* Los Angeles: Author.

Luke, A., & Freebody, P. (1999). A map of possible practices: Further notes on the four resources model. *Practically Primary, 4,* 2.

Luria, A. R. (1976). *Cognitive development: Its cultural and social foundations.* Cambridge, MA: Harvard University Press.

Macrorie, Ken. (1988) *The I-Search paper-revised edition of "Searching Writing."* Portsmouth, NH: Heinemann.

Mann, V. A., Tobin, P., & Wilson, R. (1987). Measuring phonological awareness through the invented spellings of kindergarten children. *Merrill-Palmer Quarterly, 33,* 365–391.

Manzo, A. V. (1969). The ReQuest procedure. *Journal of Reading, 13,* 123–126.

Markle, S. (2000). *Outside and inside dinosaurs.* New York: Atheneum Books for Young Readers.

Marsh, G. (1977). Developmental changes in reading strategies. *Journal of Reading Behavior, 9*(4): 391–394.

Marshall, E. (1994). *Fox and his friends.* Illustrated by James Marshall. New York: Puffin.

Martinez, M., & Roser, N. (1991). Children's responses to literature. In J. Flood, J. Jensen, J. Lapp, & J. Squire (Eds.), *Handbook of research in teaching the English language arts.* New York: Macmillan.

McCafferty, S. G., & Iddings, C. (2001). *Carnival: Putting a round peg in a square hole.* Paper presented at the meeting of the National Reading Conference, San Antonio, TX.

McCartney, K. (1984). Effect of quality of day care environment on children's language development. *Developmental Psychology, 20,* 244–260.

McCauley, D. (1982). *Castle.* New York: Houghton Mifflin Co.

McCutcheon, M. (2000). *Descriptionary: A thematic dictionary,* (2nd Ed.). New York: Checkmark Books.

McGee, L. M., & Richgels, D. J. (2000). *Literacy's beginnings: Supporting young readers and writers* (3rd ed.). Boston: Allyn & Bacon.

McKeown, M. G., & Beck, I. L. (1988). http://www.indiana.edu/~eric_rec/ieo/digests/d126bib.html *Remedial and Special Education, 9*(1), 42–46.

McKissack, P. C. (1997). *Ma Dear's aprons.* New York: Alladin Paperbacks.

McQuillan, J., & Tse, L. (1998). What's the story? Using the narrative approach in beginning language classrooms. *TESOL Journal, 7,* 18–23.

McTighe, J., & Lyman, F. T. (1988). Cueing thinking in the classroom: The promise of theory-embedded tools. *Educational Leadership, 45,* 18–24.

Mehan, J. (1979). *Learning lessons.* Cambridge, MA: Harvard University Press.

Mitsumasa, Anno. (1997). *Anno's journey.* New York: Penguin Putnam Books for Young Readers.

Modiano, N. (1968). Bilingual education for children of linguistic minorities. *American Indígena, 28,* 405–414.

Moffett, J. (1976). *Teaching the universe of discourse.* New York: Holt, Rinehart, & Winston.

Moffett, J., & Wagner, B. J. (1983). *Student-centered language arts and reading, K–13: A handbook for teachers* (3rd ed.). Boston: Houghton Mifflin.

Mohr, H. (1987). *How to talk Minnesotan, a visitor's guide.* New York: Penguin Books.

Moje, E. B., Young, J. P., Readence, J. E., & Moore, D.W. (2000). Reinventing adolescent literacy for new times: Perennial and millennial issues. *Journal of Adolescent and Adult Literacy, 43,* 400–410.

Moore, D. W., Bean, T., Berdyshaw, D., & Lycis, J. (1999). *Adolescent literacy: A position statement for the commission on adolescent literacy of the International Reading Association.* Newark, DE: International Reading Association.

Moore, D. W. (1996). Contexts for literacy in secondary schools. In D. J. Leu, C. K. Kinzer, & K. A. Hinchman (Eds.), *Literacies for the 21st century: Research and practice* (45th Yearbook of the National Reading Conference, pp. 15–46). Chicago, IL: National Reading Conference.

Moore, D. W., Alvermann, D. E., & Hinchman, K. A. (2000). *Struggling adolescent readers: A collection of teaching strategies.* Newark, DE: International Reading Association.

Morris, R. D. (1992). What constitutes "at risk": The Early Reading Screening Inventory. Best practices in speech pathology.

Morris, R. D. (1998). *Case studies in beginning reading.* New York: Guilford Press.

Morris, R. D. (1999). *The Howard Street tutoring manual.* New York: Guilford Press.

Morris, W. (1962). *Dictionary of word and phrase origins.* New York: Harper & Row.

Morrow, L., & Weinstein, C. S. (1982). Increasing children's use of literature through program and physical design changes. *The Elementary School Journal, 83,* 131–137.

Moustafa, M. (1997). *Beyond traditional phonics.* Portsmouth, NH: Heinemann.

Moustafa, M., & Penrose, J. (1985). Comprehensible input PLUS the language experience approach: Reading instruction for limited English speaking students. *The Reading Teacher, 38,* 640–647.

Munsch, R. (1992). *The paper bag princess.* Toronto: Annick Press.

Murray, D. (1985). *A writer teaches writing.* Boston: Houghton Mifflin.

NAEYC. (1998). *Learning to read and write: Developmentally appropriate practices for young children.* A joint position statement of the International Reading Association (IRA) and National Association for the Education of Young Children (NAEYC). *Young Children 23*(4) 30–46.

Nagy, W. E., Anderson, R. C., & Herman, P. A. (1987). Learning word meanings from context during normal reading. *American Educational Research Journal, 24,* 237–270.

Nagy, W. E., et al. (1985). http://www.indiana.edu/~eric_rec/ieo/digests/d126bib.html? (Technical Report No. 347). Urbana, IL: Center for the Study of Reading.

Nagy, W. E., García, G. E., Durgunoglu, A. Y., & Hancin-Bhatt, B. (1993). Spanish-English bilingual students' use of cognates in English reading. *Journal of Reading Behavior, 25,* 241–259.

Nagy, W., & Anderson, R. C. (1984). How many words are there in printed school English? *Reading Research Quarterly, 19,* 304–330.

Nagy, W., Herman, P., & Anderson, R. (1985). Learning words from context. *Reading Research Quarterly, 20,* 233-253.

Nathan, R., Temple, F., Juntunen, K., & Temple, C. (1988). *Classroom strategies that work: An elementary teacher's guide to process writing.* Portsmouth, NH: Heinemann.

Nathenson-Mejia, S. (1989). Writing in a second language: Negotiating meaning through invented spelling. *Language Arts, 66,* 516–526.

National Center for Education Statistics. (1999). *Digest of education statistics, 1998.* Washington, DC: U.S. Department of Education.

National Center for Educational Statistics (NCES). (1993). *Adult literacy in America: A first look at the National Adult Literacy Survey.* Washington, DC: U.S. Department of Education.

National Center for Educational Statistics (NCES). (1994). *National assessment of educational progress.* Washington, DC: U.S. Department of Education.

National Center for Educational Statistics. (1999, 2002). *The condition of education.* Washington, DC: U.S. Government Printing Office. Web site: http://nces.ed.gov/programs/coe/.

National Center for Educational Statistics. (2000). *Elementary and secondary education: An international perspective.* Washington, DC: U.S. Department of Education. (On the web at http://nces.ed.gov/pubs2000/2000033.pdf).

National Council for the Accreditation of Teacher Education. (2000). *Standards for reading.* Web site: www.ncate.org/standard/m_stds.htm.

National Geographic World. Washington, DC: National Geographic.

National Reading Panel website. (2003). *Reports.* On the web at *http://www.nationalreadingpanel.org.*

National Reading Panel. (2000, December). *Teaching children to read: An evidence-based assessment of the sci-* *entific research literature on reading and its implications for reading instruction.* (Reports of the Subgroups). Washington, DC: National Institute of Child Health and Human Development, National Institutes of Health.

Nelson-Herber, J. (1986). http://www.indiana.edu/~eric_rec/ieo/digests/d126bib.html *Journal of Reading, 29,* 626–633.

Nessel, D. D., & Jones, M. B. (1981). *The language-experience approach to reading.* New York: Teachers College Press.

Neuman, S. B., & Celano, D. (2001). Access to print in low-income and middle-income communities: An ecological study of four neighborhoods. *Reading Research Quarterly, 56,* 8–28.

Neuman, S. B., & Dickenson, D. K. (2001). *Handbook of early literacy research.* New York: Guilford.

Neuman, S., & Rosko, K. (1991). The influence of literacy-enriched play centers on preschoolers' conceptions of the functions of print. In J. Christie (Ed.), *Play and early literacy development* (pp. 167–187). Albany: State University of New York Press.

New Standards for Primary Literacy Committee. (1999). *Reading and writing grade by grade: Primary literacy standards for kindergarten through third grade.* New York: Board of Education of the City of New York.

New York State Education Department. (2002). *English language arts resource guide.* Albany, NY: Author. (On the web at http://www.emsc.nysed.gov/ciai/ela/pub/elals.pdf).

Newport, E. L., Gleitman, H., & Gleitman, L. (1977). Mother, I'd rather do it myself: Some effects and non-effects of maternal speech style. In C. E. Snow & A. Ferguson (Eds.), *Talking to children: Language input and acquisition.* Cambridge, England: Cambridge University Press.

Nolan, S. B., Haladyna, T. M., & Haas, N. S. (1992). Uses and abuses of achievement test scores. *Educational Measurement: Issues and Practice, 11,* 9–15.

O'Connor, R. E., Jenkins, J. R., & Slocum, T. A. (1995). Transfer among phonological tasks in kindergarten: Essential instructional content. *Journal of Educational Psychology, 87,* 202–217.

O'Leary, D. (2002). *2002 widening achievement gap.* Tucson: League of Latin American Citizens (LULAC).

Office of Economic and Community Development. (2001). *The OECD programme for international student assessment.* New York: Author.

Ogden, C. K., & Richards, I. A. (1923). *The meaning of meaning: A study of the influence of language on thought and the science of symbolism.* New York: Harcourt Brace.

Ogle, D., & Blachowicz, C. (2001). Beyond literature circles: Helping students comprehend informational texts. In C. C. Block, & M. Pressley (Eds.) *Comprehension Instruction: Research-based practices.* New York: Guilford Press.

Ogle, D. (1986). K-W-L: A teaching model that develops active reading of expository text. *Reading Teacher, 40,* 564–570.

Ogle, D. (1991). The know, want to know, learn strategy. In N. Muth (Ed.), *Children's comprehension of text: Research and practice* (pp. 22–23). Newark, DE: International Reading Association.

Ogle, D. (2000). Make it visual: A picture is worth a thousand words. In M. McLaughlin & M. Vogt (Eds.), *Creativity and innovation in content area teaching.* Norwood, MA: Christopher-Gordon Publishers, Inc.

Ogle, D., & Blachowicz, C. (2001). Beyond literature circles: Helping students comprehend informational texts. In C. C. Block & M. Pressley (Eds.), *Comprehension instruction: Research-based best practices.* New York: Guilford.

Oldfather, P., & McLaughlin, H. J. (1993). Gaining and losing voice: A longitudinal student's continuing impulse to learn across elementary and middle school contexts. *Research in Middle Level Education, 3,* 1–25.

Olson, M. W., & Gee, T. C. (1988). A review of story grammar research. *Childhood Education, 64*(4), 302–306.

Organisation for Economic Co-operation and Development. (1995). *Employment outlook.* Paris: Author.

Organisation for Economic Co-operation and Development. (2001). *Knowledge and skills for life: First results from PISA 2000.* Paris, France: Author.

Organization of Economic and Community Development. (2000). *Program for international student assessment.* New York: The United Nations. http://www.pisa.oecd.org/.

Palincsar, A. S., & Brown, A. L. (1984). Interactive teaching to promote independent learning from text. *The Reading Teacher, 39,* 771–777.

Palincsar, A. S., & Brown, A. L. (1984). Reciprocal teaching of comprehension-fostering and monitoring activities. *Cognition and Instruction, 1*(2), 117–175.

Paris, S. G., & Oka, E. R. (1986). Children's reading strategies, metacognition, and motivation. *Developmental Review, 6,* 25–56.

Parrish, P. (1992). *Amelia Bedelia.* Illustrated by Fritz Siebel. New York: HarperCollins.

Paterson, K. (1994). *Lyddie.* New York: Puffin.

Pearson, P. D. (1985). Changing the face of reading comprehension instruction. *The Reading Teacher, 38,* 724–738.

Peck, J. (1989). Using storytelling to promote language and literacy development. *The Reading Teacher, 43,* 138–141.

Pellegrini, A. D., & Galda, L. (2000). Children's pretend play and literacy. In D. S. Strickland & L. M. Morrow (Eds.), *Beginning reading and writing, language and literacy series.* Newark, DE: International Reading Association.

Pennycook, A. (1985). Actions speak louder than words: Paralanguage, communication, and education. *TESOL Quarterly, 19,* 259–282.

Perfetti, C. (1992). *Reading ability.* New York: Oxford University Press.

Perfetti, C. A. (1986). Cognitive and linguistic components of reading ability. In B. Foorman & A. Siegel (Eds.), *Acquisition of reading skills, cultural constraints and cognitive universals* (pp. 11–40). Hillsdale, NJ: Erlbaum.

Perrone, V. (1990). How did we get here? In C. Kamii (Ed.), *Achievement testing in the early grades.* Washington, DC: National Association for the Education of Young Children.

Peters, C. (1995). *At the zoo.* Boston: Houghton Mifflin.

Piaget, J. (1926). *The language and thought of the child.* London: Routledge & Kegan Paul.

Pilkey, D. (2000). *Captain underpants boxed set.* New York: Scholastic.

Pinker, S. (1994). *The language instinct.* New York: HarperPerennial.

Pinnell, G. S., & Fountas, I. C. (2001). *Leveled books for readers, grades 3–6.* Portsmouth, NH: Heinemann.

Pinnell, G. S., & Fountas, I. C., with Giacobbe, M. E. (1998). *Word matters: Teaching phonics and spelling in the reading/writing classroom.* Portsmouth, NH: Heinemann.

Pinnell, G. S., Bridges, L. B., & Fountas, I. C. (1999). *Matching books to readers: Using leveled books in guided reading.* Portsmouth, NH: Heinemann.

Pittelman, S. D., Heimlich, J. E., Berglund, R. L., & French M. P. (1991). *Semantic feature analysis: Classroom applications.* Newark, DE: International Reading Association.

Plecha, J. (1992). Shared inquiry: The Great Books method of interpretive reading and discussion. In D. Temple & P. Collins (Eds.), *Stories and readers: New perspectives on literature, the elementary classroom* (pp. 103–114). Norwood, MA: Christopher-Gordon.

Powell, R., Cantrell, S. C., & Adams, S. (2001). Saving Black Mountain: The promise of critical literacy in a multicultural democracy. *The Reading Teacher, 54,* 772–781.

Pressley, M. (1998). *Reading instruction that works: The case for balanced instruction.* New York: Guilford.

Pressley, M. (1999). Self-regulated comprehension processing and its development through instruction. In L. B. Gambrell, L. M. Morrow, S. B. Neuman, & M. Pressley (Eds.), *Best practices in literacy instruction.* New York: Guilford.

Pressley, M. (2000). "What should comprehension instruction be the instruction of?" In M. L. Kamil, P. B. Mosenthal, P. D. Pearson, & R. Barr (Eds.), *Handbook of reading research* (Vol. III, pp. 545–562). Mahwah, NJ: Erlbaum.

Pressley, M. (2002). Metacognition and self-regulated comprehension. In A. E. Farstrup & S. J. Samuels (Eds.), *What research has to say about reading instruction* (pp. 291–309). Newark, DE: International Reading Association.

Pressley, M., et al. (1994). Transactional instruction of reading comprehension strategies. *Perspectives in Reading Research, No. 5,* Fall. Athens, GA: National Reading Research Center Brookline Books.

Pressley, M., & Afflerbach, P. (1995) *Verbal protocols of reading: The nature of constructively responsive reading.* Hillsdale, NJ: Erlbaum.

Pressley, M., Allington, R. L., Wharton-McDonald, R., Block, C. C., & Morrow, L. M. (Eds.). (2001). *Learning to read: Lessons from exemplary first-grade classrooms.* New York: Guilford.

Pressley, M., Rankin, J., & Yokoi, L. (1996). A survey of instructional practices of primary teachers nominated as effective in promoting literacy. *Elementary School Journal, 96,* 363–384.

Pressley, M., Wharton-McDonald, R., Mistretta, J., & Echevarria, M. (1998). The nature of literacy instruction in ten grade 4/5 classrooms in upstate New York. *Scientific Studies of Reading, 2,* 159–191.

Public Agenda On-Line. (2002). *Reality check, 2002.* New York: Public Agenda (On the web at http://www.publicagenda.org/specials/rcheck2002/reality.htm).

Purcell-Gates, V. (1991). Ability of well-read-to kindergartners to decontextualise/ recontextualise experience into a written-narrative register. *Language and Education: An International Journal, 5*(3), 177–188.

Purcell-Gates, V. (1995). *Other people's words: The cycle of low literacy.* Cambridge, MA: Harvard University Press.

Purcell-Gates, V., L'Allier, S., & Smith, D. (1995). Literacy at the Harts' and the Larsons': Diversity among poor inner city families. *The Reading Teacher, 48,* 572–578.

Purcell-Gates, V., McIntyre, E., & Freppon, P. A. (1995). Learning written storybook language in school: A comparison of low-SES children in skills-based and whole language classrooms. *American Educational Research Journal, 32*(3), 659–685.

Raffi. (1996). The more we get together. *Raffi Sampler.* [CD]. Cambridge, MA: Rounder Records.

Ramírez, J. D. (1991). *Final report: Longitudinal study of structured English immersion strategy, early-exit and late-exit bilingual education programs.* NTIS, 300-87-0156. Washington, DC: U.S. Department of Education.

Randell, B. (1996a). *Baby bear goes fishing.* Crystal Lake, IL: Rigby.

Randell, B. (1996b). *Ben's tooth.* Crystal Lake, IL: Rigby.

Randell, B. (1996c). *Wake up, Dad.* Crystal Lake, IL: Rigby.

Raphael, T. E. (1982). Question-answering strategies for children. *The Reading Teacher, 36,* 186–191.

Raphael, T. E. (1986). Teaching question answer relationships, revisited. *The Reading Teacher, 39*(6), 516–522.

Raphael, T. E. (1998). Balanced instruction and the role of classroom discourse. In J. Osborn, & F. Lehr (Eds.), *Literacy for all: Issues in teaching and learning.* New York: Guilford.

Raphael, T. E., Goatley, V., McMahon, S., & Woodman, D. (1995). Teaching literacy through student book clubs. In N. Roser & M. Martinez (Eds.), *Book talk and beyond: Children and teachers respond to literature* (pp. 66–79). Newark, DE: International Reading Association.

Raphael, T. E., & McMahon, S. I. (1994). Book club: An alternative framework for reading instruction. *The Reading Teacher, 48,* 102–117.

Rasinsky, T. (2000). Speed does matter in reading. *Reading Teacher, 54,* 146–151.

Read, C. (1975). *Children's categorization of speech sounds in English* (Research Report No. 17). Urbana, IL: National Council of Teachers of English.

Rébsamen, E. C. (1949). *La enseñanza de la escritura y lectura en el primer año escolar: Guía metodológica.* Paris: Librería de la Vda de Ch. Bouret.

Reed, C. (1971). Preschool children's knowledge of English phonology. *Harvard Educational Review, 41,* 1–34.

Reid, D. K., Hresko, W. P., & Hammill, D. D. (1989). *TERA-2: Test of Early Reading Ability.* Austin, TX: PRO-ED.

Reutzel, D. R., & Hollingsworth, P. M. (1991). Reading comprehension skills: Testing the skills distinctiveness hypothesis. *Reading Research and Instruction, 30,* 32–46.

Richard-Amato, P., & Snow, M. A. (1992). *The multicultural classroom: Readings for content content area teachers.* New York: Longman.

Richards, I. A. (1929). *Practical criticism.* New York: Harcourt, Brace.

Rickford, R. R., & Rickford, A. E. (1995). Dialect readers revisited. *Linguistics and Education, 7,* 107–128.

Riley, J. (1996). *The teaching of reading.* London: Paul Chapman.

Robb, L., Klemp, R., & Schwartz, W. (2002). *Reader's handbook: A student guide for reading and learning.* Wilmington, MA: Great Source Education Group.

Rodríguez Fuenzalida, E. (1982). *Metodologías de alfabetización en América Latina.* Pátzcuaro, Michoacán, México: UNESCO/CREFAL.

Roop, P., & Roop, C. (1985). *Keep the lights burning, Abbie.* Minneapolis, MN: Carolrhoda Books.

Rosen, M. (2003). *We're going on a bear hunt.* Illustrated by H. Oxenbury. New York: Alladin.

Rosenblatt, L. (1978). *The reader, the text, and the poem.* Carbondale, IL: Southern Illinois University Press.

Roser, N., & Hoffman, J. V. (1995). Language charts: A record of story time talk. In N. Roser & M. Martinez (Eds.), *Book talk and beyond: Children and teachers respond to literature* (pp. 66–79). Newark, DE: International Reading Association.

Roth, R., Speece, D. H., & Cooper, D. H. (2002). A longitudinal analysis of the connection between oral language and early reading. *Journal of Educational Reasearch, 95,* 259–272.

Routman, R. (1996). *Literacy at the crossroads: Crucial talk about reading, writing, and other teaching dilemmas.* Portsmouth, NH: Heinemann.

Rowe, M. B. (1974). Wait-time and rewards as instructional variables: Their influence on language, logic and fate control: Part one—Wait time. *Journal of Research in Science Teaching, 11*(2), 81–94.

Rupley, W. H., & Willson, V. L. (1997). The relationship between reading comprehension and components of word recognition: Support for developmental shifts. *Journal of Research and Development in Education, 30*(4), 255–260.

Rylant, C. (1987). *Henry and Mudge.* New York: Simon & Schuster.

Sachar, L. (1998). *Holes.* New York: Farrar, Strauss, & Giroux.

Sainsbury, M. (2001). *The 2001 IEA progress in international reading literacy study.* Paper presented at the 12th European Conference on Reading. Dublin, July 2001.

Salmon, K. (1995). *Lenguaje integral: Una alternativa para la enseñanza-aprendizaje de la lecto-escritura.* Quito, Ecuador: Abrapalabra Editores.

Samuels, S. J. (1971). Letter-name versus letter-sound knowledge in learning to read. *The Reading Teacher, 24,* 604–608.

Samuels, S. J. (1979). The method of repeated readings. *The Reading Teacher, 34*(4), 403–408.

Saville, M. R., & Troike, R. C. (1971). *A handbook of bilingual education.* Washington, DC: Teachers of English to Speakers of Other Languages.

Scarcella, R. (1990). *Teaching language minority students in multicultural classrooms.* New York: Longman.

Schifini, A. (1985). *Sheltered English: Content area instruction for limited English proficient students.* Los Angeles: Los Angeles County Office of Education.

Schifini, A. (1996). Reading instruction for the pre-literate and struggling older student. *NABE News, 20,* 5–6, 20, 30.

Schon, I. (2000). *Recommended books in Spanish for children and young adults, 1996–1999.* Lanham, MD: Scarecrow Press.

Schon, I. (2001). Los niños y el mundo: Children's books in Spanish from around the world. *The Reading Teacher, 54,* 692–698.

Schon, I. (2002). From Pulgarcito to Shakespeare. *Language, 2,* 28–30.

Schon, I., & Corona Berkin, S. (1996). *Introducción a la literatura infantil y juvenil.* Newark, DE: International Reading Association.

Schwartz, A. (1982). *The cat's elbow and other secret languages.* New York: Farrar, Straus and Giroux.

Schwartz, R. M., & Taffy, R. (1985). http://www.indi-ana.edu/~eric_rec/ieo/digests/d126bib.html *Reading Teacher, 39*(2), 198–205.

Scragg, D. G. (1974). *A history of English spelling.* London: Longman.

Searle, J. (1969). *Speech acts.* Cambridge, MA: Harvard University Press.

Selinker, L., Swain, M., & Dumas, G. (1975). The interlanguage hypothesis extended to children. *Language Learning, 25,* 129–152.

Sepúlveda, L. (1989). *The old man who read love stories.* New York: Harcourt Brace.

Seymour, E. (1984). *Hobble De Hoy!: The word game for geniuses.* New York: W. W. Norton.

Sharmat, C. (1972). *Nate the Great and the Pillowcase.* New York: Dell Random House.

Shaywitz, S. E., Escobar, M. D., Shaywitz, B. A., Fletcher, J. M., & Makuch, J. R. (1992). Evidence that dyslexia may represent the lower tail of a normal distribution of reading ability. *New England Journal of Medicine, 326,* 145–150.

Shipley, J. T. (1960). *Playing with words.* Englewood Cliffs, NJ: Prentice-Hall.

Short, K., & Kauffman, G. (1995). So what do I do? The role of the teacher in literature circles. In N. Roser & M. Martinez (Eds.), *Book talk and beyond: Children and teachers respond to literature* (pp. 140–149). Newark, DE: International Reading Association.

Short, K., Harste, J., & Burke, C. (1996). *Creating classrooms for authors and inquirers.* Portsmouth, NH: Heinemann.

Shostak, J. (1988). *Vocabulary workshop.* New York: Oxford Books.

Siegel, M., & Fernandez, S. L. (2000). Critical approaches. In M. L. Kamil, P. B. Mosenthal, P. D. Pearson, & R. Barr (Eds.), *Handbook of reading research* (Vol. III). Mahwah, NJ: Lawrence Erlbaum.

Silvaroli, N. J., & Wheelock, W. H. (2000). *Classroom reading inventory.* New York: McGraw-Hill.

Simon, S. (1955). *Sharks.* New York: HarperCollins.

Simpkins, G., Holt, G., & Simpkins, C. (1974). *Bridge: A cross-culture reading program.* Boston: Houghton Mifflin.

Skinner, B. F. (1957). *Verbal behavior.* Englewood Cliffs, NJ: Prentice Hall.

Sleeter, C. E., & Grant, C. A. (1999). *Making choices for multicultural education.* Upper Saddle River, NJ: Merrill.

Smith, C. B. (1997). Vocabulary instruction and reading comprehension. *ERIC Digest.*

Smith, F. (1973). *Psycholinguistics and reading.* New York: Holt, Rinehart, and Winston.

Smith, F. (1985). *Reading without nonsense.* New York: Teachers College Press.

Smith, F. (1986). *Keynote address: How education backed the wrong horse.* Presented at meeting of the California Reading Association, Fresno, California.

Smith, M. C. (2000). The real-world reading practices of adults. *Journal of Literary Research, 32*(1), 25–32.

Snow, C. E., Burns, M. S., & Griffin, P. (Eds.). (1998). *Preventing reading difficulties in young children.* Committee on the Prevention of Reading Difficulties in Young Children. Commission on Behavioral and Social Sciences and Education, National Research Council. Washington, DC: National Academy Press.

Snow, C. E., Tabors, P. O., & Dickenson, D. K. (2001). Language development in the preschool years. In D. K. Dickinson & P. O. Tabors (Eds.), *Beginning literacy with language.* Baltimore: Brookes.

Solé, I. (1994). *Estrategias de lectura.* Barcelona, Spain: Graó Editorial.

Souriau, E. (1955). *Les deux cent milles situations dramatiques.* Paris: Flamarion.

Spache, G. (1981). *Diagnosing and correcting reading disabilities* (2nd ed.). Boston: Allyn & Bacon.

Spandel, V. (1996). *Seeing with new eyes.* Portland, OR: Northwest Regional Educational Laboratory.

Spandel, V. (2000). *Creating writers through 6-Trait writing assessment and instruction* (3rd ed.). Boston: Allyn & Bacon.

Spinelli, J. (1990a). *Maniac Magee.* Boston: Little, Brown.

Spinelli, J. (1990b). *Maniac Magee.* New York: Scholastic. Large-print version from Library Reproduction Service, ISBN 0-590-45203-7.

Spolin, V. (1986). *Theater games for the classroom: A teacher's handbook.* Chicago: Northwestern University Press.

Stanovich, K. E. (1986). Matthew effects in reading: Some consequences of individual differences in the acquisition of literacy. *Reading Research Quarterly, 21,* 360–407.

Stanovich, K. E. (1992). Are we overselling literacy? In C. Temple & P. Collins (Eds.), *Stories and readers.* Norwood, MA: Christopher Gordon.

Stanovich, K. E., & Siegel, L. S. (1994). Phenotypic performance profiles of children with reading disabilities: A regression-based test of the phonological core variable-difference model. *Journal of Educational Psychology, 86,* 24–53.

Stauffer, R. (1975). *The language experience approach to the teaching of reading.* New York: Harper.

Stein, N. L., & Glenn, C. F. (1979). An analysis of story comprehension in elementary school children. In R. O. Freedle (Ed.), *New directions in discourse processing: Vol. 2. Advances in discourse processes* (pp. 53–120). Norwood, NJ: Ablex.

Stieglitz, E. L. (2001). *The Stieglitz informal reading inventory: Assessing reading behaviors from emergent to advanced levels.* New York: Allyn & Bacon.

Stoll, D. R. (Ed.). (1977). *Magazines for kids and teens.* Newark, DE: International Reading Association.

Stoll, D. R. (Ed.). (1994). *Magazines for kids and teens: A resource for parents, teachers, librarians and kids!* Glassboro, NJ: Educational Press of America.

Strauss, S. L. (2001). An open letter to Reid Lyon. *American Educational Research Association, 30,* 26–33.

Strickland, D. S. (1991). Cooperative, collaborative learning for children and teachers (emerging readers and writers). *Reading Teacher, 44,* 600–602.

Sulzby, E. (1985). Kindergarteners as writers and readers. In M. Farr, (Ed.), *Advances in writing research: Vol. I. Children's early writing development* (pp. 127–199). Norwood, NJ: Ablex.

Sulzby, E. (1985). Children's emergent reading of favorite storybooks: A developmental study. *Reading Research Quarterly, 20,* 458–479.

Suro, R., & Singer, A. (2002). *Latino growth in metropolitan America: Changing patterns, new locations.* Washington, DC: Brookings.

Sutherland-Smith, W. (2002). Weaving the literacy web: Changes in reading from page to screen. *The Reading Teacher, 55,* 662–669.

Szymborski, J. A. (1995). http://www.indiana.edu/ ~eric_rec/ieo/digests/d126bib.html M.A. Project, Kean College of New Jersey.

Tattershaw, S., & Prendeville, J. (1995). *Using familiar routines in language assessment and intervention.* San Antonio, TX: Communication Skill Builders.

Taylor, B. M., Pearson, P. D., Clark, K. F., & Walpole, S. (1999). *CIERA Inquiry 2: Home and School. What schoolwide practices characterize schools in which at-risk learners are beating the odds? What instructional practices are used by the most accomplished primary-grade teachers and by teachers in the most effective schools?* Ann Arbor, MI: CIERA.

Taylor, B., & Beach, R. (1984). The effects of text structure instruction on middle-grade students' comprehension and production of expository text. *Reading Research Quarterly, 19,* 134–146.

Taylor, B., Pearson, P. D., Clark, K., & Walpole, S. (1999). *Beating the odds in teaching all children to read.* Ann Arbor, MI: CIERA.

Taylor, B. M., Graves, M. F., & Ven Den Broek, P. (Eds.). (2000). *Reading for meaning: Fostering comprehension in the middle grades.* New York: Teachers College Press.

Taylor, M. *Roll of thunder, hear my cry.* New York: Puffin, 1997.

Teaching the English language arts: A sample standards-based lesson plan. (2002). In *Orientation to K–12 English language arts standards.* Unpublished work. (Available from Literacy Specialists Project Office, John Carroll University, 20700 North Park Boulevard. University Heights, OH 44118).

Teale, W. (1986). Home background and children's literacy development. In W. Teale & E. Sluzby (Eds.), *Emergent literacy: Writing and reading* (pp. 173–206). Norwood, NJ: Ablex.

Teale, W. H., & Sulzby, E. (1986). *Emergent literacy: Writing and reading.* Upper Saddle River, NJ: Ablex.

Teale, W. H., & Sulzby, E. (1987). Literacy acquisition in early childhood: The roles of access and mediation in storybook reading. In D. Wagner (Ed.), *The future of literacy in a changing world* (pp. 111–130). New York: Pergamon Press.

Temple, C., Meredith, K., & Steele, J. (1997). *How children learn.* Washington, DC: The Reading & Writing for Critical Thinking Project.

Temple, C., & Gillet J. (1996). *Language and literacy: A lively approach.* New York: HarperCollins.

Temple, C., Martinez, M., Yokota, J., & Naylor, A. (2002). *Children's books in children's hands* (2nd ed.). Boston: Allyn & Bacon.

Temple, C., Nathan, R., Burris, N., & Temple, F. (1993). *The beginnings of writing* (3rd ed.). Boston: Allyn & Bacon.

Temple, F. (1992). *Tiger soup.* New York: Orchard.

Temple, F. (1995). *Tonight, by sea.* New York: Harper Trophy.

Templeton, S. (1983). Using the spelling/meaning connection to develop word knowledge in older students. *Journal of Reading, 27,* 8–14.

Templeton, S. (1989). Tacit and explicit knowledge of derivational morphology: Foundations for a unified approach to spelling and vocabulary development in the intermediate grades and beyond. *Reading Psychology, 10,* 233–253.

Templeton, S. (1991). Teaching and learning the English spelling system: Reconceptualizing method and purpose. *Elementary School Journal, 92,* 183–199.

Templeton, S., & Morris, D. (2000). Spelling: Reconceptualizing spelling development and instruction. In M. Kamil, P. B. Mosenthal, P. D. Pearson, & R. Barr (Eds.), *Handbook of reading research* (Vol. 3, pp. 525–539). Mahwah, NJ: Erlbaum.

Terrell, T. D. (1977). A natural approach to second language acquisition and learning. *Modern Language Journal, 6,* 325–337.

Terrell, T. D. (1981). The natural approach in bilingual education. In California State Department of Education (Ed.), *School and language minority students: A theoretical framework* (pp. 117–146). California State University, Los Angeles, Los Angeles: Evaluation, Dissemination and Assessment Center.

Terrell, T. D. (1982). The natural approach to language teaching: An update. *Modern Language Journal, 66,* 121–122.

Terrell, T. D. (1986). Acquisition in the natural approach: The binding/access framework. *Modern Language Journal, 70,* 212–227.

TESOL. (1997). *Policy Statement of the TESOL Board on African American Vernacular English.* Arlington, VA: Center for Applied Linguistics.

Texas Education Agency. (1996). *Comprehensive biennial report on Texas public schools: A report to the 75th Texas Legislature.* Austin: Author.

Texas Education Agency. (1998). *Texas essential knowledge and skills for English language arts and read-*

ing: Subchapter A. Elementary. Austin: Author. Available at www.tea.state.tx.us/rules/tac/chapter110/ch110a.html#110.1).

The Children's Partnership. (2000). *Online content for low-income and underserved Americans: The digital divide's new frontier.* Santa Monica, CA: Author.

Theodorou, R. (1996). *The animals went to bed.* Crystal Lake, IL: Rigby.

Thomas, W. P., & Collier, V. (1997). *School effectiveness for language minority students.* Washington, DC: National Clearinghouse for Bilingual Education.

Thomas, W. P., & Collier, V. P. (2002). *A national study of school effectiveness for language minority students' long-term academic achievement final report: Project 1.1.* Santa Cruz, CA: Center for Research on Education, Diversity and Excellence.

Tinajero, J. V., & Nagel, G. (1995). "I never knew I was needed until you called!": Promoting parent involvement in schools. *The Reading Teacher, 48,* 614–617.

Tompkins, G. (2000). *Teaching writing: Balancing process and product.* Columbus, OH: Merrill.

Torres Quintero, G. (1976). *Método onomatopéyico.* Mexico City, Mexico: Editorial Patria.

Trieman, R. (1985). Onsets and rimes as units of spoken syllables: Evidence from children. *Journal of Experimental Child Psychology, 39,* 161–181.

U.S. Census Bureau. (2000). *U.S. Census 2000.* Washington, DC: U.S. Department of Commerce.

U.S. Department of Education. (2001). *No child left behind.* (On the web at http://www.ed.gov/offices/OESE/esea/).

U.S. Department of Education. (2003). *The facts about . . . reading achievement.* (On the web at http://www.nclb.gov/start/facts/reading.html).

UNESCO. (1953). *The use of vernacular languages in education.* Paris: UNESCO.

University of Wisconsin–Eau Claire. (2000). *Hmong population research project.* Retrieved from www.uwec.edu/Academic/Econ/HmongResearch/HPopulation.htm on August 3, 2001.

Urrea, L. A. (1996). *By the lake of sleeping children: The secret life of the Mexican border.* New York: Anchor Books.

Vacca, R., & Vacca, J. (1986). *Content area reading.* Boston: Allyn & Bacon.

Vacca, R., & Vacca, J. (1996). *Content area reading,* 5th ed. New York: HarperCollins.

Van Buren, T. (n.d.). "Six Trait writing evaluation sheet." (Available at http://coe.west.asu.edu/students/tvanburen/sixtreval.htm).

Veatch, J. (1996). From the vantage of retirement. *The Reading Teacher, 49,* 510–516.

Veatch, J., Sawicki, F., Elliott, G., Flake, E., & Blakey, J. (1979). *Key words to reading: The language experience approach begins.* Columbus, OH: Merrill.

Vellutino, F. R. (1979). *Dyslexia: Theory and research.* Cambridge: MIT Press.

Vellutino, F. R., Scanlon, D. M., Sipay, E. R., Small, S. G., Pratt, A., Chen, R., & Denckla, M. B. (1996). Cognitive profiles of difficult-to-remediate and readily remediated poor readers: Early intervention as a vehicle for distinguishing between cognitive and experiential deficits as a basic cause of specific reading disability. *Journal of Educational Psychology, 88,* 601–638.

Vellutino, F., & Scanlon, D. (2001). Emergent literacy skills, early instruction, and individual differences as determinants of difficulties in learning to read: The case for early intervention. In S. B. Newman & D. K. Dickinson (Eds.), *Handbook of early literacy research.* New York: Guilford Press.

Venezky, R. L. (1999). *The American way of spelling: The structure and origins of American English orthography.* New York: Guilford.

Virginia State Department of Education. (2002). *English standards of learning for Virginia public schools.* Richmond, VA: Author. (On the web at http://www.pen.k12.va.us/VDOE/Superintendent/Sols/2002/EnglishK-12.doc).

Vogt, M. E. (2000). Content learning for students needing modifications: An issue of access. In M. McLaughlin & M. E. Vogt (Eds.), *Creativity and innovation in content area teaching* (pp. 329–351). Norwood, MA: Christopher-Gordon.

Vukelich, C., Christie, J., & Enz, B. (2002). *Helping young children learn language and literacy.* Boston: Allyn & Bacon.

Vygotsky, L. (1986). *Thought and language.* A. Kozulin, Trans. Cambridge, MA: MIT Press.

Vygotsky, L. S. (1978). *Mind in society: The development of higher psychological processes*. Cambridge, MA: Harvard University Press.

Wagner, B. (1999). *Dorothy Heathcote: Drama as a learning medium*. Portland, ME: Calendar Islands Publishers.

Walsh, D., Price, G., & Gillingham M., (1988). The critical but transitory importance of letter naming. *Reading Research Quarterly, 23*(1), 108–122.

Walton, R., & Miglio, P. (1998). *So many bunnies: A bedtime counting book*. New York: Scholastic.

Ward, C. (1997). *Cookie's week*. Illustrated by T. dePaola. New York: Paperstar Book.

Webb, S. (2000). *My season with penguins*. Boston: Houghton Mifflin.

Wepner, W. B., Valmont, W. J., & Thurlow, R. (Eds.). (2000). *Linking literacy and technology: A guide for K–8 classrooms*. Newark, DE: International Reading Association.

Wharton-McDonald, R. (2001). Andy Schultheis. In M. Pressley, R. L. Allington, R. Wharton-McDonald, C. Collins Block, & L. Mandel Morrow (Eds.), *Learning to read*. New York: Guilford.

Wheelock, A., & Dorman, G. (1988). *Before it's too late: Dropout prevention in the middle grades*. Boston: Massachusetts Advocacy Center and Chapel Hill Center for Early Adolescence.

White, E. B. (1952/1980). *Charlotte's web*. New York: Harper Trophy.

Whitehurst, G. J. (1994). *Dialogic reading for parents: Headstart, K, and pre-K*. (Available from G. J. Whitehurst, State University of New York at Stony Brook, Stony Brook, NY 11794–2500).

Whitehurst, G. J., & Lonigan, C. J. (2001). Emergent literacy: From pre-readers to readers. In S. B. Neuman & D. K. Dickinson (Eds.), *Handbook of early literacy research*. New York: Guilford Press.

Wilhelm, Jeffrey D. (2001). *Improving comprehension with think-aloud strategies*. New York: Scholastic Professional Books.

Williams, S. (1991). Classroom use of African American Language: Educational tool or social weapon? In C. Sleeter (Ed.), *Empowering through multicultural education* (pp. 199–215). New York: State University of New York.

Willms, J. D. (1999). *International adult literacy survey: Inequalities in literacy skills among youth in Canada and the United States*. Ottawa, Ontario: Ministry of Industry.

Winner, E. (1982). *Invented worlds: A psychology of the arts*. Cambridge, MA: Harvard University Press.

Wise, W. (2000). *Dinosaurs forever*. New York: Dial Books for Young Readers.

Wood, J. M. (2000). *A marriage waiting to happen: Computers and process writing*. Newton, MA: Education Development Center.

Woodcock, R. W. (1987). *Woodcock Reading Mastery Test Revised*. Circle Pines, MN: American Guidance Service.

Worthy, J., & Broaddus, K. (2002). Fluency beyond the primary grades: From group performance to silent, independent reading. *The Reading Teacher, 55,* 334–343.

Wylie, R. E., & Durrell, D. D. (1970). Teaching vowels through phonograms. *Elementary English Journal, 47,* 787–791.

Yolen, J. (1997). *Sleeping ugly*. New York: Puffin.

Young, J. P., & Brozo, W. G. (2001). Boys will be boys, or will they?: Literacy and masculinities. *Reading Research Quarterly, 36,* 316–325.

Zarrillo, J. (1994). *Multicultural literature, multicultural teaching: Units for the elementary grades*. Fort Worth, TX: Harcourt Brace College Publishers.

Zutell, J. (1999). Sorting it out through word sorts. In I. C. Fountas & G. S. Pinnell (Eds.), *Voices on word matters* (pp. 103–113). Portsmouth, NH: Heinemann.

Zutell, J., & Rasinski, T. (1991). Training teachers to attend to their students' oral reading fluency. *Theory into Practice, 30,* 212–217. Paperstar Book.

Appendix

Standards for Reading Professionals:
IRA and NCTE

Throughout this book, the impact of standards on the Literacy profession is discussed in various chapters and particularly in a special "Standards & Literacy" feature. Discussions are intended to promote an understanding of how standards affect curriculum and instruction throughout the country. Two sets of standards of particular interest to reading professionals are the International Reading Association's "Standards for Reading Professionals—Revised 2003" and the National Council of Teachers of English (NCTE) Standards for Language Arts. In this appendix, we will try to help you understand how the new International Reading Association standards have changed, as well as provide you with a listing of the NCTE Standards for Language Arts and a correlation of where the NCTE standards are addressed within *All Children Read*.

How Does *All Children Read* Correlate to the IRA Standards for Reading Professionals—Revised 2003?

In 2003, the Professional Standards and Ethics Committee of the International Reading Association issued new criteria for the development and training of new reading professionals. The focus of the new standards is on knowledge and skills and identifies what new reading professionals should "know and be able to do." The 2003 revised standards represent a fairly significant change from the 1998 version of the *Standards for Reading Professionals*, to which *All Children Read* correlates very carefully.

Change 1: **Greater focus on candidate performance, with the criteria being much more performance-based than ever before.**

All Children Read: Every chapter contains numerous in-class examples and case studies, as well as ongoing assessment and special teaching strategies that provide you with all the tools necessary for teaching literacy skills to all students. Every chapter contains a special "Standards & Literacy" feature that discusses various state and national performance-based standards that address pertinent literacy skills and help you plan instruction.

Change 2: **Reduction in the number of core standards from sixteen to five:**

- **Foundational Knowledge**
- **Instructional Strategies and Curriculum Materials**

- **Assessment, Diagnosis, and Evaluation**
- **Creating a Literate Environment, and**
- **Professional Development**

Each standard includes several elements that specify particular knowledge and skills relevant for each type of reading professional.

All Children Read: A full listing of the "Standards for Reading Professionals—Revised 2003" and where *All Children Read* correlates to these standards is included on the inside of the cover of this book. As you can see, *All Children Read* has been written to correlate tightly to the new IRA standards.

Change 3:   **The complete IRA standards table identifies standards and elements for five reading professional categories.** Individuals in each of these categories have various degrees of responsibility for supporting and meeting the needs of all students and for interacting with colleagues in a school community to ensure that every student receives appropriate reading instruction. For a complete breakdown of the elements for each category of professional, visit IRA online at www.reading.org/advocacy/standards/standards03_revised/index.html.

- **The Paraprofessional**
  - Assists in classrooms and in after-school and summer programs
  - Two-year postsecondary degree with an emphasis on human development and educational processes and a concentration on reading and reading instruction

- **The Classroom Teacher**
  - Teaches reading and writing or literacy instruction in preschool, school, or adult education
  - Undergraduate or graduate degree that includes a concentration in reading and reading instruction

- **The Reading Specialist/Literacy Coach**
  - Provides specialized reading and writing instruction, assessment, and diagnosis to students
  - May serve as a professional resource, work with other professionals in planning programs, provide professional development opportunities at the local and state levels, and provide leadership in student advocacy
  - Has previous teaching experience
  - Master's degree with concentration in reading education

- **The Teacher Educator**
  - Provides instruction to candidates at the graduate and undergraduate levels
  - Participates in scholarly activities
  - Forges partnerships with other educational agencies to promote the advancement of literacy
  - Minimum of three years' teaching experience including the teaching of reading
  - Terminal degree that focuses on reading and reading instruction

- **The Administrator**
  - Includes principals, superintendents, and reading curriculum specialists

- Recognizes and supports reading professionals as they plan, implement, and evaluate effective reading instruction
- Master's degree that includes a focus on reading and reading instruction and a concentration in instructional leadership and administration

All Children Read: A primary focus of the book is on the skill development of the first three categories of literacy professionals: paraprofessional, the classroom teacher, and the reading specialist/literacy coach. Throughout this book and in the special *Teach It!* booklet, you are provided with an abundance of strategies and activities that are ready to use in the classroom.

Change 4: **Inclusion of references to research that support each of the elements, an acknowledgment of the shift toward an emphasis on the use of research-based practices in schools.**

All Children Read: All content and recommended strategies are rooted in the latest research and represent proven practices, from author Donna Ogle's own KWL to Ehri's work in linguistics.

Change 5: **A primary focus on the changing population demographic and the effect this has had on the cultural and linguistic diversity of today's classrooms.**

All Children Read: Special ELL sections in every chapter and two unique chapters (Chapters 2 and 12) that examine the changing demographic of today's schools, the changing needs of these students, and special considerations for teaching in a culturally and linguistically diverse classroom and community. Use these chapters and activities to utilize the diversity of your children and their families in a way that empowers your instruction.

Change 6: **A much heavier emphasis on the use of technology for teaching children and preparing teachers to use technology effectively and efficiently.**

All Children Read: The use of technology in the classroom and all aspects of daily living is growing rapidly, and you and your children need to learn to make good use of the technology available. This book contains numerous suggestions of technology options—ranging from educational programs to simple technology applications that can be used to encourage reading and writing. These suggestions appear in the written narrative of each chapter as well as within the special Technology Connections activities at the end of each chapter.

Source: Professional Standards and Ethics Committee, International Reading Association. (2003). Standards for reading professionals—revised 2003. Newark, DE: International Reading Association. Available: http://www.reading.org/advocacy/standards/standards03_revised/

How Does *All Children Read* correlate to the National Council of Teachers of English Standards for Language Arts?

On the following page is a listing of the NCTE Standards for the Assessment of Reading and Writing and a correlation of where those standards are addressed within *All Children Read.*

NCTE STANDARD	CHAPTER COVERAGE
1. Students read a wide range of print and non-print texts to build an understanding of texts, of themselves, and the culture of the United States and the world; to acquire new information; to respond to the needs and demands of society and the workplace; and for personal fulfillment. Among these texts are fiction and nonfiction, classic and contemporary works.	2, 6, 7
2. Students read a wide range of literature from many periods in many genres to build an understanding of the many dimensions (e.g., philosophical, ethical, aesthetic) of human experience.	1, 2, 5, 6, 7
3. Students apply a wide range of strategies to comprehend, interpret, evaluate, and appreciate texts. They draw on their prior experience, their interactions with other readers and writers, their knowledge of word meaning and of other texts, their word identification strategies, and their understanding of textual features (e.g., sound-letter correspondence, sentence structure, context, graphics).	2–12
4. Students adjust their use of spoken, written, and visual language (e.g., conventions, style, vocabulary) to communicate effectively with a variety of audiences and for different purposes.	3–5, 8–12
5. Students employ a wide range of strategies as they write and use different writing process elements appropriately to communicate with different audiences for a variety of purposes.	3, 4, 8, 11
6. Students apply knowledge of language structure, language conventions (e.g., spelling and punctuation), media techniques, figurative language, and genre, to create, critique, and discuss print and non-print texts.	3, 4, 9–11
7. Students conduct research on issues and interests by generating ideas and questions, and by posing problems. They gather, evaluate, and synthesize data from a variety of sources (e.g., print and non-print texts, artifacts, people) to communicate their discoveries in ways that suit their purpose and audience.	6, 7, 10, 11
8. Students use a variety of technological and informational resources (e.g., libraries, databases, computer networks, video) to gather and synthesize information and to create and communicate knowledge.	All chapters
9. Students develop an understanding of and respect for diversity in language use, patterns, and dialects across cultures, ethnic groups, geographic regions, and social roles.	2, 3, 5, 9, 10, 12
10. Students whose first language is not English make use of their first language to develop competency in the English language arts and to develop understanding of content across the curriculum.	2, 4–12
11. Students participate as knowledgeable, reflective, creative, and critical members of a variety of literacy communities.	All chapters
12. Students use spoken, written, and visual language to accomplish their own purposes (e.g., for learning, enjoyment, persuasion, and the exchange of information).	2–12

Photo Credits

P. 1, left, © Ellen B. Senisi; right, Lindfors Photography; middle, Skjold Photographs; p. 2, Lindfors Photography; p. 6, © Michael Newman/PhotoEdit, Inc.; p. 16, © Ron Chapple/Getty Images; p. 22, Nancy Sheehan Photography; p. 30, © Gary Conner/PhotoEdit, Inc.; p. 49, © Ellen B. Senisi; p. 55, © Michael Newman/PhotoEdit, Inc.; p. 63, © Bill Aron/PhotoEdit, Inc.; p. 68 Nancy Sheehan Photography; p. 76 © Charles Temple; p. 81, © Richard Hutchings/PhotoEdit, Inc.; p. 104, Nancy Sheehan Photography; p. 107, © Will Hart; p. 117, left and right, Lindfors Photography; middle, Stephanie Maze/Corbis/Bettmann; p. 118, © Ellen B. Senisi; pp. 124, 134, Lindfors Photography; p. 145, © Ellen B. Senisi; pp. 156, 179, 181, 186, 190, Lindfors Photography; p. 204, © Bob Daemmrich/The Image Works; p. 212, Lindfors Photography; p. 220, Getty Images Inc.–Stone Allstock; p. 234, © Mary Kate Denny/PhotoEdit, Inc.; p. 252, Lindfors Photography; p. 262, © Ellen B. Senisi/The Image Works; p. 278, left and right, Charles Temple; p. 290, © Mary Kate Denny/ PhotoEdit, Inc.; p. 302, © Bob Daemmrich/The Image Works; p. 319, Lindfors Photography; p. 334, left, © Ellen B. Senisi/The Image Works; right © Ellen B. Senisi; p. 343, left, © Carl J. Single/The Image Works; right, © Cindy Charles/PhotoEdit, Iinc; middle, © Genna Naccache/Getty Images, Inc.-Taxi; p. 344, © Will Hart; p. 349, Lindfors Photography; pp. 367 left and right, 370 © Linda Headings; pp. 376, 377, Lindfors Photography; p. 380 © Ulricke Welsch/PhotoEdit, Inc.; p. 394, © Paul Conklin/PhotoEdit, Inc.; p. 400 © David Young-Wolff/PhotoEdit, Inc.; p. 415, Lindfors Photography; p. 424, © Michael Newman/PhotoEdit, Inc.; p. 432, Lindfors Photography; p. 437, © Brian Smith; p. 444, © Chip Henderson/Tony Stone Images; p. 455, © Myrleen Ferguson Cate/PhotoEdit, Inc.; pp. 471, 479 © Will Hart/PhotoEdit, Inc.; p. 483, © Paul Conklin/PhotoEdit Inc.; p. 494, © Michael Newman, PhotoEdit, Inc.; p. 508, © Paul Conklin/PhotoEdit, Inc.; p. 517, © Michael Newman, PhotoEdit, Inc.; p. 533, © Will Hart.

Name Index

Achilles, C. M., 62
Adams, M. J., 18–19, 123, 163, 354
Adams, S., 414
Adler, M., 452
Afflerbach, P., 214, 218, 264, 385
Aitchison, J., 104
Alexander, P., 264
Allard, H., 217
Allen, R. V., 190, 376, 422
Allington, R., 358
Allington, R. L., 21, 61, 62, 66, 263, 267, 295, 358, 380, 385
Allison, A., 473
Almasi, J. F., 477
Anderson, R. C., 5, 8, 18, 71, 172, 210, 460
Andrade, A., 524
Aramburo, D., 63
Archambault, J., 324
Asher, J. J., 482, 507
Ashton-Warner, S., 17, 141
Atwell, N., 18, 314, 479
Austin, J. L., 106
Avi, 481
Ayers, W., 349
Baca, L., 63
Baker, S., 9, 63
Bamman, 457
Banks, C. A., 66
Banks, J. A., 66
Barone, D., 213, 324
Barthes, R., 236
Bartlett, J. R., 457
Beamon, G. W., 485
Bean, T., 449
Beane, J., 264, 485
Bear, D. R. 45, 165–166, 181, 187, 193, 423, 427, 457
Beaver, J., 388
Beck, I., 5, 81, 151, 171, 172, 173, 185, 187, 191, 192, 223, 285, 455, 460

Becker, H. J., 68
Beers, C., 356
Berdyshaw, D., 449
Berninger, 45
Berthoff, A., 227, 324
Bettelheim, B., 239
Biber, D., 503, 515, 517
Biklen, D., 214
Blachowicz, C., 259, 295, 455, 457, 463, 465
Bleich, D., 211, 213
Block, C. C., 219
Bloom, B., 219
Bode, J., 473
Bond, G. L., 357
Bormuth, 487
Bradley, L., 89, 90
Bridges, L. B., 400
Britton, J., 321
Broaddus, K., 402
Brock, C. H., 5
Bromley, K., 315
Bronfenbrenner, U., 379
Brown, A. L., 284
Brown, H., 412
Brown, M., 275
Brown, R., 5, 81, 82, 97, 101, 171
Browne, N., 213
Brozo, W. G., 65
Bruner, J., 405
Bryant, 45
Bryant, P., 89, 90
Buehl, D., 405
Burke, C. L., 45, 125, 137, 193, 227, 230, 387, 418
Burnett, F. H., 214
Burns, M. S., 6, 84, 501
Burns, P. C., 420, 431
Burris, N., 14, 121, 126, 127, 128
Butler, A., 18
Caldwell, J. S., 381, 385, 389

California Commission on Teacher Credentialing, 82
California State Board of Education, 47
Calkins, L., 18, 307, 309, 321, 322
Calkins, L. M., 311
Cambourne, B., 412
Campbell, J., 239
Campo-Flores, A., 53
Cantrell, S. C., 414
Carjuzaa, J., 63
Carle, E., 376, 400
Carr, E. M., 281, 459
Carroll, L., 102
CATESOL, 512
Caverly, D. C., 287
Celano, D., 66
Chall, J., 17, 162, 163
Chastain, K., 504, 505
Children's Partnership, 68
Chinn, P. C., 49
Chomsky, N., 79, 84, 89
Christie, J., 365, 377
Clark, L. K., 177
Clay, M. M., 14, 15, 123, 126, 129, 146, 193, 333, 378
Cleary, B., 233
Coleman, J. S., 61
Collier, V. P., 55, 498, 500, 501, 506, 507, 517
Collins, J. L., 320
Conrad, P., 220, 321
Cooper, D. H., 374
Corona Berkin, S., 66
Corson, D., 424
Cowley, J., 374
Crawford, A. N., 61, 190, 191, 196, 376, 402, 405, 408, 410, 411, 412, 420, 422, 423, 424, 425, 426, 427, 428, 429, 435, 505, 506, 509, 510, 514, 517, 527, 528
Crawford, J., 53

Subject Index